7th Workshop on NLP for Similar Languages, Varieties and Dialects (VarDial '2020)

Held online due to COVID-19

Barcelona, Spain
13 December 2020

ISBN: 978-1-7138-2842-6

Printed from e-media with permission by:

Curran Associates, Inc.
57 Morehouse Lane
Red Hook, NY 12571

Some format issues inherent in the e-media version may also appear in this print version.

Copyright© (2020) by the Association for Computational Linguistics
All rights reserved.
Copyright for individual papers remains with the authors and are licensed under a Creative Commons 4.0
license, CC-BY. (https://creativecommons.org/licenses/by/4.0/)

Printed with permission by Curran Associates, Inc. (2021)

For permission requests, please contact the Association for Computational Linguistics
at the address below.

Association for Computational Linguistics
209 N. Eighth Street
Stroudsburg, Pennsylvania 18360

Phone: 1-570-476-8006
Fax: 1-570-476-0860

acl@aclweb.org

Additional copies of this publication are available from:

Curran Associates, Inc.
57 Morehouse Lane
Red Hook, NY 12571 USA
Phone: 845-758-0400
Fax: 845-758-2633
Email: curran@proceedings.com
Web: www.proceedings.com

COLING 2020

Proceedings of the 7th VarDial Workshop
on NLP for Similar Languages, Varieties and Dialects,

**Co-located with the 28th International Conference
on Computational Linguistics COLING'2020**

VarDial '2020

December 13, 2020
Barcelona, Spain (Online)

Copyright of each paper stays with the respective authors (or their employers).

Preface

These proceedings include the 27 papers presented at the Seventh Workshop on NLP for Similar Languages, Varieties and Dialects (VarDial)[1], co-located with the 28th International Conference on Computational Linguistics (COLING). VarDial and COLING were scheduled to take place in Barcelona, Spain, but both were changed to a virtual format due to the COVID-19 outbreak.

We are glad to see that VarDial keeps growing in popularity, reaching its seventh edition. Moreover, this year, we received an all-time high number of regular submissions —21 papers —, and we accepted 15 of them to be presented at the workshop. These papers deal with various topics related to the processing of diatopic language variation in both text and speech. This volume includes papers on topics such as automatic speech recognition, corpus building, pre-processing, syntactic parsing, language identification, and machine translation, to name a few.

Diversity is innate to VarDial due to its focus on dialects and under-resourced languages. We are happy that the workshop continues to bring together researchers working on different languages, sharing ideas and contributing to advancing the state of the art of NLP for dialects, low-resource languages, and language varieties. This year, we accepted papers dealing with languages such as Armenian, Basque, German, Italian, Kurdish, and Occitan, as well as groups of dialects and low-resource languages from families such as Dravidian, Slavic, and Zaza-Gorani.

As in previous years, together with the workshop, we organized another iteration of the popular VarDial Evaluation Campaign with three shared tasks: Romanian Dialect Identification (RDI), Social Media Variety Geolocation (SMG), and Uralic Language Identification (ULI). These tasks addressed important challenges in dialect and language identification, attracting many teams who submitted runs across the three competitions. Eleven teams prepared system description papers that are included in this volume, along with a report paper summarizing the results and the main findings of the evaluation campaign written by the campaign organizers.

Finally, we would like to take this opportunity to thank the amazing VarDial program committee members for their thorough reviews. They have been playing a very important role in making the VarDial workshop series a success and we are fortunate to have them on board. We further thank the VarDial Evaluation Campaign shared task organizers and the participants for their hard work.

The VarDial workshop organizers:

Marcos Zampieri, Preslav Nakov, Nikola Ljubešić, Jörg Tiedemann, and Yves Scherrer

`http://sites.google.com/view/vardial2020/`

---

[1] https://sites.google.com/view/vardial2020/home

Organizers:

Marcos Zampieri - Rochester Institute of Technology (USA)
Preslav Nakov - Qatar Computing Research Institute, HBKU (Qatar)
Nikola Ljubešić - Jožef Stefan Institute (Slovenia) and University of Zagreb (Croatia)
Jörg Tiedemann - University of Helsinki (Finland)
Yves Scherrer - University of Helsinki (Finland)

Program Committee:

Željko Agić (Corti, Denmark)
Cesar Aguilar (Pontifical Catholic University of Chile, Chile)
Laura Alonso y Alemany (University of Cordoba, Argentina)
Eric Atwell (University of Leeds, United Kingdom)
Jorge Baptista (University of Algarve and INESC-ID, Portugal)
Eckhard Bick (University of Southern Denmark, Denmark)
Johannes Bjerva (University of Copenhagen, Denmark)
Francis Bond (Nanyang Technological University, Singapore)
Aoife Cahill (Educational Testing Service, United States)
David Chiang (University of Notre Dame, United States)
Paul Cook (University of New Brunswick, Canada)
Marta Costa-Jussà (Universitat Politècnica de Catalunya, Spain)
Jon Dehdari (Think Big Analytics, United States)
Liviu Dinu (University of Bucharest, Romania)
Stefanie Dipper (Ruhr University Bochum, Germany)
Sascha Diwersy (University of Montpellier, France)
Mark Dras (Macquarie University, Australia)
Tomaž Erjavec (Jožef Stefan Institute, Slovenia)
Pablo Gamallo (University of Santiago de Compostela, Spain)
Binyam Gebrekidan Gebre (Phillips Research, The Netherlands)
Cyril Goutte (National Research Council, Canada)
Nizar Habash (New York University Abu Dhabi, UAE)
Chu-Ren Huang (Hong Kong Polytechnic University, Hong Kong)
Radu Ionescu (University of Bucharest, Romania)
Jeremy Jancsary (Nuance Communications, Austria)
Tommi Jauhiainen (University of Helsinki, Finland)
Surafel Melaku Lakew (FBK , Italy)
Ekaterina Lapshinova-Koltunski (Saarland University, Germany)
Lung-Hao Lee (National Taiwan Normal University, Taiwan)
John Nerbonne (University of Groningen, Netherlands and University of Freiburg, Germany)
Kemal Oflazer (Carnegie-Mellon University in Qatar, Qatar)
Maciej Ogrodniczuk (IPAN, Polish Academy of Sciences, Poland)
Petya Osenova (Bulgarian Academy of Sciences, Bulgaria)
Santanu Pal (Saarland University, Germany)
Francisco Rangel (Autoritas Consulting, Spain)
Taraka Rama (University of North Texas, United States)
Reinhard Rapp (University of Mainz, Germany and University of Aix-Marsaille, France)
Paolo Rosso (Technical University of Valencia, Spain)
Rachel Edita O. Roxas (National University, Phillipines)

Fatiha Sadat (Université du Québec à Montréal (UQAM), Canada)
Tanja Samardžić (University of Zurich, Switzerland)
Kevin Scannell (Saint Louis University, United States)
Serge Sharoff (University of Leeds, United Kingdom)
Miikka Silfverberg (University of Helsinki, Finland)
Kiril Simov (Bulgarian Academy of Sciences, Bulgaria)
Milena Slavcheva (Bulgarian Academy of Sciences, Bulgaria)
Marko Tadić (University of Zagreb, Croatia)
Liling Tan (Rakuten Institute of Technology, Singapore)
Joel Tetreault (Dataminr, United States)
Francis Tyers (Indiana University, United States)
Taro Watanabe (Google Inc., Japan)
Pidong Wang (Google Inc., United States)

Invited Speaker:

Barbara Plank (IT University of Copenhagen, Denmark)

Table of Contents

Conference Program

Sunday, December 13, 2020

14:00–14:05   ***Opening Remarks***

14:05–14:20   *A Report on the VarDial Evaluation Campaign 2020*
Mihaela Gaman, Dirk Hovy, Radu Tudor Ionescu, Heidi Jauhiainen, Tommi Jauhiainen, Krister Lindén, Nikola Ljubešić, Niko Partanen, Christoph Purschke, Yves Scherrer and Marcos Zampieri

14:30–15:30   *Invited Talk by Barbara Plank*

Oral presentations

16:00–16:15   *ASR for Non-standardised Languages with Dialectal Variation: the case of Swiss German*
Iuliia Nigmatulina, Tannon Kew and Tanja Samardzic

16:15–16:30   *LSDC - A comprehensive dataset for Low Saxon Dialect Classification*
Janine Siewert, Yves Scherrer, Martijn Wieling and Jörg Tiedemann

16:30–16:45   *Machine-oriented NMT Adaptation for Zero-shot NLP tasks: Comparing the Usefulness of Close and Distant Languages*
Amirhossein Tebbifakhr, Matteo Negri and Marco Turchi

16:45–17:00   *Character Alignment in Morphologically Complex Translation Sets for Related Languages*
Michael Gasser, Binyam Ephrem Seyoum and Nazareth Amlesom Kifle

17:30-18:30   **Poster presentations**

Bilingual Lexicon Induction across Orthographically-distinct Under-Resourced Dravidian Languages
Bharathi Raja Chakravarthi, Navaneethan Rajasekaran, Mihael Arcan, Kevin McGuinness, Noel E. O'Connor and John P. McCrae

Building a Corpus for the Zaza–Gorani Language Family
Sina Ahmadi

Dealing with dialectal variation in the construction of the Basque historical corpus
Ainara Estarrona, Izaskun Etxeberria, Ricardo Etxepare, Manuel Padilla-Moyano and Ander Soraluze

Recycling and Comparing Morphological Annotation Models for Armenian Diachronic-Variational Corpus Processing
Chahan Vidal-Gorène, Victoria Khurshudyan and Anaïd Donabédian-Demopoulos

Neural Machine Translation for translating into Croatian and Serbian
Maja Popović, Alberto Poncelas, Marija Brkic and Andy Way

A Tokenization System for the Kurdish Language
Sina Ahmadi

Rediscovering the Slavic Continuum in Representations Emerging from Neural Models of Spoken Language Identification
Badr M. Abdullah, Jacek Kudera, Tania Avgustinova, Bernd Möbius and Dietrich Klakow

A Four-Dialect Treebank for Occitan: Building Process and Parsing Experiments
Aleksandra Miletic, Myriam Bras, Marianne Vergez-Couret, Louise Esher, Clamença Poujade and Jean Sibille

Vulgaris: Analysis of a Corpus for Middle-Age Varieties of Italian Language
Andrea Zugarini, Matteo Tiezzi and Marco Maggini

Towards Augmenting Lexical Resources for Slang and African American English
Alyssa Hwang, William R. Frey and Kathleen McKeown

Uralic Language Identification (ULI) 2020 shared task dataset and the Wanca 2017 corpora
Tommi Jauhiainen, Heidi Jauhiainen, Niko Partanen and Krister Lindén

Sunday, December 13, 2020 (continued)

18:30–19:00   Discussion and Closing

A Report on the VarDial Evaluation Campaign 2020

Mihaela Găman[1], Dirk Hovy[2], Radu Tudor Ionescu[1], Heidi Jauhiainen[3]
Tommi Jauhiainen[3], Krister Lindén[3], Nikola Ljubešić[4,5], Niko Partanen[3]
Christoph Purschke[6], Yves Scherrer[3], Marcos Zampieri[7]

[1]University of Bucharest, [2]Bocconi University, [3]University of Helsinki,
[4]Jožef Stefan Institute, [5]University of Ljubljana, [6]University of Luxembourg,
[7]Rochester Institute of Technology

vardialworkshop@gmail.com

Abstract

This paper presents the results of the VarDial Evaluation Campaign 2020 organized as part of the seventh workshop on Natural Language Processing (NLP) for Similar Languages, Varieties and Dialects (VarDial), co-located with COLING 2020. The campaign included three shared tasks each focusing on a different challenge of language and dialect identification: Romanian Dialect Identification (RDI), Social Media Variety Geolocation (SMG), and Uralic Language Identification (ULI). The campaign attracted 30 teams who enrolled to participate in one or multiple shared tasks and 14 of them submitted runs across the three shared tasks. Finally, 11 papers describing participating systems are published in the VarDial proceedings and referred to in this report.

1 Introduction

The VarDial Evaluation Campaign 2020[1] is the most recent iteration of a series of evaluation campaigns featuring multiple shared tasks organized together with the Workshop on Natural Language Processing (NLP) for Similar Languages, Varieties and Dialects (VarDial). It follows three editions organized in 2017 (Zampieri et al., 2017) featuring four shared tasks and in 2018 (Zampieri et al., 2018) and 2019 (Zampieri et al., 2019) featuring five shared tasks.

Co-located with international NLP conferences such as COLING, EACL, and NAACL, VarDial is a forum for researchers interested in diatopic language variation from a computational perspective. Since its first edition in 2014, VarDial hosted shared tasks on various topics such as morphosyntactic tagging, cross-lingual dependency parsing, and language and dialect identification. Most shared tasks organized at VarDial have addressed dialect and language identification on newspaper texts, social media posts, speech transcriptions, and many other genres and domains (Malmasi et al., 2016; Goutte et al., 2016). A large number of languages and dialects from different families have been included in the VarDial shared tasks: national language varieties of Chinese, English, French, Spanish, and Portuguese, pairs or groups of similar languages such as Bosnian, Croatian, and Serbian and Malay and Indonesian, and dialects of languages such as Arabic and German. Some of the datasets made available in these tasks, such as the ArchiMob for Swiss German dialects and the multilingual DSLCC, have been used outside these competitions evidencing the interest of the NLP community in the topic (Tan et al., 2014; Samardžić et al., 2016; Kumar et al., 2018).[2]

In this paper, we present the results and the main findings of the VarDial Evaluation Campaign 2020. Three tasks addressing different aspects of language and dialect identification have been organized this year. The Romanian Dialect Identification (RDI) shared task is described in Section 4, the Social Media Variety Geolocation (SMG) task is presented in Section 5, and finally the Uralic Language Identification (ULI) shared task is described in Section 6. We include references to the 11 system description papers written by the participants of the campaign in Table 1.

This work is licensed under a Creative Commons Attribution 4.0 International License. License details: http://creativecommons.org/licenses/by/4.0/.

[1]https://sites.google.com/view/vardial2020/evaluation-campaign

[2]For recent surveys on these topics see Zampieri et al. (2020) and Jauhiainen et al. (2019c).

Proceedings of the 7th VarDial Workshop on NLP for Similar Languages, Varieties and Dialects, pages 1–14
Barcelona, Spain (Online), December 13, 2020

2 Shared Tasks at VarDial 2020

Romanian Dialect Identification (RDI):   In the Romanian Dialect Identification (RDI) shared task, we provided participants with the MOROCO data set (Butnaru and Ionescu, 2019) for training, which contains Moldavian (MD) and Romanian (RO) samples of text collected from the news domain. The task was a binary classification by dialect, in which a classification model is required to discriminate between the Moldavian (MD) and the Romanian (RO) dialects. The task was closed, therefore, participants are not allowed to use external data to train their models. The test set contained newly collected text samples from a different domain, not previously included in MOROCO, resulting in a cross-domain dialect identification task.

Social Media Variety Geolocation (SMG):   In contrast to most past and present VarDial tasks, the SMG task is framed as a geolocation task: given a text, the participants have to predict its geographic location in terms of latitude/longitude coordinates. This setup addresses the common issue that defining a set of discrete labels is not trivial for many language areas where there is a continuum between varieties rather than clear-cut borders. The SMG task is split into three subtasks covering different language areas: the **BCMS** subtask is focused on geolocated tweets published in the area of Croatia, Bosnia and Herzegovina, Montenegro and Serbia in the HBS macro-language (Ljubešić et al., 2016); the **DE-AT** subtask focuses on conversations from the microblogging platform Jodel initiated in Germany and Austria, which are written in standard German but commonly contain regional and dialectal forms; the **CH** subtask is based on Jodel conversations initiated in Switzerland, which were found to be held majoritarily in Swiss German dialects (Hovy and Purschke, 2018). All three subtasks used the same data format and evaluation methodology. Both constrained and unconstrained submissions were allowed, but only one participating team made use of the latter.

Uralic Language Identification (ULI):   This shared task focused on discriminating between endangered languages of the Uralic group. In addition to 29 Uralic minority languages, the shared task also featured 149 non-relevant languages. For training, we provided texts from the Wanca 2016 corpora (Jauhiainen et al., 2019a) for the relevant languages while the texts for the non-relevant languages came from the Leipzig corpora collection (Goldhahn et al., 2012). The test set for the relevant languages included sentences from the forthcoming Wanca 2017 corpora (Jauhiainen et al., 2020b) that were not present in the Wanca 2016 corpora. The sentences for the non-relevant languages were from the Leipzig corpora collection. The ULI shared task was divided into three separate tracks using the same training and test data. The difference between the tracks was based on how the submissions were scored: track 1 focused on macro-averaged F-score for the 29 relevant languages, track 2 on micro-averaged F-score for the relevant languages, and track 3 on macro-averaged F-score for all 178 languages. All the tracks were closed, so no other data or models were to be used for training in addition to the pre-defined training sets.

3 Participating Teams

A total of 30 teams enrolled to participate in this year's VarDial evaluation campaign and 14 of them submitted results to one or more shared tasks. In Table 1, we list the teams that participated in the shared tasks, including references to the 11 system description papers written by the participants. We include detailed information about these submissions in each respective task section of this report.

The RDI task attracted 8 teams followed by the SMG task with 7 teams who submitted runs to one or more of its three language tracks: BCMS, DE-AT, and CH. This is a similar number of teams that have participated in the most popular shared tasks from the VarDial evaluation campaign 2019. Only the NRC team submitted results to the ULI shared task, which is rather unusual, as tasks in past VarDial evaluation campaign have all received a very good number of submissions. It should be noted that the 2020 campaign run from April 20 to July 30 during the early stages of the COVID-19 pandemic. Lock downs and restrictive measures in many countries during this period have impacted universities and research centers worldwide causing significant disruption. We believe that this situation is very likely to have discouraged more teams to participate in this year's evaluation campaign.

Team	RDI	SMG	ULI	System Description Paper
Akanksha	✓			
Anumiți	✓			(Popa and Ștefănescu, 2020)
CUBoulder-UBC		✓		*
Phlyers	✓			(Ceolin and Zhang, 2020)
HeLju		✓		(Scherrer and Ljubešić, 2020)
NRC			✓	(Bernier-Colborne and Goutte, 2020)
Piyush Mishra		✓		(Mishra, 2020)
SUKI	✓	✓		(Jauhiainen et al., 2020a)
The Linguistadors	✓	✓		
Tübingen	✓			(Çöltekin, 2020)
UAIC	✓			(Rebeja and Cristea, 2020)
UnibucKernel		✓		(Găman and Ionescu, 2020a)
UPB	✓			(Zaharia et al., 2020)
ZHAW-InIT		✓		(Benites et al., 2020)
Total	**8**	**7**	**1**	**11**

Table 1: The teams that participated in the VarDial Evaluation Campaign 2020 along with their system description papers. *The system description paper by team CUBoulder-UBC does not appear in the VarDial workshop proceedings. CUBoulder-UBC reused a system described in Hulden et al. (2015).

4 Romanian Dialect Identification RDI

4.1 Dataset

The training data is composed of news articles from the Moldavian and Romanian Dialectal Corpus (MO-ROCO)[3] (Butnaru and Ionescu, 2019). MOROCO was collected from the top five news websites from Romania and the Republic of Moldova, using each country's web domain (*.ro* or *.md*) to automatically separate the news articles by dialect.

The test data consists of short text samples from MOROCO-Tweets[4] (Găman and Ionescu, 2020b). The tweets are collected from Romania and the Republic of Moldova, the labels being assigned based on the geographical location of tweets.

Dialect	Training Set Size	Development Set Size		Test Set Size
		News Articles	Tweets	
Romanian	18,161	3,205	102	2,523
Moldavian	15,403	2,718	113	2,499
Total	**33,564**	**5,923**	**215**	**5,022**

Table 2: Number of text samples in the training, the development and the test sets considered for the RDI shared task.

The chosen training and test corpora allowed us to evaluate participants on a challenging cross-genre binary dialect identification task: Romanian (RO) versus Moldavian (MD). However, participants were provided with development data comprising both news articles and tweets. The number of samples in the training, the development and the test sets are listed in Table 2. All text samples were automatically pre-processed to replace each named entity with the token NE.

---

[3] https://github.com/butnaruandrei/MOROCO
[4] https://github.com/raduionescu/MOROCO-Tweets

4.2 Participants and Approaches

Akanksha. The Akanksha team fine-tuned a reformer model (Kitaev et al., 2019) on the provided data, considering character-level and phrase-level tokens. Then, a binary classifier is trained on top of the fine-tuned reformer model. The team submitted only one run.

Anumiți. The Anumiți team (Popa and Ștefănescu, 2020) submitted three runs using fine-tuned Romanian BERT models (Dumitrescu et al., 2020). They started from BERT models that are pre-trained on Romanian corpora. For the first two runs, the team submitted individual models, the first one being a cased BERT model and the second one being an uncased BERT model, respectively. For the third run, the team proposed an SVM ensemble of five different transformer-based models, some being multilingual and others being specifically trained on Romanian corpora.

Phlyers. All the submissions made by the Phlyers (Ceolin and Zhang, 2020) are based on Naïve Bayes models applied on character n-grams. Before applying the models, the team preprocessed the text samples by removing numbers, punctuation and common Twitter tags such as "LIVE", "FOTO" and "VIDEO", as well as the \$NE\$ tag (which was used to replace named entities). For the first run, the Phlyers tuned the model on the news development set, obtaining optimal results with $\alpha = 10^{-4}$ and n-grams in the range 5-8 that occur less than 1000 times. For the second and third runs, the Phlyers tuned the model on the tweets development set. The best model uses $\alpha = 10^{-3}$ and n-grams in the range 6-8 that occur less than 250 times, while the second best model uses $\alpha = 10^{-3}$ and n-grams in the range 5-7 that occur less than 200 times.

The Linguistadors. The Linguistadors proposed a character-level CNN architecture, which was trained using ground-truth and pseudo-labels. For the first run, the model is fine-tuned using pseudo-labels for the validation set. For the second run, the model is fine-tuned using pseudo-labels for both validation and test sets. For the third run, the CNN is fine-tuned using pseudo-labels for a subset of the validation set that includes samples with 95% confidence of being correct.

Tübingen. The runs submitted by the Tübingen team (Çöltekin, 2020) consist of multiple linear SVM classifiers based on sparse character and word n-gram features, including a domain adaptation method proposed in their earlier shared task participation (Wu et al., 2019). For the first run, a base SVM model (trained only on the target development set) is first applied on the test set. Then, the model is retrained by adding the test predictions for which the classifier is confident (distance from the decision boundary is higher than 0.5) to the training set. As the final predictions, the authors take the majority vote of five classifiers trained with (slightly) different hyperparameters. For the second run, the Tübingen team used an ensemble of 20 classifiers trained on disjoint parts of the training data, while also splitting the news articles into sentences. The training data for the second submission is formed of the training and the development sets, assigning $25\times$ higher weights to tweets than to sentences taken from news articles. The third run of the Tübingen team is very similar to the second, the only difference being the filtering of the source documents based on the confidence of another classifier trained on the target development set.

UAIC. The UAIC team (Rebeja and Cristea, 2020) proposed a model based on TF-IDF encoders trained on each dialect, independently. The TF-IDF encodings are concatenated into a single tensor and provided as input to a deep learning architecture that learns to classify each data sample. The architecture is trained using categorical cross-entropy. The UAIC team submitted two runs with slightly different hyperparameters.

UPB. Similar to Anumiți, the UPB team (Zaharia et al., 2020) submitted three runs using the Romanian BERT model (Dumitrescu et al., 2020). For the first submission, the model is trained for three epochs on text chunks of 512 tokens taken with an overlap of 128 tokens. For the second run, the Romanian BERT model is trained using an adversarial technique that alters certain examples in the data set. For the third run, the model is trained for four epochs on text chunks of 480 tokens.

SUKI. The SUKI team (Jauhiainen et al., 2020a) submitted a single run to the RDI shared task. The authors employed a custom Naïve Bayes model based on relative frequencies of character 4-grams and 5-grams as features. They removed NE tags and non-alphabetic characters from all data samples. Then, they changed the remaining characters to lowercase. The SUKI team trained the submitted model on both training and development samples.

4.3 Results

Rank	Team	Run	Method	F1 (macro)
1	Tübingen	1	SVM ensemble based on word and char n-grams	0.787592
	Tübingen	2	SVM ensemble based on word and char n-grams	0.784317
2	Anumiţi	3	SVM ensemble based on five BERT embeddings	0.775178
	Anumiţi	2	Fine-tuned uncased Romanian BERT	0.762677
	Tübingen	3	SVM ensemble based on word and char n-grams	0.756461
	Anumiţi	1	Fine-tuned cased Romanian BERT	0.746005
3	Phlyers	1	Naïve Bayes based on word n-grams	0.666090
4	SUKI	1	Naïve Bayes based on char n-grams	0.658437
	Phlyers	2	Naïve Bayes based on word n-grams	0.650884
5	UPB	1	Fine-tuned Romanian BERT	0.647577
	Phlyers	3	Naïve Bayes based on word n-grams	0.644527
	UPB	2	Fine-tuned Romanian BERT	0.563287
	UPB	3	Fine-tuned Romanian BERT	0.557496
6	UAIC	1	Deep network based on TF-IDF encodings	0.555044
	UAIC	2	Deep network based on TF-IDF encodings	0.486896
7	Akanksha	1	Character-level and phrase-level reformer	0.481325
8	The Linguistadors	2	Character-level CNN with pseudo-labels	0.429412
	The Linguistadors	3	Character-level CNN with pseudo-labels	0.411571
	The Linguistadors	1	Character-level CNN with pseudo-labels	0.396090

Table 3: Macro F_1-scores attained by the participating teams on the RDI shared task. A summary of methods and features used by participants are also included.

The runs submitted by each participant in the RDI shared task are presented in Table 3. The systems are ranked according to the macro F_1-scores. Interestingly, we observe that the top scoring system is a shallow approach based on an SVM ensemble applied on word and character n-grams. The best model, which is submitted by the Tübingen team, is closely followed by an SVM ensemble applied on fine-tuned multilingual and monolingual BERT embeddings. The results show that Tübingen and Anumiţi are the only two teams surpassing the 70% threshold. Their very good results compared with the rest of the participants are likely due to the idea of splitting the news articles in sentences. This hypothesis is also supported by the following observation. Although both Anumiţi and UPB fine-tuned the same Romanian BERT model, their results are significantly different, probably because the Anumiţi team fine-tuned the model on sentences, while UPB fine-tuned it on text chunks. Considering the domain gap between news articles and tweets, which is also caused by the high difference in the average number of tokens per sample – see (Găman and Ionescu, 2020b) – we believe that the idea of splitting the news articles into sentences to reduce the domain gap is quite useful.

4.4 Summary

In the Romanian Dialect Identification challenge, we proposed a shared task on cross-domain binary classification by dialect. A total of 8 teams participated in the competition, each submitting between 1 and 3 runs. This resulted in a total of 19 submissions, which represents an increase of almost 100% compared with last year's Moldavian vs. Romanian Cross-Dialect Topic Identification (MRC) shared task (Zampieri et al., 2019). An interesting difference compared with the results reported for the MRC shared task is that, in the RDI shared task, the best performance is obtained by a shallow approach based on word and character n-grams. This is consistent with the results observed in previous VarDial evaluation campaigns (Zampieri et al., 2017; Zampieri et al., 2018), where some of the winners employed shallow approaches based on character n-grams (Butnaru and Ionescu, 2018; Ionescu and Butnaru, 2017). In summary, we conclude that the battle between deep and shallow approaches is still open, at least when it comes to dialect identification.

5 Social Media Variety Geolocation SMG

5.1 Datasets

The SMG task is based on three datasets from two Social Media platforms, Jodel and Twitter.

- The **BCMS subtask** is focused on geolocated tweets published in the area of Croatia, Bosnia and Herzegovina, Montenegro and Serbia in the so-called BCMS macro-language (ISO acronym HBS, code 639-3). While the independent status of the specific languages is rather disputed, there is significant variation between them.

- The **DE-AT subtask** focuses on Jodel conversations initiated in Germany and Austria, which are written in standard German but commonly contain regional and dialectal forms. Jodel is a mobile chat application that lets people anonymously talk to other users within a 10km-radius around them.

- The **CH subtask** focuses on Jodel conversations from Switzerland, which were found to be held majoritarily in Swiss German dialects. This dataset is considerably smaller, but we expect it to contain more dialect-specific cues than the DE-AT one.

The BCMS Twitter dataset is described in Ljubešić et al. (2016). The two Jodel datasets are subsets of the corpus collected by Hovy and Purschke (2018). Some additional cleaning and filtering steps have been applied to these corpora, and they have been split into training, development and test sets (see Table 4 for key figures). All three subtasks use the same data format: each instance consists of three fields, the unprocessed text of the message (BCMS) or conversation (DE-AT and CH), the latitude coordinate and the longitude coordinate. Figure 1 shows the geographic distribution of training instances.

Subtask	Number of instances			Average number of
	Training	**Development**	**Test**	**tokens per instance**
BCMS	320,042	39,750	39,723	13
DE-AT	336,983	46,582	48,239	71
CH	22,600	3,068	3,097	55

Table 4: SMG datasets.

5.2 Participants and Approaches

We received submissions from seven teams, with five teams participating in all three subtasks. The HeLju team submitted both unconstrained and constrained systems, whereas all other participants focused on constrained systems (i.e., not using any external training data).

The participating systems can be classified into two approaches to geolocation: a direct one which frames the problem as a double regression, and an indirect one which converts the coordinates into a finite set of dialect areas and uses a classification model to predict one of the areas.

CUBoulder-UBC. This approach is based on earlier work described in Hulden et al. (2015). It divides each geographic area into a fixed grid and uses a Naive Bayes classifier with bag-of-words features for prediction, together with kernel density estimation to avoid data sparsity. The submissions include a single system, a mean-based ensemble of 10, and a median-based ensemble of 10.

Figure 1: Geographic distribution of training instances in the three SMG datasets: DE-AT (top), CH (bottom left), BCMS (bottom right).

HeLju.   The HeLju systems (Scherrer and Ljubešić, 2020) rely on the BERT architecture, where the classification output is replaced by a double regression output. For the constrained submissions (C), the BERT models are trained from scratch using the SMG training data, whereas pre-trained models are used for the unconstrained submissions (UC). The unconstrained submissions named *UC ext* include additional training data from the development set.

Piyush Mishra.   This submission is based on a bidirectional LSTM that is fed with FastText embeddings (Mishra, 2020). Latitudes and longitudes are predicted by double regression with quantile loss.

SUKI.   This approach divides each geographic area into a fixed grid with 81 areas and uses a n-gram language model to predict the most likely area (Jauhiainen et al., 2020a).

The Linguistadors.   These submissions are based on classic regression methods (linear regression, lasso regression, and ridge regression) and rely on TF-IDF weighted input features.

UnibucKernel.   The UnibucKernel team (Găman and Ionescu, 2020a) submitted two single systems, a character-level CNN (Zhang et al., 2015) with double regression output, and a Nu-SVR model trained on top of n-gram string kernels (Ionescu et al., 2016). The third system is an ensemble approach based on XGBoost, trained on the predictions provided by the two previously mentioned systems and an LSTM-based one. The LSTM is trained on top of fine-tuned German BERT embeddings.

ZHAW-InIT.   The ZHAW-InIT team (Benites et al., 2020) uses unsupervised k-means clustering to infer a set of dialect classes which are then used in a classification architecture. Their systems are based either on SVMs with TF-IDF weighted word and character n-gram features, or on the HELI language modeling architecture (ZHAW-InIT (HELI)). The SVM submission to the CH subtask (ZHAW-InIT (META)) is in fact a meta-classifier combining several SVMs with different features, whereas single SVMs are used for BCMS and DE-AT (ZHAW-InIT (SVM)).

5.3 Results

The test set predictions were evaluated on the basis of median and mean distance to the gold coordinate. Submissions are ranked by decreasing median distance, which is the official metric. For comparison, we also mention the distance values obtained from a simple centroid baseline, which predicts the center point (measured on the training data) for each test instance. Results and rankings for the three tasks are presented in Tables 5, 6, and 7 respectively. Ranks are attributed only to the best-ranked submission of each team.

Rank	Team (Run)	Median distance	Mean distance
1	HeLju (UC)	41.54	80.89
	HeLju (UC ext)	41.61	80.24
	HeLju (C)	48.99	86.83
2	ZHAW-InIT (SVM)	57.24	100.42
3	SUKI	61.01	105.11
4	CUBoulder-UBC (single)	64.76	106.67
	CUBoulder-UBC (med. ens.)	64.92	106.45
	CUBoulder-UBC (mean ens.)	66.36	102.85
5	Piyush Mishra	85.70	112.65
6	The lingustadors (Linear)	97.16	141.88
	The lingustadors (Ridge)	105.54	141.58
	The lingustadors (Lasso)	107.04	145.68
	Centroid baseline	*107.10*	*145.72*
	ZHAW-InIT (HELI)	111.40	130.23

Table 5: SMG shared task - BCMS results. Unconstrained submissions above the horizontal line, constrained ones below.

Rank	Team (Run)	Median distance	Mean distance	Dialect area accuracy
1	HeLju (UC ext)	143.30	166.64	36.1%
	HeLju (UC)	143.85	168.45	34.8%
	HeLju (C)	159.59	183.97	29.5%
2	Piyush Mishra	183.99	204.93	21.8%
3	CUBoulder-UBC (mean ens.)	198.27	218.51	25.1%
	Centroid baseline	*201.34*	*221.55*	*17.7%*
4	ZHAW-InIT (SVM)	205.81	230.78	27.7%
	CUBoulder-UBC (median ens.)	214.72	235.62	25.4%
	ZHAW-InIT (HELI)	217.80	241.33	19.5%
	CUBoulder-UBC (single)	219.08	239.47	25.7%
5	SUKI	243.12	266.85	24.4%

Table 6: SMG shared task - DE-AT results. Unconstrained submissions above the horizontal line, constrained ones below.

For the DE-AT and CH subtasks, we also provide a dialect area accuracy measure. These are based on partitions of the areas into different dialectal areas based on previous dialectological research (Lameli,

Rank	Team (Run)	Median distance	Mean distance	Dialect area accuracy
1	HeLju (UC ext)	15.45	22.45	72.6%
	HeLju (UC)	15.72	22.67	72.9%
2	ZHAW-InIT (META)	15.93	25.06	72.6%
	ZHAW-InIT (HELI)	17.66	26.21	69.4%
	HeLju (C)	17.97	26.04	68.7%
3	CUBoulder-UBC (mean ens.)	19.49	27.63	66.9%
	CUBoulder-UBC (median ens.)	19.66	28.83	66.4%
	CUBoulder-UBC (single)	19.99	29.09	66.2%
4	SUKI	23.96	34.59	57.0%
5	UnibucKernel (ens.)	25.57	30.52	53.9%
6	The Linguistadors (Ridge)	26.70	31.21	50.3%
	UnibucKernel (SVR)	26.78	31.49	51.1%
7	Piyush Mishra	27.31	33.20	53.3%
	The Linguistadors (Linear)	35.70	39.66	33.6%
	UnibucKernel (CNN)	40.23	42.87	29.8%
	Centroid baseline	*41.38*	*48.16*	*15.8%*
	The Linguistadors (Lasso)	41.60	48.19	15.8%

Table 7: CH results. Unconstrained submissions above the horizontal line, constrained ones below.

2013; Scherrer and Stoeckle, 2016).[5] Dialect area accuracy represents the percentage of test instances whose predicted coordinates lie inside the same area as the gold coordinates.

Rather unsurprisingly, the unconstrained approaches outperform the constrained ones, but only by a small margin in the CH subtask. There is no clear winning approach among the constrained submissions. BERT (HeLju) works well in large-data settings, but underperforms on the CH subtask where classical approaches are more competitive. The ZHAW-InIT and CUBoulder-UBC systems show that a classification strategy with a fixed set of classes can outperform a regression strategy that learns to predict longitudes and latitudes directly. This finding may be due to the fact that social media posts are not randomly scattered across space, but tend to gather around a relatively small number of larger cities and agglomerations.

More generally, the DE-AT subtask has turned out to be the hardest one: only half of the submitted systems managed to beat the baseline, and unlike in the other subtasks, no system managed to halve the baseline distance. This suggests that the regional features in the DE-AT Jodel corpus are too sparse to be learned reliably.

In terms of evaluation measures, the median and mean distances are highly correlated. Dialect area accuracy also yields a similar picture overall, but some differences are noteworthy. For DE-AT, all systems clearly outperform the baseline on this measure, and the ZHAW-InIT (SVM) submission turns out to be much more competitive than the distance measures suggest. This submission confirms its advantage on the CH task, where it is indistinguishable from the unconstrained submissions in terms of dialect area accuracy.

5.4 Summary

For the first time at VarDial, we have proposed a dialect geolocation task, in which the prediction outputs are coordinate pairs rather than variety labels. The SMG task attracted a total of seven participants across three subtasks, a number that is comparable with other VarDial tasks in recent years. We received a wide range of technical solutions: solutions based on deep learning as well as traditional machine learning, constrained as well as unconstrained solutions, and regression-based as well as classification-

---

[5]The DE-AT areas are based on those used in (Hovy and Purschke, 2018), augmented with a single area covering the territory of Austria. The CH areas correspond to the 10-cluster solution presented in (Scherrer and Stoeckle, 2016).

based approaches. The best scores were obtained by unconstrained solutions based on pre-trained BERT models, on all three subtasks. Thanks to its reliance on easily available geolocated messages from social media services, another edition of the SMG task could be envisaged, possibly focusing on different language areas.

6 Uralic Language Identification ULI

The first edition of the ULI shared task was a language identification task focusing on differentiating between minority Uralic languages and distinguishing them from a large number of other languages.

We define minority Uralic languages as those languages that are not official state languages in the countries where they are spoken. This definition excludes Estonian, Finnish and Hungarian. The remaining Uralic languages are all endangered. They can also be characterized as extremely diverse, at least when it comes to their use and current situation. Some of the languages in the shared task are extinct, while others have very young and varying orthographies that are still becoming established. Nevertheless, the task also includes languages that are widely used in the modern society and have a large online presence. Most of the Uralic languages spoken in Russia are written using the Cyrillic alphabet, often with additional individual characters that differ from the character set used for Russian. Since the Uralic languages form a large and old language family, the varieties in the task are generally far apart from one another. At the same time, the task also contains closely related Uralic languages from individual branches, which share a large percentage of their vocabulary and features.

The shared task included a total of 178 languages, of which 29 were Uralic minority languages. The 29 endangered Uralic languages were considered relevant and the 148 languages non-relevant. The ULI task consisted of three tracks using the same training and testing data. The tracks differed from each other in how they were scored.

The motivation behind including the non-relevant languages in the shared task was to simulate the situation we faced when we were automatically searching for minority Uralic languages on the Internet during the Finno-Ugric Languages and the Internet project (Jauhiainen et al., 2015). The different ways of scoring the tracks was also designed to highlight the inherent difficulties of such a search. The third track did not especially focus on the relevant languages, the second track focused on the relevant languages as a group, and the first track forced the participants to consider even the most rare of the relevant languages.

The first track, ULI-RLE (Relevant languages as equals), considered all the relevant languages equal in value and the aim was to maximize their average F-score. This is important when one is interested in finding rare languages on, for example, the Internet. The F-score was calculated as a macro-averaged F1 score over the relevant languages in the training set.

The second track, ULI-RSS (Relevant sentences as equals), considered each sentence in the test set that was written in or was predicted to be in a relevant language as equals. When compared with the first track, this track gave less importance to the very rare languages as their precision was not as important when the resulting F-score was calculated. The resulting F-score was calculated as a micro-F1 over the sentences in the test set for both the sentences in the relevant languages and the ones that were predicted to be in relevant languages.

In the first two tracks, there was no difference between the non-relevant languages. All the non-relevant languages could have been labeled as English in the submissions and it would not have changed the resulting F1-scores. The third track, ULI-178 (All 178 languages as equals), however, did not focus on the 29 relevant languages, but instead the target was to maximize the average F-score over all the 178 languages present in the training set. The ULI shared task, and especially this track, was the language identification shared task with the largest number of languages used so far. The F-score was calculated as a macro-F1 score over all the languages in the training set.

6.1 Dataset

For training, we provided texts from the Wanca 2016 corpora (Jauhiainen et al., 2019a) for the relevant languages and from the Leipzig corpora collection (Goldhahn et al., 2012) for the non-relevant languages.

The number of lines for the non-relevant languages in the training data varied from 10,000 lines of Cebuano and Corsican to 3 million lines of Indonesian. As relevant language sentences in the test set from the forthcoming Wanca 2017 corpora (Jauhiainen et al., 2020b), we chose those sentences that were not present in the Wanca 2016 corpora which have been published in the Language Bank of Finland. The sentences for the non-relevant languages were from the Leipzig corpora collection. We did not create a separate set for development so the participants had to decide themselves how to use the given training material for that as well. The dataset used in the ULI shared task, as well as its creation, is described in detail by Jauhiainen et al. (2020b).

6.2 Participants and Approaches

Unfortunately, the ULI shared task had only one team submitting results to the tracks. The NRC team submitted three runs for each of the shared task tracks. All the runs used BERT-related deep neural networks taking sequences of characters as input similar to what the NRC team used when they won the CLI shared task (Jauhiainen et al., 2019b) in the previous VarDial Evaluation Campaign (Bernier-Colborne et al., 2019). The encoders of the networks were pre-trained on masked language modeling (MLM) and sentence pair classification (SPC) tasks (Devlin et al., 2019). The third run on each track was using only the information on the training set as opposed to the second run, in which the MLM was also done on the unlabeled test set in order to adapt the model. The first run on each track was a plurality voting ensemble of the six models used in the second and third runs of all the tracks.

6.3 Results

For the baseline, we used an implementation of the HeLI method equal to the one we used when evaluating language identification methods for 285 languages (Jauhiainen et al., 2017). The baseline and the NRC teams results are listed in Tables 8, 9, and 10.

Rank	Team	Run	Method	Relevant macro F_1
	baseline		HeLI	0.8004
1	NRC	2	deep neural network with adaptation to the test set	0.2996
	NRC	1	ensemble of 6 deep neural networks	0.2872
	NRC	3	deep neural network	0.2514

Table 8: ULI shaed task - RLE results.

Rank	Team	Run	Method	Relevant micro F_1
	baseline		HeLI	0.9632
1	NRC	1	ensemble of 6 deep neural networks	0.2596
	NRC	2	deep neural network with adaptation to the test set	0.1547
	NRC	3	deep neural network	0.1359

Table 9: ULI shared task - RSS results.

Rank	Team	Run	Method	Macro F_1
	baseline		HeLI	0.9252
1	NRC	2	deep neural network with adaptation to the test set	0.6751
	NRC	3	deep neural network	0.6628
	NRC	1	ensemble of 6 deep neural networks	0.6356

Table 10: ULIshared task - 178 results.

All the results submitted by the NRC team are well below the baselines. After the shared task results were announced, the NRC team investigated reasons for the low performance of their classifiers and found that the low scores were mostly due to a flaw in the function they used to sample the data for training and evaluation (Bernier-Colborne and Goutte, 2020).

6.4 Summary

Needless to say, we were not happy that the ULI task attracted the submissions of only one team. The shared tasks at VarDial have historically attracted a good number of submissions but, as previously mentioned, the VarDial Evaluation Campaign 2020 run during the early stages of the COVID-19 pandemic, a period in which significant disruption has been observed in universities and research centers worldwide. This is likely to have precluded more teams from participating. Furthermore, we acknowledge that we did not make the task easy to participate with the larger than normal training sets. The results of the participating team also suggest that the task might have been more difficult than we anticipated. Due to the low number of participants in the shared task and the challenges caused by the COVID-19 pandemic, we have decided to continue accepting submissions until the next edition of the ULI shared task. Thus, we are not yet publishing the gold-labeled test set. Instead, we will set up a web-page[6] with information on how to request the training and the test sets. The web-page will also feature a table with all the results submitted so far.

7   Conclusion

In this paper we present the results and findings of the shared tasks organized as part of the VarDial Evaluation Campaign 2020. Three shared tasks were organized this year: Romanian Dialect Identification (RDI), Social Media Variety Geolocation (SMG), and Uralic Language Identification (ULI). Each of these tasks tackled an important challenge in language and dialect identification on different languages and dialects. Furthermore, in these tasks we provided participants with new datasets that will be made freely available to the research community after the competitions.

A total of 14 teams submitted runs across the three shared tasks. We included short descriptions for each team's systems in this report and references to all 11 system description papers in Table 1. A complete description of these systems is available in the system description papers published in the VarDial workshop proceedings.

Acknowledgments

We would like to thank the shared task participants for their participation, support, and the feedback provided. We further thank the VarDial program committee for reviewing all submissions.

References

Fernando Benites, Manuela Hürlimann, Pius von Däniken, and Mark Cieliebak. 2020. ZHAW-InIT - Social Media Geolocation at VarDial 2020. In *Proceedings of VarDial*.

Gabriel Bernier-Colborne and Cyril Goutte. 2020. Challenges in neural language identification: NRC at VarDial 2020. In *Proceedings of VarDial*.

Gabriel Bernier-Colborne, Cyril Goutte, and Serge Léger. 2019. Improving cuneiform language identification with BERT. In *Proceedings of VarDial*.

Andrei M. Butnaru and Radu Ionescu. 2018. UnibucKernel Reloaded: First Place in Arabic Dialect Identification for the Second Year in a Row. In *Proceedings of VarDial*.

Andrei M. Butnaru and Radu Tudor Ionescu. 2019. MOROCO: The Moldavian and Romanian Dialectal Corpus. In *Proceedings of ACL*.

Andrea Ceolin and Hong Zhang. 2020. Discriminating between standard Romanian and Moldavian tweets using filtered character ngrams. In *Proceedings of VarDial*.

---

[6]http://urn.fi/urn:nbn:fi:lb-2020102201

Çağrı Çöltekin. 2020. Dialect identification under domain shift: Experiments with discriminating Romanian and Moldavian. In *Proceedings of VarDial*.

Jacob Devlin, Ming-Wei Chang, Kenton Lee, and Kristina Toutanova. 2019. Bert: Pre-training of deep bidirectional transformers for language understanding. In *Proceedings of NAACL*.

Ştefan Daniel Dumitrescu, Andrei-Marius Avram, and Sampo Pyysalo. 2020. The birth of Romanian BERT. In *Findings of EMNLP*.

Dirk Goldhahn, Thomas Eckart, and Uwe Quasthoff. 2012. Building Large Monolingual Dictionaries at the Leipzig Corpora Collection: From 100 to 200 Languages. In *Proceedings of LREC*.

Cyril Goutte, Serge Léger, Shervin Malmasi, and Marcos Zampieri. 2016. Discriminating Similar Languages: Evaluations and Explorations. In *Proceedings of LREC*.

Mihaela Găman and Radu Tudor Ionescu. 2020a. Combining deep learning and string kernels for the localization of Swiss German tweets. In *Proceedings of VarDial*.

Mihaela Găman and Radu Tudor Ionescu. 2020b. The Unreasonable Effectiveness of Machine Learning in Moldavian versus Romanian Dialect Identification. *arXiv preprint arXiv:2007.15700*.

Dirk Hovy and Christoph Purschke. 2018. Capturing regional variation with distributed place representations and geographic retrofitting. In *Proceedings of EMNLP*.

Mans Hulden, Miikka Silfverberg, and Jerid Francom. 2015. Kernel density estimation for text-based geolocation. In *Proceedings of AAAI*.

Radu Tudor Ionescu and Andrei Butnaru. 2017. Learning to identify Arabic and German dialects using multiple kernels. In *Proceedings of VarDial*.

Radu Tudor Ionescu, Marius Popescu, and Aoife Cahill. 2016. String kernels for native language identification: Insights from behind the curtains. *Computational Linguistics*, 42(3):491–525.

Heidi Jauhiainen, Tommi Jauhiainen, and Krister Lindén. 2015. The Finno-Ugric Languages and The Internet Project. In *Proceedings of IWCLUL*.

Tommi Jauhiainen, Krister Lindén, and Heidi Jauhiainen. 2017. Evaluation of Language Identification Methods Using 285 Languages. In *Proceedings of NoDaLiDa*.

Heidi Jauhiainen, Tommi Jauhiainen, and Krister Linden. 2019a. Wanca in Korp: Text corpora for underresourced Uralic languages. In *Proceedings of RDHUM*.

Tommi Jauhiainen, Heidi Jauhiainen, Tero Alstola, and Krister Lindén. 2019b. Language and dialect identification of cuneiform texts. In *Proceedings of VarDial*.

Tommi Jauhiainen, Marco Lui, Marcos Zampieri, Timothy Baldwin, and Krister Lindén. 2019c. Automatic Language Identification in Texts: A Survey. *Journal of Artificial Intelligence Research*, 65:675–782.

Tommi Jauhiainen, Heidi Jauhiainen, and Krister Lindén. 2020a. Experiments in language variety geolocation and dialect identification. In *Proceedings of VarDial*.

Tommi Jauhiainen, Heidi Jauhiainen, Niko Partanen, and Krister Lindén. 2020b. Uralic Language Identification (ULI) 2020 shared task dataset and the Wanca 2017 corpora. In *Proceedings of VarDial*.

Nikita Kitaev, Lukasz Kaiser, and Anselm Levskaya. 2019. Reformer: The Efficient Transformer. In *Proceedings of ICLR*.

Ritesh Kumar, Bornini Lahiri, Deepak Alok, Atul Kr. Ojha, Mayank Jain, Abdul Basit, and Yogesh Dawar. 2018. Automatic Identification of Closely-related Indian Languages: Resources and Experiments. In *Proceedings of LREC*.

Alfred Lameli. 2013. *Strukturen im Sprachraum: Analysen zur arealtypologischen Komplexität der Dialekte in Deutschland*. Walter de Gruyter.

Nikola Ljubešić, Tanja Samardžić, and Curdin Derungs. 2016. TweetGeo - a tool for collecting, processing and analysing geo-encoded linguistic data. In *Proceedings of COLING*.

Shervin Malmasi, Marcos Zampieri, Nikola Ljubešić, Preslav Nakov, Ahmed Ali, and Jörg Tiedemann. 2016. Discriminating between Similar Languages and Arabic Dialect Identification: A Report on the Third DSL Shared Task. In *Proceedings of VarDial*.

Piyush Mishra. 2020. Geolocation of tweets with a BiLSTM regression model. In *Proceedings of VarDial*.

Cristian Popa and Vlad Ștefănescu. 2020. Applying multilingual and monolingual Transformer-based models for dialect identification. In *Proceedings of VarDial*.

Petru Rebeja and Dan Cristea. 2020. A dual-encoding system for dialect classification. In *Proceedings of VarDial*.

Tanja Samardžić, Yves Scherrer, and Elvira Glaser. 2016. ArchiMob–A corpus of spoken Swiss German. In *Proceedings of LREC*.

Yves Scherrer and Nikola Ljubešić. 2020. HeLju@VarDial 2020: Social media variety geolocation with BERT models. In *Proceedings of VarDial*.

Yves Scherrer and Philipp Stoeckle. 2016. A quantitative approach to Swiss German – Dialectometric analyses and comparisons of linguistic levels. *Dialectologia et Geolinguistica*, 1(24):92–125.

Liling Tan, Marcos Zampieri, Nikola Ljubešic, and Jörg Tiedemann. 2014. Merging Comparable Data Sources for the Discrimination of Similar Languages: The DSL Corpus Collection. In *Proceedings of BUCC*.

Nianheng Wu, Eric DeMattos, Kwok Him So, Pin-zhen Chen, and Çağrı Çöltekin. 2019. Language discrimination and transfer learning for similar languages: Experiments with feature combinations and adaptation. In *Proceedings of VarDial*.

George-Eduard Zaharia, Andrei-Marius Avram, Dumitru-Clementin Cercel, and Traian Rebedea. 2020. Exploring the power of Romanian BERT for dialect identification. In *Proceedings of VarDial*.

Marcos Zampieri, Shervin Malmasi, Nikola Ljubešić, Preslav Nakov, Ahmed Ali, Jörg Tiedemann, Yves Scherrer, and Noëmi Aepli. 2017. Findings of the VarDial Evaluation Campaign 2017. In *Proceedings of VarDial*.

Marcos Zampieri, Shervin Malmasi, Preslav Nakov, Ahmed Ali, Suwon Shon, James Glass, Yves Scherrer, Tanja Samardžić, Nikola Ljubešić, Jörg Tiedemann, Chris van der Lee, Stefan Grondelaers, Nelleke Oostdijk, Dirk Speelman, Antal van den Bosch, Ritesh Kumar, Bornini Lahiri, and Mayank Jain. 2018. Language Identification and Morphosyntactic Tagging: The Second VarDial Evaluation Campaign. In *Proceedings of VarDial*.

Marcos Zampieri, Shervin Malmasi, Yves Scherrer, Tanja Samardžić, Francis Tyers, Miikka Silfverberg, Natalia Klyueva, Tung-Le Pan, Chu-Ren Huang, Radu Tudor Ionescu, Andrei Butnaru, and Tommi Jauhiainen. 2019. A Report on the Third VarDial Evaluation Campaign. In *Proceedings of VarDial*.

Marcos Zampieri, Preslav Nakov, and Yves Scherrer. 2020. Natural Language Processing for Similar Languages, Varieties, and Dialects: A Survey. *Natural Language Engineering*, 26:595–612.

Xiang Zhang, Junbo Zhao, and Yann LeCun. 2015. Character-level Convolutional Networks for Text Classification. In *Proceedings of NIPS*, pages 649–657.

ASR for Non-standardised Languages with Dialectal Variation: the case of Swiss German

Iuliia Nigmatulina[1], Tannon Kew[2], Tanja Samardžić[1]
[1]URPP Language and Space, University of Zurich
[2]Department of Computational Linguistics, University of Zurich
{iuliia.nigmatulina, tanja.samardzic}@uzh.ch, kew@cl.uzh.ch

Abstract

Strong regional variation, together with the lack of standard orthography, makes Swiss German automatic speech recognition (ASR) particularly difficult in a multi-dialectal setting. This paper focuses on one of the many challenges, namely, the choice of the output text to represent non-standardised Swiss German. We investigate two potential options: a) *dialectal* writing – approximate phonemic transcriptions that provide close correspondence between grapheme labels and the acoustic signal but are highly inconsistent and b) *normalised* writing – transcriptions resembling standard German that are relatively consistent but distant from the acoustic signal. To find out which writing facilitates Swiss German ASR, we build several systems using the Kaldi toolkit and a dataset covering 14 regional varieties. A formal comparison shows that the system trained on the normalised transcriptions achieves better results in word error rate (WER) (29.39%) but underperforms at the character level, suggesting dialectal transcriptions offer a viable solution for downstream applications where dialectal differences are important. To better assess word-level performance for dialectal transcriptions, we use a flexible WER measure (FlexWER). When evaluated with this metric, the system trained on dialectal transcriptions outperforms that trained on the normalised writing. Besides establishing a benchmark for Swiss German multi-dialectal ASR, our findings can be helpful in designing ASR systems for other languages without standard orthography.

Index Terms: speech recognition, human-computer interaction, Swiss German dialects

1 Introduction

Over the last few years, advancements in speech technology (word error rates (WER) less than 5%, (Chiu et al., 2018; Xiong et al., 2018; Wang et al., 2019)) have lead to an increased demand for automatic speech recognition (ASR) systems outside of a small set of standardised, high resource languages. However, developing ASR systems for non-standard languages and dialects is difficult since, in addition to the lack of a writing standard, one has to deal with a high degree of regional variation coupled with limited training resources. Thus, in such settings, WERs of more than 40% are common (Ali et al., 2017).

Swiss German is a typical case of a non-standard language for which there is a growing interest in ASR technology. The term *Swiss German* describes a family of mutually intelligible Allemanic dialects spoken in the northern two-thirds of Switzerland. Despite carrying the official status of a dialect, Swiss German is spoken in all spheres of oral communication and has long enjoyed a high degree of cultural value and prestige, unlike many other dialects (Hogg et al., 1984). In the past, the linguistic situation in the region has been described as a case of 'medial diglossia' (Kolde, 1981), in which standard German is used for written communication and spoken in formal settings, while Swiss German is primarily used for everyday spoken communication. Being the primary language for approximately five million people in the region, Swiss German has a growing demand for automatic processing and in particular ASR. However, without a single orthography it is difficult to determine not only how to convert speech to text, but also *which* text to convert it to.

This work is licensed under a Creative Commons Attribution 4.0 International Licence. Licence details: http://creativecommons.org/licenses/by/4.0/.

Proceedings of the 7th VarDial Workshop on NLP for Similar Languages, Varieties and Dialects, pages 15–24
Barcelona, Spain (Online), December 13, 2020

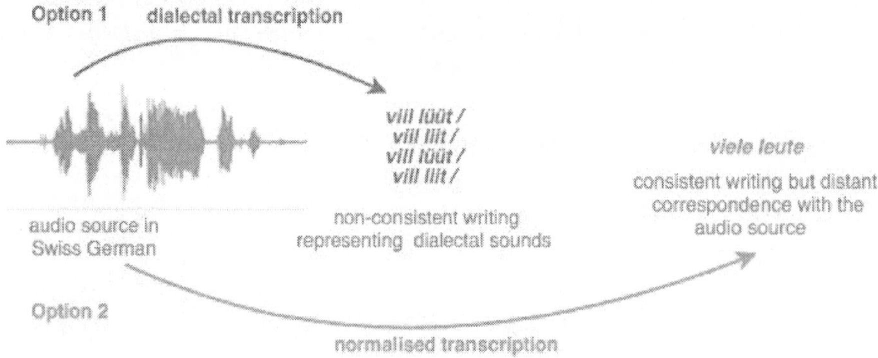

Figure 1: Two potential approaches to Swiss German ASR for the phrase *'viele Leute'* ('many people').

In this paper, we propose the first multi-dialect speech-to-text (STT) framework for Swiss German dialects[1] and explore the efficacy of two potential target textual representations. The first uses *dialectal transcriptions* (option 1 in Figure 1), a writing system proposed by (Dieth, 1986) intended to accommodate all dialects of Swiss German in a manner which closely reflects the sound of the spoken language, while still being easily readable. This is a loosely phonemic spelling system that draws on familiar spelling norms from standard German, restricting the space of possible writings for a given word. It is, however, often subject to transcribers' interpretation leading to considerable intra- and inter-dialectal inconsistency. The second option is to use *normalised transcriptions* (option 2 in Figure 1), a word-level many-to-one mapping between Swiss variants and a single canonical writing resembling standard German whenever possible. Using a normalised transcription should aid ASR by reducing the effect of lexical variability on the target side. On the other hand, it might be harder to establish alignments between the dialectal sound and the standard writing which does not represent the original pronunciation. There is currently no conclusive evidence as to which of the two options yields better results.

The experiments presented in this paper are intended to identify an optimal approach to dealing with Swiss German and non-standard languages in general. The resulting ASR systems, featuring a single unified acoustic model (AM) trained with the time-delay neural network (TDNN) architecture (Waibel et al., 1989) following Kaldi's[2] WSJ *chain* recipe (Peddinti et al., 2015), are the first multi-dialectal solutions for Swiss German and constitute a baseline for future improvements.

2 Related Work

In addressing the topic of multi-dialectal ASR for non-standard languages, our work draws on previous studies carried out in the context of Arabic dialects (e.g. Ali et al. (2014; 2016)). In particular, Khurana et al. (2016) successfully trained a multi-dialect ASR system with a single acoustic model (AM) using approximately 1,200 hours of dialectal Arabic speech data. Leveraging a combination of TDNNs and (bidirectional) long-short term memory networks (bi-LSTMs), trained on speed and volume perturbed data, they reported a WER of 14.7% on held-out test data sampled from different dialects.

In the context of Swiss German, previous studies on ASR have typically focused on one particular regional variety. For example, Imseng et al. (2012) trained an ASR system on the MediaParl corpus, containing Swiss German speech data from the canton of Valais with text transcriptions in standard German. The authors used a triphone-based AM trained with Gaussian mixture models and Hidden Markoc Models (GMM-HMM) and a bigram language model (LM), reporting WER scores of 68.4%. Following this, more advanced AMs have been applied to the same dataset, namely a three-layer ANN-HMM (Razavi et al., 2014), a three-layer CNN-HMM (Palaz, 2016), and a three-layer sMBR discriminative ANN-HMM optimised towards the state-level error rate (Dubagunta and Doss, 2019), with WERs of

---

[1] `https://github.com/yunigma/Kaldi-for-ASR-of-Swiss-German` (10.10.20).
[2] `http://kaldi-asr.org/doc/index.html` (13.08.20).

25.5%, 23.5% and 18.7%, respectively. In another study, Garner et al. (2014) trained an ASR system on a corpus of radio news broadcasts in Valais German annotated with approximate dialectal transcriptions, achieving 19.4% WER. Note though that the language model used (LM) was trained on the training and evaluation data together and thus failed to provide an accurate estimation of performance on unseen data. Finally, Stadtschnitzer and Schmidt (2018) adapted a standard German ASR system to better handle Swiss German varieties given a small corpus of weather reports, reporting WERs of 23.8% on a challenge corpus of dialectal and standard German speech developed by Baum et al. (2010).

An important aspect of non-standardised-language speech recognition is its evaluation. Usual metrics such as WER and character error rate (CER) assume that only one word or character is correct for each particular position in a sequence. For languages without a standardised orthography, there can be multiple permissible spelling variants for the same word. Therefore, neither WER nor CER are flexible enough to provide an accurate picture of system performance. Ali et al. (2017) proposed WERd (word error rate for dialects) for evaluating dialectal Arabic ASR. They gathered a large collection of potential spelling variants from social media, using a small context window for a given target word or phrase. Valid variants were then found according to occurrence frequencies and normalised with edit distance scores. Then, when comparing the system hypothesis to the reference transcription, a word was considered correct if deemed a valid spelling variant of the corresponding word in the reference. In line with this approach, we exploit the many-to-one mappings provided by the normalised transcriptions in our corpus to better evaluate performance on the dialectal transcriptions.

3   Data

For our experiments, we used the second release of the ArchiMob corpus of Swiss German (Samardžić et al., 2016; Scherrer et al., 2019). The corpus consists of 43 interview recordings with native speakers in 14 different Swiss German dialects, totaling approximately 70 hours of raw speech data.[3] These interviews have been manually transcribed by five native-speaker annotators, with the audio signals aligned to utterance segments typically of around 4-8 seconds in length.

3.1   Transcription Types

The ArchiMob corpus provides two types of transcriptions. Firstly, the Dieth orthography, which constitutes the dialectal transcriptions, is intended to convey the true sound of spoken Swiss German using spelling conventions from standard German (Dieth, 1986). This spelling 'system' essentially guides the writer towards producing relatively consistent spellings, making it easier for anyone familiar with German to read, while still representing the variety and pronunciations of *all* Swiss German dialects. Thus, this orthography can be considered a loosely phonemic textual representation, albeit with considerable variation. Despite the fact that it has not been adopted for use by native speakers, it is commonly used by trained annotators for the purpose of manually transcribing Swiss German speech material according to their intuition of correct pronunciation.

The second type of transcription is a semi-automatically normalised version of the original Dieth transcriptions, where all surface form spelling variants of the same word are mapped to a single normalised form that more closely resembles standard German. This normalisation layer was attained by applying character-level machine translation trained on a small amount of manually normalised transcriptions from the corpus (see Samardžić et al. (2015) , Scherrer et al. (2019)). While this layer by no means constitutes a translation into standard German, it provides a word-level annotation layer that is intended to facilitate automatic processing. Comparing the distinct word types of these two transcriptions shows a considerable effect, reducing the number of distinct word forms (types) from 73,899 to 31,755. Table 1 provides some example instances where multiple Swiss German surface forms in the dialectal transcriptions are mapped to a single standard German form.

---

[3]Note, dialects are not equally represented in the ArchiMob dataset. The approximate amount of speech data per regional variety is given as follows: Zurich (20hrs), Aargau (10hrs), Bern (8hrs), Lucerne (8hrs), Basel-Stadt (6.5hrs), Glarus (3.3hrs), Uri (1.6hrs), Schwyz (1.6hrs), Valais (1.6hrs), Nidwalden (1.6hrs), Graubünden (1.6hrs), Basel-Landschaft (1.6hrs), Schaffhausen (1.6hrs), St. Gallen (1.6hrs).

Normalised	Dialectal
abbauen	abbaue, abboue, abbuue
abend	aabe, aabed, aaben, aabet, aabid, aabig, abed, abend, abet, abig,
	abud, obet, obig, oobig, zabig, äbig, òòbed, òòbig
mitbekommen	mitbecho, mitbechoo, mitbichoo, mitbikho

Table 1: Examples of normalisation on dialectal surface variants in the Dieth orthography.

3.2 Data Preparation

For the purpose of our experiments, we split the corpus into training, development and evaluation sets so that they all have a balanced distribution of dialects and speakers. After preprocessing and removing utterances containing overlapping speech signals and anonymised personal names, the sets were reduced to 67,693, 1,710, 1,486 speech utterances, respectively, totalling slightly more than 60 hours of speech data. The small size of the development and evaluation sets was motivated in order to leverage as much data as possible for AM training.

4 Methods

In this section, we describe our approach to building a multi-dialectal ASR system for Swiss German which follows the classical pipeline approach depicted in Figure 2. In particular, we discuss the steps taken to establish a suitable pronunciation lexicon, our choices in training AMs and LMs and the evaluation set up.

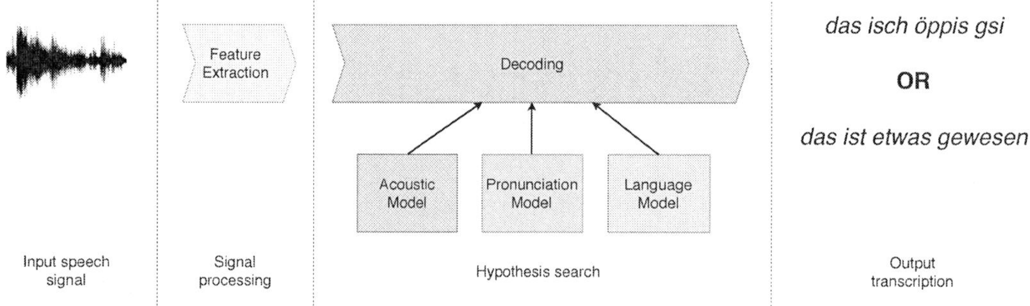

Figure 2: Standard ASR pipeline for Swiss German with potential target textual representations. Note, the output transcription of an input utterance is intended to be either *dialectal* (top) or *normalised* (bottom) depending on the system, not both.

4.1 Pronunciation Lexicon

We took different approaches in establishing pronunciation lexicons for each of the two target textual representations. First, in the case of dialectal writing, we relied on the loosely phonemic representation and derived a pronunciation string for each written word in the training set by segmenting its constituent graphemes with simple heuristics. For example, Swiss German *schwiirigkait* (German *Schwierigkeit*, English 'difficulty') is mapped to the pronunciation string 'sch w i r i g k ai t'.

Second, in the case of normalised writing, we exploited an 11,000-word pronunciation dictionary, mapping standard German words to their Swiss German pronunciations (Schmidt et al., 2020). This dictionary contains manually annotated pronunciation strings (in the SAMPA alphabet (Wells and others, 1997)) for six major regional varieties, namely Zurich, St. Gallen, Bern, Basel, Visp and Nidwalden. To complete the coverage of our data set, we trained a transformer-based a grapheme-to-phoneme (g2p) model[4] on the available pairs (standard German, Swiss SAMPA) and applied it on the words for which

---

[4] `https://github.com/cmusphinx/g2p-seq2seq` (12.08.20).

manual Swiss SAMPA annotation is missing. We trained the g2p model with the default settings[5] using the pronunciations given for only one of the regional varieties, namely Zurich.

While the overall word-level accuracy of the g2p model, estimated on a held out test set, was only 51.6%, the output still proved useful for the ASR pipeline since it provided good coverage with plausible g2p mappings confirmed by manual inspection of the output. Table 2 shows the percentage of lexical coverage in the train, validation and test sets for each transcription type after these steps.

Split	Dialectal	Normalised
Train	100%	99.9%
Dev	80.2%	82.7%
Test	79.9%	84.8%

Table 2: Pronunciation lexicon coverage on dataset splits. Note, while coverage of the normalised training set is almost complete, a small number of words were missed due to a mismatch in graphemes between the g2p training data and the ArchiMob training set.

4.2 Language Model

The language modeling component in all systems is a statistical N-gram LM. An intrinsic evaluation of several techniques, using test set perplexity (PPL) as a metric, revealed that 3-gram LMs with interpolated modified Kneser-Ney smoothing (Chen and Goodman, 1999), as implemented with MITLM (Hsu and Glass, 2008)[6], consistently yielded the best performance for the dialectal transcriptions. Meanwhile, 5-gram LMs provided additional improvement for the normalised transcriptions. We used these settings for our experiments with varied size of the training data.

The ArchiMob corpus training set provides a total of 76K text utterances which we used for training our base LMs. To test the impact of a larger LM, we created an additional LM trained on the ArchiMob corpus plus some out-of-domain (OOD) data. In order to derive the optimum LM, we gradually concatenated utterances from additional corpora selected for each transcription type individually and trained a series of 3-gram LMs, each time increasing the number of training utterances by 10,000. We first added Swiss corpora and then proceeded with standard German. In order to ensure comparability between LMs, the vocabulary must be consistent (Buck et al., 2014). Therefore, we restricted it to match that of the ArchiMob corpus.

Figure 3 depicts the resulting test set PPL scores with the variable increase in training utterances. As expected, dialectal spelling LMs have considerably higher PPLs than their normalised counterparts. This indicates the challenge of handling a high degree of lexical variety. For both transcription types, however, slight improvements in test set PPL are attained by including a small amount of OOD data from the additional corpora. For dialectal spelling, the minimum PPL is achieved with up to 90,000 utterances, while for normalised text, PPL starts to increase slowly after 80,000 utterances. Following these tests, we selected larger LMs for our ASR experiments, namely the 90k-utterance LM for dialectal writing and the 80k-utterance LM for normalised writing.

4.3 Flexible Evaluation: FlexWER

To score the performance of the systems, besides using the standard metrics of WER and CER, we introduce a soft evaluation measure called FlexWER. The general idea follows Ali et al. (2017), however, we rely on the word-level mapping between the dialectal and the normalised transcriptions provided in the ArchiMob corpus rather than using external sources. Since in our test set we dealt with a closed vocabulary from the corpus, we do not introduce any further metrics, such as an edit distance threshold. Using this measure, a word in the system output hypothesis transcription is considered correct if it shares the same normalised word as the corresponding word in the ground-truth transcription.

---

[5] Default settings for g2p-seq2seq are as follows: size of each hidden layer = 256, number of layers = 3, size of the filter layer in a convolutional layer = 512, number of heads in multi-attention mechanism = 4.

[6] https://github.com/mitlm/mitlm (10.08.20).

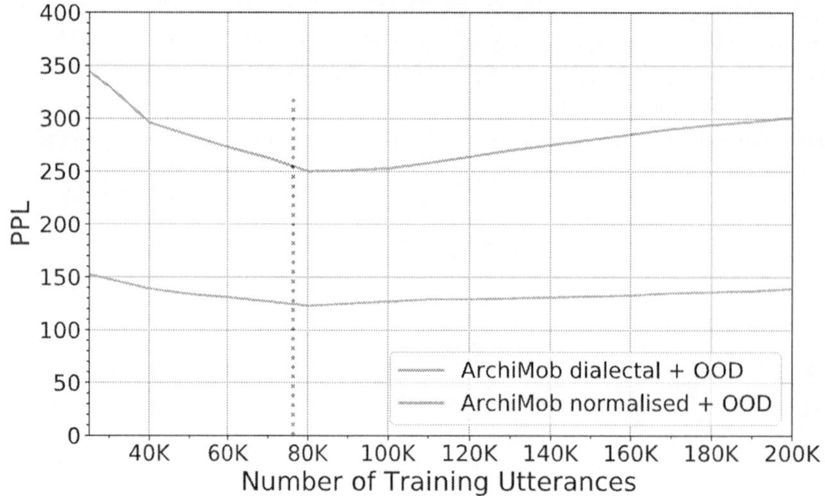

Figure 3: Test set PPL scores for LMs trained on the dialectal transcriptions and normalised transcriptions with additional OOD data. The grey dotted line indicates the upper limit of in-domain utterances (76K).

4.4 Experimental Setup

As a baseline, we built an ASR system based on the WSJ recipe[7] provided in the Kaldi toolkit. We used 13-dimensional Mel-Frequency Cepstral Coefficients (MFCC) features with cepstral mean-variance normalisation (CMVN), the first and second derivatives, and Linear Discriminative Analysis (LDA) and Maximum Likelihood Linear Transform (MLLT) transformations. The AM was discriminatively trained using a DNN with state-level minimum bayes risk (sMBR) criterion. The alignment between acoustic signal segments and transcriptions was attained with the GMM-HMM discriminative model with 4,000 senones and 40,000 Gaussians. Since no multi-dialectal ASR baseline exists for Swiss German, we decided to use this simple Kaldi setup as a starting point for our experiments as it allows for comparison between the contributions made by both the AM and LM components. We trained one AM on the dialectal transcriptions and a second AM on the normalised transcriptions and combined these with the pronunciation lexicons and LMs described above to derive our final systems.

For the main models, the TDNN architecture from the WSJ *chain* recipe was adapted (Peddinti et al., 2015) based on the GMM-HMM alignment from Kaldi pipeline. To increase the amount of training data and improve its robustness, we performed audio speed perturbation with speed factors of 0.9, 1.0, 1.1, followed by volume perturbation. In addition to the features used in the baseline model, we also included 100-dimensional iVectors extracted from each speech frame in order to normalise the variation between speakers and dialectal varieties.

In total, we trained six different systems (three for each transcription type): (i) **NNET-DISC-baseLM** (baseline) — discriminatively trained NN AM with the base LM trained on the ArchiMob data only; (ii) **TDNN-iVector-baseLM** — TDNN AM with the base LM; (iii) **TDNN-iVector-dial90k** — TDNN AM with the LM trained on the ArchiMob and OOD data; (iv) **NNET-DISC-baseLM normalised** — similar to the baseline set up but trained with the normalised transcriptions; (v) **TDNN-iVector-baseLM normalised** — similar to the TDNN-iVector-baseLM set up but trained with the normalised transcriptions; (vi) **TDNN-iVector-norm80k** — TDNN AM with the LM trained on the normalised ArchiMob transcriptions and OOD data.

All the systems are evaluated with the standard WER measure on both development and test sets. The systems trained on the dialectal transcription were additionally evaluated with FlexWER measure to account for permissible spelling variation. Finally, we report CER scores too. While this measure

---

[7]`https://github.com/kaldi-asr/kaldi/tree/master/egs/wsj` (01.05.20).

Transcription	AM	LM	Dev			Test		
			WER	FlexWER	CER	WER	FlexWER	CER
dialectal	NNET-DISC (baseline)	dial-baseLM	54.85	32.87	22.7	54.39	32.09	22.19
dialectal	TDNN-iVector	dial-baseLM	43.18	23.3	15.23	42.38	21.53	14.81
dialectal	TDNN-iVector	dial90k	41.88	21.94	14.97	42.16	**21.27**	**14.64**
normalised	NNET-DISC	norm-baseLM	43.30	–	24.82	40.81	–	23.19
normalised	TDNN-iVector	norm-baseLM	31.96	–	16.97	29.91	–	15.20
normalised	TDNN-iVector	norm80k	31.65	–	16.48	**29.39**	–	14.77

Table 3: WER/FlexWER (where applicable) and CER evaluation of the models.

is typically used when the word boundaries are unclear, we use CER as an indicator of subword-level matches, which are potentially interesting for capturing dialectal variation.

Note that the main goal of our experimental setup is not to establish the advantage of one model over another (e.g. TDNN over NNET-DISC), but to investigate the effect of the writing choice on the target side. To observe this effect, one should compare each dialectal setting with its corresponding normalised setting in Table 3.

5 Results & Discussion

The evaluation results presented in Table 3 indicate that according to the standard WER metric, the best system for multi-dialectal ASR for Swiss German is the one trained on the normalised transcriptions, with a test set WER of 29.39% (see the Appendix for examples of model predictions). Normalised transcriptions effectively reduce the high degree of noise in the transcriptions, allowing for more reliable and robust LMs and also reducing the amount of OOV words in our automatically extended lexicon. The better performance of these models on the test set compared to the development set may be explained by a slightly higher lexicon coverage for the test set: 84.8% vs. 82.7% (see Table 2).

If we consider the FlexWER evaluation measure, which accounts for permissible spelling variants, the best scores are achieved by the dialectal system TDNN-iVector-dial90k (21.27%). The major disadvantage of systems trained on dialectal transcriptions is that the higher degree of lexical variability hinders the contribution of the LM and, for getting more reliable performance estimation, additional normalisation of the results, or even manual evaluation, should be performed. At the same time, the normalised models trained on transcriptions that poorly reflect the pronunciation and thus rely on a simple g2p-based pronunciation lexicon generally miss more subword-level information. According to CER, which is more sensitive to more precise correspondence between the acoustic signal and the annotation than WER, the systems trained on the dialectal transcriptions perform slightly better than their normalised counterparts. This is most noticeable on the development set, where TDNN-iVector-dial90k and TDNN-iVector-norm80k systems score 14.97% and 16.48%, respectively. Therefore, these models may be preferable when dialectal variability is desirable in the output transcriptions.

For the normalised transcriptions, leveraging a slightly larger LM results in only minor improvements in WER over the baseline. We hypothesise that this is a consequence of the restricted domain of the ArchiMob dataset, which limits the effectiveness of any additional information provided by extending LM training data. Further evaluation on OOD data is still needed to answer the question of how well the system is able to adapt to new domains given improved LMs.

The evaluation results can differ between dialects depending on how well a dialect is represented in training data and the degree to which certain dialects differ from the majority of the training data. To attain an impression of these effects, we report WER scores as a distribution over individual dialects (see Figure 4).

Firstly, the effect of the proportion of a corresponding dialect in the training data does not seem to be borne out. The Graubünden dialect has the lowest WER but is represented in the ArchiMob corpus with only a single interview. Similarly, Basel-Landschaft and Schaffhausen varieties, which also have

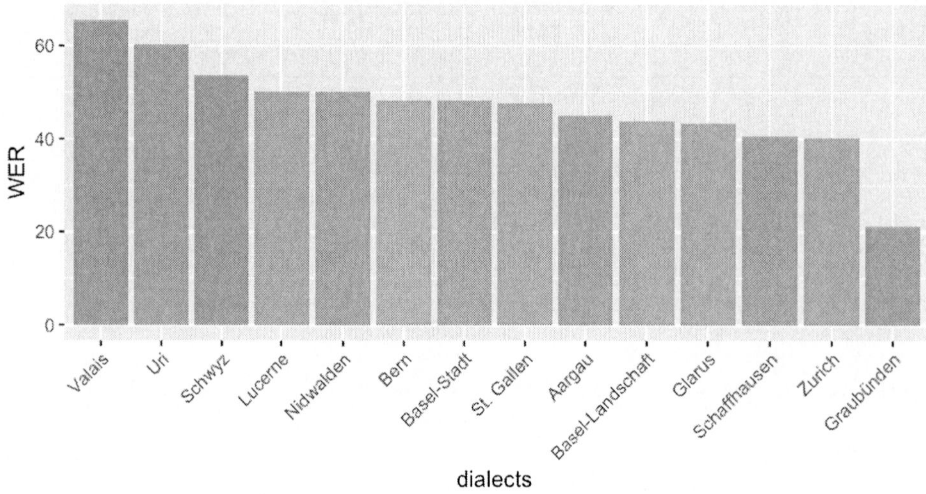

Figure 4: WER of the dialectal TDNN-iVector system evaluated on different dialects.

only one interview each in the corpus, show lower error rates than regional varieties which are well-represented in the corpus (e.g. Aargau, Bern and Lucerne).

Secondly, the degree of similarity between different dialects demands further investigation and is out of the scope of the current paper. Some tendencies, however, can be noticed from the plot: the system performs considerably worse when evaluated on the Valais dialect compared to other dialects. This observation reflects the fact that Swiss German from the canton of Valais is further removed from the other varieties.

Most notably, evaluation on the Graubünden dialect is consistently good, outperforming the results on the Zurich dialect which comprises the largest part of the training data (12 interviews). This peculiarity may be due to the fact that recognition of a dialect, in our case, is very speaker specific. In the ArchiMob corpus, many dialects have only one interview. This means that they are also represented by only a single speaker. Therefore, in order to attain a more reliable picture of dialect-specific speech recognition with a unified ASR system, more speakers are needed for under-represented dialects.

A general limitation of our work is that it uses a relatively closed domain covered by the ArchiMob corpus (personal narratives on a similar topic). To get an idea of how our models perform outside of this domain, we perform an additional OOD evaluation for our dialectal systems using a small data set with appropriate Dieth orthography transcriptions. The results of this evaluation are predictably worse: 59.81% WER and 37.83% FlexWER for the TDNN-iVector-baseLM system. We suspect that potential improvements can be gained by (a) applying advanced training architectures including end-to-end systems; and, of course, (b) increasing the amount of training data to cover more domains and speakers. Since this paper focuses on the efficacy of the target textual representation and the corresponding pronunciation lexicons, we leave further investigations of these factors for future work.

6 Conclusion

In this paper, we have introduced the first multi-dialect ASR framework for Swiss German that exploits a single unified acoustic model. We have tested currently popular techniques for dealing with noisy data and established a solid baseline for future studies in ASR for Swiss German. We have shown a clear benefit of working with normalised transcriptions (provided a suitable pronunciation lexicon is at hand), but also that loosely phonemic dialectal writing yields output potentially interesting for downstream applications specifically targeting regional variation in non-standard languages.

References

Ahmed Ali, Yifan Zhang, Patrick Cardinal, Najim Dahak, Stephan Vogel, and James Glass. 2014. A complete kaldi recipe for building arabic speech recognition systems. In *2014 IEEE spoken language technology workshop (SLT)*, pages 525–529. IEEE.

Ahmed Ali, Peter Bell, James Glass, Yacine Messaoui, Hamdy Mubarak, Steve Renals, and Yifan Zhang. 2016. The mgb-2 challenge: Arabic multi-dialect broadcast media recognition. In *2016 IEEE Spoken Language Technology Workshop (SLT)*, pages 279–284. IEEE.

Ahmed Ali, Preslav Nakov, Peter Bell, and Steve Renals. 2017. Werd: Using social text spelling variants for evaluating dialectal speech recognition. In *2017 IEEE Automatic Speech Recognition and Understanding Workshop (ASRU)*, pages 141–148. IEEE.

Doris Baum, Daniel Schneider, Jochen Schwenninger, Barbara Samlowski, Thomas Winkler, and Joachim Köhler. 2010. Disco-a german evaluation corpus for challenging problems in the broadcast domain. *LREC 2010*.

Christian Buck, Kenneth Heafield, and Bas Van Ooyen. 2014. N-gram Counts and Language Models from the Common Crawl. In *Proceedings of the Ninth International Conference on Language Resources and Evaluation (LREC)*, Reykjavik, Iceland. European Language Resources Association.

Stanley F Chen and Joshua Goodman. 1999. An Empirical Study of Smoothing Techniques for Language Modeling. *Computer Speech & Language*, 13(4):359–394.

Chung-Cheng Chiu, Tara N Sainath, Yonghui Wu, Rohit Prabhavalkar, Patrick Nguyen, Zhifeng Chen, Anjuli Kannan, Ron J Weiss, Kanishka Rao, Ekaterina Gonina, et al. 2018. State-of-the-art speech recognition with sequence-to-sequence models. In *2018 IEEE International Conference on Acoustics, Speech and Signal Processing (ICASSP)*, pages 4774–4778. IEEE.

Eugen Dieth. 1986. *Schwyzertütschi Dialäktschrift: Dieth-Schreibung*, volume 1. Sauerländer.

S Pavankumar Dubagunta and Mathew Magimai Doss. 2019. Segment-level training of anns based on acoustic confidence measures for hybrid hmm/ann speech recognition. In *ICASSP 2019-2019 IEEE International Conference on Acoustics, Speech and Signal Processing (ICASSP)*, pages 6435–6439. IEEE.

Philip N Garner, David Imseng, and Thomas Meyer. 2014. Automatic speech recognition and translation of a swiss german dialect: Walliserdeutsch. In *Proceedings of Interspeech*, number CONF.

Michael A Hogg, Nicholas Joyce, and Dominic Abrams. 1984. Diglossia in switzerland? a social identity analysis of speaker evaluations. *Journal of language and social psychology*, 3(3):185–196.

Bo-June (Paul) Hsu and James R. Glass. 2008. Iterative language model estimation: Efficient data structure & algorithms. In *In Proceedings of the Ninth Annual Conference of the International Speech Communication Association*, pages 841–844, Brisbane, Australia.

David Imseng, Hervé Bourlard, Holger Caesar, Philip N Garner, Gwénolé Lecorvé, and Alexandre Nanchen. 2012. Mediaparl: Bilingual mixed language accented speech database. In *2012 IEEE Spoken Language Technology Workshop (SLT)*, pages 263–268. IEEE.

Sameer Khurana and Ahmed Ali. 2016. Qcri advanced transcription system (qats) for the arabic multi-dialect broadcast media recognition: Mgb-2 challenge. In *2016 IEEE Spoken Language Technology Workshop (SLT)*, pages 292–298. IEEE.

Gottfried Kolde. 1981. *Sprachkontakte in Gemischtsprachigen Städten: Vergleichende Untersuchungen Über Voraussetzungen Und Formen Sprachlicher Interaktion Verschiedensprachiger Jugendlicher in Den Schweitzer Städten Biel/Bienne Und Fribourg/Freiburg*, volume 37. Steiner Franz Verlag.

Dimitri Palaz. 2016. Towards end-to-end speech recognition. Technical report, EPFL.

Vijayaditya Peddinti, Daniel Povey, and Sanjeev Khudanpur. 2015. A time delay neural network architecture for efficient modeling of long temporal contexts. In *Sixteenth Annual Conference of the International Speech Communication Association*.

Marzieh Razavi, Ramya Rasipuram, and Mathew Magimai-Doss. 2014. On modeling context-dependent clustered states: Comparing hmm/gmm, hybrid hmm/ann and kl-hmm approaches. In *2014 IEEE international conference on acoustics, speech and signal processing (ICASSP)*, pages 7659–7663. IEEE.

Tanja Samardžić, Yves Scherrer, and Elvira Glaser. 2015. Normalising orthographic and dialectal variants for the automatic processing of Swiss German. In *Proceedings of the 7th Language and Technology Conference*.

Tanja Samardžić, Yves Scherrer, and Elvira Glaser. 2016. ArchiMob - a corpus of spoken Swiss German. In Nicoletta Calzolari (Conference Chair), Khalid Choukri, Thierry Declerck, Sara Goggi, Marko Grobelnik, Bente Maegaard, Joseph Mariani, Helene Mazo, Asuncion Moreno, Jan Odijk, and Stelios Piperidis, editors, *Proceedings of the Tenth International Conference on Language Resources and Evaluation (LREC 2016)*, Paris, France, may. European Language Resources Association (ELRA).

Yves Scherrer, Tanja Samardžić, and Elvira Glaser. 2019. Digitising swiss german: how to process and study a polycentric spoken language. *Language Resources and Evaluation*, pages 1–35.

Larissa Schmidt, Lucy Linder, Sandra Djambazovska, Alexandros Lazaridis, Tanja Samardžić, and Claudiu Musat. 2020. A swiss german dictionary: Variation in speech and writing.

Michael Stadtschnitzer and Christoph Schmidt. 2018. Data-driven pronunciation modeling of swiss german dialectal speech for automatic speech recognition. In *Proceedings of the Eleventh International Conference on Language Resources and Evaluation (LREC 2018)*.

Alex Waibel, Toshiyuki Hanazawa, Geoffrey Hinton, Kiyohiro Shikano, and Kevin J Lang. 1989. Phoneme recognition using time-delay neural networks. *IEEE transactions on acoustics, speech, and signal processing*, 37(3):328–339.

Dong Wang, Xiaodong Wang, and Shaohe Lv. 2019. An overview of end-to-end automatic speech recognition. *Symmetry*, 11(8):1018.

John C Wells et al. 1997. Sampa computer readable phonetic alphabet. *Handbook of standards and resources for spoken language systems*, 4.

Wayne Xiong, Lingfeng Wu, Fil Alleva, Jasha Droppo, Xuedong Huang, and Andreas Stolcke. 2018. The microsoft 2017 conversational speech recognition system. In *2018 IEEE international conference on acoustics, speech and signal processing (ICASSP)*, pages 5934–5938. IEEE.

Appendix

Dialectal TDNN-iVector + dial90k

---

reference   glòüb ìch echli organisiert uf al fäl am aabig **wo de** vatter **hai cho isch** isch aifach **niit me** daa gsii
prediction   glòüb ìch echli organisiert uf al fäl am aabig *** **oder** vatter *** *** **haichoo** isch aifach *** **nimi** daa gsii
operation   C C C C C C C C C D S C D D S C C D S C C

reference   han ich **den min maa isch drìssgi** gsii und **ìich** äbe *** **zwaijezwänzgi guet**
prediction   han ich **de mim ja esch driissgi** gsii und **ich** äbe **zwai zwänzgi guet**
operation   C C S S S S S C C S C I S C

Normalised TDNN-iVector + norm80k

---

reference   glaube ich ein_klein organisiert auf alle fälle am abend **wo der** vater **heim gekommen ist** ist einfach **nicht** mehr da gewesen
prediction   glaube ich ein_klein organisiert auf alle fälle am abend *** **oder** vater *** *** *** ist einfach **nichts** mehr da gewesen
operation   C C C C C C C C C D S C D D D C C S C C C

reference   habe ich dann *** **mein mann** ist dreissig gewesen und ich eben zweiundzwanzig gut
prediction   habe ich dann **meine man ja** ist dreissig gewesen und ich eben zweiundzwanzig gut
operation   C C C I S S C C C C C C C C

Table 4: Examples of predictions on test data by models trained on 1) dialectal and 2) normalised transcriptions. Asterisk symbols are used in cases of model *deletions* and *insertions* instead of absent words.

LSDC – A comprehensive dataset for Low Saxon Dialect Classification

Janine Siewert
University of Helsinki
`janine.siewert@helsinki.fi`

Yves Scherrer
University of Helsinki
`yves.scherrer@helsinki.fi`

Martijn Wieling
University of Groningen
`m.b.wieling@rug.nl`

Jörg Tiedemann
University of Helsinki
`jorg.tiedemann@helsinki.fi`

Abstract

We present a new comprehensive dataset for the unstandardised West-Germanic language Low Saxon covering the last two centuries, the majority of modern dialects and various genres, which will be made openly available in connection with the final version of this paper. Since so far no such comprehensive dataset of contemporary Low Saxon exists, this provides a great contribution to NLP research on this language. We also test the use of this dataset for dialect classification by training a few baseline models comparing statistical and neural approaches. The performance of these models shows that in spite of an imbalance in the amount of data per dialect, enough features can be learned for a relatively high classification accuracy.

1 Introduction

Compared with the dominant languages of larger countries, minority languages tend to be underrepresented in terms of access to NLP tools. Availability of such tools however is of vital importance, since a lack of these indirectly forces groups already under pressure of language shift to resort to tools in the dominant language, with the consequence of a further decrease in the proportion of domains where the language can be used in daily life (Kornai, 2013). This is especially true for unstandardised languages like Low Saxon, where the lack of a written norm poses challenges for the development of modern NLP applications, which typically rely on large amounts of, ideally, orthographically uniform data. While a reference corpus exists for Middle Low Saxon (ReN-Team, 2019), the few datasets of modern Low Saxon available so far tend to either be very restricted content-wise (e.g. the DSA data (Wrede et al., 1927–1956)) or only represent a fraction of the language area without indication of the dialect (e.g. the OPUS data (Tiedemann, 2012)). In addition, both the DSA data and most of the OPUS data consist of content translated into Low Saxon instead of original texts, which will affect the naturalness of the language. The aim of this dataset for Low Saxon is thus to provide open and for the most part original data in Low Saxon covering nearly the whole language area in order to foster research and facilitate the development of NLP tools.

The composition of this dataset and testing the suitability of language recognition tools is a first step in our larger research project on processing Low Saxon data and modelling the historical development of the language-internal variation. Successful dialect recognition could thus be a useful step in a preprocessing pipeline where it would then be followed by normalisation to one of the writing systems in use, before applying tools developed for standardised languages to Low Saxon text.

In this paper, we will first give an overview of the societal and historical background as well as characteristic features of Low Saxon dialects, followed by a description of the dataset.[1] We will conclude with the presentation of a few baseline models for dialect identification trained on this data and an analysis of their results.

This work is licensed under a Creative Commons Attribution 4.0 International Licence. Licence details: `http://creativecommons.org/licenses/by/4.0/`.

[1]The dataset is made available under a CC NC-BY-SA licence at `https://github.com/Helsinki-NLP/LSDC/`.

Proceedings of the 7th VarDial Workshop on NLP for Similar Languages, Varieties and Dialects, pages 25–35
Barcelona, Spain (Online), December 13, 2020

2 Background

Low Saxon is an unstandardised West-Germanic language with most of its around 5 million speakers today living in the north of Germany and the north-eastern parts of the Netherlands (Moseley, 2010). Starting from the 20th century, the usage of Low Saxon and its intergenerational transmission have been in decline but in the late 20th and in the 21st century, minor revitalisation and popularisation efforts have emerged, e.g. by introducing Low Saxon as a school subject and encouraging young musicians to produce songs in the language. Furthermore, especially since the advent of social media, more people have started to use Low Saxon as a written language for communication in daily life, as described e.g. by Palmiotta (2019) in his PhD thesis on Low Saxon speaking communities on Facebook.

Even though Low Saxon has some official status in several federal states of Germany, e.g. in Schleswig-Holstein (Landesregierung Schleswig-Holstein, 1992), and is protected under the European Charter for Regional and Minority Languages in both Germany and the Netherlands (Council of Europe, 2020), there is no official standard variety in use. This is why characteristics of local dialects tend to be rather well reflected in modern written Low Saxon, not only in terms of lexicon and syntax, but also in the writing system employed. These local writing traditions are based to different degrees and in different ways on the majority language orthography, i.e. German or Dutch. Some of their characteristics will be explained in more detail below.

2.1 Historical background an modern Low Saxon dialects

During the late Middle Ages, Low Saxon, as the main language spoken by Hanseatic merchants, played a major role as a language of international trade in Central and Northern Europe. However, in spite of the interregional influence of the writing tradition of Lübeck, the capital of the Hanseatic League, the Middle Low Saxon written language never became fully uniform (Stellmacher, 1990), and when the Hanseatic League lost its influence in the 16th and 17th century, the literary language started to fade out of use and was gradually replaced by Dutch and German in most written domains (Gabrielson, 1983).

While occasional Low Saxon texts were produced in the 17th and 18th century, the renaissance of Low Saxon as a written language is generally considered to have taken place in the 19th century, led by authors like Klaus Groth and Fritz Reuter, both represented in the LSDC ("Low Saxon Dialect Classification") corpus.

Low Saxon today exists in the form of a dialect continuum without a common overarching written form. There are various ways of classifying these dialects based for instance on historical or current political units or certain isoglosses such as the usage of specific inflectional suffixes or particular vowel mergers.

Our classification of the Dutch Low Saxon dialects follows the division used by Bloemhoff et al. (2008) and the dialects from the German side were divided according to the traditional classification presented e.g. by Schröder (2004) and Stellmacher (1983). Table 2 and Figure 1 show which dialects are spoken in which country. This traditional classification is based on certain developments in the phoneme system and particular morphological features, and is still widely in use and often cited in standard works (Schröder, 2004, 51–52). As data for all subdialects from Germany was not easily obtainable or identifiable, in several cases, only the larger dialect group was used as category. For instance, whereas for Westphalia, all of the data could clearly be identified as belonging to either of three out of the four subdialects (MON, OWL and SUD), this was not the case for most of the other regions.

2.2 Phonological and morphological differences

Low Saxon is known for not having a differentiation into 1st, 2nd and 3rd person in the plural of verbs, but the dialects differ as to which suffix occurs. (Schröder, 2004, 43–44) A morphological feature commonly used in Low Saxon dialect classification thus is the plural suffix of verbs in the present tense. In eastern Low Saxon (MKB, MAR, NPR), East Frisian (OFR) and Gronings (GRO), the plural suffix is *-(e)n*, whereas the remaining dialects in this dataset use the suffix *-(e)t*. A characteristic morphological feature contrasting Eastphalian with the other dialects are the inflected forms of the personal pronouns, where e.g. *mik* 'me' and *dik* 'you-SG ("thee")' are used instead of variants of *mi* and *di* elsewhere (Schröder,

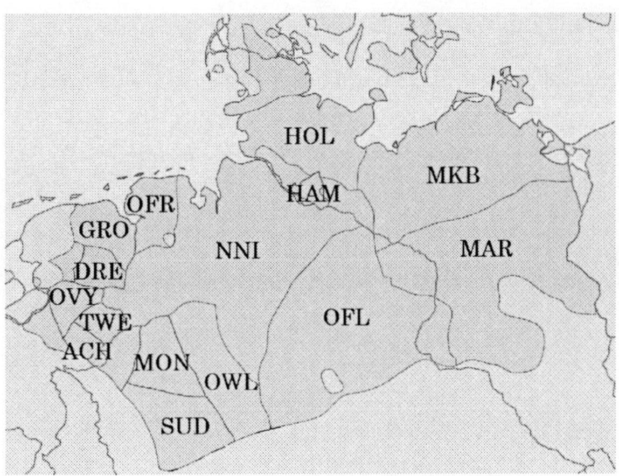

Figure 1: The geographic situation of the Low Saxon dialects covered in this article. The area of the Lower Prussian ('NPR') dialects, previously spoken further to the east along the coast of the Baltic Sea, is missing from the map. The dialect borders added (ACH, DRE, HAM, MON, OVY, OWL, SUD and TWE) are not meant to be precise delineations of the dialect areas, but are intended to give an impression of the position in relation to the other dialects. Map source: `https://commons.wikimedia.or g/wiki/File:Low_Saxon_dialects.png`

2004, 49). In Dutch Low Saxon, a morphological change is attested in the dataset. In most Dutch Low Saxon dialects, the old second person singular *doe~du* and its corresponding verb inflection have fallen out of use today and have been replaced by the counterparts of Dutch *jij* 'you-SG' and *jullie* 'you-PL'. In texts from the 19th century, however, the old second person singular is still encountered.

On the phonological level, a feature usually employed for dialect classification is the development of stressed old short vowels in open syllable. These old short vowels in open syllable, e.g. Old Saxon *fugal* 'bird' and *etan* 'to eat' (Orel, 2003), were diphthongised in Middle Low Saxon time and either preserved as diphthongs or monophthongised (Lasch, 1914). Examples of these developments are the diphthongs in *Vuëgel* and *iäten* in the Münsterland dialect (Kahl, 2009) contrasting with *Vågel* and *äten* in Mecklenburg-Vorpommern (Herrmann-Winter, 2006). Subsequently, mergers occurred in several dialects. While the Westphalian dialects (MON, OWL and SUD) have preserved seven distinct reflexes of the lengthened/diphthongised short vowels, the northern dialects (HAM, HOL, MKB and NNI) only know a threefold distinction and Eastphalian (OFL) takes an intermediate position with five phonemes (Schröder, 2004, 53). According to map 8 in Panzer and Thümmel (1971), some of the central Dutch Low Saxon dialects have preserved a differentiation similar to the Westphalian dialects in Germany, while the remainder takes a more intermediate position similar to Eastphalian with 4–5 distinct phonemes.

2.3 Differences in writing systems

In addition to the above-mentioned differences in the dialects themselves, the influence of the majority language orthography introduces further divergences on the text level. The different grapheme usage in the German and the Dutch orthography thus causes the same pronunciation to appear clearly distinct in written form on the other side of the border: E.g. while according to the East Frisian online dictionary (Ostfriesische Landschaft, 2020), one should write *Huus* 'house', *för* 'for' and *südelk* 'southern', this corresponds to *hoes*, *veur* and *zudelk* on the other side of the border in Groningen (Reker, 2020). These divergent written forms do not represent different phonemes, but are a result of different graphemes used to represent the same phoneme following the usage in the Dutch and the German orthography.

Furthermore, there are also differences in the way the majority language orthography functions as a reference. This is expecially noticeable in the German Low Saxon writing systems. While the writing systems of the northern Low Saxon dialects in Germany use the written form of lexemes in the German orthography as a reference, the Westphalian writing systems more consistently adopt phoneme-grapheme

ACH:	Ziene olders hadden altied hard ewarkt en wazzen gezene leu in den naoberschop.
DE:	*Seine Eltern hatten immer hart gearbeitet und waren geschätzte Leute in der Nachbarschaft.*
NL:	*Zijn ouders hadden altijd hard gewerkt en waren voorname mensen in de gemeenschap.*
GRO:	Daor, kiek man ijs goud, 't kan best wezen, dat 't nog familie van die is.
DE:	*Da, guck nur mal gut, es kann gut sein, dass das noch Familie von dir ist.*
NL:	*Daar, kijk maar even goed, het kan best zijn dat 't nog familie van je is.*
HOL:	Arfest neem twe Kaarten to de eerst Klaß, un as ik daröver grote Ogen maak, lach he un meen, dat kunn darop staan, ik schull man instigen.
DE:	*Arfest nahm zwei Karten für die erste Klasse und als ich darüber große Augen machte, lachte er und sagte, das könne darauf stehen, ich solle nur einsteigen.*
NL:	*Arfest nam twee kaarten voor de eerste klasse, en toen ik daarover grote ogen opzette, lachte hij en zei, het kan erop staan, maar ik zou gewoon instappen.*
MAR:	Unn so wo de Doot dat den Fischer vertellt hett, isset ook ekåmen; dat ganze Dörp is uutstorven, man de Fischer is aarbliiwen unn issen riiken riiken Mann wåren, unn siene Kinger leewen noch bett upp dissen Dach in Göttin unn sinn riike Lüüe.
DE:	*Und so, wie der Tod es dem Fischer erzählt hat, ist es auch gekommen; das ganze Dorf ist ausgestorben, aber der Fischer ist übriggeblieben und ist ein reicher Mann geworden, und seine Kinder leben noch bis auf diesen Tag in Göttin und sind reiche Leute.*
NL:	*En zo, hoe de dood het de visser verteld heeft, is het ook gebeurd; het hele dorp is uitgestorven, maar de visser is overgebleven en is een rijke man geworden, en z'n kinderen leven nog tot op de dag van vandaag in Göttin en zijn rijke mensen.*
OFL:	Ik kann nich sä güt wiet lupen un dorumme schölle mik miene Fründin hier ne Parkbuchte friehulen.
DE:	*Ich kann nicht so gut weit gehen und darum sollte mir meine Freundin hier eine Parkbucht freihalten.*
NL:	*Ik kan niet zo goed ver lopen en daarom moet mijn vriendin hier een parkeerplaats vrijhouden.*
SUD:	Eunige Dage später frogere de Magister, biu de veuer Johrestyien herren: Hiärmen sprank op, un de Magister mennte all, hai härr' et wieten.
DE:	*Einige Tage später fragte der Magister, wie die vier Jahreszeiten hießen: Harmen sprang auf und der Magister dachte schon, dass er es gewusst hätte.*
NL:	*Enige dagen later vroeg de magister, hoe de vier jaargetijden heetten: Harmen sprong op en de magister dacht al dat hij het had geweten.*

Table 1: Example sentences from six dialects and added translations into German (DE) and Dutch (NL).

correspondences from the German orthography: E.g. the SASS writing system (Kahl and Thies, 2009), nowadays used for part of the north-western dialects, and the writing system for Mecklenburg-Vorpommern (Herrmann-Winter, 2006) prescribe the usage of <h> as a vowel-length marker, if the same is used in the German cognate, as in *föhlen* and *fäuhlen* 'to feel' following German *fühlen*. Similarly, in the same writing systems, the Low Saxon phoneme /d/ is represented by the grapheme <t> or <tt> word finally, if this grapheme occurs in the German cognate. Examples of this are the words *Brett* 'board' and *wiet* 'wide', corresponding to German *Brett* and *weit*. In contrast, in the Münsterland writing system (Kahl, 2009), one would write *fölen*, *Bräd* and *wied*, according to the Low Saxon phonemes instead. However, most texts from the northern dialects included in the LSDC corpus predate these writing systems, so the authors did not necessarily adhere to the same rules. As a consequence of these differences in spelling, the LSDC dataset is not suitable for measuring distances between dialects without introducing a normalisation step. In order to illustrate the dialectal and orthographical variation, a selection of example sentences from LSDC is shown in Table 1.

3   The LSDC dataset

We have gathered a comprehensive data set of Low Saxon dialects covering nearly the whole language area. The collection includes historical texts from the 19th and 20th century as well as contemporary Low Saxon and therefore spans a period of around 200 years with most dialects being presented in at least two centuries. The total size is 105 876 sentences with an average sentence length of 20.16 words and a total word count of 2 134 753. This LSDC dataset presents a unique resource for modern Low Saxon which will be made openly available together with the final version of the paper. In the following subsections, we will provide background on the original text sources and the characteristics of the data.

3.1 Text sources

Most of the data for German Low Saxon dialects is copyright-free material from Wikisource. This is true for the dialects of Holstein, Hamburg, Mecklenburg-Vorpommern, Mark-Brandenburg, Lower Prussia and the north of Lower Saxony. The data for the Sauerland dialect originates from the Christine Koch Mundartarchiv and the Eastern Westphalian data consists partially of works written by Heinrich Stolte and made publicly available online by Olaf Bordasch, partially of texts from the website Lippisch Platt. Eastphalian and East Frisian data was provided by local authors and for the Münsterland dialects, we were given permission to use the data from Dr. Klaus-Werner Kahl's website.

The Groningen data originates from the online magazine Kreuze. Except for several older texts found on Wikisource, the remainder of data in Dutch Low Saxon dialects (Achterhoeks, Drents, Western Overijssels and Twents) was directly sent to us by different Low Saxon institutions or authors.

The links to the websites where the publicly accessible data can be found are listed in Table 5.

3.2 Description of the data

While a reference corpus for Middle Low Saxon (spanning the period 1200–1650 and excluding the dialects from today's Netherlands) exists (ReN-Team, 2019), so far no balanced corpus of more modern Low Saxon is available, which is why we hope that the LSDC dataset will greatly improve the possibilities for Low Saxon NLP research. The dataset spans the whole period from the renaissance of Low Saxon as a written language in the 19th century until today, covers nearly the whole of the current language area, and in addition one (nearly) extinct dialect, and presents the language in various genres. With the exception of passages from the Bible and other occasional translated works, the majority of texts was originally written in Low Saxon and therefore provides an authentic picture of the kind of language used in contemporary Low Saxon literature.

The most common genre in the dataset are short stories and short novels, and – especially in texts from the 19th and early 20th century – also fairytales and legends. In addition, the corpus contains genres as varied as religious texts, historical accounts, journal articles, poetry and songs, political speeches and simple texts for school children. An overview of the genres represented in the different dialects can be found in Table 2. Due to time restrictions, we however could not annotate the genres yet to make use of them in the experiments described in section 4.

The original text sources were not readily available in plain text format, but needed to be converted, and in particular the PDF documents required manual correction. Sentence splitting was performed using Python's NLTK tokenize package[2]. Moreover, we removed larger passages in other languages and performed careful manual cleaning of the test set.

3.3 Placenames

In addition to actual text data, we also collected Low Saxon place names from the two Low Saxon Wikipedia versions[3] and for the German side also from the websites of the district of Lüneburg and the local organisation Fehrs-Gill, also to be found in Table 5. These placenames will be included in the Low Saxon dataset to be published in connection with the article. The idea behind this setting is to test whether placenames could play a major role in dialect classification for Low Saxon, that we will discuss in more detail in the next section below. For the Lower Prussian region, we only found less than 30 placenames, so we excluded this dialect from the purely placename-based tests. Issues concerning the placename-based testing are on the one hand the incomplete lists on Wikipedia and furthermore the fact that the lack of standardisation of course also applies to the written form of placenames, so they do not necessarily occur in the same form in the lists and in the actual text data. Moreover, in the eastern regions of the Low Saxon language area, many placenames are of Slavonic origin, reflecting their history of settlement, and hence do not correspond to regular Low Saxon words.

---

[2] https://www.nltk.org/

[3] https://nds-nl.wikipedia.org/wiki/ for Dutch Low Saxon and https://nds.wikipedia.org/wiki/ for German Low Saxon.

Dialect region	Abbr.	Country	Sentences in train and test set		Tokens	Types	Centuries covered	Genres covered
Achterhoek	ACH	NL	500	488	20253	4020	20th, 21st	N
Drenthe	DRE	NL	5659	1000	97311	10538	19th, 21st	N
Groningen	GRO	NL	15999	1000	260477	28654	20th, 21st	various
Hamburg	HAM	DE	6095	1000	100590	9740	19th, 20th	N, T
Holstein	HOL	DE	11818	1000	263084	19554	19th, 20th	F, N
Mark-Brandenburg	MAR	DE	100	72	7102	1959	19th	F
Mecklenburg-Vorpommern	MKB	DE	14432	1000	541273	33122	19th	F, N
Münsterland	MON	DE	400	361	13468	3482	20th, 21st	N, S
Northern Lower Saxony	NNI	DE	401	377	18812	3592	20th, 21st	F, A
Lower Prussia	NPR	DE	200	155	9059	2751	19th, 20th	F, N, S
Eastphalia	OFL	DE	8377	1000	176187	15074	19th, 20th, 21st	various
East Frisia	OFR	DE	150	90	4051	1158	19th, 21st	N, A, S
Overijssel (west)	OVY	NL	800	547	21397	3267	21st	N, S
Eastern Westphalia	OWL	DE	14131	1000	260612	16319	20th, 21st	various
Sauerland	SUD	DE	16056	1000	329920	38831	19th, 20th, 21st	various
Twente	TWE	NL	368	300	11562	3231	21st	various

Table 2: Dialects and training set size. Abbreviations used: A = administration, announcements and politics, F = fairytales and legends, N = (short) stories and (short) novels, S = songs and poetry, T = theatre plays. Subcorpora marked with 'various' cover more than three genres, in addition to the ones mentioned above including e.g. religious texts, meta-discussions about language (usually about Low Saxon) and discussions of history.

4 Dialect identification

So far, Low Saxon is still an underresearched language within the field of NLP, which probably at least partly is due to its lack of a standardised form. We are not aware of any comparable previous work on dialect identification for this language, but Birkenes (2018) conducted n-gram-based measurements of the distance between dialects of German Low Saxon for dialect classification and identification of dialect areas using the Wenker atlas data (Wrede et al., 1927–1956).

For testing the usability of the dataset, we chose the fastText and langID toolkits to train baseline models. Both are supervised classifiers where the classes are predefined, but otherwise they differ in both the way the language data is represented and their general architecture.

4.1 Approaches to automatic language identification

There is a vast amount of literature on language identification and most approaches base their predictions on character n-gram statistics and language model features such as estimated token probabilities. A comprehensive overview of approaches is provided by Jauhiainen et al. (2018). There are also recent approaches based on neural models and representation learning. In our work we focus on two popular tools representing purely statistical models (langID, Lui and Baldwin (2011)) and neural models (fastText, Joulin et al. (2016)).

While fastText is also used for language identification, it is designed as a general text classification model, which is used for tasks like sentiment analysis as well. This orientation towards general text classification presumably is the reason for choosing a language representation based on bag of words and bag of word n-grams. If Low Saxon had a unified orthography, one would expect such a model to be more useful for dialect identification, which in this case would have to rely more on differences in lexicon and syntax.

The basic structure is a linear classifier which is combined with a rank constraint supposed to improve the generalisation of the model in case that some classes only have a small amount of examples. They use stochastic gradient descent, a linearly decreasing learning rate and hierarchical softmax in order to reduce training time. The best performance was achieved with word n-grams up to 5, but for our experiments we kept the default of 1.

The langID model is specifically designed for language identification controlling for divergent language use in different genres by choosing features with a high information gain related to language, but a low information gain in relation to domain. Since our data however is not (yet) divided according to domain, a possibly useful functionality could thus not be taken advantage of.

In addition, a bias towards more high-resource varieties is supposed to be prevented by choosing a fixed number of features per variety. Unlike the fastText model, the features selected by langID for creating a document vector are not complete words, but character n-grams (1 to 4 grams), and no assumption is made concerning word delimitation. Due to the lack of a standard orthography, the same word may easily appear in slightly divergent spellings within the same dialects, which is why a character-based model seems more appropriate. However, Jauhiainen et al. (2018, 17) had determined that a larger unit, namely syllables and syllable n-grams are particularly suitable if the varieties to be identified are closely related. For classification, langID applies a multinomial naïve Bayes model with feature selection based on an information gain measure.

4.2 Discriminating Low Saxon from other Germanic languages

We originally chose the fasttext model because it includes a pretrained language model for Low Saxon ('nds'). This pretrained model however performed poorly on the majority of dialects, which were mis-classified most frequently as Dutch or German, in all likelihood depending on whether they were written with a Dutch- or a German-based spelling. An exception are the north-western dialects from the German side, with a classification accuracy of more than 50% achieved for the dialects from East Frisia, Northern Lower Saxony, Hamburg and Schleswig-Holstein. This is unsurprising given that apparently the language model was trained on data from the German Low Saxon Wikipedia. Therefore, we eventually decided to train new Low Saxon models completely from scratch in order to not propagate the apparent north-western bias towards the dialect models.

4.3 Identifying Low Saxon dialects

The division into train and test set was based on the amount of dialect data. While the test set of more high-resource dialects was given a fixed size of 1000 sentences with the remainder being used for training, the test set size for the dialects with less than 1000 sentences of overall data was set to be at roughly 1-1.5:2 compared with the train set. The ratio however changed a little after removing duplicates from both the train and the test set. Furthermore, sentences of length three words or shorter, as well as sentences mostly or fully in a language other than Low Saxon were moved from the test set to the train set and replaced by fully Low Saxon sentences taken from the train set. The final size of the train and test sets per dialect is shown in Table 2.

During testing, the models were to classify the sentences separately instead of as a whole document. We considered this a meaningful size, since Low Saxon data for future research could be collected from social media platforms such as Facebook, Instagram or WhatsApp, where messages often do not exceed this length either.

Sampled training data

Since the fastText model exhibited a strong bias in favour of more resource-rich dialects, we decided to balance out the amount of training data. Thus, the train sets were either over- or undersampled to 10,000 sentences for each dialect. For oversampling, the same train sentences were copied over until a number of 10,000 or higher was reached. Subsequently, the train sets with a number higher than 10,000 were shuffled and cut off at 10,000 sentences. This was repeated three times to create three train sets per dialect, one for each of the three runs, as to not overly influence the final result by which part of the train set is dropped.

Placenames

In order to control for the effect of placenames on classification accuracy, we built a simple classifier where the dialect identification only depended on whether a placename from the list occurs in the sentence to be classified. This classifier's overall accuracy remained below 1%, which is unsurprising given the spelling variation and that most sentences do not contain any placenames to begin with. Therefore, placenames alone probably do not play a major role for dialect classification in our experiments.

	fastText		langID		placenames
	recall	precision	recall	precision	in train set
ACH	$0.0^{\pm0.0}$	$0.0^{\pm0.0}$	$0.0^{\pm0.0}$	$0.0^{\pm0.0}$	196
DRE	$4.0^{\pm2.5}$	$10.0^{\pm2.3}$	$3.4^{\pm0.6}$	$15.9^{\pm1.5}$	527
GRO	$23.3^{\pm10.0}$	$66.6^{\pm16.7}$	$12.7^{\pm3.0}$	$24.5^{\pm2.9}$	505
HAM	$0.1^{\pm0.1}$	$33.3^{\pm47.1}$	$0.0^{\pm0.0}$	$0.0^{\pm0.0}$	113
HOL	$7.6^{\pm3.0}$	$13.1^{\pm0.7}$	$8.3^{\pm2.5}$	$20.0^{\pm3.6}$	2288
MAR	$23.1^{\pm17.1}$	$2.1^{\pm0.2}$	$2.2^{\pm1.1}$	$1.1^{\pm0.6}$	494
MKB	$0.0^{\pm0.0}$	$0.0^{\pm0.0}$	$0.0^{\pm0.0}$	$0.0^{\pm0.0}$	157
MON	$0.5^{\pm0.7}$	$0.4^{\pm0.5}$	$0.0^{\pm0.0}$	$0.0^{\pm0.0}$	328
NNI	$22.9^{\pm4.0}$	$3.3^{\pm0.1}$	$69.8^{\pm3.9}$	$4.4^{\pm0.0}$	4564
OFL	$38.6^{\pm1.3}$	$9.4^{\pm0.0}$	$19.0^{\pm3.6}$	$6.7^{\pm0.7}$	2804
OFR	$0.7^{\pm1.0}$	$1.0^{\pm1.4}$	$0.0^{\pm0.0}$	$0.0^{\pm0.0}$	379
OVY	$10.6^{\pm10.2}$	$7.3^{\pm0.1}$	$1.3^{\pm0.5}$	$8.1^{\pm1.3}$	334
OWL	$2.7^{\pm3.9}$	$2.6^{\pm3.6}$	$1.6^{\pm0.8}$	$26.7^{\pm4.6}$	652
SUD	$0.0^{\pm0.0}$	$0.0^{\pm0.0}$	$0.2^{\pm0.1}$	$0.5^{\pm0.6}$	452
TWE	$0.0^{\pm0.0}$	$0.0^{\pm0.0}$	$0.7^{\pm0.7}$	$9.4^{\pm10.3}$	196
Macro F-score	9.4		7.9		

Table 3: Results of the placename-based models.

Subsequently, we used the placename list to train fastText and langID models in order to test if enough information on e.g. common letter combinations for successful classification can be extracted from placenames alone (see Table 3). An interesting observation here is the noticeable bias towards the more high-resource dialects in both the fastText and the langID models, while langID results appear to be more stable over several training runs. These classifiers, too, only attain a low F-score, so it seems that one can safely conclude that the placenames alone do not provide a major contribution for Low Saxon dialect identification. For more detailed results cf. Table 3.

Results of the dialect identification models

In the discussion of the results, we will focus on three aspects: the performance on low-resource vs. more high-resource data, the overall correctness, and which dialects tend to be confused.

When examining the performance of the first fastText model which was trained on the unsampled data (cf. the 'basic' columns in Table 4), a striking difference can be observed between the low-resource and more high-resource dialects: The model only attained a mean recall of between 0 and 6.2% on dialects with less than 500 sentences training data, it stayed below 50% for dialects with less than 1000 sentences and achieved decent results of over 90% for most dialects with over 5000 train sentences. The only exception are the neighbouring dialects of Hamburg and Holstein which relatively often are confused with each other. At the same time, the precision remains low, at 59.8–70.9%, for most of the high-resource dialects, since data in the low-resource dialects tends to be misclassified as one of the more resource-rich geographically close dialects. This is well reflected by the low macro F-scores of the fastText models on the original train set, as can be seen in the last row of Table 4.

With sampled training data, the fastText model shows a clear improvement in the macro F-score. As is evident from the 'sampled' columns in Table 4, even though the low-resource dialects' recall still falls behind the other dialects, a noticeable gain compared with the models trained on unsampled data can be observed. In the precision of dialect detection, no apparent difference related to the amount of distinct training data can be seen, and with the exception of the Holstein dialect, which again often was confused with the Hamburg dialect, a score between 82.2 and 98.0% is attained. The langID model is more stable across different training runs, which is apparent both from the macro F-scores and from the lower standard deviation scores. Interestingly, the sampling of the train set does not lead to noticeable improvements in the langID models. Clearly, the langID models manage to extract the features just as well without copied data, but nevertheless, do not attain the accuracy of the sampled fastText models.

Generally, it can be observed that it is possible for the models, for the sampled fastText one even more so than for the langID models, to learn to distinguish between the different Low Saxon dialects relatively well. Furthermore, dialects are rarely confused across the Dutch-German border. This is expected, as the different writing traditions increase the grapheme-level distance between otherwise close dialects.

	fastText				langID			
	basic		sampled		basic		sampled	
	recall	precision	recall	precision	recall	precision	recall	precision
ACH	$28.2^{\pm15.4}$	$56.3^{\pm6.3}$	$77.0^{\pm5.6}$	$89.3^{\pm4.0}$	$73.8^{\pm4.7}$	$78.7^{\pm1.8}$	$80.9^{\pm3.1}$	$75.0^{\pm0.7}$
DRE	$93.1^{\pm6.4}$	$64.1^{\pm7.6}$	$92.5^{\pm3.7}$	$90.1^{\pm2.1}$	$85.3^{\pm1.3}$	$78.4^{\pm0.4}$	$83.4^{\pm0.4}$	$83.8^{\pm0.5}$
GRO	$97.0^{\pm1.5}$	$73.3^{\pm13.1}$	$95.8^{\pm2.3}$	$89.4^{\pm5.9}$	$89.4^{\pm0.1}$	$83.5^{\pm2.0}$	$89.5^{\pm0.8}$	$86.9^{\pm1.2}$
HAM	$59.8^{\pm30.5}$	$82.9^{\pm17.3}$	$77.3^{\pm12.8}$	$86.3^{\pm7.4}$	$73.6^{\pm0.5}$	$75.2^{\pm0.6}$	$70.9^{\pm0.3}$	$77.0^{\pm0.3}$
HOL	$87.1^{\pm12.3}$	$66.8^{\pm18.9}$	$95.4^{\pm4.1}$	$63.2^{\pm11.8}$	$80.8^{\pm0.3}$	$71.7^{\pm0.6}$	$77.9^{\pm0.3}$	$73.0^{\pm0.8}$
MAR	$0.0^{\pm0.0}$	$0.0^{\pm0.0}$	$63.9^{\pm2.3}$	$97.3^{\pm2.4}$	$60.2^{\pm2.6}$	$62.8^{\pm1.4}$	$66.7^{\pm0.0}$	$41.3^{\pm0.4}$
MKB	$96.9^{\pm1.2}$	$72.0^{\pm6.6}$	$80.3^{\pm9.6}$	$95.7^{\pm2.9}$	$86.0^{\pm0.7}$	$77.0^{\pm0.7}$	$84.2^{\pm1.1}$	$80.2^{\pm2.4}$
MON	$3.1^{\pm2.3}$	$29.6^{\pm40.9}$	$61.9^{\pm7.7}$	$96.4^{\pm3.4}$	$65.2^{\pm1.7}$	$77.0^{\pm2.1}$	$68.6^{\pm1.0}$	$76.2^{\pm0.7}$
NNI	$2.4^{\pm2.7}$	$32.8^{\pm29.7}$	$49.2^{\pm7.8}$	$91.9^{\pm4.9}$	$42.4^{\pm0.4}$	$60.6^{\pm2.0}$	$51.8^{\pm0.6}$	$54.8^{\pm1.3}$
NPR	$6.2^{\pm0.6}$	$80.6^{\pm14.6}$	$74.2^{\pm1.1}$	$95.0^{\pm0.6}$	$77.4^{\pm1.4}$	$68.1^{\pm1.3}$	$80.4^{\pm1.1}$	$61.0^{\pm0.7}$
OFL	$90.9^{\pm6.6}$	$94.4^{\pm3.2}$	$95.5^{\pm1.3}$	$91.9^{\pm1.6}$	$81.8^{\pm0.1}$	$86.6^{\pm0.7}$	$80.5^{\pm0.6}$	$86.9^{\pm0.7}$
OFR	$1.1^{\pm0.9}$	$11.8^{\pm8.5}$	$54.4^{\pm5.5}$	$83.9^{\pm9.0}$	$39.6^{\pm2.1}$	$64.2^{\pm4.0}$	$45.2^{\pm1.9}$	$39.4^{\pm1.7}$
OVY	$45.8^{\pm25.4}$	$83.7^{\pm2.8}$	$89.9^{\pm1.6}$	$89.9^{\pm2.8}$	$78.4^{\pm2.4}$	$84.8^{\pm3.0}$	$81.8^{\pm1.3}$	$87.9^{\pm1.3}$
OWL	$97.7^{\pm1.1}$	$91.9^{\pm2.7}$	$96.3^{\pm1.7}$	$98.0^{\pm1.1}$	$88.0^{\pm0.4}$	$92.4^{\pm0.2}$	$88.2^{\pm0.1}$	$93.4^{\pm0.0}$
SUD	$97.4^{\pm0.8}$	$78.6^{\pm5.8}$	$95.0^{\pm1.6}$	$90.0^{\pm3.5}$	$84.9^{\pm0.9}$	$82.0^{\pm0.6}$	$86.1^{\pm0.8}$	$85.4^{\pm0.7}$
TWE	$0.6^{\pm0.4}$	$19.4^{\pm14.2}$	$69.9^{\pm4.8}$	$87.1^{\pm4.0}$	$59.9^{\pm1.1}$	$75.4^{\pm2.5}$	$68.8^{\pm2.6}$	$70.5^{\pm1.8}$
macro-avg.	50.5	58.6	79.3	89.7	72.9	76.2	75.3	73.3
avg. F-scores	$55.0^{\pm3.7}$		$84.2^{\pm0.6}$		$74.5^{\pm0.6}$		$74.3^{\pm0.1}$	

Table 4: Mean and standard deviation for recall and precision of the three training runs of the different models and F-scores separately for the three training runs.

Furthermore, the confusion of dialects tends to correlate with geographical closeness. In the langID models, this is even more evident than in the fastText models, which seem to have a stronger bias towards particular dialects. E.g. the Münsterland dialect is most often misclassified as the neighbouring Sauerland dialect. We also observed that the low-resource Markish-Brandenburgish dialect is most often confused with the dialects from the northern neighbouring region Mecklenburg-Vorpommern. Also the fact that the most prominent confusion between high-resource dialects can be observed between Hamburg and Holstein suggests that the models do in fact learn relevant features and that some dialects simply are harder to classify correctly due to their greater similarity.

The performance of the models also correlates roughly with the intuition of the Low Saxon speaker in our group, who e.g. would judge the dialects from Holstein, Hamburg and Northern Lower Saxony present in the dataset to be comparatively similar and would have an easier time distinguishing the three Westphalian subdialects of Eastern Westphalia, the Sauerland and the Münsterland, even given that they speak a northern dialect themself. This may at least partly be due to the writing systems employed, since while there are distinct writing systems for at least Eastern Westphalia and the Münsterland, authors from Holstein, Hamburg and Northern Lower Saxony follow approximately the same tradition.

5   Conclusions, discussions and future work

The LSDC dataset presented in this paper is a comprehensive dataset for contemporary Low Saxon. With nearly all modern dialect groups being included and two centuries as well as various genres being covered, this dataset provides a unique new resource for NLP research on and application development for this minority language. We have tested the resource on a dialect identification task, demonstrating its use for further collections and classifications of dialectal data. Even though the amount of data per dialect is not balanced in LSDC, we have seen that sampling makes it possible to achieve a comparable precision for both high- and low-resource dialects with a neural classification model and that the performance of that model even approximately resembles native speaker intuition.

One central aspect affecting dialect identification are the various ways of writing Low Saxon. As no normalisation of spelling was included, we need to acknowledge that we cannot fully discern in how far the models classify the dialects based on the local writing system or based on actual dialect features such as lexicon, inflectional suffixes and syntax. As a consequence, it would be meaningful to conduct additional dialect identification experiments with orthographically normalised Low Saxon text data. In addition, one could test the effect of grouping the dialects according to similarity in writing systems and training separate models for instance for Dutch Low Saxon, northern German Low Saxon and southern German Low Saxon.

The next steps in our research project on the historical development of the language internal variation in Low Saxon will require us to expand the corpus. First of all, more data in the low-resource dialects will be needed and the time coverage for all dialects needs to be improved, so that roughly the same amount of data is available for each dialect and century. Ideally, each dialect should additionally be represented by a variety of genres for each century and have the genre included as part of the annotation. This will allow us to investigate to what extent characteristics of a specific domain are misinterpreted as dialect features. Lastly, we will need to increase the time depth in order to close the gap between the Middle Low Saxon reference corpus and our modern Low Saxon dataset, so that the development of Middle Low Saxon into contemporary Low Saxon can be traced.

Acknowledgements

We would like to express our gratitude to the *Lännerzentrum för Nedderdüütsch* and the *Oostfreeske Landskupp* for establishing contact with Low Saxon authors, and especially to the authors themselves who provided us with data that would not have been accessible online: Diana Abbink from the *Erfgoedcentrum Achterhoek en Liemers*, Rolf Ahlers, Erich Bolinius, Marieke Dannenberg from the *Twentehoes*, Jan Germs from the *Huus van de Taol*, Joop Hekkelman, Dr. Harrie Scholtmeijer from the *IJsselacademie* and Gerard Uwland. Furthermore, we would like to thank the Discovery group lead by Prof. Hannu Toivonen at the department of Computer Science at the University of Helsinki for financing Janine Siewert's summer internship in 2019 in connection with which the collection of the dataset presented here was started.

References

Magnus Breder Birkenes. 2018. N-Gramm-basierte Ähnlichkeitsmessungen als dialektometrische Methode: Die Fragebögen des Wenker-Atlas. Linguistisches Kolloquium, University of Munich, Germany.

Henk Bloemhoff, Jurjen van der Kooi, Hermann Niebaum, and Siemon Reker, editors. 2008. *Handboek Nedersaksische Taal- en Letterkunde*. Koninklijke van Gorcum, Assen, Netherlands.

Council of Europe. 2020. Reservations and Declarations for Treaty No.148 - European Charter for Regional or Minority Languages.

Artur Gabrielson. 1983. Die Verdrängung der mittelniederdeutschen durch die neuhochdeutsche Schriftsprache. In Gerhard Cordes and Dieter Möhn, editors, *Handbuch zur niederdeutschen Sprach- und Literaturwissenschaft*, pages 119–153. Erich Schmidt Verlag, Berlin, Germany.

Renate Herrmann-Winter. 2006. *Hör- und Lernbuch für das Plattdeutsche*. Hinstorff, Rostock, Germany.

Tommi Jauhiainen, Marco Lui, Marcos Zampieri, Timothy Baldwin, and Krister Lindén. 2018. Automatic language identification in texts: A survey. *Journal of Artificial Intelligence Research*, 65, 04.

Armand Joulin, Edouard Grave, Piotr Bojanowski, and Tomas Mikolov. 2016. Bag of tricks for efficient text classification. *arXiv preprint arXiv:1607.01759*.

Heinrich Kahl and Heinrich Thies. 2009. *der neue SASS – Plattdeutsches Wörterbuch*. Wachholtz Verlag, Neumünster, Germany.

Klaus-Werner Kahl. 2009. *Wörterbuch des Münsterländer Platt*. Aschendorff Verlag, Münster, Germany.

András Kornai. 2013. Digital language death. *PLOS ONE*, 8(10):1–11, 10.

Landesregierung Schleswig-Holstein. 1992. Allgemeines Verwaltungsgesetz für das Land Schleswig-Holstein (Landesverwaltungsgesetz - LVwG -) in der Fassung der Bekanntmachung vom 2. Juni 1992 § 82 b Regional- und Minderheitensprachen vor Behörden.

Agathe Lasch. 1914. *Mittelniederdeutsche Grammatik*. Max Niemeyer Verlag, Tübingen, Germany. Unchanged reprint from 1974.

Marco Lui and Timothy Baldwin. 2011. Cross-domain feature selection for language identification. In *Proceedings of 5th International Joint Conference on Natural Language Processing*, pages 553–561, Chiang Mai, Thailand, November. Asian Federation of Natural Language Processing.

Christopher Moseley, editor. 2010. *Atlas of the World's Languages in Danger.* UNESCO Publishing, Paris, 3 edition. Online version: `http://www.unesco.org/culture/en/endangeredlanguages/atlas`.

Vladimir Orel. 2003. *A Handbook of Germanic Etymology.* Brill, Leiden and Boston.

Ostfriesische Landschaft. 2020. Plattdeutsch-Hochdeutsches Wörterbuch für Ostfriesland. `https://www.platt-wb.de/`.

Michele Palmiotta. 2019. *Social network e lingue minoritarie: il gruppo Facebook come spazio di discussione e costruzione dell'identità linguistica del Niederdeutsch.* Ph.D. thesis, Università degli Studi di Bari Aldo Modo.

Baldur Panzer and Wolf Thümmel. 1971. *Die Einteilung der niederdeutschen Mundarten auf Grund der strukturellen Entwicklung des Vokalismus.* Max Hueber Verlag, München, Germany.

Siemon Reker. 2020. Groninger zakwoordenboek. `http://www.groningsonline.nl/woordenboek`.

ReN-Team. 2019. Referenzkorpus Mittelniederdeutsch/Niederrheinisch (1200-1650). Archived in Hamburger Zentrum für Sprachkorpora. Version 1.0. Publication date 2019-08-14.

Ingrid Schröder. 2004. Niederdeutsch in der Gegenwart - Sprachgebiet – Grammatisches – Binnendifferenzierung. In Dieter Stellmacher, editor, *Niederdeutsche Sprache und Literatur der Gegenwart*, pages 35–97. Georg Olms Verlag, Hildesheim and Zürich and New York.

Dieter Stellmacher. 1983. Neuniederdeutsche Grammatik – Phonologie und Morphologie. In Gerhard Cordes and Dieter Möhn, editors, *Handbuch zur niederdeutschen Sprach- und Literaturwissenschaft*, pages 238–278. Erich Schmidt Verlag, Berlin, Germany.

Dieter Stellmacher. 1990. *Niederdeutsche Sprache – Eine Einführung.* Peter Lang, Bern, Frankfurt am Main, New York and Paris.

Jörg Tiedemann. 2012. Parallel data, tools and interfaces in OPUS. In *Proceedings of the 8th International Conference on Language Resources and Evaluation (LREC'2012)*. Data available at: `http://opus.nlpl.eu/`.

Ferdinand Wrede, Walther Mitzka, and Berhard Martin, editors. 1927–1956. *Deutscher Sprachatlas auf Grund des Sprachatlas des Deutschen Reiches von Georg Wenker. Begonnen von Ferdinand Wrede, fortgesetzt von Walther Mitzka und Bernhard Martin.* N.G. Elwert'sche Verlagsbuchhandlung, Marburg (Lahn), Germany.

Dialect	Web address
GRO	`http://kreuzekeuze.nl/kreuzewebstee/index.html`
HOL placenames	`https://sass-platt.de/plattdeutsche-ortsnamen-schleswig-holstein/index.html`
MON	`https://www.plattdeutsch.net/pages/platt-lesen/gedichte-und-geschichten.php` `http://www.sauerlandmundart.de/daunlots.html`
NNI placenames	`https://www.landkreis-lueneburg.de/Home-Landkreis-Lueneburg/Bildung-Soziales-und-Gesundheit-Landkreis/Bildung-und-Kultur/Kultur/Plattdeutsch.aspx`

OWL	`http://www.plattdeutsch-niederdeutsch.net/der_bauernhof_um_1870/index.htm`
	`http://www.plattdeutsch-niederdeutsch.net/neues_testament/index.htm`
	`http://www.lippischplatt.de/`

SUD	`http://www.sauerlandmundart.de/daunlots.html`

Table 5: Origin of the Low Saxon data from online sources other than Wikisource and Wikipedia.

Machine-oriented NMT Adaptation for Zero-shot NLP tasks: Comparing the Usefulness of Close and Distant Languages

Amirhossein Tebbifakhr
FBK, Trento, Italy
University of Trento, Italy
atebbifakhr@fbk.eu

Matteo Negri
FBK, Trento, Italy
negri@fbk.eu

Marco Turchi
FBK, Trento, Italy
turchi@fbk.eu

Abstract

Neural Machine Translation (NMT) models are typically trained by considering humans as end-users and maximizing human-oriented objectives. However, in some scenarios, their output is consumed by automatic NLP components rather than by humans. In these scenarios, translations' quality is measured in terms of their "fitness for purpose" (i.e. maximizing performance of external NLP tools) rather than in terms of standard human fluency/adequacy criteria. Recently, reinforcement learning techniques exploiting the feedback from downstream NLP tools have been proposed for "machine-oriented" NMT adaptation. In this work, we tackle the problem in a multilingual setting where a single NMT model translates from multiple languages for downstream automatic processing in the target language. Knowledge sharing across close and distant languages allows to apply our machine-oriented approach in the zero-shot setting where no labeled data for the test language is seen at training time. Moreover, we incorporate multilingual BERT in the source side of our NMT system to benefit from the knowledge embedded in this model. Our experiments show coherent performance gains, for different language directions over both *i)* "generic" NMT models (trained for human consumption), and *ii)* fine-tuned multilingual BERT. This gain for zero-shot language directions (e.g. Spanish–English) is higher when the models are fine-tuned on a closely-related source language (Italian) than a distant one (German).

1 Introduction

With the rapid growth of cloud computing, there are plenty of online services for a variety of natural language processing (NLP) tasks such as document classification, sentiment analysis, and spam detection. However, building them from scratch typically requires a massive amount of labeled data, which is not always publicly available and, for many tasks, is limited to high-resource languages like English. A possible solution to leverage these services in low-resource settings is using Neural Machine Translation (NMT) in the so-called "translation-based" approach, where a text in the low-resource language is first translated into a high-resource one for which dedicated NLP tools exist. Then, the translated text is processed by these downstream tools and, finally, the results are propagated back to the source language.

Although the translation-based approach shows promising results in low-resource settings (Conneau et al., 2018), it still has drawbacks. First, the output quality of current NMT models is not perfect yet (Koehn and Knowles, 2017). Second, even a good translation can alter some traits in the text, which are essential for the downstream NLP tool. This, for instance, is typical for sentiment traits, whose loss can result in final performance drops in sentiment classification tasks (Mohammad et al., 2016). Finally, state-of-the-art NMT models are trained considering humans as end-users and hence optimized to maximize human-oriented objectives like fluency and semantic equivalence of the translation with respect to the source sentence. However, these objectives are not necessarily the optimal ones to exploit an NLP tool at its best. Machines, in fact, are still worse than humans in handling ambiguous or overly complex sentences. This observation calls for strategies that are alternative to the human-oriented enhancement

This work is licensed under a Creative Commons Attribution 4.0 International License. License details: http://creativecommons.org/licenses/by/4.0/.

Proceedings of the 7th VarDial Workshop on NLP for Similar Languages, Varieties and Dialects, pages 36–46
Barcelona, Spain (Online), December 13, 2020

of NMT. Rather, models should be adapted in a *machine-oriented* way that is optimal for automatic processing of their output.

Traditionally, NMT models are trained using parallel corpora, consisting of sentences in the source language and their human translations in the target language. Recently, Tebbifakhr et al. (2019) proposed Machine-Oriented Reinforce (MO-Reinforce), a method based on Reinforcement Learning to pursue machine-oriented objectives for sentence-level classification tasks. In a nutshell: given the output of the downstream classifier (i.e. a probability distribution over the labels), MO-Reinforce considers the probability given to the true class as the collected reward from the downstream classifier. By maximizing the expected value of the collected reward, MO-Reinforce adapts the NMT model's behavior to generate outputs that are easier to label by the downstream classifier.

Although NMT models adapted with MO-Reinforce show promising results compared to the "generic" ones trained by only pursuing human-oriented objectives, they still need a small amount of labeled data in the source language to compute the reward that may not be available for some languages. To address this problem, we exploit multilingual NMT models (Johnson et al., 2017), the MO-Reinforce algorithm and a small quantity of data in closely-related languages. Starting from a multilingual NMT system used to translate texts from n low-resource languages into a resource-rich one, the MO-Reinforce algorithm is run in three different conditions by using source data in: *i)* the same language of the test set (tuning on Italian - testing on Italian); *ii)* a different language, but closely related to the one of the test set, (Italian - Spanish), and *iii)* a different and distant language (German - Spanish). The main goal of these experiments is to show that MO-Reinforce leveraging a multilingual NMT and data in a closely-related language is able to overcome the lack of source labelled data in a specific task.

Moreover, recently, multilingual BERT (Devlin et al., 2019) has shown good performance when fine-tuned for downstream tasks. Multilingual BERT is a pre-trained model built on the union of unlabeled data for more than 100 languages. The availability of unlabeled text in significant quantities in different languages helps this model to extract valuable knowledge about the languages resulting in good performance for different tasks. To strengthen the capability of the NMT system to represent the source sentence, we try different approaches to incorporate multilingual BERT in the NMT system's encoder. Our goal, in this case, is to show that BERT-based NMT systems can benefit from the knowledge embedded in BERT, particularly in zero-shot language directions.

We focus on a 4-class sentence classification task (news classification), which is harder compared to the binary task (polarity detection) chosen in (Tebbifakhr et al., 2019). We evaluate the translation-based approach from German, Italian, and Spanish (simulating low-resource language settings) into English. It is important to remark that, although our source languages are not low-resource ones, their choice is motivated by the availability of standard benchmark for a comparative evaluation in a simulated low-resource scenario. The results show that:

- Closely-related languages can help to cope with the lack of annotated data for specific NLP tasks (in this case for document classification into four domains).

- MO-Reinforce is able to take advantage of these data to outperform the classification performance of the generic NMT system and Multilingual BERT.

- Although the addition of Multilingual BERT does not yield improvements in translation quality, its capability of generating good source-sentence representations helps MO-Reinforce to achieve better performance.

2   Related Works

Reinforcement Learning methods have been mainly proposed to address the *exposure bias* problem inside sequence-to-sequence models, which refers to the discrepancy between training and inference time in NMT systems. During training, in fact, the model is exposed to the reference translations, while at inference time the model generates the translation based on its own (typically sub-optimal) predictions, at the risk of cumulative errors at each step. In (Ranzato et al., 2016), the authors proposed a gradual shifting from token-level maximum likelihood to sentence-level BLEU score to expose the model to its prediction instead of the reference translation. Shen et al. (2016) extended this idea by adopting minimum risk training (Goel and Byrne, 2000) to directly optimize task-specific metrics like BLEU or TER in NMT. Bahdanau et al. (2017) optimized the policy using the actor-critic algorithm. In another line of research, in situations where the reference translation is not available, (Kreutzer et al., 2017) proposed bandit structured prediction, which describes a stochastic optimization framework to leverage "weak" feedbacks collected from the user (e.g. Likert scores about output quality). A common trait of all the above-mentioned works is that they all consider *humans* as the end-users of NMT system's output, which should hence adhere to the human criteria of fluency and adequacy. Tebbifakhr et al. (2019) recently proposed a paradigm shift by considering *machines* as the final consumers on machine-translated text, which should hence maximize "fitness for purpose" criteria (i.e. providing easy-to-process input to downstream NLP components). To this aim, they adopted the REINFORCE (Williams, 1992) approach to leverage the feedback from a downstream task (e.g. classification accuracy in a polarity detection task) to update the agent's policy (the probability of taking a certain action α when in state s). This approach was extended in (Tebbifakhr et al., 2020) to address different NLP tasks in parallel, with a single NMT engine using the same policy. Both works showed that leveraging the downstream classifier's feedback adapts the NMT system to output translations that are easier to be classified by the downstream tool. None of them, however, explored the application of the approach in zero-shot settings, nor focused on how language closeness/distance affects final performance as done in this paper.

Pre-training a neural network or parts of it with existing models is a common approach in several NLP tasks and it allows developers to speed up the training, to leverage different types of training data and to improve the overall performance of the learning system. Among various solutions, *word2vec* (Mikolov et al., 2013) and its variants (Pennington et al., 2014; Levy and Goldberg, 2014) have been the first resources used to pre-training the embeddings in an NMT system. They provide embedded vectors of individual words and have been widely used in NLP.

Recently, pre-trained Language Models (LM) showed better performance when fine-tuned for downstream tasks. ELMo (Peters et al., 2018) is among the first pre-trained LMs, which is based on Bi-LSTM architecture trained on monolingual data. The authors showed that combining the representations from different layers obtains contextual-aware word representations that can be used for other NLP tasks. Right after ELMo, BERT (Devlin et al., 2019) was proposed based on the encoder of Transformer (Vaswani et al., 2017). This model was trained on unlabeled data using two loss functions: *i)* Masked Language Model (MLM) and *ii)* Next Sentence Prediction (NPS). This pre-trained model showed outstanding performance when fine-tuned for a variety of NLP tasks. There are many variants of BERT proposed after, among them: Conneau and Lample (2019) add cross-lingual data and only use MLM loss function, and Yang et al. (2019) train the model on the permuted data.

Specifically for NMT, different attempts have been done to integrate pre-trained LMs in the sequence-to-sequence model. Among others, ELMo was used for initializing the embedding layer in the NMT system (Edunov et al., 2019). Clinchant et al. (2019) used BERT for initializing the encoder or embedding layer of the NMT systems. Then the BERT models are fixed or fine-tuned along with other variables of the model. In (Zhu et al., 2020), a method was proposed to fuse the representations obtained from BERT with each layer of the encoder and decoder in the NMT model through attention mechanisms. We take a similar approach to (Clinchant et al., 2019) in initializing source embedding or the encoder of the NMT system while training a generic NMT systems. Here, this is done for the first time in a machine-oriented setting and in zero-shot conditions.

3 Background and Methodology

3.1 Neural Machine Translation

State-of-the-art NMT models are based on the encoder-decoder architecture (Bahdanau et al., 2015; Vaswani et al., 2017). In this architecture, the encoder encodes the sentence in the source language into vector representations. Then, the decoder autoregressively decodes these representations into a sentence in the target language, emitting a token at each time step until the end-of-sentence token is generated.

More formally, at time step i the NMT model generates a probability distribution $p_\theta(.|\mathbf{y}_{\{0..i-1\}}, \mathbf{x})$ based on the source sentence $\mathbf{x}$ and the already generated translation prefix $\mathbf{y}_{\{0..i-1\}}$, where θ is the model's parameter set. So, for a given translation pair $(\mathbf{x}, \mathbf{y})$ the probability of generating reference translation $\mathbf{y}$ for the given source sentence $\mathbf{x}$ can be computed as follows:

$$P(\mathbf{y}|\mathbf{x}) = \prod_{i=1}^{N} p_\theta(\mathbf{y}_i|\mathbf{y}_{\{0..i-1\}}, \mathbf{x}) \tag{1}$$

where N is the length of $\mathbf{y}$. These models are usually trained by maximizing the likelihood of a given parallel corpus containing S translation pairs $\{\mathbf{x}^s, \mathbf{y}^s\}_{s=1}^{S}$. The Maximum Likelihood Estimation (MLE) objective function can be written as follows:

$$\begin{aligned}
\mathcal{L}_{MLE} &= \sum_{s=1}^{S} \log P(\mathbf{y}^s|\mathbf{x}^s) \\
&= \sum_{s=1}^{S} \sum_{i=1}^{N^s} \log p_\theta(\mathbf{y}_i^s|\mathbf{y}_{\{0..i-1\}}^s, \mathbf{x})
\end{aligned} \tag{2}$$

The parameters of the model can be optimized by applying stochastic gradient descent to maximize MLE objective function. As mentioned in §1, this approach indirectly maximizes the *human-oriented* translation criteria embedded in the parallel corpora used for training.

3.2 Multilingual Machine-Oriented REINFORCE

Tebbifakhr et al. (2019) proposed an approach based on Reinforce (Williams, 1992) that, instead of maximizing the likelihood of the training data, maximizes the expected value of the reward on the output of the NMT system. Formally, the NMT model defines an agent that chooses an action, i.e. generating a translation candidate $\hat{\mathbf{y}}$, and gets a reward $\Delta(\hat{\mathbf{y}})$ according to the action taken. This reward is external to the NMT system and can be collected either from humans (Ranzato et al., 2016; Kreutzer et al., 2017) or, as in MO-Reinforce, from a downstream NLP tool (Tebbifakhr et al., 2019). This objective function can be written as follows:

$$\begin{aligned}
\mathcal{L}_{RL} &= \sum_{s=1}^{S} E_{\hat{\mathbf{y}} \sim P(.|\mathbf{x}^{(s)})} \Delta(\hat{\mathbf{y}}) \\
&= \sum_{s=1}^{S} \sum_{\hat{\mathbf{y}} \in \mathbf{Y}} P(\hat{\mathbf{y}}|\mathbf{x}^{(s)}) \Delta(\hat{\mathbf{y}})
\end{aligned} \tag{3}$$

where $\mathbf{Y}$ is the set containing all the possible translations. Since the size of this set is exponentially large, the expected value is usually estimated by sampling one or few candidates from $\mathbf{Y}$. In (Ranzato et al., 2016), the expected value is estimated by sampling only one candidate using multinomial sampling:

$$\hat{\mathcal{L}_{RL}} = \sum_{s=1}^{S} P(\hat{\mathbf{y}}|\mathbf{x}^s) \Delta(\hat{\mathbf{y}}), \hat{\mathbf{y}} \sim P(.|\mathbf{x}^s) \tag{4}$$

In MO-Reinforce, the reward is computed as the probability given to the true class by the downstream classifier. The maximum value of this reward is 1 when the downstream classifier assigns the correct label to the translation candidate with total confidence. Also, to increase the contribution of the reward, MO-Reinforce exploits a sampling strategy (Algorithm 1) where: *i)* K translation candidates are sampled from the output probability distribution of the NMT system, *ii)* the reward is computed for each of them, and *iii)* the one with the highest reward is chosen as final candidate. Although MO-Reinforce shows promising results in adapting NMT models to pursue machine-oriented objectives, it still needs a small amount of labeled data for computing the reward. These data, however, are not always available in the low-resource settings for which it is proposed. To tackle this problem, we extend MO-Reinforce to

---

Algorithm 1 Machine-Oriented Reinforce

1: **Input:** $\mathbf{x}^{(s)}$ s-th source sentence in training data, K number of sampled candidates
2: **Output:** sampled candidate $\hat{\mathbf{y}}^{(s)}$
3: $C = \emptyset$ {Candidates set}
4: **for** $k = 1$ **to** K **do**
5:     $\mathbf{y}_0 = BOS$ {Beginning-Of-Sentence token}
6:     $i = 0$
7:     **repeat**
8:       $i = i + 1$
9:       $\mathbf{y}_i \sim p_\theta(.|\mathbf{x}^s, \mathbf{y}_{\{0..i-1\}})$
10:       $\mathbf{y}_{\{0..i\}} = \mathbf{y}_{\{0..i-1\}} + \mathbf{y}_i$
11:     **until** $\mathbf{y}_i$ is EOS {End-Of-Sentence token}
12:     $\mathbf{y} = \mathbf{y}_{\{1..i-1\}}$
13:     $\mathbf{r} = \Delta(\mathbf{y})$ {Reward from the classifier}
14:     $C = C \cup (\mathbf{y}, \mathbf{r})$
15: **end for**
16: $\hat{\mathbf{y}}^{(s)} = \max_{\mathbf{r}}(C)$ {Candidate with maximum reward}

---

the multilingual setting. We train a multilingual NMT model (Ha et al., 2016), which translates from different low-resource languages (S_1, S_2,...S_n) to a high-resource one (T). This model is trained on the union of (S_i, T) parallel corpora in which the source language differs. This unification of corpora results in learning a language-agnostic representation on the encoder side and enables knowledge transfer from language for which labeled data exist to the (zero-shot) language without labeled data (Eriguchi et al., 2018). The fact that multilingual NMT results in a single model covering multiple languages (as opposed to relying on dedicated models for each language pair) represents an architectural advantage that makes it scalable, easy to maintain and, in turn, particularly appealing for real-world applications.

3.3 BERT-Based NMT

Recently, the pre-trained BERT has shown outstanding results when it is fine-tuned for a downstream task. This superiority comes from the fact that this model has been trained on a huge amount of unlabeled data, which helps it to learn valuable knowledge about the language. The multilingual version of BERT has been trained on the union of the unlabeled data from more than 100 different languages. This multilingual information motivated us in incorporating the multilingual BERT in our NMT system to take advantage of its embedded knowledge. In our setting, where the NMT system serves the downstream tool having a better representation of the input can be beneficial to generate a better and more useful translation, in particular in zero-shot languages.

We employ two different approaches to incorporating BERT in our NMT system based on Transformer (Vaswani et al., 2017). In the standard Transformer, all the variables of the model are randomly initialized and then trained. In our implementation of this model, we use Byte-Pair Encoding (BPE) (Sennrich et al., 2016) to extract the vocabulary from the source and target side of the parallel data. The following paragraphs explains the details of each BERT-based NMT implementations.

BERT Encoder   The first approach to incorporating BERT in our NMT system is initializing the encoder of the NMT system using the weights of the multilingual BERT. In this approach instead of using BPE, we tokenize the input sentence to sub-words using the BERT tokenizer and add special tokens **[CLS]** and **[SEP]** to the beginning and the end of the sentence. Then the tokenized sentence is encoded with multilingual BERT and the encoded representations are passed to the decoder of the NMT system.

BERT Embedding   In the second approach, we use the output of multilingual BERT as contextualized embeddings of the source sentence. Then these embeddings are passed to the encoder of the NMT system to encode the source sentence. Finally, the output of the encoder is passed to the decoder of the NMT system.

The next Section will explain how the BERT-based NMT systems and MO-Reinforce are used in our experiments to address the lack of source data in a specific language.

4   Experiments

Experimental Settings   We pre-train the two NMT systems described in § 3.3 and the standard Transformer using the Maximum-Likelihood Estimation on the parallel corpora for the human-oriented translation task. Their translation performance are evaluated in § 5.1. The outputs of these NMT systems are then passed to the downstream classifier and its classification performance is evaluated in § 5.2. We compare the performance of these approaches (different NMT + Downstream classifier) with the multilingual BERT trained on English data. In this set of experiments, the NMT systems and the BERT classifier are not tuned on any kind of source language classification training data (e.g. using the MO-Reinforce algorithm for the NMT systems), so we consider this setting a zero-shot scenario.

For training the NMT systems using multilingual BERT, we freeze the variables of BERT. We use six layers of the encoder (if any) and six layers of the decoder. We keep the hyper-parameters of the model similar to the original settings (Vaswani et al., 2017). We train each model with the effective batch size equal to 25K tokens.

We then consider the condition when a minimum amount of downstream labeled data is available for a closely-related language to Spanish (Italian) and a distant one (German). We use these data to adapt each NMT system using the Multilingual MO-Reinforce approach described in § 3.2. We evaluate the downstream classifier's performance on the output of each adapted NMT system. We compare the Multilingual MO-Reinforce approach with the multilingual BERT fined-tuned for the downstream task using the same limited amount of the labeled data (see § 5.3). Similar to (Tebbifakhr et al., 2020), we adapt the NMT systems using MO-Reinforce by disabling and enabling the dropout while generating the translation candidates. We keep the parameter K in MO-Reinforce equal to 5, and adapt each NMT system for 50 epochs and choose the best checkpoint based on the performance on the development set. For simulating the downstream classifier we use English BERT fine-tuned for the downstream task using the English labeled data.

Data   For pre-training the NMT systems, we use the parallel corpora reported in Table 1, and we evaluate the Spanish and Italian translation performance of the NMT systems on the Ubuntu parallel corpus (Tiedemann, 2012). For the Transformer model, we tokenize and encode each side of the parallel corpora with 32K byte-pair encoding rules. For the other Bert-based NMT systems, on the source side, we use the BERT encoder setting to split the sentences to the tokens.

We evaluate our translation-based classification approaches on a multilingual document classification task where Spanish and Italian news documents have to be automatically annotated with domain labels. Our classification data consists of the first sentence of each document that, according to (Bell, 1991) is a good proxy to determine the domain of news texts. The data used (Schwenk and Li, 2018) cover 4 domains: Corporate/Industrial, Economics, Government/Social, and Markets. The training, development, and test sets for each language respectively contain 10K, 1K, and 4K documents, equally distributed in the 4 classes. For the English downstream classifier we use whole 10K documents while, to simulate the low-resource setting, we sample 100 documents for each class from the Italian training set. In addition, we collect the same amount of data also for German. This data is used to fine-tune the Spanish system on a distant language and compare downstream performance results achieved by our approach in the two fine-tuning conditions (close – Es-It – vs distant – Es-De – languages).

Evaluation metrics   We evaluate the translation performance of the NMT systems using BLEU Score (Papineni et al., 2002) and the classification performance with macro average F1 Score.

5   Results

5.1   The NMT systems' translation performance

We start the evaluation by comparing the translation performance of the three different NMT systems. The performance of the NMT systems in terms of BLEU score is reported in Table 2. As shown, *BERT*

	Europarl	JRC	Wikipedia	ECB	TED	KDE	News11	News	Total
Es-En	2M	0.8M	1.8M	0.1M	0.2M	0.2M	0.3M	0.2M	5.6M
It-En	2M	0.8M	1M	0.2M	0.2M	0.3M	0.04M	0.02M	4.56M
De-En	2M	0.7M	2.5M	0.1M	0.1M	0.3M	0.2M	0.2M	6.1M

Table 1: Number of sentences in the parallel corpora used for training the generic NMT systems.

	BERT Encoder	BERT Embedding	Transformer
Italian	20.19	21.88	**25.56**
German	17.18	19.04	**21.86**
Spanish	26.15	28.12	**32.02**

Table 2: Translation performance of the different NMT systems in terms of BLEU score.

Encoder has lower performance compared to *Transformer* (-5.37 in Italian, -4.68 in German, and -5.87 in Spanish). This is due to the fact that the encoder of the NMT system is the fixed multilingual BERT and only the weights on the decoder side (embeddings, decoder weights, and linear projection to vocabulary) are trained in this setting. *BERT Embedding* outperforms *BERT Encoder* in translation task (+1.69 in Italian, +1.86 in German, +1.97 in Spanish). This improvement was expected, because in this setting the weights in the encoder are also trained along with the parameters on the decoder side. However, the performance of this systems is still lower than *Transformer* (-3.68 in Italian, -2.82 in German, and -3.90 in Spanish). This is because multilingual BERT is trained only on monolingual data. Compared to *Transformer*, in which all the weights are trained on parallel data, its output representations are hence less effective for translation tasks. These results are mainly in line with those reported in (Clinchant et al., 2019) when using BERT as fixed encoder. However, while they showed improvements using BERT as embedding matrix on the encoder side in some settings, this is not visible in our experiments.

5.2 The classification performance on the output of the NMT systems

We continue the evaluation, by using these three NMT systems in our translation-based classification approach for the downstream task. All the NMT systems are not aware of the downstream task and are not fine-tuned on any task-specific data in the source and target languages. For these reasons, we consider these experiments as in zero-shot conditions. Table 3 shows the downstream classification task's performance using the different NMT systems. We also compare them with the multilingual BERT fine-tuned for the downstream task using the English labeled data. As shown in the table, except for the *BERT Encoder* in German (-0.9 F1 Score), the translation-based classification approach in all the other settings has better performance in the zero-shot settings than the multilingual BERT. Among the BERT-based NMT systems, except Spanish in which the results are similar (85.9 for *BERT Encoder* and 85.8 for *BERT Embedding*), *BERT Embedding* outperforms *BERT Encoder* in the other two languages (+0.8 in Italian and +2.8 in German). These results are in line with BERT-based NMT systems' translation performance reported in Table 2. However, when comparing the BERT-based NMT systems with the *Transformer*, the translation gap showed in Table 2 in favour of Transformer is minimized for Italian and German in terms of classification performance and overturned for Spanish (+1.6 F1 Score). This analysis shows that the translation quality in terms of human-oriented scores (like the BLEU score) does not have a high correlation with the performance of the downstream task in the translation-based classification scenario.

5.3 MO-Reinforce adaptation

Table 4 reports the performance of Multilingual BERT and the three NMT systems when testing on Italian and Spanish. The systems are fine-tuned using the Italian and German labeled data. This set of experiments covers the conditions when the NMT system is fine-tuned by MO-Reinforce on the data belonging to a) the same language of the test set (Italian - Italian, second column); b) a different language,

	Italian	German	Spanish
Multilingual BERT	70.2	87.0	80.6
BERT Encoder	74.5	86.1	85.9
BERT Embedding	75.3	88.9	85.8
Transformer	76.1	88.8	84.2

Table 3: Document classification performance in terms of F1 Score using only English labeled data.

	Fine-tuned on labeled data in Italian		*Fine-tuned on labeled data in German*
	Italian	Spanish	Spanish
Multilingual BERT	82.9	80.7	73.2
BERT Encoder	76.7	85.3	83.3
BERT Embedding	76.8	**86.7**	**86.3**
Transformer	77.8	86.1	84.3
(enabled dropout)			
BERT Encoder	83.6	83.4	76.8
BERT Embedding	**84.0**	82.7	76.0
Transformer	82.5	82.3	75.7

Table 4: Document classification performance in terms of F1 Score by fine-tuning on labeled data in close and distant languages.

but closely-related (Italian - Spanish, third column) and c) a different and distant language (German - Spanish, fourth column), the more extreme case. The NMT systems do not use the dropout during the MO-Reinforce fine-tuning in the top part of the table, while it is enabled in the bottom experiments.

In the top part of Table 4, comparing the performance of all the systems tested on Spanish (third and fourth columns), fine-tuning on Italian and German shows coherent performance gains when the systems are trained on the closely-related language (Italian) over the distant language (German). The NMT systems adapted using MO-Reinforce, except for *BERT Encoder*, have performance improvement over the generic NMT systems (Table 3), showing that MO-Reinforce can alter the output of the translation system to benefit more from the knowledge embedded in the downstream classifier. Also, MO-Reinforce outperforms multilingual BERT in both cases (fine-tuning on close and distant languages), thanks to the language-agnostic representation of the NMT encoder , which is not the case in multilingual BERT trained only on monolingual data. The best result for Spanish is obtained when *BERT Embedding* is fine-tuned on Italian labeled data. It confirms our hypothesis that the better representation of the language by multilingual BERT trained on huge amount of data can be beneficial compared to *Transformer*, which has seen only the limited parallel data. When testing on Italian, as expected, all the systems have an increase in performance compared to the results in Table 3. The best result is obtained by multilingual BERT (82.19 F1 Score) showing that it is able to better leverage the labeled data. Our intuition is that the NMT systems without enabling the dropout during fine-tuning do not properly explore the searching space. On one side, this allows the system to better transfer the source-language data knowledge to the other languages, but, on the other, it limits the learning capability on the language for which the labelled data is available.

To test this hypothesis and similar to (Tebbifakhr et al., 2020), we repeat the adaption of the NMT systems using MO-Reinforce by enabling the dropout while generating the translation candidates. This adds some noise to the translation outputs that helps the system to avoid possible local optima and favours a deeper exploration of the probability space. The bottom part of Table 4 reports the performance of the translation-based approaches for the downstream classification task for NMT systems adapted by

MO-Reinforce on Italian and German labeled data using the dropout while generating the translation candidates. The first noticeable change in the result is the boost in the Italian language's performance. This difference is higher for *BERT Encoder* and *BERT Embedding* (83.6 and 84.0 F1 score respectively) outperforming the multilingual BERT (82.9 F1 Score). However, this improvement in Italian comes at the cost of lower performance in Spanish (zero-shot language). This drop is smaller for the systems fine-tuned on Italian confirming the advantage of using closely-related languages. Indeed, the more the NMT system becomes specialized on German (distant language), the lower the performance are on Spanish. However, even with this drop in performance on the zero-shot language, the performance of all the systems are higher than the multilingual BERT. This observation confirms that NMT systems have a more language-agnostic representation of the input text, which results in easier knowledge transfer between languages, in particular the closer ones.

6 Conclusion

In this paper, we proposed a multilingual extension of the MO-Reinforce algorithm able to work in zero-shot settings. Our solution takes advantage of a multilingual NMT model, which translates texts from different low-resource languages into English. To mitigate the lack of data in zero-shot languages, we also incorporated the multilingual BERT with different approaches in the NMT model. Our evaluation shows that using generic NMT systems in the translation-based approach works better than the multilingual BERT in zero-shot settings. Furthermore, the shared knowledge between the source languages allows MO-Reinforce to leverage the labeled data in one language to adapt the NMT model to pursue machine-oriented objectives in other languages, even in zero-shot settings. Our results show that data in closely-related languages can help to cope with the lack of task-specific resources and confirm the capability of MO-Reinforce to leverage and transfer information across languages. The best result in zero-shot settings is obtained with the NMT system by incorporating multilingual BERT as embeddings adapted on closely-related language. However, for the language with a small amount of data, the best approach uses the multilingual BERT as the embedding for the source side of the NMT system by enabling the dropout while generating the translation candidates. Our future works will consider fine-tuning the multilingual BERT variables along with other variables of the model in NMT systems, which can obtain a language-agnostic representation in the BERT model and be helpful in zero-shot settings.

References

Dzmitry Bahdanau, Kyunghyun Cho, and Yoshua Bengio. 2015. Neural machine translation by jointly learning to align and translate. In *3rd International Conference on Learning Representations, Conference Track Proceedings*, San Diego, California, USA, May.

Dzmitry Bahdanau, Philemon Brakel, Kelvin Xu, Anirudh Goyal, Ryan Lowe, Joelle Pineau, Aaron C. Courville, and Yoshua Bengio. 2017. An actor-critic algorithm for sequence prediction. In *5th International Conference on Learning Representations, Conference Track Proceedings*, Toulon, France, April.

A. Bell. 1991. *The Language of News Media*. Language in society. Blackwell.

Stephane Clinchant, Kweon Woo Jung, and Vassilina Nikoulina. 2019. On the use of BERT for neural machine translation. In *Proceedings of the 3rd Workshop on Neural Generation and Translation*, pages 108–117, Hong Kong, November.

Alexis Conneau and Guillaume Lample. 2019. Cross-lingual language model pretraining. In *Advances in Neural Information Processing Systems 32*, pages 7059–7069. Vancouver, Canada, December.

Alexis Conneau, Ruty Rinott, Guillaume Lample, Adina Williams, Samuel Bowman, Holger Schwenk, and Veselin Stoyanov. 2018. XNLI: Evaluating cross-lingual sentence representations. In *Proceedings of the 2018 Conference on Empirical Methods in Natural Language Processing*, pages 2475–2485, Brussels, Belgium, October-November.

Jacob Devlin, Ming-Wei Chang, Kenton Lee, and Kristina Toutanova. 2019. BERT: Pre-training of deep bidirectional transformers for language understanding. In *Proceedings of the 2019 Conference of the North American Chapter of the Association for Computational Linguistics: Human Language Technologies, Volume 1 (Long and Short Papers)*, pages 4171–4186, Minneapolis, Minnesota, June.

Sergey Edunov, Alexei Baevski, and Michael Auli. 2019. Pre-trained language model representations for language generation. In *Proceedings of the 2019 Conference of the North American Chapter of the Association for Computational Linguistics: Human Language Technologies, Volume 1 (Long and Short Papers)*, pages 4052–4059, Minneapolis, Minnesota, June.

Akiko Eriguchi, Melvin Johnson, Orhan Firat, Hideto Kazawa, and Wolfgang Macherey. 2018. Zero-shot cross-lingual classification using multilingual neural machine translation. *CoRR*, abs/1809.04686.

Vaibhava Goel and William J Byrne. 2000. Minimum bayes-risk automatic speech recognition. *Comput. Speech Lang.*, 14(2):115–135, April.

Thanh-Le Ha, Jan Niehues, and Alexander H. Waibel. 2016. Toward multilingual neural machine translation with universal encoder and decoder. *CoRR*, abs/1611.04798.

Melvin Johnson, Mike Schuster, Quoc V. Le, Maxim Krikun, Yonghui Wu, Zhifeng Chen, Nikhil Thorat, Fernanda Viégas, Martin Wattenberg, Greg Corrado, Macduff Hughes, and Jeffrey Dean. 2017. Google's multilingual neural machine translation system: Enabling zero-shot translation. *Transactions of the Association for Computational Linguistics*, 5:339–351.

Philipp Koehn and Rebecca Knowles. 2017. Six challenges for neural machine translation. In *Proceedings of the First Workshop on Neural Machine Translation*, pages 28–39, Vancouver, Canada, August.

Julia Kreutzer, Artem Sokolov, and Stefan Riezler. 2017. Bandit structured prediction for neural sequence-to-sequence learning. In *Proceedings of the 55th Annual Meeting of the Association for Computational Linguistics (Volume 1: Long Papers)*, pages 1503–1513, Vancouver, Canada, July.

Omer Levy and Yoav Goldberg. 2014. Neural word embedding as implicit matrix factorization. In Z. Ghahramani, M. Welling, C. Cortes, N. D. Lawrence, and K. Q. Weinberger, editors, *Advances in Neural Information Processing Systems 27*, pages 2177–2185.

Tomas Mikolov, Ilya Sutskever, Kai Chen, Greg S Corrado, and Jeff Dean. 2013. Distributed representations of words and phrases and their compositionality. In C. J. C. Burges, L. Bottou, M. Welling, Z. Ghahramani, and K. Q. Weinberger, editors, *Advances in Neural Information Processing Systems 26*, pages 3111–3119.

Saif M. Mohammad, Mohammad Salameh, and Svetlana Kiritchenko. 2016. How translation alters sentiment. *Journal of Artificial Intelligence Research*, 55(1):95–130, January.

Kishore Papineni, Salim Roukos, Todd Ward, and Wei-Jing Zhu. 2002. Bleu: a method for automatic evaluation of machine translation. In *Proceedings of the 40th Annual Meeting of the Association for Computational Linguistics*, pages 311–318, Philadelphia, Pennsylvania, USA, July.

Jeffrey Pennington, Richard Socher, and Christopher Manning. 2014. GloVe: Global vectors for word representation. In *Proceedings of the 2014 Conference on Empirical Methods in Natural Language Processing*, pages 1532–1543, Doha, Qatar, October.

Matthew Peters, Mark Neumann, Mohit Iyyer, Matt Gardner, Christopher Clark, Kenton Lee, and Luke Zettlemoyer. 2018. Deep contextualized word representations. In *Proceedings of the 2018 Conference of the North American Chapter of the Association for Computational Linguistics: Human Language Technologies, Volume 1 (Long Papers)*, pages 2227–2237, New Orleans, Louisiana, USA, June.

Marc'Aurelio Ranzato, Sumit Chopra, Michael Auli, and Wojciech Zaremba. 2016. Sequence level training with recurrent neural networks. In *4th International Conference on Learning Representations, Conference Track Proceedings*, San Juan, Puerto Rico, May.

Holger Schwenk and Xian Li. 2018. A corpus for multilingual document classification in eight languages. In *Proceedings of the Eleventh International Conference on Language Resources and Evaluation*, Miyazaki, Japan, May.

Rico Sennrich, Barry Haddow, and Alexandra Birch. 2016. Neural machine translation of rare words with subword units. In *Proceedings of the 54th Annual Meeting of the Association for Computational Linguistics (Volume 1: Long Papers)*, pages 1715–1725, Berlin, Germany, August.

Shiqi Shen, Yong Cheng, Zhongjun He, Wei He, Hua Wu, Maosong Sun, and Yang Liu. 2016. Minimum risk training for neural machine translation. In *Proceedings of the 54th Annual Meeting of the Association for Computational Linguistics (Volume 1: Long Papers)*, pages 1683–1692, Berlin, Germany, August.

Amirhossein Tebbifakhr, Luisa Bentivogli, Matteo Negri, and Marco Turchi. 2019. Machine translation for machines: the sentiment classification use case. In *Proceedings of the 2019 Conference on Empirical Methods in Natural Language Processing and the 9th International Joint Conference on Natural Language Processing*, pages 1368–1374, Hong Kong, China, November.

Amirhossein Tebbifakhr, Matteo Negri, and Marco Turchi. 2020. Automatic translation for multiple nlp tasks: a multi-task approach to machine-oriented nmt adaptation. In *Proceedings of the 22nd Annual Conference of the European Association for Machine Translation*, pages 235–244, Virtual, November.

Jörg Tiedemann. 2012. Parallel data, tools and interfaces in OPUS. In *Proceedings of the Eighth International Conference on Language Resources and Evaluation*, pages 2214–2218, Istanbul, Turkey, May.

Ashish Vaswani, Noam Shazeer, Niki Parmar, Jakob Uszkoreit, et al. 2017. Attention is all you need. In *Advances in Neural Information Processing Systems 30*, pages 5998–6008. Long Beach, California, USA, December.

Ronald J Williams. 1992. Simple statistical gradient-following algorithms for connectionist reinforcement learning. *Machine learning*, 8(3-4):229–256.

Zhilin Yang, Zihang Dai, Yiming Yang, Jaime Carbonell, Russ R Salakhutdinov, and Quoc V Le. 2019. Xlnet: Generalized autoregressive pretraining for language understanding. In *Advances in Neural Information Processing Systems 32*, pages 5753–5763. Vancouver, Canada, December.

Jinhua Zhu, Yingce Xia, Lijun Wu, Di He, Tao Qin, Wengang Zhou, Houqiang Li, and Tieyan Liu. 2020. Incorporating bert into neural machine translation. In *8th International Conference on Learning Representations, Conference Track Proceedings*, Virtual, April.

Character Alignment in Morphologically Complex
Translation Sets for Related Languages

Michael Gasser
Indiana University
gasser@indiana.edu

Nazareth Amlesom Kifle
Østfold University College
nazareth.a.kifle@hiof.no

Binyam Ephrem
Addis Ababa University
binephrem@gmail.com

Abstract

For languages with complex morphology, word-to-word translation is a task with various potential applications, for example, in information retrieval, language instruction, and dictionary creation, as well as in machine translation. In this paper, we confine ourselves to the subtask of character alignment for the particular case of families of related languages with very few resources for most or all members. There are many such families; we focus on the subgroup of Semitic languages spoken in Ethiopia and Eritrea. We begin with an adaptation of the familiar alignment algorithms behind statistical machine translation, modifying them as appropriate for our task. We show how character alignment can reveal morphological, phonological, and orthographic correspondences among related languages.

1 Background

Languages such as Turkish, Arabic, and Swahili are characterized by a wide variety of productive ways in which morphemes are combined to form words. In these *morphologically complex languages* (MCLs) —and there are thousands of them— many more specific word forms are possible than in languages such as English and Chinese. This very high type-to-token ratio results in a severe data sparsity problem, leading the field of machine translation (MT) to begin to take morphology seriously once such languages were considered (El-Kahlout et al., 2019). As far as we know, however, no one has investigated the translation of individual words between MCLs. Why would such a task be worth pursuing? First, in MCLs, words may correspond to entire phrases in languages such as English or Chinese. Thus when translating from, say, Arabic to Turkish, the capacity to translate individual nouns or verbs, segmented into their constituent morphemes, could play a significant role. We suspect this will be especially true for translation between closely related MCLs. In such cases, syntactic differences may be limited, with word order and long-distance dependencies largely preserved, while the within-word differences may remain challenging. Second, focusing on word translation pairs may reveal other potentially useful information, especially for related languages, such as language distance or correspondences between characters or phonemes. Finally, a system that translates complex words can support applications such as cross-linguistic information retrieval, dictionary creation, and language instruction.

In this paper, we consider the more general problem of translation among a *set* of words in related MCLs. As an illustration, see the words in column (b) of Figure 1, each a translation of 'I was listening' in one of four closely related Romance languages of the Iberian Peninsula. By examining multiple related languages, we eventually hope to be able to capitalize on inter-relationships among the languages. We are specifically interested in the word translation task for languages with few computational resources.

Our task is related to other work in MT. We could, for example, approach the translation of pairs of words within a set using one of the state-of-the-art neural sequence-to-sequence methods, which have also been shown to be applicable to other morphological tasks (Cotterell et al., 2018; McCarthy et al., 2019). However, we may be just as interested in the details of what is learned — where the boundaries between

This work is licensed under a Creative Commons Attribution 4.0 International License. License details: http://creativecommons.org/licenses/by/4.0/.

Proceedings of the 7th VarDial Workshop on NLP for Similar Languages, Varieties and Dialects, pages 47–56
Barcelona, Spain (Online), December 13, 2020

morphemes are, what morphophonological rules apply — as we are in the performance itself, and it may be difficult or impossible to extract this knowledge from a neural system. For now, we will look for inspiration in earlier MT work, specifically variants of statistical MT (SMT) and leave comparison with neural approaches to future work.

A further related area of work, which actually resembles our task more closely, concerns morphological paradigms (Erdmann et al., 2020; Jin et al., 2020; Cotterell et al., 2018; McCarthy et al., 2019). A partial example of a Spanish paradigm appears in column (a) of Figure 1. Of particular interest to us is the "paradigm cell filling" problem, that of learning the inflections that comprise a paradigm given all forms for a set of lemmas (Durrett and DeNero, 2013).

If we compare word translations in a set of related languages with cells in a morphological paradigm within one language, the relationship between our task and the paradigm cell filling problem becomes clear. However, this is only the case for the translation of words with similar roots. Figure 1 illustrates this point with an example paradigm from Spanish and two example translation sets from four Romance languages.[1] When the roots are related, as in the translation set in column (b), the set resembles a paradigm; when they aren't (or aren't obviously), as in the translation set in column (c), only the affixes resemble one another. We will be focusing on the case where roots are similar; thus we will need to address the question of how to distinguish such sets from those like the one in column (c).

	(a)		**(b)**		**(c)**
PRES	*escucho*		*escuchaba*	ES	*hablaba*
IMPF	*escuchaba*		*escoltava*	PT	*falava*
PRET	*escuché*		*escutava*	CA	*parlava*
FUT	*escucharé*		*escoitaba*	GL	*falaba*
	escuchar 'to listen': 1pers.sing.		'I was listening'		'I was speaking'
	PARADIGM		WORD TRANSLATION SETS		

Figure 1: Paradigm (Spanish); word translation sets (Spanish, Portuguese, Catalan, Galician)

Our longer-term goal is translation: given a word in one language, generate a plausible word in one or more of the other related training languages. In this paper, however, we focus on the subtask that Durrett and Denero (2013) begin with in their paradigm cell filling research, that of aligning the characters of the words in a translation set.

The rest of the paper is organized as follows. In Section 2, after an introduction to the Ethio-Eritrean Semitic (EES) languages, we define our task in more detail, looking specifically at possible types of morphological relationships between related languages, with focus on the EES languages. Next, in Section 3, we discuss how some cross-linguistic morphological relationships can be captured in terms of character alignment and show how character alignment within word translation pairs in closely related languages can be be constrained. Next, in Section 4, we outline our approach to character alignment within word translation sets, in particular, how we adapt SMT word alignment methods to handle character-level alignment. Then, in Section 5, we describe our experiments applying the method to data from the Semitic languages. In Section 5.4, we discuss results, both in terms of alignment performance and in terms of useful information that the alignments provide. Finally, in Section 6, we conclude, looking forward to the next steps in the long-term project of the translation of morphologically complex words.

2 Semitic languages of Ethiopia and Eritrea

The languages of the world differ greatly with respect to how much morphological elaboration they make available to speakers (Stump, 2017). What is interesting for our purposes (and those of this workshop) is the apparent tendency for languages within a closely related family to *agree* in morphological complexity, though not necessarily in the morphological details.

---

[1] Without the benefit of context, there is a much greater potential for translation ambiguity for words than for sentences. Here and elsewhere in this paper, we assume that "translation of a word" refers to a translation in *some possible context*.

In this paper we focus on one of these families, the Ethio-Eritrean Semitic (EES) languages, consisting of the subgroup of Semitic languages spoken in Ethiopia and Eritrea (Demeke, 2001). There is no general agreement on the number of EES languages, but, judged by mutual intelligibility, there are between 10 and 15. Of these, two, Tigrinya (hereafter, Ti) and Tigre (hereafter, Te), are spoken in Eritrea, by roughly 85% of the population, and the remainder, in addition to Ti, are spoken in Ethiopia, as native languages of roughly 38% of the population. These include Amharic (hereafter Am), the official language of the Federal Government of Ethiopia. The EES languages are divided into northern and southern subgroups, with Ge'ez, Ti, and Te in the northern subgroup, Am and the remaining languages in the southern subgroup.

2.1 Morphology

The languages exhibit many features common to other Semitic languages, especially very complex verbal morphology, including subject agreement suffixes and prefixes, object agreement suffixes, and the templatic morphology that Semitic languages are famous for. Verb roots consist of sequences of consonants, organized in a number of root classes. Verb stems consist of patterns of particular vowel and consonant gemination that are overlaid on the consonantal roots. For an Am, Ti, and Te example, see Figure 3a.

2.2 Orthography

The EES languages are written using the Ge'ez writing system, an abugida system in which each character represents either a consonant-vowel sequence (the onset and nucleus of a syllable) or a single consonant (the coda of a syllable). The characters are usually presented in a table, in which each row contains the characters for a single consonant. Figure 2 shows three rows from this table, the symbols representing the consonants /l/, /b/, and /g/ followed by vowels or alone. In addition to their realization as a single consonant, the characters in the sixth column can also represent the consonant followed by the epenthetic vowel [ɨ].[2] For example, the Am word *bəlibb* 'by heart' is written በልብ. Of the two sixth-column characters, the first, ል, is pronounced with a following vowel, while the second, ብ, is not. This example also illustrates the only significant deviation of the orthography from the phonological form of a word: consonant gemination (length) is not indicated.

	ə	u	i	a	e	−	o
l	ለ	ሉ	ሊ	ላ	ሌ	ል	ሎ
b	በ	ቡ	ቢ	ባ	ቤ	ብ	ቦ
g	ገ	ጉ	ጊ	ጋ	ጌ	ግ	ጎ

Figure 2: Three rows from the table of Ge'ez characters.

In our experiments we work with both the *orthographic* representations of words and a *phonemic* transcription in which gemination is indicated (marked with ":"). Because the orthography obscures the boundaries between consonants and vowels, it may also obscure the boundaries between morphemes. An example is shown in Figure 3a. Circles surround affixes; rectangles surround stems. In multiple cases, morpheme boundaries are between consonants and vowels, so a single Ge'ez character spans two morphemes. For example, the final character in each word, በ /bə/, includes the last stem consonant /b/ and the perfective 3sm suffix /ə/. We include gemination in our phonemic representation because of its role in EES verb morphology as well as its importance for speech synthesis in the languages.

2.3 Previous work

Like most African languages, EES languages suffer from a lack of resources. With the exception of Am and Ti (Abate et al., 2018), corpora in the languages are very limited, in some cases non-existent. However, we do have the advantage of bilingual root lexica (Am-Ti, Ti-Te) and dedicated morphological analyzers and generators for three of the languages, Am, Ti, and Te, within the HornMorpho project (Gasser, 2011).[3] HornMorpho consists of weighted finite-state transducers constructed by hand. Using HornMorpho and our bilingual root lexica, we can generate data for the morphological translation task.

---

[2]Linguists disagree on whether this vowel represents a phoneme, and its status may vary between the languages.
[3]Te has been added to HornMorpho for the purpose of this project.

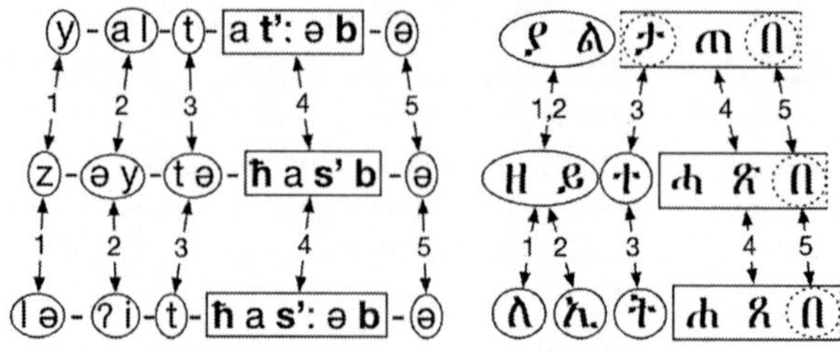
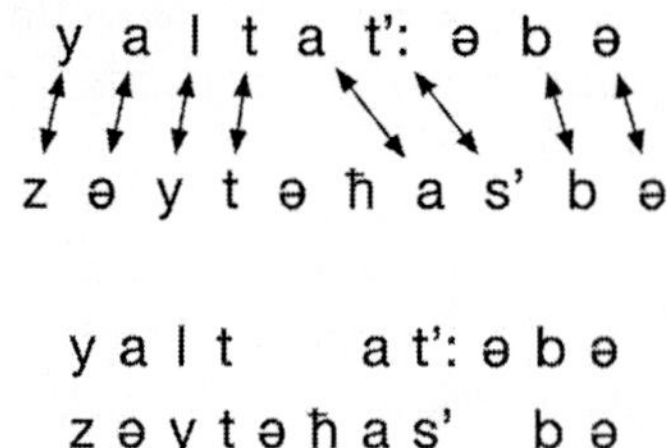

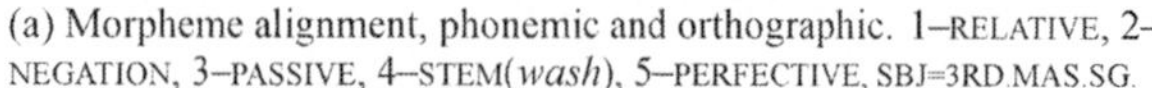

(a) Morpheme alignment, phonemic and orthographic. 1–RELATIVE, 2– NEGATION, 3–PASSIVE, 4–STEM(*wash*), 5–PERFECTIVE, SBJ=3RD.MAS.SG.

(b) Monotonic character alignment (Am, Ti only), diagrammed in two ways.

Figure 3: Alignment within an Am-Ti-Te translation set. Gloss: 'which was not washed.'

3 Morphological alignment and character alignment

It is beyond the scope of this paper to discuss morphological complexity (Stump, 2017). We base our consideration of morphology in the remainder of the paper on the structure of verbs in EES languages and on general notions familiar from basic morphological research. We assume that for each word in a MCL, there is a stem, based on a root; zero or more affixes; and possibly instances of reduplication. For each of these elements in a word, there may be a correspondence within the word's translation in another language. There may be similarities in the order of the morphemes, their forms, and the morphophonological processes that take place at their boundaries. Some of these correspondences are illustrated in Figure 3a for an Am-Ti-Te translation set. The arrows indicate corresponding morphemes, with the phonetic relationships relatively clear, except in the case of the first prefix. Within the stem, the root consonants appear in boldface. Though this may not be apparent, the Am and Ti roots in this case are systematically related: the Ti consonant /ħ/ corresponds regularly to zero in Am, and the Ti consonant /s'/ corresponds often (though not always) to /t'/.

Clearly translation between words such as those in Figure 3a can benefit from recognizing the relationships indicated by the arrows in the figure. Alignment is the process of determining such relationships.

Alignment—identifying corresponding elements in source and target—is fundamental to the training of MT systems; the progress in neural MT resulting from the inclusion of attention mechanisms is just the most recent example (Bahdanau et al., 2015; Vaswani et al., 2017). Within SMT, alignment is a separate step, and because everything else depends on the quality of the alignment, a great deal of emphasis is given to alignment mechanisms (Och and Ney, 2003).

How is character alignment constrained for word translation pairs in closely related languages? With rare exceptions (see below), we can expect it to be *monotonic*. That is, for word translation pair s and t, if the character in position i in s is associated with the character in position j in t, then the character in position $i + 1$ in s is either (1) not associated with any character in t or (2) associated with a character in position k in t such that $k >= j$. This is illustrated for the Am-Ti pair in Figure 3b. Informally, monotonicity means that none of the association arrows (as in the upper diagram in Figure 3b) cross one another. Given this constraint, we can represent character alignments in the simpler format shown in the lower diagram in the figure, with aligned characters above one another.

What would it mean for the monotonicity constraint to be violated for word pairs in related languages? As far as we can tell, the only situation where this could occur is one in which one of the languages has undergone a diachronic or synchronic metathesis process, by which a pair of characters has swapped their positions. For example, imagine a word *gabla* in language 1, which translates as the word *galba* in language 2. While we are not aware of any such cases, they are certainly possible, but in this paper we restrict ourselves to the computationally simpler, and obviously much more common, monotonic cases.

Morphemes can of course consist of multiple characters, and a morpheme in one language can correspond to a morpheme of a different length in another; there are several examples in Figure 3a. However, as in Durrett and DeNero's (2013) approach to paradigm cell filling, we begin with the *alignment of single characters*, constraining the alignment to be one-to-one in both directions. As can be seen from the alignment shown in Figure 3b, these one-to-one character alignments usually do not represent morpheme correspondences, but they do represent a step towards the identification of corresponding morphemes.

Following character alignment, Durrett and DeNero merge neighboring aligned characters into candidate morphemes. This step will be the topic of the next phase of the project and a future paper.

4 Approach

Durrett and DeNero (2013) realize the alignment step in their paradigm cell filling system as an iterated edit-distance algorithm. However, the word translation problem does not lend itself to this approach because of the number of associated characters that are not identical. We applied Durrett and DeNero's algorithm to our task but were only able to achieve reasonable results by modifying it to include explicit character categories, such as consonants and vowels, affecting the probabilities of the edit operations. For example, we treated the substitution of a vowel for a vowel as more likely than the substitution of a vowel for a consonant. In general, we cannot expect to have this kind of knowledge of character categories for arbitrary orthographic systems, so it is desirable to develop a less knowledge-intensive approach to alignment. Since the early SMT work makes no assumptions at all about the categories of source and target words, we looked to this work for inspiration in designing an approach to our task that makes no assumptions about the categories of source and target characters.

4.1 IBM word alignment models

Nearly all SMT research relies on the original insights from Brown et al. (1993). Alignment is implemented through a set of parameters whose values are determined by maximizing the likelihood of a training corpus of sentence pairs. The maximization is performed using the expectation maximization (EM) algorithm (Dempster et al., 1977). In the expectation (E) step of each iteration, a set of "expected counts" of co-occurring source and target words within the corpus is calculated, weighted by the current values of the parameters. In the maximization (M) step of each iteration, new values of the parameters are calculated on the basis of the expected counts from the E-step.

4.2 Character association probabilities

In the simplest SMT alignment model (IBM Model 1), the only parameters involved are word-word translation probabilities. The goodness of an alignment of the words in a pair of sentences depends only on the probabilities that the aligned words are translations of one another, not on position in the sentences. There is the additional assumption that each word in the source sentence can be aligned with at most one word in the target sentence.

For our word translation task, we start with IBM Model 1, with words replaced by characters. That is, for each pair of source and target language characters, there is a *character association probability*, representing the probability of the source character given the target character. Each source character also has a probability of being "deleted," that is, of no association at all in the target word. However, we start with a bit more knowledge here than in the case of sentence translation. Specifically characters that are identical should have relatively high association probabilities. Thus we initialize the probabilities with a high value for identical characters (a meta-parameter that we set to 0.5) and equal low probabilities for all other character pairs. As with IBM Model 1 for sentence translation, we make the assumption that each source word character is associated with at most one target word character. In addition, we assume the inverse constraint as well: that each target word character is associated with at most one source word character. During the E-step of this simple version of our model, for each word pair in the corpus, for each combination of source and target language character, we count the ways they can be aligned (if they occur at all in the words), weighted by their current association probabilities. During the M-step we recalculate the probabilities based on the counts. The E- and M-steps are repeated until the parameters converge within some criterion.

4.3 Position and length effects

IBM Model 1 is clearly inadequate for sentence translation because a target language word is equally likely to be aligned with a source language word wherever it appears in the sentence; the order of the words is irrelevant. Succeeding models in the IBM series include additional parameters to handle position, as well as relative sentence length.

We also add additional parameters to handle position, but because our task is more constrained than the sentence translation task, we diverge here from the IBM models. Specifically, given our monotonicity constraint, we expect a character at a particular relative position within the source word to be associated with a character at a similar relative position with the target word. For example, in the pair of words in Figure 3b, even though the Am *l* and the Ti *y* are not equivalent, they should have a relatively high probability of association because of their positions within the word.

To operationalize this notion, we view an alignment as either "left-justified" or "right-justified," as proceeding from one or the other end of the word. Thus rather than relative distance within the words, we are actually comparing their absolute distances from one end of the word or the other. We include a set of parameters representing the probability of a left-justified alignment given the difference in the lengths of the two words. That is, for each of the possible differences in word length (there are about 20 of these in a typical dataset for our languages), the system is trained on a *left justification probability* (the right justification probability is just one minus this value).

During the E-step in this modified version of the model, the expected counts for each word pair depend not only on the current association probabilities for each character pair but also on the positions of the associated characters and on the left justification probabilities. That is, separate counts are calculated starting at the left and right ends of the word pairs, each weighted by the justification parameters. In addition, expected counts are also calculated for left justified and right justified alignments of each word pair, to use in updating the left justification parameters during the M-step.

Finally, the number of characters in a source word that are associated with characters in the target word depends not only on the difference in the lengths of the words but also on the number of target characters that are "deleted," that is, not associated with any source language characters. For example, consider the example in Figure 3b. The source word has nine characters, the target word ten characters. The number of deleted characters in the source word not only depends on the length difference (-1) but also on the likelihood that target characters are deleted. In particular the Ti phoneme /h/ is nearly always deleted. Thus we include a separate set of *target character deletion probabilities*, which are also trained during EM.

In summary, we define three sets of parameters governing alignments over word translation pairs and learn the values of the parameters that maximize the likelihood of the training set: (1) character association parameters, (2) left justification parameters, and (3) target character deletion parameters. We train the system using the EM algorithm. During the E-step, expected counts are calculated for each of the parameter types over the whole training set using the current parameter values as weights. During the M-step, new values for each of the parameters are calculated on the basis of the counts from the E-step. Following training, we align a given pair of words by searching for the alignment with the highest probability given the parameter values.

4.4   Possible data sources

Where would the sets of word translations for training the parameters come from? In the most general case, we are interested in languages with little or no available data, but for related languages there is often a community of multilinguals, especially when one of the languages is a lingua franca or an official regional or national language. Thus one source of data would be elicitation of word translations from multilinguals. In other cases, we might benefit from limited corpora. For the purposes of this paper, however, we wish to show only that the framework is viable, so we work with a set of languages for which we have the morphological and lexical resources necessary to generate the data automatically. Below, we describe the generation of the datasets in detail.

Applying the method to a language with few or no resources at all, through a combination of elicitation of translated words from multilinguals or word alignment in limited corpora, will wait for future work.

5   Experiments

The goal of the experiments reported on below is to investigate whether our EM alignment algorithm (1) results in character alignments that reflect the correspondences between affixes and root consonants

CATEGORY		Tense-Aspect	Polarity	Subordination	Subject Agr	Object Agr
PROPERTIES		perfective imperfective	affirmative negative	main clause relative clause	1s, 3sm, 2p(f)[6]	0, 3sm, 3sf
EXAMPLES						
Am: አልመከራችጊትም		perfective	negative	main clause	2p	3sf
Ti: እቅድስ		imperfective	affirmative	main clause	1s	3sm
Te: ለኢልበሽል		imperfective	negative	relative clause	3sm	0

Table 1: Morphological properties used in generating datasets.

and (2) yields parameters that embody the known phonetic relationships between the languages.

5.1 Training and test data

We generate the data for the experiments automatically using our multilingual root lexica and the morphological generators available in HornMorpho (Gasser, 2011). Because our initial assumption is that alignment will succeed only for words with similar roots, using our root lexica for the languages, we first extract a set of verbs in the three languages with the same or similar meanings that have the same or similar roots.[4]

The result is a set of 42 roots for each of the three languages.[5] For each of the roots, we generate a set of word forms, yielding all combinations of a set of morphological properties that are common to the three languages. These properties are shown in Table 1. This results in 1488 word translation sets. We reserve 298 of these for validation and testing, yielding a training set of 1190 translation sets. Each translation set appears in an orthographic form and a phonemic form. We also isolated a separate set of 42 *dissimilar* root pairs for Am and Ti (see below for the motivation), for example, the pair Am $<č'fr>$ Ti $<sʕsʕ>$ 'dance'. For each of these roots, we generated word forms using the same set of morphological properties. The result is a separate dissimilar training set consisting of 1488 word translation pairs and a "mixed" training set of 2,380 pairs consisting of both similar and dissimilar pairs.

The number of distinct characters in the orthographic data sets is as follows: Am–72, Ti–76, Te–57. The phonemic data sets include separate characters for the geminated and labialized forms of consonants; for example, k, $k:$, k^w, and $k^w:$ all appear in the Am data as "characters". The number of distinct characters in the phonemic data sets is as follows: Am–47, Ti–40, Te–39.

5.2 Training

For all conditions, we trained eight iterations of the EM algorithm. Following training, we aligned the test items on the basis of the learned parameters and evaluated the alignments on the basis of the constraints described below.

We first trained the Am-to-Ti and Ti-to-Te translation pairs, separately for the orthographic and phonemic training sets. Next, we trained each of these translation pairs in the opposite direction. Then, inspired by symmetrization techniques applied to alignment in SMT (Och and Ney, 2003), we aligned the test set on the basis of the union and the intersection of alignments based on the parameters learned in the two directions. In the union case, characters were considered aligned if they would have been aligned in either of the two directions. In the intersection case, characters were considered aligned if they would have been aligned in both of the two directions.

Finally, we attempted to address the artificiality of our training set by training on the "mixed" training set described above. For the mixed condition, the test set was the same one used for the similar roots condition.

---

[4]Phonetic "similarity" here takes into account known relationships among the languages, for example, the fact that the root consonants h, $ħ$, $ʔ$, and $ʕ$ in Ti and Te correspond to zero in Am roots. Of course these are relationships that must be discovered by the alignment mechanism.

[5]More precisely, each "root" is a combination of a consonantal root, its root category, and one of the set of derivational categories that characterize EES verbs, for example, passive-reflexive or transitive. An example is the Ti "root" $<lʔk>$:A:ps 'be sent', consisting of root consonant sequence $lʔk$ in root class A and in the passive-reflexive derivational category.

5.3 Evaluation

We annotated each phonemic and orthographic test set of 149 word pairs by hand, based on our knowledge of the morphology of the languages; see the upper portion of Figure 4. For the phonemic translation pairs, we indicate specific character-to-character alignments for root consonants, where these are present in both words, and for affixes, when there are clear correspondences between the characters. In cases where corresponding affixes do not clearly map onto one another, we constrain the characters in the two affixes to overlap. That is, each character within the shorter affix should align with some character in the longer affix. For the orthographic translation pairs, we indicate corresponding root characters (sharing a consonant but not necessarily a vowel), where these are present in both words. For affixes, annotation is as for the phonemic pairs. There are no constraints associated with affixes in one language that correspond to nothing in the other language. The upper part of Figure 4 shows an example, the Am-Ti translation pair from the previous figures, translating 'which was not washed'. Root consonant correspondences are indicated by arrows, affix correspondences by boxes. There are seven alignment constraints in the phonemic pair, five constraints in the orthographic pair.

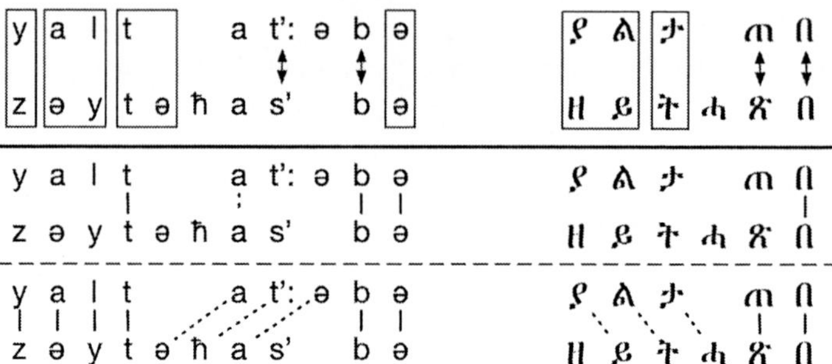

Figure 4: Alignment constraints (above), possible parameter-based alignments (below) for an Am-Ti translation pair.

We evaluated the performance of the system for both recall, the proportion of alignment constraints that were satisfied, and precision, the proportion of aligned characters that satisfied the constraints. The lower part of Figure 4 shows two alignments for the phonemic and two for the orthographic pair in the upper part of the figure. Correct alignments are indicated with solid lines, incorrect alignments with dashed lines. The upper alignments are like those we would expect early in training; only identical characters are aligned. (Recall that the character association probabilities for identical characters are initialized with much higher values than those for other character pairs.) Note that precision is high in this case: 0.75 for the phonemic pair, 1.0 for the orthographic pair. Because many correct alignments are missed, however, recall is low: 0.43 for the phonemic pair, 0.2 for the orthographic pair. The lower alignments are of a sort we would expect later in training. In both the phonemic and orthographic pairs, the system is confused because of the similarities (based on the trained parameters) of characters that should not be aligned. Recall is 0.86 for the phonemic example, 0.4 for the orthographic example. Precision is 0.67 for the phonemic example, 0.4 for the orthographic example.

5.4 Results and discussion

Results of the experiments are shown in Table 2. From these results, we may notice the following points.

First, note the relatively high baseline precision scores, especially for the orthographic data. This is not surprising, given alignments based almost entirely on character identity (see Figure 4).

Second, as we might expect, we see somewhat higher recall and precision for the more closely related languages, Ti and Te, than for Am and Ti. This suggests that the alignment mechanism might function as a measure of morphological relatedness between languages or dialects.

Third, clearly both recall and precision improve a great deal with training; this can be also be seen in the uniformly increasing F-scores. Since the system starts with no knowledge of character similarity, this is significant in and of itself. Recall improves in all four cases when alignments are formed from the union of the alignments in the two directions ("$L1 \overset{\cup}{\leftrightarrow} L2$" in the table). Somewhat surprisingly, we do not

	Orthographic						Phonemic					
	Recall		Precision		F-score		Recall		Precision		F-score	
	Base	Train	Base	Train	Base	Train	Base	Train	Base	Train	Base	Train
Am→Ti	0.405	0.906	0.865	0.959	0.552	0.932	0.581	0.925	0.650	0.813	0.614	0.865
Ti→Am	0.405	0.926	0.870	0.976	0.553	0.950	0.496	0.893	0.625	0.824	0.553	0.857
Am$\overset{\cup}{\leftrightarrow}$Ti	−	0.960	−	0.976	−	0.968	−	0.940	−	0.821	−	0.876
Am$\overset{\cap}{\leftrightarrow}$Ti	−	0.896	−	0.961	−	0.927	−	0.925	−	0.813	−	0.865
Am$\overset{\cup}{\leftrightarrow}$Ti (mixed)	−	−	−	−	−	−	−	0.894	−	0.770	−	0.827
Ti→Te	0.484	0.973	0.868	0.979	0.621	0.976	0.659	0.976	0.773	0.864	0.711	0.917
Te→Ti	0.515	0.974	0.880	0.977	0.650	0.975	0.756	0.981	0.797	0.858	0.776	0.915
Ti$\overset{\cup}{\leftrightarrow}$Te	−	0.981	−	0.980	−	0.980	−	0.989	−	0.856	−	0.918
Ti$\overset{\cap}{\leftrightarrow}$Te	−	0.973	−	0.979	−	0.976	−	0.976	−	0.864	−	0.917

Table 2: Experimental results.

see the same sort of improvement with precision, which we would expect to benefit from the intersection of the alignments ("$L1 \overset{\cap}{\leftrightarrow} L2$" in the table).

Fourth, with dissimilar roots included along with similar roots in training ("mixed" in the table, reported only for the union of the alignments and for Am and Ti translation pairs), recall is not as high as with only similar roots, but there is still significant improvement over the baseline. Of the expected correspondences between root consonants and affix segments, 0.894 are correctly aligned. Even with as many dissimilar as similar roots, the alignment algorithm is not confused.

To further investigate the value of what has been learned, we looked at the trained character association probabilities, which should reflect the morphological and phonological relationships between characters in the two languages. Focusing on the Am-Ti case, we first isolated those character pairs with character association probabilities of 0.01 or greater. We then took the intersection of the set of such characters found in the two translation directions. We performed this analysis for both the phonemic and orthographic conditions. Not surprisingly, Am characters tend to be associated with the identical Ti characters. Other intriguing relationships are also found. Because gemination operates quite differently in the two languages, ten of the consonants in the phonemic conditions are associated with their geminated variants (recall that these take the form of different characters in the data). In addition, in both the phonemic and orthographic conditions, the Am phoneme /t'/ is clearly associated with the Ti phoneme /s'/, a frequent and familiar correspondence between the languages. Similarly, the Am phonemes k and k' correspond, when ungeminated, to fricative versions of these phonemes in Ti, and again these correspondences are found, in both the phonemic and orthographic conditions. Finally, in the orthographic condition, 27 of the characters are associated with other characters in the same row in the Ge'ez character table, that is, with characters representing the same consonant followed by different vowels (see Figure 2).

6 Conclusions

The main contributions of this paper are (1) the introduction of a new task, that of translation of sets of words in morphologically complex, closely related languages and (2) the demonstration that a simple alignment algorithm, based on work within SMT, is a promising first step in approaching this task. In particular, we have shown that the parameters that are learned during EM training support alignments that reveal (1) correspondences between affixes and root consonants in pairs of EES languages and (2) relationships between orthographic or phonetic segments that we know to be valid.

Of course we have not yet shown to what extent alignment actually supports translation of morphologically complex words. To that end, our next step will be to proceed roughly as in the work of Durrett and DeNero (2013), extracting a set of transformation rules based on the alignments and then using a discriminative sequence model to learn the contexts for the rules.

References

Solomon Teferra Abate, Michael Melese Woldeyohannis, Martha Yifiru Tachbelie, Million Meshesha, Solomon Atinafu, Wondwossen Mulugeta, Yaregal Assabie, Hafte Abera, Biniyam Ephrem, Tewodros Abebe, Wondimagegnehu Tsegaye, Amanuel Lemma, Tsegaye Andargie, and Seifedin Shifaw. 2018. Parallel corpora for bi-directional statistical machine translation for seven Ethiopian language pairs. In *Proceedings of the First Workshop on Linguistic Resources for Natural Language Processing*, pages 83–90, Santa Fe, NM, USA.

Dzmitry Bahdanau, Kyunghyun Cho, and Yoshua Bengio. 2015. Neural machine translation by jointly learning to align and translate. In Yoshua Bengio and Yann LeCun, editors, *3rd International Conference on Learning Representations, ICLR 2015, San Diego, CA, USA, May 7-9, 2015, Conference Track Proceedings*.

Peter F. Brown, Stephen A. Della Pietra, Vincent J. Della Pietra, and Robert L. Mercer. 1993. The mathematics of statistical machine translation: Parameter estimation. *Computational Linguistics*, 19(2):263–311.

Ryan Cotterell, Christo Kirov, John Sylak-Glassman, Géraldine Walther, Ekaterina Vylomova, Arya D. McCarthy, Katharina Kann, Sabrina J. Mielke, Garrett Nicolai, Miikka Silfverberg, David Yarowsky, Jason Eisner, and Mans Hulden. 2018. The CoNLL–SIGMORPHON 2018 shared task: Universal morphological reinflection. In *Proceedings of the CoNLL–SIGMORPHON 2018 Shared Task: Universal Morphological Reinflection*, pages 1–27, Brussels, October. Association for Computational Linguistics.

Girma A. Demeke. 2001. The Ethio-Semitic languages (re-examining the classification). *Journal of Ethiopian Studies*, 34(2):57–93.

A. P. Dempster, N. M. Laird, and D. B. Rubin. 1977. Maximum likelihood from incomplete data via the EM algorithm. *Journal of the Royal Statistical Society. Series B (Methodological)*, 39(1):1–38.

Greg Durrett and John DeNero. 2013. Supervised learning of complete morphological paradigms. In *Proceedings of the 2013 Conference of the North American Chapter of the Association for Computational Linguistics: Human Language Technologies*, pages 1185–1195, Atlanta, Georgia, June. Association for Computational Linguistics.

Ilknur Durgar El-Kahlout, Emre Bektaş, Naime Şeyma Erdem, and Hamza Kaya. 2019. Translating between morphologically rich languages: An Arabic-to-Turkish machine translation system. In *Proceedings of the Fourth Arabic Natural Language Processing Workshop*, pages 158–166.

Alexander Erdmann, Micha Elsner, Shijie Wu, Ryan Cotterell, and Nizar Habash. 2020. The paradigm discovery problem. In *Proceedings of the 58th Annual Meeting of the Association for Computational Linguistics*, pages 7778–7790.

Michael Gasser. 2011. HornMorpho: a system for morphological processing of Amharic, Oromo, and Tigrinya. In *Proceedings of the Conference on Human Language Technology for Development*, Alexandria, Egypt.

Huimin Jin, Liwei Cai, Yihui Peng, and Xia. 2020. Unsupervised morphological paradigm completion. In *Proceedings of the 58th Annual Meeting of the Association for Computational Linguistics*, pages 6696–6707.

Arya D. McCarthy, Ekaterina Vylomova, Shijie Wu, Chaitanya Malaviya, Lawrence Wolf-Sonkin, Garrett Nicolai, Christo Kirov, Miikka Silfverberg, Sabrina J. Mielke, Jeffrey Heinz, Ryan Cotterell, and Mans Hulden. 2019. The SIGMORPHON 2019 shared task: Morphological analysis in context and cross-lingual transfer for inflection. In *Proceedings of the 16th Workshop on Computational Research in Phonetics, Phonology, and Morphology*, pages 229–244, Florence, Italy, August. Association for Computational Linguistics.

Franz Josef Och and Hermann Ney. 2003. A systematic comparison of various statistical alignment models. *Computational Linguistics*, 29(1):19–51.

Gregory Stump. 2017. The nature and dimensions of complexity in morphology. *Annual Review of Linguistics*, 3:65–83.

Ashish Vaswani, Noam Shazeer, Niki Parmar, Jakob Uszkoreit, Llion Jones, Aidan N. Gomez, Lukasz Kaiser, and Illia Polosukhin. 2017. Attention is all you need. *CoRR*, abs/1706.03762.

Bilingual Lexicon Induction across Orthographically-distinct Under-Resourced Dravidian Languages

Bharathi Raja Chakravarthi♛, Navaneethan Rajasekaran♥,
Mihael Arcan♛, Kevin McGuinness♥, Noel E. O'Connor♥, John P. McCrae♛
♛,♥Insight SFI Research Centre for Data Analytics,
♛Data Science Institute, National University of Ireland Galway, Galway, Ireland
♥Dublin City University, Dublin, Ireland
`bharathi.raja@insight-centre.org`

Abstract

Bilingual lexicons are a vital tool for under-resourced languages and recent state-of-the-art approaches to this leverage pretrained monolingual word embeddings using supervised or semi-supervised approaches. However, these approaches require cross-lingual information such as seed dictionaries to train the model and find a linear transformation between the word embedding spaces. Especially in the case of low-resourced languages, seed dictionaries are not readily available, and as such, these methods produce extremely weak results on these languages. In this work, we focus on the Dravidian languages, namely Tamil, Telugu, Kannada, and Malayalam, which are even more challenging as they are written in unique scripts. To take advantage of orthographic information and cognates in these languages, we bring the related languages into a single script. Previous approaches have used linguistically sub-optimal measures such as the Levenshtein edit distance to detect cognates, whereby we demonstrate that the longest common sub-sequence is linguistically more sound and improves the performance of bilingual lexicon induction. We show that our approach can increase the accuracy of bilingual lexicon induction methods on these languages many times, making bilingual lexicon induction approaches feasible for such under-resourced languages.

1 Introduction

Bilingual lexicon induction (BLI) is the process of creating lexicons for two or more languages from monolingual corpora (Irvine and Callison-Burch, 2017). It is a time-consuming process to do it manually so automatically inducing bilingual lexicons based on edit-distance (Haghighi et al., 2008), comparable corpora (Turcato, 1998), bilingual corpora (Rosner and Sultana, 2014) or pretrained embeddings from monolingual corpora (Vulić and Moens, 2015) is more suitable. However, sentence-aligned parallel data is not available for all languages. Methods based on unsupervised or semi-supervised learning can utilise readily available monolingual data to induce bilingual lexicons. Artetxe et al. (2018) showed that an iterative self-learning method could bootstrap this approach without the need of a seed dictionary by utilising numbers as seed dictionary through adversarial training. However, Patra et al. (2019) showed that with even a small seed dictionary, the results could be improved considerably. This task is further complicated by the fact that many languages use distinct scripts, and as such learning the similarities between cognates is a non-trivial task. As such, BLI is a challenging task for under-resourced languages due to lack of seed dictionaries and large monolingual corpora. For this work, we proposed to use the IndoWordNet as a seed dictionary for the closely related Dravidian languages, namely Tamil, Telugu, Kannada, and Malayalam, which use different scripts.

BLI between closely-related languages has shown to perform better than unrelated languages (Irvine and Callison-Burch, 2017), since closely related languages often share similar linguistics properties and cognates (Nasution et al., 2016). Cognates are words that have a similar meaning and similar orthography based on etymological relationships (Kondrak et al., 2003). Computational models of monolingual embeddings also exhibit isomorphism across closely related languages (Mikolov et al., 2013b; Ormazabal

This work is licensed under a Creative Commons Attribution 4.0 International Licence. Licence details: `http://creativecommons.org/licenses/by/4.0/`.

Proceedings of the 7th VarDial Workshop on NLP for Similar Languages, Varieties and Dialects, pages 57–69
Barcelona, Spain (Online), December 13, 2020

et al., 2019) based on the assumption that word embeddings in different languages have approximately the same structure. This isomorphic property was exploited by Artetxe et al. (2018) and Lample et al. (2018) to map monolingual word embeddings in different languages to a shared space through a linear transformation. For closely-related languages, it follows that cognates can be used as a form of alignment as words that have a similar form are quite likely to be cognates and therefore could be used as a weak seed dictionary. Given previous work on the use of seed dictionaries (Patra et al., 2019), the usage of such alignments is likely to improve performance of BLI. Previous works used the Levenshtein distance (Riley and Gildea, 2018); however, this is not linguistically well-motivated as it allows for multiple changes that are not consistent with the kinds of changes seen etymologically.

The goal of this work is to exploit the orthographic information between languages that use a different script. For that purpose, we bring the languages into a single script, which allows us to take advantage of the cognate properties of closely related languages. This paper has two principal contributions: first, we study the use of transliteration, and we demonstrate that it is an effective and necessary step which yields more isomorphic embeddings and obtains more robust BLI. Second, we show that the use of the longest common subsequence (LCS) is a superior method of assessing the cognate similarity.

2 Dravidian Languages

Dravidian languages are the common terminology (Caldwell, 1856) used to represent the South Indian languages, which consist of around 26 languages divided into four branches: 11 in the Southern group, 7 in the South-Central group, 5 in the Central group and 3 in the Northern group (Krishnamurti, 2003; Chakravarthi et al., 2018). Out of the 26 Dravidian languages, many of them are non-literary languages except the four languages chosen for this paper. Indigenous minority populations primarily use the non-literary languages. The modern society widely uses the four literary languages in literature, public communications, government institutions, academic settings and many other places in the day-to-day life of an ordinary person (Chakravarthi et al., 2020b; Chakravarthi et al., 2020a). For many natural language processing tasks such as machine translation (MT) systems, it is essential to have a corpus of written documents, as well as well-defined lexicons and grammar for the selected languages (Chakravarthi et al., 2020c). Hence in this work, we will focus on the four chosen Dravidian languages Tamil, Malayalam, Kannada and Telugu which are spoken by approximately 210 million people (Steever, 2015) across the world either as their first or second language.

ISO 639-3	tam	mal	kan	tel	eng
Script	Tamil	Malayalam	Kannada	Telugu	Latin
	உப்பு(Uppu)	ഉപ്പ് (Uppu)	ಉಪ್ಪು (Uppu)	ఉ ప్పు (Upp)	Salt
	நாணயம் (Nanayam)	നാണയം (Nanayam)	ನಾಣ್ಯ (Nanya)	నాణెం (Nanem)	Coin
	வாகணம்(Vakanam)	വാഹനം(Vahanam)	ವಾಹನ (Vahan)	వాహనం (Vahanam)	Vehicle
	நடை(Nadai)	നട (Nada)	ನಡಿ (Nadi)	నడిచి (Nadici)	Walk

Figure 1: Example of cognate words for the Dravidian language

Even though these languages share a common root, they cannot be termed as regional dialects of a language of the same origin (Caldwell, 1856). Tamil and Malayalam are more closely related such that a regional speaker of one language can understand another without translation (Burrow and Emeneau, 1961). Figure 1 illustrates the words for 'salt', 'coin', 'vehicle', 'walk' are similar in both Tamil and Malayalam. The Tamil, Malayalam and Telugu languages have their own written script symbols whereas Telugu and Kannada have significant similarities in their script symbols. Though Telugu and Kannada have these similarities, they are not readily intelligible for speakers of the language. The study of languages suggests that these languages formed a single language around late 4000 BCE and then started evolving on their own (Steever, 2015). Since the languages evolved sharing geographical, etymological and political borders, the cognates may have evolved similar meanings or borrowed words from each other. Chakravarthi et al. (2019a) have compared the Latin script and the International Phonetic Alphabet (IPA) for multilingual translation systems and shown that bringing the Dravidian languages into Latin script outperforms a multilingual neural machine translation system trained on native script and IPA. Inspired by this, we transform the Dravidian language monolingual corpora into a single script (Latin script).

3 Our Approach

3.1 Bilingual Lexicon Induction

State-of-the-art approaches to BLI use monolingual (Haghighi et al., 2008) or comparable corpora (Fung, 1995; Tamura et al., 2012) to identify pairs of translated words with or without a seed dictionary (Vulić and Korhonen, 2016). The induced translation can improve MT systems (Golan et al., 1988) to expand the coverage of translation models by translating Out-Of-Vocabulary (OOV) words. Nevertheless, prior work in BLI treated it as stand-alone task (Irvine and Callison-Burch, 2017).

Using monolingual word embeddings for BLI has attracted significant attention in recent years. State-of-the-art BLI results are based on bilingual word embedding models (Irvine and Callison-Burch, 2017). Given the source and target language word embeddings trained independently on monolingual data, unsupervised models (Vulić and Moens, 2015; Artetxe et al., 2016; Zhang et al., 2017; Artetxe et al., 2017; Artetxe et al., 2018; Riley and Gildea, 2018; Artetxe et al., 2019) learn a linear mapping W between the source and target space such that:

$$W^* = \arg\min_{W} \sum_{i} \sum_{j} D_{ij} \left\| X_{i*}W - Z_{j*} \right\|^2 , \tag{1}$$

where X and Z are two aligned matrices of embedding size d containing the embeddings of the words in the parallel vocabulary. The vocabulary of each language are V_s and V_t, and $D \in \{0,1\}^{|V_s| \times |V_t|}$ is a binary matrix representing a dictionary such that $D_{ij} = 1$ if the i-th word in the source language is aligned with the j-th word in the target language. Equation (1) is equivelent to:

$$W^* = \arg\max_{W} \mathrm{Tr}\left(XWZ^T D^T \right) , \tag{2}$$

where $\mathrm{Tr}(\cdot)$ is the trace operator (the sum of all diagonal entries). The optimal solution to this equation is $W^* = UV^T$, where $X^T DZ = U\Sigma V^T$ is the singular value decomposition of $X^T DZ$. To get this required seed dictionary D, Artetxe et al. (2018) introduced an iterative, self-learning framework that uses numerals as a seed dictionary for the first time to determine W and uses it to calculate D. From the next iteration on, it appends D to the seed dictionary to learn as shown in the Algorithm 1. However, it suffers from the non-availability of seed dictionary.

Algorithm 1: Self-learning framework

Input: X (source embeddings)
Input: Z (target embeddings)
Input: D (seed dictionary)
  1: **repeat**
    2:   $W \leftarrow$ LEARN-MAPPING (X, Z, D)
    3:   $D \leftarrow$ LEARN-DICTIONARY (X, Z, W)
  4: **until** convergence criterion
  5: EVALUATE-DICTIONARY(D)

The goal of the function LEARN-MAPPING (X, Z, D) is to find the optimal mapping matrix W^* so that the sum of squared Euclidean distances between the mapped source embeddings $X_{i*}W$ and target embeddings Z_{j*} for the dictionary entries D_{ij} is minimised as per Equation (1) and (2).

LEARN-DICTIONARY (X, Z, W) uses the dot product between the mapped source language embeddings and the target language embeddings as the similarity measure, which is roughly equivalent to cosine similarity. Then D_{ij} is set to 1, if $j = \mathrm{argmax}_k (X_{i*}W) \cdot Z_{k*}$ and D_{ij} is set to 0 otherwise.

We evaluate our process by using D to create a translation for words from test set and then compare it with the true values. EVALUATE-DICTIONARY(D) calculates translation accuracy on the test set:

$$\text{Translation Accuracy} = \frac{\text{Correct Translations}}{\text{All Samples}}, \tag{3}$$

where the *'Correct Translation'* is the number of correct target words in the source translation from the test set. *'All Samples'* is the total number of samples in the test set.

Riley and Gildea (2018) proposed two methods to utilise the orthographic information to improve the BLI. The first method is an orthographic extension of word embeddings, where each word embedding in the monolingual embedding is appended with a vector of length equal to the size of the union of the two language alphabets.

Mathematically, let A be an ordered set of alphabet containing all characters appearing in both language's alphabets:

$$A = A_{\text{source}} \cup A_{\text{target}}. \tag{4}$$

Let O_{source} and O_{target} be the orthographic extension matrices for each language, containing counts of the characters appearing in each word w_i, scaled by a constant factor c_e:

$$O_{ij} = c_e \cdot \text{count}\left(A_j, w_i\right), \quad O \in \left\{O_{\text{source}}, O_{\text{target}}\right\}. \tag{5}$$

Then embedding matrices were concatenated with orthographic matrices as below:

$$X' = [X; O_{\text{source}}], \quad Z' = [Z; O_{\text{target}}]. \tag{6}$$

Finally, in the normalized embedding matrices X'' and Z'', each row has magnitude 1:

$$X''_{i*} = \frac{X'_{i*}}{\|X'_{i*}\|}, \quad Z''_{i*} = \frac{Z'_{i*}}{\|Z'_{i*}\|}. \tag{7}$$

X'' and Z'' are new matrices that are used in the place of X and Z to include orthographic information.

The second approach of Riley and Gildea (2018) modifies the similarity score to include orthographic information for each word pair during the dictionary induction phase of the self-learning phase. Instead of using the dot product of the words' embeddings to quantify similarity, the approach modifies the similarity score by adding a measure of orthographic similarity, which is a function of Levenshtein distance (Levenshtein, 1966) divided by the length of the longer word. The normalised Levenshtein distance, denoted NL, is:

$$\text{NL}\left(w_1, w_2\right) = \frac{\text{L}\left(w_1, w_2\right)}{\max\left(|w_1|, |w_2|\right)}. \tag{8}$$

The Orthographic similarity of two words w_1 and w_2 is $\log\left(2.0 - \text{NL}\left(w_1, w_2\right)\right)$. The edit distance for a subset of possible word pairs is just considered as by how far most of word sets are orthographically unique, resulting in a normalised edit distance close to 1 and an orthographic similarity close to 0.

3.2 Longest Common Subsequence

The Levenshtein distance is a standard measure of the distance between two sequences by a minimum number of single-character edits required to map one string from another based on deletions, additions and substitution. This approach makes a binary decision about whether a pair of characters match. LCS (Paterson and Dančík, 1994; Melamed, 1999) is a similarity measure of two or more strings to find the longest subsequence common to all sequence in two or more strings. LCS was previously used to extract the morphological variations and generate lexicons (Hulden et al., 2014; Sorokin, 2016). LCS was also used to identify cognate candidates during the construction of N-best translation lexicons from parallel texts (Melamed, 1995; Kondrak et al., 2003), and for the automatic evaluation of translation quality (Lin and Och, 2004). Recent work on the creation of a large-scale multilingual lexical database based on cognates was introduced by Batsuren et al. (2019), called CogNet, which uses LCS ratio to find cognates.

Karakanta et al. (2018) also used the LCS ratio to extract cognate pairs from Wikipedia titles between Russian and Belarusian. Inspired by this, we use LCS for our work.

A sequence $Z = [z_1, z_2, \ldots, z_n]$ is a subsequence of another sequence $X = [x_1, x_2, \ldots, x_m]$, if there exists a sequence $[i_1, i_2, \ldots, i_k]$ of indices of X such that for all $j = 1, 2, \ldots, k$, where $x_{ij} = z_j$. Given two sequences X and Y, the LCS of X and Y is a common subsequence with maximum length. More formally:

$$\text{LCS}\,(X_i, Y_j) = \begin{cases} \emptyset & \text{if } i = 0 \text{ or } j = 0 \\ \text{LCS}\,(X_{i-1}, Y_{j-1})'\, x_i & \text{if } i, j > 0 \text{ and } x_i = y_j \\ \max\left\{\text{LCS}\,(X_i, Y_{j-1}), \text{LCS}\,(X_{i-1}, Y_j)\right\} & \text{if } i, j > 0 \text{ and } x_i \neq y_j \end{cases} \tag{9}$$

In previous works, Artetxe et al. (2018) uses the dot product of two words embeddings to quantify similarity. Riley and Gildea (2018) uses normalised string edit distance based on Levenshtein distance during the dictionary induction phase of the self-learning framework. In our method, we used LCS during the dictionary induction phase of self-learning framework. LCS is used to measure the orthographic similarity of the languages (Melamed, 1995; Nakov and Ng, 2012). Dravidian languages have rich morphological features, which will be beneficial in comprehending their cognate information by LCS. To include LCS, we modify the Riley and Gildea (2018) similarity score for each word pair during the dictionary induction phase. The normalised edit distance of Equation (8) is modified as to become:

$$\text{NLCS}\,(w_1, w_2) = 1 - \frac{\text{LCS}\,(w_1, w_2)}{\max\,(|w_1|, |w_2|).} \tag{10}$$

Now the orthographic similarity of two words w_1 and w_2 is $\log\,(2.0 - \text{NLCS}\,(w_1, w_2))$.

3.3 Phonetic Transcription

Phonetic transcription is used for describing a speech by means of symbols. The most common type of phonetic transcription uses a phonetic alphabet, such as the International Phonetic Alphabet (IPA); however, transcribing into the Latin script or non-native script is prevalent due to the ubiquity of the US/UK keyboard. The IPA is an evolving standard initially developed by the International Phonetic Association in 1888 with the goal of transcribing the sounds of all human languages. Transliteration is used to help language learners to read words written in foreign scripts, by writing the sound of the word using the equivalent letters. Romanisation remains a popular technique for transliteration of various languages (Hermjakob et al., 2018). The use of the Latin script for text entry of South Asian languages is common, even though there is no standard orthography for these languages in the script (Wolf-Sonkin et al., 2019). The 107 symbols used for writing the IPA are taken primarily from the Latin and Greek scripts some are novel creations. Diacritics are used for subtle distinctions in sounds and to show nasalisation of vowels, length, stress, and tones. Using IPA symbols, one can represent the pronunciation of words. Nevertheless, the study by Chakravarthi et al. (2019a) and Chakravarthi et al. (2019c) shows that transliteration into the Latin Script is best suited to take advantage of cognate information from closely related languages.

For example, LCS of the input sequence "AABCDH" and "AABHEDE" is "AAB" of length 3. However, LCS might be zero even though the Dravidian languages share a common root. This is due to the difference in the orthography of these languages. They must be converted to a single script to take advantage of the closeness of these languages. The phonetic transcription of Dravidian languages by Chakravarthi et al. (2019b) showed improvement in the translation of WordNet entries and compared the results with IndoWordNet. Chakravarthi (2020) showed that the usage of Latin script outperforms the IPA for Multilingual NMT for Dravidian languages. This was proven with a cosine similarity of the corpus showing that transcribing the text into the Latin script retain more similarity. Inspired by this, we used the Indic-trans library by Bhat et al. (2015) to transliterate. We show the example of a comparison of NLCS and NL between languages for examples of cognate words in Table 1.

Previous methods based on edit-distance and orthographic similarity are proposed for using linguist features for word alignments by supervised and unsupervised methods (Dyer et al., 2011; Berg-Kirkpatrick et al., 2010; Hauer et al., 2017). Hauer et al. (2017) created a seed dictionary based on the cognates of

Language Pairs	Word Pair	English Translation	NLCS	NL
kan-mal	hajaradant-hajarulla	arriving	0.4545	0.6363
kan-mal	rahasyadaan-rahasyadan	secret	0.2307	0.3076
kan-tam	navratn-navmani	nine gems	0.3750	0.5000
kan-tam	tandeilladant-tacoppanillat	having no living father	0.4285	0.7857
kan-tel	poojaniyavadantah-poojyaniyulu	worthy of adoration	0.5555	0.6666
kan-tel	atyagatyavadant-atyavasaramin	primary	0.5000	0.5625
mal-tam	navaratnam-navmani	nine gems	0.5454	0.6363
mal-tam	tatanillat-tacoppanillat	having no living father	0.3571	0.4285
mal-tel	navaratnam-navratnalu	nine gems	0.2727	0.3636
mal-tel	tatanillat-tandriless	having no living father	0.5454	0.7272
tam-tel	tacoppanillat-tandriless	having no living father	0.6428	0.7857
tam-tel	sammadam-samardhinchada	approval	0.6000	0.6666

Table 1: Example training set comparison of NLCS and NL

the related languages using orthographic information. They have shown that approaches that include orthographic information outperform the previous approaches for closely related languages. Unlike our work, previous works did not study languages that have different scripts, and used Levenshtein distance without considering morphological properties.

3.4 Data

Lexicons such as WordNet (Miller, 1995; Miller, 1998) for English or EuroWordNet for European languages are lexical resources which were used to improve MT quality. EuroWordNet is a cross-lingual synonym resource that linked WordNet synsets across European languages (Vossen, 1997). Similarly, IndoWordNet (Bhattacharyya, 2010) links WordNet synsets across major Indian languages from the Indo-Aryan, Dravidian and Sino-Tibetan families. An online multilingual dictionary for Indian languages was developed by Redkar et al. (2015) from IndoWordNet. However, this dictionary is not publicly accessible. To train and evaluate the quality of BLI, a seed dictionary and a test set of the bilingual lexicon is required. For the Dravidian languages, there is no existing seed dictionary, so we used the IndoWordNet. To create a seed dictionary, we used the IndoWordNet ID to link the WordNet entries for Tamil, Telugu, Malayalam and Kannada. We map the one-to-many word mapping from IndoWordNet to one-to-one word mapping by replicating the source word. Table 2 shows the seed dictionary statistics and Table 3 shows the statistics for the test set. The test set was randomly chosen among the mapping from IndoWordNet for languages under study. Even though IndoWordNet is not perfect, it is one of the resources readily available for the under-resourced Dravidian language experiments.

Language Pair	Number of entries
Tamil-Telugu	11,666
Tamil-Kannada	4,353
Tamil-Malayalam	18,731
Telugu-Kannada	12,769
Telugu-Malayalam	3,791
Kannada-Malayalam	4,639

Table 2: Number of entries in the initial bilingual lexicons used as a seed dictionary for the experiment

Wikipedia is a free online encyclopedia that created by volunteers from a different regions of the world. It has contents in more than 200 languages. Wikipedia dumps (Wikidump)[1] for Tamil, Telugu, Malayalam

---
[1] https://dumps.wikimedia.org/

Language Pair	Number of entries
Tamil-Telugu	1,982
Tamil-Kannada	1,930
Tamil-Malayalam	1,918
Telugu-Kannada	2,000
Telugu-Malayalam	2,000
Kannada-Malayalam	1,999

Table 3: Number of entries in the test set for the experiment

and Kannada were downloaded to create a monolingual embedding for each language. Wikidumps were downloaded from July 2019. Wikiextractor[2] was used to extract the documents from the Wikidump. The total number of sentences and the number of tokens from Wikidump is given in Table 4. Even if Wikipedia is available for more than 200 languages, many dumps are relatively small in size compared to other high resourced language such as English. The Wikidumps for Dravidian languages are considerably smaller corpora than that of the pre-trained embeddings for other high resourced languages studied by Artetxe et al. (2017) and Riley and Gildea (2018). We used the indic-trans library[3] to transliterate the corpus into Latin script. We trained the embedding based on the skip-gram model with 300 dimensions and default parameters.

Language	Number of sentences	Number of tokens
Tamil	1,088,753	18,761,579
Telugu	1,423,448	27,229,563
Kannada	416,764	11,109,735
Malayalam	539,755	10,501,347

Table 4: Number of sentences and number of tokens extracted from wikimedia.org for Dravidian languages

4 Experimental Settings

Words that share a similar context are semantically related. Based on their word embeddings, methods represent words in a vector space by grouping semantically similar words near each other. Word embeddings are useful for several lexical-semantic tasks such as detecting synonyms and disambiguating word sense. Several pre-trained embedding models are publicly available such as word2vec[4] (Mikolov et al., 2013a; Mikolov et al., 2013b), global word representation-based models (GloVe)[5] (Pennington et al., 2014) and FastText[6] (Bojanowski et al., 2017; Grave et al., 2018). FastText was used to create monolingual embeddings from Wikipedia articles. FastText enhances traditional word-based vectors by representing each word as a bag of character n-grams. Incorporating this subword information from FastText embeddings as well as semantic relatedness allows the capturing of orthographic and morphological similarity. We did not use the pre-trained embeddings from FastText since we also created embedding for transliteration. Given that the main focus of our work is on bringing closely related languages into a single script, we transcribed the Wikidump corpus before creating word embeddings and training seed dictionary. We conducted an experiment on BLI on language pairs, Tamil-Telugu, Tamil-Kannada, Tamil-Malayalam, Telugu-Malayalam, Telugu-Kannada, and Kannada-Malayalam.

---

[2]https://github.com/attardi/wikiextractor

[3]https://github.com/libindic/indic-trans

[4]https://github.com/tmikolov/word2vec

[5]https://nlp.stanford.edu/projects/glove/

[6]https://fasttext.cc/

Similar to Riley and Gildea (2018)[7], we stop training when the improvement on the average cosine similarity for the induced dictionary is below 10^{-6} between successive iterations. We compare our methods with baselines with and without a seed dictionary. An automatically-generated dictionary consisting only of numeral identity translations such as 4-4, 8-8, as in Artetxe et al. (2017), was used as a training set as the input dictionary to the baseline system without a seed dictionary.

5 Results and Discussion

We show results of all eight cases studied for BLI in Table 5. First, we added the seed dictionary created from IndoWordNet to the work by Artetxe et al. (2017) while maintaining the corpora in native script. Adding the seed dictionary showed small improvement over the baseline. Further, we did an experiment with the methodology proposed by Riley and Gildea (2018) as another comparable baseline still maintaining the corpora in the native script, which showed improvement over baselines. In our approach, we first transliterate the corpora work with numerals only and a seed dictionary. In the final experiment, we used LCS to improve baseline methodology with transliteration numerals only and a seed dictionary.

Once the dictionary D is learned by the self-learning process, we use the dictionary D to create translations for source words from the test set, and compare it against the target words within the evaluation set to calculate translation accuracy. Translation accuracy is the proportion of correct predictions among the total number of cases examined in the test set given in Equation 3. The total number of cases examined for language pairs under study is given in Table 3. Translation accuracy is our evaluation measure since most of the state-of-the systems are evaluated using accuracy. For example, our method with LCS-transliterated+seed dictionary for the Tamil-Malayalam language pair yields 220 correct word translations of a total of 2,000, giving a translation accuracy of 11.00%. The experimental results indicate a seed dictionary and transliteration improve accuracy. We further investigate our result to explicate the effects of cognates from similar languages.

	Approach	tam-tel	kan-tam	tam-mal	tel-kan	mal-tel	kan-ml
(Artetxe et al., 2017)	N-Numerals	0.00	0.00	0.00	0.00	0.00	0.00
	N-Seed-Dict	2.61	1.22	1.33	2.45	2.11	1.45
(Riley and Gildea, 2018)	N-Numerals	4.06	3.08	4.01	4.80	3.20	3.66
	N-Seed-Dict	5.67	4.66	6.35	6.24	4.64	4.65
T-with NL	T-Numerals	8.93	6.03	10.34	9.24	4.98	5.02
	T-Seed-Dict	10.11	6.20	10.56	9.16	5.01	5.13
T-with NLCS	T-Numerals	9.01	6.10	10.38	9.28	5.05	5.02
	T-Seed-Dict	10.12	6.36	11.00	9.74	6.04	5.36

Table 5: Performance comparison of bilingual lexicon induction on test data for Dravidian languages. Translation accuracy is represented in percentage. N: native script, T: transliteration, seed-dict: seed dictionary.

As it can be seen from Table 5, our approach with LCS outperforms the baseline methods within their groups for all four languages. Moreover, the proposed transliteration approach gives the best accuracy compared against all baseline methods for all six language pairs (Table 1). Our method with a transliteration and LCS outperforms all baselines on Tamil-Telugu. Interestingly, the transliteration and LCS fails on Malayalam-Kannada with the numerals seed dictionary, since the monolingual corpus for these languages is very small compared with the high-resourced languages such as English, Spanish and German studied by Artetxe et al. (2018). For example, 1.3 billion + 65 billion tokens for German, 702 million + 36 billion tokens for Italian, and 127 million + 6 billion tokens for Finnish from Wikipedia

---

[7]https://github.com/Luminite2/vecmap

and Common Crawl respectively are used in training word vectors, a very high number compared to tokens in Dravidian languages as shown in Table 4. The results for the IndoWordNet seed dictionaries show that our method is comparable or even better than the baseline systems. As another reference, the best-published results using orthographic information used by Riley and Gildea (2018) for high-resource languages reported accuracy of 55.53% for English-German, 46.27% for English-Italian, and 41.78% for English-Finnish dictionary. In any case, the main focus of our work is on under-resourced languages, and it is under this setting that our method stands out.

As it can be seen, our method with LCS obtains the best results in all language pairs and directions, with a highest accuracy of 11.00% for the Tamil-Malayalam language pair and lowest of 5.36% for the Kannada-Malayalam language pair. These results are very consistent across all translation directions. This suggests that, while previous methods did not focus on languages with different scripts, there is a substantial margin of improvement when orthographic information is taken into consideration. We believe that, beyond the substantial gains in this particular task, our work has important implications for future research in MT and cross-lingual word embeddings mapping between languages that use different scripts.

All approaches do better with the transliteration corpora, indicating that this may be suitable for under-resourced closely related languages in different scripts. We observed that providing IndoWordNet as a seed dictionary helps with the training process when compared to purely a unsupervised approach using only numbers as the seed dictionary. When the word vectors are not rich enough, the baseline methods fail entirely to map the embeddings without a seed dictionary. Orthographic information added to the BLI does not face this problem. As can be observed, the model performs reasonably well even with numerals only as a seed dictionary.

6 Conclusion

In this paper, we have explored bringing closely related languages into a single script and their impact on the task of BLI from monolingual word embeddings. We created a seed dictionary for Tamil, Telugu, Malayalam and Kannada from IndoWordNet. Our initial experiments with 'off-the-shelf' BLI, based on the alignment of numbers, produced very poor results, showing that these methods were not possible to apply directly to these under-resourced languages. We found that mapping these languages to a single character system helps the system to discover cognates in these closely-related under-resourced languages. Further, we showed that LCS is more linguistically sound for cognate detection by quantitative evaluation and in application to BLI. This paper shows that importance of evaluating methodologies directly on under-resourced languages as the challenges related to these languages may require modification to existing methodologies so as to make them work effectively, as demonstrated in this paper.

Acknowledgements

This publication has emanated from research supported in part by a research grant from Science Foundation Ireland (SFI) under Grant Number SFI/12/RC/2289_P2 (Insight_2), co-funded by the European Regional Development Fund as well as by the EU H2020 programme under grant agreements 825182 (Prêt-à-LLOD), and Irish Research Council grant IRCLA/2017/129 (CARDAMOM-Comparative Deep Models of Language for Minority and Historical Languages).

References

Mikel Artetxe, Gorka Labaka, and Eneko Agirre. 2016. Learning principled bilingual mappings of word embeddings while preserving monolingual invariance. In *Proceedings of the 2016 Conference on Empirical Methods in Natural Language Processing*, pages 2289–2294.

Mikel Artetxe, Gorka Labaka, and Eneko Agirre. 2017. Learning bilingual word embeddings with (almost) no bilingual data. In *Proceedings of the 55th Annual Meeting of the Association for Computational Linguistics (Volume 1: Long Papers)*, pages 451–462, Vancouver, Canada, July. Association for Computational Linguistics.

Mikel Artetxe, Gorka Labaka, and Eneko Agirre. 2018. A robust self-learning method for fully unsupervised cross-lingual mappings of word embeddings. In *Proceedings of the 56th Annual Meeting of the Association for*

Computational Linguistics (Volume 1: Long Papers), pages 789–798, Melbourne, Australia, July. Association for Computational Linguistics.

Mikel Artetxe, Gorka Labaka, and Eneko Agirre. 2019. Bilingual lexicon induction through unsupervised machine translation. In *Proceedings of the 57th Annual Meeting of the Association for Computational Linguistics*, pages 5002–5007, Florence, Italy, July. Association for Computational Linguistics.

Khuyagbaatar Batsuren, Gabor Bella, and Fausto Giunchiglia. 2019. CogNet: A large-scale cognate database. In *Proceedings of the 57th Annual Meeting of the Association for Computational Linguistics*, pages 3136–3145, Florence, Italy, July. Association for Computational Linguistics.

Taylor Berg-Kirkpatrick, Alexandre Bouchard-Côté, John DeNero, and Dan Klein. 2010. Painless unsupervised learning with features. In *Human Language Technologies: The 2010 Annual Conference of the North American Chapter of the Association for Computational Linguistics*, pages 582–590, Los Angeles, California, June. Association for Computational Linguistics.

Irshad Ahmad Bhat, Vandan Mujadia, Aniruddha Tammewar, Riyaz Ahmad Bhat, and Manish Shrivastava. 2015. IIIT-H system submission for FIRE2014 shared task on transliterated search. In *Proceedings of the Forum for Information Retrieval Evaluation*, FIRE '14, pages 48–53, New York, NY, USA. ACM.

Pushpak Bhattacharyya. 2010. IndoWordNet. In *Proceedings of the Seventh International Conference on Language Resources and Evaluation (LREC'10)*, Valletta, Malta, May. European Language Resources Association (ELRA).

Piotr Bojanowski, Edouard Grave, Armand Joulin, and Tomas Mikolov. 2017. Enriching word vectors with subword information. *Transactions of the Association for Computational Linguistics*, 5:135–146.

Thomas Burrow and Murray Barnson Emeneau. 1961. *A Dravidian etymological dictionary: supplement*. Oxford University Press.

Robert Caldwell. 1856. A comparative grammar of the Dravidian or south-Indian family of languages.(Madras: University of Madras. 1961).

Bharathi Raja Chakravarthi, Mihael Arcan, and John P McCrae. 2018. Improving wordnets for under-resourced languages using machine translation. In *Proceedings of the 9th Global WordNet Conference (GWC 2018)*, page 78.

Bharathi Raja Chakravarthi, Mihael Arcan, and John P. McCrae. 2019a. Comparison of Different Orthographies for Machine Translation of Under-Resourced Dravidian Languages. In *2nd Conference on Language, Data and Knowledge (LDK 2019)*, volume 70 of *OpenAccess Series in Informatics (OASIcs)*, pages 6:1–6:14, Dagstuhl, Germany. Schloss Dagstuhl–Leibniz-Zentrum fuer Informatik.

Bharathi Raja Chakravarthi, Mihael Arcan, and John P. McCrae. 2019b. WordNet gloss translation for under-resourced languages using multilingual neural machine translation. In *Proceedings of the Second Workshop on Multilingualism at the Intersection of Knowledge Bases and Machine Translation*, pages 1–7, Dublin, Ireland, August. European Association for Machine Translation.

Bharathi Raja Chakravarthi, Ruba Priyadharshini, Bernardo Stearns, Arun Jayapal, Sridevy S, Mihael Arcan, Manel Zarrouk, and John P McCrae. 2019c. Multilingual multimodal machine translation for Dravidian languages utilizing phonetic transcription. In *Proceedings of the 2nd Workshop on Technologies for MT of Low Resource Languages*, pages 56–63, Dublin, Ireland, August. European Association for Machine Translation.

Bharathi Raja Chakravarthi, Navya Jose, Shardul Suryawanshi, Elizabeth Sherly, and John Philip McCrae. 2020a. A sentiment analysis dataset for code-mixed Malayalam-English. In *Proceedings of the 1st Joint Workshop on Spoken Language Technologies for Under-resourced languages (SLTU) and Collaboration and Computing for Under-Resourced Languages (CCURL)*, pages 177–184, Marseille, France, May. European Language Resources association.

Bharathi Raja Chakravarthi, Vigneshwaran Muralidaran, Ruba Priyadharshini, and John Philip McCrae. 2020b. Corpus creation for sentiment analysis in code-mixed Tamil-English text. In *Proceedings of the 1st Joint Workshop on Spoken Language Technologies for Under-resourced languages (SLTU) and Collaboration and Computing for Under-Resourced Languages (CCURL)*, pages 202–210, Marseille, France, May. European Language Resources association.

Bharathi Raja Chakravarthi, Priya Rani, Mihael Arcan, and John P McCrae. 2020c. A survey of orthographic information in machine translation. *arXiv preprint arXiv:2008.01391*.

Bharathi Raja Chakravarthi. 2020. *Leveraging orthographic information to improve machine translation of under-resourced languages*. Ph.D. thesis, NUI Galway.

Chris Dyer, Jonathan Clark, Alon Lavie, and Noah A. Smith. 2011. Unsupervised word alignment with arbitrary features. In *Proceedings of the 49th Annual Meeting of the Association for Computational Linguistics: Human Language Technologies - Volume 1*, HLT '11, page 409–419, USA. Association for Computational Linguistics.

Pascale Fung. 1995. Compiling bilingual lexicon entries from a non-parallel English-Chinese corpus. In *Third Workshop on Very Large Corpora*.

Igal Golan, Shalom Lappin, and Mori Rimon. 1988. An active bilingual lexicon for machine translation. In *Coling Budapest 1988 Volume 1: International Conference on Computational Linguistics*.

Edouard Grave, Piotr Bojanowski, Prakhar Gupta, Armand Joulin, and Tomas Mikolov. 2018. Learning word vectors for 157 languages. In *Proceedings of the International Conference on Language Resources and Evaluation (LREC 2018)*.

Aria Haghighi, Percy Liang, Taylor Berg-Kirkpatrick, and Dan Klein. 2008. Learning bilingual lexicons from monolingual corpora. In *Proceedings of ACL-08: HLT*, pages 771–779, Columbus, Ohio, June. Association for Computational Linguistics.

Bradley Hauer, Garrett Nicolai, and Grzegorz Kondrak. 2017. Bootstrapping unsupervised bilingual lexicon induction. In *Proceedings of the 15th Conference of the European Chapter of the Association for Computational Linguistics: Volume 2, Short Papers*, pages 619–624, Valencia, Spain, April. Association for Computational Linguistics.

Ulf Hermjakob, Jonathan May, and Kevin Knight. 2018. Out-of-the-box universal romanization tool uroman. In *ACL*.

Mans Hulden, Markus Forsberg, and Malin Ahlberg. 2014. Semi-supervised learning of morphological paradigms and lexicons. In *Proceedings of the 14th Conference of the European Chapter of the Association for Computational Linguistics*, pages 569–578, Gothenburg, Sweden, April. Association for Computational Linguistics.

Ann Irvine and Chris Callison-Burch. 2017. A comprehensive analysis of bilingual lexicon induction. *Computational Linguistics*, 43(2):273–310, June.

Alina Karakanta, Jon Dehdari, and Josef Genabith. 2018. Neural machine translation for low-resource languages without parallel corpora. *Machine Translation*, 32(1–2):167–189, June.

Grzegorz Kondrak, Daniel Marcu, and Kevin Knight. 2003. Cognates can improve statistical translation models. In *Companion Volume of the Proceedings of HLT-NAACL 2003 - Short Papers*, pages 46–48.

Bhadriraju Krishnamurti. 2003. *The Dravidian languages*. Cambridge University Press.

Guillaume Lample, Alexis Conneau, Marc'Aurelio Ranzato, Ludovic Denoyer, and Hervé Jégou. 2018. Word translation without parallel data. In *6th International Conference on Learning Representations, ICLR 2018, Vancouver, BC, Canada, April 30 - May 3, 2018, Conference Track Proceedings*.

Vladimir Iosifovich Levenshtein. 1966. Binary codes capable of correcting deletions, insertions and reversals. *Soviet Physics Doklady*, 10(8):707–710, Feb. Doklady Akademii Nauk SSSR, V163 No4 845-848 1965.

Chin-Yew Lin and Franz Josef Och. 2004. Automatic evaluation of machine translation quality using longest common subsequence and skip-bigram statistics. In *Proceedings of the 42nd Annual Meeting on Association for Computational Linguistics*, ACL '04, page 605–es, USA. Association for Computational Linguistics.

I. Dan Melamed. 1995. Automatic evaluation and uniform filter cascades for inducing n-best translation lexicons. In *Third Workshop on Very Large Corpora*.

I. Dan Melamed. 1999. Bitext maps and alignment via pattern recognition. *Comput. Linguist.*, 25(1):107–130, March.

Tomas Mikolov, Kai Chen, Greg Corrado, and Jeffrey Dean. 2013a. Efficient estimation of word representations in vector space. In *1st International Conference on Learning Representations, ICLR 2013, Scottsdale, Arizona, USA, May 2-4, 2013, Workshop Track Proceedings*.

Tomas Mikolov, Google Inc, Mountain View, Quoc V. Le, Google Inc, Ilya Sutskever, and Google Inc. 2013b. Exploiting similarities among languages for machine translation.

George A. Miller. 1995. Wordnet: A lexical database for English. *Commun. ACM*, 38(11):39–41, November.

George A Miller. 1998. *WordNet: An electronic lexical database*. MIT press.

Preslav Nakov and Hwee Tou Ng. 2012. Improving statistical machine translation for a resource-poor language using related resource-rich languages. *J. Artif. Int. Res.*, 44(1):179–222, May.

Arbi Haza Nasution, Yohei Murakami, and Toru Ishida. 2016. Constraint-based bilingual lexicon induction for closely related languages. In *Proceedings of the Tenth International Conference on Language Resources and Evaluation (LREC'16)*, pages 3291–3298, Portorož, Slovenia, May. European Language Resources Association (ELRA).

Aitor Ormazabal, Mikel Artetxe, Gorka Labaka, Aitor Soroa, and Eneko Agirre. 2019. Analyzing the limitations of cross-lingual word embedding mappings. In *Proceedings of the 57th Annual Meeting of the Association for Computational Linguistics*, pages 4990–4995, Florence, Italy, July. Association for Computational Linguistics.

Mike Paterson and Vlado Dančík. 1994. Longest common subsequences. In Igor Prívara, Branislav Rovan, and Peter Ruzička, editors, *Mathematical Foundations of Computer Science 1994*, pages 127–142, Berlin, Heidelberg. Springer Berlin Heidelberg.

Barun Patra, Joel Ruben Antony Moniz, Sarthak Garg, Matthew R. Gormley, and Graham Neubig. 2019. Bilingual lexicon induction with semi-supervision in non-isometric embedding spaces. In *Proceedings of the 57th Annual Meeting of the Association for Computational Linguistics*, pages 184–193, Florence, Italy, July. Association for Computational Linguistics.

Jeffrey Pennington, Richard Socher, and Christopher Manning. 2014. GloVe: Global vectors for word representation. In *Proceedings of the 2014 Conference on Empirical Methods in Natural Language Processing (EMNLP)*, pages 1532–1543, Doha, Qatar, October. Association for Computational Linguistics.

Hanumant Redkar, Sandhya Singh, Nilesh Joshi, Anupam Ghosh, and Pushpak Bhattacharyya. 2015. IndoWordNet dictionary: An online multilingual dictionary using IndoWordNet. In *Proceedings of the 12th International Conference on Natural Language Processing*, pages 71–78, Trivandrum, India, December. NLP Association of India.

Parker Riley and Daniel Gildea. 2018. Orthographic features for bilingual lexicon induction. In *Proceedings of the 56th Annual Meeting of the Association for Computational Linguistics (Volume 2: Short Papers)*, pages 390–394, Melbourne, Australia, July. Association for Computational Linguistics.

Michael Rosner and Kurt Sultana. 2014. Automatic methods for the extension of a bilingual dictionary using comparable corpora. In *Proceedings of the Ninth International Conference on Language Resources and Evaluation (LREC'14)*, pages 3790–3797, Reykjavik, Iceland, May. European Language Resources Association (ELRA).

Alexey Sorokin. 2016. Using longest common subsequence and character models to predict word forms. In *Proceedings of the 14th SIGMORPHON Workshop on Computational Research in Phonetics, Phonology, and Morphology*, pages 54–61, Berlin, Germany, August. Association for Computational Linguistics.

Sanford B Steever. 2015. *The Dravidian Languages*. Routledge.

Akihiro Tamura, Taro Watanabe, and Eiichiro Sumita. 2012. Bilingual lexicon extraction from comparable corpora using label propagation. In *Proceedings of the 2012 Joint Conference on Empirical Methods in Natural Language Processing and Computational Natural Language Learning*, pages 24–36, Jeju Island, Korea, July. Association for Computational Linguistics.

Davide Turcato. 1998. Automatically creating bilingual lexicons for machine translation from bilingual text. In *36th Annual Meeting of the Association for Computational Linguistics and 17th International Conference on Computational Linguistics, Volume 2*, pages 1299–1306, Montreal, Quebec, Canada, August. Association for Computational Linguistics.

Piek Vossen. 1997. EuroWordNet: a multilingual database for information retrieval. In *Proceedings of the DELOS workshop on Cross-language Information Retrieval, March 5-7, 1997 Zurich*. Vrije Universiteit. Proceedings of the DELOS workshop on Cross-language Information Retrieval, March 5-7, 1997, Zurich.

Ivan Vulić and Anna Korhonen. 2016. On the role of seed lexicons in learning bilingual word embeddings. In *Proceedings of the 54th Annual Meeting of the Association for Computational Linguistics (Volume 1: Long Papers)*, pages 247–257, Berlin, Germany, August. Association for Computational Linguistics.

Ivan Vulić and Marie-Francine Moens. 2015. Bilingual word embeddings from non-parallel document-aligned data applied to bilingual lexicon induction. In *Proceedings of the 53rd Annual Meeting of the Association for Computational Linguistics and the 7th International Joint Conference on Natural Language Processing (Volume 2: Short Papers)*, pages 719–725, Beijing, China, July. Association for Computational Linguistics.

Lawrence Wolf-Sonkin, Vlad Schogol, Brian Roark, and Michael Riley. 2019. Latin script keyboards for south Asian languages with finite-state normalization. In *Proceedings of the 14th International Conference on Finite-State Methods and Natural Language Processing*, pages 108–117, Dresden, Germany, September. Association for Computational Linguistics.

Meng Zhang, Yang Liu, Huanbo Luan, and Maosong Sun. 2017. Adversarial training for unsupervised bilingual lexicon induction. In *Proceedings of the 55th Annual Meeting of the Association for Computational Linguistics (Volume 1: Long Papers)*, pages 1959–1970, Vancouver, Canada, July. Association for Computational Linguistics.

Building a Corpus for the Zaza–Gorani Language Family

Sina Ahmadi
Insight Centre for Data Analytics
National University of Ireland Galway, Ireland
ahmadi.sina@outlook.com

Abstract

Thanks to the growth of local communities and various news websites along with the increasing accessibility of the Web, some of the endangered and less-resourced languages have a chance to revive in the information era. Therefore, the Web is considered a huge resource that can be used to extract language corpora which enable researchers to carry out various studies in linguistics and language technology. The Zaza–Gorani language family is a linguistic subgroup of the Northwestern Iranian languages for which there is no significant corpus available. Motivated to create one, in this paper we present our endeavour to collect a corpus in Zazaki and Gorani languages containing over 1.6M and 194k word tokens, respectively. This corpus is publicly available[1].

1 Introduction

A language corpus refers to a collection of data in a specific language or languages which can be utilized as a sample of the language for linguistic purposes. With a significant number of tokens and sentences, a corpus contains various word forms and therefore, is beneficial in the linguistic analysis of a language, for instance in morphology and syntax. Moreover, the recent advances in applying statistical and neural methods in natural language processing (NLP) have proved the importance of language resources, including large corpora, in improving various tasks, particularly using language models. However, language resources are not evenly available for all languages; given the number of the human languages around the globe, most of the languages are still considered less-resourced, i.e. languages for which there are only general grammar and few electronic texts available.

Zaza-Gorani languages, a subgroup of the Northwestern Iranian languages, are not only less-resourced but are also deemed as endangered languages (Aryadoust et al., 2008; Arslan, 2016; Arslan, 2017). Zazaki and Gorani are two of the main and most known languages belonging to this family. Zazaki, also known as Dimlî, is spoken by an estimated number of 2 million speakers in various regions in Turkey (Paul, 1998; Extra and Gorter, 2001, p 418). On the other hand, Gorani[2], also written as Gurani, is the language of ∼300,000 speakers in the parts of the Iranian of Iraqi Kurdistan (Paul, 2007). Historically, Gorani was the high literary language within the Sorani Kurdish speaking regions in such a way that it played a great role in the formation of modern Sorani Kurdish and literature (Edmonds, 2013).

In this study, we present a corpus for Zazaki and Gorani. Shabaki, as the last language in this language family could not be included due to it being extremely under-documented and least known (Sultan, 2011). The corpus is built on the news articles from various sources in several topics such as science, politics, culture and art, and contains 1,633,770 tokens in Zazaki and 194,563 tokens in Gorani. We believe that this resource can pave the way for further developments in the processing of Zaza-Gorani languages in various NLP tasks such as automatic language and dialect identification (Hassani and Medjedovic, 2016) and spelling and grammatical error correction. Given the similarities between these languages and Kurdish, this corpus can also be beneficial to take use of available resources and tools of Kurdish, such as named-entity recognition (Littell et al., 2016).

---

[1] https://github.com/sinaahmadi/ZazaGoraniCorpus
[2] Not to be confused with the Gorani people in the Balkans
This work is licensed under a Creative Commons Attribution 4.0 International License (CC-BY).

Proceedings of the 7th VarDial Workshop on NLP for Similar Languages, Varieties and Dialects, pages 70–78
Barcelona, Spain (Online), December 13, 2020

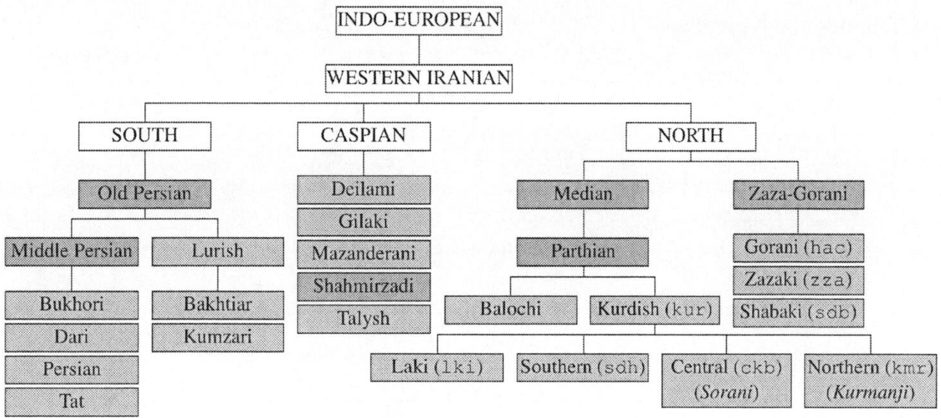

Figure 1: The place of the Kurdish and Zaza-Gorani languages in the Western Iranian language family. Dead and alive languages are respectively specified in red and green and, ISO 639-3 language codes are provided in parentheses

2   Kurdish vs. Zaza-Gorani

The question of dialects and languages in the Kurdish inhabitant regions has been a matter of discussion both in academia and among people. Although some have suggested that Northern and Central Kurdish, also widely known by their endonyms, respectively, Kurmanji[3] and Sorani, are two distinct languages given the structural differences between them, they are more uncontroversially accepted as two dialects of Kurdish (Haig and Matras, 2002). Despite the common belief that Zazaki and Gorani are two dialects of Kurdish (Hassanpour, 1998), studies indicate a consensus among linguists that those two are two distinct languages on their own (MacKenzie, 1966; Minorsky, 1943). That said, there is generally a close feeling among all the three ethnic groups, Kurds, Goranis and Zazas, with respect to the Kurdish identity and culture with many centuries living together (Yavuz, 1998; Schmidinger, 2013). However, the formation of new identities among Gorani and Zazas to distinguish themselves from Kurds has been also studied more recently (Kane, 2003; Hassanpour et al., 2012; Sheyholislami, 2017).

Kurdish, Zazaki and Gorani languages are all in the Northwestern branch of the Iranian languages within the Indo-European language family. Regarding the Kurdish dialects, Kurmanji is spoken in all the regions of Kurdistan in Iraq, Iran, Syria and Turkey, with a predominant population in the two latter regions. Sorani and Southern Kurdish are both spoken by the Kurdish populations of Iraq and Iran. While the majority of the Southern Kurdish speakers are located in the southern parts of the Iranian Kurdistan, particularly in Kermanshah and Ilam provinces, Sorani is the most widely spoken dialect in both Kurdish regions of Iran and Iraq. On the other hand, Zazaki is spoken only in the Kurdish region of Turkey, mostly in Tunceli, Bingöl, Urfa, Elazığ and north of Diyarbakır in various dialects of *Dimli*, *Kirdki*, *Kirmanjki* and *Kirmanji* (White, 1995). Finally, Gorani is mostly spoken in the Iranian Kurdistan and smaller parts of the Iraqi Kurdistan in various dialects, including *Bajelani*, *Sarli*, *Gawrajuyi* and *Hawrami* (also known as *Awromani* or *Awramani*), among which the latter is the most popular and known dialect (MacKenzie, 2002; Mahmoudveysi et al., 2012).

These languages and dialects have linguistically influenced each other in various ways, including phonetics, vocabulary and morphology. More specifically, the mutual influence is observed between Kurmanji Kurdish and Zazaki (Haig and Matras, 2002; Karacan, 2020), and also, between Sorani Kurdish and Gorani (Leezenberg, 1993; Chaman Ara and Amiri, 2018). In order to better compare these languages, we discuss some of the major common features of Kurdish, Zazaki and Gorani from a comparative perspective. Additionally, we present the alphabets used for writing. We regret that Southern Kurdish, Laki and Shabaki could not be included due to scarcity of resources and grammar books (Fattah, 2000).

---

[3]*Badini* is also used to refer to the Kurmanji spoken in the Iraqi Kurdistan

2.1 Phonetics and Alphabets

		b	t͡ʃ	d͡ʒ	d	f	g	h	ʒ	k	l	ɬ	m	n	p	q	ɾ	r	ɻˠ	s	sˤ	ʃ	tˤ	t	v	w	x	j	z	ʕ	ħ	ɣ	ʔ
IPA		b	t͡ʃ	d͡ʒ	d	f	g	h	ʒ	k	l	ɬ	m	n	p	q	ɾ	r	ɻˠ	s	sˤ	ʃ	tˤ	t	v	w	x	j	z	ʕ	ħ	ɣ	ʔ
Zazaki		b	ç	c	d	f	g	h	j	k	l	'l	m	n	p	q	r	rr		s	's	ş	't	t	v	w	x	y	z	'	'h	ğ	'
Kurdish	Latin	b	ç	c	d	f	g	h	j	k	l	l/ll	m	n	p	q	r	ř/rr		s		ş		t	v	w	x	y	z	ë/'	ḧ/'h	ẍ	'
	Arabic	ب	ج	چ	د	ف	گ	ھ	ژ	ک	ل	ڵ	م	ن	پ	ق	ر	ڕ		س		ش		ت	ف	و	خ	ی	ز	ع	ح	غ	ئ
Gorani		ب	ج	چ	د	ف	گ	ھ	ژ	ک	ل	ڵ	م	ن	پ	ق	ر	ڕ	ذ	س		ش		ت	ف/ۆ	و	خ	ی	ز	ع	ح	غ	ئ

(a) Consonants

		aː	æ	e	eː	ɪ	iː	oː	uː	ʊ	ɔ
IPA		aː	æ	e	eː	ɪ	iː	oː	uː	ʊ	ɔ
Zazaki		a	e		ê	i/ı	î/i	o	û	u	
Kurdish	Latin	a	e		ê	i	î	o	û	u	
	Arabic	ا	ە		ێ		ی	ۆ	وو	و	
Gorani		ا	ە	ێ/ئێ	ێ		ی	ۆ	وو	و	ۆ/ژۆ

(b) Vowels

Table 1: A comparison of the Kurdish, Zazaki and Gorani alphabets

Historically, many scripts have been used for writing Kurdish, Zazaki and Gorani, namely, Cyrillic, Armenian, Arabic and Latin among which the latter two are still widely used (Ahmadi et al., 2019). Although the standardization of alphabets and orthographies has been widely discussed among scholars, to date it is considered an unsolved problem (Tavadze, 2019). The choice of scripts seems to be influenced by the administration where the language is spoken. For instance, the Kurmanji speakers of Iraqi Kurdistan still use the Arabic-based script while the majority of the Kurmanji speakers, who are in Turkey and Syria, use the Latin-based alphabet. Similarly, Zazaki uses the Latin-based alphabet (Werner, 2012). Regarding the Gorani language, the Arabic-based alphabet of Sorani Kurdish is used along with new graphemes for phonemes unique to Gorani. It should be noted that all these alphabets are used with phonemic orthographies, i.e. each phoneme is associated with a grapheme.

Table 1 presents the alphabets used in each language with their corresponding phonemes in the International Phonetic Alphabet (IPA). One can say that all the common vowels and consonants are identical in all languages, with a few subtle but audible differences (Haig, 2018; Odden, 2005, p 131). Regarding the number of consonants and vowels, Zaza-Gorani languages outnumber Kurdish. This is particularly because of the presence of pharyngalized consonants in Zazaki ([sˤ] and [tˤ]), the more diverse vowels ([e] and [ɔ]) and the approximant interdental plosive [ɻˠ] in Gorani (Naghshbandi, 2020; Karacan, 2020). The latter is unique to Gorani language and is also known as the Zagros [d] (Haig and Khan, 2018, p 386). Although [ɪ] exists in all languages, there is no grapheme for it in the Arabic-based script. It is worth noting that as we did not find any formal description of the Gorani alphabet, the alphabet described in the Wişename dictionary (Habiballah (Bedar), 2010) and (Kord Zafaranlu Kambuziya and Sajjadi, 2013) are used as reference. Moreover, in cases where more than a variation is found for a grapheme, they are specified with "/".

2.2 Grammar

All the languages have a system of tense-aspect-modality along with person marking (Haig and Matras, 2002) with subject-object-verb (SOV) positioning. In addition, similar to some of the other Western Iranian languages, there is a common feature in morphosyntactic alignment of all those languages and that is ergativity (Scheucher, 2019). Ergativity refers to the morphosyntactic property where the subject of a transitive verb is marked by an agentive, i.e. oblique case, which is distinct from the nominative case. In all Kurdish, Zazaki and Gorani languages the ergative-absolutive alignment appears only in the past tenses of transitive verbs.

Regarding passive voice, Kurmanji expresses passive forms periphrastically, using the auxiliary verb *hatin* 'to come' while Sorani Kurdish, Zazaki and Gorani apply morphological changes to the verb stem.

Language	Passive	Gender	Case	Alignment
Kurmanji Kurdish	periphrastic with *hatin* (to come) (Thackston, 2006a)	feminine, masculine (Thackston, 2006a)	nominative, oblique, Izafa, vocative (Thackston, 2006a)	nominative–accusative, only in past transitive ergative–absolutive (Matras, 1997)
Sorani Kurdish	morphological (Thackston, 2006b)	no gender (Thackston, 2006b)	nominative, oblique, locative, vocative (McCarus, 2007)	nominative–accusative, only in past transitive ergative–absolutive (Karimi, 2014)
Gorani	morphological (Aryadoust et al., 2008)	feminine, masculine (Sadjadi, 2019)	nominative, oblique, Izafa (MacKenzie, 1966)	nominative–accusative, only in past transitive ergative–absolutive (Rasekh Mahand and Naghshbandi, 2014)
Zazaki	morphological (Selcan, 1998; Todd, 2003)	feminine, masculine (Todd, 2003)	nominative, oblique, oblique of kinship terms, locative, vocative, double Izafe (Todd, 2003; Larson and Yamakido, 2006)	nominative–accusative, only in past transitive ergative–absolutive (Todd, 2003)

Table 2: A comparison of the Sorani and Kurmanji dialects of Kurdish with Zazaki and Gorani languages

In regards to the grammatical cases, all languages have four major noun cases, namely nominative, oblique, locative and vocative. Additionally, like some other languages in the Iranian language family, Kurdish, Zazaki and Gorani have a linker morpheme called *Izafa* (also known as *Ezafe*) which appears between a head and its dependents in a noun phrase and is usually recognized as a specific grammatical case known as construct. Izafa is widely used for creating attributive adjectives and possessive constructions. In the latter, it can be translated as 'of' in English. Similar to Kurmanji Kurdish, Izafa in Gorani and Zazaki has several realizations. In Gorani, [-i], [-æ], [-e], [-ʊ] are used based on the modifier and the presence of those elements which require a grammatical agreement, such as definiteness and number (Holmberg and Odden, 2008). Likewise, Zazaki has various morphological forms for Izafa depending on the relationship between the noun and its dependents, namely *-o*, *-a*, *-ê* (Werner, 2012; Ludovico et al., 2015, p 322). Moreover, Zazaki has a special type of Izafa, called doubled-Izafa, which happens when an Izafa construction is used within another Izafa phrase (Larson and Yamakido, 2006). For this purpose, morphemes *-da* and *-de* are used depending on gender and number. In comparison to the aforementioned languages, Sorani dialect of Kurdish has a simpler Izafa construction where only *-î* and its allomorph *-e* are used (Salehi, 2018, p 53).

Language		Noun						Verb				Adjective	
		DEF			INDEF			INF	PROG	SBJV	NEG	COMP	SUPL
		M	F	PL	M	F	PL						
Kurdish	Sorani	-eke		-ekan	-êk		-an, -gel	-in	de-, e-	bi-	ne-, na-, me-	-tir	-tirîn
	Kurmanji	-	-	-	-ek	-ek	-in	-in	di-	bi-	ne-, na-	-tir	-tirîn
Gorani		-[(æ)kæ]	-[(æ)ke]	-[(æ)ke], -[(æ)kan]	-[ew], -[ewæ]	-[ewæ], -[evæ]	-[e], -[aː], -[aːn]	-[æj]	[mæ]-	[bɪ]-	[næ]-	-[tær]	-[tæriːn]
Zazaki		-	-	-	-ê	-ê	-ê	-iş, -ene	-	bi-	nê-, ni-, me-, çi-	-êrî	-

Table 3: Some inflectional morphemes in Zazaki, Gorani and Kurdish. Nominal morphemes are provided in nominative and morphophonological alternations are excluded. Sorani Kurdish does not have gender.

Tables 2 and 3 provide some of the major morphological and syntactic characteristics of Kurdish (Sorani and Kurmanji dialects), Zazaki and Gorani languages. Regarding nouns, definiteness is not specified with markers in Kurmanji Kurdish and Zazaki while Gorani and Sorani Kurdish use markers. The fully-marked article system is a distinct feature of Gorani and Sorani (Jugel, 2014). As Sorani does not have any grammatical gender, it has a simpler combination of noun markers in comparison to Kurmanji, Zazaki and Gorani. Regarding verbs and adjectives, Sorani and Kurmanji use identical prefixes, except in a few cases. However, such a similarity is less observed in Zazaki and Gorani. In Zazaki, *da, ra* and *-êrî* are used with adjectives among which only the latter appears as a suffix. Moreover, superlative adjectives are implicit without any specific morpheme (Todd, 2003). Zazaki also has a different oblique case for kinship terms, such as *cenî* 'wife'. Affixes in Kurmanji and Zazaki are compared in more detail in Malmîsanîj and Mosa (2017).

It is worth mentioning that the description of the grammar in this section may vary depending on the dialects. For instance, in some dialects of Sorani Kurdish, namely Ardalani and Babani, oblique case does not exist while in some other dialects, such as Mukryani, nouns are specified with oblique markers.

3 Methodology

Similar to the methodology proposed by Esmaili and Salavati (2013) to create the first standard test collection for the Kurdish language, we used the material published on news websites in Zazaki and Gorani languages to build the first corpus for those two languages. In comparison to the Sorani and Kurmanji dialects of Kurdish for which many websites are available, there are a very limited number of websites for Zaza-Gorani languages. Among the available websites, we selected Zazaki.net[4] for Zazaki and Firat News Agency[5] for both languages. Our selection criteria were the number of the available articles, availability of metadata in pages' source and the diversity of the covered topics. Regarding the topics, the first website focuses on cultural issues and is composed of analytical articles in humanities and provides interviews in such fields. On the other hand, the latter addresses a wider range of news in topics such as women, politics, world, Kurdistan, science, culture and art.

After crawling the websites, we extract the content of the HTML pages and further clean them by removing non-relevant information such as URLs, hashtags, contact details and cited sentences in languages other than our target ones, e.g. Koranic verses in Arabic. In most cases, the page's address schema enabled us to identify the language. However, in none of the websites specific tags were found to explicitly identify the language or the dialect in which the article is written. As such, we use a simple classifier to exclude English, Turkish and Kurdish articles from the Zazaki and Gorani ones. For this purpose, we manually selecte a list of the most frequent and unique words in each language as features. For instance, *ziwan/zan/zon* 'language', *kerd* 'did' and *zî* 'too, also' are unique to Zazaki while *ziman, kir* and *jî* are respectively used in Kurmanji Kurdish. In the case of Sorani Kurdish and Gorani, in addition to the frequent words, we use unique characters as features as well. This step is followed by a manual verification of the documents.

#	Zazaki	Gorani
articles	4,855	428
word tokens	1,633,770	194,563
word types	102,665	41,454
characters	10,802,266	2,246,425
average word length	4.84	5.50

Table 4: Basic statistics of the Zaza-Gorani corpus

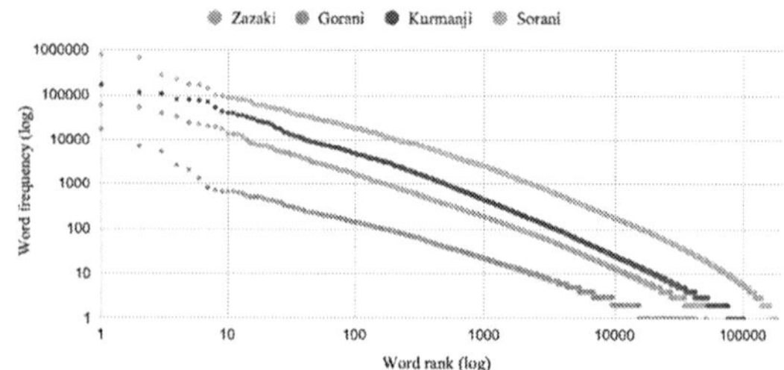

Figure 2: Zipfian distribution of the Zaza-Gorani and Kurdish corpora

---

[4]http://www.zazaki.net/

[5]https://anfsorani.com, https://anfkirmancki.com

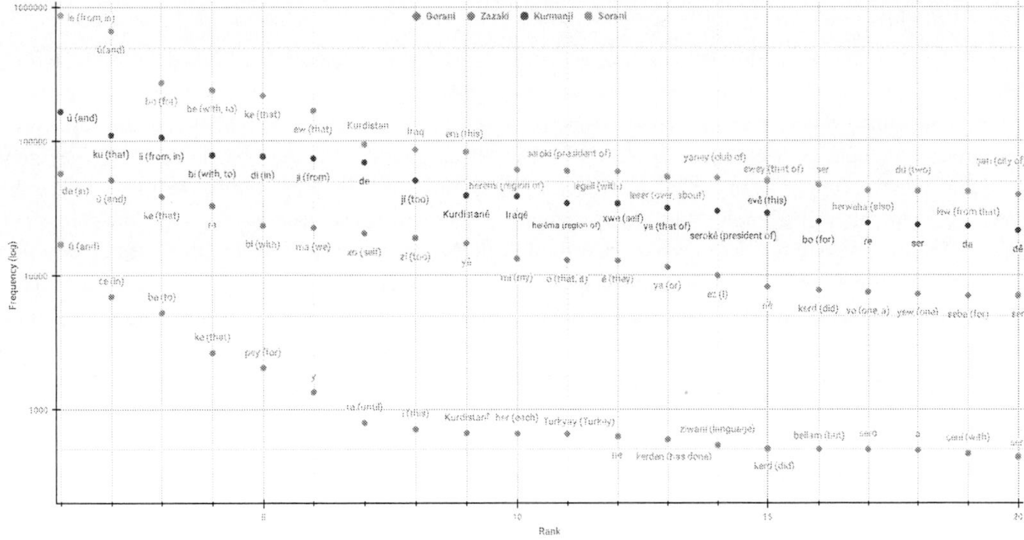

Figure 3: The 20 most frequent words in the Zaza-Gorani and Kurdish corpora

In order to keep the document-level information, we collected the cleaned documents in two directories based on the language. We provide further metadata such as topic, original source of the article and date of publication in a separate JSON file that can be associated to each document. Regarding the date of publication, the Zazaki articles dated between 2009 and 2020 while the Gorani ones are more recent (2018-2020).

4   Results

We carry out an intrinsic evaluation based on the statistics and the most frequent words in our corpus with comparison to Esmaili and Salavati's PEWAN corpus (2013). This corpus contains 18M tokens in Sorani and 4M tokens in Kurmanji Kurdish.

4.1   Frequency

Table 4 provides the basic statistics of the corpus in Zazaki and Gorani. 6.28% of the Zazaki words, i.e. 102,665 words, and 21.3% of the Gorani words, i.e. 41,454 words, are distinct in the corpus. Such ratios of word types with respect to word tokens demonstrate the richness of the corpora and the diversity of the words if the corpora are of the same size. Regarding the average word length, Esmaili and Salavati (2013) report 4.8 and 5.6 for Kurmanji and Sorani, respectively, which are almost identical to Zazaki and Gorani averages. This can be explained by the usage of the Arabic-based alphabets in both Gorani and Sorani where words, particularly one-letter morphemes such as present copula, are often concatenated with other words.

Figure 3 provides the 20 most frequent words in our corpus in comparison with the Kurdish corpus. Conjunctions ('and', 'that'), demonstratives ('this', 'that') and prepositions ('in', 'from', 'until') appear in all the languages. Postpositions *de*, *re* and *da*, which appear mostly as a part of circumpositions, are among the most frequent words in the Kurmanji and Zazaki corpora as well. The same cannot be observed in Gorani and Sorani as postpositions are mostly attached to the previous word in the Arabic-based script. For the same reason, the counterparts of the emphatic clitics *jî* in Kurmanji and *zî* in Zazaki, namely *îş* in Sorani and *îç* in Gorani, do not appear among the most frequent words. These clitics are usually translated as 'also', 'too' and 'even' in English. In Zazaki and Gorani, the past form of the verb 'to do' (*kerd*) is of high frequency. Finally, the occurrence of non-function words such as *Kurdistan* and *Iraq*, indicates the tendency of the news content towards Kurdish-related issues.

4.2 Zipf's law

Zipf's Law, also known as the rank-size distribution, states that in a reasonably huge data set, including language corpus, there is a correlation between word frequencies and word ranks, both in logarithmic scales, that follows a power law function. Using data of 50 languages, Yu et al. (2018) demonstrate that the patterns of such a correlation, i.e. Zipf's law, in all their studied languages share a three-segment structural pattern: upper segment where the most frequent words appear, middle segment where the curve gets smoother and finally, the lower segment where the rest of the words with low frequency appear. Figure 2 illustrates the rank-size distribution in the Zaza-Gorani and Kurdish corpora where a similar three-segment pattern is observed. The first 10 most frequent words in all the languages appear in the upper segment. While Zazaki and Kurmanji closely follow the same pattern, there is a sharp drop between the upper and the middle segments in Sorani and Gorani. Zipf's law is beneficial to understand the significance of words in a language with various applications in information retrieval and computational psycholinguistics (Powers, 1998).

5 Conclusion and Future Work

In this paper, we presented our efforts in creating a language corpus for two endangered languages of the Zaza-Gorani language family. Zazaki, Gorani and Shabaki are the three languages belonging to this language family and are popularly believed to belong to Kurdish. We briefly discuss how these languages are different from Kurdish, Sorani and Kurmanji dialects, in terms of phonetics, morphology and syntax. We also report our efforts in collecting documents in various topics from news websites and create the first corpus for Zazaki and Gorani. We believe that this corpus can pave the way for further developments in linguistics and computer science, particularly in information retrieval and NLP where language modeling is beneficial to various applications such as grammatical and spell checking.

As a future work, we suggest a better documentation of the Kurdish and Zaza-Gorani languages, particularly Shabaki, Southern Kurdish and Laki, by promoting the usage of those languages within local communities, websites and social media platforms. In the same vein, we invite researchers and native speakers to pay further attention to these languages, both in linguistics and NLP, by providing more analytical grammars, particularly in Gorani and Southern Kurdish, and developing basic language processing tools, such as tokenization, stemming and lemmatization, and resources, such as WordNet (Aliabadi et al., 2014) and parallel corpora.

Acknowledgements

The author would like to thank the constructive comments of Dr. Ilyas Arslan and Mesut Keskin regarding Zazaki and the invaluable insights of Dr. Parvin Mahmoudveysi regarding Gorani. Likewise, the comments of the anynomous reviewers are very much appreciated.

References

Sina Ahmadi, Hossein Hassani, and John P. McCrae. 2019. Towards electronic lexicography for the Kurdish language. In *Proceedings of the sixth biennial conference on electronic lexicography (eLex)*, pages 881–906, Sintra, Portugal, 10.

Purya Aliabadi, Mohammad Sina Ahmadi, Shahin Salavati, and Kyumars Sheykh Esmaili. 2014. Towards building Kurdnet, the Kurdish wordnet. In *Proceedings of the Seventh Global Wordnet Conference*, pages 1–6.

Ilyas Arslan. 2016. *Verbfunktionalität und Ergativität in der Zaza-Sprache*. Ph.D. thesis, Heinrich-Heine-Universität Düsseldorf.

Zeynep Arslan. 2017. Zazaki–yesterday, today and tomorrow. *Survival and standardization of a threatened language. Dieter Halwachs: Grazer Plurlingualismus Studien (GPS 04). Graz: GLM*.

Seyed Vahid Aryadoust, Narges Marandi, and Masoud Aryadoust. 2008. A contrastive analysis of modern Hawrami Kurdish and Persian verbs and tenses. *National Institute of Education, Singapore*.

Behrooz Chaman Ara and Cyrus Amiri. 2018. Gurani: practical language or Kurdish literary idiom? *British Journal of Middle Eastern Studies*, 45(4):627–643.

Alexander Johannes Edmonds. 2013. The Dialects of Kurdish. *Ruprecht-Karls-Universität Heidelberg*.

Kyumars Sheykh Esmaili and Shahin Salavati. 2013. Sorani Kurdish versus Kurmanji Kurdish: an empirical comparison. In *Proceedings of the 51st Annual Meeting of the Association for Computational Linguistics (Volume 2: Short Papers)*, pages 300–305.

Guus Extra and Durk Gorter. 2001. *The other languages of Europe: Demographic, sociolinguistic, and educational perspectives*, volume 118. Multilingual Matters.

Ismaïl Kamandâr Fattah. 2000. *Les dialectes kurdes méridionaux: étude linguistique et dialectologique*. Acta Iranica : Encyclopédie permanente des études iraniennes. Peeters.

Jamal Habiballah (Bedar). 2010. *Wişename (Hawrami-Sorani Kurdish dictionary)*. Aras Publishing and Printing House.

Geoffrey Haig and Geoffrey Khan. 2018. *The Languages and Linguistics of Western Asia: An Areal Perspective*. The World of Linguistics. De Gruyter.

Geoffrey Haig and Yaron Matras. 2002. Kurdish linguistics: a brief overview. *STUF-Language Typology and Universals*, 55(1):3–14.

Geoffrey Haig. 2018. The Iranian languages of Northern Iraq. *The Languages and Linguistics of Western Asia: An Areal Perspective*, 6:267.

Hossein Hassani and Dzejla Medjedovic. 2016. Automatic Kurdish dialects identification. *Computer Science & Information Technology*, 6(2):61–78.

Amir Hassanpour, Jaffer Sheyholislami, and Tove Skutnabb-Kangas. 2012. Introduction. Kurdish: Linguicide, resistance and hope. *De Gruyter Mouton*.

Amir Hassanpour. 1998. The identity of Hewrami speakers: Reflections on the theory and ideology of comparative philology. *Anthology of Gorani Kurdish poetry*, 35:49.

Anders Holmberg and David Odden. 2008. The noun phrase in Hawrami. *Aspects of Iranian linguistics*, 12952.

Thomas Jugel. 2014. On the linguistic history of Kurdish. *Kurdish Studies*, 2(2):123–142.

Andrew Kane. 2003. The Reality of Intra-Kurdish Rivalry Undermines the Notion of Pan-Kurdish Nationalism. *Geopolitics*, 8(1):48.

Hasan Karacan. 2020. Kurmanji and Zazaki Dialects: Comparative Study on their Phonetics. *International Journal of Kurdish Studies*, 6(1):35–51.

Yadgar Karimi. 2014. On the syntax of ergativity in Kurdish. *Poznan Studies in Contemporary Linguistics*, 50(3):231–271.

Aliye Kord Zafaranlu Kambuziya and Seyed Mehdi Sajjadi. 2013. Syllable Structure in Hawrami (Takht Dialect) [In Persian]. *The journal of Western Iranian Languages and Dialects*, 1(2):57–78.

Richard K Larson and Hiroko Yamakido. 2006. Zazaki "double Ezafe" as double case-marking. In *annual meeting of the Linguistic Society of America, Albuquerque, NM*.

Michiel Leezenberg. 1993. *Gorani influence on Central Kurdish: Substratum or prestige borrowing?* Universiteit van Amsterdam. Instituut voor Taal, Logica en Informatie (ITLI).

Patrick Littell, David R Mortensen, Kartik Goyal, Chris Dyer, and Lori Levin. 2016. Bridge-language capitalization inference in western Iranian: Sorani, Kurmanji, Zazaki, and Tajik. In *Proceedings of the Tenth International Conference on Language Resources and Evaluation (LREC'16)*, pages 3318–3324.

Franco Ludovico, M Rita Manzini, and Leonardo M Savoia. 2015. Linkers and agreement. *The Linguistic Review*, 32(2):277–332.

David Neil MacKenzie. 1966. *The Dialect of Awroman (Hawraman-i Luhon): Grammatical Sketch, Texts, and Vocabulary*. E. Munksgaard.

David Neil MacKenzie. 2002. Gurāni. *Encyclopaedia Iranica*, XI:401–403.

Parvin Mahmoudveysi, Denise Bailey, Ludwig Paul, and Geoffrey Haig. 2012. The Gorani language of Gawrajū, a village of West Iran. *Wiesbaden: Reichert.*

Mehmet T Malmîsanîj and Abdulwahab X Mosa. 2017. Prefixes, suffixes and infixes in Kurmanji (Zazaki) (Comparative descriptive study) [In Kurdish]. *Humanities Journal of University of Zakho*, 5(2):508–526.

Yaron Matras. 1997. Clause combining, ergativity, and coreferent deletion in Kurmanji. *Studies in Language. International Journal sponsored by the Foundation "Foundations of Language"*, 21(3):613–653.

Ernst M McCarus. 2007. Kurdish morphology. *Morphologies of Asia and Africa*, 2:1021–1049.

Vladmir Minorsky. 1943. The Gūrān. *Bulletin of the School of Oriental and African Studies*, 11(1):75–103.

Shahram Naghshbandi. 2020. The Approximantization of Alveolar Plosives in Hawrami (Paveh Variety) [In Persian]. *Language Related Research, Tarbiat Modares University Press*, 11(1).

David Odden. 2005. *Introducing phonology*. Cambridge university press.

Ludwig Paul. 1998. The position of Zazaki among West Iranian languages. *Old and Middle Iranian Studies*, pages 163–176.

Ludwig Paul. 2007. Zur Lage der Gōrānī-Dialekte im Iran und ihrer Erforschung. *Iranian Languages and Texts from Iran and Turan–Ronald E. Emmerick Memorial*, pages 285–296.

David MW Powers. 1998. Applications and explanations of Zipf's law. In *New methods in language processing and computational natural language learning*.

Mohammad Rasekh Mahand and Zaniar Naghshbandi. 2014. The effect of discourse factors on case system in Hawrami. *Language Related Research*, 4(4):87–109.

Mahdi Sadjadi. 2019. Grammatical Gender in Arabic and Hawrami. *International Journal of Language and Linguistics*, 6(2).

Ali Salehi. 2018. Constraints on Izāfa in Sorani Kurdish. In *Theses and Dissertations–Linguistics. 31.*

Bernhard Scheucher. 2019. Ergativity in New West Iranian. *Essays on Typology of Iranian Languages*, 328:5.

Thomas Schmidinger. 2013. The Kurdish diaspora in Austria and its imagined Kurdistan. *The Kurdish Spring: Geopolitical Changes and the Kurds (308-338). Costa Mesa, California: Mazda Publishers.*

Zılfi Selcan. 1998. *Grammatik der Zaza-Sprache: Nord-Dialekt (Dersim-Dialekt)*. Wiss.-und-Technik-Verlag.

Jaffer Sheyholislami. 2017. Language Status and Party Politics in Kurdistan-Iraq: The case of Badini and Hawrami Varieties. *Zazaki–yesterday, today and tomorrow. Survival and standardization of a threatened language. Dieter Halwachs: Grazer Plurlingualismus Studien (GPS 04). Graz: GLM.*

Abbas Sultan. 2011. An account of light verb constructions in Shabaki. *Acta Linguistica Journal*, 5(2).

Givi Tavadze. 2019. Spreading of the Kurdish Language Dialects and Writing Systems Used in the Middle East. *Bull. Georg. Natl. Acad. Sci*, 13(1).

Wheeler M Thackston. 2006a. *Kurmanji Kurdish:A Reference Grammar with Selected Readings*. Harvard University.

Wheeler M Thackston. 2006b. *Sorani Kurdish: A Reference Grammar with Selected Readings*. Harvard University.

Terry Lynn Todd. 2003. *A grammar of Dimili: also known as Zaza*. Ph.D. thesis, UMI Ann Arbor.

Brigitte Werner. 2012. Morphological Sketch of Southern Zazaki. *SIL International.*

Paul J White. 1995. Ethnic Differentiation among the Kurds: Kurmanci, Kızılbaş and Zaza. *Journal of Arabic, Islamic & Middle Eastern Studies*, 1:67–90.

M Hakan Yavuz. 1998. A preamble to the Kurdish question: The politics of Kurdish identity. *Journal of Muslim Minority Affairs*, 18(1):9–18.

Shuiyuan Yu, Chunshan Xu, and Haitao Liu. 2018. Zipf's law in 50 languages: its structural pattern, linguistic interpretation, and cognitive motivation. *arXiv preprint arXiv:1807.01855.*

Dealing with dialectal variation in the construction of the Basque historical corpus

Ainara Estarrona[1], Izaskun Etxeberria[1], Ricardo Etxepare[2],
Manuel Padilla-Moyano[2], Ander Soraluze[1]
[1]HiTZ Center - Ixa, University of the Basque Country (UPV/EHU)
[2]CNRS - IKER (UMR 5478)
{ainara.estarrona}{izaskun.etxeberria}{ander.soraluze}@ehu.eus
{r.etxepare}{manuel.padilla}@iker.cnrs.fr

Abstract

This paper analyses the challenge of working with dialectal variation when semi-automatically normalising and analysing historical Basque texts. This work is part of a more general ongoing project for the construction of a morphosyntactically annotated historical corpus of Basque called *Basque in the Making (BIM): A Historical Look at a European Language Isolate,* whose main objective is the systematic and diachronic study of a number of grammatical features. This will be not only the first tagged corpus of historical Basque, but also a means to improve language processing tools by analysing historical Basque varieties more or less distant from present-day standard Basque.

1 Introduction

In many languages other than Basque, different historical corpora exist which are annotated morphologically and syntactically, and allow lexical, morphological or syntactic searches in historical texts, e.g. the *Penn Parsed Corpora of Historical English* (Kroch and Taylor, 2000; Kroch et al., 2004; Kroch et al., 2016), the *Tycho Brahe Corpus* [historical corpus of Portuguese] (Galves et al., 2017), the *Icelandic Parsed Historical Corpus* (Wallenberg et al., 2011) or the *Parsed Old and Middle Irish Corpus* (Lash, 2014). However, no appropriate instruments of this type have ever been developed for Basque.

In this paper we present the work we are carrying out in the construction of a historical corpus of Basque considering the dialectal variation of historical texts. This work is part of a more general ongoing project called *Basque in the Making (BIM): A Historical Look at a European Language Isolate*[1], which has two main objectives: First, an exhaustive diachronic study of different grammatical features of the Basque language; second, the creation of a morphosyntactically annotated historical corpus that will enable comprehensive diachronic analysis.

The final output of our project will be a search interface to browse the corpus. This interface must be useful for analysing diachronic syntax. Therefore, it must be able to perform complex searches, both in terms of metadata (period, dialect, author, gender, etc.) and morphosyntactic characteristics (original form, lemma, part-of-speech, case ending, auxiliary verb root, time, aspect, mode, etc.), as well as any combination of them. Taking all this into account, BIM is an interdisciplinary project, where experts on Linguistics (IKER centre)[2] and Natural Language Processing (HiTZ centre)[3] work together.

This being the general scenario of the project, in this article we will focus on how we are dealing with dialectal variation in text normalisation. Together with that, we will also mention the first steps taken towards the adaptation of the morphosyntactic analyser of standard Basque developed by the Ixa group to be able to correctly analyse historical texts (by definition dialectal ones).

After having presented the overview of the project, in Section 2 we will make an exposition of the related work. In Section 3 we will present the corpus we are working with. The first steps taken in the

---

This work is licensed under a Creative Commons Attribution 4.0 International Licence. Licence details: http://creativecommons.org/licenses/by/4.0/.

[1]http://ixa2.si.ehu.es/bim/en
[2]https://www.iker.cnrs.fr/?lang=fr
[3]http://hitz.eus/en

Proceedings of the 7th VarDial Workshop on NLP for Similar Languages, Varieties and Dialects, pages 79–89
Barcelona, Spain (Online), December 13, 2020

adaptation of the morphosyntactic analyser will be presented in Section 4. Section 5 will be dedicated to the text normalisation process. In Section 6 we will outline and discuss the main experimental results and the normalisation strategy adopted in the light of the results. Finally, we will review the main conclusions and future work in Section 7.

2   Related work

Historical and dialectal texts present problems from an NLP point of view, since NLP tools developed for contemporary standard language often fail in handling the linguistic varieties encountered in such texts. A majority of NLP tools are designed to process newspaper texts written in contemporary language, but the characteristics of the standardised modern texts are not shared by historical texts: standard variants adhere to orthographic and grammatical norms which may be comparatively recent in the written corpus of the language. Therefore, the creation of a morphosyntactically annotated historical corpus using standard NLP tools needs a previous step such as normalisation of the texts.

Text normalisation has attracted a lot of interest over the past years, particularly normalisation of historical and dialectal texts, but also of informal texts such as those collected on Twitter (Alegria et al., 2014). Several techniques have been used for this task, but it can be said that nowadays machine-learning based techniques are the most popular ones, that is, systems that learn from examples of standard-variant pairs. First methods used for automatic normalisation of historical texts were rule-based methods. For instance, in the construction of the *Tycho Brahe Corpus of Historical Portuguese*, re-write rules were used to normalise historical texts (Hirohashi, 2005). These methods do not need hand-annotating training data, but they do need linguist experts to detect which rules to apply in the normalisation process, which is costly and not always successful.

Character level Statistical Machine Translation techniques (CSMT) have been applied by Pettersson et al. (2013) by treating normalisation task as a translation problem. Then, in Pettersson et al. (2014) they evaluate and compare their approach with a memory-based filtering and a Levenshtein-based approach considering five languages. The SMT-based approach generally works best.

Using the same CSMT approach Scherrer and Erjavec (2016) develop a language-independent word normalisation method and test it on a task of modernising historical Slovene words. They perform two sets of experiments: supervised and unsupervised. In the first one, they use the lexicon of word pairs as training data to build a CSMT system. In the second one, they simulate a scenario in which word pairs are not available. They show that both methods produce significantly better results than the baselines.

In our previous works (Etxeberria et al., 2016; Etxeberria et al., 2019) a different approach is presented. The method learns to map phonological changes using a noisy channel model that combines weighted finite-state transducers (WFST) and language models. In Etxeberria et al. (2019) our approach is compared with the CSMT methods explained in Pettersson et al. (2014) and in Scherrer and Erjavec (2016) using same historical corpora. The results show that the WFST approach produces similar or better scores for the six languages tested.

Lately, neural network architectures have become popular for a variety of NLP tasks, and they have been also applied to text normalisation (Korchagina, 2017; Bollmann, 2018; Tang et al., 2018). The results obtained by deep learning are good. However, these methods usually train on a lot of manually labelled data. In Tang et al. (2018) eight different NMT models are applied to the spelling normalisation task in several languages (English, German, Hungarian, Icelandic, and Swedish). The authors carry out particular experimentation on Swedish by increasing the size of the training set and they conclude that the performance of NMT models is highly related to the size.

3   The corpus

The Basque historical corpus covers the most representative written production between the 15th and the 18th century. It is a time span within which all historical dialects of Basque are represented and it is also the temporal span that divides Archaic and Old Basque from Early Modern Basque[4]. Texts have been

---

[4]We are already working on another project called SAHCOBA and funded by Spanish Ministry of Science and Innovation (MICINN, RTI2018-098082-J-I00) which addresses both Early and Late Modern Basque.

selected on the basis of: 1) their representativeness; 2) the existence of reliable editions; and 3) their social context.

As far as corpus size is concerned, our goal is to get as much text as possible, because the wider the corpus, the more relevant the results of the research become. At the time being, we are creating a reference corpus of around one million words. Given the problems and limitations associated to the written past of languages, specially in a language like Basque, this range is considered acceptable for a historical corpus (Claridge, 2009).

3.1 The reference sub-corpus

Basque is an extremely fragmented language; a number of dialects and sub-dialects spread over an area of 10,000 km2 (see Figure 1). The dialectal split began in the early Middle Ages (Mitxelena, 1981), and during the last centuries, the linguistic distance between dialects has been increasing to the extent that today peripheral varieties are not mutually intelligible in oral speech by non-trained speakers.

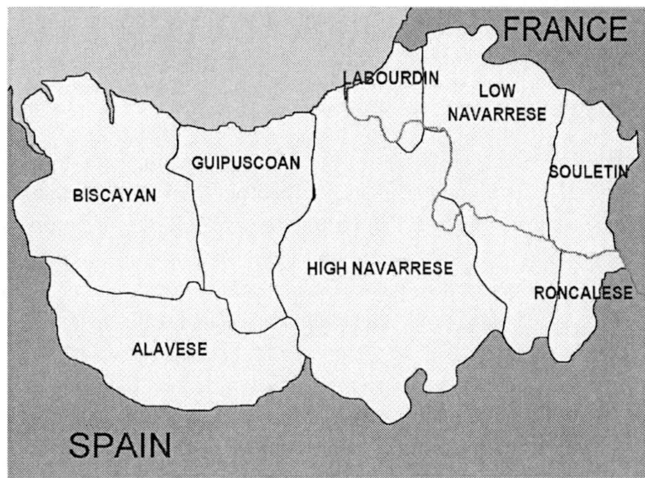

Figure 1: Historical Basque dialects. Alavese and Roncalese are extinct varieties. The green line represents the French-Spanish border.

At this point mention must be made to standard Basque, also known as unified Basque. Standard Basque is a literary variety constructed upon central dialects of the language. It was formulated in the 1960's, and today it has become the reference for speakers of all dialects, as well as the official form of the language. The Royal Academy of the Basque Language (1919) is the institution charged for the construction of unified Basque, and its decisions have normative character. The basis of standard Basque is formed by a spelling system, paradigms of noun- and verb morphology, syntactic rules, and an official dictionary. Historical dialects differ from standard Basque to different degrees; the most distant varieties are Biscayan in the West, and Souletin in the East.

Hence, in this corpus we are working with texts from different periods and dialects, and such diversity of materials adds complexity to the normalisation task. Consequently, we are carrying out this normalisation process in two phases. In the first phase we perform a manual normalisation of a sample of each text, and in the second phase, based on this manual work, we use computational techniques for the automatic normalisation of the rest of the text (see Section 5.2 for more details).

The manual work of normalising the whole corpus would take too much time. For this reason, we have created a sub-corpus which includes one or two texts representative of each dialect at each period. These works will be annotated semi-automatically and based on the results obtained in this sub-corpus the rest of the corpus will be annotated fully automatically. The works included in this sub-corpus are works that are relevant to the history of Basque and that, moreover, reflect the main characteristics of each historical dialect. This sub-corpus contains about 675,000 words, which is just over half of the total corpus. In

Table 1 we can see graphically each work included in the sub-corpus in its corresponding century and dialect[5]:

	G	B	Al	L	LN	HN	S
16th cent.		*RS*	Lazarraga / Bet	Lç	E		
17th cent.		Cap		Ax / Mat	Tt, *Onsa*	Ber, *Doc*	Bp
18th cent.	Lar, *ET*	Arz		He / Ch	AR	El	Mst

Table 1: G > Gipuscoan; B > Biscayan; Al > Alavese; L > Labourdin; LN > Low Navarrese; HN > High Navarrese, and S > Souletin.

Table 1 does not display the small 15th century texts compiled in two collections that will be mentioned in Section 5.1 (*TAV* and *Contr*). The gaps in the table mean that there are no works for that dialect and that century.

With regard to this paper in Section 6 we will present the results of normalisation for texts corresponding to the 16th and 17th centuries[6]

4 Adaptation of the morphosyntactic analyser

The morphosyntactic analyser was created for standard Basque, but dialectal texts show significant differences at all linguistic levels. First, there is an array of morpho-phonological phenomena, which confer a particular shape to every dialect; second, there are divergences in the inventory of case markers and other elements of noun morphology; third, extreme degree of variation in verbal morphology, which involves even different auxiliary verbs; last, but not least, specific lexical items.

Therefore, when we face the challenge of analysing historical and dialectal texts using natural language processing tools, we have two main tasks. On the one hand, to adapt the tools available for the standard so that they are capable of analysing historical texts, and on the other hand, to normalise or standardise historical texts so that the NLP tools are able to work with them. We believe it is necessary to undertake both tasks and in this section we will explain the preliminary work we have done for the adaptation of the morphosyntactic analyser of Basque.

The main reference for normalisation has been the dictionary of the Royal Academy of the Basque Language[7], but as far as morphology is concerned, we have followed two different criteria: i) concerning noun morphology, to prioritise the standard forms of case markers: *-rano* → *-raino* (terminative marking), *-rekilako* → *-rekiko* (comitative and relational suffix agglutination), *-akgatik* → *-engatik* (causal case); ii) with regards to verbal morphology, to preserve the roots of auxiliary verbs not belonging to standard Basque. And it is in this second point where we have had to carry out an adaptation work on the morphosyntactic analyser Eustagger (Alegria et al., 2002).

Standard Basque has four auxiliary verbs: two transitives (**edun*[8] "to have" and **ezan* [obscure semantics][9]) and two intransitives (*izan* "to be" and **edin* "to become"). Nevertheless, the historical dialects were much richer and more complex. Our goal has been to make our tools capable of collecting and correctly analysing all that complexity and that is why we have included the paradigms of five more auxiliary verbs in the morphosyntactic analyser. These auxiliary verbs are the following: *egin* "to do", **eradun* [causative of **edun*], **erazan* [causative of **ezan*], *eutsi* "to keep" and **iron* [obscure semantics][10]. This task has involved exhaustive philological and linguistic work, since three of these five

---

[5]For the abbreviations of the works we refer to the *Basque General Dictionary* of the Royal Academy of the Basque Language (*Orotariko Euskal Hiztegia*): https://www.euskaltzaindia.eus/components/com$_o$ehberria/pdf/02 − erreferentzia − bibliografikoak.pdf

[6]Due to time constraints we cannot present the results of Tt, *Onsa* as we have not yet finished the manual annotation of this work.

[7]https://www.euskaltzaindia.eus/en/

[8]We use the symbol '*' to refer to reconstructed or unattested forms.

[9]Reconstructed form, its semantics is not clear, although some etymological connection with the verbal root *za "to be" can be postulated.

[10]Reconstructed verb. The forms of *iron are restricted to the expression of modal meanings with transitive verbs.

dialectal verbal paradigms (*eradun, *erazan* and *iron*) have been standardised for the first time. By including them, on the one hand, NLP tools for Basque improve significantly their performance when processing historical and dialectal texts, and on the other hand, we are able to collect this dialectal variation to enable linguists to search for these auxiliary verbs that no longer exist in standard Basque. For this process the standard transducer used by Eustagger is extended with new lexical entries and phonological rules obtained after the philological and linguistic work. It should be mentioned that this extended version of the analyser is only used to analyse historical texts, while the previous version is the one used for standard Basque, i.e. we now have two analysers, one for standard and one for historical texts.

5 Methodology for text normalisation

As we said before text normalisation is a necessary step in this project. Once ancient and dialectal texts are normalised, the NLP tools developed for standard Basque could be applied for the linguistic analysis of corpora.

The normalisation method used is the WFST-based method presented in Etxeberria et al. (2016) and Etxeberria et al. (2019) and used also in Estarrona et al. (2019). This approach uses *Phonetisaurus*, a WFST-driven phonology tool (Novak et al., 2012; Novak et al., 2016), based on OpenFST (Allauzen et al., 2007), which learns mapping of phonological changes, using a noisy channel model. It is the strongest method found in previous work with dialect normalisation in Basque (Etxeberria et al., 2014) and when it has been tested with other languages in order to be compared with the CSMT methods proposed in Pettersson et al. (2014) and Scherrer and Erjavec (2016) it has obtained similar results (Etxeberria et al., 2019). For the moment we have ruled out neural methods due to the features mentioned of our corpus: several historical periods, several dialects and short texts. Further research is necessary for a robust solution based on neural methods.

The process of text normalisation will be carried out in two phases. First, part of the text will be manually annotated, and then, the rest of the text will be automatically normalised.

The purpose of this article is not to explain the normalisation process that has already been explained in detail in Etxeberria et al. (2019) and Estarrona et al. (2019); therefore here we will only give a brief summary of each of the normalisation phases.

5.1 Manual normalisation

Previous work on normalisation of Basque historical texts (Etxeberria, 2016) has shown that manual normalisation of 10% of the text is sufficient to obtain satisfactory results in automatic normalisation. Thus, we have randomly collected 10% of each of the texts. However, we have also found that it is necessary for the work to be of a minimum length for the results to be acceptable, so we have decided that works with less than 6,000 tokens will be normalised manually in their entirety. Following this criterion, we have manually normalised two works of the 16th century: i) the anonymous compendium of sayings *Refranes y Sentencias* (3,078 tokens) written in an archaic Biscayan dialect, and ii) the Christian doctrine of Betolaza (1,050 tokens) written in the Old Alavese dialect. In addition to these two works, three collections which include small texts from the 15th, 16th and 17th centuries written in different dialects have been manually labelled: *Textos Arcaicos Vascos* (TAV) by Michelena, *Contribución al estudio de Textos Arcaicos Vascos* (Contr) by Sarasola and *Euskal Testu Zaharrak* (ETZ) by Satrustegi.

The previous step to manual normalisation is to pre-process the text. This pre-processing consists of three phases: tokenization, named-entity recognition and lexical recognition. After this pre-processing, all the words that have not been recognised and that are therefore likely to have to be normalised will be marked in the text with an OOV ('out of vocabulary') tag. The task of the linguistic annotator is to normalise all those words marked as OOV, that is, to assign to each of them its corresponding standard based on the dictionary of the Royal Academy of the Basque Language, and also to check the rest of the words to identify possible false friends.

The manual normalisation is done using the BRAT tool (Stenetorp et al., 2012)[11] and the task is carried out by a single linguistic annotator with training in historical texts. The time needed to manually

---

[11] http://brat.nlplab.org/index.html

annotate the whole corpus has been estimated and it can be seen that about 143 words per hour are labelled. Therefore, a person would need about 4 years to label the entire corpus manually, and this is obviously why we plan to implement computational techniques to normalise the corpus.

5.2   Automatic normalisation

For the automatic normalisation process we have reapplied the method previously cited in Etxeberria et al. (2019). This method uses *Phonetisaurus*[12], a Weighted Finite State Transducer (WFST) driven phonology tool (Novak et al., 2012; Novak et al., 2016).

After collecting the word pairs (variant-standard) tagged in the manual normalisation process into a dictionary, the application of the tool requires three steps: a) sequence alignment: in this step the historical and standard words are aligned, obtaining a joint grapheme/grapheme chunks used in the next step; b) model training: using the aligned data obtained in the previous step, a model is trained and converted to a WFST; c) decoding: given the WFST obtained in the previous step, the decoder finds the best hypothesis for the input words.

We use the *Phonetisaurus* tool to learn the changes that occur within the word pairs (variant-standard) in the learning set, which by itself produces a grapheme-to-grapheme system. Once this model is trained and converted to a WFST format, it can be used to generate correspondences between previously unseen words and modern standard forms.

6   Results and discussion

In our previous work (Estarrona et al., 2019), the phonological induction inspired method we have chosen has been evaluated on three works of the 16th century selected from the sub-corpus: *Refranes y Sentencias*, Leizarraga's translation of the New Testament and Etxepare's *Linguae Vasconum Primitiae*.

The method achieved an accuracy value between 80% and 95% in the experiments and the results suggested, on the one hand, that automatic normalisation should be done taking into account for the learning process texts from the same dialect or nearby dialects and, on the other hand, that the more text we have for the learning process the better the results we get.

The main objective of the set of experiments presented below is to validate these hypotheses in order to define the normalisation strategy to be followed in the texts that will not be manually tagged.

6.1   Experiments and results

In order to evaluate the quality of the automatic normalisation method used we have performed 10-fold cross-validation experiments on the manually annotated text. The text selected for manual annotation has been divided into 10 files, therefore getting the 10 sets for learning and testing has been straightforward.

We have carried out the same experiments for all the works included in the 16th and 17th centuries[13]. To compare the improvements of our method, first we have calculated the baseline values using two approaches: 1) by giving the input word as output; 2) by looking at the memorised word pairs (variant-standard) and if there is an input word form, providing its normalised version. In case the word form is not memorised, we give as output the input word.

After the baseline has been set, in the first experiment we have evaluated the normalisation considering only the evaluated work. The second experiment has consisted in using for the learning process texts from the same dialectal region of the evaluated work, and for that purpose we have defined two major dialectal groups, the Eastern dialects (Labourdin, Low Navarrese and High Navarrese) on the one hand, and the Western dialects (Biscayan and Alavese) on the other (see Figure 1). Finally, in the third experiment, we have used for learning all the texts manually normalised so far.

All the word pairs in the learning set are taken into account for the learning process. However, we have prepared two different lists of word pairs for the test set: the first one contains all the word pairs in the test set including those which do not need to be normalised, and the second one contains only the

---

[12]https://github.com/AdolfVonKleist/Phonetisaurus

[13]Except *Refranes y Sentencias* which was manually tagged in its entirety and Tt, *Onsa* which we have not labelled yet.

word pairs labelled as variants, those which need to be normalised. Nevertheless, we have to point out that the real scenario we will always work on is that of considering all the words in the text.

Results are given based upon accuracy, i.e., the percentage of words that have been normalised correctly, and are presented in Table 2.

	Baseline1	Baseline2	Test-all	Test-variants
Leizarraga	63.08	82.13	**94.24**	**87.68**
Leizarraga + 1	-	-	94.10	87.87
Leizarraga + 3	-	-	92.67	88.00
Axular	72.89	87.51	**96.75**	**90.87**
Axular + 1	-	-	96.57	90.53
Axular + 3	-	-	94.35	88.74
Materra	72.43	82.32	93.11	77.86
Materra + 1	-	-	**96.56**	**89.42**
Materra + 3	-	-	94.42	89.17
Etxepare	56.45	72.54	73.88	59.58
Etxepare + 1	-	-	87.63	73.69
Etxepare + 3	-	-	**90.90**	**84.01**
Beriain	61.43	80.43	91.69	81.31
Beriain + 1	-	-	**92.73**	**82.88**
Beriain + 3	-	-	91.71	85.11
Belapeire	44.09	68.43	**87.82**	**81.40**
Belapeire + 1	-	-	87.69	80.07
Belapeire + 3	-	-	86.28	80.50
Lazarraga	47.57	64.30	77.71	64.00
Lazarraga + 2	-	-	81.13	70.00
Lazarraga + 3	-	-	**84.13**	**75.06**
Kapanaga	41.76	61.94	80.08	70.87
Kapanaga + 2	-	-	**84.50**	**78.35**
Kapanaga + 3	-	-	84.21	77.31

Table 2: 1= Eastern dialect works (Labourdin, Low Navarrese, High Navarrese); 2= Western dialect works (Biscayan and Alavese); 3= All the works.

6.2 Discussion

As we can see in Table 2 our normalisation method improves in all cases the two baselines we have defined for the task. In the case of Etxepare the improvement between Baseline2 and our method is only slightly more than one point. This may be due to the fact that this work is very short (6,842 tokens) and therefore we do not have enough volume of manually annotated text for the learning process. This would be confirmed by the fact that in this case the best results are obtained by including all the texts we have in the learning process (90.90% and 84.01%).

As we have said in Section 6.1 before starting the experiments we had raised two main hypotheses: i) normalisation should be done taking into account for the learning process the nearby dialects, and ii) the more text for learning, the better the results.

The main conclusion we have drawn from this set of experiments is that the performance of normalisation improves substantially when treating texts of the same dialect or dialectal group for learning purposes which validates our first hypothesis. Nevertheless, in the case of Leizarraga and Axular, the results do not improve (rather they worsen somewhat) by including more texts in the learning process, perhaps because, being two long texts (77,780 and 102,000 tokens respectively) and both of them close to standard Basque as shown by the Baseline1, the results obtained in the first experiment leave little room for improvement. In addition, the fact that they are two works very close to standard Basque means that including variants of other dialects has a negative influence on the results. Materra's work also reflects a variety very close to the standard, however it is a short work (6,750 tokens) and probably for this reason, the results of the second experiment benefit from increasing the volume of text in the learning process.

This leads us to the second major hypothesis of this normalisation work: the more volume of text we have for learning, the better the results. We have validated this hypothesis in the case of short texts as Etxepare's which achieves the best results in the third experiment when we use all the texts we have for the learning process. However, we have also seen in the rest of the works that including more text in the learning process without taking into account the dialectal variety does not improve the results. In the case of Lazarraga the results also improve with experiment 3. We have two possible explanations for this. On the one hand, it is not a very extensive work (12,500 tokens) and it benefits from the increase of text in the learning process. On the other hand, it is a work that reflects a rather archaic variety of the Alavese dialect and in experiment 3 we have incorporated all the works manually annotated up to now including the two collections that involve the more archaic texts: *TAV* and *Contr*. In addition, this work is written in a more eastern variety of the Alavese dialect and this would make the texts that do not belong to the Western dialect group help in the results.

We can therefore conclude that the second hypothesis alone would not be sufficient to achieve the best results, i.e. including more text in the learning process without taking into account dialectal variety, does not ensure improved results.

Consequently, instead of having a system for each work or a single general system for all works, we will implement a system for each dialect or dialects that are linguistically proximate, including for learning what is learned in all the works that belong to that group of dialects.

In the case of the Souletin dialect, as we can see in Table 2, the best results for Belapeire's work, written in this variety, are obtained by using the text itself. It is true that the same occurs in both Leizarraga and Axular, although the main difference between these works and Belapeire's, apart from the size, is that the first two are very close to the standard, while the third differs considerably as shown by Baseline1.

These results are coherent with the marginal character of this language variety; indeed, Souletin differs to a great extent from the rest of the Basque dialects, because it has countless specific distinctive features at all linguistic levels: phonology, morphology, syntax and lexicon.

In order to validate this fact we wanted to test the influence of including Souletin in the learning process to normalise other works of the group of eastern texts. The two works linguistically closest to Souletin are those of Etxepare and Beriain, written in Low and High Navarrese respectively, as they are the most eastern varieties outside Souletin. For this reason, we think that if Souletin could be of help in normalisation, it would be in these two works.

Nevertheless, the results shown in Table 3 did not confirm our hypothesis, since the inclusion of Souletin in the learning process did not improve the results obtained for the works of Etxepare and Beriain which curiously remain at exactly the same value. This reinforces the thesis of historical dialectology that characterises Souletin as a marginal dialect with respect to the other varieties of Basque.

	Test-all	Test-variants
Etxepare + 1	87.63	73.69
Etxepare + 1 + Bp	87.63	73.69
Beriain + 1	92.73	82.88
Beriain + 1 + Bp	92.73	82.88

Table 3: 1= Eastern dialect works (Labourdin, Low Navarrese, High Navarrese); Bp= Belapeire.

In view of the results obtained in the experiments, we have decided for our normalisation strategy to treat Souletin separately from the other eastern dialects.

7   Conclusions and future work

In this paper we have presented the results obtained in the normalisation of Basque historical texts using a Weighted Finite State Transducer (WFST) driven phonology tool and taking into account the dialectal variation when designing the experiments. Our initial hypotheses were two: i) by using texts from linguistically close dialects in the learning process, the results would improve, and ii) the results would improve as more text is fed. The results presented confirm the first hypothesis, since, in general, they are substantially improved by including in the learning process texts from the same dialectal group. However, the second hypothesis is not validated by the results, since in most cases by including all the texts available in the learning process, the results are worse than those obtained with texts from nearby dialects. This is with the exception of Etxepare and Lazarraga, but in both there are reasons that would explain these results and which have been discussed in Section 6.2. These results have led us to conclude that the best normalisation strategy for texts that will be normalised in a fully automatic way is to create a normaliser for each dialectal group. In the same way, the results obtained with the work written in Souletin have confirmed that given the marginal character of this dialect, the normalisation must be done separately from the rest of the eastern dialects.

We would like to underline that the results obtained reinforce the theories of historical dialectology in a way that has not been explored so far, that is, using computational methods. We would like to continue exploring this line of research in future work and in collaboration with dialectologists.

On the other hand, we have presented the preliminary work carried out to adapt the morphosyntactic analyser for standard Basque in order to correctly recognise and analyse the historical and dialectal variation of auxiliary verbs. Thanks to this work we have included five new paradigms in the lexicon used by the analyser. We have to emphasise that from the philological and linguistic point of view this has been a significant work, since three of these five dialectal verbal paradigms have been standardised for the first time.

The next steps in this project are the following: i) the semi-automatic normalisation of the 18th century works included in the reference sub-corpus; ii) the automatic normalisation of the rest of the corpus, and finally, iii) the morphosyntactic analysis of the corpus. For the normalisation we have already defined the strategy to follow, and for the automatic morphosyntactic analysis of the corpus we will use the Eustagger tool. A sample of this automatic analysis will be revised manually to detect errors and to proceed to the annotation of interesting morphosyntactic phenomena from the point of view of diachronic syntax. This syntactically annotated corpus will facilitate the systematic study of a number of grammatical features of the Basque in a diachronic way by means of a search interface, on which we are already working, and it will be the only tool of these characteristics existing for the Basque language. The annotated corpus and the search interface will be public and freely available to the research community.

Finally, we think it might be interesting to test the performance of different methods of normalisation based on neural networks. We are aware of the limitations of our corpus, in terms of its extension, in order to achieve adequate results using methods based on neural networks. For this reason, we have decided to work on this line of research in the elaboration of the corpus that will include the next stages in the history of the Basque language, Early and Late Modern Basque. We are already working on the choice of the works that will make up this new corpus. With this new project, we plan to extend the historical corpus to 12 million words, which would allow us to work with more guarantees on methods based on neural networks. In any case, there are authors (Moeller et al., 2019) who have tried different strategies to deal with these types of limitations and we believe that it would be an interesting line of investigation in the case of the Basque language.

Acknowledgements

The research leading to these results was carried out as part of the *Basque in the Making (BIM): A Historical Look at a European Language Isolate* project (ANR-17-CE27-0011 - BIM, Agence Nationale de la Recherche, France) and the *Syntactically Annotated Historical Corpus in Basque* (SAHCOBA, RTI2018-098082-J-I00) project (Ministry of Science and Innovation (MICINN), Spain).

References

I. Alegria, M.J. Aranzabe, N. Ezeiza, A. Ezeiza, and R. Urizar. 2002. Robustness and customisation in an analyser/lemmatiser for basque. In *LREC-2002 Customizing knowledge in NLP applications workshop*, pages 1–6.

I. Alegria, N. Aranberri, P. Comas, V. Fresno, P. Gamallo, L. Padró, I. San Vicente, J. Turmo, and A. Zubiaga. 2014. Tweetnorm_es: an annotated corpus for spanish microtext normalization. In *Proceedings of the Ninth International Conference on Language Resources and Evaluation (LREC'14)*, pages 2274–2278. European Language Resources Association (ELRA).

C. Allauzen, M. Riley, J. Schalkwyk, W. Skut, and M. Mohri. 2007. OpenFst: A general and efficient weighted finite-state transducer library. In *Implementation and Application of Automata*, pages 11–23. Springer.

M. Bollmann. 2018. *Normalization of historical texts with neural network models*. Ph.D. thesis, Bochum, Ruhr-Universität Bochum.

C. Claridge. 2009. Historical corpora. In A. Lüdeling and M. Kytö, editors, *Corpus linguistics. An International Handbook*, page 242–259. Berlin: Mouton de Gruyter.

A. Estarrona, I. Etxeberria, A. Soraluze, and M. Padilla-Moyano. 2019. Spelling Normalisation of Basque Historical Texts. *Procesamiento del Lenguaje Natural*, 63:59–66.

I. Etxeberria, I. Alegria, M. Hulden, and L. Uria. 2014. Learning to map variation-standard forms using a limited parallel corpus and the standard morphology. *Procesamiento del Lenguaje Natural*, 52:13–20.

I. Etxeberria, I. Alegria, L. Uria, and M. Hulden. 2016. Evaluating the Noisy Channel Model for the Normalization of Historical Texts: Basque, Spanish and Slovene. In *Proceedings of the Tenth International Conference on Language Resources and Evaluation (LREC 2016)*, pages 1064–1069.

I. Etxeberria, I. Alegria, and L. Uria. 2019. Weighted finite-state transducers for normalization of historical texts. *Natural Language Engineering*, 25(2):307–321.

I. Etxeberria. 2016. *Aldaera linguistikoen normalizazioa inferentzia fonologikoa eta morfologikoa erabiliz*. Ph.D. thesis, Universidad del Pais Vasco / Euskal Herriko Unibertsiatea.

Ch. Galves, A. Andrade, and P. Faria. 2017. Tycho Brahe Parsed Corpus of Historical Portuguese. url: http://www.tycho.iel.unicamp.br/ tycho/corpus/texts/psd.zip.

A. Hirohashi. 2005. *Aprendizado de regras de substituição para normatização de textos históricos*. Ph.D. thesis.

N. Korchagina. 2017. Normalizing Medieval German Texts: from rules to deep learning. In *Proceedings of the NoDaLiDa 2017 Workshop on Processing Historical Language*, pages 12–17.

A. Kroch and A. Taylor. 2000. The Penn-Helsinki Parsed Corpus of Middle English (PPCME2). url: http://www.ling.upenn.edu/ppche-release-2016/PPCME2-RELEASE-4.

A. Kroch, B. Santorini, and L. Delfs. 2004. The Penn-Helsinki Parsed Corpus of Early Modern English (PPCEME). url: http://www.ling.upenn.edu/ppche-release-2016/PPCEME-RELEASE-3.

A. Kroch, B. Santorini, and A. Diertani. 2016. The Penn Parsed Corpus of Modern British English (PPCMBE2). url: http://www.ling.upenn.edu/ppche-release-2016/PPCMBE2-RELEASE-1.

E. Lash. 2014. The Parsed Old and Middle Irish Corpus (POMIC). url: https://www.dias.ie/celt/celt-publications-2/celt-the-parsed-old-and-middle-irishcorpus-pomic/.

K. Mitxelena. 1981. Lengua común y dialectos vascos. *International Journal of Basque Linguistics and Philology*, 15:291–313.

S. Moeller, G. Kazeminejad, A. Cowell, and M. Hulden. 2019. Improving Low-Resource Morphological Learning with Intermediate Forms from Finite State Transducers. In *Proceedings of the Workshop on Computational Methods for Endangered Languages*, volume 1, pages 81–86.

J.R. Novak, N. Minematsu, and K. Hirose. 2012. WFST-Based Grapheme-to-Phoneme Conversion: Open Source tools for Alignment, Model-Building and Decoding. In *Proceedings of the 10th International Workshop on Finite State Methods and Natural Language Processing*, pages 45–49.

J.R. Novak, N. Minematsu, and K. Hirose. 2016. Phonetisaurus: Exploring grapheme-to-phoneme conversion with joint n-gram models in the WFST framework. *Natural Language Engineering*, 22(6):907–938.

E. Pettersson, B. Megyesi, and J. Tiedemann. 2013. An SMT approach to automatic annotation of historical text. In *Proceedings of the Workshop on Computational Historical Linguistics at NODALIDA 2013, NEALT Proceedings Series*, volume 18, pages 54–69.

E. Pettersson, B. Megyesi, and J. Nivre. 2014. A multilingual evaluation of three spelling normalisation methods for historical text. *Proceedings of LaTeCH*, pages 32–41.

Y. Scherrer and T. Erjavec. 2016. Modernising historical Slovene words. *Natural Language Engineering*, 22(6):881–905.

P. Stenetorp, S. Pyysalo, G. Topić, T. TOhta, S. Ananiadou, and J. Tsujii. 2012. Brat: A web-based tool for NLP-assisted text annotation. In *Proceedings of the Demonstrations at the 13th Conference of the European Chapter of the Association for Computational Linguistics*, EACL '12, pages 102–107, Stroudsburg, PA, USA. Association for Computational Linguistics.

G. Tang, F. Cap, E. Pettersson, and J. Nivre. 2018. An evaluation of neural machine translation models on historical spelling normalization. *arXiv preprint arXiv:1806.05210*.

J.C. Wallenberg, A.K. Ingason, E.F. Sigurosson, and E. Rögnvaldsson. 2011. Icelandic Parsed Historical Corpus (IcePaHC). url: http://www.linguist.is/icelandic$_t reebank$.

Recycling and Comparing Morphological Annotation Models for Armenian Diachronic-Variational Corpus Processing

Chahan Vidal-Gorène
École Nationale des Chartes-PSL
65 rue de Richelieu
75003 Paris
chahan.vidal-gorene@chartes.psl.eu

Victoria Khurshudyan
SeDyL, UMR8202,
INALCO, CNRS, IRD
65 rue des Grands Moulins
75013 Paris
victoria.khurshudyan@inalco.fr

Anaïd Donabédian-Demopoulos
SeDyL, UMR8202,
INALCO, CNRS, IRD
65 rue des Grands Moulins
75013 Paris
anaid.donabedian@inalco.fr

Abstract

Armenian is a language with significant variation and unevenly distributed NLP resources for different varieties. An attempt is made to process an RNN model for morphological annotation on the basis of different Armenian data (provided or not with morphologically annotated corpora), and to compare the annotation results of RNN and rule-based models. Different tests were carried out to evaluate the reuse of an unspecialized model of lemmatization and POS-tagging for under-resourced language varieties. The research focused on three dialects and further extended to Western Armenian with a mean accuracy of 94,00 % in lemmatization and 97,02% in POS-tagging, as well as a possible reusability of models to cover different other Armenian varieties. Interestingly, the comparison of an RNN model trained on Eastern Armenian with the Eastern Armenian National Corpus rule-based model applied to Western Armenian showed an enhancement of 19% in parsing. This model covers 88,79% of a short heterogeneous dataset in Western Armenian, and could be a baseline for a massive corpus annotation in that standard. It is argued that an RNN-based model can be a valid alternative to a rule-based one giving consideration to such factors as time-consumption, reusability for different varieties of a target language and significant qualitative results in morphological annotation.

1 Introduction

So far rule-based (RB) approaches prevailed in the annotation of the Armenian varieties which proved to show very good results provided that the system is sufficiently complete and refined (see Khurshudyan et al. (2020) for Modern Eastern Armenian [henceforth MEA]), or more modest ones if the system is perturbed by certain factors (see Vidal-Gorène and Kindt (2020) for Classical Armenian). However, RB systems have the drawback of being considerably time-consuming and not sufficiently reusable for other varieties of the target language.

The current research aims at exploring an alternative recurrent neural network (RNN) approach to annotate Armenian varieties favored for its flexibility and application rapidity on linguistically and structurally various datasets, as well as for the possibility of making predictions on unknown tokens (predominantly on very different corpora) and contextual disambiguation (Dereza, 2018).

RNN approach has already been applied to some Armenian varieties [(Vidal-Gorène and Kindt, 2020) for Classical Armenian and (Arakelyan et al., 2018; Yavrumyan, 2019) for MEA], highlighting competitive advantages for tagging Armenian data. Trained on more modest (Universal Dependencies [UD]) or specialized (GREgORI project) datasets, the results described are equivalent in lemmatization to Eastern Armenian National Corpus (EANC) rule-based approach and more precise in POS-tagging. The experiments (currently limited to POS tagging and lemmatization) are extended to three Armenian dialect varieties and to the two Modern Armenian Standards and the results are compared to EANC rule-based tools.

The article is structured as follows: *Armenian language preliminaries* give a highlight to Armenian variation in diachronic and synchronic perspectives; the chapter on the *Armenian ressources online* make a state of the art of existing Armenian online open-access corpora and databases. The chapter on the *datasets* focuses on the target datasets designed and used for current research experiment, whereas the

Proceedings of the 7th VarDial Workshop on NLP for Similar Languages, Varieties and Dialects, pages 90–101
Barcelona, Spain (Online), December 13, 2020

chapters on *methodology and results, lemmatization results, POS-tagging results* spotlight the lemmatisation and POS-tagging results which are furthermore compared in RNN and RB approaches. Finally, the last chapter on *MWA model* explores the feasibility of MWA tagging with a MEA model.

2 Armenian language preliminaries

Armenian is an Indo-European language with a nominative-accusative alignment, predominantly with an agglutinative nominal system and with a more fusional verbal one. It is a left-branching language with flexible word order (SVO/SOV).

The periodization of the Armenian language includes: Classical Armenian (henceforth CA)[1] (5th-10th cen. A.D), Middle Armenian (11th-17th cen.) and Modern Armenian (17th cen. – up to present). Modern Armenian includes two standards: Modern Eastern Armenian and Modern Western Armenian, both standardized in the 19th century. MEA is the official language of the Republic of Armenia and it is also spoken by the Armenian communities of Iran and ex-Soviet republics. MWA is spoken by traditional Armenian communities in Europe, Americas and Middle East originating mainly from Ottoman Empire. Aside from the two standards the Armenian language continuum includes various dialects as well as vernacular forms (Figure 1). Classical Armenian is preserved exclusively for canonical uses. The variation in Armenian continuum can vary from light to significant with or without mutual intelligibility. In particular, MEA can vary from MWA less than from certain Armenian dialects which sometimes lack mutual intelligibility [for more details on Armenian varieties and variation see Donabedian-Demopoulos (2018) and Donabedian-Demopoulos and Sitaridou (2021)].

Different classifications exist for the Armenian dialects depending on the criteria applied (e.g. areal (Aytənean, 1866), morphological (Adjarian, 1909), phonological (Gharibyan, 1953), typological-statistical (Jahukyan, 1972), etc.). In our research the morphological criteria prevail due to their importance in annotation processing.

One of the main distinguishing morphological features for Armenian dialects is the formation of the present indicative according to which three main groups (*-um*, *kə* and *-l* branches)[2] can be outlined as shown in Figure 1 [for more details on the Armenian dialects see Martirosyan (2018) as well as Greppin and Khachaturian (1986)].

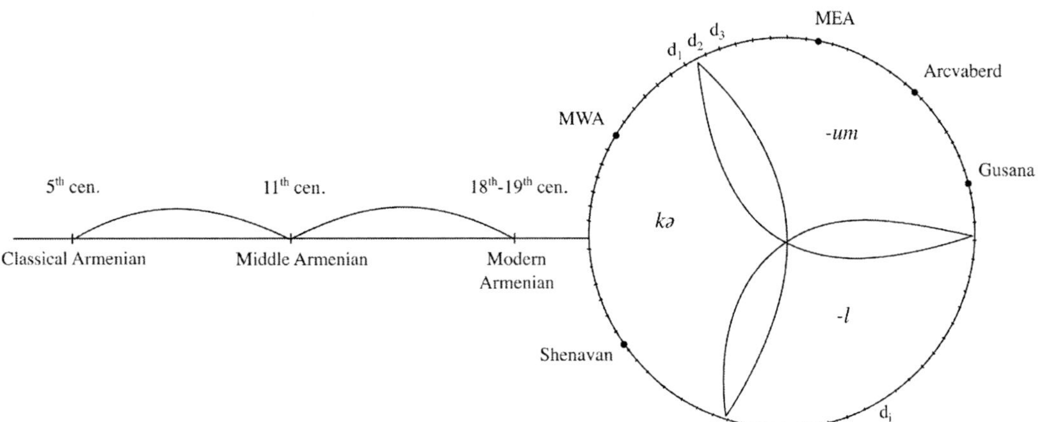

Figure 1: Armenian diachronic and synchronic varieties with d_i corresponding to a dialectal variety

One of the important issues for dialect corpora is how to transcribe the recordings and how to annotate

---

[1] Classical Armenian traces back to the creation of the Armenian alphabet attributed to the monk Mashtots at the beginning of the 5th century A.D. Currently, the Armenian alphabet is composed of 39 graphemes and it is the only alphabet used for Armenian. At the beginning of the 20th century an orthography reform was carried out in (Eastern/Soviet) Armenia alongside with her sovietization. Currently, two spellings exist for Armenian, since the traditional Armenian diaspora (both Western and Eastern Armenian speakers) continued to preserve the traditional orthographic standard. Technically it requires a conversion system to avoid annotation "noise". Several conversion tools have been developed.

[2] According to this criterion, MEA belongs to the *-um*, whereas MWA belongs to the *kə* branch.

the transcripts. Except for rare specialized dialect corpora, it is usually very difficult (often impossible in case of big corpora) and time-consuming to get a reliable phonetic transcription. An alternative to a phonetic transcription is either a complete standardized (orthographized) transcription (with the condition to have sound alignment) or a semi-standardized (orthographized) one with certain adjustments proper to the target dialect. The most important advantage of the standardized transcription would be the possibility to apply the NLP resources of the standard variety to dialects [for more details on different approaches see Arkhangelskiy and Georgieva (2018) and von Waldenfels et al. (2014)].

3   Armenian resources online

Heterogeneous texts representing various Armenian varieties can be found in a number of online resources which vary in their accessibility, formatting and linguistic background.

1. Classical Armenian. Currently, the most important corpus project with full morphological annotation for Classical Armenian is the Classical Armenian Bible project with parallel King James Version realized by Arak29 foundation[3]. The corpus database contains approximately 630.000 tokens (60.000 unique tokens, 12.000 lexemes) covering a very specific lexicon in Classical Armenian.
GREgORI project (UCLouvain)[4] is mainly specialized on Hellenophile Classical Armenian texts (6th-7th cen.), thus, Armenian translated texts from Greek. The public database of the project is more modest and it counts 66.812 tokens (16.000 unique tokens) with full morphological annotation and context-disambiguation (Vidal-Gorène and Kindt, 2020).
Several other Classical Armenian text databases exist among which the most significant one is the project of Digital Library of Armenian Literature (American University of Armenia)[5]. The database covers nearly all Classical Armenian texts from the 5th to 18th centuries.
The projects TITUS for Classical Armenian (Johann Wolfgang Goethe University)[6] and the Leiden Armenian Lexical Textbase (University of Leiden)[7] provide searchable databases of the Bible as well as certain historical and hagiographical texts with limited annotation.
The Calfa project[8] is a comprehensive online reference dictionary platform for Classical Armenian with particularly the ongoing project of New Dictionary of the Armenian Language (Awetik'ean et al., 1836 1837) including 54.000 headwords with 150.000 examples (1.3 million tokens, 190.000 unique tokens) drawn from various Classical Armenian texts provided with full context-disambiguated morphological annotation (Vidal-Gorène et al., 2020).
2. Middle Armenian. No dedicated Middle Armenian corpus or database exists. Certain texts can be randomly found in different databases.
3. a. Modern Western Armenian. No annotated corpus is publicly available for MWA with the exception of a small fully annotated corpus by Nooj (Donabedian-Demopoulos and Boyacioglu, 2007). The Digital Library of Armenian Literature offers the biggest database of MWA texts of the 19th and 20th centuries (1850-2000) with the complete works of 75 authors (about 8.400.000 tokens).
3. b. Modern Eastern Armenian. The largest resource for MEA is the open-access Eastern Armenian National Corpus[9]. EANC is designed as a comprehensive corpus with about 110 million tokens, covering MEA written and oral discourses from the mid-19th century to the present. The texts/transcripts have full morphological, semantic and metatext annotation and they are provided by English translations[10] for frequent tokens searchable for making complex lexical morphological queries. Besides the corpus, EANC proposes also an electronic library with full-view access for over hundreds of works by classical

---

[3] https://www.arak29.am/bible_28E/index.htm
[4] https://gregoriproject.com
[5] http://digilib.aua.am
[6] http://titus.uni-frankfurt.de/indexe.htm
[7] http://sd-editions.com/LALT/index.html
[8] https://calfa.fr
[9] http://eanc.net
[10] EANC allows search by an English lexeme (for about 85%) with the same functionality as for an Armenian lexeme, e.g. grammatical and lexical features, sentence position, punctuation etc.

authors in public domain. The library provides the same morphological analysis and translation as the rest of the corpus. The EANC annotation relies on a rule-based approach, combining a wordlist (about 80.000 lexemes composed of a combination of different dictionaries (Galstyan, 1985; Aġayan, 1976; Grgearyan and Harutyunian, 1987 1989; Gyurdjinyan and Hekekyan, 2007) and a morphological model. Overall, 92,5% of all tokens are recognized and annotated with 72,6% analyzed unambiguously, 17% ambiguously, and 7,5% not recognized[11] [for more details on EANC see Khurshudyan et al. (2020)].

The Universal Dependencies project includes MEA[12] (Yavrumyan, 2019) providing 2.502 manually annotated sentences in MEA (about 53.000 tokens [v. 2.5]) with morphological and syntactic annotations in the form of a complete dependency tree bank.

Several other databases (not always searchable) provide MEA and MWA texts: Armenian Wikisource project, Fundamental Scientific Library of the National Academy of Sciences of the Republic of Armenia, etc.

3. c. Armenian Dialects. Except for some rare scanned books containing dialectal texts[13] with various types of linguistic accuracy and transcription approaches (not always reusable for linguistic research), no dedicated dialectal resources exist online. The Armenian dialectology started developing from the mid-19th century and has recorded important advances during the 20th century with a number of dedicated dialect descriptions, important attempts to collect dialectal data with a systematic approach through-out fieldworks as well as various types of researches carried out by the Institute of Language, National Academy of Sciences of Armenia. After the collapse of the Soviet Union the scientific thrust was significantly stopped. An attempt to set up a dialectal corpus was made in the framework of EANC research grant project during 2008-2009. Three dialects were chosen (1. Arcvaberd dialect (Shamshadin, Tavush region), 2. Shenavan dialect (Aparan, Aragatsotn region), and 3. Gusana dialect (Maralik, Shirak region) for each of which about 15 hours of recordings were made and transcribed entirely by the grantees[14] (about 100.000 tokens for each dialect corpus, see *infra* Datasets). For each corpus a list of unique word-forms was processed and the grantees provided full morphological annotation manually. The pilot version of the three dialectal corpora is available online[15].

Project	Tokens	Variety	Contextual annotation	Annotation type	Accessibility
Arak29	630.000	CA	no	full	OD
GREgORI	66.812	CA	yes	lemma, pos	O
Calfa	1,3 million	CA	yes	full	O
EANC	110 million	MEA	no	full	O
UD	53.000	MEA	yes	full	OD
EANC	300.000	dialects	no	full	O

Table 1: Target annotated corpora used in datasets (O = open access, D = downloadable)

Besides the lack of disambiguation for certain target corpora used in our datasets (e.g. in Arak only interlexical homonymy is disambiguated), different projects rely on various tagging systems for POS and morphological annotation (see annotation differences in Table 2 from the examples (1) and (2) for CA and MEA respectively) and sometimes on a various level of lemma annotation (e.g. GREgORI and Calfa consider *mardoyn* as a polylexical wordform because of the definite article). The datasets were automatically standardized, however, the lack of interoperability can have an impact on the results (see *infra*).

---

[11]EANC original analyzer was updated by Timofey Arkhangelskiy and Aleksei Fedorenko and current open source version is available at https://bitbucket.org/timarkh/uniparser-grammar-eastern-armenian/.

[12]https://universaldependencies.org/hy/

[13]E.g. one can find the scanned 18 volumes of Armenian folk tales (1959-2016) available at the site of the Fundamental Scientific Library of the National Academy of Sciences of the Republic of Armenia http://serials.flib.sci.am/.

[14]Shushan Asilbekian (Institute of Linguistics, Armenian Academy of Sciences); Garik Mkrtchian (Yerevan State University); Susanna Davtian (Yerevan State University).

[15]http://web-corpora.net/EANC_dialects/search/

(1) Mk 7:20

or	inč'	i	**mardoyn**	elan-ē
which	what	PREP	**man.ABL.SG.DEF**	go.out-3SG

"That which cometh out of the man ..."

(2) UD

ergel	em	Iṙlandiay-um
sing-PFV	be.AUX.1SG	Ireland-LOC

"I have sung in Ireland."

	Variety	Wordform	Annotation
Arak29	CA	*mardoyn*	*mard* noun.gen.dat.abl.sg.def
GREgORI	CA	*mardoyn*	*mard@n* N+Com:Âs
Calfa	CA	*mardoyn*	*mard@n* 1. NOUN:abl.sg@DEF 2. N+COM:Âs@DEF
UD	MEA	*ergel*	*ergel* Aspect=Perf, Polarity=Pos, VerbForm=Part, Voice=Act
EANC	MEA	*ergel*	1. *ergel* (V,intr/tr) cvb, pfv 'sing' 2. *ergel* (V,intr/tr) inf 'sing'

Table 2: Target corpora annotation samples

4   Datasets

Five datasets were set up to conduct experiments (see Figure 2 and Table 3): three dialect variety and
two Modern Armenian standard datasets. Besides, three mixed datasets were constituted to assess
the potential advantages of mixed data drawn from EANC database. All the datasets have full token
morphological analysis (lemma, POS and morphological features).

D-Ab: Arcvaberd dialect (Shamshadin, Tavush region) dataset includes the transcripts of about 15 hours
of recordings (16 informants) and 120.258 manually annotated wordforms (14.405 unique). This is the
most important and yet the least varied dialect dataset with only 4.120 unique lemmata. **D-Ab** has a
significant number of ambiguous forms due to free-form (vs. context-based) annotation. Arcvaberd
dialect belongs to the *-um* branch, like the dialect of Gusana, and is considered to be a blend of two *-um*
type dialects (Ararat and Karabakh).

D-Ga: Gusana dialect (Maralik, Shirak region) dataset is composed of the transcripts of about 15
hours of recordings (26 informants) and 100.352 manually annotated wordforms (20.647 unique).
Although it is equivalent to **D-Ab** by its volume, it is much more varied with 9.087 unique lemmata.
As a consequence, much more unknown tokens are found in the associated test set which makes **D-Ga**
an interesting benchmark for the evaluation of predictions on unknown tokens. Although the main
population of Gusana originates from Kars, Van and partly Mush (immigrated at the beginning of the
19th century) and the village is areally situated in a *kə* branch region, the dialect is of *-um* type (like
Arcvaberd dialect) with certain mixed features.

D-Shn: Shenavan dialect (Aparan, Aragatsotn region) includes the transcripts of about 15 hours
of recordings (18 informants) and 89.632 manually annotated wordforms (17.940 unique). Proportionally, this is the most varied dataset with 7.568 unique lemmata, thus, with many ambiguous and unknown

forms. Shenavan population immigrated from Mush at the beginning of the 19th century and the dialect originates from Western *kə* branch Mush dialect. However, being in contact with *-um* branch varieties for almost two centuries certain contact-induced changes are present.

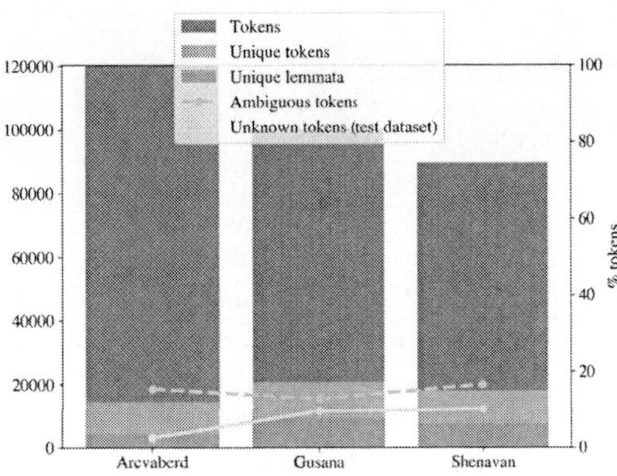

Figure 2: Dialect datasets composition

D-MEA: This dataset is the reference representative dataset for MEA, a subset drawn from EANC database. It counts 5.111.614 tokens (201.710 unique). The sentences are taken from heterogeneous sources: press (2.037.629 tokens), fiction (1.453.894 tokens) and non-fiction (2.031.055 tokens).

D-MWA: This dataset is an experimental dataset for MWA designed for assessing the reuse and reproducibility relevance of the models. The database counts 3.531 tokens (1.788 unique). The sentences are drawn from miscellaneous data such as press, fiction, non-fiction and the Bible.

	D-MEA	**D-Ab**	**D-Ga**	**D-Shn**	**D-MWA**
Wordforms	5.111.614	120.258	100.352	89.632	3.531
Unique tokens	201.710	14.405	20.647	17.940	1.788
Unique lemmata	-	4.120	9.087	7.568	1.311
Ambiguous tokens	-	18.584	12.883	14.844	250
Unknown tokens (test dataset)	13.145	364	1.968	1.810	1.080

Table 3: Dedicated dataset composition

Three more mixed datasets were created: **D-Ab+MEA, D-Ga+MEA** and **D-Shn+MEA** composed of the target dialect dataset and increased by a third of its volume with varied data from **D-MEA**.

Finally, three other external datasets were considered for the creation of the models: Universal Dependencies (**D-UD**) for MEA, and GREgORI (**D-CA1**) and Arak29 (**D-CA2**) for Classical Armenian (see *supra* Armenian resources online).

Unlike **D-UD, D-CA1** and **D-CA2**, the annotations for **D-Ab, D-GA** and **D-Shn** are not context-based (matching between the list of wordforms and the corpus) and its influence on the annotation is discussed below. The evaluation of the different models (see *infra*) showed less considerable results, since **D-Ab, D-GA** and **D-Shn** have a phonetic transcription based on the Armenian alphabet and figures[16]. Finally, **D-Ab, D-Ga, D-Shn, D-MEA, D-UD** use reformed orthography, while **D-MWA, D-CA1** and **D-CA2** use the traditional one. Orthography conversion with some limitations has been performed to allow the evaluation[17].

---

[16]E.g. հըվընդächäv '[he/she] fell ill' (vs. the MEA wordform հիվանդացավ hivandacʰav).

[17]The orthography conversion was processed by the converter designed by Arak29 foundation available at

5 Methodology and results

A number of tests were carried out to develop an RNN annotation model for three dialects (with manually annotated corpora available) and MWA (no annotated corpus available). Three sets of neural networks have been trained and evaluated:

1. univariational targeted variety RNN model;

2. mixed model (2/3 dialect model +1/3 MEA);

3. univariational non-targeted variety RNN model.

The RNN relies on Pie (Manjavacas et al., 2019), which offers a highly modular architecture particularly designed to process historical (cf. Classical Armenian) and non-standard languages (cf. Armenian dialects). The RNN model adopted in this research was successfully tested on Classical Armenian [for more details on the RNN model used see Vidal-Gorène and Kindt (2020)]. Generally, Pie learning ability exploits fully sentence context to increase the lemmatization accuracy and POS-tagging tasks, particularly in case of ambiguous tokens (Eger et al., 2016; Sprugnoli et al., 2020). However, in our experiments Pie learning ability has been limited because of the unresolved ambiguity of the annotations in **D-Ab**, **D-Ga** and **D-Shn**. Consequently, the RNN preserves either all possible categories or only the most probable one. Although the linear decoder showed better results for Classical Armenian POS-tagging, it was compared with the CRF decoder provided by MarMoT and LEMMING (Mueller et al., 2013; Müller et al., 2015), which obtained convincing results on equivalent datasets at the last Evalatin Evaluation Campaign (Sprugnoli et al., 2020; Stoeckel et al., 2020). The model of the lemmatizer and POS-tagger has been trained jointly using a single multitask architecture.

Finally, the relevance of the architecture was evaluated for a standard language (MEA) on the basis of two datasets (**D-MEA** and **D-UD**). COMBO (Rybak and Wróblewska, 2018) trained with **D-UD** (v. 2.3) is at 88.05% for lemmatization and 85.07% for POS-tagging (Arakelyan et al., 2018; Yavrumyan, 2019). The present architecture (**m-UD**) trained with **D-UD** (v. 2.5) obtains 91.56% in lemmatization (74.35% for the ambiguous tokens and 61,85% for the unknown tokens) and 92.54% in POS-tagging (87,81% ambiguous tokens and 83,56% unknown tokens).

5.1 Lemmatization results

Arcvaberd and Gusana being morphologically of *-um* branch, thus, closer to each other, as well as to MEA, a working hypothesis could be to have more positive annotation overlapping between these two dialect data. On the contrary, Shenavan belonging to the *kə* branch would be morphologically more distinct from the two other dialects and MEA, and closer to MWA (see Figure 1), thus the two other dialect and MEA models could be expected to be less relevant for the annotation of its data.

Specialized models: The results of lemmatization of all the dialect tokens (known and unknown) vary between 92.05% and 97.69% (see Table 4) with greater discrepancy for unknown tokens (from 46.52% to 66.87%) (see Table 5). The **m-Ab** model (trained with **D-Ab** which is the biggest dialect dataset) turns out to be the best performer in the general task (97.69%), but the lack of token and lemma variety leads to poor predictions on unknown tokens, whereas **m-Ga** and **m-Shn** prove to be more robust. The confusion matrix shows that **m-Ab** mostly fails on the verbal forms with no phonetic particularity in the transcript (i.e. formally similar to the standard language forms). **m-Ga** and **m-Shn** generate much more false forms for the same token, in addition to being penalized by the wide variety of phonetic transcriptions reproduced in the corpora. Despite being very robust, **M-MEA** suffers from the ambiguity of the data. The model proves to be more efficient for generating all the possible analyses rather than just one (unlike **m-UD** described previously). It processes successfully 94.34% of **D-UD**.

Mixed models: Adding data from **D-MEA** to **D-Ab**, **D-Ga** and **D-Shn** for training mixed models is relatively advantageous for the Arcvaberd dialect (+ 0.64% in accuracy and + 4.4% in precision and

https://www.arak29.am/template/_msconv.php/

recall), including the prediction on unknown tokens ranging from 46.52% to 51.10%. On the other hand, this disadvantages Gusana and Shenavan dialects (see *infra* Non-specialized models for a possible explanation).

Non-specialized models: Similar to the models trained on Classical Armenian (**m-CA1** and **m-CA2**) a model strictly trained on MEA (**m-MEA** and **m-UD**) does not currently allow dialect lemmatization. However, these results should be nuanced, since **D-MEA**, **D-Ab**, **D-Ga** and **D-Shn** are transcribed very differently and in reformed spelling. **D-CA1** and **D-CA2** also have differences at lemma description level (e.g. lemmas in -em and not in -el for verbs) which results in a large number of false negatives despite automatic smoothing. Arcvaberd and Gusana dialects being linguistically close to each other (see *supra*) show right lemmatization for less than 50% (49.47% and 46.38% respectively), which, nevertheless, is a better result than **D-Ab** annotation by **m-Shn** (42.90%). **M-Shn** correctly annotates **D-Ga** at 58.45%, while **D-Shn** annotated by **m-Ga** is at 52.32%. Mixed models provide better results (see Table 4 and Table 5).

Models	Lem. **D-MEA**	POS-t. **D-MEA**	Lem. **D-Ab**	POS-t. **D-Ab**	Lem. **D-Ga**	POS-t. **D-Ga**	Lem. **D-Shn**	POS-t. **D-Shn**
m-MEA	A: 0.9870 P: 0.8859 R: 0.8774	0.9974 P: 0.9989 R: 0.9976	A: 0.3576	-	0.3219	-	0.4264	-
m-Ab	-	-	0.9769 P: 0.7795 R: 0.7796	0.9894 P: 0.992 R: 0.9893	0.4947	0.6288	0.4695	0.6487
m-Ga	-	-	0.4638	0.6627	0.9228 P: 0.6332 R: 0.6229)	0.9645 P: 0.74 R: 0.7019	0.5232	0.7553
m-Shn	-	-	0.4290	0.7452	0.5845	0.8173	0.9205 P: 0.6509 R: 0.6398	0.9569 P: 0.8384 R: 0.8218
m-Ab+MEA	-	-	0.9833 P: 0.8235 R: 0.8219	0.9912 P: 0.9959 R: 0.9899	0.5010	0.6744	0.5010	0.6579
m-Ga+MEA	-	-	0.4856	0.6833	0.9151 P: 0.6205 R: 0.6064	0.9700 P: 0.7867 R: 0.7793	0.5460	0.7534
m-Shn+MEA	-	-	0.4337	0.7684	0.5650	0.8222	0.9166 P: 0.6396 R: 0.6246	0.9645 P: 0.7479 R: 0.7268
m-UD	0.6508	-	0.2035	-	0.2117	-	0.2513	-
m-CA1	0.2616	-	0.1364	-	0.1607	-	0.1787	-
m-CA2	0.2930	-	0.2104	-	0.2435	-	0.2397	-

Table 4: Lemmatization and POS-tagging evaluation of the models on **D-MEA**, **D-Ab**, **D-Ga**, and **D-Shn** for all tokens (A = accuracy, P = precision and R = recall)

5.2 POS-tagging results

Taking into account the limits exposed for the lemmatization task described above, the results in POS-tagging are much more regular. All the POS-tagging evaluations could not be performed due to the excessive conventional variation in the annotation of the corpora (morphological and lexical tagging, formatting, transcription etc.). The conventional discrepancies existing in different projects is an important issue for conducting additional experiments.

Specialized models: POS-tagging models provided significant results (> 95%) for all the dialects including unknown tokens. **M-Ab** is the least efficient because of its diversity. More than two thirds of the errors are caused by the confusion between noun and adjective, which can be explained by the absence of context and especially by the potential homonymy between these two categories, since in Armenian adjectives (and other parts of speech functioning as an attribute) can be easily nominalized, thus having formal endings similar to nouns. In EANC nominalized adjectives are tagged as A, NMLZ which facilitates the search of the target matches.

Mixed models: Adding MEA data to the dialects improves significantly the results for POS-tagging annotation, in particular for unknown tokens (see Table 3).

Non-specialized models: The reuse of models between dialects prove viable in particular for Gusana and Shenavan. The two target dialects do not belong to the same linguistic branch (see *supra*), and yet **m-Shn+MEA** provides 82.22% for **D-Ga**. Moreover, even though **m-Ga** covers only 66.27% for **D-Ab** it may provide a considerable basis for faster annotation of dialect corpora.

Models	Lem. **D-MEA**	POS-t. **D-MEA**	Lem. **D-Ab**	POS-t. **D-Ab**	Lem. **D-Ga**	POS-t. **D-Ga**	Lem. **D-Shn**	POS-t. **D-Shn**
m-MEA	A: 0.9239 P: 0.8487 R: 0.8455	0.9614 P: 0.9108 R: 0.9497	A: 0.1950	-	0.1996	-	0.1937	-
m-Ab	-	-	0.4652 P: 0.2984 R: 0.2897	0.7406 P: 0.3299 R: 0.3284	0.3758	0.5474	0.3856	0.5280
m-Ga	-	-	0.2504	0.5278	0.6687 P: 0.4861 R: 0.468	0.8318 P: 0.4862 R: 0.3992	0.4067	0.6729
m-Shn	-	-	0.2929	0.5933	0.5468	0.7456	0.6547 P: 0.4700 R: 0.4547	0.8083 P: 0.3369 R: 0.3292
m-Ab+MEA	-	-	0.5110 P: 0.3170 R: 0.3064	0.7634 P: 0.4016 R: 0.4020	0.3803	0.5853	0.3799	0.5097
m-Ga+MEA	-	-	0.3241	0.5629	0.6660 P: 0.4826 R: 0.4639	0.8507 P: 0.3850 R: 0.4074	0.4135	0.6609
m-Shn+MEA	-	-	0.2986	0.6365	0.5043	0.7508	0.6459 P: 0.4553 R: 0.4347	0.8358 P: 0.4726 R: 0.3994
m-UD	0.5545	-	0.0916	-	0.1162	-	0.1301	-
m-CA1	0.1991	-	0.1161	-	0.1599	-	0.1553	-
m-CA2	0.2371	-	0.2072	-	0.2240	-	0.2165	-

Table 5: Lemmatization and POS-tagging evaluation of the models on **D-MEA**, **D-Ab**, **D-Ga**, and **D-Shn** for the unknown tokens (A = accuracy, P = precision and R = recall)

5.3 MWA Model

D-MWA was first processed by **m-MEA** model after which the predicted lemmata were checked and manually corrected. The results were compared to the rule-based EANC parser predictions (see Table 4).

ID	Original	Converted	Lemma GT	Lemma RNN	Lemma RB-EANC	POS GT	POS RNN	POS RB-EANC
1	aɫjikə	aɫjikə	aɫjik	aɫjik	aɫjik	N	N	N
2	grkac	grkac	grkel	grkel	grkel	V	V	V
3	ēr	ēr	ē	ē	ē	V	V	V
4	etewi	etewi	etev	etev	etew	N	V	N
5	koɫnən	koɫnən	koɫm	koɫmel	koɫnel	N	N	V
6	t'ewerə	t'ewerə	t'ev	t'ev	t'ew	N	N	N
7	anut'nerən	anut'nerən	anut'	anut'	anut'nerel	N	N	V
8	anc'uc'ac	anc'uc'ac	ancənel	anc'uc'el	anc'uc'el	V	V	V
9	u	u	u	u	u	CONJ	CONJ	CONJ
10	ir	ir	ink'ə	ir	ink'ə	PRON	N	PRON
11	k'it'ə	k'it'ə	k'it'	k'it'	k'it'	N	N	N
12	hetzhetə	hetzhetə	hetzhete	hetzhete	hetzhete	ADV	ADV	ADV
13	aweli	aweli	aveli	aveli	aveli	A	V	ADV
14	ke mxrčuer	kmxrčver	mxrčvil	mxrčvel	kmxrčvel	V	V	V
15	anor	anor	an	aner	aner	PRON	N	N
16	akanǰin	akanǰin	akanǰ	akanǰ	akanǰ	N	N	N
17	etew	etew	etev	etev	etew	N	N	N
18	zmayleli	zmayleli	zmayleli	zmayleli	zmayleli	A	A	A
19	anušahotut'əamb	anušahotut'yamb	anušahotut'yun	anušahotut'yun	anušahotut'yun	N	N	N
20	mə	mə	mə	mə	mə	INDEF	NUM	N
21	glxə	glxə	glux	glxel		N	A	
22	elac	elac	elnel	elnel	elnel	V	V	V
23	:	:	:	:	:	PUNCT	PUNCT	

Table 6: **m-MEA** and EANC rule-based parser comparison of lemmatization and POS-Tagging for **D-MWA** data

The **m-MEA** model provides 88.79% correct lemmatization and 87.33% correct POS-tagging on the **D-MWA**. EANC parser (RB-EANC) obtains 74.09% and 68.57% respectively for the same dataset. As shown in Table 6, the original spelling of the text was converted in order to make **m-MEA** operational. The errors are focused on radically different lemmas between MWA and MEA (e.g. ըլլալ əllal/ լինել linel "to be", certain pronouns (#10 and #15 in Table 6), indefinite article (#20 in Table 6), etc.) which are easily identifiable and could be corrected in the future. **M-MEA** processes successfully lemmas from unknown declined forms (e.g. ablative forms, #7 in Table 6).

The **m-MEA** model can allow rapid corpus processing. Manual correction of such a corpus can provide a specialized MWA model which is of utmost importance for MWA documentation, an endangered language with crucially decreasing native speakers (Donabedian-Demopoulos, 2000; Donabedian-Demopoulos and Al-Bataineh, 2014). **D-MWA** was first processed by **m-MEA** model and predicted lemmata were further checked and manually corrected. The results were compared to the rule-based EANC parser predictions (see Table 6).

6 Conclusion

Different experiments were carried out to illustrate for the first time the automatic morphological annotation of Armenian dialect varieties, and the possible reuse of non-specialized models for rapid corpus processing. The first results are more than relevant with very accurate models specialized on the dialects and MEA showing more than 92% accuracy in lemmatization and 95% in POS-tagging.

The mixed and non-specialized models prove to be insignificant for the annotation rate improvement. These models lack interoperability between the target databases which is detrimental to the models and results in producing many false negatives.

The experiments show considerable relevance in model reuse for Armenian diachronic and variational data, as illustrated more particularly by MWA target test (88.79% in lemmatization and 87.33% in POS-tagging).

The standardization and harmonization of annotation conventions is one of the further challenges. The upcoming experiments will be extended to context-based and full morphological annotation. The experimental data show that parallel to the rule-based approaches RNN models can be a sound alternative to process Armenian diachronic and variational corpora.

No precise estimations are available for the models trained on RB tagged corpora to assess RNN time-consumption. However, current tagging results for MWA and CA allow to take into account an iterative and mixed approach which can partially cover the annotation of non-specialized models reducing the time-consumption for new corpora design.

Language varieties have usually fragile vitality when lacking the "standard" status (cf. dialects) and/or natural regenerating native speakers' rotation and evolution (cf. MWA). The first is true for the Armenian dialects which have always "secondary" status as compared to the standard language with which they coexist. MWA is a standard language and yet it has become mainly a diaspora/heritage language for more than a century. Therefore, the documentation of these Armenian varieties as well as the processing of the documented data is of foremost importance not only in NLP but also and especially in linguistic, anthropological and social perspectives.

References

Hratchia Adjarian. 1909. *Classification des dialectes arméniens*. H. Champion, Paris, France.

Gor Arakelyan, Karen Hambardzumyan, and Hrant Khachatrian. 2018. Towards JointUD: Part-of-speech Tagging and Lemmatization using Recurrent Neural Networks. In *Proceedings of the CoNLL 2018 Shared Task: Multilingual Parsing from Raw Text to Universal Dependencies*, pages 180–186, Brussels, Belgium. Association for Computational Linguistics.

This work is licensed under a Creative Commons Attribution 4.0 International Licence. Licence details: `http://creativecommons.org/licenses/by/4.0/`.

Timofey Arkhangelskiy and Ekaterina Georgieva. 2018. Sound-aligned corpus of Udmurt dialectal texts. In *Proceedings of the Fourth International Workshop on Computational Linguistics of Uralic Languages*, pages 26–38, Helsinki, Finland. Association for Computational Linguistics.

Gabriēl Awetik'ean, Xač'atur Siwrmēlean, and Mkrtič' Awgerean. 1836–1837. *New Dictionary of the Armenian Language*. Tparan i Srboyn Łazaru, Venice, Italia.

Arsēn Aytənean. 1866. *K'nnakan k'erakanowt'iwn ašxarhabar kam ardi hayerēn lezowi [Critical Grammar of the Vernacular or Modern Armenian Language]*. Vienna, Austria.

Eduard Aġayan. 1976. *Ardi hayereni bac'atrakan baṙaran [Explanatory dictionary of Modern Armenian language]*. Yerevan, Armenia.

Oksana Dereza, 2018. *Lemmatization for Ancient Languages: Rules or Neural Networks?*, pages 35–47. Springer International Publishing, Cham.

Anaïd Donabedian-Demopoulos and Anke Al-Bataineh. 2014. L'arménien occidental en France : dynamiques actuelles. Research report, SeDyL UMR8202 (Inalco, CNRS, IRD).

Anaïd Donabedian-Demopoulos and Nisan Boyacioglu. 2007. La lemmatisation de l'arménien occidental avec NooJ. In S. Koeva, D. Maurel, and M. Silberztein, editors, *Formaliser les langues avec l'ordinateur, de INTEX à NooJ*, pages 55–75. Presses Universitaires de Franche Comté.

Anaïd Donabedian-Demopoulos and Ioanna Sitaridou. 2021. Anatolia. In E. Adamou and Y. Matras, editors, *The Routledge Handbook of Language Contact*, pages 404–433. Routledge, London, England.

Anaïd Donabedian-Demopoulos. 2000. Langues de diaspora, langues en danger : le cas de l'arménien occidental. In *Les langues en danger*, Mémoires de la Société de Linguistique de Paris, Nouvelle Série, t. VIII, pages 137–156. Société de Linguistique de Paris, Paris, France.

Anaïd Donabedian-Demopoulos. 2018. Middle East and Beyond - Western Armenian at the crossroads : A sociolinguistic and typological sketch. In Christiane Bulut, editor, *Linguistic minorities in Turkey and Turkic-speaking minorities of the periphery*, volume 111 of *Turcologica*, pages 89–148. Harrazowitz Verlag, Wiesbaden, Allemagne.

Steffen Eger, Rüdiger Gleim, and Alexander Mehler. 2016. Lemmatization and Morphological Tagging in German and Latin: A comparison and a survey of the state-of-the-art. In *Proceedings of the Tenth International Conference on Language Resources and Evaluation (LREC'16)*, pages 1507–1513, Portorož, Slovenia. European Language Resources Association (ELRA).

E. Galstyan. 1985. *Hay-ṙuseren baṙaran [Armenian-Russian dictionary]*. Yerevan, Armenia.

Ararat Gharibyan. 1953. *Hay barbaṙagitut'yun [Armenian Dialectology]*. Yerevan, Armenia.

John A. C. Greppin and Amalya Khachaturian. 1986. *A handbook of Armenian dialectology*. Caravan Books, Delmar N.Y., USA.

Hagop Grgearyan and Nora Harutyunian. 1987-1989. *Ašxarhagrakan anunneri baṙaran [Dictionary of Geographic Names]*. Yerevan.

Davit Gyurdjinyan and Narine Hekekyan. 2007. *Hayerenum gorcacvoł taṙayin hapavumneri baṙaran [Dictionary of acronyms used in Armenian]*. Yerevan, Armenia.

Gevorg Jahukyan. 1972. *Hay barbaṙagitut'yan neracut'yun [Introduction to Armenian Dialectology]*. Yerevan, Armenia.

Victoria Khurshudyan, Timofey Arkhangelskiy, Michael Daniel, Dmitri Levonian, Vladimir Plungian, Alex Polyakov, and Sergey Rubakov. 2020. Introduction to Eastern Armenian National Corpus: www.eanc.net. *Études arméniennes contemporaines*. submitted.

Enrique Manjavacas, Kádár Ákos, and Kestemont Mike. 2019. Improving Lemmatization of Non-Standard Languages with Joint Learning. In *Proceedings of the 2019 Conference of the North American Chapter of the Association for Computational Linguistics: Human Language Technologies, Volume 1 (Long and Short Papers)*, pages 1493–1503, Minneapolis, Minnesota, USA. Association for Computational Linguistics.

Hrach Martirosyan. 2018. The Armenian Dialects. In Geoffrey Haig and Geoffrey Khan, editors, *The languages and linguistics of Western Asia: an areal perspective*, The world of linguistics, 6, pages 46–105. De Gruyter Mouton, Berlin, Boston, USA.

Thomas Mueller, Helmut Schmid, and Hinrich Schütze. 2013. Efficient Higher-Order CRFs for Morphological Tagging. In *Proceedings of the 2013 Conference on Empirical Methods in Natural Language Processing*, pages 322–332, Seattle, Washington, USA. Association for Computational Linguistics.

Thomas Müller, Ryan Cotterell, Alexander Fraser, and Hinrich Schütze. 2015. Joint Lemmatization and Morphological Tagging with Lemming. In *Proceedings of the 2015 Conference on Empirical Methods in Natural Language Processing*, pages 2268–2274, Lisbon, Portugal. Association for Computational Linguistics.

Piotr Rybak and Alina Wróblewska. 2018. Semi-Supervised Neural System for Tagging, Parsing and Lematization. In *Proceedings of the CoNLL 2018 Shared Task: Multilingual Parsing from Raw Text to Universal Dependencies*, pages 45–54, Brussels, Belgium. Association for Computational Linguistics.

Rachele Sprugnoli, Marco Passarotti, Flavio Massimiliano Cecchini, and Matteo Pellegrini. 2020. Overview of the EvaLatin 2020 Evaluation Campaign. In *Proceedings of LT4HALA 2020 - 1st Workshop on Language Technologies for Historical and Ancient Languages*, pages 105–110, Marseille, France. European Language Resources Association (ELRA).

Manuel Stoeckel, Alexander Henlein, Wahed Hemati, and Alexander Mehler. 2020. Voting for POS tagging of Latin texts: Using the flair of FLAIR to better Ensemble Classifiers by Example of Latin. In *Proceedings of LT4HALA 2020 - 1st Workshop on Language Technologies for Historical and Ancient Languages*, pages 130–135, Marseille, France. European Language Resources Association (ELRA).

Chahan Vidal-Gorène and Bastien Kindt. 2020. Lemmatization and POS-tagging process by using joint learning approach. Experimental results on Classical Armenian, Old georgian, and Syriac. In *Proceedings of LT4HALA 2020 - 1st Workshop on Language Technologies for Historical and Ancient Languages*, pages 22–27, Marseille, France. European Language Resources Association (ELRA).

Chahan Vidal-Gorène, Aliénor Decours-Perez, Baptiste Queuche, Agnès Ouzounian, and Thomas Riccioli. 2020. Digitalization and Enrichment of the Nor Baṙgirkʻ Haykazean Lezui: Work in Progress for Armenian Lexicography. *Journal of the Society of Armenian Studies*, 27. submitted.

Ruprecht von Waldenfels, Michael Daniel, and Nina Dobrushina. 2014. Why standard orthography? Building the Ustya River Basin corpus, an online corpus of a Russian dialect. In *Компьютерная лингвистика и интеллектуальные технологии*, pages 720–728.

Marat Yavrumyan. 2019. Tekʻsti mekʻenakan hatuytʻavorumə arewelahayereni šarahyusakan caṙeri UD Armenian-ArmTDP bankum [Tokenization and Word Segmentation in the UD ARMENIAN-ArmTDP Treebank]. *Banber Erewani hamalsarani*, pages 52–65.

Neural Machine Translation for translating into Croatian and Serbian

Maja Popović, Alberto Poncelas, Andy Way
ADAPT Centre, School of Computing
Dublin City University, Ireland
`name.surname@adaptcentre.ie`

Marija Brkić Bakarić
Department of Informatics
University of Rijeka, Croatia
`mbrkic@uniri.hr`

Abstract

In this work, we systematically investigate different set-ups for training of neural machine translation (NMT) systems for translation into Croatian and Serbian, two closely related South Slavic languages. We explore English and German as source languages, different sizes and types of training corpora, as well as bilingual and multilingual systems. We also explore translation of English IMDb user movie reviews, a domain/genre where only monolingual data are available.

First, our results confirm that multilingual systems with joint target languages perform better. Furthermore, translation performance from English is much better than from German, partly because German is morphologically more complex and partly because the corpus consists mostly of parallel human translations instead of original text and its human translation. The translation from German should be further investigated systematically.

For translating user reviews, creating synthetic in-domain parallel data through back- and forward-translation and adding them to a small out-of-domain parallel corpus can yield performance comparable with a system trained on a full out-of-domain corpus. However, it is still not clear what is the optimal size of synthetic in-domain data, especially for forward-translated data where the target language is machine translated. More detailed research including manual evaluation and analysis is needed in this direction.

1 Introduction

Whereas South Slavic languages are generally less supported and investigated in natural language processing, they have been explored in the field of machine translation (MT). Nevertheless, a large part of the work deals with the previous state-of-the-art approach, namely phrase-based statistical machine translation (PBSMT) (Popović and Ljubešić, 2014; Toral et al., 2014; Popović and Arčan, 2015; Arčan et al., 2016; Popović et al., 2016; Sánchez-Cartagena et al., 2016; Maučec and Brest, 2017), while much less work can be found about the new state-of-the-art, neural machine translation (NMT) (Lakew et al., 2018; Lohar et al., 2019).

In this work, we focus on NMT into Croatian and Serbian, two very closely related South Slavic languages. We explore two source languages, English and German. The main goals of our research are to explore two source languages, each of them with different sizes and types of training corpora, as well as to test our systems on translating English user reviews, a challenging domain/genre where no parallel training data are available. For these purposes, we train bilingual and multilingual NMT systems on different publicly available parallel training corpora. For translating English user reviews, we also explore different types of synthetic parallel in-domain data (Sennrich et al., 2016a; Zhang and Zong, 2016; Burlot and Yvon, 2018; Poncelas et al., 2018a), which is a widely used practice in NMT. We explored two types of synthetic data: back-translated (BT) and forward-translated (FT). BT data consist of in-domain target language data and their machine translations into English, whereas FT data consist of English data and their machine translations into Serbian and Croatian. All our experiments were carried out on publicly available data sets.

This work is licensed under a Creative Commons Attribution 4.0 International Licence.
Licence details: `http://creativecommons.org/licenses/by/4.0/`.

Proceedings of the 7th VarDial Workshop on NLP for Similar Languages, Varieties and Dialects, pages 102–113
Barcelona, Spain (Online), December 13, 2020

For all our systems, we present three distinct automatic MT evaluation scores, training corpus size, percentage of the particular target language in the training corpus, as well as training time. In order to get a broader picture about the current state of NMT into these two languages, we also present automatic scores for MT outputs[1] of two on-line systems: Google Translate[2] and Amazon Translate.[3]

1.1 Related work

As already mentioned, a large number of publications deal with the PBSMT approach for South Slavic languages. An overview of Slavic languages and PBSMT is given in (Maučec and Brest, 2017). Translating from Croatian into English for tourism domain is presented in (Toral et al., 2014), while factor models for the same language pair were explored in (Sánchez-Cartagena et al., 2016). Similarities and differences between Serbian and Croatian in terms of building PBMT systems were investigated in (Popović and Ljubešić, 2014) for news domain, as well as in (Popović et al., 2016) for the educational domain. Linguistic phenomena posing problems for PBSMT systems between Serbian and Slovenian on one side and English and German on the other side were investigated in (Popović and Arčan, 2015). Publicly available on-line PBSMT systems for translating between English on one side and Croatian, Slovenian and Serbian on another are described in (Arčan et al., 2016).

With the emergence of NMT, several publications have compared its performance with PBSMT. Translation errors from English into Croatian are analysed in (Klubička et al., 2018) and discourse phenomena for the same language pair in (Šoštarić et al., 2018), while (Popović, 2018) explores linguistically motivated issues for the English–Serbian language pair.

Different training set-ups for NMT from English into Serbian and Croatian were first investigated in (Lakew et al., 2018). They explored individual bilingual systems for each language, systems built on merged unlabelled data, as well as multilingual systems built on merged labelled data, namely with a language identifier in each source sentence. In addition, they investigated combinations of unlabelled and labelled data. Their results showed that the multilingual approach with a language identifier is the most promising. However, they carried out the experiments only on a very small TED corpus consisting of about 100k segments for each target language. In our work, we systematically investigate different corpora with sizes in the range of 300k to 40M segments.

NMT for translating English user reviews into Serbian has been addressed in (Lohar et al., 2019). They compared PBSMT and NMT systems trained on out-of-domain data, and then further investigated the NMT system with additional synthetic data. However, they explored only Serbian as a target language, and their baseline system was built on a very small News corpus of 200k segments. In this work, we also include Croatian, and we build the systems on more data, both out-of-domain as well as in-domain.

2 Data sets

2.1 OPUS parallel data

For all our systems, we use the publicly available OPUS[4] parallel data (Tiedemann, 2012). The vast majority of these resources for the desired language combinations consists of *OpenSubtitles*. For English and both target languages, we also used *SETIMES News*, *Bible*, *Tilde*, *EU-bookshop*, *QED*, and *Tatoeba* corpora. In addition, we used *GlobalVoices* for Serbian, and *hrenWac*, *TED* and *Wikimedia* for Croatian. For German, we only used *OpenSubtitles* because other corpora are rather sparse. However, including these corpora might be interesting for future work.

The original parallel data were filtered in order to eliminate noisy parts: too long segments (more than 100 words), segment pairs with disproportional sentence lengths, segments with more than 1/3 of non-alphanumeric characters, as well as duplicate segment pairs were removed. Table 1 shows the number of remaining segments which were used for training and testing the systems. For testing English systems,

---

[1] The outputs were generated at the beginning of August 2020.

[2] `https://translate.google.com/`

[3] `https://aws.amazon.com/translate/`

[4] `http://opus.nlpl.eu/`

domain	en-hr		en-sr		de-hr		de-sr	
	# of sentences		# of sentences		# of sentences		# of sentences	
	training	test	training	test	training	test	training	test
Subtitles	23 956 612	800	29 445 286	800	9 816 820	1044	10 620 905	1062
News	202 133	200	221 109	200	/	/	/	/
Other	856 594	/	92 357	/	/	/	/	/

Table 1: Statistics of the parallel OPUS data: English–Croatian (en-hr), English–Serbian (en-sr), German–Croatian (de-hr) and German–Serbian (de-sr).

we used 800 segments from *Subtitles* and 200 segments from *News*. For testing German systems, we used only *Subtitles*.

2.2 Movie reviews

Translation from English is also tested on publicly available texts[5] consisting of English user movie reviews from IMDb and their human translations into Serbian and Croatian. This test set, also used in (Lohar et al., 2019), was compiled from the publicly available IMDb corpus[6] created for sentiment analysis. For this test set, we explored the use of synthetic data obtained from the following monolingual in-domain data:

Movies: Croatian and Serbian texts collected from web sites dedicated to movie overviews and cinema programmes. This corpus is very small, consisting of about 100k Serbian segments and 5k Croatian segments.

Selected: Extracted from the mixed Croatian and Serbian web data *hrWac* and *srWac* (Ljubešić and Erjavec, 2011; Ljubešić and Klubička, 2014) using the Feature Decay Algorithm (FDA) (Biçici and Yuret, 2011; Biçici and Yuret, 2015; Poncelas et al., 2018b; Poncelas, 2019). FDA selects sentences from an initial set S based on the number of n-grams which overlap with an in-domain text *Seed* and adds these sentences to a selected set *Sel*. In addition, in order to promote a diversity, the n-grams are penalized proportionally to the number of instances present in *Sel*. During the execution of FDA, candidate sentences from the set S are selected one by one according to the score defined in (1):

$$score(s, Seed, Sel) = \frac{\sum\limits_{ngr \in \{s \cap Seed\}} 0.5^{C_{Sel}(ngr)}}{\text{length}(s)} \tag{1}$$

The sentence with the highest score is removed from S and added to Sel. The count of occurrences of n-gram ngr in the selected set Sel, $C_{Sel}(ngr)$, is updated so that in the following iterations this n-gram contributes less to the scoring of one sentence. The process is executed iteratively, adding a single sentence from the set S to the selected set Sel at a time, and it stops after enough sentences have been extracted.

For our experiment, the *hrWac* and *srWac* corpora represented the set S, and the *Movies* data were used as *Seed*. Before applying FDA, the undesirable sentences were removed from S: those containing URLs, those with more than 1/3 of non-alphanumeric characters, duplicates, as well as too long (more than 60 words) and too short (less than 5 words) sentences. In this way, we obtained about 500k selected segments for each target language.

IMDb: English data consisting of about 600k IMDb movie reviews which were not used as a test set.

Amazon: English Amazon movie reviews from the Amazon product review collection[7] (McAuley et al., 2015). We used the first 1M segments (from about 15M in total) for the experiments described in this work. Using more of these data could be an interesting direction for future work.

---

[5] https://github.com/m-popovic/imdb-corpus-for-MT
[6] https://ai.stanford.edu/~amaas/data/sentiment/
[7] http://jmcauley.ucsd.edu/data/amazon/

corpus		en→hr			en→sr	
			# of sentences			# of sentences
	languages	training	test	languages	training	test
Movies	hr-en(BT)	5 357	/	sr-en(BT)	117 768	/
Selected	hr-en(BT)	449 388	/	sr-en(BT)	549 756	/
IMDb	en-hr(FT)	306 874	485	en-sr(FT)	306 874	485
Amazon	en-hr(FT)	500 000	/	en-sr(FT)	500 000	/

Table 2: Statistics of the movie reviews data.

BT and FT synthetic parallel corpora The Serbian and Croatian data *Movies* and *Selected* were translated into English by an NMT system in order to create BT synthetic parallel corpora. The English *IMDb* and *Amazon* data were translated into Serbian and Croatian by an NMT system thus providing FT synthetic parallel corpora. In order to obtain a balanced corpus in terms of the two target languages, we translated half of the *IMDb* (about 300k segments) and half of the *Amazon* (about 500k segments) corpora into Croatian, and the other two halves into Serbian. More details about the NMT systems used for BT and FT can be found in the next section. Detailed statistics for all movie reviews can be seen in Table 2.

3   NMT systems

All our systems are based on the Transformer architecture (Vaswani et al., 2017) and built using the Sockeye implementation (Hieber et al., 2018). The systems operate on sub-word units generated by byte-pair encoding (BPE) (Sennrich et al., 2016b). We set the number of BPE merge operations at 32000 both for the source and for the target language texts. We do not use shared vocabularies between the source (English, German) and the target (Serbian, Croatian) languages because they are distinct. For multilingual systems, on the other hand, we build a joint vocabulary for the two target languages (Serbian and Croatian) because they are very similar. These systems are built using the same technique as (Johnson et al., 2017) and (Aharoni et al., 2019), namely adding a target language label "SR" or "HR" to each source sentence.

All the systems have Transformer architecture with 6 layers for both the encoder and decoder, model size of 512, feed forward size of 2048, and 8 attention heads. For training, we use Adam optimiser (Kingma and Ba, 2015), initial learning rate of 0.0002, and batch size of 4096 (sub)words. Validation perplexity is calculated after every 4000 batches (at so-called "checkpoints"), and if this perplexity does not improve after 20 checkpoints, the training stops. For set-ups with less than two million segments,[8] following the recommendations for low-resource settings in (Sennrich and Zhang, 2019), we changed the following parameters: training stops after 10 checkpoints instead of 20, initial learning rate is 0.0001 instead of 0.0002, and checkpoint interval is 100 batches instead of 4000.

3.1   Systems for translating from English

The following set-ups were investigated for translating from English into Croatian and Serbian:

Clean data only The bilingual (EN→HR_CLEAN, EN→SR_CLEAN) and multilingual (EN→HR+SR_CLEAN) low-resourced systems are trained only on *News* and *Other* data from Table 1. The segments in these texts are mainly properly aligned, so we refer to it as "clean". It is worth noting that this corpus is rather unbalanced in the terms of target languages, as can be observed from Table 1: there are only about 300k segments for Serbian and about 1M for Croatian.

Subtitles only (first 2M segments) In order to compare bilingual and multilingual systems in a balanced scenario, a small sub-set of *Subtitles* is used. The bilingual systems EN→HR_SUBS2M and

---

[8]This threshold was chosen intuitively. Systematic experiments with different corpus sizes and different parameters should be carried out in order to determine the exact threshold for the low-resourced scenario.

EN→SR_SUBS2M are trained on the first 2M segments for each target language. For the multilingual system EN→HR+SR_SUBS2M, the duplicates were removed after joining the corpora so that 3.6M segments remained.

Cleaning: *Subtitles* contain a number of misaligned segments even after the basic filtering. Therefore, a multisource system in the opposite direction[9] "*hr+sr→en_subs2M*" was trained on the same data and was used for removing segment pairs with the negative log-probability larger than 2 from its own training corpus. The threshold of 2 was chosen after a qualitative manual inspection of parallel segments and their log-probabilities. The opposite translation direction was used for cleaning because of different complexity levels of the languages; probabilities provided by an MT system are usually more reliable when translating from more complex languages into less complex ones. After cleaning, the number of parallel segments is reduced to 2.7M and this cleaned corpus is used to train a cleaned multilingual system EN→HR+SR_CLEANED.

***Subtitles* (cleaned first 2M segments) + clean data** The multilingual system EN→HR+SR_CLEAN/ED is trained on the cleaned 2.7M segments from *Subtitles* merged with the low-resourced clean data, consisting in total of 4.1M segments. This system is used as a baseline for translating English movie reviews.

A multisource system in the opposite direction "*hr+sr→en_clean/ed*" is trained on the same data and is used for cleaning the full *Subtitles* corpus as well as for back-translation of movie reviews.

Full data As mentioned above, in order to reduce noise in the whole *Subtitles* corpus, the multisource "*hr+sr→en_clean/ed*" system was used with the log-probability threshold of 3 (again, established after a manual qualitative inspection of the parallel segments and their log-probabilities). The multilingual system EN→HR+SR_FULL_CLEAN/ED is then built on all clean and all cleaned *Subtitles*. For the sake of completeness, bilingual systems EN→HR_FULL and EN→SR_FULL are trained on all data from Table 1, without any cleaning.

3.2 Systems for translating from German

The following set-ups were investigated for translating from German into Croatian and Serbian:

***Subtitles* (first 2M segments)** The bilingual systems DE→HR_SUBS2M and DE→SR_SUBS2M are trained on the first 2M segments from *Subtitles* for each target language. For the multilingual system DE→HR+SR_SUBS2M, the duplicates were removed so that 3.5M segments remained.

Cleaning: Analogously to translation from English, a multisource system in the opposite direction "*hr+sr→de_subs2M*" was used for removing misaligned segments from its own training corpus. Although German is morphologically more complex than English, it is still less complex than Serbian and Croatian, so we also used the opposite translation direction for cleaning. After cleaning, the number of segments is reduced to 2.3M, and the cleaned multilingual system DE→HR+SR_CLEANED is trained on this corpus.

Multisource German+English: Because the corpora including German are smaller than those including English, we wanted to check the potential of joining German and English corpora in order to build a multisource system. As the first step, we wanted to test it on a more or less balanced corpus in terms of source languages. For this purpose, we built a multilingual system DE+EN→HR+SR_CLEAN/ED by merging the cleaned German *Subtitles* with the English clean data and cleaned (first 2M) *Subtitles*.

Full *Subtitles* Again, the multisource "*sr+hr→de_clean*" system was used with the translation score threshold of 3. The multilingual system DE→HR+SR_FULL_CLEANED is then built on all cleaned *Subtitles* data. Also, two bilingual systems DE→HR_FULL and DE→SR_FULL are trained on all *Subtitles* data from Table 1, without any cleaning.

---

[9]It is worth noting that the multilingual system is better than the bilingual systems also for the opposite translation direction.

3.3 Systems for translating English movie reviews

The main challenge when translating this test set is that there are no readily available parallel corpora of movie reviews which could be used for in-domain training. Therefore, we apply the following strategy: we start from the multilingual EN→HR+SR_CLEAN/ED system trained on 4.1M clean segments as the baseline, and enrich it with different types and amounts of synthetic parallel movie reviews. The following systems are trained:

baseline EN→HR+SR CLEAN/ED: on the clean data together with the cleaned first 2M segments from OpenSubtitles.

+MOVIES-BT: on the baseline system data enriched with back-translated *Movies* data. The system used for back-translation is the same "*hr+sr-en_clean/ed*" system used for cleaning the full *Subtitles* data. This system can be seen as the baseline system in the opposite translation direction.

+SELECTED-BT: the baseline system data enriched with back-translated *Movies* and *Selected* data.

+IMDB-FT: on the data of the system "+SELECTED-BT" enriched with forward-translated *IMDb* data. Forward translation was performed by the system "+SELECTED-BT".

+AMAZON-FT: on the data used for the system "+IMDB-FT" enriched with forward-translated *Amazon* data. Forward translation was performed by the system "+IMDB-FT".

In addition to these mid-resourced partially in-domain systems, we also translate the movie reviews test set by the three systems trained on full out-of-domain OPUS data (EN→HR_FULL, EN→SR_FULL, EN→HR+SR_FULL_CLEAN/ED).

4 Results

We evaluate our systems using the following three automatic overall evaluation scores: sacreBLEU (Post, 2018), chrF (Popović, 2015) and characTER (Wang et al., 2016). The BLEU score is based on word n-gram (n in range from 1 to 4) precision and brevity penalty which should replace recall. The chrF score is based on character n-gram matching (n in range from 1 to 6) instead of word n-gram matching. It is F-score which weights recall two times more than precision. The characTER score is based on edit distance which takes into account not only substitutions, insertions and deletions, but also word sequence reorderings and character sequences in unmatched words. We use the BLEU score because of the long tradition of using it for MT evaluation despite well-known faults, and the two character level scores because they are shown to correlate much better with human assessments (Bojar et al., 2017; Ma et al., 2018). Recently, the chrF score is recommended as a replacement for BLEU (Mathur et al., 2020).

In addition to the automatic MT evaluation scores, for each of the systems we report the size of the training corpus, the percentage of particular target language data in this corpus, as well as the training time in terms of days.

4.1 Translation from English

The results for translation from English are presented in Table 3. As expected, multilingual systems are better than bilingual for all set-ups, even for the unbalanced clean low-resourced corpus. However, the improvements are smaller for Croatian, the language with more data (77.1% of segments). Another observation is that multilingual systems trained on cleaned data, with reduced corpus size and similar or shorter training time, demonstrate better translation performance in terms of three automatic scores than bilingual systems trained on uncleaned data.

Adding the first 2M cleaned segments from *Subtitles* to the small clean data (EN-HR+SR_CLEAN/ED) results in scores which are approaching those obtained by full data, although the corpus size is 6 to 10 times smaller (4.1M vs. 26/30/39M). The training time is more than two times shorter (two days vs. five days). This could be interesting for cases when a trade-off between performance and resources can play a role. Adding German data does not prolong the training time, but it slightly deteriorates all scores.

(a) Translation from English into Croatian

system	training			test, en→hr, subs+news		
	size	%hr	time	BLEU↑	chrF↑	chrTER↓
EN→HR_CLEAN	0.9M	100	<12h	22.3	48.5	52.1
EN→HR+SR_CLEAN	1.3M	77.1	<12h	22.6	48.7	51.8
EN→HR_SUBS2M	2.0M	100	<1d	20.0	44.4	49.9
EN→HR+SR_SUBS2M	3.6M	45.7	<1d	22.1	47.2	46.8
EN→HR+SR_SUBS2M_CLEANED	2.7M	44.8	<12h	20.9	45.6	48.2
EN→HR+SR_CLEAN/ED	4.1M	55.5	<2d	**32.4**	**56.7**	**43.4**
DE+EN→HR+SR_CLEAN/ED	6.4M	56.1	<2d	31.8	56.2	43.7
EN→HR_FULL	26M	100	∼5d	33.0	57.4	41.6
EN→HR+SR_FULL_CLEAN/ED	39M	39.1	∼5d	**33.7**	**58.2**	**41.0**
Google	*n.a.*	*n.a.*	*n.a.*	*26.9*	*53.4*	*46.2*
Amazon	*n.a.*	*n.a.*	*n.a.*	***31.7***	***57.1***	***42.5***

(b) Translation from English into Serbian

system	training			test, en→sr, subs+news		
	size	%sr	time	BLEU↑	chrF↑	chrTER↓
EN→SR_CLEAN	0.3M	100.0	<12h	19.3	43.6	60.4
EN→HR+SR_CLEAN	1.3M	22.9	<12h	22.8	47.0	58.0
EN→SR_SUBS2M	2.0M	100	<1d	19.2	43.1	55.0
EN→HR+SR_SUBS2M	3.6M	54.3	<1d	22.2	46.5	52.1
EN→HR+SR_SUBS2M_CLEANED	2.7M	55.2	<12h	20.7	45.2	52.4
EN→HR+SR_CLEAN/ED	4.1M	44.5	<2d	**33.8**	**56.6**	**47.6**
DE+EN→HR+SR_CLEAN/ED	6.4M	43.9	<2d	32.6	55.6	48.4
EN→SR_FULL	30M	100	∼5d	**35.5**	57.6	46.1
EN→HR+SR_FULL_CLEAN/ED	39M	60.9	∼5d	35.2	**57.7**	**45.6**
Google	*n.a.*	*n.a.*	*n.a.*	24.4	50.8	51.5
Amazon	*n.a.*	*n.a.*	*n.a.*	26.5	52.5	51.1

Table 3: Results for translation from English into Croatian (above) and Serbian (below): corpus size, percentage of the target language, training time, and the three automatic MT evaluation scores: BLEU (higher values are better), chrF (higher values are better) and characTER (lower values are better).

Apart from this, it can be seen that only Amazon Translate for Croatian is comparable to our best systems while all other on-line systems are clearly outperformed.[10]

4.2 Translation from German

Table 4 shows the results for translation from German. First of all, it can be noted that, as expected, the scores for translating from German are generally much worse than for translating from English. Due to this discrepancy in performance, the multisource system including both English and German data DE+EN-HR+SR_CLEAN/ED improves the scores for German although it slightly deteriorates the scores for English (Table 3).

One possible reason for the discrepancy is that the German language is morphologically more complex than English, although it has more similarities with the target languages (such as grammatical gender, cases, verb prefixes, etc.). Still, these general similarities often cannot be mapped (such as usage of different cases for the same constructions, different grammatical gender of the same noun, etc.), which is not very helpful for the translation process. Another factor, namely the nature of the corpus, could also play an important role. The majority of non-English texts in *OpenSubtitles* are human translations from English original sentences. Therefore, for translation from English, the source language is the original one and the target language is its human translation. In contrast, for translation from German, both sides are human translations, which can have a strong impact on performance (Kurokawa et al., 2009; Vyas et al., 2018; Zhang and Toral, 2019). A thorough investigation of the data should be carried out in future work in order to better understand these results.

Apart from this, it is once more confirmed that multilingual systems yield better scores than bilingual.

---

[10]On one hand, our systems were trained on in-domain data. On the other hand, the companies providing on-line systems have access to huge amounts of data and computer resources.

(a) Translation from German into Croatian

system	training			test, de→hr, subs		
	size	%hr	time	BLEU↑	chrF↑	chrTER↓
DE→HR_SUBS2M	2.0M	100.0	<1d	15.8	36.6	60.5
DE→HR+SR_SUBS2M	3.5M	56.6	<1d	18.2	39.1	57.9
DE→HR+SR_SUBS2M_CLEANED	2.3M	57.2	<12h	16.5	37.3	58.9
DE+EN→HR+SR_CLEAN/ED	6.4M	56.1	<2d	**18.6**	**39.4**	**57.6**
DE→HR_FULL	9.8M	100.0	~3d	20.7	41.9	55.4
DE→HR+SR_FULL_CLEANED	12.6M	55.6	~3d	**21.4**	**42.4**	**55.3**
Google	*n.a.*	*n.a.*	*n.a.*	*14.8*	*38.2*	*59.7*
Amazon	*n.a.*	*n.a.*	*n.a.*	*18.5*	*40.6*	*57.1*

(b) Translation from German into Serbian

system	training			test, de→sr, subs		
	size	%sr	time	BLEU↑	chrF↑	chrTER↓
DE→SR_SUBS2M	2.0M	100.0	<1d	14.7	34.9	60.8
DE→HR+SR_SUBS2M	3.5M	43.4	<1d	16.1	36.4	59.5
DE→HR+SR_SUBS2M_CLEANED	2.3M	42.8	<12h	14.9	35.4	59.8
DE+EN→HR+SR_CLEAN/ED	6.4M	43.9	<2d	**15.7**	**36.8**	**59.1**
DE→SR_FULL	10.6M	100.0	~3d	18.2	39.1	56.9
DE→HR+SR_FULL_CLEANED	12.6M	44.4	~3d	**18.5**	**39.4**	**56.7**
Google	*n.a.*	*n.a.*	*n.a.*	*11.6*	*34.8*	*61.9*
Amazon	*n.a.*	*n.a.*	*n.a.*	*12.4*	*35.6*	*60.5*

Table 4: Results for translation from German into Croatian (above) and Serbian (below): corpus size, percentage of the target language, training time, and the three automatic MT evaluation scores: BLEU (the higher the better), chrF (the higher the better) and characTER (the lower the better).

Furthermore, our systems result in better scores than on-line systems.

4.3 Translation of English movie reviews

Table 5 shows the results for the IMDb test set. The multisource system including German also deteriorates the scores for this test set. As for synthetic parallel data, it can be noted that, as expected, the BT data improve the scores, especially for Serbian because there are many more movie reviews in this language. FT data further improves the scores at the cost of slightly prolonged training. In contrast, simply including all out-domain data results in better scores although there is no in-domain data. In addition, contrary to all other test sets, bilingual system for Croatian results in better automatic scores than the multilingual cleaned system. For all these reasons, it is still hard to draw conclusions about translating user reviews, so further systematic research including manual evaluation and analysis of MT outputs is needed to find an optimal set-up.

As for on-line systems, again only Amazon Translate into Croatian is comparable with our best system. All other on-line systems are outperformed both by our best system as well as by our second and third best systems.

5 Summary and outlook

This work presents a systematic investigation of different set-ups for training NMT systems for translation into Serbian and Croatian, two closely related South Slavic languages. We explore English and German as source languages, different sizes and types of training corpora, as well as bilingual and multilingual systems. We also explore translation of English IMDb user movie reviews, a domain/genre where only monolingual data are available.

Our results confirm that multilingual systems with joint target languages perform better. The performance of translation from English is generally much better than from German, partly because German is morphologically more complex and partly because the corpus consists mostly of parallel human translations instead of original text and its human translation. More research should be carried out on translation from German (as well as on more languages other than English) in order to better understand the poten-

(a) Translation of English IMDb movie reviews into Croatian

| system | training | | | test, en→hr, imdb | | |
	size	%hr in domain	time	BLEU↑	chrF↑	chrTER↓
EN→HR+SR_CLEAN/ED	4.1M	0	<2d	27.4	53.9	41.9
+MOVIES-BT	4.2M	4.4	<2d	27.4	54.1	41.6
+SELECTED-BT	5.2M	45.0	<2d	27.4	55.0	40.9
+IMDB-FT	5.8M	50.0	<3d	28.2	55.9	40.2
+AMAZON-FT	6.8M	50.0	~3d	**29.2**	**56.6**	**39.8**
DE+EN→HR+SR_CLEAN/ED	6.4M	0	<2d	26.7	53.4	42.4
EN→HR_FULL	25.5M	0	~5d	**31.8**	**57.6**	**39.3**
EN→HR+SR_FULL_CLEAN/ED	39M	0	~5d	30.6	56.7	39.8
Google	*n.a.*	*n.a.*	*n.a.*	*28.6*	*55.7*	*40.6*
Amazon	*n.a.*	*n.a.*	*n.a.*	*30.9*	*57.6*	*38.9*

(b) Translation of English IMDb movie reviews into Serbian

| system | training | | | test, en→sr, imdb | | |
	size	%sr in domain	time	BLEU↑	chrF↑	chrTER↓
EN→HR+SR_CLEAN/ED	4.1M	0	<2d	26.5	53.3	42.2
+MOVIES-BT	4.2M	95.6	<2d	28.0	54.7	41.1
+SELECTED-BT	5.2M	55.0	<2d	28.8	55.6	40.0
+IMDB-FT	5.8M	50.0	<3d	29.6	56.3	39.4
+AMAZON-FT	6.8M	50.0	~3d	**30.2**	**56.5**	**39.0**
DE+EN→HR+SR_CLEAN/ED	6.4M	0	<2d	26.5	53.3	42.0
EN→SR_FULL	30M	0	~5d	31.5	56.9	39.3
EN→HR+SR_FULL_CLEAN/ED	39M	0	~5d	**31.6**	**57.2**	**39.1**
Google	*n.a.*	*n.a.*	*n.a.*	*26.4*	*54.2*	*40.9*
Amazon	*n.a.*	*n.a.*	*n.a.*	*26.7*	*54.6*	*40.8*

Table 5: Results for translation of English IMDb movie reviews into Croatian (above) and Serbian (below): corpus size, percentage of the target language in the in-domain training corpus, training time, and the three automatic MT evaluation scores (BLEU, chrF and characTER)

tials and limits of the approaches tested here. Still, for both source languages, our best systems perform better than the two online-systems, Google Translate and Amazon Translate, whereby the Amazon systems for translating English into Croatian are comparable with ours.

For translating user reviews, creating synthetic in-domain parallel data through back- and forward-translation and adding them to a small out-of-domain parallel corpus can yield performance comparable with a system trained on a full out-of-domain corpus. Our experiments still leave some important questions open, such as the impact of the size of synthetic FT data and impact of performance of MT system which generated this data. Therefore, more detailed research including manual evaluation and analysis of translated reviews is needed in this direction.

Apart from this, removing misaligned segments by log-probabilities provided by MT systems should be investigated systematically, by comparing different NMT systems for cleaning together with different thresholds for log-probabilities.

Acknowledgements

The ADAPT SFI Centre for Digital Media Technology is funded by Science Foundation Ireland through the SFI Research Centres Programme and is co-funded under the European Regional Development Fund (ERDF) through Grant 13/RC/2106. This research was partly funded by financial support of the European Association for Machine Translation (EAMT) under its programme "2019 Sponsorship of Activities".

References

Roee Aharoni, Melvin Johnson, and Orhan Firat. 2019. Massively multilingual neural machine translation. In *Proceedings of the 2019 Conference of the North American Chapter of the Association for Computational Linguistics: Human Language Technologies (NAACL-HLT 2019)*, pages 3874–3884, Minneapolis, Minnesota, June.

Mihael Arčan, Maja Popović, and Paul Buitelaar. 2016. Asistent – A Machine Translation System for Slovene, Serbian and Croatian. In *Proceedings of the Tenth Conference on Language Technologies and Digital Humanities (JDTH 2016)*, pages 13–20, Ljubljana, Slovenia, September.

Ergun Biçici and Deniz Yuret. 2011. Instance selection for machine translation using feature decay algorithms. In *Proceedings of the Sixth Workshop on Statistical Machine Translation (WMT 2011)*, pages 272–283, Edinburgh, Scotland.

Ergun Biçici and Deniz Yuret. 2015. Optimizing instance selection for statistical machine translation with feature decay algorithms. *IEEE/ACM Transactions on Audio, Speech, and Language Processing*, 23(2):339–350.

Ondřej Bojar, Yvette Graham, and Amir Kamran. 2017. Results of the WMT17 metrics shared task. In *Proceedings of the Second Conference on Machine Translation (WMT 2017)*, pages 489–513, Copenhagen, Denmark, September.

Franck Burlot and François Yvon. 2018. Using Monolingual Data in Neural Machine Translation: a Systematic Study. In *Proceedings of the 3rd Conference on Machine Translation (WMT 2018)*, pages 144–155, Belgium, Brussels, November.

Felix Hieber, Tobias Domhan, Michael Denkowski, David Vilar, Artem Sokolov, Ann Clifton, and Matt Post. 2018. The sockeye neural machine translation toolkit at AMTA 2018. In *Proceedings of the 13th Conference of the Association for Machine Translation in the Americas (AMTA 2018)*, pages 200–207, Boston, MA, March.

Melvin Johnson, Mike Schuster, Quoc V. Le, Maxim Krikun, Yonghui Wu, Zhifeng Chen, Nikhil Thorat, Fernanda Viégas, Martin Wattenberg, Greg Corrado, Macduff Hughes, and Jeffrey Dean. 2017. Google's multilingual neural machine translation system: Enabling zero-shot translation. *Transactions of the Association for Computational Linguistics*, 5:339–351.

Diederik P. Kingma and Jimmy Ba. 2015. Adam: A method for stochastic optimization. In *Proceedings of the 3rd International Conference on Learning Representations (ICLR 2015)*, San Diego, CA, May.

Filip Klubička, Antonio Toral, and Víctor M. Sánchez-Cartagena. 2018. Quantitative Fine-grained Human Evaluation of Machine Translation Systems: A Case Study on English to Croatian. *Machine Translation*, 32(3):195–215, September.

David Kurokawa, Cyril Goutte, and Pierre Isabelle. 2009. Automatic detection of translated text and its impact on machine translation. In *In Proceedings of MT Summit XII*, pages 81–88, Ottawa, Canada, August.

Surafel Melaku Lakew, Aliia Erofeeva, and Marcello Federico. 2018. Neural machine translation into language varieties. In *Proceedings of the Third Conference on Machine Translation (WMT 2018)*, pages 156–164, Brussels, Belgium, October.

Nikola Ljubešić and Tomaž Erjavec. 2011. hrWaC and slWac: Compiling Web Corpora for Croatian and Slovene. In *Proceedings of the 14 Conference on Text, Speech and Dialogue (TSD 2011)*, Lecture Notes in Computer Science, pages 395–402, Pilsen, Czech Republic, September. Springer.

Nikola Ljubešić and Filip Klubička. 2014. {bs,hr,sr}WaC – web corpora of Bosnian, Croatian and Serbian. In *Proceedings of the 9th Web as Corpus Workshop (WaC-9)*, pages 29–35, Gothenburg, Sweden, April.

Pintu Lohar, Maja Popović, and Andy Way. 2019. Building English-to-Serbian Machine Translation System for IMDb Movie Reviews. In *Proceedings of the 7th Workshop on Balto-Slavic Natural Language Processing (BSNLP 2019)*, pages 105–113, Florence, Italy, August.

Qingsong Ma, Ondřej Bojar, and Yvette Graham. 2018. Results of the WMT18 metrics shared task: Both characters and embeddings achieve good performance. In *Proceedings of the Third Conference on Machine Translation (WMT 2018)*, pages 671–688, Belgium, Brussels, October.

Nitika Mathur, Timothy Baldwin, and Trevor Cohn. 2020. Tangled up in BLEU: Reevaluating the evaluation of automatic machine translation evaluation metrics. In *Proceedings of the 58th Annual Meeting of the Association for Computational Linguistics*, pages 4984–4997, Online, July.

Mirjam Sepesy Maučec and Janez Brest. 2017. Slavic languages in phrase-based statistical machine translation: a survey. *Artificial Intelligence Review*, 51(1):77–117, May.

Julian McAuley, Christopher Targett, Qinfeng Shi, and Anton van den Hengel. 2015. Image-Based Recommendations on Styles and Substitutes. In *Proceedings of the 38th International ACM SIGIR Conference on Research and Development in Information Retrieval (SIGIR 2015)*, pages 43–52, Santiago, Chile.

Alberto Poncelas, Dimitar Shterionov, Andy Way, Gideon Maillette de Buy Wenniger, and Peyman Passban. 2018a. Investigating Back translation in Neural Machine Translation. In *Proceedings of the 21st Annual Conference of the European Association for Machine Translation (EAMT 2018)*, pages 249–258, Alicante, Spain, May.

Alberto Poncelas, Dimitar Shterionov, Andy Way, Gideon Maillette de Buy Wenniger, and Peyman Passban. 2018b. Investigating backtranslation in neural machine translation. In *21st Annual Conference of the European Association for Machine Translation*, pages 249–258, Alicante, Spain.

Alberto Poncelas. 2019. *Improving transductive data selection algorithms for machine translation*. Ph.D. thesis, Dublin City University.

Maja Popović and Mihael Arčan. 2015. Identifying main obstacles for statistical machine translation of morphologically rich south Slavic languages. In *Proceedings of the 18th Annual Conference of the European Association for Machine Translation (EAMT 2015)*, pages 97–104, Antalya, Turkey, May.

Maja Popović and Nikola Ljubešić. 2014. Exploring cross-language statistical machine translation for closely related south Slavic languages. In *Proceedings of the EMNLP'2014 Workshop on Language Technology for Closely Related Languages and Language Variants (LT4CloseLang 2014)*, pages 76–84, Doha, Qatar, October. Association for Computational Linguistics.

Maja Popović, Kostadin Cholakov, Valia Kordoni, and Nikola Ljubešić. 2016. Enlarging scarce in-domain English-Croatian corpus for SMT of MOOCs using Serbian. In *Proceedings of the Third Workshop on NLP for Similar Languages, Varieties and Dialects (VarDial3)*, pages 97–105, Osaka, Japan, December.

Maja Popović. 2015. chrF: character n-gram f-score for automatic MT evaluation. In *Proceedings of the Tenth Workshop on Statistical Machine Translation (WMT 2015)*, pages 392–395, Lisbon, Portugal, September. Association for Computational Linguistics.

Maja Popović. 2018. Language-related issues for NMT and PBMT for English–German and English–Serbian. *Machine Translation*, 32(3):237–253.

Matt Post. 2018. A call for clarity in reporting BLEU scores. In *Proceedings of the Third Conference on Machine Translation (WMT 2018)*, pages 186–191, Brussels, Belgium, October.

Victor M. Sánchez-Cartagena, Nikola Ljubešić, and Filip Klubička. 2016. Dealing with data sparseness in SMT with factured models and morphological expansion: a case study on Croatian. In *Proceedings of the 19th Annual Conference of the European Association for Machine Translation (EAMT 2016)*, pages 354–360, Riga, Latvia.

Rico Sennrich and Biao Zhang. 2019. Revisiting low-resource neural machine translation: A case study. In *Proceedings of the 57th Annual Meeting of the Association for Computational Linguistics (ACL 2019)*, pages 211–221, Florence, Italy, July.

Rico Sennrich, Barry Haddow, and Alexandra Birch. 2016a. Improving Neural Machine Translation Models with Monolingual Data. In *Proceedings of the 54th Annual Meeting of the Association for Computational Linguistics (ACL 2016)*, pages 86–96, Berlin, Germany, August.

Rico Sennrich, Barry Haddow, and Alexandra Birch. 2016b. Neural machine translation of rare words with subword units. In *Proceedings of the 54th Annual Meeting of the Association for Computational Linguistics (ACL 2016)*, pages 1715–1725, Berlin, Germany, August.

Margita Šoštarić, Christian Hardmeier, and Sara Stymne. 2018. Discourse-related language contrasts in English-Croatian human and machine translation. In *Proceedings of the Third Conference on Machine Translation (WMT 2018)*, pages 36–48, Brussels, Belgium, October.

Jörg Tiedemann. 2012. Parallel data, tools and interfaces in OPUS. In *Proceedings of the Eighth International Conference on Language Resources and Evaluation (LREC 2012)*, pages 2214–2218, Istanbul, Turkey, May.

Antonio Toral, Raphael Rubino, Miquel Esplá-Gomis, Tommi Pirinen, Andy Way, and Gema Ramirez-Sanchez. 2014. Extrinsic Evaluation of Web-Crawlers in Machine Translation: a Case Study on Croatian–English for the Tourism Domain. In *Proceedings of the 17th Annual Conference of the European Association for Machine Translation (EAMT 2014)*, pages 220–224, Dubrovnik, Croatia, June.

Ashish Vaswani, Noam Shazeer, Niki Parmar, Jakob Uszkoreit, Llion Jones, Aidan N Gomez, Lukasz Kaiser, and Illia Polosukhin. 2017. Attention is all you need. In *Proceedings of the 31st Conference on Neural Information Processing Systems (NeurIPS 2017)*, pages 5998–6008, Long Beach, CA, December.

Yogarshi Vyas, Xing Niu, and Marine Carpuat. 2018. Identifying semantic divergences in parallel text without annotations. In *Proceedings of the 2018 Conference of the North American Chapter of the Association for Computational Linguistics: Human Language Technologies (NAACL-HLT 2018)*, pages 1503–1515, New Orleans, Louisiana, June.

Weiyue Wang, Jan-Thorsten Peter, Hendrik Rosendahl, and Hermann Ney. 2016. CharacTer: Translation Edit Rate on Character Level. In *Proceedings of the 1st Conference on Machine Translation (WMT 2016)*, pages 505–510, Berlin, Germany, August.

Mike Zhang and Antonio Toral. 2019. The effect of translationese in machine translation test sets. In *Proceedings of the Fourth Conference on Machine Translation (WMT 2019)*, pages 73–81, Florence, Italy, August. Association for Computational Linguistics.

Jiajun Zhang and Chengqing Zong. 2016. Exploiting source-side monolingual data in neural machine translation. In *Proceedings of the 2016 Conference on Empirical Methods in Natural Language Processing (EMNLP 2016)*, pages 1535–1545, Austin, Texas, November.

A Tokenization System for the Kurdish Language

Sina Ahmadi
Insight Centre for Data Analytics
National University of Ireland Galway, Ireland
ahmadi.sina@outlook.com

Abstract

Tokenization is one of the essential and fundamental tasks in natural language processing. Despite the recent advances in applying unsupervised statistical methods for this task, every language with its writing system and orthography represents specific challenges that should be addressed individually. In this paper, as a preliminary study of its kind, we propose an approach for the tokenization of the Sorani and Kurmanji dialects of Kurdish using a lexicon and a morphological analyzer. We demonstrate how the morphological complexity of the language along with the lack of a unified orthography can be efficiently addressed in tokenization. We also develop an annotated dataset for which our approach outperforms the performance of unsupervised methods[1].

1 Introduction

A text, as the input of text processing applications, is composed of a string of characters and is interpreted based on the way it is segmented. Words and sentences are two segments in a text which carry meaning at different levels. Although the boundaries of words and sentences are specified to some extent in some scripts, e.g. by using whitespaces and punctuation marks, finding such boundaries is a non-trivial task (Guo, 1997). For instance, in scripts where spaces are not widely used or the *scriptio continua* style is used, such as Japanese, Chinese and Classical Latin, or languages where words are concatenated to create compound forms as in German, word boundary may not be explicitly specified.

In natural language processing (NLP), tokenization generally refers to the task of finding segment boundaries in a text. More specifically, retrieving the boundary of words and sentences are respectively known as word tokenization and sentence tokenization. Given a string of characters, a tokenization system, also known as lexical analyzer or tokenizer, splits the input into tokens, i.e. words or sentences (Kaplan, 2005). Tokenization is one of the most important and fundamental language processing tasks with many applications, such as part-of-speech tagging and machine translation (Webster and Kit, 1992).

Given the recent advances in NLP and artificial intelligence, tokenization is considered a solved problem and has been efficiently addressed for many languages (Habert et al., 1998; Forst and Kaplan, 2006). Although methodologies and approaches in tokenization of one language might be applicable to and beneficial for another language, linguistic and orthographic issues can make tokenization a language-specific problem (Lebart et al., 1997). For instance, although whitespaces are generally used in Arabic-based scripts, such as Urdu, Persian and Arabic, the joining and non-joining characteristics of graphemes create further complexity in tokenizing compound words, i.e. words consisted of more than one word, and various morphemes, such as affixes and clitics (Rehman et al., 2013; Shamsfard et al., 2009).

In this paper, we carry out a preliminary study on the task of tokenization for the Kurdish language with a particular focus on two of the Kurdish dialects, i.e. Kurmanji and Sorani, for which Latin and Arabic-based scripts are respectively used. We show how the Kurdish scripts and their lack of standardized orthographies create variations in writing words, especially compound forms. To address this task, we develop a tokenization system using a basic morphological analyzer and a lexicon and demonstrate that it outperforms regular expression based and unsupervised neural methods.

---

[1]The tool and the resources are publicly available at https://github.com/sinaahmadi/KurdishTokenization
This work is licensed under a Creative Commons Attribution 4.0 International License (CC-BY).

Proceedings of the 7th VarDial Workshop on NLP for Similar Languages, Varieties and Dialects, pages 114–127
Barcelona, Spain (Online), December 13, 2020

2   Related Work

The notion of word is one of the most basic concepts in various fields and therefore can be defined in different ways. Generally speaking, a word refers to a building block of a sentence. However, from a morphological point of view, a word, which is also known as word-token, is defined based on its form and meaning. If a word carries a concrete meaning, it is defined as a word-form such as *drives, driving, drove,* while a word with an abstract meaning is known as a lexeme or lexical item, e.g. DRIVE (Haspelmath and Sims, 2013, p 15). Lexemes are also distinguished by their function as headwords in dictionaries. It is worth mentioning that in addition to lexemes, lemmas are used to refer to the canonical forms of the lexemes. For instance, although خواردن (*xwardin*) EAT and خواردنەوە (*xwardinewe*) DRINK are two distinct lexemes in Kurdish, they both have one lemma and that is *xwardin*. The task of retrieving word lemmata is called lemmatization and is of importance in NLP.

Analogous to the distinction between word-forms and lexemes in morphology, corpus linguistics distinguishes a word as token and type based on their distinctness in a text. While a token can frequently occur, a type is considered the unique form of the token which can also be used as a dictionary entry (McEnery and Wilson, 2003). Additionally, Habert et al. (1998) describe tokens based on the lexico-graphic information, the context such as sub-languages and terminologies and, the applications. The application-based definition suggests that word boundary depends on the underlying application for which the tokenization task is required. For instance, the performance of tokenization methods have been studied in various tasks, such as statistical and neural machine translation (Zalmout and Habash, 2017; Domingo et al., 2018), text classification (Hiraoka et al., 2019) and named-entity recognition (Bai et al., 2001).

Being a basic task in information retrieval, text processing and NLP, the task of tokenization has been widely previously studied for many languages. A wide range of techniques are used for the task, particularly rule-based (Marcus et al., 1993; Dridan and Oepen, 2012; Waldron et al., 2006), statistical (Kiss and Strunk, 2006; McNamee and Mayfield, 2004) and more recently, neural networks (Kudo and Richardson, 2018; Schweter and Ahmed, 2019). The latter are particularly beneficial to alleviate open vocabulary problems independent of the language. Moreover, given the importance of tokenization in downstream applications, tokenization tools are usually also provided within NLP frameworks such as Moses (Koehn et al., 2007) and OpenNMT (Klein et al., 2017) for machine translation.

As the earliest work that addresses tokenization for Kurdish language, Rezaie (2001) discusses some of the issues in word boundary in the Arabic-based scripts. Although Kurdish tokenization has been partially addressed in the context of other tasks, such as text classification (Rashid et al., 2017), machine translation (Forcada et al., 2011) and syntactic analysis (Gökırmak and Tyers, 2017), no previous study is found to explicitly focus on Kurdish tokenization. For Kurdish as a less-resourced language, we believe that the current study will pave the way for further developments in Kurdish language processing.

3   An Overview of the Kurdish Language

Kurdish is a less-resourced Indo-European language spoken by 20-30 million speakers in the Kurdish regions of Iran, Iraq, Turkey and Syria (Ahmadi et al., 2019). There are various points of view regarding the classification of the dialects of Kurdish (Matras, 2017). However, Northern Kurdish, also known as Kurmanji, Central Kurdish, also known as Sorani and, Southern Kurdish are less controversially accepted as the Kurdish dialects (Matras, 2019). Historically, many alphabets have been used for writing Kurdish among which the Latin-based and Arabic-based scripts are still widely in use (Chyet and Schwartz, 2003). Although the standardization of the language, in the written and spoken forms, have been a matter of discussion in academia and also among Kurdish people, there is no consensus regarding what is meant by a standard writing system or orthography for Kurdish (Tavadze, 2019). Due to the lack of standardization, different scripts may be used for writing in various dialects. Regarding the popularity of the scripts, the Arabic-based alphabet is widely used for Sorani and Southern Kurdish while the Latin-based is used for Kurmanji. Due to Southern Kurdish being an under-documented dialect (Fattah, 2000), we only focus on the Sorani and Kurmanji dialects in this study.

Table 1 provides a comparison between the Latin-based and Arabic-based alphabets of Sorani and Kurmanji Kurdish. It should be noted that the vowel *i* does not have an equivalent grapheme in the Arabic-based alphabet. On the other hand, some of the consonants in the Latin-based alphabet are composed of a punctuation mark, usually an apostrophe as in 'e. In addition to the consonants and vowels, some of the punctuation marks in the two alphabets are provided in Table 1c. Variations are specified by "/".

Similar to the Arabic-based scripts of Persian and Urdu, the Arabic-based script of Kurdish has a zero width non joiner (ZWNJ, U+200C) character which enables joining characters be written in their non-joining grapheme. For instance, the character ل in هەلگرتن (*helgirtin*) 'to lift' appears as هەل گرتن when followed by a ZWNJ. Moreover, to further add to the length of the joining between graphemes, a dual-joining grapheme known as *Tatweel* or *Kashida* (U+0640) is used. This grapheme does not represent any phoneme but only elongates characters for justification and alignment of the text.

Latin	b	ç	c	d	f	g	h	j	k	l	ł/ll	m	n	p	q	r	ř/rr	s	ş	t	v	w	x	y	z	'/e/ë	h/'h	ẍ/x	'
Arabic	ب	چ	ج	د	ف	گ	ە	ژ	ک	ل	ڵ	م	ن	پ	ق	ر	ڕ	س	ش	ت	ڤ	و	خ	ی	ز	ع	ح	غ	ئ

(a) consonants

Latin	a	e	ê	i	î	o	û	u		Latin	.	;	,	%	!	?	:		
Arabic	ا	ە	ێ		ی	ۆ	وو	و		Arabic	.	؛	،	٪	!	؟	:	(U+200C)	ـ (U+0640)

(b) vowels   (c) punctuation marks

Table 1: A comparison of the two common scripts of Kurdish, Latin-based and Arabic-based

4 Word Boundary in Kurdish

In both the Latin-based and Arabic-based scripts of Kurdish, whitespaces are used for delimiting word boundaries. In addition, the ZWNJ in the Arabic-based script is also commonly used for separating words, particularly verbs that are consisted of more than one word. Having said that, none of these delimiters are deterministic for word boundary in Kurdish (Esmaili, 2012) due to the issues addressed in this section.

4.1 Orthographic Inconsistencies

Despite the efforts within the Kurdish linguistic community to raise awareness regarding orthography and to promote writing guidelines, such as (Hashemi, 2016) for Sorani and (Aydoğan, 2012) for Kurmanji, there is no unified orthography for Kurdish (Ahmadi, 2019). As such, various variations are found with respect to writing a specific word in Kurdish texts. For instance, numbers followed by a morpheme, as in "di 18ê Adarê" "on March 18th", may be separated by an apostrophe as in *18'ê*, a hyphen as in *18-ê* or without any punctuation mark.

4.2 Excessive Concatenation

Characters in the Latin script have only one grapheme without changing form. However, depending on the position within the word, characters in the Arabic script may have four different graphemes, namely initial, middle, final and isolated. According to their joining property, characters are categorized into right-joining as ر , dual-joining as ب and non-joining as digits. This characteristic of the Arabic script may result the reckless concatenation of words without proper spacing. For instance, the word لەوێشدایه (*lewêşdaye*) "(it) is also there" is composed of five words written as one single word, namely لە (*le*) 'from', وێ (*wê*) 'there', ش (*ş*) '*also*', دا (*da*, postposition) and یە (*ye*) 'is'. Such an excessive concatenation creates larger number of tokens represented as one and further complicates the tokenization task.

4.3 Compound Words

Having a relatively few number of around 300 single-word verbs, i.e. verbal lexemes, Kurdish extensively uses compound forms to develop its vocabulary (Walther and Sagot, 2010; Traida, 2007). A compound, also known as multi-word expression (MWE), is a more complex type of word which is consisted of two or more base words. Compound forms represent various challenges in many NLP tasks, including tokenization (Sag et al., 2002; Nasr et al., 2015). Due to the aforementioned issues, finding boundary of compound forms is a non-trivial task as well. In Kurdish, compound forms are written in many different ways, with and without space, using ZWNJ and rarely, using hyphen.

Compound type	Construction	Example		Gloss
		Sorani	Kurmanji	
Verb (v)	particle + v	*rŏ-nîstin* ڕۆنیشتن	*rû-niştin*	(over-sit) "to sit down"
	ADJ + V	*germ-kirdin* گەرم-کردن	*germ-kirin*	(warm-do) "to heat"
	N + V	*masî-girtin* ماسی-گرتن	*masî-girtin*	(fish-take) "to fish"
	preposition + V (+ postposition)	*lê-kewtin* لێ-کەوتن	*lê-ketin*	(to that-fall) "to hit"
	v + postposition	*kirdin-ewe* کردنەوە		(do-again) "to open"
	coord. comp. + v	*cê-be-cê-kirdin* جێ-بە-جێ-کردن	*cê-bi-cê-kirin*	(place-to-place-do) "to move"
Noun (N)	infinitive of comp. verbs	*beşdar-bûn* بەشدار-بوون	*beşdar-bûn*	(participate-be) "involvement"
	N + ADJ	*girê-kwêr* گرێ-کوێر	*girê-hişk*	(knot-blind) "hard knot"
	coord. comp.	*cil-û-berg* جل-و-بەرگ	*cil-û-berg*	(cloth-and-cover) "clothes"
	N + present stem	*goranî-bêj* گۆرانی-بێژ	*stran-bêj*	(song-sing.PRS.STEM) "singer"
Adjective (ADJ)	preposition + N	*bê-tam* بێ-تام	*bê-çêj*	(without-taste) "bland"
	coord. comp.	*dûr-û-dirêj* دوور-و-درێژ	*dûr-û-dirêj*	(far-and-long) "detailed"
	ADJ + N	*ciwan-mêr* جوان-مێر	*xweş-mêr*	(young-man) "affable"
Adverb (ADV)	preposition + N	*be-başî* بە-باشی	*bi-başî*	(with-goodness) "nicely"
	preposition + ADJ (+ postposition)	*le-zû-ewe* لە-زوو-ەوە	*ji-zû-ve*	(from-early) "long ago"
	preposition + coord. comp.	*be-lez-û-bez* بە-لەز-و-بەز	*bi-lez-û-bez*	(with-haste-and-race) "hurriedly"
Preposition	preposition + preposition	*be-ser* بە-سەر	*bi-ser*	(with-over) "over"
Conjunction	conjunction + conjunction	*heta-kû* هەتا-کوو	*heta-ku*	(until-that) "so that"

Table 2: Some of the formal constructions of compound (comp.) forms in Kurdish that are consisted of free morphemes. For consistency in writing, composing words are separated by a hyphen

In addition to the verbal compounds, Kurdish widely takes use of coordinative compounds (coord. comp.), i.e. compounds which are formed with conjunction و (*û*) 'and'. Since compound forms carry one meaning, they are usually considered as one token. Moreover, phrasal words are frequently used in Kurdish, such as مردوو-مراو (*mirdû-miraw*) "hapless (adj)"[2] or خوا-خراو-بۆ-کردگ (*xwa-xiraw-bo-kirdig*) "cursed (adj)"[3] respectively in Babani and Ardalani subdialects of Sorani.

Table 2 provides some of the frequent constructions used to create compound forms in Sorani and Kur-

---

[2]Literally meaning *the one whose dead is dead*
[3]Literally meaning *the one who is cursed by god*

manji Kurdish. It is worth noting that only compound forms which are consisted of free morphemes are provided. Many Kurdish compound forms are produced using inflectional and derivational morphemes which are not covered in this study. In addition, the current formal constructions can be further combined and form more complex compounds, such as دەست-تێ-وەردان (*dest-tê-wer-dan*) 'to manipulate'.

5 Approach

As a preliminary study, we focus on the application of a lexicon of lemmata and morphological analysis for tokenization of Kurdish texts. Moreover, we follow the common practices in tokenization, such as detecting digits, dates, URLs and punctuation marks as distinct tokens. This sub-task is called "normalization prior to tokenization" (Dridan and Oepen, 2012). Given the complexity of detecting word boundaries in Kurdish, particularly in the Arabic-based script of the Sorani dialect, we carry out the task of tokenization based on the syntactic property of the words. In other words, if a sequence of characters, whether delimited by spaces or not, can have a syntactic role, we consider them as a distinct token. Therefore, tokens in Kurdish can be words such as *bira* 'brother', compound words such as *germ kirin* 'to heat (something) up', clitics such as تان =*tan* (2.PL pronominal endoclitic) and affixes such as ەکان -*ekan* (definite plural marker). The following shows an example of how the input sentences in Sorani and Kurmanji are tokenized in our system:

- Sorani
    - Raw: "دواکەوتنی شێوازەکانی بەرهەمهێنان"
    - Tokenized: ['_دوا-کەوتن_ـی_' , '_شێواز_ەکان_ـی_' , '_بەرهەم-هێنان_']
- Kurmanji
    - Raw: "endamên encûmena wezîrên herêma Kurdistanê"
    - Tokenized: ['_endam_ên_', 'encûmen_a', '_wezîr_ên_', '_herêm_a_', '_Kurdistan_ê_']

5.1 Lexicon

To develop a lexicon for our task, we use the lexicographic material of FREEDICTS[4] and the Kurdish Wiktionary, WÎKÎFERHENG[5]. The two resources are available for Sorani and Kurmanji in the Latin-based and Arabic-based scripts of Kurdish. After merging these two resources, we further clean the data by removing the duplicates and normalizing the characters such as diacritical characters 'ř' and 'ł'. We also transliterate the Sorani lexicon into the Arabic-based script using WERGOR[6] (Ahmadi, 2019). Overall, 8,180 and 9,970 headwords are collected in Sorani and Kurmanji among which 1,513 and 1,507 lemmata are compound forms in Sorani and Kurmanji, respectively.

Using simple regular expressions, the headwords which are consisted of more than one word with a space are retrieved. If the compound form can undergo orthographic inconsistency, the words in such compound forms are separated by a figure dash, i.e. ‒. Using this special character, we can distinguish the compound forms which can possibly be written differently from the headword in the dictionary. For instance, the words in ولایەتە یەکگرتووەکانی ئەمەریکا (*Wilayete Yekgirtûwekanî Emerika*) "the United States of America" are considered to be consistently separated using a whitespace while the space in *birîndar bûn* "to be wounded" can be kept or omitted based on the writer's choice as in *birindar bûn* or *birindarbûn*.

Given that there are various ways to write compound words in Kurdish and due to the lack of a unified orthography, we generate all the possible forms, with and without a whitespace, for each compound entry in our lexicon. The generated forms are then saved in JSON where each compound headword is associated with the possible forms. Listing 1 provides an example of the compound headword *bi-can-û-bên* 'eagerly' in Kurmanji and ئاخر-و-تۆخر 'end' in Sorani and their corresponding forms.

---

[4] https://freedict.org
[5] https://ku.wiktionary.org
[6] https://github.com/sinaahmadi/wergor

```
{
    "bi-can-û-bên": {
        "token_forms": [
            "bicanûbên",
            "bi canûbên",
            "bican ûbên",
            "bi can ûbên",
            "bicanû bên",
            "bi canû bên",
            "bican û bên",
            "bi can û bên"
]}}
```

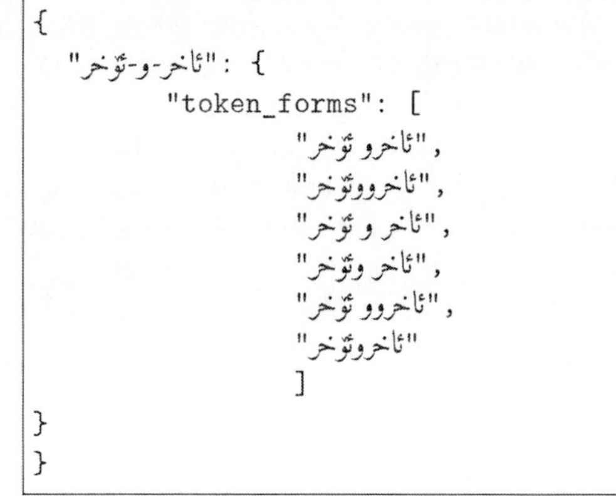

```
{
    "ئاخر-و-تۆخر": {
        "token_forms": [
            "ئاخرو تۆخر",
            "ئاخرووتۆخر",
            "ئاخر و تۆخر",
            "ئاخر وتۆخر",
            "ئاخرو تۆخر",
            "ئاخروتۆخر"
        ]
}
}
```

| Listing 1: A Kurmanji compound lemma and its possible forms in the lexicon in JSON | Listing 2: A Sorani compound lemma and its possible forms in the lexicon in JSON |

5.2 Morphological Analyzer

In order to retrieve the lemma form, retrieving inflectional morphemes is required. To do so, we first create a list of the clitics and inflectional affixes used in Kurmanji and Sorani. This list is provided in Table 3. In addition to the given form of the morphemes, some of them can be concatenated and appear in compound forms of two or more morphemes. For instance, the comparative suffix ـتر (-tir) in Sorani can be concatenated with the article maker ەکە (-eke) and result the compound form تەرەکە (-tireke) as in بەرزترەکە *berztireke* 'the higher one'. In addition, some of the clitics appear in an erratic pattern, i.e. depending on their syntactic function they can appear as proclitic, enclitic or endoclitic (Walther, 2012). This is particularly the case of the Sorani pronominal clitics and یش-ش (*îş, ş*). The latter can be translated as 'also, even' and is equivalent to *ji* in Kurmanji (Thackston, 2006). Given such complexities, we create a list of possible forms of the combination of these bound morphemes according to the Kurdish morphology and categorize them based on their position in the word, i.e. before or after the host word. This way, the task of morphological analysis can be carried out in a more simplified way with fewer particular cases to directly consider. The list contains 161 Sorani and 46 Kurmanji compound bound morphemes that can appear after the host and, 11 Sorani and 17 Kurmanji morphemes that can appear before the host. Once a compound morpheme retrieved in a word, it is then replaced by the composing morphemes as in بەرزترەکە → بەرز + تەرەکە → بەرز + تر + ەکە (*berztireke* → *berz* + *tireke* → *berz* + *tir* + *eke*) where the bound morphemes are shown in bold.

5.3 Tokenization System

Given a text in Kurdish, our tokenization approach is carried out following these steps.

1. **Text preprocessing**: In this step, we unify the encoding of characters, add spaces around punctuation marks, numbers, dates and URLs and remove ZWNJ.
2. **Compound word tokenization**: We append a space before and after the compound lemmas in the lexicon, delimit any occurrence in the text using two ▁ (U+2581). The figure dashes in the compound lemmas are replaced with whitespace. In addition to the lemma, the forms associated with each lemma are to be searched and delimited accordingly.
3. **Word tokenization**: Given the text with compound tokens, we split the text by space and delimit the words that match an entry in the lexicon using one ▁. If a word is not found in the lexicon, we proceed to the next step.
4. **Morphological analysis**: Given the sorted list of the morphemes based on length (longest to shortest), we retrieve the prefixes and suffixes in the word. A prefix or suffix is considered valid only if applying steps 1 and 2 on the remaining of the word returns a match in the lexicon. If so, two tokens consisting of the affix and the word are separated and delimited by a ▁. The affix is accordingly replaced by the composing parts, if any.

This procedure is illustrated in the flowchart in Figure A.4. The output of the tokenization system is a list of tokens. If a word is not delimited throughout this process, it is returned in the original form. Retrieving words based on the their length, which is used in the morphological analysis, is also known as the maximum matching algorithm and has been previously used for the same task (Webster and Kit, 1992). In addition to the word tokenization, we also provide a simple sentence tokenizer using punctuation marks, line breaks, URLs and abbreviations such as هتد (*htd*) in Sorani and *hwd* in Kurmanji for 'etc'.

Description	Morphemes	
	Sorani	Kurmanji
preposition	*le, we, de, ře, be* به - ڕه - ده - وه - له	*ba, berî, beyî, bê, bi,* *der, di, ji, li, ve*
postposition	*da, řa, ewe, we* وه - ەوه - ڕا - دا	*de, re, ve, da, ra, va*
absolute prepositions and postpositions	*pê, lê, tê, wê, ê* ئێ - وێ - تێ - لێ - پێ	*pê - tê - jê - lê*
reciprocal verbal particles	*pêk, řêk, têk, lêk, wêk* لێک - تێک - ڕێک - پێک وێک	*lêk, jêk, pêk, têk*
article marking suffixes	*êk, an, gel, ekan, yekan,* *ek, yek, eke, yeke, ekan,* *yekan, ane, e, gele* ەکان - گەل - ان - ێک - ەکە - یەک - ەک - یەکان - ە - انه - یەکان - ەکان - یەکە گەله	*ê, î, y, an, ek, yek, ekî,* *ekê, yekî, yekê, in, ine,* *inan, ên*
Izafa	*î, y, e /* ی - ە	*ê, a, yê, ya, yên*
locative and vocative suffixes	*îne, o, ê, yê* یێ - ێ - ۆ - ینه	*o, ê, ên, no*
pronominal cliticcs	*im,m,it,t,man,tan,yan* یان - تان - مان - ی - ت - م	*min, te, wî, wê, vî, vê,* *me, we, wan, van*
present copula	*im,m,î,y,ît,e,ye,în,in,n* ن - ین - یه - ە - یت - ی - م	*im, î, e, in, me, yî, ye, ne*
superlative and comparative suffixes	*tir, tirîn /* ترین - تر	*tir, tirîn*
other endoclitics	*îş, ş /* ش - یش	

Table 3: The morphemes used in our morphological analyzer to extract tokens from word forms. The morphemes in the Latin-based and Arabic-based alphabets are respectively separated by a comma and a hyphen

6   Experiments

6.1   Data Annotation

In order to evaluate the performance of our tokenization system, we create a gold-standard dataset by annotating 100 sentences from the KTC corpus (Abdulrahman et al., 2019) for Sorani and 100 sentences from the Pewan corpus (Esmaili et al., 2013) for Kurmanji. In the annotation process, we followed the same guidelines regarding the definition of tokens in Kurdish depicted in this study. The datasets are available in the Text Corpus Format (TCF) (Heid et al., 2010) and can be further enriched by adding annotations regarding lemmata, part-of-speech and constituent parse trees. Table 4 provides basic statistics of the annotated datasets and the samples of two Sorani and Kurmanji sentences are provided in Figure A.2.

Dataset	# sentences	# word types	# space-delimited words	# annotated tokens
Kurmanji	100	727	1378	2066
Sorani	100	904	1201	1994

Table 4: Statistics of the annotated datasets for the evaluation of the tokenization system. # denotes the number

6.2 Tokenization Models

We create our baseline model using the WordPunct tokenizer of NLTK (Loper and Bird, 2002). This technique tokenizes text into a sequence of alphabetic and non-alphabetic characters using the regular expression "\w+|[^\w\s]+". In addition, we train a few unsupervised neural models using Hugging-Face Tokenizers[7] and SentencePiece[8] (Wu et al., 2016). In the first case, we use WordPiece which is a subword tokenization algorithm used for BERT language model (Devlin et al., 2018). In the latter, we train tokenization models using Byte Pair Encoding (BPE) (Sennrich et al., 2016), unigram language model (Unigram) (Kudo, 2018) and Word model types. It is worth noting that the Word tokenization model is in fact a language model trained on data pre-tokenized with the WordPunct tokenizer.

The unsupervised neural models are trained with various vocabulary sizes and a character coverage of 1.0 using the available Sorani Kurdish raw corpora, namely PEWAN corpus containing 18M Sorani words and 4M Kurmanji words (Esmaili et al., 2013), the Kurdish Textbooks Corpus (KTC) containing 693K Sorani words (Abdulrahman et al., 2019), Veisi et al. (2020)'s Sorani corpus containing 8.1M words and the Sorani Kurdish folkloric lyrics corpus containing 49K words (Ahmadi et al., 2020). Due to the limited size of the Kurmanji data, we also used the raw text of the Kurmanji Wikipedia containing 3M words[9]. The corpora are preprocessed by unifying character encoding according to the alphabets in Table 1.

6.3 Evaluation Metrics

The performance of tokenization methods is more meaningful to be evaluated within an end-to-end scenario such as machine translation and syntactic parsing (Resnik and Lin, 2010, p 275). Due to the limited advances in Kurdish language processing, we evaluate our tokenization as a component alone. To this end, we calculate accuracy (acc) by comparing the gold-standard tokens versus the output of each system and dividing the number of correctly-tokenized tokens by the whole number of tokens. In addition to this overall accuracy, we evaluate the accuracy of the systems with respect to compound words ($acc_{comp.}$) where only the compound lemmata in the lexicon is evaluated.

In addition to accuracy, we use the Bilingual Evaluation Understudy Score, more commonly known as BLEU (Papineni et al., 2002). This scoring method is widely used for evaluation purposes in machine translation and has also many applications in evaluating the quality of a generated text with comparison to a reference one. In our case, we calculate the cumulative n-gram case-sensitive BLEU score (BLEU-n) (Yang et al., 2018) on the gold-standard tokens and the output of the various tokenization methods. The cumulative n-gram considers individual n-gram scores from 1 to n, in our case 4 and using their weighted geometric mean, calculates the overall BLEU score. This way, the performance of single-word tokens, i.e. BLEU-1, as well as compound words are taken into account.

6.4 Results

Table 5 presents the evaluation results of the unsupervised models with comparison to the baseline and our approach. In all the models, the BLEU scores decrease gradually from BLEU-1 to BLEU-4. This indicates that the models perform relatively better with respect to the tokenization of words which are composed of one single token and are accompanied with few morphemes while, a compound word with richer morphological form is more challenging to be tokenized correctly. On the other hand, by increasing the vocabulary size, the overall accuracy, i.e. acc increases in most cases. Figure 1 illustrates this

---

[7]https://github.com/huggingface/tokenizers

[8]https://github.com/google/sentencepiece

[9]Based on May 2020 dump

Model type	#Vocab.	Sorani						Kurmanji					
		BLEU-1	BLEU-2	BLEU-3	BLEU-4	$acc\,\%$	$acc_{comp.}\,\%$	BLEU-1	BLEU-2	BLEU-3	BLEU-4	$acc\,\%$	$acc_{comp.}\,\%$
BPE	4000	0.94	0.85	0.77	0.7	7.78	20.04	0.93	0.85	0.77	0.71	7.07	12.03
	8000	0.97	0.89	0.83	0.77	12.89	35.63	**0.98**	0.92	0.87	0.82	15.28	25.97
	16000	**0.98**	0.92	0.86	0.81	13.68	50.03	0.97	0.92	0.88	0.84	17.19	39.59
	32000	0.97	0.92	0.87	0.83	14.87	62.77	0.96	0.92	0.89	0.85	18.82	50.83
Unigram	4000	0.95	0.88	0.82	0.76	11.55	24.29	0.94	0.86	0.8	0.74	10.89	13.62
	8000	0.97	0.92	0.87	0.82	14.38	40.15	**0.98**	0.93	0.89	0.84	15.71	30.4
	16000	**0.98**	0.93	0.89	0.85	15.37	51.36	0.97	0.93	0.89	0.86	18.62	42.89
	32000	0.97	0.93	0.9	0.86	17.3	62.64	0.96	0.93	0.9	**0.87**	19.39	51.88
Word	4000	0.88	0.83	0.79	0.74	5.75	81.22	0.91	0.87	0.84	0.81	8.21	87.64
	8000	0.89	0.84	0.8	0.76	6.1	92.5	0.92	0.88	0.85	0.82	8.55	89.95
	16000	0.89	0.85	0.81	0.77	6.59	94.89	0.92	0.88	0.85	0.82	9.12	92.2
	32000	0.9	0.85	0.81	0.77	6.35	**96.35**	0.92	0.89	0.86	0.82	9.12	**94.32**
WordPiece	4000	0.94	0.86	0.78	0.71	9.17	17.32	0.85	0.80	0.75	0.70	13.94	19.43
	8000	0.93	0.87	0.8	0.75	13.29	34.04	0.83	0.79	0.75	0.71	13.90	34.96
	16000	0.92	0.87	0.82	0.77	13.73	47.78	0.81	0.78	0.75	0.72	13.09	47.65
	32000	0.9	0.86	0.82	0.78	13.29	59.99	0.81	0.78	0.75	0.72	12.13	58.63
WordPunct (baseline)		0.93	0.91	0.88	0.85	9.72		0.95	0.92	0.9	**0.87**	15.09	
Our system		**0.98**	**0.95**	**0.91**	**0.87**	**30.44**		0.97	**0.94**	**0.91**	**0.87**	**31.38**	

Table 5: Evaluation of various unsupervised methods and our tokenization system

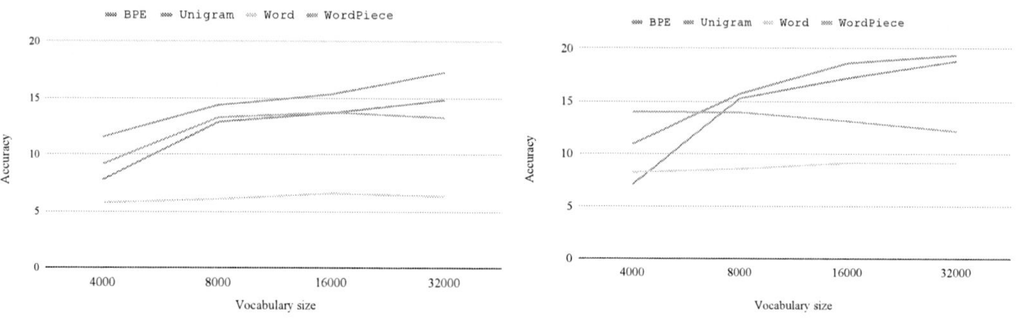

Figure 1: Accuracy of the unsupervised tokenization models in Sorani (left) and Kurmanji (right)

correlation in the various models. In almost all cases, the results of our system outperforms the other methods with a remarkable difference in the accuracy. It is worth mentioning that the accuracy of the baseline with respect to compound forms, i.e. $acc_{comp.}$ is either 100% or 0% depending on adding a whitespace between composing parts or not. Figure A.3 presents an example of the output of the models.

7   Conclusion and Future Work

In this paper, we presented a tokenization system for the Sorani and Kurmanji dialects of Kurdish. Having a complex morphology and various compound form constructions, Kurdish represents non-trivial challenges to the tokenization task. Using a lexicon and a morphological analyzer, our system outperforms unsupervised neural methods and can also be used to detect compound forms efficiently.

One limitation of the current study is the tokenization of compound verbs. In addition to tense, aspect, person and mood, verbs are inflected according to the patient, i.e. object of transitive verbs, and can be accompanied by other affixes such as هوه (-ewe) to indicate repetition and یش/ش ($=\hat{\imath}\c{s}/=\c{s}$) to indicate emphasis. Some clitics appear within the root of the verb, therefore called endoclitic, and create more complex forms. If in the tokenization task, such parts of the verbs are split into tokens, the compound verb is also split into its composing parts instead of being tokenized as one.

Given the relatedness of lemmatization to the current task, we believe that extending the current study can be beneficial to create a lemmatization system for Kurdish as well. Moreover, enriching the lexicons, particularly by including further compound form constructions, should also be considered in the future by integrating further collaboratively-curated open resources.

Acknowledgements

The author would like to thank the four anonymous reviewers for their constructive comments.

References

Roshna Omer Abdulrahman, Hossein Hassani, and Sina Ahmadi. 2019. Developing a Fine-Grained Corpus for a Less-resourced Language: the case of Kurdish. *arXiv preprint arXiv:1909.11467.*

Sina Ahmadi, Hossein Hassani, and John P. McCrae. 2019. Towards Electronic Lexicography for the Kurdish Language. In *Proceedings of the eLex 2019 conference*, pages 881–906, Sintra, Portugal, 1–3 October. Brno: Lexical Computing CZ, s.r.o.

Sina Ahmadi, Hossein Hassani, and Kamaladdin Abedi. 2020. A Corpus of the Sorani Kurdish Folkloric Lyrics. In *Proceedings of the 1st Joint Spoken Language Technologies for Under-resourced languages (SLTU) and Collaboration and Computing for Under-Resourced Languages (CCURL) Workshop at the 12th International Conference on Language Resources and Evaluation (LREC)*, Marseille, France.

Sina Ahmadi. 2019. A rule-based Kurdish text transliteration system. *Asian and Low-Resource Language Information Processing (TALLIP)*, 18(2):18:1–18:8.

Mustafa Aydoğan. 2012. *Rêbera rastnivîsînê*. Weşanxaneya Rûpelê. Ziman. Rûpel.

Shuanhu Bai, Horng Jyh Paul Wu, Haizhou Li, and Gareth Loudon. 2001. System for Chinese tokenization and named entity recognition, October 30. US Patent 6,311,152.

Michael L Chyet and Martin Schwartz. 2003. *Kurdish-English Dictionary*. Yale University Press.

Jacob Devlin, Ming-Wei Chang, Kenton Lee, and Kristina Toutanova. 2018. Bert: Pre-training of deep bidirectional transformers for language understanding. *arXiv preprint arXiv:1810.04805.*

Miguel Domingo, Mercedes García-Martínez, Alexandre Helle, Francisco Casacuberta, and Manuel Herranz. 2018. How Much Does Tokenization Affect Neural Machine Translation? *arXiv preprint arXiv:1812.08621.*

Rebecca Dridan and Stephan Oepen. 2012. Tokenization: Returning to a long solved problem—a survey, contrastive experiment, recommendations, and toolkit—. In *Proceedings of the 50th Annual Meeting of the Association for Computational Linguistics (Volume 2: Short Papers)*, pages 378–382.

Kyumars Sheykh Esmaili, Donya Eliassi, Shahin Salavati, Purya Aliabadi, Asrin Mohammadi, Somayeh Yosefi, and Shownem Hakimi. 2013. Building a test collection for Sorani Kurdish. In *Computer Systems and Applications (AICCSA), 2013 ACS International Conference on*, pages 1–7. IEEE.

Kyumars Sheykh Esmaili. 2012. Challenges in Kurdish text processing. *arXiv preprint arXiv:1212.0074.*

Ismaïl Kamandâr Fattah. 2000. *Les dialectes kurdes méridionaux: étude linguistique et dialectologique*. Acta Iranica : Encyclopédie permanente des études iraniennes. Peeters.

Mikel L Forcada, Mireia Ginestí-Rosell, Jacob Nordfalk, Jim O'Regan, Sergio Ortiz-Rojas, Juan Antonio Pérez-Ortiz, Felipe Sánchez-Martínez, Gema Ramírez-Sánchez, and Francis M Tyers. 2011. Apertium: a free/open-source platform for rule-based machine translation. *Machine translation*, 25(2):127–144.

Martin Forst and Ronald M Kaplan. 2006. The importance of precise tokenizing for deep grammars. In *LREC*, pages 369–372.

Memduh Gökırmak and Francis M Tyers. 2017. A dependency treebank for Kurmanji Kurdish. In *Proceedings of the Fourth International Conference on Dependency Linguistics (Depling 2017)*, pages 64–72.

Jin Guo. 1997. Critical tokenization and its properties. *Computational Linguistics*, 23(4):569–596.

Benoit Habert, Gilles Adda, Martine Adda-Decker, P Boula de Marëuil, Serge Ferrari, Olivier Ferret, Gabriel Illouz, and Patrick Paroubek. 1998. Towards tokenization evaluation. In *Proceedings of LREC*, volume 98, pages 427–431.

Dyako Hashemi. 2016. Kurdish orthography [In Kurdish]. http://yageyziman.com/Renusi_Kurdi.htm. Accessed: 2020-07-25.

Martin Haspelmath and Andrea D Sims. 2013. *Understanding morphology*. Routledge.

Ulrich Heid, Helmut Schmid, Kerstin Eckart, and Erhard Hinrichs. 2010. A Corpus Representation Format for Linguistic Web Services: The D-SPIN Text Corpus Format and its Relationship with ISO Standards. In *Proceedings of the Seventh International Conference on Language Resources and Evaluation (LREC'10)*.

Tatsuya Hiraoka, Hiroyuki Shindo, and Yuji Matsumoto. 2019. Stochastic tokenization with a language model for neural text classification. In *Proceedings of the 57th Annual Meeting of the Association for Computational Linguistics*, pages 1620–1629.

Ronald M Kaplan. 2005. A method for tokenizing text. *Inquiries into words, constraints and contexts*, 55.

Tibor Kiss and Jan Strunk. 2006. Unsupervised multilingual sentence boundary detection. *Computational linguistics*, 32(4):485–525.

Guillaume Klein, Yoon Kim, Yuntian Deng, Jean Senellart, and Alexander M Rush. 2017. Opennmt: Open-source toolkit for neural machine translation. *arXiv preprint arXiv:1701.02810*.

Philipp Koehn, Hieu Hoang, Alexandra Birch, Chris Callison-Burch, Marcello Federico, Nicola Bertoldi, Brooke Cowan, Wade Shen, Christine Moran, Richard Zens, et al. 2007. Moses: Open source toolkit for statistical machine translation. In *Proceedings of the 45th annual meeting of the ACL on interactive poster and demonstration sessions*, pages 177–180. Association for Computational Linguistics.

Taku Kudo and John Richardson. 2018. Sentencepiece: A simple and language independent subword tokenizer and detokenizer for neural text processing. *arXiv preprint arXiv:1808.06226*.

Taku Kudo. 2018. Subword regularization: Improving neural network translation models with multiple subword candidates. *arXiv preprint arXiv:1804.10959*.

Ludovic Lebart, André Salem, and Lisette Berry. 1997. *Exploring textual data*, volume 4. Springer Science & Business Media.

Edward Loper and Steven Bird. 2002. NLTK: the natural language toolkit. *arXiv preprint cs/0205028*.

Mitch Marcus, Beatrice Santorini, and Mary Ann Marcinkiewicz. 1993. Building a Large Annotated Corpus of English: The Penn Treebank. *Computational Linguistics*, 19(2):313–330.

Yaron Matras. 2017. Revisiting Kurdish dialect geography: Preliminary findings from the Manchester Database. http://kurdish.humanities.manchester.ac.uk/wp-content/uploads/2017/07/PDF-Revisiting-Kurdish-dialect-geography.pdf. [Online; accessed 02-Aug-2020].

Yaron Matras. 2019. Revisiting Kurdish dialect geography: Findings from the Manchester Database. *Current issues in Kurdish linguistics*, 1:225.

Tony McEnery and Andrew Wilson. 2003. Corpus linguistics. *The Oxford handbook of computational linguistics*, pages 448–463.

Paul McNamee and James Mayfield. 2004. Character n-gram tokenization for European language text retrieval. *Information retrieval*, 7(1-2):73–97.

Alexis Nasr, Carlos Ramisch, José Deulofeu, and Andre Valli. 2015. Joint Dependency Parsing and Multiword Expression Tokenization. In *Proceedings of the 53rd Annual Meeting of the Association for Computational Linguistics and the 7th International Joint Conference on Natural Language Processing (Volume 1: Long Papers)*, pages 1116–1126.

Kishore Papineni, Salim Roukos, Todd Ward, and Wei-Jing Zhu. 2002. BLEU: a method for automatic evaluation of machine translation. In *Proceedings of the 40th annual meeting of the Association for Computational Linguistics*, pages 311–318.

Tarik A Rashid, Arazo M Mustafa, and A Saeed. 2017. A robust categorization system for Kurdish Sorani text documents. *Inf. Technol. J*, 16(1):27–34.

Zobia Rehman, Waqas Anwar, Usama Ijaz Bajwa, Wang Xuan, and Zhou Chaoying. 2013. Morpheme matching based text tokenization for a scarce resourced language. *PloS one*, 8(8):e68178.

Philip Resnik and Jimmy Lin. 2010. Evaluation of NLP Systems. *The handbook of computational linguistics and natural language processing*, 57.

Siamak Rezaie. 2001. Tokenizing an Arabic script language. *Arabic language processing: Status and prospects, ACL/EACL*.

Ivan A Sag, Timothy Baldwin, Francis Bond, Ann Copestake, and Dan Flickinger. 2002. Multiword expressions: A pain in the neck for NLP. In *International conference on intelligent text processing and computational linguistics*, pages 1–15. Springer.

Stefan Schweter and Sajawel Ahmed. 2019. Deep-EOS: General-Purpose Neural Networks for Sentence Boundary Detection. In *KONVENS*.

Rico Sennrich, Barry Haddow, and Alexandra Birch. 2016. Neural machine translation of rare words with subword units. In *Proceedings of the 54th Annual Meeting of the Association for Computational Linguistics (Volume 1: Long Papers)*, pages 1715–1725, Berlin, Germany, August. Association for Computational Linguistics.

Mehrnoush Shamsfard, Soheila Kiani, and Yaseer Shahedi. 2009. STeP-1: standard text preparation for Persian language. In *Third Workshop on Computational Approaches to Arabic Script-based Languages*, pages 859–865.

Givi Tavadze. 2019. Spreading of the Kurdish Language Dialects and Writing Systems Used in the Middle East. *Bull. Georg. Natl. Acad. Sci*, 13(1).

Wheeler M. Thackston. 2006. *Kurmanji Kurdish:-A Reference Grammar with Selected Readings*. Harvard University.

Sandrine Traida. 2007. *Morphosyntactic Study of the compound verbs in Sorani Kurdish Étude morpho-syntaxique des verbes composés (nom-verbe) en kurde (dialecte sorani) [in French]*. PhD thesis at the Université Paris 3 - Sorbonne Nouvelle.

Hadi Veisi, Mohammad MohammadAmini, and Hawre Hosseini. 2020. Toward Kurdish language processing: Experiments in collecting and processing the AsoSoft text corpus. *Digital Scholarship in the Humanities*, 35(1):176–193.

Benjamin Waldron, Ann A Copestake, Ulrich Schäfer, and Bernd Kiefer. 2006. Preprocessing and Tokenisation Standards in DELPH-IN Tools. In *LREC*, pages 2263–2268.

Géraldine Walther and Benoît Sagot. 2010. Developing a large-scale lexicon for a less-resourced language: General methodology and preliminary experiments on Sorani Kurdish. In *Proceedings of the 7th SaLTMiL Workshop on Creation and use of basic lexical resources for less-resourced languages (LREC 2010 Workshop)*.

Géraldine Walther. 2012. Fitting into morphological structure: accounting for Sorani Kurdish endoclitics. In *Mediterranean Morphology Meetings*, volume 8, pages 299–321. [Online; accessed 02-Aug-2020].

Jonathan J Webster and Chunyu Kit. 1992. Tokenization as the initial phase in NLP. In *COLING 1992 Volume 4: The 15th International Conference on Computational Linguistics*.

Yonghui Wu, Mike Schuster, Zhifeng Chen, Quoc V Le, Mohammad Norouzi, Wolfgang Macherey, Maxim Krikun, Yuan Cao, Qin Gao, Klaus Macherey, et al. 2016. Google's neural machine translation system: Bridging the gap between human and machine translation. *arXiv preprint arXiv:1609.08144*.

An Yang, Kai Liu, Jing Liu, Yajuan Lyu, and Sujian Li. 2018. Adaptations of ROUGE and BLEU to Better Evaluate Machine Reading Comprehension Task. In *Proceedings of the Workshop on Machine Reading for Question Answering*, pages 98–104.

Nasser Zalmout and Nizar Habash. 2017. Optimizing tokenization choice for machine translation across multiple target languages. *The Prague Bulletin of Mathematical Linguistics*, 108(1):257–269.

A Appendix

Figure A.2: An example of the annotated tokens of two different sentences in Sorani (left) and Kurmanji (right) in the Text Corpus Format

Reference	دواکوتن ی شێواز ەکان ی بەرهەمهێنان لەم ئابووری انه دا دەگەرێتەوه بۆ : نەبوون ی هۆیەکان ی تەکنیکی ی تازه ی هاوردە تا بەرهەمهێن ەکان بە کاری بێن ی .
Our system	دواکوتن ی شێواز ەکان ی بەرهەمهێنان لەم ئابووریانەدا دەگەرێتەوه بۆ : نەبوونی هۆیەکان ی تەکنیکی تازه ی هاوردە تا بەرهەمهێنەکان بەکاری بێن ن .
BPE	دواکوتنی شێوازەکانی بەرهەمهێنان لەم ئابووری انەدا دەگەرێتەوه بۆ : نەبوونی هۆیەکانی تەکنیک یی تازەی هاوردە تا بەرهەمهێن ەکان بەکاری بێن .
Unigram	دواکوتنی شێوازەکانی بەرهەمهێنان لەم ئابووری انەدا دەگەرێتەوه بۆ : نەبوونی هۆیەکانی تەکنیکی ی تازەی هاوردە تا بەرهەمهێن ەکان بەکاری بێن .
Word	دواکوتنی شێوازەکانی بەرهەمهێنان لەم ئابووریانەدا دەگەرێتەوه بۆ: نەبوونی هۆیەکانی تەکنیکی تازەی هاوردە تا بەرهەمهێنەکان بەکاری بێن.
WordPiece	دواکوتنی شێوازەکانی بەرهەمهێنان لەم دەگەرێتەوه بۆ : نەبوونی هۆیەکانی تەکنیکی ی تازەی هاوردە تا بەرهەمهێن ەکان بەکاری بێن .
WordPunct	دواکوتنی شێوازەکانی بەرهەمهێنان لەم ئابووریانەدا دەگەرێتەوه بۆ : نەبوونی هۆیەکانی تەکنیکی تازەی هاوردە تا بەرهەمهێنەکان بەکاری بێن .

(a) Sorani

Reference	di evê peywendî ya telefonî de , behsa peywendî yên navber a Baxdad ê û Parîs di hemû biwaran de hatîye kirin .
Our system	di ev ê peywend îya telefonî de , behs a peywendî yên navbera Baxdadê û Parîs di hemû biwaran de hatîye kirin .
BPE	di evê peywendîya telefonî de , behsa peywendîyên navbera Baxdadê û Parîs di hemû biwaran de hatîye kirin .
Unigram	di evê peywendîya telefonî de , behsa peywendîyên navbera Baxdadê û Parîs di hemû biwaran de hatîye kirin .
Word	di evê peywendîya telefonî de, behsa peywendîyên navbera Baxdadê û Parîs di hemû biwaran de hatîye kirin.
WordPiece	di evê peywendîya telefonî de , behsa peywendîyên navbera û di hemû biwaran de hatîye kirin .
WordPunct	di evê peywendîya telefonî de , behsa peywendîyên navbera Baxdadê û Parîs di hemû biwaran de hatîye kirin .

(b) Kurmanji

Figure A.3: The output of the unsupervised neural tokenization models with vocabulary size 32000, the baseline (WordPunct) and our system

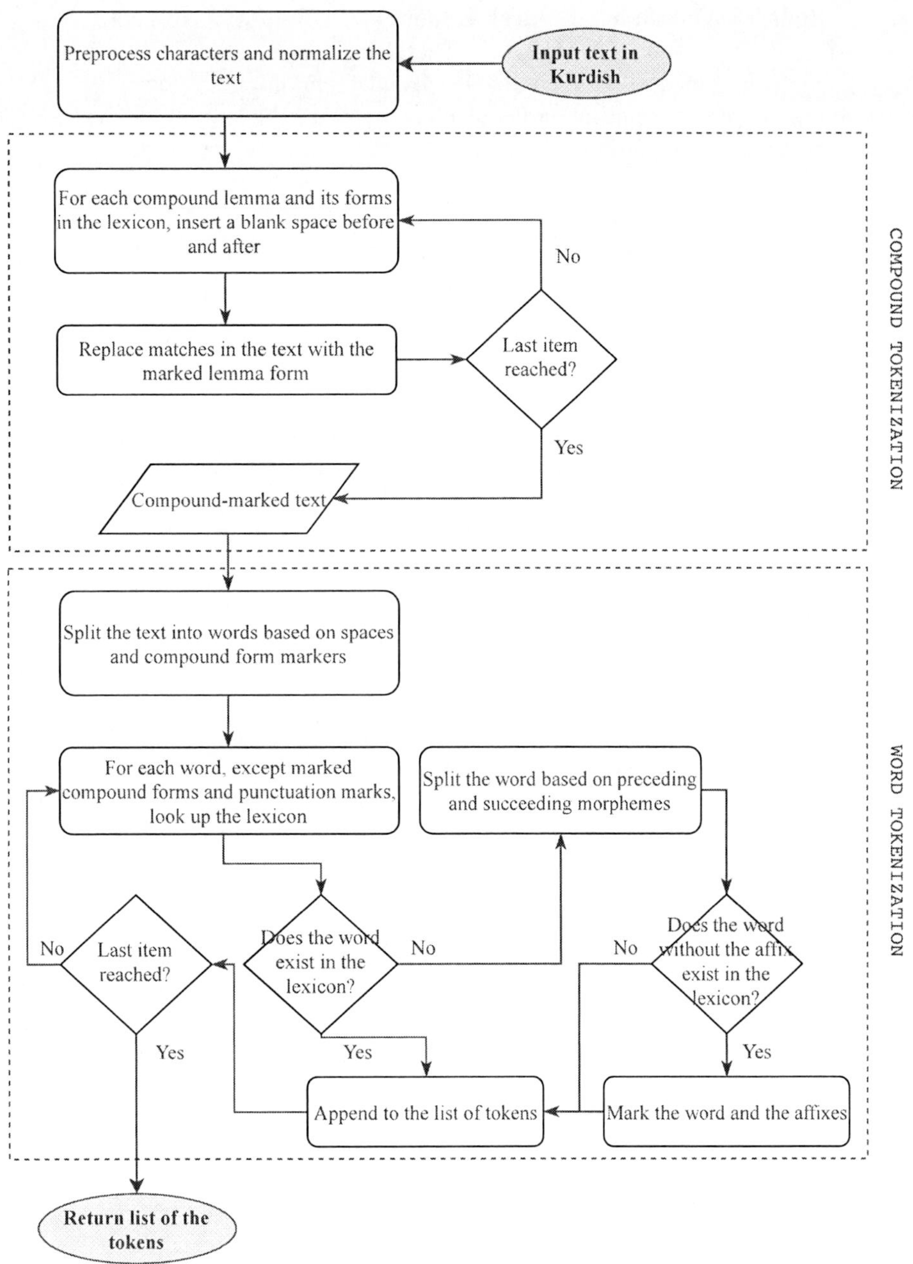

Figure A.4: The flowchart of the Kurdish tokenization system proposed in this paper. Marking action refers to appending ___ (U+2581) before and after a token

Rediscovering the Slavic Continuum in Representations Emerging from Neural Models of Spoken Language Identification

Badr M. Abdullah **Jacek Kudera** **Tania Avgustinova**
Bernd Möbius **Dietrich Klakow**
Department of Language Science and Technology (LST)
Saarland Informatics Campus, Saarland University, 66123 Saarbrücken, Germany
Corresponding author: `babdullah@lsv.uni-saarland.de`

Abstract

Deep neural networks have been employed for various spoken language recognition tasks, including tasks that are multilingual by definition such as spoken language identification. In this paper, we present a neural model for Slavic language identification in speech signals and analyze its emergent representations to investigate whether they reflect objective measures of language relatedness and/or non-linguists' perception of language similarity. While our analysis shows that the language representation space indeed captures language relatedness to a great extent, we find perceptual confusability between languages in our study to be the best predictor of the language representation similarity.

1 Introduction

The relationship between a group of human languages can be characterized across several dimensions of variation (Skirgård et al., 2017), including (1) the temporal dimension, wherein languages have diverged from a common historical ancestor as in the case of Romance languages; (2) the spatial dimension, wherein the speaker communities are geographically adjacent as in the case of the Indo-Aryan and Dravidian languages of India; and (3) the socio-political dimension, wherein languages have evolved under shared political and/or religious forces as in the case of Arabic and Swahili. Languages, or language varieties, can be related across all these dimensions, which often results in a dialect continuum. Speakers of languages that constitute a dialect continuum can usually communicate with each other efficiently using their own mother tongue. The degree of intercomprehensibility between speakers of different language varieties within a continuum is mainly determined by linguistic similarities. A notable case of this phenomenon is the mutual intelligibility among the Slavic languages, which we study in this paper.

One of the goals of linguistics is to study and categorize languages based on objective measures of linguistic distance. The degrees of similarity at different levels of the linguistic structural organization can be seen as preconditions for, as well as predictors of, successful oral intercomprehension. For closely-related languages, similarities at the pre-lexical, that is the acoustic-phonetic and phonological, level have been found to be better predictors of cross-lingual speech intelligibility than lexical similarities (Gooskens et al., 2008; Heeringa et al., 2009). In a different, yet relevant research direction, Skirgård et al. (2017) have investigated non-linguists' perception of language variation using data from the popular spoken language guessing game, the Great Language Game (GLG). By analyzing the confusion patterns of the GLG's human participants, the authors have shown that factors predicting players' confusion in the game correspond to objective measures of similarity established by linguists. For example, both phylogenetic relatedness and overlap in phoneme inventories have been identified as factors of perceptual confusability (and by implication, similarity) of languages in GLG.

This work is licensed under a Creative Commons Attribution 4.0 International License. License details: `http://creativecommons.org/licenses/by/4.0/`.

Proceedings of the 7th VarDial Workshop on NLP for Similar Languages, Varieties and Dialects, pages 128–139
Barcelona, Spain (Online), December 13, 2020

The development of automatic systems that determine the identity of the language in a speech segment has received attention in the speech recognition community (see Li et al. (2013) for an overview). State-of-the-art approaches for automatic spoken language identification, henceforth LID, are based on multilayer deep neural networks (DNNs). DNN-based LID systems are parametric models that learn a mapping from spectral acoustic features of (untranscribed) speech to high-level feature representations in geometric space where languages are linearly separable. These models have shown tremendous success not only in discriminating between distant languages but also closely-related language varieties (Gelly et al., 2016; Shon et al., 2018; Mateju et al., 2018). Nevertheless, none of the previous works in spoken language recognition has analyzed the emerging representations from neural LID models for related languages. Thus, it is still unknown whether the distances in these representation spaces correspond to objective measurements of linguistic similarity and/or to non-linguists' perception of language variation. In this paper, we aim to fill this gap and consider the family of Slavic languages as a case study. Our key contribution is two-fold:

(1) We present an LID model for Slavic languages based on convolutional neural networks. Our model incorporates a domain-adversarial training strategy to improve its robustness against non-language sources of variability in speech signals. We show that our approach significantly improves generalization across datasets that differ in their recording conditions (§3 and §4).

(2) We analyze and visualize the emergent representations from our robust LID model for 11 Slavic languages, five of which are not observed (held-out) during training. We show that the distances in the representation space correspond to measures of linguistic distance to a great extent (§5).

In this paper, we attempt to bridge different lines of research that have so far remained unconnected. On the one hand, we employ neural architectures from the field of spoken language recognition and build a robust model to identify languages in contemporary acoustic realizations of Slavic speech. On the other hand, we analyze the emerging language representations using techniques established by previous research in multilingual natural language processing (NLP). We consequently shed light on the speech modality and show how (untranscribed) speech signals can complement research done in computational studies of linguistic typology and language variation.

2 Background and Related Work

2.1 Slavic Languages

The Slavic language family is a branch of Indo-European languages that is conventionally divided into three subgroups: West-, East-, and South-Slavic. Apart from being related across the temporal dimension by sharing a common ancestor, Slavic languages form a spatial continuum of variation in a relatively connected geographic area across Europe and Northern Asia, except for the region where the Romance and Finno-Ugric wedge separates the South-Slavic from the West- and East-Slavic subgroups. Beside this traditional division (see Ethnologue, 23ed.), alternative classifications can be found in the Slavistics literature (cf. Bednarczuk, 2018; Pianka and Tokarz, 2000; Dalewska-Greń, 2020; Lehr-Spławiński et al., 1954; Nalepa, 1968; Mańczak, 2004). Nevertheless, and despite differences in taxonomies among various proposals, the development of contemporary Slavic languages from a common historical ancestor is uncontroversial. The supporting arguments are based on historical phonology and comparative studies of the phoneme inventories (Sawicka, 1991), as well as on studies of loanwords and Slavic toponyms. The high number of cognates as well as cross-linguistically shared features, such as lexical aspect, phonemic jotation and complex consonant clusters, provide strong evidence for common roots. In terms of diachronic phonology, the Common-Slavic era ends with the vocalization and reduction of the *yers* – the so-called "half-vowels" or "reduced vowels", [ъ] and [ь]. The outcomes of these alternations consistently define the most common division of Slavic. Similarly, the reflexes of *yat* [ě] provide a clear distinction between East-, West- and South-Slavic. The results of common phonological processes, such as liquid metathesis, palatalization and sibilarization, also support the tripartite division. Moreover, these regularities of sound changes allow us to precisely trace the phonological development within the language family not only in the core standardized varieties but also in vernaculars and dialects. One of the objectives of our work is to assess the extent to which neural models of spoken language learn to detect such regularities from acoustic realizations of contemporary Slavic speech.

2.2 Language Identification in Speech Signals

Research in automatic identification of the language in a speech signal (Li et al., 2013) is mainly concerned with the development of computational models that take an acoustic realization of a short utterance (usually a few seconds of speech) and predict the spoken language as output. Currently, end-to-end deep neural networks are the predominant paradigm for LID and have shown tremendous success in previous works (Lopez-Moreno et al., 2014; Gonzalez-Dominguez et al., 2014; Gelly and Gauvain, 2017). In this paradigm, the LID problem has usually been modelled as a temporal sequence classification problem in which a spectro-temporal representation of a spoken utterance (e.g., a sequence of spectral feature vectors) is transformed via a multi-layer neural network into a high-level vector representation that captures language-ID features. Other works in the literature have addressed LID for closely-related spoken language varieties including Arabic dialects (Shon et al., 2018; Gelly et al., 2016), Iberian languages (Gelly et al., 2016), and Slavic languages (Mateju et al., 2018; Abdullah et al., 2020).

At the intersection of speech recognition and linguistic typology, Gutkin et al. (2018) have trained a neural network on a large-scale multilingual speech database to predict typological features of the World Atlas of Language Structure (WALS) (Dryer and Haspelmath, 2013) for a language given a speech segment. The authors have shown that the speech modality contains enough signals to predict typological features of a held-out set of languages without explicit linguistic annotations. Their findings indicate that neural networks trained on multilingual speech could capture linguistic regularities and generalize beyond the languages observed in the training data.

2.3 Language Representations in Continuous Vector Spaces

Inspired by the advances in representation learning for NLP, multilingual neural models have been explored in the literature to induce real-valued language vectors, also known as *language representations* or *language embeddings*, where a single vector ($\mathbf{v} \in \mathbb{R}^d$) is associated with each language. Even though it has been motivated from different points of view, the main idea of this stream of research is to train a single NLP model on many languages whereby the language representation space is learned by exploiting the multilingual signal. For example, Johnson et al. (2017) introduced a multilingual neural machine translation (NMT) model in which the required target language of the translation was specified by the language embedding. Other works have either scaled this approach to a massively multilingual setting (Östling and Tiedemann, 2017; Malaviya et al., 2017) or explored other NLP tasks such as linguistic structure prediction (Bjerva et al., 2019) and grapheme-to-phoneme conversion (Peters et al., 2017). Furthermore, Rabinovich et al. (2017) and Bjerva et al. (2019) have analyzed the learned language representations and shown that the distance in the representation space reflects the phylogenetic distance between Indo-European languages. However, Bjerva et al. (2019) have argued that structural syntactic similarities between languages are a better predictor of the language representation similarities than phylogenetic similarities.

The most relevant analysis to ours is the recent work by Cathcart and Wandl (2020), in which the authors have trained a neural sequence-to-sequence model on a Slavic etymological dictionary. Their model was trained to consume a reconstructed Proto-Slavic word form and a language embedding, then emit a word form in the modern language specified by the language embedding. The authors have applied a clustering analysis on the learned language embeddings and successfully reconstructed the phylogenetic Slavic family tree. Our work complements this line of research with one fundamental difference: we perform our analysis on contemporary realizations of Slavic speech instead of the historically reconstructed phonological data without explicitly training our model to capture systematic sound changes.

3 Methodology

3.1 Slavic Speech Data

The data we use in this research are drawn from two different datasets:

(1) **Radio Broadcast Speech (RBS)**   A large collection of Slavic speech recordings were collected by crawling online radio stations in previous work (Nouza et al., 2016; Mateju et al., 2018). The dataset includes speech segments in 11 Slavic languages from the three subgroups: (1) South-Slavic: Bulgarian (BUL), Croatian (HRV), Serbian (SRP), Slovene (SLV), and Macedonian (MAC). (2) West-Slavic: Czech (CZE), Polish (POL), and Slovak (SLO). (3) East-Slavic: Russian (RUS), Ukrainian (UKR), and Belorussian (BEL). The audio recordings are either segments of professional news reports or of spontaneous speech during discussions. The recording conditions are diverse and the utterances occasionally include background music. We sample 8,000 and 500 utterances per language from the training split as our training and validation sets, respectively, and use the test set in Mateju et al. (2018) as our evaluation set.

(2) **GlobalPhone Read Speech (GRS)**   We also use the Slavic portion of the multilingual Global-Phone speech database (Schultz et al., 2013) which includes read speech recordings from native speakers of six Slavic languages: Bulgarian, Croatian, Czech, Polish, Russian, and Ukrainian. The utterances vary in length and quality across languages. Our final GRS training subset consists of 8,000 utterances per language.

3.2 Signal Representations of Speech

Human speech can be modelled with various signal representations. For automatic speech recognition (ASR), the conventional approach is to convert time-varying speech waveforms into time-frequency, or spectro-temporal, representations using a standard signal processing pipeline based on the short-time Fourier transform. An example of such representations is the mel-frequency spectral coefficients (MF-SCs) representation, whose development has been inspired by the human auditory system. MFSCs describe the spectral envelope along the temporal dimension in a way that reflects the shape of the human vocal tract during speech production at each timepoint. In this paper, we use MFSCs for all presented experiments.

3.3 Neural LID Model

Our problem definition and LID models are based on the work of Abdullah et al. (2020). The LID task is defined as an instance of temporal sequence classification. A speech segment is first converted into a sequence of acoustic events $\mathbf{X} = (\mathbf{x}_1, \ldots, \mathbf{x}_T)$, where $\mathbf{x}_t \in \mathbb{R}^k$ is a spectral feature vector at timestep t. Then, the goal is to predict the spoken language $\hat{y}$ given the sequence $\mathbf{X}$. This definition can be formalized using a deep neural network as a parameterization of the model as follows

$$\hat{y} = \arg\max_{y \in \mathcal{Y}} P(y \mid \mathbf{X}; \boldsymbol{\theta})$$

where $\mathcal{Y}$ is the set of languages, $\boldsymbol{\theta}$ is the model's parameters learned from a labelled dataset, and $P(y|\mathbf{X}; \boldsymbol{\theta})$ is the posterior probability of the language label y.

Baseline.   We use an end-to-end convolutional neural network (CNN) with three convolutional layers followed by three feed-forward layers (see Fig. 1 for full description of the model). Our baseline LID model can be viewed as two components that are jointly trained: a *segment-level feature extractor* (F) and a *language classifier* (G), each associated with two sets of parameters $\boldsymbol{\theta}_F$ and $\boldsymbol{\theta}_G$, respectively. The parameters of the network $\boldsymbol{\theta}_F$ and $\boldsymbol{\theta}_G$ are learned in a supervised approach given a source dataset $\mathcal{D}_\mathcal{S} = \{(\mathbf{X}_i, y_i)\}_{i=1}^{N_\mathcal{S}}$ of $N_\mathcal{S}$ labelled samples and an optimization algorithm that minimizes cross-entropy loss.

Robust LID.   To improve the robustness of our model against non-linguistic sources of variability in speech signals, we employ a well-established adversarial domain adaptation strategy (Ganin and Lempitsky, 2015), which has been shown to be effective for LID (Abdullah et al., 2020). Adversarial domain adaptation aims to minimize the discrepancy between the representations of the model given speech samples from two sources that differ in their recording conditions or spoken genre. This approach only requires a target dataset $\mathcal{D}_\mathcal{T} = \{(\mathbf{X}_i)\}_{i=1}^{N_\mathcal{T}}$ of $N_\mathcal{T}$ unlabelled samples, in addition to the labelled samples of the source dataset $\mathcal{D}_\mathcal{S}$ to train the model. To this end, an adversarial *domain classifier* (D) with

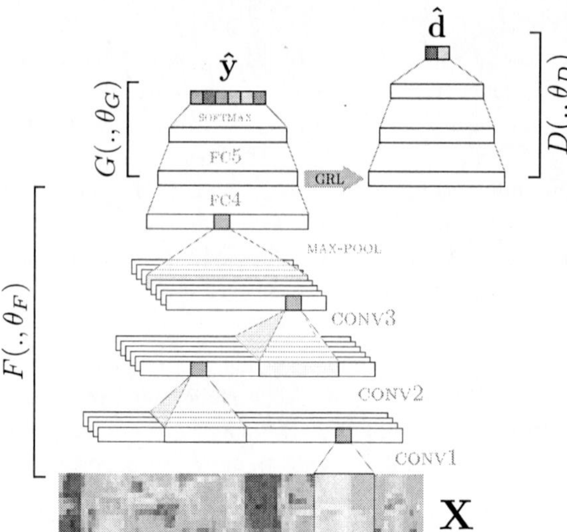

Figure 1: A schematic view of our LID model. A 3-layer 1-dimensional convolutional network followed by 3-layer fully-connected feed-forward network. The segment-level feature extractor $F(., \boldsymbol{\theta}_F)$ maps the input sequence $\mathbf{X}$ into a d-dimensional feature vector $\mathbf{f} \in \mathbb{R}^d$, i.e. $\mathbf{f} = F(\mathbf{X}; \boldsymbol{\theta}_F)$. Then, the language classifier $G(., \boldsymbol{\theta}_G)$ maps $\mathbf{f}$ into a probability distribution over the language space, i.e. $\hat{\mathbf{y}} = G(\mathbf{f}; \boldsymbol{\theta}_G)$. In the robust LID model, the domain classifier $D(., \boldsymbol{\theta}_D)$ is connected to the network through a gradient reversal layer (GRL) to predict the domain given $\mathbf{f}$.

parameters $\boldsymbol{\theta}_D$ is connected to the network with the objective of predicting the dataset of each speech sample in the training data. Now the goal is to encourage the segment-level feature extractor F is to produce representations that are language-discriminative but invariant with respect to the non-linguistic sources of variability in speech signals. We refer the reader to previous work to get a detailed overview of adversarial training for domain adaptation in the context of the LID task (Abdullah et al., 2020).

4 Experiments and Results

4.1 Training and Evaluation Data

We train our LID models to discriminate between the six Slavic languages that are shared by the RBS and GRS datasets, namely: Bulgarian, Czech, Croatian, Polish, Russian, and Ukrainian. The labelled speech samples are drawn from the RBS dataset (source dataset) while the unlabelled speech samples, which are used to improve our model robustness against non-language sources of variability, are drawn from the the GRS dataset (target dataset). For each language, we sample a balanced subset of 3-second 8,000 segments from each dataset to ensure our models are not effected by undesirable biases due to imbalanced conditions. We evaluate our models in two conditions: (1) in-domain evaluation, in which the evaluation samples come from the source dataset (i.e., the test split of RBS), and (2) cross-domain evaluation, in which the evaluation samples come from the target dataset whose labels are not observed during training (i.e., the development split of GRS).

4.2 Feature Extraction

In our experiments, we use the first 12 mel-frequency spectral coefficients (MFSCs) and frame-level averaged energy as low-level speech features. We extract frames of 25ms with 10ms overlap. Then, each speech sample is normalized with utterance-level mean and variance normalization.

4.3 Model Architecture and Hyperparameters

CNN Architecture. We employ three 1-dimensional convolutional layers over the temporal dimension with 128, 256, and 512 filters and filter widths of 5, 10, and 10 for each layer with strides of 1 step for each layer. Batch normalization and ReLU non-linearity are applied after each convolutional operation. We downsample the representation by applying a single max pooling operation at the end of the convolution block. For the language classifier, we use three fully-connected layers ($512 \rightarrow 512 \rightarrow 512 \rightarrow 6$) before the softmax for both the baseline and the robust LID models.

LID Model	In-domain				Cross-domain			
	1-sec	2-sec	3-sec	Full	1-sec	2-sec	3-sec	Full
Baseline LID	72.93	91.10	95.48	97.38	30.18	47.61	55.91	65.45
Robust LID	64.25	88.55	94.77	97.35	51.59	76.76	86.94	93.29
Δ	-11.9	-2.80	-0.74	-0.03	70.94	61.23	55.50	42.54

Table 1: In-domain and cross-domain evaluation of our LID models in balanced accuracy (%). Δ is the relative percentage difference in accuracy scores of baseline and robust LID models.

Adversarial Classifier. For our robust LID model, we add a 3-layer fully-connected feed-forward block ($512 \rightarrow 1024 \rightarrow 1024 \rightarrow 2$) to the network as the adversarial domain classifier D. The adversarial classifier takes the output of the segment-level feature extractor $\mathbf{f}$ (the output of layer FC4) and predicts the domain of the input sample. The adversarial loss is realized with a special layer, that is, a gradient reversal layer (GRL). The GRL behaves as an identity function during the forward pass but reverses the direction of the gradient signal during backpropagation.

Training Details. The cross-entropy loss is used for both the language classifier loss and the adversarial classifier loss. We use the Adam optimizer with a learning rate of 1×10^{-3} and train our models with a batch size of 256 samples. For the robust model, half of the samples within a mini-batch are drawn from the training split of the RBS dataset while the rest are drawn from the training split of the GRS dataset. Both the baseline and the robust models are trained for 50 epochs and the best models are selected based on the performance on the validation set. We do not use the early stopping criterion in our experiments.

4.4 Experimental Results

In this section, we report the evaluation results and show the effect of the adversarial training on the model's robustness. Since the GRS evaluation data is imbalanced, we use balanced accuracy (Brodersen et al., 2010) as our evaluation metric to obtain a better estimate of the models' performance. Table 1 shows our results for speech segments of various lengths. It can be observed from the cross-domain evaluation that the performance of the baseline model drops by a substantial factor. On the other hand, our robust model significantly improves cross-domain performance with little effect on the performance on the in-domain evaluation dataset, especially for longer utterances.

To get further insight into why adversarial training improves cross-domain performance, we analyze the predictions of the GRS evaluation samples made by the baseline and robust models by computing the F_1 score per language. The results of this analysis are shown in Table 2. For our baseline, we observe a much higher variance between languages compared to the robust model. The performance drop is more pronounced in the case of Ukrainian with a significant decrease in F_1. However, our robust model boosts the F_1 score on Ukrainian from 14.66% to 94.49%.

LID Model	BUL	HRV	CZE	POL	RUS	UKR	macro Avg.	micro Avg.
Baseline LID	59.73	64.86	76.50	61.93	41.79	14.66	53.25	54.17
Robust LID	85.12	83.32	89.36	83.96	87.66	94.49	87.32	88.26
Δ	42.51	28.46	16.81	35.57	109.76	544.54	63.98	62.93

Table 2: F_1 score (%) per language. Predictions were obtained by feeding 3-second segments from GRS evaluation dataset to the LID models. Δ is the relative percentage difference in F_1 scores of baseline and robust LID models.

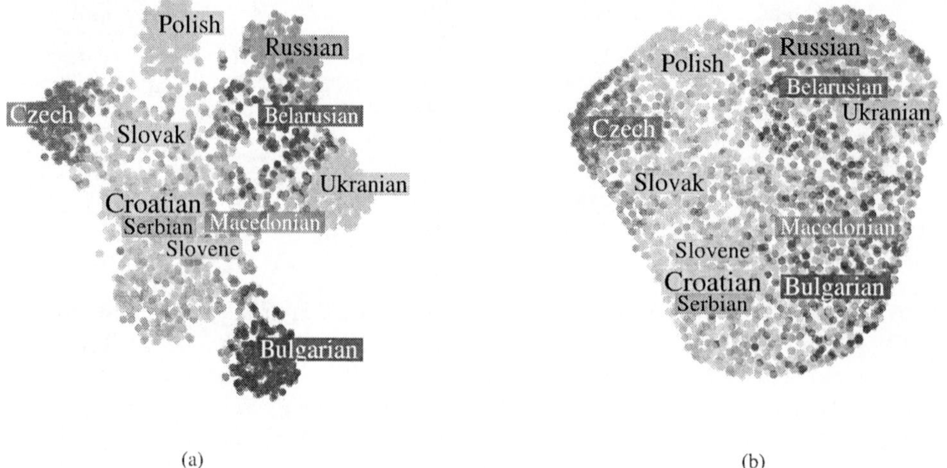

(a)   (b)

Figure 2: Two-dimensional visualization of representations of evaluation speech segments: (a) t-SNE projections, and (b) UMAP projections (best viewed in color).

5 Representation Similarity Analysis

In this section, we present our representation similarity analysis. From the robust LID model presented in the previous section, we obtain 512-dimensional representations for the 11 languages from the RBS evaluation set (500 5-second speech segments for each language). These representations are the output of the last fully-connected layer of the language classifier (i.e., layer FC5) before the softmax output layer.[1] It is worth pointing out that our LID model has been trained on a subset of only six languages out of the 11 languages that we analyze in this section.

5.1 Language Representation Visualizations

As our first analysis, we use dimensionality reduction techniques to obtain 2-dimensional projections from representations of the evaluation set and visualize the resulting data points. We use two dimensionality reduction techniques; t-SNE (Maaten and Hinton, 2008) and UMAP (McInnes et al., 2018). The resulting graphs are illustrated in Fig. 2. The motivation for using two different techniques in this analysis is that t-SNE and UMAP have different optimization objectives that complement each other. That is, the t-SNE algorithm preserves the local structure of the space; thus, it mainly reveals the cluster structure within the representation space. On the other hand, the UMAP algorithm preserves the global structure of the space. Nevertheless, both t-SNE and UMPA plots in Fig. 2 show very similar trends since the emerging subspaces shown in the figure correspond to the conventional sub-grouping of Slavic languages into East-, West-, and South-Slavic.

5.2 Correlation with Geographic Proximity

Following Bjerva et al. (2019), we investigate whether the language representations reflect the geographic proximity of their respective speaker communities. To perform this analysis, we first obtain a single prototypical vector representation for each Slavic language in our study by taking the average over the representations of the evaluation speech segments as

$$\mathbf{v}_L = \frac{1}{|\mathcal{E}_L|} \sum_{\mathbf{X} \in \mathcal{E}_L} \text{NN}(\mathbf{X})$$

---

[1]In the speaker and language recognition community, these representations are usually referred to as x-vectors, while the emerging geometric space is referred to as the x-vector space.

134

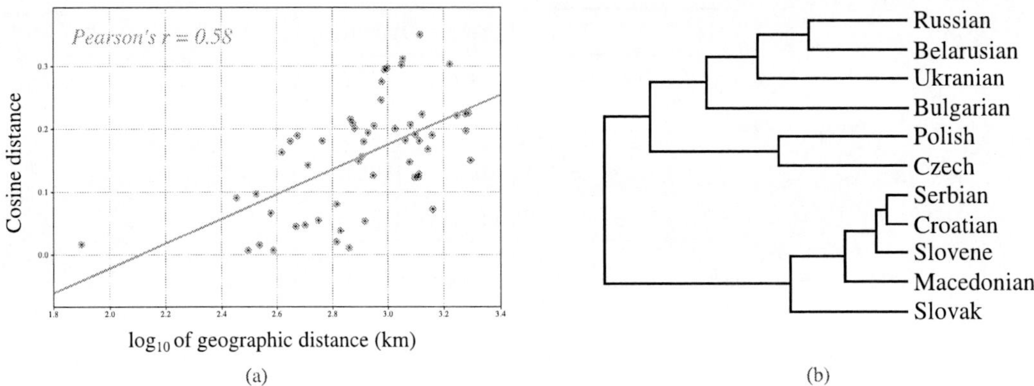

(a)   (b)

Figure 3: (a) Correlation between geographic distance and distances between prototype language representations measured by cosine similarity, and (b) a genetic tree generated from the pairwise distance matrix of the language prototype representations from our LID model.

where $\mathbf{v}_L \in \mathbb{R}^{512}$ is a prototypical vector representation for language L, $\mathcal{E}_L$ is the evaluation speech segments for language L, and NN(.) is the output of the last non-linear layer (layer FC5) of the robust LID model. The distance in the representation space between two languages is computed using cosine distance. For geographic distance, we follow a similar approach as in Skirgård et al. (2017). First, each language is characterized by a point location on the map given the latitude and longitude information in the ASJP linguistic database (which is intended to represent the cultural or historical center of the language). We then compute the pairwise distances between the points on the map (in kilometers) and convert them into $\log_{10}$ scale. Fig. 3(a) shows a scatter plot between the data points in which the x-axis represents the geographic distance and the y-axis represents the cosine distance in the representation space. We observe a positive correlation between the two distance measures (Pearson's $r = 0.58$). This clearly shows that the distance in the representation space does indeed reflect the geographic distance.

5.3 Genetic Signal in the Representation Space

Similar to the analysis in Bjerva et al. (2019) and Cathcart and Wandl (2020), we investigate the genetic signal in the representation space. To this end, the pairwise cosine distances computed in the previous section are first converted into a confusion matrix. Then, we generate a tree by performing hierarchical clustering on the confusion matrix using the Ward algorithm. The resulting tree is depicted in Fig. 3(b). We observe that the generated tree shows many similarities to phylogenetic trees that correspond to the widely accepted tripartite division of Slavic languages (that is, the 3-way categorization of Slavic languages into East-, West-, and South-Slavic). However, we observe two notable discrepancies between the widely-accepted Slavic tree and our generated tree: (1) the placement of Bulgarian (a South-Slavic language) within the East-Slavic group, and (2) the placement of Slovak (a West-Slavic language) within the South-Slavic group.

5.4 Fine-grained Analysis of Similarities

Although we have shown that the distances in the representation space of our LID model correlate with geographic distances and have adequately reconstructed the Slavic genetic tree, we seek to understand the factors that could better explain the similarities. To this end, we compare our generated tree with various genetic trees of Slavic languages presented in previous studies.[2]

(1) **Levenshtein distance-based tree** Serva and Petroni (2008) have automatically generated a phylogenetic tree for 50 Indo-European languages using a renormalized Levenshtein distance based on a

---

[2]Although a correlation analysis on confusion matrices would have been more optimal, we instead apply tree similarity analysis because not all underlying confusion matrices are available.

Tree	Distance
Levenshtein distance-based	0.270
Glottochronology-based	0.132
Geographic distance-based	0.140
GLG Confusion-based	**0.084**
Random	0.371

Table 3: Tree distance evaluation. Lower values correspond to smaller distances.

Swadesh list of 200 words that have the same word meanings across languages. We take the Slavic branch from this tree for our similarity analysis.

(2) **Glottochronology-based tree** Novotná and Blažek (2007) have used a classical glottochronological approach to generate a genetic a tree for the Balto-Slavic languages. Their approach employs a manual calculation of pairwise distances between languages based on the recognition of cognates.

(3) **Geographic distance-based tree** Using the geographic distance matrix we obtained from the ASJP database, we apply the same hierarchical clustering as we applied on our prototype language vectors to obtain a tree based on geographic distance.

(4) **GLG Confusion-based tree** Skirgård et al. (2017) have applied hierarchical clustering on their player confusion data and their resulting tree shows that the Slavic languages form a pure cluster. We consider this tree to be a good approximation of non-linguist's perception of language variation and similarity.

(5) **Randomly generated tree** To give a reference point for a worst case scenario in our analysis, we generate a tree using the Ward hierarchical clustering on a random confusion matrix.

First, and to facilitate the measurement of distance between different trees, we consider Croatian and Serbian as a single node in our tree (i.e., Serbo-Croatian) and keep only the nodes that represent languages shared by all trees. This leaves us with eight languages: Bulgarian, Serbo-Croatian, Slovene, Czech, Polish, Slovak, Russian, and Ukrainian. Second, we compute the distances between the tree generated from the representation distances of our LID model and each of the aforementioned trees using the unweighted tree distance metric introduced by Rabinovich et al. (2017). The result of this evaluation is presented in Table 3. We observe that the most similar tree to our tree is the one based on the player confusion data from the GLG. These findings suggest that the factor that best explains the similarities within the emerging representations from our LID model is the perceptual similarity between Slavic languages, approximated by the confusability obtained from the GLG participants.

6   Discussion

Many recent works have shown that deep neural networks are good models of human perception. For example, Zhang et al. (2018) and Peterson et al. (2018) have shown that emerging representations from neural models trained on visual recognition tasks are predictive of human similarity judgments. For auditory recognition, neural speech recognition models have been shown to capture human-like behavior in cross-lingual phonetic perception (Schatz and Feldman, 2018). Following the same spirit, our objective is to the investigate the extent to which neural models of spoken language identification capture language similarity. Nevertheless, and because of the complex space in which language variation can be realized, the similarity between two languages is a multidimensional phenomenon that cannot be expressed in a single number (Van Heuven, 2008). We therefore do not consider a single reference as a "ground truth" in our analysis, but consider several reference criteria of distance including genetic, geographic, and perceptual distance.

Our representation similarity analysis shows that emerging representations in our spoken LID model capture language similarity. The representation visualization illustrated in Fig. 2 demonstrates the generalization ability of our model to project speech segments of non-observed (held-out) languages into subspaces of their respective subgroups. Given that the data in our study constitute contemporary realizations of Slavic speech that do not explicitly encode diachronic sound changes, we first hypothesized that the geographic distances between the linguistic communities would be a good predictor of the distances in the representation space of the LID model. This turns out to indeed be the case as we observe a high positive correlation between geographic distances and cosine distances within prototype language representations.

On the other hand, we were less optimistic about our LID model capturing the genetic signal between Slavic languages (that is, whether the language representations encode the historical relationships between languages). Earlier works that have investigated computational approaches to generating genetic language trees have either employed historical etymological data capturing phonological sound changes (Cathcart and Wandl, 2020), sequences reflecting syntactic patterns in different languages (Rabinovich et al., 2017; Bjerva et al., 2019), or word lists reflecting lexical similarity (Serva and Petroni, 2008). Arguably, these sources of language data are more likely to preserve the relationship between languages across the temporal dimension than the contemporary Slavic speech we use in this study. Therefore, our initial intuition was that the resulting tree would reflect variation across the spatial dimension and not the temporal dimension. Nevertheless, the tree generated by our analysis is an adequate approximation of the Slavic genetic tree given the contemporary nature of the data sources.

Finally, it is striking to observe the similarity between our generated tree and the Slavic subtree constructed from player confusion patterns of GLG participants (Skirgård et al., 2017). There are two main factors that contribute to this similarity of our analysis to that of Skirgård et al. (2017): (1) West-Slavic and East-Slavic branches are clustered together before joining the South-Slavic branch to form a single Slavic cluster, and (2) the deviations from the widely accepted Slavic grouping are present in both analyses at approximately the same node locations since Bulgarian is grouped with East-Slavic and Slovak is grouped with South-Slavic. These findings provide evidence that the perceived language similarity is the factor that can best predict the geometric distance between languages in the emerging representation space from neural models of spoken language identification.

7   Conclusion

We have presented a convolutional neural model for Slavic language identification in speech signals and analyzed the extent to which its emerging representations reflect language similarity. Our analysis has shown that the distances in the emergent language representations reflect language variation across the temporal (phylogenetic) and spatial (geographic) dimensions. Moreover, by comparing our clustering analysis to the confusion patterns of the Great Language Game participants, we have shown that perceptual confusability is a better predictor of language representation similarities than phylogenetic and geographic distances.

Acknowledgements

We would like to thank Nicole Macher for assisting with the research presented in this paper. We extend our gratitude to anonymous reviewers for their insightful suggestions and comments. This research is funded by the Deutsche Forschungsgemeinschaft (DFG, German Research Foundation), Project ID 232722074, SFB 1102.

References

Badr M. Abdullah, Tania Avgustinova, Bernd Mobius, and Dietrich Klakow. Cross-domain adaptation of spoken language identification for related languages: The curious case of slavic languages. In *Interspeech*, 2020.

Leszek Bednarczuk. *Poczkatki i pogranicza polszczyzny*. Lexis, 2018.

Johannes Bjerva, Robert Östling, Maria Han Veiga, Jörg Tiedemann, and Isabelle Augenstein. What do language representations really represent? *Computational Linguistics*, 45(2):381–389, 2019.

Kay Henning Brodersen, Cheng Soon Ong, Klaas Enno Stephan, and Joachim M Buhmann. The balanced accuracy and its posterior distribution. In *International Conference on Pattern Recognition*, pages 3121–3124. IEEE, 2010.

Chundra Cathcart and Florian Wandl. In search of isoglosses: continuous and discrete language embeddings in Slavic historical phonology. In *Proceedings of the 17th SIGMORPHON Workshop on Computational Research in Phonetics, Phonology, and Morphology*, Online, July 2020. Association for Computational Linguistics.

Hanna Dalewska-Greń. *Języki słowiańskie*. Wydawnictwo Naukowe PWN, Warszawa, second edition, 2020.

Matthew S. Dryer and Martin Haspelmath, editors. *WALS Online*. Max Planck Institute for Evolutionary Anthropology, Leipzig, 2013. URL https://wals.info/.

Yaroslav Ganin and Victor Lempitsky. Unsupervised domain adaptation by backpropagation. In *International Conference on Machine Learning*, pages 1180–1189, 2015.

Gregory Gelly and Jean-Luc Gauvain. Spoken language identification using lstm-based angular proximity. In *Interspeech*, 2017.

Gregory Gelly, Jean-Luc Gauvain, Lori Lamel, Antoine Laurent, Viet Bac Le, and Abdel Messaoudi. Language recognition for dialects and closely related languages. In *Odyssey*, volume 2016, pages 124–131, 2016.

Javier Gonzalez-Dominguez, Ignacio Lopez-Moreno, Haşim Sak, Joaquin Gonzalez-Rodriguez, and Pedro J Moreno. Automatic language identification using long short-term memory recurrent neural networks. In *Interspeech*, 2014.

Charlotte Gooskens, Wilbert Heeringa, and Karin Beijering. Phonetic and lexical predictors of intelligibility. *International journal of humanities and arts computing*, 2(1-2):63–81, 2008.

Alexander Gutkin, Tatiana Merkulova, and Martin Jansche. Predicting the features of world atlas of language structures from speech. In *Proc. The 6th Intl. Workshop on Spoken Language Technologies for Under-Resourced Languages*, pages 248–252, 2018.

Wilbert Heeringa, Keith Johnson, and Charlotte Gooskens. Measuring norwegian dialect distances using acoustic features. *Speech Communication*, 51(2):167–183, 2009.

Melvin Johnson, Mike Schuster, Quoc V Le, Maxim Krikun, Yonghui Wu, Zhifeng Chen, Nikhil Thorat, Fernanda Viégas, Martin Wattenberg, Greg Corrado, et al. Google's multilingual neural machine translation system: Enabling zero-shot translation. *Transactions of the Association for Computational Linguistics*, 5:339–351, 2017.

Tadeusz Lehr-Spławiński, Władysław Kuraszkiewicz, and Franciszek Sławski. *Przegląd i charakterystyka języków słowiańskich*. Państwowe Wydawn. Naukowe, 1954.

Haizhou Li, Bin Ma, and Kong Aik Lee. Spoken language recognition: from fundamentals to practice. *Proceedings of the IEEE*, 101(5):1136–1159, 2013.

Ignacio Lopez-Moreno, Javier Gonzalez-Dominguez, Oldrich Plchot, David Martinez, Joaquin Gonzalez-Rodriguez, and Pedro Moreno. Automatic language identification using deep neural networks. In *2014 IEEE international conference on acoustics, speech and signal processing (ICASSP)*, pages 5337–5341. IEEE, 2014.

Laurens van der Maaten and Geoffrey Hinton. Visualizing data using t-sne. *Journal of machine learning research*, 9(Nov):2579–2605, 2008.

Chaitanya Malaviya, Graham Neubig, and Patrick Littell. Learning language representations for typology prediction. In *Proceedings of the 2017 Conference on Empirical Methods in Natural Language Processing*, Copenhagen, Denmark, September 2017. Association for Computational Linguistics.

Witold Mańczak. *Przedhistoryczne migracje Słowian i pochodzenie języka staro-cerkiewno-słowiańskiego*. Nakładem Polskiej Akad. Umiejętności, 2004.

Lukas Mateju, Petr Cerva, Jindrich Zdánskỳ, and Radek Safarik. Using deep neural networks for identification of slavic languages from acoustic signal. In *Interspeech*, 2018.

Leland McInnes, John Healy, Nathaniel Saul, and Lukas Großberger. Umap: Uniform manifold approximation and projection. *Journal of Open Source Software*, 3(29):861, 2018.

Jerzy Nalepa. *Słowiańszczyzna północno-zachodnia: podstawy jedności i jej rozpad*, volume 25. Państwowe Wydawn. Naukowe; Oddz. w Poznaniu, 1968.

Jan Nouza, Radek Safarik, and Petr Cerva. Asr for south slavic languages developed in almost automated way. In *Interspeech*, 2016.

Petra Novotná and Václav Blažek. Glottochronology and its application to the balto-slavic languages. *Baltistica*, 42(2):185–210, 2007.

Robert Östling and Jörg Tiedemann. Continuous multilinguality with language vectors. In *Proceedings of the 15th Conference of the European Chapter of the Association for Computational Linguistics: Volume 2, Short Papers*, Valencia, Spain, April 2017. Association for Computational Linguistics.

Ben Peters, Jon Dehdari, and Josef van Genabith. Massively multilingual neural grapheme-to-phoneme conversion. In *Proceedings of the First Workshop on Building Linguistically Generalizable NLP Systems*, Copenhagen, Denmark, September 2017. Association for Computational Linguistics.

Joshua C Peterson, Jordan W Suchow, Krisha Aghi, Alexander Y Ku, and Thomas L Griffiths. Capturing human category representations by sampling in deep feature spaces. Proceedings of the 40th Annual Conference of the Cognitive Science Society., 2018.

Włodzimierz Pianka and Emil Tokarz. *Gramatyka konfrontatywna języków słowiańskich. 1 (2000)*. Śląsk, 2000.

Ella Rabinovich, Noam Ordan, and Shuly Wintner. Found in translation: Reconstructing phylogenetic language trees from translations. In *Proceedings of the 55th Annual Meeting of the Association for Computational Linguistics (Volume 1: Long Papers)*, Vancouver, Canada, July 2017. Association for Computational Linguistics.

Irena Sawicka. Problems of the phonetic typology of the slavic languages. *Studies in the Phonetic Typology of the Slavic Languages. Warszawa: Slawistyczny Osrodek Wydawniczy przy Instytucie Slowianoznawstwa PAN*, 1991.

Thomas Schatz and Naomi H Feldman. Neural network vs. hmm speech recognition systems as models of human cross-linguistic phonetic perception. In *Proceedings of the Conference on Cognitive Computational Neuroscience*, 2018.

Tanja Schultz, Ngoc Thang Vu, and Tim Schlippe. Globalphone: A multilingual text & speech database in 20 languages. In *2013 IEEE International Conference on Acoustics, Speech and Signal Processing*, pages 8126–8130. IEEE, 2013.

Maurizio Serva and Filippo Petroni. Indo-european languages tree by levenshtein distance. *EPL (Europhysics Letters)*, 81(6):68005, 2008.

Suwon Shon, Ahmed Ali, and James Glass. Convolutional neural network and language embeddings for end-to-end dialect recognition. In *Proc. Odyssey 2018 The Speaker and Language Recognition Workshop*, pages 98–104, 2018.

Hedvig Skirgård, Seán G Roberts, and Lars Yencken. Why are some languages confused for others? investigating data from the great language game. *PloS one*, 12(4), 2017.

Vincent J Van Heuven. Making sense of strange sounds:(mutual) intelligibility of related language varieties. a review. *International journal of humanities and arts computing*, 2(1-2):39–62, 2008.

Richard Zhang, Phillip Isola, Alexei A Efros, Eli Shechtman, and Oliver Wang. The unreasonable effectiveness of deep features as a perceptual metric. In *Proceedings of the IEEE conference on computer vision and pattern recognition*, pages 586–595, 2018.

A Four-Dialect Treebank for Occitan: Building Process and Parsing Experiments

Aleksandra Miletic
CNRS UMR 5263 CLLE
University of Toulouse, France
aleksandra.miletic@univ-tlse2.fr

Myriam Bras
CNRS UMR 5263 CLLE
University of Toulouse, France
myriam.bras@univ-tlse2.fr

Marianne Vergez-Couret
EA 3816 FoReLLIS
University of Poitiers, France
marianne.vergez.couret@univ-poitiers.fr

Louise Esher
CNRS UMR 5263 CLLE
University of Toulouse, France
louise.esher@univ-tlse2.fr

Jean Sibille
CNRS UMR 5263 CLLE
University of Toulouse, France
jean.sibille@univ-tlse2.fr

Clamença Poujade
CNRS UMR 5263 CLLE
University of Toulouse, France
clamenca.poujade@univ-tlse2.fr

Abstract

Occitan is a Romance language spoken mainly in the south of France. It has no official status in the country, it is not standardized and displays important diatopic variation resulting in a rich system of dialects. Recently, we created a first treebank for this language (Miletic et al., 2020). However, this corpus is based exclusively on texts in the Lengadocian dialect. Our paper describes the work aimed at extending the existing corpus with content in three new dialects, namely Gascon, Provençau and Lemosin. We describe both the annotation of initial content in these new varieties of Occitan and experiments allowing us to identify the most efficient method for further enrichment of the corpus. We observe that parsing models trained on Occitan dialects achieve better results than a delexicalized model trained on other Romance languages despite the latter training corpus being much larger (20K vs 900K tokens). The results of the native Occitan models show an important impact of cross-dialectal lexical variation, whereas syntactic variation seems to affect the systems less. We hope that these results, as well as the associated corpus, incorporating several Occitan varieties, will facilitate the training of robust NLP tools, capable of processing all kinds of Occitan texts.

1 Introduction

Occitan is a Romance language spoken in southern France (except in the Basque and Catalan areas), in several valleys of the Italian Piedmont and in the Val d'Aran in Spain. It does not have the status of an official language, and as many such languages, it is not standardized. It displays a rich system of diatopic varieties, organized into dialects. The variation can be appreciated at all levels of linguistic structure: it can be lexical or phonetic, but also morphological and syntactical (see Section 2). Also, there are two different spelling norms in use today, one called the classical, based on the Occitan troubadours' medieval spelling, and the other closer to the French language conventions (Sibille, 2002).

Since all these factors contribute to data sparsity, they make Occitan particularly challenging for natural language processing (hereafter NLP). In fact, Occitan is still relatively low-resourced, although recent efforts have started to remedy this situation. The firsts of them was the creation of the BaTelÒc text base (Bras and Vergez-Couret, 2016) and the RESTAURE project, which resulted in the creation

This work is licensed under a Creative Commons Attribution 4.0 International Licence. Licence details: http://creativecommons.org/licenses/by/4.0/.

Proceedings of the 7th VarDial Workshop on NLP for Similar Languages, Varieties and Dialects, pages 140–149
Barcelona, Spain (Online), December 13, 2020

of an electronic lexicon (Vergez-Couret, 2016; Bras et al., 2020) and a POS tagged corpus (Bernhard et al., 2018). Even more recently, the first treebank for Occitan was created (Miletic et al., 2020) following Universal Dependencies guidelines[1]. Whereas the RESTAURE corpus contains several dialects, the Loflòc lexicon and the treebank are based on only one dialect – the Lengadocian. However, our goal is to be able to train robust machine learning tools capable of successfully processing texts in all varieties of Occitan. There are two main possible solutions to this: we need either training corpora representative of all Occitan varieties or extensive compensation methods for NLP which would allow us to adapt tools across varieties, such as delexicalized cross-lingual parsing. This technique consists in training a parsing model on a delexicalized corpus of a source language (i.e., using only POS tags and morphosyntactic features while ignoring tokens and lemmas) and then using the model to process data in the target language. It has been successfully used on a number of language pairs in the past (McDonald et al., 2013; Lynn et al., 2014; Duong et al., 2015; Tiedemann, 2015), including on Occitan (Miletic et al., 2019b). Both the corpus building solution and the parsing transfer solution are explored in the remainder of the paper.

In Section 2, we give a brief description of the linguistic properties of Occitan and of its main dialects. Section 3 describes the addition of three new dialects to the existing treebank and the resulting corpus. Section 4 is dedicated to experiments looking to identify the most effective method for training a robust parsing model for all Occitan dialects in the corpus. Finally, in Section 5, we give our conclusions and directions for future work.

2 Occitan: Main Linguistic Properties and Diatopic Variation

Occitan belongs to the Gallo-Romance group of Romance languages, together with standard French and "langues d'oïl", Francoprovençal and Catalan. It is closer to Catalan than to French and forms with Catalan a subgroup called occitano-roman (Bec, 1970). It is a null subject language with tense, person and number inflection marks on finite verbs for each person. Many dialects mark number and gender inflection on all components of the noun phrase. Unlike contemporary French, Occitan maintains the use of the preterite (*passat simple*), which contrasts with the perfect tense (*passat compausat*), and the use of the imperfect subjunctive, even in oral colloquial speech. An example in Lengadocian illustrating some of these properties is given in Example 1.

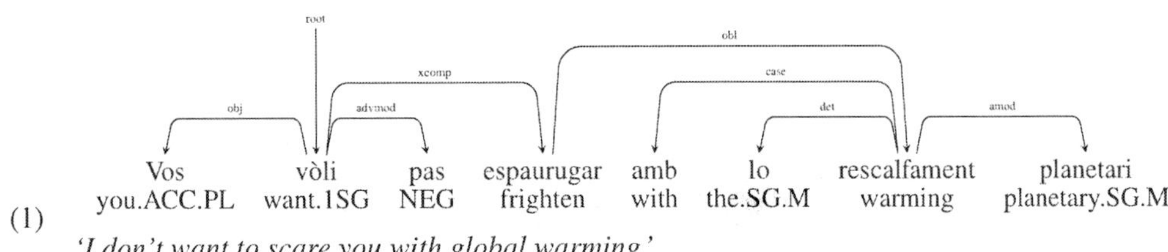

(1)

'I don't want to scare you with global warming.'

As mentioned above, Occitan has several diatopic varieties, organized into dialects. The most widely accepted classification proposed by Bec (1995) includes Auvernhat, Gascon, Lengadocian, Lemosin, Provençau and Vivaroaupenc (see Figure 1), but these dialects are not homogeneous: they form a continuum with areas of greater or lesser variation. In this article we focus on four of them: Lengadocian, Gascon, Provençau and Lemosin[2], since they are the ones for which the greatest number and variety of texts are currently available. Differences in dialects can be appreciated at different levels (lexical, phonological, morphological and syntactical), as shown below.

The variation can be lexical: e.g., the word *potato* translates as *mandòrra* in some Gascon varieties, but as *trufa/trufet* or *patana/patanon* in Lengadocian. A large part of this type of variation stems from different phonological processes, many of which appear in Gascon: the aspirated *h* in word-initial position in

---

[1] https://universaldependencies.org/
[2] Names of dialects are given in Occitan (each one in its dialect) as there is no standardized orthographic form for those names in English.

Figure 1: Occitan dialects map

words such as *hilh* 'son', *hèsta* 'celebration' (cf. *filh* in Lengadocian and Lemosin, *fiu* in Provençau and Vivaroaupenc, *fèsta* in Lengadocian and Provençau, *festa* in Lemosin, Auvernhàt and Vivaroaupenc), the drop of the intervocalic *n* in words such as *lua* 'moon' (cf. *luna* in Lengadocian) and the *r* metathesis in words such as *craba* 'goat', *dromir* 'to sleep' (cf. respectively *cabra, dormir/durmir* in a large part of the Lengadocian area). It is also caused by the existence of several spelling norms. Since the 19th century, two major spelling conventions can be distinguished: the first was influenced by French; the second, called the "classical spelling" and inspired by the medieval troubadour spelling, appeared in the 20th century. The latter is a unified spelling convention distributed across all of the Occitan territories (Sibille, 2002).

On the morpho-syntactic level, verb inflection varies from one dialect to another as illustrated in Table 1, which gives the present indicative of the verb *èsser/èstre* 'to be' in the most common paradigm for each of the four dialects (there is also intradialectal variation).

Number	Person	Gascon	Lemosin	Lengadocian	Provençau
sg	1st	soi	sei	soi	siáu
	2nd	ès	ses	ès/siás	siás
	3rd	ei/es	es	es	es
pl	1st	èm	sem	sèm	siam
	2nd	ètz	setz	sètz	siatz
	3rd	son	son	son	son

Table 1: Verb *èsser/èstre* 'to be' in present indicative across dialects

When it comes to syntax, there is more homogeneity across dialects, but Gascon exhibits several important specificities. First, it has enunciative particles which mark the sentence modality: the most frequent are *que* for affirmative sentences, *be* and *ja* for exclamative sentences and *e* for interrogative sentences and subordinate clauses. They appear between the subject and the verb and their presence is even obligatory in some Gascon areas. They have no equivalent in the Lengadocian, Provençau and Lemosin dialects (cf. Example 2.a). The interrogative and relative pronoun *qui* 'who'(cf. Example 2.b), which is scarcely used in Lengadocian, Provençau and Lemosin and only as an interrogative pronoun, has many functions in Gascon, such as the subject or direct object functions (where the other dialects use *que*), and it can be precedeed by the preposition *de* regardless of the verbal rection (cf. Example 2.c), which does not occur in other dialects. *Qui* and *de qui* can also be a subordinating conjunction introducing a completive clause. Furthermore, object clitics and reflexive pronouns are more often found in post-verbal position than it is the case in Lengadocian, in which they are typically pre-verbal (cf. Example 2.d). Finally, unlike in other dialects, there are no indefinite or partitive articles in Gascon (cf. Example 2.e).

(2)

a.
| Lo | vent | **que** | s' | èra | lhevat | e | **que** | hasó | drin | fresc. |
| the.SG.M | wind | PART | REFL | was | risen | and | PART | did | slightly | cold |

'*The wind had started blowing and it was a bit cold.*'
Leng.: '*lo vent s'èra levat e fasiá un pauc freg.*'

b.
| l' | atge | **qui** | a |
| the | age | that | has |

lit. '*the age he has*', '*his age*'
Leng.: '*l'atge qu'as / que as*'

c.
| los | guardians | d' | un | concèpte | de | civilizacion | **de** | **qui** | calèva | preservar |
| the.PL.M | guardians | of | a.M.SG | concept | of | civilization | PREP | which | ought | preserve |

'*the guardians of a concept of civilization that needed to be preserved*'
Leng.: '*los gardians d'un concèpte de civilizacion que caliá preservar*'

d.
| Ne | cau | pas | està | **'s** | darrèr | mieidia |
| NEG | ought | NEG | stay | REFL | after | noon |

'*You shouldn't stay after noon*'
Leng.: '*vos cal pas demorar après miègjorn*'

e.
| entà | véner | Ø | objècts | de | pietat. |
| in.order.to | sell | | objects | of | piety |

'*in order to sell objects of piety*'
Leng.: '*per vendre d'objèctes de pietat*'

It is important to note the potential impact of these characteristics on NLP tools based on machine learning. The lexical and morpho-syntactical variation is potentially problematic, but it is mostly a question of coverage: it can be alleviated either by a carefully engineered training corpus, representative of as many dialects as possible, or by an extensive, dialect-diversified lexicon. If a combination of the two were available, we could reasonably suppose that the effect of the variation would be minimized and that a tool trained and used in such conditions would be able to POS-tag, lemmatize and parse texts independently of dialect. However, the syntactic variation has a potentially more profound effect: a Gascon corpus can be expected to have more ambiguity related to relative pronouns, but also a different distribution of POS tags (i.e., more particles, fewer determiners) and of syntactic structures (i.e., more right-branching verb dependents) than corpora in other dialects. This could compromise the transfer of parsers trained on other dialects to Gascon and *vice versa*.

3 Extending the Existing Corpus with Content in Other Dialects

3.1 Initial Treebank in Lengadocian

The first treebank for Occitan (TTB: Tolosa Treebank) was created recently (Miletic et al., 2020). It contains 19K tokens of Lengadocian texts spanning 5 different genres (literature, newspaper, encyclopedia, scientific text and blog) (cf. row *Lengadocian* in Table 2). It is annotated for POS-tags, lemmas and syntactic dependencies. The annotation was done according to the Universal Dependencies (UD) guidelines, with some adaptations (see (Miletic et al., 2020) for a detailed description). A part of the content was taken from the RESTAURE project and the initial GRACE tagset was converted automatically to the UD tags (Miletic et al., 2019a). The remainder was tagged and lemmatized manually.

As for the syntactic annotation, the whole Lengadocian corpus was processed following the same procedure. We offer here a quick overview of the experiment; for a detailed account, see (Miletic et al., 2019b). Given the absence of training data for Occitan at the start of our project, we explored delexicalized cross-lingual parsing based on existing UD corpora for Romance languages. We trained a total of 21 models and evaluated them on a manually annotated Occitan sample. The top 5 models achieved LAS between 70.0 and 71.6 points[3]. These models were trained on individual or combined UD treebanks in Italian (ISDT, ISDT+ParTUT), French (GSD, GSD+ParTUT+Sequoia), and Portuguese (Bosque). One model per language was selected (Italian ISDT, French ParTUT+GSD+Sequoia, Portuguese Bosque) for manual pre-annotation of new samples in Occitan. During manual validation of their output, the human annotator observed that their performances were rather homogeneous. In the following stages of our work, we therefore decided to train a delexicalized model on a merged trilingual corpus (bringing the train size to 900K tokens) in an effort to further improve the performances. Using this model for pre-annotation brought the mean manual validation time from 340 tokens/h (for a fully manual annotation) to 650 tokens/h.

The quality of the manual annotation was regularly evaluated through inter-annotator agreement both in terms of Cohen's *kappa* and as a simple agreement ratio (raw percentage of consistent annotations between annotators)[4] (Miletic et al., 2020). The values stabilized around 0.87 for Cohen's *kappa* and 88% for the agreement ratio during the last stages of annotation.

	literature	newspaper	encyclopedia	science	blog	TOTAL
Lengadocian	13056	974	3546	776	621	18973
Gascon	1672	2379	-	-	-	4051
Lemosin	1323	-	-	-	-	1323
Provençau	1275	-	-	-	-	1275
TOTAL	17326	3353	3546	776	621	25622

Table 2: Distribution of the TTB corpus content by dialect and by genre

3.2 Adding Gascon, Lemosin and Provençau

In order to enrich the existing Lengadocian corpus with initial samples of other dialects, we draw on the RESTAURE corpus described above. More precisely, we transferred all available texts in Gascon, Lemosin and Provençau to the TTB corpus. The samples contain around 4K, 1,3K and 1,2K tokens respectively. There is less genre diversity than in the Lengadocian corpus: the Gascon sample contains literature and newspaper content, whereas the Lemosin and Provençau sections of the corpus are limited to literary texts. The distribution of content by genre is given in Table 2.

The content in the new dialects was lemmatized and POS-tagged as part of the RESTAURE project, and the initial GRACE tagset was converted to the Universal Dependencies tags. The syntactic annotation method we used is the same one used for the initial Lengadocian subcorpus: we pre-annotated the samples using the delexicalized parsing model trained on French, Italian and Portuguese UD corpora described above and then corrected manually. The manual annotation stage was relatively fast and simple. No significant performance decrease was noted by the annotators[5] compared to the Lengadocian subcorpus. This brought the total size of the corpus to 25K tokens. Table 3 gives some basic statistics for the whole corpus and by dialect. Tables 4 and 5 give counts for POS tags and syntactic labels, respectively, for the whole corpus.

It should be noted that the added samples remain fairly small, especially given their intended use as training and evaluation data for NLP tools based on machine learning, whose performances notoriously depend on the size of the data. This is due to two factors. First, as with many non-standardized varieties that are most often not written, it was not easy to acquire content in these dialects, especially if the licensing issues are taken into account. We therefore worked with the content that was already available, leaving further extensions to later efforts. Second, we wanted to identify promising methods

---

[3]LAS (labelled attachment score): the percentage of tokens for which the parser correctly identifies both the head and the label.

[4]We are aware that both of these measures have their deficiencies: the former is intended for classification tasks and dependency annotation is more complex, whereas the latter does not correct for chance agreement. However, both have been used in treebank building projects (cf. (Uria et al., 2009; Bhat and Sharma, 2012; Urieli, 2013) for Cohen's *kappa*, (Skjærholt, 2013; Voutilainen and Purtonen, 2011) for the agreement ratio) and they allow to estimate the agreement level in the corpus.

[5]The annotation campaign was managed by the first author of this paper, whereas the remaining authors acted as annotators.

for the annotation process as early as possible in order to simplify the work of our annotators. From our experience, this has an important impact on ergonomic issues during the annotation stage.

	All	Lengadocian	Gascon	Limousin	Provençal
Tokens	25622	18973	4051	1323	1275
Types	5786	4191	1333	570	547
Lemmas	4196	3045	1088	474	472
No. of sentences	1522	1113	255	77	77
Mean sent. length	16.83	17.04	15.89	17.18	16.56

Table 3: Annotated corpus information

Tag	Count	Tag	Count
ADJ	1056	NUM	298
ADP	3174	PART	148
ADV	1360	PRON	1915
AUX	671	PROPN	707
CCONJ	769	PUNCT	3706
DET	3560	SCONJ	449
INTJ	90	VERB	3233
NOUN	4468	X	18

Table 4: POS tag counts in the corpus

Label	Meaning	Count
acl	adjectival clause	520
advcl	adverbial clause	379
advmod	adverbial modifier	1224
amod	adjectival modifier	798
appos	apposition	99
aux	auxiliary	350
case	case mark	2661
cc	coordinating conjunction	754
ccomp	clausal complement	174
compound	compound word element	5
conj	coordination conjunct	964
cop	copula	335
csubj	clausal subject	12
dep	dependency	10
det	determiner	3556
discourse	discourse element	62
dislocated	dislocated element	85
expl	expletive element	506
fixed	element of a fully grammaticalized MWE	271
flat	element of an exocentric construction	191
iobj	indirect object	275
mark	subordination mark	803
nmod	nominal modifier	1159
nsubj	nominal subject	1070
nummod	numeral modifier	172
obj	direct object	1382
obl	oblique dependent	1509
orphan	element orphaned by ellipsis	47
parataxis	paratactic element	305
punct	punctuation	3706
reparandum	overriden speech disfluency	5
root	sentence root	1496
vocative	vocative	69
xcomp	open clausal complement	535

Table 5: Dependency labels in the corpus

4 Exploring Methods for Expanding the Multi-Dialect Part of the Corpus

4.1 Evaluation Setup

In order to further enrich our treebank with content in different dialects, we explore several possibilities to improve the quality of the automatic pre-annotation. As stated above, the delexicalized model trained on Italian, Portuguese and French corpora from the UD collection was useful in the first round of annotation. However, given the Occitan content at our disposal, we examined if parsing models trained on the same language (although on much smaller amounts of text) yielded better results. We consider three main scenarios:

1. delexicalized cross-lingual parsing with the model trained on UD corpora in Italian, Portuguese and French;

2. direct parsing transfer with a lexicalized model trained on Occitan;

3. delexicalized cross-dialectal parsing with a delexicalized model trained on Occitan.

The first scenario is our point of comparison, given the fact that it has already been used in pre-processing Occitan texts. The second scenario (direct transfer of lexicalized models trained on Occitan) corresponds to the most straightforward strategy: since all the varieties belong to the same language, a model trained on one of them should be able to process others. In the third scenario, we are looking to investigate if the delexicalization benefits the model by allowing it to abstract the lexical variation or hurts it by the fact that it reduces the amount of information available for learning.

We further refine the second and third scenario by using Lengadocian as the basis for the training corpus, then adding training material in each of the other dialects. This is done in order to evaluate if these additions lend robustness to the model so as to make it sufficient for processing all Occitan varieties or if variety-based parsing should be considered in the future.

4.2 Results and Discussion

Each of the models (9 in total) is evaluated on a test sample in each of the dialects. Train and test sample sizes are given in Table 6. The results are given in Table 7 as LAS and UAS scores[6]. Since the CoNLL shared tasks in 2006 (Buchholz and Marsi, 2006) and 2007 (Nivre et al., 2007), these metrics are widely used in dependency parsing evaluations and can be considered as a *de facto* standard in the domain. In our context (automatic pre-annotation intended for manual validation), both metrics can help estimate the extent of human intervention needed: the LAS gives us the percentage of tokens that need no correction, whereas UAS indicates how much of the tree structure will need no modification. Since correcting the tree structure is more time-consuming than simply changing a syntactic label, if a model has lower LAS, but significantly higher UAS than another, it can be more adapted to our purpose.

For each dialect, the best-performing model in terms of LAS is given in bold, and the worst in italics.

Sample	Lengadocian	Gascon	Lemosin	Provençau	UD
train	17 081	3 635	905	867	912 121
test	1 894	416	418	408	na

Table 6: Train and test sample sizes for each of the subcorpora (in tokens)

The best results for Lengadocian and Provençau were achieved by the delexicalized model trained on a combination of Lengadocian and Gascon, whereas the best scores for Gascon and Lemosin were achieved by the lexicalized models trained on the combination of Lengadocian and the dialect in question. However, the delexicalized model trained on Lengadocian and Gascon was on par with the best performing model for Lemosin in UAS, and it scored second best in LAS and UAS on Gascon. It can therefore be considered as the most useful across the board.

---

[6]LAS (labelled attachment score): see section 3.1. UAS (unlabelled attachment score): the percentage of tokens for which the parser correctly identifies the head, regardless of the label.

Model	Lengadocian		Gascon		Lemosin		Provençau	
	LAS	UAS	LAS	UAS	LAS	UAS	LAS	UAS
Lex_Leng	79.1	88.6	77.2	87.7	80.6	85.6	73.3	83.4
Lex_Leng+Gasc	79.4	88.4	**79.1**	**89.9**	80.6	**86.1**	76.2	86.0
Lex_Leng+Lem	78.5	88.2	75.7	86.8	**81.3**	**86.1**	74.0	84.3
Lex_Leng+Prov	79.0	88.6	77.6	88.0	80.7	85.9	74.7	85.0
Delex_Leng	79.5	88.9	77.9	87.8	80.6	85.4	76.7	85.5
Delex_Leng+Gasc	**80.2**	**89.2**	77.9	87.7	80.1	**86.1**	**77.0**	**86.3**
Delex_Leng+Lem	79.6	88.7	76.7	86.8	80.6	85.4	76.7	85.3
Delex_Leng+Prov	79.0	88.2	77.9	87.5	79.4	84.7	76.5	84.8
Delex_UD	*66.5*	*76.4*	*65.4*	*76.6*	*71.0*	*77.9*	*67.4*	*78.0*

Table 7: Parsing evaluation results

It is also interesting to note that despite the observed non-lexical variation in Gascon, this dialect does not seem to be the hardest to parse. Somewhat surprisingly, it is on Provençau that the models almost systematically obtain the lowest results. It remains to be determined if this is due to the properties of the dialect itself or potentially to the properties of the test sample.

More globally, the delexicalized models almost systematically outperformed their lexicalized counterparts. This seems to indicate that abstracting away from the lexical level allows for better generalization when dealing with different varieties of Occitan. However, this effect could also be due to other factors, such as the limited sample size and some genre variation in Lengadocian and Gascon data. We will therefore repeat these evaluations once the samples are extended. It is also interesting to note that the addition of Gascon seems to make the model the most robust, but this can also be due to the fact that the Gascon train sample is larger than the other two (3K tokens vs around 900 tokens).

Another interesting observation that can be made is that the delexicalized cross-lingual model trained on UD corpora in Italian, Portuguese and French scored systematically the worst, with 10-15 points of difference compared to the best-performing model for the given dialect. It is worth pointing out that the cross-lingual model's training corpus is an order of magnitude greater than for the models trained on Occitan: it contains 912K tokens, whereas the various training samples in Occitan contain between 17,5K and 20,5K tokens. This indicates once again that a small amount of annotated data in the target language can be as useful (or more useful, as we can see here) than a truly large corpus in a related language. This fact underlines the importance of developing data sets for under-resourced languages: even though transfer techniques for NLP tasks are useful, resources in each given language can be particularly valuable in achieving solid processing results.

5 Conclusion

In this paper we presented an extension of an existing Occitan treebank based on the Lengadocian dialect with content in three additional dialects, namely Gascon, Lemosin and Provençau. The resulting corpus contains 25K tokens, it is annotated following Universal Dependencies guidelines and will be made available as part of the November 2020 release.

Our experiments in parsing show that parsing models trained on dialects of Occitan achieve better results than a delexicalized model trained on UD corpora of Romance languages even though the latter is much larger (20k vs 900K tokens). This underlines once again the need to foster development of corpora for low-resourced languages: our results indicate that even a small amount of data in the target language can be expected to yield important improvements. We also observe that delexicalized models trained on Occitan dialects perform better than their lexicalized counterparts. While this is in line with the observed degree of lexical variation across Occitan dialects, it remains to be confirmed on larger amounts of data. On the other hand, contrary to our expectations, the syntactic variation observed in Gascon did not seem to overly affect the models' performance. The most useful model across the board was the delexicalized model trained on a combination of Lengadocian and Gascon content. Thanks to these experiments, we will be able to continue our work on corpus enrichment using a more efficient parsing model. Hopefully, this will further simplify the work of human annotators and allow for faster and easier additions to the treebank, ultimately leading to the creation of robust parsing models capable of processing all Occitan texts.

Acknowledgements

The present work is supported by the EFA 227/16 LINGUATEC Project, financed by the POCTEFA Interreg European funds.

References

Pierre Bec. 1970. *Manuel pratique de philologie romane*, volume Vol. 1. Picard.

Pierre Bec. 1995. *La langue occitane*. PUF, 6th edition.

Delphine Bernhard, Anne-Laure Ligozat, Fanny Martin, Myriam Bras, Pierre Magistry, Marianne Vergez-Couret, Lucie Steiblé, Pascale Erhart, Nabil Hathout, Dominique Huck, Christophe Rey, Philippe Reynés, Sophie Rosset, Jean Sibille, and Thomas Lavergne. 2018. Corpora with Part-of-Speech Annotations for Three Regional Languages of France: Alsatian, Occitan and Picard. In *International Conference on Language Resources and Evaluation*, Miyazaki, Japan, May.

Riyaz Ahmad Bhat and Dipti Misra Sharma. 2012. A dependency treebank of Urdu and its evaluation. In *Proceedings of the Sixth Linguistic Annotation Workshop (LAW 2012)*, pages 157–165, Jeju Island, South Korea. Association for Computational Linguistics (ACL).

Myriam Bras and Marianne Vergez-Couret. 2016. BaTelÒc : a Text Base for the Occitan Language. In Vera Ferreira and Peter Bouda, editor, *Language Documentation and Conservation in Europe*, pages 133–149. Honolulu: University of Hawaï Press .

Myriam Bras, Marianne Vergez-Couret, Nabil Hathout, Jean Sibille, Aure Séguier, and Benazet Dazéas. 2020. Loflòc : Lexic obèrt flechit occitan. In Jean-François Courouau, editor, *Fidélités et dissidences (Actes du XIIe congrès de l'Association Internationale d'Études Occitanes)*, Albi. Centre d'Etude de la Littérature Occitane.

Sabine Buchholz and Erwin Marsi. 2006. CoNLL-X shared task on multilingual dependency parsing. In *Proceedings of the 10th Conference on Computational Natural Language Learning (CoNLL2006)*, pages 149–164, New York City, USA. Association for Computational Linguistics (ACL).

Long Duong, Trevor Cohn, Steven Bird, and Paul Cook. 2015. Low resource dependency parsing: Cross-lingual parameter sharing in a neural network parser. In *Proceedings of the 53rd Annual Meeting of the Association for Computational Linguistics and the 7th International Joint Conference on Natural Language Processing (Volume 2: Short Papers)*, volume 2, pages 845–850.

Teresa Lynn, Jennifer Foster, Mark Dras, and Lamia Tounsi. 2014. Cross-lingual transfer parsing for low-resourced languages: An Irish case study. In *Proceedings of the First Celtic Language Technology Workshop*, pages 41–49.

Ryan McDonald, Joakim Nivre, Yvonne Quirmbach-Brundage, Yoav Goldberg, Dipanjan Das, Kuzman Ganchev, Keith Hall, Slav Petrov, Hao Zhang, Oscar Täckström, et al. 2013. Universal dependency annotation for multilingual parsing. In *Proceedings of the 51st Annual Meeting of the Association for Computational Linguistics (Volume 2: Short Papers)*, volume 2, pages 92–97.

Aleksandra Miletic, Delphine Bernhard, Myriam Bras, Anne-Laure Ligozat, and Marianne Vergez-Couret. 2019a. Transformation d'annotations en parties du discours et lemmes vers le format Universal Dependencies : étude de cas pour l'alsacien et l'occitan. TALN19, July. Poster.

Aleksandra Miletic, Myriam Bras, Louise Esher, Jean Sibille, and Marianne Vergez-Couret. 2019b. Building a treebank for Occitan: what use for Romance UD corpora? In *Proceedings of the Third Workshop on Universal Dependencies (UDW, SyntaxFest 2019)*, pages 2–11, Paris, France, August. Association for Computational Linguistics.

Aleksandra Miletic, Myriam Bras, Marianne Vergez-Couret, Louise Esher, Clamença Poujade, and Jean Sibille. 2020. Building a Universal Dependencies Treebank for Occitan. In *Proceedings of The 12th Language Resources and Evaluation Conference*, pages 2932–2939, Marseille, France, May. European Language Resources Association.

Joakim Nivre, Johan Hall, Sandra Kübler, Ryan McDonald, Jens Nilsson, Sebastian Riedel, and Deniz Yuret. 2007. The CoNLL 2007 shared task on dependency parsing. In *Proceedings of the CoNLL shared task session of EMNLP-CoNLL*, pages 915–932. Association for Computational Linguistics (ACL).

Jean Sibille. 2002. Ecrire l'occitan : essai de présentation et de synthèse. In Dominique Caubet, Salem Chaker, and Jean Sibille, editors, *Les langues de France et leur codification. Ecrits divers – Ecrits ouverts*, Paris, France, May. Inalco / Association Universitaire des Langues de France, L'Harmattan.

Arne Skjærholt. 2013. Influence of preprocessing on dependency syntax annotation: speed and agreement. In *Proceedings of the 7th Linguistic Annotation Workshop and Interoperability with Discourse*, pages 28–32.

Jörg Tiedemann. 2015. Cross-lingual dependency parsing with universal dependencies and predicted PoS labels. In *Proceedings of the Third International Conference on Dependency Linguistics (Depling 2015)*, pages 340–349.

Larraitz Uria, Ainara Estarrona, Izaskun Aldezabal, Maria Jesús Aranzabe, Arantza Díaz De Ilarraza, and Mikel Iruskieta. 2009. Evaluation of the syntactic annotation in EPEC, the reference corpus for the processing of Basque. In *International Conference on Intelligent Text Processing and Computational Linguistics*, pages 72–85. Springer.

Assaf Urieli. 2013. *Robust French syntax analysis: reconciling statistical methods and linguistic knowledge in the Talismane toolkit*. Ph.D. thesis, Université Toulouse le Mirail-Toulouse II.

Marianne Vergez-Couret. 2016. Description du lexique Loflòc. Research report, CLLE-ERSS, Apr.

Atro Voutilainen and Tanja Purtonen. 2011. A double-blind experiment on interannotator agreement: The case of dependency syntax and finnish. In *Proceedings of the 18th Nordic Conference of Computational Linguistics (NODALIDA 2011)*, pages 319–322.

Vulgaris: Analysis of a Corpus for Middle-Age Varieties of Italian Language

Andrea Zugarini[1,2] and **Matteo Tiezzi**[2] and **Marco Maggini**[2]
[1]DINFO, University of Florence
[2]DIISM, University of Siena
andrea.zugarini@unifi.it, {mtiezzi,maggini}@diism.unisi.it

Abstract

Italian is a Romance language that has its roots in Vulgar Latin. The birth of the modern Italian started in Tuscany around the 14th century, and it is mainly attributed to the works of Dante Alighieri, Francesco Petrarca and Giovanni Boccaccio, who are among the most acclaimed authors of the medieval age in Tuscany. However, Italy has been characterized by a high variety of dialects, which are often loosely related to each other, due to the past fragmentation of the territory. Italian has absorbed influences from many of these dialects, as also from other languages due to dominion of portions of the country by other nations, such as Spain and France. In this work we present Vulgaris, a project aimed at studying a corpus of Italian textual resources from authors of different regions, ranging in a time period between 1200 and 1600. Each composition is associated to its author, and authors are also grouped in families, i.e. sharing similar stylistic/chronological characteristics. Hence, the dataset is not only a valuable resource for studying the diachronic evolution of Italian and the differences between its dialects, but it is also useful to investigate stylistic aspects between single authors. We provide a detailed statistical analysis of the data, and a corpus-driven study in dialectology and diachronic varieties.

1 Introduction

Understanding the evolution of a language is a challenging problem. When a language originated? What are the influences coming from dialects and other languages? These are crucial questions that the study of language evolution aims to face.

Natural Language Processing techniques are powerful tools that can support researchers in the analysis of dialects and diachronic language varieties (Zampieri and Nakov, 2020; Ciobanu and Dinu, 2020). There exists several lines of research that approach the problem of defining distances between languages or varieties. Linguistic phylogenetics (Borin, 2013) aim at determining a rooted tree to describe the evolution of a group of languages or varieties. Trees are built based on the so called *lexicostatistics* technique, that takes into account words with common origin to determine a taxonomic organization of the languages. Language distance approaches instead rely on the distributional hypothesis of words and require cross-lingual corpora. Similarity is based on word co-occurrences (Asgari and Mofrad, 2016; Liu and Cong, 2013), or using perplexity-based methods (Basile et al., 2016; Gamallo et al., 2017; Campos et al., 2018; Campos et al., 2020). Perplexity is estimated from Language Models, typically n-grams LMs of characters, trained on one corpus and evaluated on another variety.

Differently from previous work, we consider Neural Language Models (NLMs) (Bengio et al., 2003; Mikolov et al., 2010), that are more robust estimators well known for their generalization capabilities and currently the state-of-the-art approaches in Language Modeling tasks. There is a vast literature on NLMs. Many works also address the problem of character language modeling (Jozefowicz et al., 2016; Hwang and Sung, 2017) or character-aware LMs (Marra et al., 2018; Kim et al., 2016).

In this work we focus on Italian, a Romance language derived from Vulgar Latin. The uniquely fragmented political situation that occurred in Italy during the middle age makes Italian an extremely

This work is licensed under a Creative Commons Attribution 4.0 International Licence. Licence details: http://creativecommons.org/licenses/by/4.0/.

Proceedings of the 7th VarDial Workshop on NLP for Similar Languages, Varieties and Dialects, pages 150–159
Barcelona, Spain (Online), December 13, 2020

variegate and complex case of study, rich of dialects that are still spoken nowadays. We consider a corpus of medieval text collections, with the purpose of easing the research activity on diachronic varieties. Moreover, the dataset can be also a valid resource to study the problem Text Generation in low-data and variegate styles conditions. Similar corpora have been already collected for other languages. Colonia (Zampieri and Becker, 2013), is a Portuguese diachronic dataset of about 5 milion tokens grouped by century in five sub-corpora. In (Campos et al., 2020) they gathered three corpora for English, Spanish and Portuguese.

In summary, the contributions of this paper are: (1) we present a project, *Vulgaris*, that studied a text corpus consisting of vulgar Italian language literary resources, organized in such a way to ease language research, (2) studying the historical and geographical background, the statistical properties of the collected data and its composition and (3) deepening our analysis through a corpus-driven study in dialectology and diachronic varieties exploiting perplexity-based distances. In particular, we introduce Neural Language Models to estimate the perplexity and provide a new indicator, named as Perplexity-based Language Ratio (PLR), to analyse the historical evolution process of the varieties.

The rest of the paper is organized as follows. In Section 2, we describe in detail *Vulgaris*, its composition and we report several statistics on it. Then, in Section 3, we introduce perplexity-based metrics combined with neural language models that are then used to carry out experiments on the diachronic varieties within *Vulgaris*.

2 Vulgaris

The main goal of project *Vulgaris*[1] is the analysis of the diachronic evolution and variance of the vulgar italian language. In order to do so, we collected an heterogeneous literary text corpus, comprehensive of poetry, prose, epistles and correspondence by the most important Italian authors ranging from the dawn of the vulgar language to the Reinassance Age. Henceforth, for compactness, we refer to such data as *Vulgaris*. The dataset represents a fundamental timeframe for the Italian language, including the first steps and diachronic evolutions departing from the Latin language. Moreover, through *Vulgaris* it is possible to gain evidence of the early language fragmentation deriving from the complex historical geo-political context of the Middle Age.

2.1 Hystorical background and families

The earliest years of the 13th century were characterized by a novel and complex civilisation. The rise of medieval Communes, associations among citizens of towns belonging to the same social class, influenced the rise of a novel school of secular thought increasingly unhindered by the religious influences. For these reasons, along with the establishment of the first universities, beside latin literature the vulgar Italian language started to appear in various literary works. The heterogeneous political and geographical context led to a linguistic fragmentation, characterized by various contact points. The first literary evidence of vulgar poetic, which we denote as belonging to the **Archaic text** family, is a collection of verses still connected with religious and moral themes, written in regions of the central Italy, in particular Umbria and Tuscany. Amongst the main authors, we mention *Francesco d'Assisi*. Inspired by this works, in the middle of the century (about 1250) some vulgar authors (e.g. *Jacopone da Todi* et al.), in the same geographical zone, composed several **Laude**, enriching the religious and mystical poetry theme.

The **Northern Didactic poetry** family, flourished in the same years, was influenced by these religious and moral guidelines. We point out *Bonvesin da la Riva* from Milan and *Giacomino da Verona* among the representatives, having the goal to instruct readers about morality, philosophy and doctrine.

The prosperous and thriving Imperial court of Federico II fostered the birth of a **Sicilian School** (1230-1250), where the figure of an angelic woman and the stereotype of love play a central role. This group laid the foundations of modern poetry, introducing a specific metric and organization in *Stanzas*, creating Sonnets and unifying the language lexicon and structure. Among the authors we highlight *Giacomo da Lentini* and *Pier della Vigna*.

---

[1]The project is available at `https://sailab.diism.unisi.it/vulgaris/`.

With the death of Federico II, the cultural axis moved to Tuscany, thanks to the proliferation of Communes. Differently from the Sicilian School we cannot talk of a unique literary school. Indeed, in several important cities, such as Pisa, Lucca, Arezzo, Siena, other than Florence, which became only afterwards the most important cultural center, emerged themes inspired by the Sicilian similar ones.

The **Northern/Tuscan Courtly poetry** arises from poets belonging to the Sicilian school who moved after the decadence of the Svevian Empire, influencing the themes and style of local authors (*Guittone D'Arezzo, Bonagiunta Orbicciani, Compiuta Donzella*). In the meanwhile, **Central Italy Didactic poetry** (*Brunetto Latini*) and **Realistic Tuscan poetry** (*Cecco Angiolieri, Folgòre da San Gimignano, Cenne de la Chitarra*) emerged, differentiated by the themes, goal of the poetry, and style. Departing from the literature inspired by court life, a more popular and playful genre, the **Folk and Giullaresca Poetry**, was mainly due to jesters such as *Ruggieri Apuliese*.

Finally, thanks to the influence of Sicilian School and Tuscan poetry, the **Stilnovisti** family (*Guido Guinizzelli, Dante Alighieri, Guido Cavalcanti, Lapo Gianni, Gianni Alfani, Dino Frescobaldi, Cino da Pistoia*) and some authors close to them (**Similar to Stilnovisti** - *Lippo Pasci de Bardi*) evolved and refined the poetry of their predecessors. Metaphors, a noble symbolism and introspection characterize this movement, which was born in Bologna and developed in Florence reaching its climax.

Boccaccio and **Petrarca** compose, together with Dante, the three *Crowns* of Italian literature. Their poetry and prose are inspired by *Dolce Stil Novo*, with an evolution toward a more wordily thematic, rather than spiritual. Their linguistic style is the offspring of an evolved society.

The works developed by these families highly influenced following authors. In particular, **Ariosto** and **Tasso**, at the beginning of the 16th century, were deeply inspired by Petrarca and the Stilnovisti, respectively. However, their different temporal context was reflected in their literary works.

Therefore, the vulgar Italian language, starting from the beginning of the 13th century, became more and more popular amongst various authors, evolving during the following years in several families, which we summarize in Fig.1. The highly fragmented geo-political context gave rise to different schools, groups, communities (depicted in Fig. 1) and hence many language varieties, dialects, that even nowadays are noticeable.

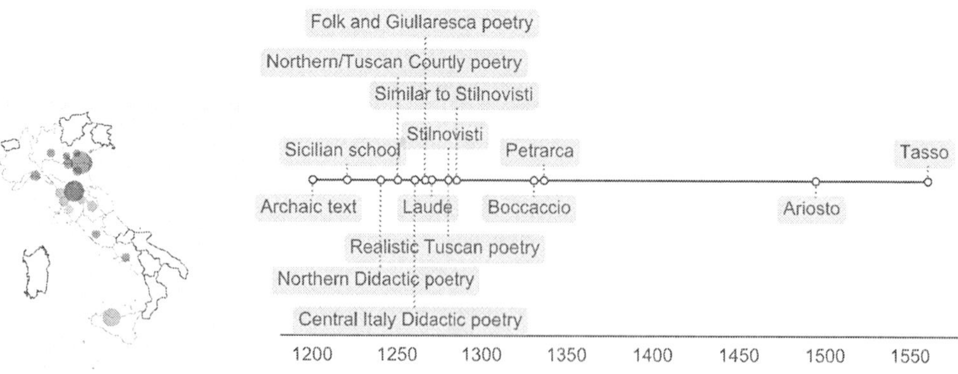

Figure 1: On the left side, a geographical map of the Italian peninsula with the biggest cultural centers marked (the map is attributed to https://freevectormaps.com/italy/IT-EPS-01-0004). On the right, a timeline representing the temporal sequence of the different families we described in the main text.

Through the Vulgaris project, we aim to provide a rich resource to analyze the diachronic evolution of the early Italian language, in particular in poetry, prose and correspondence texts.

Family	Authors	#Texts	#Poetry	#Prose
Archaic text	Francesco d'Assisi, Ritmo Laurenziano, Ritmo Cassinese	5	5	-
Sicilian School	Giacomo da Lentini, Guido delle Colonne, Pier della Vigna, Pronotaro da Messina	46	46	-
Northern Didactic poetry	Girardo Patecchio Da Cremona, Bonvesin Da La Riva, Giacomino Da Verona, Anonimo Genovese	29	29	-
Northern/Tuscan Courtly poetry	Guittone D'Arezzo, Bonagiunta Orbicciani, Chiaro Davanzati, Monte Andrea Da Firenze	101	101	-
Central Italy Didactic poetry	Brunetto Latini,Garzo, Detto Del Gatto Lupesco Dal Bestiario Moralizzato Di Gubbio	8	8	-
Folk and Giullaresca poetry	Ruggieri Apugliese, Castra Fiorentino, Matazone Da Caligano, Rime Dei Memoriali Bolognesi	23	23	-
Laude	Jacopone Da Todi, Laude Cortonesi, Lauda Dei Servi Della Vergine	41	41	-
Stilnovisti	Guido Guinizzelli, Guido Cavalcanti, Cino da Pistoia, Dante Alighieri, Lapo Gianni	769	704	65
Realistic Tuscan poetry	Rustico Filippi, Cecco Angiolieri, Folgore da San Gimignano, Cenne de la Chitarra	69	69	-
Similar to Stilnovisti	Dante's Friend, Lippo Pasci de' Bardi	709	70	-
Boccaccio	-	1058	296	762
Petrarca	-	872	747	125
Ariosto	-	363	144	219
Tasso	-	3366	1604	1762
Total	-	6820	3887	2933

Table 1: Analysis of the composition of the dataset. We report the families, their most representative authors, total number of provided texts and their distribution in poetry and prose.

2.2 Dataset structure

The examined corpus contains texts retrieved from Biblioteca Italiana[2], a digital library project collecting the most significant texts of the Italian literature, ranging from the Middle Age to the 20th century. The code to retrieve and analyse the data can be found in `https://github.com/sailab-code/vulgaris`. *Vulgaris* provides the following filtered type of information, extracted from the parsed data: **author, title, collection, family, type, text**. In details, the corpus is composed by **text** produced by 104 **authors** belonging to the 14 **families** described in Section 2. The corpus contains 177 *collections*, consisting of groups of poetry, single poems, personal epistles. Each item of the dataset is a single composition, for instance a poetry, a chapter or a letter. Moreover, we split the resources by the **style** attribute into *poetry* and *prose*, with the latter containing the both the prose and correspondence documents.

The structure of a poetic composition represents an important information in tasks such as Poem Generation (Lau et al., 2018; Zugarini et al., 2019; Zhang and Lapata, 2014). The verse organization of the poetry is encoded by tags denoting each line break <EOL> (end of a verse), as well as the end of each stanza <EOS>. In the case of prose, only the organization in paragraphs is represented by the tag <EOS>.

In Table 1 we report some statistics on the families (first column, ordered by date), including their most representative authors (second column), the total amount of collected texts, divided into poetry and prose (third, fourth and fifth column, respectively). Whilst the older families are underrepresented, families belonging to a later period are mostly characterized by a larger amount of texts. This fact is a good indicator of the diffusion that the Italian language has undergone during this timeline.

The corpus investigated in *Vulgaris* is extremely heterogeneous and composed by 4 million word

---

[2]`http://bibliotecaitaliana.it/`

occurrences, whose texts have been written by authors from a wide range of geographical regions and time periods, as shown in Figure 1. In Table 2 we summarize some statistics on the total amount of word occurrences, the number of unique words and the average occurrences per word for each text **type**. The total number of words in poetry and prose is almost balanced, whereas their composition is remarkably different. Indeed, poetry has a richer lexicon than prose, containing almost twice unique words.

To depict the contribution of each family to the dataset, Figure 2 reports the total number of word occurrences for each family and the poetry/prose proportion. Once more, these statistics confirm the increasing spread of the Italian language. We can also notice how vulgar spread. Initially, it was mainly used in poetry and only later vulgar prosaic forms appeared. Only 5 out of 14 families contain prose, and, as we can see from the timeline in Fig. 1, they correspond to the latest families.

	Global	*Poetry*	*Prose*
# word occurrences	4090166	1925838	2164328
# unique words	180450	136195	69135
Avg occurrences per word	22.67	14.14	31.31

Table 2: Statistics on words for each text category.

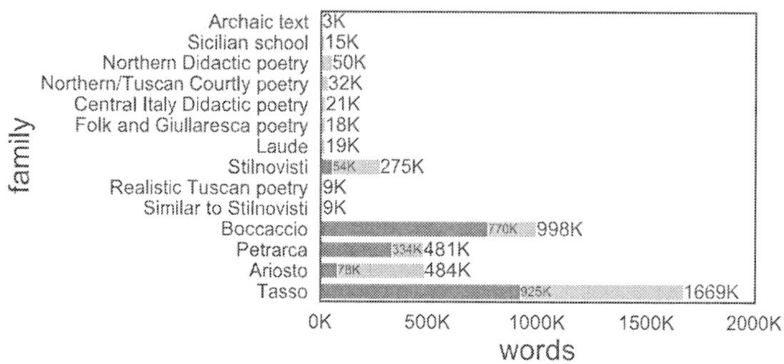

Figure 2: The figure reports the total amount of word occurrences for each family (both in poetry and prose), at the right of each family bin. The darker blue bar denotes the portion of word occurrences in prose texts only.

Finally, in the top row of Fig. 3, we report the average distribution of the text length, in both the styles (i.e, *poetry* on the left and *prose* on the right) among all the families. The bottom row of Fig. 3 shows the average number of words contained in each collection, hence texts having similar characteristics or theme.

3 Analysis of Language Varieties in Vulgaris

Vulgaris texts span over a time period of about four centuries. The diachronic varieties within the dataset are measured in terms of perplexity-based distances, taking into account the different centuries as a reference for the comparison.

3.1 Perplexity-based Language Distance

The quality of a Language Model (LM) is assessed in terms of perplexity. A good estimation by a language model for a given corpus will yield low perplexity values. LMs and perplexity have been already exploited to provide a distance between language corpora (Gamallo et al., 2017), and this approach has been effectively applied for language discrimination and the analysis of historical varieties (Campos et al., 2018; Campos et al., 2020).

Let us consider two language corpora, namely $L1$ and $L2$, and let LM_{L1}, LM_{L2} be two language models trained on $L1$ and $L2$, respectively. We can argue that the more the corpora are related to each other,

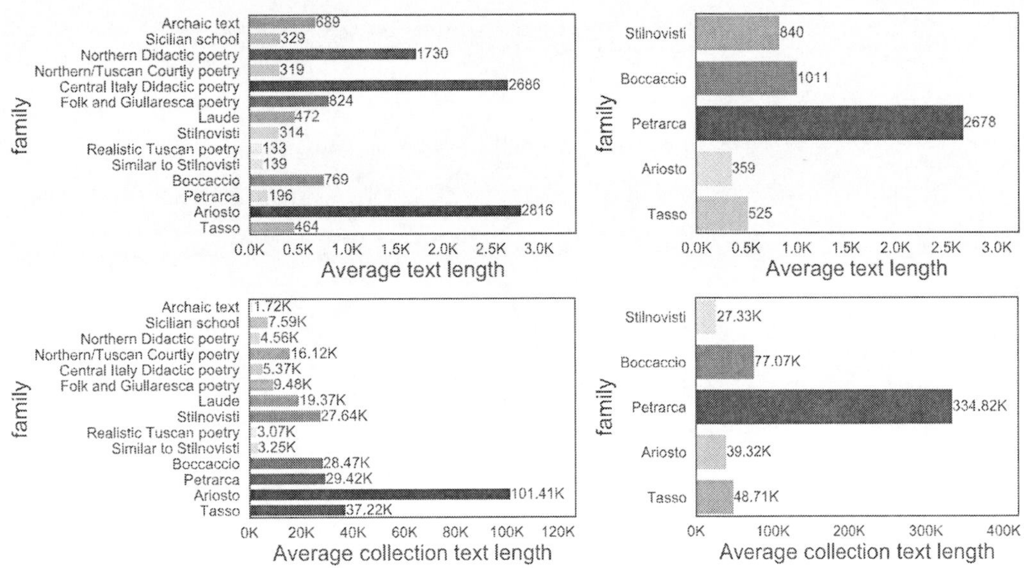

Figure 3: In the top row, the average text length of poetry (left) and prose (right) texts. On the bottom, average number of words contained in each collection in poetry (left) and prose (right).

the more accurate is the estimate provided by the LM trained on one language when evaluated on the other. By denoting the two measures of perplexity as $pp_{L1 \to L2}(L2, \text{LM}_{L1})$ and of $pp_{L2 \to L1}(L1, \text{LM}_{L2})$, the Perplexity-based Language Distance (PLD) is defined in (Gamallo et al., 2017) as the average of these two values:

$$PLD(L1, L2) = \frac{pp_{L1 \to L2}(L2, \text{LM}_{L1}) + pp_{L2 \to L1}(L1, \text{LM}_{L2})}{2}. \tag{1}$$

This metric copes with the fact that $pp_{L1 \to L2}(L2, \text{LM}_{L1})$ and $pp_{L2 \to L1}(L1, \text{LM}_{L2})$ are not symmetric, mostly because LMs are trained and tested on different data distributions. However, the asymmetry in these values can be a good indicator of the language evolution on diachronic/dialect varieties, since it can enlighten either a language compression/simplification or a language expansion over time. Indeed, in the process of language unification, words are reduced, and dialectal expressions are suppressed, thus reducing the overall richness of the language. Hence, we consider also the following Perplexity-based Language Ratio (PLR):

$$PLR(L1, L2) = \frac{pp_{L1 \to L2}(L2, \text{LM}_{L1})}{pp_{L2 \to L1}(L1, \text{LM}_{L2})}. \tag{2}$$

PLR values greater than 1 indicate that $L1$ is likely to be a more various language than $L2$, whereas values less than 1 are likely to indicate $L2$ as the more complex language.

3.2 Conditional Language Modeling

In this section we briefly describe the structure of the language models that have been exploited in the experimental evaluation. Let us consider a sequence of tokens $x = (x_1, \ldots, x_n)$ from a text corpus. The following description is general for any sequence of tokens x regardless their kind, e.g. words, characters or any token piece. The goal of the LM is to estimate the joint probability $p(x)$, that is factorized with the product of conditional probabilities as follows,

$$p(x) = \prod_{i=1}^{m} p(x_i | x_{i-1}, \ldots, x_1), \tag{3}$$

A Neural Language Model (NLM) (Bengio et al., 2003) estimates the conditional probability $p(x_i | x_{i-1}, \ldots, x_1)$ in Equation (3) with a Neural Network. We extend Equation (3) by adding other

Figure 4: Two dimensional t-SNE representation of sentences' state h_T. Different colours indicate different groups, dots for poetry, crosses for prose.

features of the text to condition the NLM. In particular, we leverage the external meta information about author a, family f and kind of composition k (prose or poetry) available in the dataset. Hence Equation (3) becomes:

$$p(\boldsymbol{x}) = \prod_{i=1}^{m} p(x_i | x_{i-1}, \ldots, x_1, a, f, k). \tag{4}$$

We model the distribution in Equation 4 by means of a recurrent neural network. Each token from the vocabulary V of size $|V|$ is associated to a latent embedding e of dimension d. The set of the $|V|$ embeddings are collected in the $|V| \times d$ matrix $\mathbf{E}$. In particular, we consider an LSTM cell (Hochreiter and Schmidhuber, 1997) to model the internal recurrent state of the network. At time t the state $\boldsymbol{h}_t$ is updated as follows,

$$\boldsymbol{h}_t = \text{LSTM}(\boldsymbol{e}_t, \boldsymbol{h}_{t-1}), \tag{5}$$

The external features (a, f, k) are concatenated to $\boldsymbol{h}_t$ and then linearly projected into a d-dimensional vector $\boldsymbol{s}_t$:

$$\boldsymbol{c}_t = [\boldsymbol{h}_t \circ \boldsymbol{a} \circ \boldsymbol{f} \circ \boldsymbol{k}],$$
$$\boldsymbol{s}_t = W \cdot \boldsymbol{c}_t + b,$$

where $\circ$ is the concatenation operator, and $\boldsymbol{a}, \boldsymbol{f}, \boldsymbol{k}$ the embedding representations associated to author a, family f and kind k, respectively. The probability distribution $\hat{\boldsymbol{y}}_t$ is the output of a softmax layer sharing the weights of the input embeddings to apply a back-projection of the contextual state $\boldsymbol{s}_t$ into the vocabulary space:

$$\boldsymbol{o}_t = \mathbf{E}^T \cdot \boldsymbol{s}_t,$$
$$\hat{\boldsymbol{y}}_t = \text{softmax}(\boldsymbol{o}_t).$$

The PLD and PLR are estimated exploiting this conditional neural language model where input tokens are characters. We chose NLMs over n-grams because of their notorious generalization capabilities. More robust LMs estimation will improve the quality of the PLD and PLR measures. The same kind of architecture is used to build and visualize the sequence representations shown in Fig. 4, learnt from a word-based language model on the entire *Vulgaris*.

3.3 Diachronic Variety

The 14 families of *Vulgaris* are arranged in four language corpora, based on their time periods, as shown in Fig. 1. The first group, referred to as XIII, includes all the families belonging to the 13th century. In this century there are 10 out of 14 families of the dataset, making this language variety the most heterogeneous one, including many authors from different areas of the Italian territory. In the second one (XIV), we consider *Petrarca* and *Boccaccio* families/authors, whereas *Ariosto* and *Tasso* constitute the third and forth corpora, respectively, XV-XVI-1 and XV-XVI-2. Clearly the boundaries are not neat, since the activity of some authors may span across two centuries. From Table 3 we can see that the diachronic corpora are unbalanced. Despite the high number of families and authors, the XIII corpus is the less represented one, followed by XV-XVI-1 that is slightly larger. They both are small compared to XIV and XV-XVI-2. However, XIII is also the dataset with lowest average number of occurrences per word, indicating a high variance of the collection caused by the rich variety of styles and authors.

	XIII	XIV	XV-XVI-1	XV-XVI-2
# words	455583	1480379	484276	1669928
dataset proportion (%)	11.14	36.19	11.84	40.83
# unique words	57343	73530	42594	72369
Avg occurrences per word	7.94	20.13	11.37	23.08

Table 3: Number of words and proportions of the four diachronic groups.

As a first qualitative analysis, we trained a word-based conditional NLM on the entire corpus, using a vocabulary of 50000 words. The final cell state h_T of a text sequence $x = (x_1, \cdots, x_T)$ is projected into a 2-dimensional representation using t-SNE (Maaten and Hinton, 2008). Fig. 4 visualizes the 2-d representation of 2000 examples, colored accordingly to the corpus they belong to, and styled differently in case of prose or poetry works. Prose and poetry are easily discriminated by the NLM. The corpus origin is also captured by the NLM, although not completely, suggesting that the diachronic varieties share a similar structure.

Then, both the PLD and the PLR described in Subsection 3.2 are computed for each pair of corpora. For the character LMs, we consider input character sequences with a maximum length of 50. The state h_t has size 256, with (a, f, k) of size 16, 16 and 32, respectively. Special tokens delimiting end of sentence, end of verse and white space are included in the vocabulary of characters. For each $L_i \rightarrow L_j$, the network is trained on 90% of the L_i corpus, whereas the remaining 10% is used for early stopping, and it is finally evaluated on the whole L_j.

	XIII	XIV	XV-XVI-1	XV-XVI-2
XIII	3.90	5.38	5.99	6.08
XIV	5.38	3.52	4.76	4.65
XV-XVI-1	5.99	4.76	3.30	4.47
XV-XVI-2	6.08	4.65	4.47	3.28

Table 4: PLD among pairs of diachronic language varieties.

Results are shown in tables 4 and 5. PLD is lower in diachronic varieties closer in time, as expected. Interestingly enough, PLR highlights a strong asymmetric behaviour on perplexity pairs involving the set XIII. Indeed, while training a language model on a heterogeneous corpus, as it is XIII, makes the LM well performing when testing on simpler varieties, a language model trained on a poorer corpus underperforms when evaluating it on a richer corpus, as XIII.

	XIII	XIV	XV-XVI-1	XV-XVI-2
XIII	1.00	0.81	0.65	0.72
XIV	**1.23**	1.00	0.86	0.95
XV-XVI-1	**1.53**	1.16	1.00	1.14
XV-XVI-2	**1.39**	1.05	0.88	1.00

Table 5: PLR among pairs of diachronic language varieties.

4 Conclusions

In this paper we described *Vulgaris*, a project that analyzes a collection of literary texts covering the production of Italian authors mainly from the middle age. The dataset contains both poetry and prose, and each document is enriched by metadata that provide both information on the text characteristics and structure (the verse and stanza organization for poems and the paragraph splitting for prose). A preliminary analysis on the dataset by means of both simple statistics and perplexity–based measures gives some insights on the main feature of the collection that reflects the complexity and diachronic properties of Italian language in the early stages of its birth.

References

Ehsaneddin Asgari and Mohammad RK Mofrad. 2016. Comparing fifty natural languages and twelve genetic languages using word embedding language divergence (weld) as a quantitative measure of language distance. *arXiv preprint arXiv:1604.08561*.

Pierpaolo Basile, Annalina Caputo, Roberta Luisi, and Giovanni Semeraro. 2016. Diachronic analysis of the italian language exploiting google ngram. *CLiC it*, page 56.

Yoshua Bengio, Réjean Ducharme, Pascal Vincent, and Christian Jauvin. 2003. A neural probabilistic language model. *Journal of machine learning research*, 3(Feb):1137–1155.

Lars Borin. 2013. The why and how of measuring linguistic differences. *Approaches to measuring linguistic differences, Berlin, Mouton de Gruyter*, pages 3–25.

José Ramom Pichel Campos, Pablo Gamallo, and Iñaki Alegria. 2018. Measuring language distance among historical varieties using perplexity. application to european portuguese. In *Proceedings of the Fifth Workshop on NLP for Similar Languages, Varieties and Dialects (VarDial 2018)*, pages 145–155.

José Ramom Pichel Campos, Pablo Gamallo Otero, and Iñaki Alegria Loinaz. 2020. Measuring diachronic language distance using perplexity: Application to english, portuguese, and spanish. *Natural Language Engineering*, 26(4):433–454.

Alina Maria Ciobanu and Liviu P Dinu. 2020. Automatic identification and production of related words for historical linguistics. *Computational Linguistics*, 45(4):667–704.

Pablo Gamallo, José Ramom Pichel Campos, and Inaki Alegria. 2017. A perplexity-based method for similar languages discrimination. In *Proceedings of the fourth workshop on NLP for similar languages, varieties and dialects (VarDial)*, pages 109–114.

Sepp Hochreiter and Jürgen Schmidhuber. 1997. Long short-term memory. *Neural computation*, 9(8):1735–1780.

Kyuyeon Hwang and Wonyong Sung. 2017. Character-level language modeling with hierarchical recurrent neural networks. In *Acoustics, Speech and Signal Processing (ICASSP), 2017 IEEE International Conference on*, pages 5720–5724. IEEE.

Rafal Jozefowicz, Oriol Vinyals, Mike Schuster, Noam Shazeer, and Yonghui Wu. 2016. Exploring the limits of language modeling. *arXiv preprint arXiv:1602.02410*.

Yoon Kim, Yacine Jernite, David Sontag, and Alexander M Rush. 2016. Character-aware neural language models. In *AAAI*, pages 2741–2749.

Jey Han Lau, Trevor Cohn, Timothy Baldwin, Julian Brooke, and Adam Hammond. 2018. Deep-speare: A joint neural model of poetic language, meter and rhyme. In *Proceedings of the 56th Annual Meeting of the Association for Computational Linguistics (Volume 1: Long Papers)*, pages 1948–1958.

HaiTao Liu and Jin Cong. 2013. Language clustering with word co-occurrence networks based on parallel texts. *Chinese Science Bulletin*, 58(10):1139–1144.

Laurens van der Maaten and Geoffrey Hinton. 2008. Visualizing data using t-sne. *Journal of machine learning research*, 9(Nov):2579–2605.

Giuseppe Marra, Andrea Zugarini, Stefano Melacci, and Marco Maggini. 2018. An unsupervised character-aware neural approach to word and context representation learning. In *International Conference on Artificial Neural Networks*, pages 126–136. Springer.

Tomáš Mikolov, Martin Karafiát, Lukáš Burget, Jan Černocký, and Sanjeev Khudanpur. 2010. Recurrent neural network based language model. In *Eleventh annual conference of the international speech communication association*.

Marcos Zampieri and Martin Becker. 2013. Colonia: Corpus of historical portuguese. *ZSM Studien, Special Volume on Non-Standard Data Sources in Corpus-Based Research*, 5:69–76.

Marcos Zampieri and Preslav Nakov. 2020. *Similar Languages, Varieties, and Dialects: A Computational Perspective*. Cambridge University Press.

Xingxing Zhang and Mirella Lapata. 2014. Chinese poetry generation with recurrent neural networks. In *Proceedings of the 2014 Conference on Empirical Methods in Natural Language Processing (EMNLP)*, pages 670–680.

Andrea Zugarini, Stefano Melacci, and Marco Maggini. 2019. Neural poetry: Learning to generate poems using syllables. In *International Conference on Artificial Neural Networks*, pages 313–325. Springer.

Towards Augmenting Lexical Resources for Slang and African American English

Alyssa Hwang
Computer Science Department
Columbia University
a.hwang@columbia.edu

William R. Frey
School of Social Work
Columbia University
w.frey@columbia.edu

Kathleen McKeown
Computer Science Department
Columbia University
kathy@cs.columbia.edu

Abstract

Researchers in natural language processing have developed large, robust resources for understanding formal Standard American English (SAE), but we lack similar resources for variations of English, such as slang and African American English (AAE). In this work, we use word embeddings and clustering algorithms to group semantically similar words in three datasets, two of which contain high incidence of slang and AAE. Since high-quality clusters would contain related words, we could also infer the meaning of an unfamiliar word based on the meanings of words clustered with it. After clustering, we compute precision and recall scores using WordNet and ConceptNet as gold standards and show that these scores are unimportant when the given resources do not fully represent slang and AAE. Amazon Mechanical Turk and expert evaluations show that clusters with low precision can still be considered high quality, and we propose the new Cluster Split Score as a metric for machine-generated clusters. These contributions emphasize the gap in natural language processing research for variations of English and motivate further work to close it.

1 Introduction

Current research in natural language processing has a fundamental gap: we lack strong resources for variations of English other than formal Standard American English (SAE), including slang and other dialects. African American English (AAE) and slang, in particular, are both very common genres of modern English, especially on social media. This lack of lexical resources prevents us from creating technology for analyzing dialects like these, which evolve quickly on social media. We already have lexical resources for understanding SAE (e.g., the Dictionary of Affect in Language for sentiment, WordNet for synonyms and antonyms, and ConceptNet for a variety of word relations), but equivalent resources for nonstandard English do not exist (Whissell, 1989; University, 2010; Speer et al., 2018). The small WordNet-like resource for slang, SlangNet, contains only 3000 words (compared to the 150000+ words in WordNet), and there are no resources for AAE at the time of this study (Dhuliawala et al., 2016). To develop tools for analyzing nonstandard English, we need lexical resources that can provide clues about the meaning of new words that appear. We also need approaches for evaluating whether the derived representations are accurate or not.

In this paper, we present a comparison of methods that combine clustering algorithms and word embeddings to group unknown words in the semantic space. We explore the use of agglomerative and k-means clustering on GloVe and Word2Vec embeddings and Brown's clustering on bigrams to create semantically related clusters of words which could then be used in downstream tasks. The overall goal is to create clusters of semantically related words found in two datasets with large amounts of AAE and slang, but we first conduct preliminary exploration on the smaller, more standard Brown Corpus. This corpus gives us a quick way to evaluate combinations of clustering algorithms and word embeddings, given that it uses a standard, formal dialect of English on which our algorithms can produce more directly

This work is licensed under a Creative Commons Attribution 4.0 International License. License details: http://creativecommons.org/licenses/by/4.0/.

Proceedings of the 7th VarDial Workshop on NLP for Similar Languages, Varieties and Dialects, pages 160–172
Barcelona, Spain (Online), December 13, 2020

interpretable clusters. After determining the optimal clustering algorithm and word embedding combination based on the preliminary exploration with the Brown corpus, we use the optimal combination to create clusters of semantically related words found in the experimental datasets.

After clustering words in the Brown corpus, we need an automatic way to determine if the clusters are accurate. We use WordNet synsets and ConceptNet "relatedto" relations as the gold standards for sets of semantically related words and calculate the precision and recall of machine-generated clusters, but we note that even SAE is better evaluated using human judgements. After evaluating these measures for all combinations of clustering algorithms and word embeddings on the Brown Corpus, we decide to move forward with GloVe embeddings and k-means clustering as the optimal combination on the two experimental corpora. The first corpus, TwitterAAE, was collected by the SLANG Lab at the University of Massachusetts at Amherst and slightly resembles SAE (Blodgett et al., 2016). The Gang Violence dataset, collected by the SAFE Lab at Columbia university, is the second corpus; it contains AAE combined with hyper-local slang that make the text especially difficult to understand (Blevins et al., 2016). We refer to the two AAE corpora as the experimental datasets.

By clustering unknown words with related known words, our approach can expand existing resources for automatically learning slang and AAE words. Throughout our work, we learn that established lexical resources like WordNet and ConceptNet need to be augmented to support slang and AAE: these resources are unable to serve as gold standards for words that have never been seen before. We also provide results from human evaluations on subsets of our machine-generated clusters. An evaluation on Amazon Mechanical Turk (AMT) over the clusters produced by the Brown Corpus shows that our machine-generated clusters are of high quality even when precision and recall scores may disagree. An expert from the Columbia University School of Social Work also evaluated a small set of example clusters from the experimental datasets because the Turkers would not be familiar with the slang in these corpora. Our efforts in combining clustering algorithms with word embeddings, automatically calculating precision and recall based on established lexical resources as gold standards, and verifying our results with human annotators show that we have made much progress towards methods for inferring the semantic meaning of slang and AAE, but much work remains to expand lexical resources for these variations of English.

This work makes the following contributions for analyzing slang and AAE:

- Methods for representing new words by clustering them with semantically related known words, which will ultimately help in augmenting lexical resources for slang and AAE,

- Exploration of clustering algorithms and word embeddings for clustering in the semantic space, and

- Automatic and human evaluation of these machine-generated clusters from three different datasets, along with the Cluster Split Score as a new metric for evaluating the clusters.

2   Related Work

Researchers have already started to work on applications of natural language processing for social media and nonstandard English. One approach includes adapting pretrained word embeddings for target domains, like social media. Recently, Chang et al. (2018) generated a lexicon and set of domain-specific word embeddings that were automatically induced from an unlabeled section of the Gang Violence dataset that is used in this work. Han and Eisenstein (2019)'s work on fine-tuning BERT embeddings for Early Modern English and Twitter supports the viability of using domain-adaptive fine-tuning for social media. Costa Bertaglia and Volpe Nunes (2016) propose an unsupervised, scalable, and language- and domain-independent method for learning word embeddings for Brazilian Portuguese. Other unsupervised methods include Hamilton et al. (2016)'s label propagation framework to induce domain-specific sentiment lexicons using seed words and Sinha and Mihalcea (2007)'s graph-based word sense disambiguation. Fine-tuning pretrained word embeddings is a promising foundation for developing completely unsupervised algorithms for semantics. In our work, we focus on simple methods using word embeddings to create clusters of semantically related words, an approach that enables interpretability of results as well as information about the meaning of new words that are just beginning to appear with low frequency.

Advancements in NLP methods related to nonstandard English could inform research in sociolinguistics and dialectology, which typically use other methods (Meyerhoff, 2016). Timestamps on social media datasets also allow for observing and predicting the evolution of language. Robust systems for tracking the appearance of new words, association of new meanings with existing words, and disappearance of old words can help us understand how, when, and why language changes. Eisenstein et al. (2014) show that language evolution in computer-mediated communication reflects geographic proximity, population size, and racial demographics. Stewart and Eisenstein (2018) find that linguistic dissemination is a strong predictor of the longevity of a new word while social dissemination is not. Change in online language is driven by social dynamics and sociocultural influence, and using natural language processing techniques on large social media datasets yields important results for sociological studies (Goel et al., 2016). Along with tracking the evolution of language, our methods can help with the use of word embeddings for lexical discovery (Roberts and Egg, 2018). Our work aims to embrace the constantly evolving nature of language and improve the representation of meanings of new words introduced over time.

3   Corpora and Linguistic Tools

This paper presents clusters of vocabulary from three corpora: Brown Corpus, TwitterAAE, and the Gang Violence dataset. We also use WordNet and ConceptNet to automatically calculate precision and recall of automatically generated clusters. We present example sentences from each corpus below.

Brown Corpus	"He's all right, Craig," Rachel said.
TwitterAAE	Whoever tryna do this tax thing to get more bread let me know
Gang Violence	people just .i.p dis [emoji] [emoji] i

3.1   Brown Corpus

The Brown Corpus is a collection of formal SAE sources printed in the mid-1900s (Francis and Kucera, 1961). The full corpus contains a million words, but we use the fiction subsection, which contains 7,000 words, for preliminary analysis. This smaller dataset mostly contains words that are widely familiar in SAE, making the results more easily interpretable. For this reason, we use the Brown Corpus as a preliminary step to test the algorithms and automatically interpret the results.

3.2   TwitterAAE

The SLANG Lab at the University of Massachusetts at Amherst has developed a corpus of 830,000 tweets (500,000 words) aligned with African American demographics. This work is provided as an extension of previous work done to identify tweets written in AAE based on geo-location and similarity to a harvested sample of tweets verified to be written in AAE (Blodgett et al., 2016). The language in these tweets is more similar to SAE than the language in the Gang Violence dataset and contains less slang, making it an ideal experimental dataset to bridge the gap between SAE and AAE.

3.3   Gang Violence

The Gang Violence dataset is a collection of 5,000 labeled tweets written by Gakirah Barnes, a deceased member of a Chicago gang, and her top communicators on Twitter (Chang et al., 2018). This corpus is an expansion of a previous corpus collected by natural language processing researchers at Columbia University in collaboration with the School of Social Work, and research assistants from Chicago neighborhoods with high rates of violence confirmed that much of the language in the corpus differed from SAE (Blevins et al., 2016). Along with giving different meanings to words already seen in SAE resources (such as "ion" as an abbreviation for "I don't" instead of a type of atom), the authors of the tweets create new words at a rapid pace to describe recently occurring events. The high rate of unknown words and familiar dialect of English make this corpus a challenging one to parse, but it will also serve as an interesting extension of TwitterAAE.

3.4   WordNet and ConceptNet

WordNet is a lexical database for English nouns, verbs, adjectives, and adverbs, which are grouped into synsets for each sense of the word (University, 2010). Synsets are composed of synonyms, or words that denote the same concept and are interchangeable in different contexts. Synsets are linked by a small number of conceptual relations. ConceptNet, on the other hand, is a crowd-sourced multilingual knowledge graph that expands on conceptual relations (Speer et al., 2018). We use the "relatedto" relation to construct the gold cluster of semantically similar words; because "relatedto" is a more general relation than synonym, the ConceptNet clusters tend to be quite large. These two tools help us automatically generate precision and recall scores of the clusters we create. See Table 1 for a comparison of sample clusters from both resources.

4   Methods

First, we evaluate three clustering algorithms (Brown's, agglomerative, and k-means) and two word embeddings (GloVe and Word2Vec) on the smaller Brown Corpus for preliminary analysis. We then use the algorithm and embedding (k-means with Word2Vec) with the best preliminary performance to cluster the TwitterAAE and Gang Violence corpora.

4.1   Clustering Algorithms

Agglomerative clustering   uses a bottom-up approach that starts with having each word in its own cluster, then pairwise combining clusters that minimize similarity distance until only one cluster containing the entire vocabulary remains (Pedregosa et al., 2011). In this case, agglomerative clustering seeks to minimize the cosine similarity between word embeddings. This recursive algorithm produces a hierarchy of clusters and allows us to examine any number of clusters from 1 to N, where N is the size of the vocabulary.

Brown's clustering   is a type of agglomerative clustering that uses context to group similar words together (Brown et al., 1992). In Brown's cluster-

	WordNet	Both	ConceptNet
Smile	[None]	smile, grin, grinning, smiling	action, smiler + *89 words*
Blue	drab, grim, Amytal + *36 words*	blue, profane, dark + *6 words*	blow, calypso, windows + *249 words*
Sword	[None]	sword, steel, brand, blade	tuck, sword-bearing + *182 words*

Table 1: The gold clusters from WordNet and ConceptNet are shown in the table above. For a query word shown in the leftmost column, the synonyms in only WordNet, related words in only ConceptNet, and words in both resources are displayed in the next columns.

ing, we use bigrams to account for context and pairwise combine clusters whose words share similar neighbors; Brown's clustering groups individual words together based on context from bigrams. This clustering algorithm can be used to assign words to classes based on the clustering results, which would allow for the categorization of new words in the future. A class can function as the high-level label for a cluster of words. The original work presents classes and clusters built from a 260,000-word vocabulary, such as:

Friday Monday Thursday Wednesday Tuesday Saturday Sunday weekends ...

mother wife father son husband brother daughter sister boss uncle

feet miles pounds degrees inches barrels tons acres meters bytes

Brown's clustering algorithm was able to group words of similar class: days of the week, family members, and units of measure, from the example taken from the original work above. It was able to group misspellings: { *that, tha, theat* } were clustered together as typos for *that*. It also accounts for "sticky pairs," pairs of words that are found in a specific order more often than alone or in reverse order, like *Humpty Dumpty*, *Ku Klux*, *Klux Klan*, and *mumbo jumbo*. These results seem promising, but the algorithm was trained on longer, more formal sources of SAE long before the rise of social media.

Lack of context, especially in short tweets, may pose an issue for Brown's clustering, but this clustering algorithm accepts raw text as input rather than vectorized representations of words. This eliminates one step of preprocessing and makes it a helpful preliminary experiment.

K-means clustering   partitions its input into k groups by randomly initiating cluster centers and determining which words are closest to those centers (Bird et al., 2009). The centers are then set to be the mean of all the data points that belong to the cluster. These two steps are repeated for a set number of iterations or until some level of stability is achieved. This clustering algorithm is well-documented, simple to implement, and scalable to large projects, but it requires choosing k manually and struggles with clusters of varying sizes. Given the variety of language in the corpora, the clusters are not likely to be of uniform size and choosing the number of clusters beforehand requires additional domain knowledge.

4.2   Word Embeddings

Word2Vec   is a neural model trained on Google News (Mikolov et al., 2013). The older of the two word embeddings, Word2Vec represents a baseline for word embedding results. Like GloVe, Word2Vec is context-independent and combines all senses of a word into a single vector.

GloVe   embeddings are similar to Word2Vec, but they are trained on a cooccurrence matrix rather than a neural network (Pennington et al., 2014). Using a context-independent word embedding loses the distinction between different senses of a word but makes the vectors immediately available for downstream tasks. We use the 50-dimensional Twitter embeddings for this task.

BERT   embeddings are the current state of the art, but we do not use them for this work. These embeddings are trained on a context-dependent neural model at the subword level, which makes BERT more robust to out-of-vocabulary words and would be useful for the constantly changing language on social media (Devlin et al., 2019). BERT embeddings, however, separate the different senses for each word, so they cannot be used without the model. The size of the BERT model and embeddings combined with the number of words for each corpus created an extremely high demand for memory that made BERT a poor candidate for this particular clustering task.

5   Results and Discussion

5.1   Preliminary Analysis: Brown Corpus

The first task for this work was to try all of the clustering algorithms and word embeddings on the smaller Brown Corpus and choose the highest performing pair for the experimental datasets. Brown's clustering with bigrams for context history yielded interesting clusters like

> that, as, when, what, which, if, where

> be, have, do, get, go, see, make, take, think, tell, find, hear

but this particular clustering algorithm is incompatible with word embeddings and poorly maintained, making it a weak choice for future work.

The results for agglomerative and k-means clustering varied distinctly in cluster size distribution (see Figure 1). Agglomerative clustering produced unbalanced clusters, with over 20% of clusters containing two words and a couple containing over 900 words. K-means clustering produced much more balanced clusters, with over half the clusters containing ten or less words. Although the results for Word2Vec and GloVe embeddings were similar, we choose to continue working with GloVe because of its faster runtime and availability of Twitter embeddings. Based on these findings, the rest of the experiments are run with k-means clustering and GloVe.

5.2   Sample Clusters from Brown, TwitterAAE, and Gang Violence Datasets

K-means clustering and GloVe embeddings produce highly interpretable clusters of semantically similar words, many of which made intuitive sense. Clusters from the Brown Corpus include

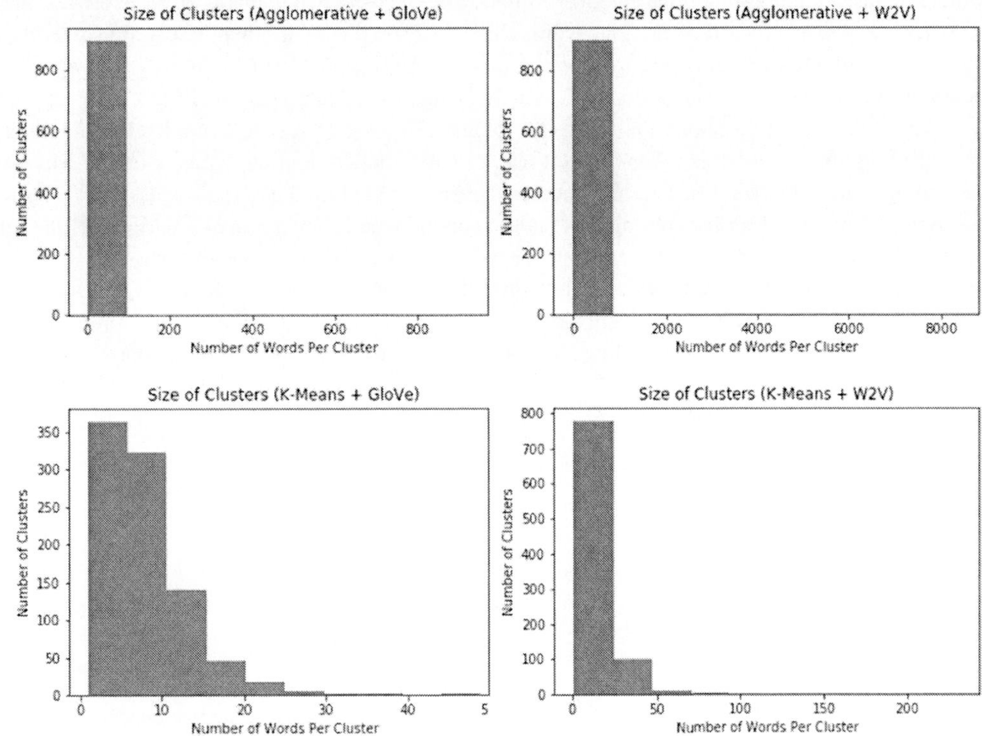

Figure 1: Sizes of word clusters for preliminary analysis on Brown Corpus with agglomerative and k-means clustering and GloVe and Word2Vec embeddings.

1. flashes, rosy

2. apple, blackberry, camera, flash, led, messenger, notebook, opera, telephone, windows

3. alors, chambre, corps, et, fille, fond, genre, lit, merveilleux, oui, petit, petits, plus, pour, repose, tout, week-end

Smaller clusters, like cluster 1, contain little interesting information, but clusters containing approximately ten words show obvious relationships. Cluster 2 contains words related to technology, like the Apple and Blackberry companies; Messenger, Windows, and Opera software; and telephone and camera. In this cluster, *led* may refer to an LED light or screen. Cluster 3 contains French words, including words that have meaning in both English and French like *fond* (Fr: to melt), *genre*, *lit* (Fr: bed), *plus* (Fr: more), *pour* (Fr: for), *repose* (Fr: to relax), and *week-end*. These results may seem disappointing, but this work was in English only and we did not use cross-lingual embeddings. Therefore, we were unable to compute semantic similarity across languages. These French words represent a very small portion of the dataset, which were clustered together as misfits that do not belong in other clusters, so it makes sense that they are seen together here.

Because of memory constraints related to the size of the TwitterAAE corpus (about 550,000 words), the clustering algorithm has to be run in sections. This generates many singleton and two-word clusters, and related words may not have been clustered together if they were in separate sections. Sample clusters are shown below:

4. ads, content, pinterest

5. pinger, iphonee, goom

6. cults, exorcisms, croak

7. lieing, talmbout, trippen

The words in cluster 4 are also familiar in SAE: *Pinterest* is a website that displays creative *content* and *ads*. Cluster 6 is also composed of familiar words that are related to each other. *Cults* are sometimes portrayed as performing *exorcisms*; the word *croak* may not make sense in this context, but it can also be a slang term for death. Cluster 5 contains mostly slang words, like a misspelling of iPhone and *pinger*, which may refer to a phone that receives "pings." The word *goom* is completely unfamiliar, but the clustering implies that it is related to cell phones (reliably determining if this is true is why we still depend on human annotation). Cluster 7 contains even more unfamiliar slang words, like *lieing* (a misspelling of lying), *talmbout* (a shortening of "talking about"), and *trippen* (an alternative spelling for "tripping," which is slang for behaving wildly). These words are related in context but show that the interpretability of these clusters requires domain knowledge on the part of the evaluator.

The individual words in the Gang Violence dataset are very unfamiliar but the clusters produced by the k-means algorithm and GloVe embeddings lend more insight to the meanings of the words:

8. chat, dm, fb, inbox, insta, offline, skype

9. app, etc, facebook, google, instagram, internet, mail, twitter, whatsapp, wifi

10. ils, ont, qui, sont

11. beto, cris, diego, felipe, fran, gabriel, lucas, manu, pedro, rafa, santos, victor

12. bla, cuba, keta, kt, mcm, mmg, mula, ni, nk, pon, pun, tk

Clusters 8 and 9 contain words that are related to social media, but cluster 8 appears to be more slang while cluster 9 contains more formal language. The words *facebook* and *instagram*, for example, appear in cluster 9 while cluster 8 contains the popular abbreviations for the two social networking sites. Cluster 10 contains exclusively French words, a repeat pattern from cluster 3 of the Brown Corpus. This may be a coincidence or a testament to the GloVe pretraining algorithm, but these words are also grammatically related: *ils* is the male plural pronoun for they, and the verbs *ont* and *sont* are the conjugations of avoir (to have) and être (to be) for *ils*. Cluster 11 appears to be a collection of men's first names of Hispanic origin. Cluster 12 is another, more powerful example of the importance of domain knowledge for clustering slang in the semantic space. These words may be slang, abbreviations, or a different language, but it is difficult to tell; current resources like WordNet and ConceptNet are also unlikely to contain much information.

5.3 Precision, Recall, and Unknown Words

The precision (Equation 1) and recall (Equation 2) for each word and cluster are calculated based on WordNet and ConceptNet as the gold standards (see Tables 2a and 2b).

$$\text{precision} = \frac{\text{size}(\text{cluster}_e \cap \text{cluster}_g)}{\text{size}(\text{cluster}_e)} \tag{1}$$

$$\text{recall} = \frac{\text{size}(\text{cluster}_e \cap \text{cluster}_g)}{\text{size}(\text{cluster}_g)} \tag{2}$$

where e = the experimental cluster and g = the gold standard from WordNet or ConceptNet.

These scores are very low and seem to increase for the Gang Violence and TwitterAAE corpora, but this pattern is more indicative of the poor quality of WordNet and ConceptNet for evaluating variations of English than the quality of machine-generated clusters. WordNet is composed of synsets, which means that the WordNet gold cluster for a word is strictly limited to synonyms. Not all related words, however, are synonyms. The low precision scores for Brown Corpus and the Gang Violence dataset show this gap in word relations. ConceptNet expands on word relations and includes words that are "relatedto" a query word, which better captures the semantic similarity we are trying to evaluate. This gives us bigger clusters per word, which causes precision scores to drop and recall scores to rise. Some scores, however, are inflated–which appears to be the case for the experimental datasets–because a large portion of words are not seen in either of these linguistic tools (see Table 3). A word is considered semantically similar to itself, so any word that is not seen in WordNet or ConceptNet would have a gold cluster of just one word: itself. This lack of data causes recall to rise, especially for small clusters.

		WordNet	ConceptNet
Brown	w	0.138	0.246
	c	0.233	0.258
GV	w	0.287	0.561
	c	0.157	0.551
TwitterAAE	w	0.686	0.686
	c	0.933	0.687

(a) Precision values.

		WordNet	ConceptNet
Brown	w	0.172	0.131
	c	0.261	0.142
GV	w	0.281	1.0
	c	0.151	1.0
TwitterAAE	w	0.872	1.0
	c	0.933	1.0

(b) Recall values.

Table 2: Precision and Recall at the word (w) and cluster (c) levels for all datasets based on WordNet and ConceptNet as gold standards.

Because the precision and recall scores depend on WordNet and ConceptNet, and both of these linguistic tools only partially represent semantic similarity or do not contain the query word at all, these scores do not completely indicate the quality of the clusters. WordNet and ConceptNet are excellent tools for other tasks involving standard English, but they misrepresent the quality of clusters of variations of English. Human annotation can help better describe the quality of these clusters.

	Total	GloVe	WN	CN
Brown	6922	0	549 (7.9%)	146 (2.1%)
GV	227223	2	9884 (4.3%)	8492 (3.7%)
Twitter AAE	53642	0	50163 (93%)	32207 (60%)

Table 3: The total number of words in each dataset along with the number of words missing from the pretrained GloVe embeddings, WordNet (WN), and ConceptNet (CN).

6 Manual
Evaluation with Amazon Mechanical Turk

To evaluate the quality of a cluster, Amazon Mechanical Turkers are given a machine-generated cluster of words and asked to split the cluster into subclusters of semantically similar words (a cluster that requires no splits would yield one subcluster: itself). Semantic similarity includes synonymy or relevance in the same context. Red and blue, for example, are not synonyms but they are relevant in the context of colors, so they would be considered semantically similar and clustered together. Turkers were given the following instructions (below) with three examples (full instructions with examples are provided in the appendix):

> You will be given a list of several words. These words will be separated with a space–there are no phrases or compound words. The goal is to group words into as few groups as possible by semantic similarity. Words may be grouped together if they have similar meaning or would make sense appearing in the same context with at least one other word in the cluster. Groups of singleton words are acceptable, but not every cluster should be singleton words.

We also define our own metric, the Cluster Split Score (see Equation 3), for evaluating Mechanical Turk annotations. The intuition is simple: a high-quality cluster would not need to be split into multiple clusters because all of the words should be similar to each other. This can be considered a top-down hierarchical approach. A high-quality cluster would have a low number of splits. Clusters with less than three words are omitted from this evaluation task and 300 clusters are randomly sampled without replacement from the remaining. The 300 clusters are divided into three batches of 100 clusters, and each batch is evaluated by three Turkers. We then take the mean number of splits as the raw score for each cluster.

We instruct the Turkers to perform the task on clusters from the Brown Corpus because these words are more familiar and the clusters are more easily interpretable. Although the task showed only slight agreement (Fleiss' kappa = 0.046, 0.066, 0.084 for each batch), the low number of mean splits indicate that the clusters are of higher quality than the automated precision scores may imply (see Figure 2). This task would benefit from rigorously defining "semantic relatedness" and selecting knowledgeable annotators, especially for tasks including slang and AAE.

After Mechanical Turk evaluations are complete, we calculate the Cluster Split Score for each cluster:

$$CSS = \text{logistic}\left(\frac{\text{number of words}}{\text{number of splits}}\right) \text{ where } \text{logistic}(x) = \frac{1}{1 + e^{-x}}. \tag{3}$$

We divide the number of words by the number of splits because we would like to reward large clusters remaining intact while penalizing clusters being divided. This number then becomes the input for the logistic equation, which squashes the range of the scores between 0 and 1, with 1 indicating the highest quality; this ensures that Cluster Split Scores can be compared for clusters of different sizes and encourages smoother steps between scores. The automated precision and CSS are reported in Figure 2.

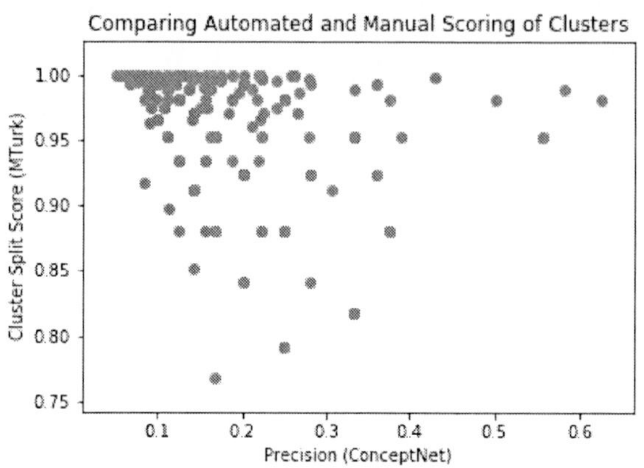

Figure 2: Automated precision scores with ConceptNet as the gold standard compared to Cluster Split Scores annotated by Mechanical Turkers.

We also ask an expert from the Columbia University School of Social Work to evaluate a small subset of clusters from both experimental datasets. Of the 14 Gang Violence clusters, he agrees with the machine generation 4 times and splits the cluster in two parts 4 times, for a mean CSS of 0.96. Of the 12 TwitterAAE clusters, he splits the cluster in two parts 12 times and never agrees with the machine-generated cluster, for a mean CSS of 0.83. The high mean Cluster Split Scores given by the expert show that machines can automatically generate high-quality clusters.

Below, we present sample clusters from the Gang Violence and TwitterAAE corpora with the expert's annotations. Each line shows one machine-generated cluster that has been split into subclusters by the expert. These clusters show many variations of English, like influences from French and Spanish and alternative spellings for existing words. Some words may be completely unfamiliar, which is why we motivate continued efforts in expanding lexical resources for slang and AAE.

Gang Violence	{ harry, mila, naya, malik, louis, payne, lou }, { hacked, dmed }, { lux }
TwitterAAE	{ shootah, bakk }, { hyz }, { bizz }
TwitterAAE	{ hungova, shleeep }, { haself }

If the automated precision scores from ConceptNet and Cluster Split Scores from AMT both reliably evaluated cluster quality, then we would see that precision and Cluster Split Scores are directly correlated. This, however, is not the case in Figure 2. The scores are skewed to the top left, showing that clusters with low precision often receive a high Cluster Split Score. This further shows that current lexical resources need to be expanded to become more inclusive of slang, AAE, and other variations of English.

7   Conclusion and Further Studies

Natural language processing resources lack representation from slang and nonstandard English that would allow us to reliably and automatically evaluate our methods. In this work, we used GloVe embeddings and k-means clustering to cluster semantically similar words in the Brown, TwitterAAE, and Gang

Violence corpora. Mechanical Turk and expert observation showed promise in the quality of automatically generated clusters and that these clusters can reveal semantic relatedness between unknown words. In contrast, precision and recall scores from WordNet and ConceptNet do not currently reflect this.

We can improve this problem by expanding lexical resources for slang and AAE. Automatic clustering with simple parameters already show great potential for automatically learning the meanings of new words. This paper presents tools for automatically and manually evaluating these new resources for slang and AAE that can be created or expanded in future work. Context-dependent training methods for sense disambiguation would make clusters more robust. In addition, another important area for improvement is using domain-adaptive fine-tuning to include words that do not have pretrained embeddings and adjusting embeddings for words that may have taken on a new meaning.

Machine-generated clusters can also be used to track the evolution of language and learn new words as they appear online. This is especially important in the age of social media since new slang terms appear so quickly. Existing words can even take on new meanings; old data for existing words can then affect results if the meaning of the word has changed. The words "terrible" and "terrific," for example, used to be synonyms—our results would certainly be different if we still assumed that.

With improved word embeddings and resources for evaluation, we can build highly interpretable clusters with an algorithm as simple as k-means clustering. These tools will help natural language processing will become more inclusive of all variations of language, not just the formal, standard features that historically gathered more attention.

Acknowledgments

We would like to thank Emily Allaway, Elsbeth Turcan, and Shinya Kondo from Columbia University for their assistance. We also thank the reviewers for their time and helpful feedback.

References

S. Bird, E. Loper, and E. Klein. *Natural Language Processing with Python*. O'Reilly Media Inc, 2009.

T. Blevins, R. Kwiatkowski, J. MacBeth, K. McKeown, D. Patton, and O. Rambow. Automatically Processing Tweets from Gang-Involved Youth: Towards Detecting Loss and Aggression. In *Proceedings of COLING 2016, the 26th International Conference on Computational Linguistics: Technical Papers*, pages 2196–2206, Osaka, Japan, Dec. 2016. The COLING 2016 Organizing Committee. URL https://www.aclweb.org/anthology/C16-1207.

S. L. Blodgett, L. Green, and B. O'Connor. Demographic Dialectal Variation in Social Media: A Case Study of African-American English. In *Proceedings of the 2016 Conference on Empirical Methods in Natural Language Processing*, pages 1119–1130, Austin, Texas, Nov. 2016. Association for Computational Linguistics. doi: 10.18653/v1/D16-1120. URL https://www.aclweb.org/anthology/D16-1120.

P. F. Brown, V. J. Della Pietra, P. V. deSouza, J. C. Lai, and R. L. Mercer. Class-Based n-gram Models of Natural Language. *Computational Linguistics*, 18(4):467–480, 1992. URL https://www.aclweb.org/anthology/J92-4003.

S. Chang, R. Zhong, E. Adams, F.-T. Lee, S. Varia, D. Patton, W. Frey, C. Kedzie, and K. McKeown. Detecting Gang-Involved Escalation on Social Media Using Context. In *Proceedings of the 2018 Conference on Empirical Methods in Natural Language Processing*, pages 46–56, Brussels, Belgium, Oct. 2018. Association for Computational Linguistics. doi: 10.18653/v1/D18-1005. URL https://www.aclweb.org/anthology/D18-1005.

T. F. Costa Bertaglia and M. d. G. Volpe Nunes. Exploring Word Embeddings for Unsupervised Textual User-Generated Content Normalization. In *Proceedings of the 2nd Workshop on Noisy User-generated Text (WNUT)*, pages 112–120, Osaka, Japan, Dec. 2016. The COLING 2016 Organizing Committee. URL https://www.aclweb.org/anthology/W16-3916.

J. Devlin, M.-W. Chang, K. Lee, and K. Toutanova. BERT: Pre-training of Deep Bidirectional Transformers for Language Understanding. In *Proceedings of the 2019 Conference of the North American*

Chapter of the Association for Computational Linguistics: Human Language Technologies, Volume 1 (Long and Short Papers), pages 4171–4186, Minneapolis, Minnesota, June 2019. Association for Computational Linguistics. doi: 10.18653/v1/N19-1423. URL https://www.aclweb.org/anthology/N19-1423.

S. Dhuliawala, D. Kanojia, and P. Bhattacharyya. Slangnet: A wordnet like resource for english slang. In *Proceedings of the Tenth International Conference on Language Resources and Evaluation (LREC'16)*, page 4329–4332. European Language Resources Association (ELRA), May 2016. URL https://www.aclweb.org/anthology/L16-1686.

J. Eisenstein, B. O'Connor, N. A. Smith, and E. P. Xing. Diffusion of Lexical Change in Social Media. *PLoS ONE*, 9(11):e113114, Nov. 2014. ISSN 1932-6203. doi: 10.1371/journal.pone.0113114. URL http://arxiv.org/abs/1210.5268. arXiv: 1210.5268.

W. N. Francis and H. Kucera. Brown Corpus Manual, 1961. URL http://icame.uib.no/brown/bcm.html.

R. Goel, S. Soni, N. Goyal, J. Paparrizos, H. Wallach, F. Diaz, and J. Eisenstein. The Social Dynamics of Language Change in Online Networks. *arXiv:1609.02075 [physics]*, Sept. 2016. URL http://arxiv.org/abs/1609.02075. arXiv: 1609.02075.

W. L. Hamilton, K. Clark, J. Leskovec, and D. Jurafsky. Inducing Domain-Specific Sentiment Lexicons from Unlabeled Corpora. In *Proceedings of the 2016 Conference on Empirical Methods in Natural Language Processing*, pages 595–605, Austin, Texas, 2016. Association for Computational Linguistics. doi: 10.18653/v1/D16-1057. URL http://aclweb.org/anthology/D16-1057.

X. Han and J. Eisenstein. Unsupervised Domain Adaptation of Contextualized Embeddings for Sequence Labeling. In *Proceedings of the 2019 Conference on Empirical Methods in Natural Language Processing and the 9th International Joint Conference on Natural Language Processing (EMNLP-IJCNLP)*, pages 4238–4248, Hong Kong, China, Nov. 2019. Association for Computational Linguistics. doi: 10.18653/v1/D19-1433. URL https://www.aclweb.org/anthology/D19-1433.

M. Meyerhoff. Methods, innovations and extensions: Reflections on half a century of methodology in social dialectology. *Journal of Sociolinguistics*, 20(4):431–452, Sep 2016. ISSN 1360-6441, 1467-9841. doi: 10.1111/josl.12195.

T. Mikolov, K. Chen, G. Corrado, and J. Dean. Efficient Estimation of Word Representations in Vector Space. *arXiv:1301.3781 [cs]*, Sept. 2013. URL http://arxiv.org/abs/1301.3781. arXiv: 1301.3781.

F. Pedregosa, G. Varoquaux, A. Gramfort, V. Michel, B. Thirion, O. Grisel, M. Blondel, P. Prettenhofer, R. Weiss, V. Dubourg, J. Vanderplas, A. Passos, D. Cournapeau, M. Brucher, M. Perrot, and E. Duchesnay. Scikit-learn: Machine Learning in Python. *Journal of Machine Learning Research*, 12: 2825–2830, 2011.

J. Pennington, R. Socher, and C. Manning. Glove: Global Vectors for Word Representation. In *Proceedings of the 2014 Conference on Empirical Methods in Natural Language Processing (EMNLP)*, pages 1532–1543, Doha, Qatar, 2014. Association for Computational Linguistics. doi: 10.3115/v1/D14-1162. URL http://aclweb.org/anthology/D14-1162.

W. Roberts and M. Egg. A large automatically-acquired all-words list of multiword expressions scored for compositionality. In *Proceedings of the Eleventh International Conference on Language Resources and Evaluation (LREC 2018)*, Miyazaki, Japan, May 2018. European Language Resources Association (ELRA). URL https://www.aclweb.org/anthology/L18-1046.

R. Sinha and R. Mihalcea. Unsupervised Graph-based Word Sense Disambiguation Using Measures of Word Semantic Similarity. page 7, 2007.

R. Speer, J. Chin, and C. Havasi. ConceptNet 5.5: An Open Multilingual Graph of General Knowledge. *arXiv:1612.03975 [cs]*, Dec. 2018. URL http://arxiv.org/abs/1612.03975. arXiv: 1612.03975.

I. Stewart and J. Eisenstein. Making "fetch" happen: The influence of social and linguistic context on nonstandard word growth and decline. *arXiv:1709.00345 [physics]*, Aug. 2018. URL `http://arxiv.org/abs/1709.00345`. arXiv: 1709.00345.

P. University. About WordNet, 2010.

C. Whissell. The dictionary of affect in language. 1989.

Appendix A. More Details on the Amazon Mechanical Turk Task

We provide more details on the evaluation task described in Section 6. We ran three batches of evaluations of 100 clusters each, with 3 Turkers evaluating each set of 100 clusters. We had three qualification requirements to help control for English fluency: (1) Location is US (2) Number of HITs Approved greater than or equal to 1000, and (3) HIT Approval Rate (%) for all Requesters' HITs greater than 97. We awarded $0.17 per assignment. See Figure A1 for an example of the user interface.

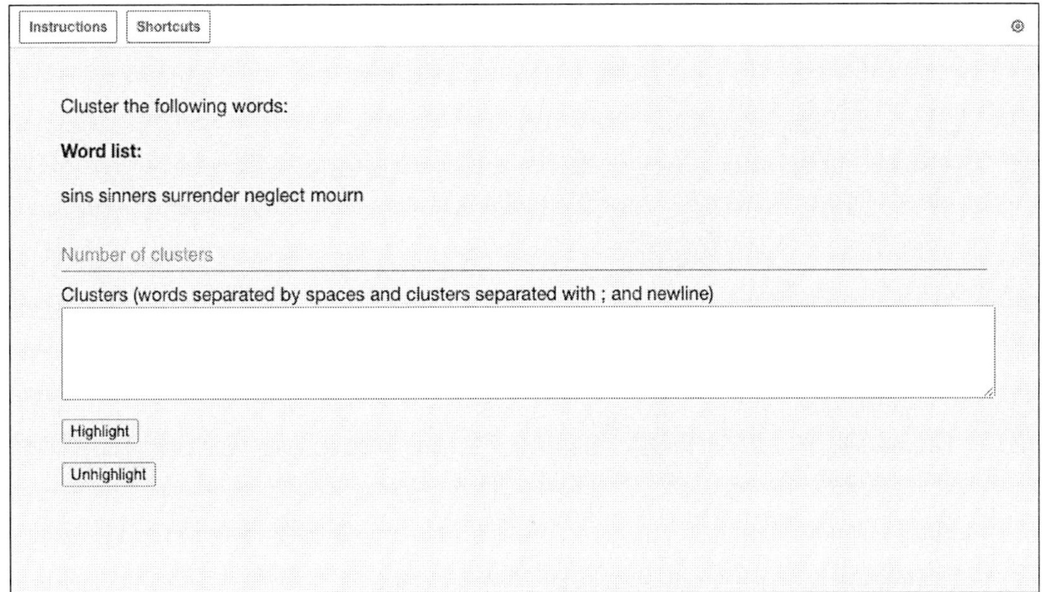

Figure A1: An example of one evaluation task on Amazon Mechanical Turk. We also included a highlight tool to help Turkers keep track of which words they have already clustered.

We provide the evaluation instructions for each task:

> Create the least number of clusters of words with similar meaning. Put a word in a cluster if at least one of its definitions is related to at least one definition of another member word. You can consider a word to be related to another if it has the same/similar meaning (like a synonym) or relate to the same topic. Sword, knife, spear, and arrow are all related to physical weapons, so they can be considered related. **You may cluster words in non-English languages with words of the same language.** You may, for example, cluster bonjour and bien together without considering the meanings of the words in the foreign language.
>
> **This task may contain foul language.**
>
> The list of words you are given will have words separated with a single space. There are no phrases or compound words. Indicate the number of clusters you make and the clusters themselves. **Separate words with a space and clusters with a semicolon (;) and newline.**

along with the examples that accompanied the instructions:

- Example 1

  - **Word List**: apple, blackberry, computer
  - **Clusters**: apple blackberry computer
  - **Number of Clusters**: 1
  - **Rationale**: Since Apple and Blackberry are technology companies and computer is a type of electronic technology, you may group all of these words in the same cluster.

- Example 2

  - **Word List**: bonjour hola oui paris
  - **Clusters**: bonjour oui paris; hola
  - **Number of Clusters**: 2
  - **Rationale**: Since this list contains French (bonjour, oui, paris) and Spanish (hola), you may split the words into two clusters.

- Example 3

  - **Word List**: blue sad red color
  - **Clusters**: blue sad red color
  - **Number of Clusters**: 1
  - **Rationale**: Blue and red are colors, but blue is also a synonmym for sadness, so the words may be grouped into one cluster.

- Example 4

  - **Word List**: shirt pants blanket book
  - **Clusters**: shirt pants; blanket; book
  - **Number of Clusters**: 3
  - **Rationale**: There should be 3 clusters (shirt, pants), (blanket), and (book). A blanket would not occur in the same context as shirt and pants (items of clothing).

- Example 5

  - **Word List**: red orange yellow green blue purple violet
  - **Clusters**: red orange yellow green blue purple violet
  - **Number of Clusters**: 1
  - **Rationale**: These words are all colors, so they can be grouped into one cluster.

Uralic Language Identification (ULI) 2020 shared task dataset and the Wanca 2017 corpora

Tommi Jauhiainen
Department of Digital Humanities
University of Helsinki
tommi.jauhiainen@helsinki.fi

Heidi Jauhiainen
Department of Digital Humanities
University of Helsinki
heidi.jauhiainen@helsinki.fi

Niko Partanen
Department of Finnish, Finno-Ugrian
and Scandinavian Studies
University of Helsinki
niko.partanen@helsinki.fi

Krister Lindén
Department of Digital Humanities
University of Helsinki
krister.linden@helsinki.fi

Abstract

This article introduces the Wanca 2017 web corpora from which the sentences written in minor Uralic languages were collected for the test set of the Uralic Language Identification (ULI) 2020 shared task. We describe the ULI shared task and how the test set was constructed using the Wanca 2017 corpora and texts in different languages from the Leipzig corpora collection. We also provide the results of a baseline language identification experiment conducted using the ULI 2020 dataset.

1 Introduction

As part of the Finno-Ugric Languages and the Internet project, (SUKI)[1] we have collected textual material for some of the more endangered Uralic languages from the Internet (Jauhiainen et al., 2015a). In this paper, we introduce the Wanca 2017 corpora which will be published in the Language Bank of Finland[2] as a downloadable package as well as through the Korp[3] concordance service. The Uralic Language Identification (ULI) 2020 shared task[4] was organized as part of the VarDial 2020 Evaluation campaign.[5] In order to create a training dataset for the shared task, we used the earlier version of the corpora, Wanca 2016[6] (Jauhiainen et al., 2019a), together with corpora available from the Leipzig corpora collection[7] (Goldhahn et al., 2012). Different corpora from the Leipzig corpora collection and a manually verified subset of the Wanca 2017 corpora were used to create the test set for the shared task. We also performed a baseline language identification experiment for the ULI dataset using the HeLI method described by Jauhiainen et al. (2017b).

In this paper, we first introduce some related work and resources for language identification and the Uralic languages in Section 2. We then describe the Wanca 2017 corpora and its creation in Section 3.

---

[1] http://www.suki.ling.helsinki.fi/eng/project.html
[2] https://www.kielipankki.fi/language-bank/
[3] https://korp.csc.fi
[4] https://sites.google.com/view/vardial2020/evaluation-campaign/uli-shared-task
[5] https://sites.google.com/view/vardial2020/evaluation-campaign
[6] http://urn.fi/urn:nbn:fi:lb-2020022901
[7] https://corpora.uni-leipzig.de

This work is licensed under a Creative Commons Attribution 4.0 International License. License details: http://creativecommons.org/licenses/by/4.0/.

Proceedings of the 7th VarDial Workshop on NLP for Similar Languages, Varieties and Dialects, pages 173–185
Barcelona, Spain (Online), December 13, 2020

In Section 4, we give a detailed description of the creation of the dataset for the ULI 2020 shared task as well as the information about the baseline language identification experiments using the dataset. Finally, we provide some error analysis for the results of those experiments.

2 Related work

In this section, we first introduce some previous work on language identification of texts, then we give a short introduction to the Uralic languages and present some of the text corpora already available for those languages.

2.1 Language identification in texts

In this paper, we focus on language identification in texts as opposed to language identification in speech. By language identification, we mean the labeling of sentences or texts by language labels from a given label set, which is the test set-up in the ULI shared task. By defining the problem this way, we have ignored two challenges in language identification: detection of unknown languages and handling multilingual texts. In unknown language detection, the language identifier can be presented with texts that are written in a language that it has not been trained in. Multilingual texts contain parts written in more than one language. Actually, in the strict sense, some of the sentences in the training and test sets of the ULI task can be considered multilingual as they may include some words in languages other than the main language of the sentence. These kind of multilingual sentences are present especially in the corpora for the non-relevant languages. In the ULI task, the target is however, to simply label the main language for each sentence.

A recent survey concerning language identification in texts by Jauhiainen et al. (2019b) gives a thorough introduction to the subject.

2.2 Uralic languages

In this section we provide a general overview to the Uralic language family, with specific attention to development of the written standards and contemporary use, as this is closely connected to the resources available for the language identification task. The Uralic language family contains 30-40 languages, and shows considerable diversity at all levels. Handbooks about the family include Abondolo (1998) and Sinor (1988), and new handbooks are currently under preparation (Bakró-Nagy et al., forthcoming; Abondolo and Valijärvi, forthcoming). The Uralic language family is one of the most reliably established old language families in the world, and can be compared with the Indo-European language family in its time depth and variation, although the exact dating of the family is a matter of on-going research.

Geographically, the Uralic languages are spoken in Northern Eurasia, with the Saami languages in the Scandinavia representing the westernmost extent, and the Nganasans at the Taimyr Peninsula being the easternmost Uralic language speakers. In the south, Hungarian, a geographical outlier, is spoken in the Central European Carpathian Basin. The majority of the Uralic languages are spoken within the Russian Federation. The wide geographical area also has resulted in different subsistence strategies and livelihoods, historically, and also in various contemporary conditions. Only three Uralic languages, Estonian, Finnish and Hungarian, are spoken as the majority language of a country. These languages are not endangered, but they have closely related varieties that often are endangered, as are all other Uralic languages.

Some Uralic languages are already extinct. This is the case with Kemi Saami, which ceased to be spoken in the 19th century, and Kamas, the last speaker of which died in 1989. The former is represented in this shared task as texts written in it were found from the Internet and they are now part of the Wanca 2016 corpora. Still spoken Uralic languages form a continuum also in their number of speakers, as the smallest languages, such as Inari Saami and Skolt Saami, have only hundreds of speakers, and Nganasan maybe slightly more than one hundred (Wagner-Nagy, 2018, 17). On the contrary, languages such as Mari or Udmurt have hundreds of thousands of speakers, and are used actively in various spheres of modern society. They are, nevertheless, endangered due to interrupted intergenerational language transmission and disruption of the traditional speech communities.

When it comes to the online presence, or generally to available textual representations of these languages, historical developments in their standardization and language planning play a very central role. This was largely outlined by Soviet language policy, described in detail in Grenoble (2003). It has also been typical for the Uralic languages spoken in Russia that their orthographies have changed numerous times. Siegl and Rießler (2015) discuss four case studies about the possible variation in the degrees of contemporary literacy and development of the written standards. There are numerous languages in the Wanca corpora for which the ortographies were developed and repeatedly changed in the late 19th or early 20th century. This pertains especially to many languages spoken in the Soviet Union, including Ingrian, Karelian, Livvi-Karelian, Vepsian, Komi-Permyak, Komi-Zyrian, Udmurt, Khanty, Mansi and Tundra Nenets. Even with very closely related languages the contemporary orthographies and the language varieties themselves contain numerous differences in their phonology and spelling conventions that make distinguishing the language of a text almost always straightforward, at least to a specialist. Such closely related languages with clearly distinct written traditions include two Komi written standards, two Mari written standards and two Mordva written standards. These differences are large enough that, from the perspective of computational linguistics, distinct infrastructure usually has to be developed for each variety, even if the actual linguistic differences would be minor. For an example of challenges in creating an infrastructure for Komi-Permyak and Komi-Zyrian see Rueter et al. (2020) and for Mordvinic languages see Rueter et al. (in press).

Some of these orthographies were more successful than others, and there is large variation in when exactly the currently used systems were established and what level of stability they have. For example, the orthography created in 1986 for Nganasan was never widely used, and in the current orthography the conventions vary with author and editor (Wagner-Nagy, 2018). For languages such as Votic, the current orthography was developed first in the 2000s (Èrnits, 2006, 3). An earlier example is Tundra Nenets, which has had the current orthography since the 1940s, and which has all in all 100 titles published. The language is also partially used in local newspapers (Nikolaeva, 2014). However, the small number of Tundra Nenets sentences in the Wanca corpora probably indicates that the online visibility of the language is relatively small. At the same time a relatively small Saami language, Skolt Saami with approximately 300 speakers, is represented in the dataset by thousands of sentences. The Skolt Saami orthography was developed in the 1970s and the knowledge of the writing standard has not reached the whole community (Feist, 2015, 26,37), but the language has been officially recognized in Finland and has received state support, which may explain why it appears to have more online presence than some other languages of the same size.

The majority of the Uralic languages spoken in Russia are nowadays written with Cyrillic orthographies. Exact orthographic conventions differ from Russian, but similar conventions are regularly employed, i.e. to express palatal or palatalized phoneme distinctions. Some languages, such as Erzya, have essentially the same character set as Russian, whereas most of the languages have additional characters. Some of these are shared by numerous languages that use Cyrillic orthography, such as *Cyrillic O with diaeresis*, which is used in Komi, Mari and Udmurt orthographies. There is also the example of *Ze with diaeresis*, which is used only in the Udmurt orthography. For the language identification task these characters can be very valuable cues about the language, but as they are not necessarily present in all keyboards, online texts are also regularly found where they are replaced with other characters or conventions. Finnic languages spoken in Russia are written with Latin orthographies, although historically also some Cyrillic orthographies have been in use.

Thereby the contemporary online presence of the Uralic languages is a complex combination of many historical factors. However, we can generally say that the languages with more widely used and taught orthographies, and with a substantial speaker base, do have enough materials online that downloading up to several million tokens is possible. With smaller languages the situation is different and much more varying. There is also the aspect of time, as continuous use accumulates increasingly larger resources. When it comes to extinct languages, their corpora have to be considered finite.

2.3 Corpora for Uralic languages

For the Uralic languages that are the majority language of a country, that is Finnish, Estonian, and Hungarian, many large text corpora already exist. For example, there is the Suomi 24 Corpus[8] with over 250 million Finnish sentences from a social networking website available from the Language Bank of Finland, and the Europarl corpus[9] with over 600,000 sentences of Hungarian and Estonian (Koehn, 2005). The Leipzig Corpora Collection[10] has texts also for some of the more rare Uralic languages: Eastern Mari, Komi, Komi-Permyak, Northern Saami, Udmurt, Võro, and Western Mari. The Giellatekno research group has three Korp installations for Uralic languages: one[11] for Saami languages, one[12] for Kven, Meänkieli, Veps, and Võro, and one[13] for Komi-Zyrian, Komi-Permyak, Udmurt, Moksha, Erzya, Hill Mari, and Meadow Mari. The Wanca in Korp corpora contain texts in all the aforementioned languages as well as some additional Uralic languages.[14] Several endangered Uralic languages also have treebanks in the Universal Dependencies project.[15] These include Northern Saami (Tyers and Sheyanova, 2017), Komi-Zyrian (Partanen et al., 2018), Komi-Permyak, Erzya (Rueter and Tyers, 2018), Moksha, and two Karelian varieties (Pirinen, 2019). Under construction in the Language Bank of Finland is also the Parallel Bible Verses for Uralic Studies corpus (PaBiVus), which contains Bible translations from different publications.[16]

Especially in the context of this shared task it is important to mention previous work that has collected online texts in the minority languages spoken in Russia. At least Orekhov et al. (2016) and Krylova et al. (2015) have collected online and social media texts in various languages, and Arkhangelskiy (2019) has published corpora of this type for Uralic languages. Wanca 2017 corpora, described next, connects well to the earlier work.

3 Wanca 2017 corpora

The aim of the SUKI project was to find texts written in Uralic minority languages from the Internet (Jauhiainen et al., 2015a). The set of relevant languages was determined as all the Uralic languages included in the ISO 639-3 standard except Finnish, Estonian, and Hungarian. In order to find the texts, we used an open-source web-crawler called Heritrix (Mohr et al., 2004) combined with different language identifiers we were developing during the project (Jauhiainen et al., 2015b; Jauhiainen et al., 2015c; Jauhiainen et al., 2016; Jauhiainen et al., 2017a; Jauhiainen et al., 2017b). In addition to collecting the texts for corpora creation, we built a crowd-sourcing portal called Wanca (Jauhiainen et al., 2019a; Jauhiainen et al., 2020).[17] The Wanca service enabled us together with a few collaborating language researchers and native speakers to easily inspect the web-pages tagged with minority languages by our language identifier. When identification mistakes were found, the wrongly set language labels were corrected manually using the service. In addition to helping us verify the language labels of the downloaded pages, Wanca functions as a collection of links for those interested in the Uralic minority languages. The service is currently maintained as a part of the Language Bank of Finland at the University of Helsinki.

The Wanca 2017 corpora are the product of a re-crawl performed by the SUKI project in October 2017. The target of the re-crawl was to download and check the availability of the then current version of the Wanca service of about 106,000 pages. This list of 106,000 http addresses was the result of several earlier web-crawls, in which we had identified the language of a total of 3,753,672,009 pages. We have listed the crawls with information about their target domains, date, and the number of pages processed in Table 1. In addition to our own crawls, we had identified the language of all the pages in the Common

---

[8]http://urn.fi/urn:nbn:fi:lb-2017021506

[9]https://www.statmt.org/europarl/

[10]https://wortschatz.uni-leipzig.de/en/download

[11]http://gtweb.uit.no/korp/

[12]http://gtweb.uit.no/f_korp/

[13]http://gtweb.uit.no/u_korp/

[14]http://urn.fi/urn:nbn:fi:lb-2019052402

[15]https://universaldependencies.org

[16]http://urn.fi/urn:nbn:fi:lb-2020021119

[17]http://wanca.fi/wanca/

Crawl archive[18] from December 2014 with almost two billion pages.

Name of crawl	Domains crawled	Date	Pages downloaded
SecondFinCrawl	.fi	22.5. – 9.6.2014	353,961,939
SweCrawl	.se	27.6. – 18.7.2014	308,130,342
NoCrawl	.no	2.8. – 23.8.2014	357,512,200
RuCrawl	.ru	7.8. – 4.9.2014	200,839,449
EeCrawl	.ee	10.9. – 14.9.2014	107,806,431
ThirdRuCrawl	.ru	17.9. – 23.9.2014	171,627,896
FourthRuCrawl	.ru	27.9. – 4.10.2014	115,419,359
FifthRuCrawl	.ru	4.10. – 22.10.2014	316,675,966
ThirdEeCrawl	.ee	15.10. – 22.10.2014	102,622,461
LVCrawl	.lv	29.10. – 18.11.2014	161,686,660
SecondNoCrawl	.no	29.10. – 20.11.2014	216,343,115
HuCrawl	.hu	29.10. – 26.11.2014	500,065,403
FinnishCrawl	.fi	18.11. – 26.11.2014	101,788,585
ComCrawl	.com, .ee, .fi, .hu, .lv, .no, .ru, .se	2.12.2014 – 20.1.2015	505,627,335
NLCrawl	.biz, .com, .org, .net	22.1. – 23.1.2015	233,564,868

Table 1: The web-crawls conducted by the SUKI-project prior to the 2017 re-crawl.

The re-crawl managed to download over 70% of the target urls. We processed the downloaded pages following the strategy presented by Jauhiainen et al. (2020) as follows.

First, all the text from each of the 78,685 downloaded pages was sent to a language set identification service we had set up for the task. The service used the HeLI language identification method together with the language set identification algorithm we had developed earlier (Jauhiainen et al., 2015c). The language set identification service used the latest language models of the SUKI project for a total of 399 languages or variants.[19] The code for the language identification service is available in GitHub with a GNU license.[20] We have not published the language models themselves as their purpose has always been to separate the small Uralic languages from the non-relevant languages and then discriminate between them. There are severe problems in discriminating between non-relevant languages, but sorting them out was not in the interest of the project as long as they did not interfere with the successful identification of the relevant languages. The training data for the ULI task will provide a better basis to train models for a language group-independent language set identifier destined for a more general use.

From the language set identified pages, we retained only those which had at least 2% text written in one of the minority Uralic languages. The relevant language that was most prominent was set as the identified language of the page. The retained pages contained a total of 1,515,068 lines and along with the lines, the identified language of the original page was kept. The lines were checked for duplicates, which left 446,233 unique lines. If the duplicates came from pages with different identified language, all those languages were set as the previously known languages of the line. Each line was then again sent to the language set identifier, which was only allowed to consider the previously known minority languages of the line as well as all non-relevant languages. Again only such lines were retained which included at least one relevant language, leaving 356,637 lines.

Next, a language-independent sentence extraction algorithm was run on each line. For this task, we had created a custom implementation of the sentence boundary disambiguation approach by Mikheev (2002) (Jauhiainen et al., 2019a). In total, 560,821 sentences were extracted using the algorithm with 477,109 of those being unique. After this, one more round of language set identifications was performed, this time for each unique sentence. Of the minority Uralic languages, the service was again allowed to consider only those in the list of the previously known languages of a sentence, but this time the absolute majority language of the identification was set as the language of the sentence. The resulting corpora contains 447,927 sentences in relevant languages divided as shown in the Wanca 2017 column of Table 2.

---

[18] https://commoncrawl.org

[19] The language models used in the project were semi-regularly updated using new or manually more checked corpora.

[20] https://github.com/tosaja/TunnistinPalveluMulti

	Wanca 2016	ULI 2020 training	Wanca 2017	ULI 2020 test
Finnic				
Estonian, Standard (**ekk**)	-	10,000	-	10,000
Finnish (**fin**)	-	1,000,000	-	10,000
Finnish, Kven (fkv)	2,156	2,156	1,499	23
Finnish, Tornedalen (fit)	5,203	5,203	4,517	100
Ingrian (izh)	81	81	80	-
Karelian (krl)	2,593	2,593	2,513	94
Liv (liv)	705	705	343	68
Livvi-Karelian (olo)	9,920	9,920	6,486	179
Ludian (lud)	771	771	411	185
Veps (vep)	13,461	13,461	9,122	2,453
Vod (vot)	20	20	11	-
Võro (vro)	66,878	66,878	61,430	443
Hungarian (**hun**)	-	1,000,000	-	10,000
Khanty (kca)	1,006	1,006	940	24
Mansi (mns)	904	904	825	1
Mari				
Mari, Hill (mrj)	30,793	30,793	22,986	18
Mari, Meadow (mhr)	110,216	110,216	38,278	3,768
Mordvin				
Erzya (myv)	28,986	28,986	16,273	1,153
Moksha (mdf)	21,571	21,571	15,170	724
Permian				
Komi-Permyak (koi)	8,162	8,162	6,104	-
Komi-Zyrian (kpv)	21,786	21,786	18,966	254
Udmurt (udm)	56,552	56,552	42,545	3,562
Saami				
Saami, Inari (smn)	15,469	15,469	14,405	228
Saami, Kemi (sjk)	19	19	-	-
Saami, Kildin (sjd)	132	132	59	13
Saami, Lule (smj)	10,605	10,605	5,644	400
Saami, North (sme)	214,226	214,226	165,009	6,009
Saami, Skolt (sms)	7,819	7,819	6,696	202
Saami, South (sma)	15,380	15,380	7,204	355
Saami, Ume (sju)	124	124	4	1
Samoyed				
Nenets (yrk)	443	443	407	58
Nganasan (nio)	62	62	-	-

Table 2: The number of sentences in Uralic languages for each dataset. The names of the relevant languages are in boldface.

4 The ULI 2020 shared task

The ULI 2020 shared task was organized as a part of the VarDial 2020 Evaluation Campaign. The evaluation campaign was the 7th incarnation of a series of shared tasks concentrating on close languages which have always incorporated some form of language identification tasks (Zampieri et al., 2014; Zampieri et al., 2015; Malmasi et al., 2016; Zampieri et al., 2017; Zampieri et al., 2018; Zampieri et al., 2019).

4.1 The dataset for the ULI shared task

The dataset for the ULI shared task consisted of two groups of languages: the relevant and the non-relevant. The relevant languages were the 29 minority Uralic languages listed in Table 2, which were present in the Wanca 2016 corpora (Jauhiainen et al., 2019a). The non-relevant languages were all the other languages for which at least two different datasets were downloadable from the Leipzig Corpora Collection (Goldhahn et al., 2012).

We used the whole Wanca 2016 corpora as training material for the for the relevant languages of the shared task and extracted a test set of new sentences from the Wanca 2017 corpora. The Wanca 2016 corpora is available from the Language Bank of Finland with a CC-BY license.[21] As Wanca 2017 was

---

[21]Helsingin yliopisto, FIN-CLARIN, Jauhiainen, H., Jauhiainen, T., & Lindén, K. (2019). Wanca 2016, source [text corpus].

not a real web-crawl, but only included downloading links already existing in the Wanca portal, it was in doubt how many completely new sentences the test set would have. For the ULI 2020 test set, we compared the Wanca 2017 corpora with the Wanca 2016 corpora and kept such sentences that were only found on the 2017 edition. This set including 25,547 sentences was then checked by us manually. We removed from the test set for relevant languages all obscure sentences as well as sentences that could have been incorrectly identified, concentrating on improving precision over recall. We were left with a total of 20,315 sentences divided between the minority Uralic languages as seen in the "ULI 2020 test" column of the Table 2.

In addition to the relevant languages, the training and test sets include sentences in 149 other languages from the Leipzig Corpora Collection. Following the goals of the SUKI-project, the three largest Uralic languages have been included in this category. The motivation for adding non-relevant languages to the shared task was to simulate the situation we faced when trying to find the texts written in minority Uralic languages on the Internet. For each page of text written in a relevant language we had found, we had identified the language of more than 50,000 pages. This kind of very unbalanced situation demands completely different levels of precision in identifying the relevant languages, when compared with any other language identification shared task so far (Grouin et al., 2011; Baldwin and Lui, 2010; Zubiaga et al., 2014; Solorio et al., 2014; Zampieri et al., 2014; Zampieri et al., 2015; Malmasi et al., 2016; Zampieri et al., 2017; Rangel et al., 2017; Ali et al., 2017; Zampieri et al., 2018; Zampieri et al., 2019). The download links for the training data for these non-relevant languages were distributed by the task organizers only to participating teams. In total, the training data for the task consisted of 63,772,445 sentences in non-relevant and 646,043 sentences in relevant languages, totaling 64,418,488 sentences. The list of the non-relevant languages is available at the Evaluation campaign website and the download links can be requested from the organizers. The Wanca 2017 corpora and the ULI test set will be published in the Language Bank of Finland with a CC-BY license after the shared task has been concluded.

4.2   Three tracks

The ULI 2020 shared task included three tracks. The tracks were not just about distinguishing between Uralic languages themselves, but also distinguishing the Uralic languages from the 149 non-relevant languages. The training and the test data for each of the tracks was the same and in each track every line in the test set was to be identified. The difference between the tracks was how the resulting scores were calculated, which significantly affects how the used classifying algorithms should be trained.

The first track of the shared task considered all the relevant languages equal in value and the aim was to maximize their average F_1-score. This is important when one is interested to find also the very rare languages included in the set of relevant languages. The results were calculated as macro-averaged F_1-scores over the small Uralic languages. In other words, for each of the 29 relevant languages present in the training set a separate recall and precision were calculated, even for those not present in the test set. The F_1-score for each language was calculated using Equation 1,

$$F_1(r, p) = \frac{2rp}{r + p} \tag{1}$$

where r is the recall and p is the precision. If the correct number of true positives for a language was zero, then precision was 100% if no false positives were predicted. If false positives were predicted, the precision was zero. So, for those five languages (Ingrian, Vod, Komi-Permyak, Kemi Saami, and Nganasan) that were part of the training set, but did not appear in the test set, the recall was always 100% and precision was either 100% (if no instances of these languages were predicted in the test set) or 0% (if even one sentence was labeled as one of them). The result was the average of the F_1-scores of the 29 relevant languages. This means that, for example, predicting one false positive sentence for Ume Saami (which has only one sentence in the test set) is equal to predicting 6,009 false positives for North Saami (which has 6,009 sentences in the test set) as far as the results of the track were concerned.

Kielipankki. Retrieved from http://urn.fi/urn:nbn:fi:lb-2020022901.

The second track considered each sentence in the test set that is written in or is predicted to be in a relevant language as equals. The resulting F_1-score was calculated as a micro-F_1 over the sentences in the test set for sentences in the relevant languages as well as those that were predicted to be in relevant languages. When compared with the first track, this track gave less importance to the very rare relevant languages as their precision was not so important when the resulting F_1-score was calculated due to their smaller number of sentences. For example, predicting 6,009 false positives for North Saami in this track had 6,009 times the effect of predicting one false positive sentence for Ume Saami.

In the first two tracks, there was no difference between the non-relevant languages when the F_1-scores were calculated. The results were not affected, for example, if Norwegian sentences were identified as Danish or vice versa. The third track, however, did not concentrate on the 29 relevant languages, but instead the target was to maximize the average F_1-score over all the 178 languages present in the training set. The F_1-score was calculated as a macro-F_1 score over all the languages in the training set. This track was the language identification shared task with the largest number of languages to date (The ALTW 2010 shared task organized by Baldwin and Lui (2010) included 74 languages).

4.3 Baseline experiments

The baseline experiments were conducted using a language identifier based on the HeLI method (Jauhiainen et al., 2016). As a method, the HeLI method belongs to the generative classification methods and is a close relative to Naive Bayes. In the earlier VarDial shared tasks (Jauhiainen et al., 2015b; Jauhiainen et al., 2016; Jauhiainen et al., 2017a), we have successfully managed to compete almost at the same level as the best discriminative classification methods (Goutte and Léger, 2015; Malmasi and Dras, 2015; Çöltekin and Rama, 2016; Bestgen, 2017). In the HeLI method, each word in the mystery text has equal weight when determining the language of a text. Each word is divided into character n-grams, where the maximum length of the character sequences, n_{max}, is determined using the training and the development sets. Other tunable parameters include a cut-off, c, for the minimum frequency of features used as well as a penalty value, p, for unseen features. Instead of tuning the parameters using the ULI 2020 training set, we used the parameters we presented in Jauhiainen et al. (2017b): $n_{max} = 6$, $c = 0.0000005$, and $p = 7$. As we did in Jauhiainen et al. (2017b), we used the relative frequency of features as a cut-off instead of a raw frequency as the training corpora were of very different sizes. Only lowercased alphabetical characters were used in the language models. Due to HeLI using space character to separate words, there was a special 'sanity check' algorithm for texts including more than 50% CJK (Chinese-Japanese-Korean) characters, which gave all non-CJK languages a high penalty. The HeLI implementation used is almost exactly the same as the "TunnistinPalveluFast" available from GitHub.[22]

We did only one common run for all three tracks of the shared task. The results are listed in Table 3.

Track	F_1-score
ULI track 1 (ULI-RLE), relevant macro F_1	0.8004
ULI track 2 (ULI-RSS), relevant micro F_1	0.9632
ULI track 3 (ULI-178), macro F_1	0.9252

Table 3: The results of the baseline language identification experiments using the HeLI method.

Table 4 displays a confusion matrix showing two of the worst performing languages on Track 1: Ingrian and Votic. There were no real instances of Ingrian in the test set, but our baseline-identifier had identified three sentences of Ludian and one sentence of Karelian as Ingrian. These three languages are all closely related, but also one sentence of Sundanese was identified as Ingrian. The sentence in question is "Unggal lempir kawengku ku tilu padalisan." Both words "ku" and "tilu" are found in the Wanca 2016 corpus for Ingrian, which gives a hint of the reason for the mistake. Another language with an F_1-score of zero was Votic. Two Ludian sentences were identified as Votic, which is again understandable due to the languages being relatives, but also one sentence in Southern Sotho was identified as Votic: "Madinayne a ja dikokwanyana." As it happens, "a" is the most common word in the Wanca 2016 corpus for Votic and "ja" the sixth most common.

---

[22]https://github.com/tosaja/TunnistinPalveluFast

Table 4 also includes Tornedalen Finnish and Kven, two variants of Finnish used in Sweden and Norway, respectively. They are extremely close to the written versions of the Finnish dialects used in northern Finland. Relatively many Finnish sentences in the test set (fin_newscrawl_2017_10K-sentences) were identified as one of them. If the Finnish test set would have included social media texts instead of news articles, the confusion would have been much greater as standard written Finnish differs clearly from the written version of the colloquial Finnish.

Language	fin	fit	fkv	hat	izh	kpv	krl	lud	sot	sun	swe	vot
Finnish (fin)	9,931	53	7				3	1			1	
Tornedalen Finnish (fit)	5	91	2	1							1	
Kven (fkv)		3	19									
Haitian (hat)				9,924								
Ingrian (izh)												
Komi-Zyrian (kpv)		1				246						
Karelian (krl)	1				1		80					
Ludian (lud)	2				3			144				2
Southern Sotho (sot)									9,962			1
Sundanese (sun)				1	1				1	5,451		
Swedish (swe)	1										9,981	
Votic (vot)												

Table 4: Confusion matrix of some of the worst performing languages on Track 1.

Table 5 shows the languages which were confused with Võro, the worst performing language on Track 2. Võro is an extremely close language to Standard Estonian, both spoken in modern Estonia. None of the sentences in Võro were identified as Standard Estonian (ekk_web_2011_10K); however, over a thousand sentences (out of 10,000) in Standard Estonian (ekk_wikipedia_2016_10K) were identified as Võro. The only mistake in identifying sentences in Võro was when the sentence "'Õdaguhe" (film) ; 20:35 . " was identified as Northern Azerbaijani. The number of false positives for Võro is explained by the domain difference between the Standard Estonian training and test sets. The training set for Standard Estonian was 10,000 sentences from news articles and the test set was 10,000 sentences from Estonian Wikipedia. The training set for Võro has a total of 66,878 sentences and 9,571 of those are from Võro language Wikipedia. The Võro and Standard Estonian Wikipedias discuss mostly the same named entities (foreign and domestic) and they were present only in the Võro training data, which resulted in a lot of sentences with those named entities being identified as Võro.

Language	azj	ekk	fin	gsw	hif	ita	lud	sun	tso	vec	vro	wuu
N. Azerbaijani (azj)	9,896											
Std. Estonian (ekk)	3	8,717	16	3	4	6	3			5	1,052	
Finnish (fin)			9,931				1				1	
Swiss German (gsw)				9,409	1	6	1			5	1	
Fiji Hindi (hif)			1	2	9,246	4		1			1	1
Italian (ita)				1	2	8,723			1	1,026	1	
Ludian (lud)		2	1				144				1	
Sundanese (sun)				2	1			5,451	4		1	
Tsonga (tso)									9,991		1	
Venetian (vec)			3			1,296				747	1	
Võro (vro)	1										442	
Wu Chinese (wuu)	1		2	9				8			1	6,103

Table 5: Confusion matrix for Võro, the worst performing language on Track 2.

To illustrate the identification errors in Track 3, we selected some of the worst performing languages and created a confusion matrix which is presented in Table 6. Bashkir and Tatar are closely related Turkic languages spoken in Russia. According to Tyers et al. (2012), their orthographical system are fairly different, which might indicate that the corpora used could be noisier than average. The extremely closely related languages Bosnian and Croatian have always been a problem for the non-discriminative HeLI method as is evidenced by the poor results for these languages in the DSL shared tasks of 2015, 2016, and 2017 (Jauhiainen, 2019). Wu Chinese was identified as Mandarin Chinese over 30% of the time. Character-based methods should be used instead of word-based methods when word-tokenization is a problem and the simple CJK algorithm included in the baseline-identifier just helps to correct some of the problems between CJK and non-CJK languages, but does not help in distinguishing between

CJK languages. The trio of close languages Indonesian, Javanese, and Sundanese got confused to the point of Indonesian being more often identified as Sundanese than Indonesian. Low German (nds-nl_wikipedia_2016_10K) was almost never identified as such (nds_wikipedia_2010_100K), but mostly as Limburgan (lim-nl_web_2015_300K). This seems to be due to the writing system of Low German being in flux and the nds.wikipedia[23] and nds-nl.wikipedia[24] being different entities.

Language	bak	bos	cmn	hrv	ind	jav	lim	nds	sun	tat	wuu
Bashkir (bak)	6,961									3,037	
Bosnian (bos)		4,403		5,593							
Mandarin Chinese (cmn)			9,562								273
Croatian (hrv)		1,134		8,864							
Indonesian (ind)					3,102	14			4,858		
Javanese (jav)					1,451	4,626			3,619		
Limburgan (lim)							9,540	10			
Low German (nds)							5,625	182			
Sundanese (sun)					87	4,330	1		5,451		
Tatar (tat)	3,784									6,215	
Wu Chinese (wuu)	1		3,610		1	2	1		8	1	6,103

Table 6: Confusion matrix of some of the worst performing languages by absolute numbers.

5 Conclusions and future work

In the beginning, we were worried about not getting enough new sentences from a simple re-crawl of the old addresses. In the end, the new sentences created an interesting setting for a language identification shared task. The three tracks highlighted different aspects of the problem of language identification.

The next edition of the ULI shared task will incorporate new sentences from the 2018 crawl performed by the SUKI project. Before processing the crawled material, we aim to improve our sentence extraction algorithm in such a way that it could allow sentences to span line-breaks. Also, as pointed out by one of the reviewers, it would be a good idea to manually inspect at least a random subset of the Wanca 2017 corpora in order to objectively assess the reliability of the language annotation process. Unlike the 2017 re-crawl, the 2018 crawl was a real crawl going beyond the addresses stored in the Wance service. Thus, we expect to find more new sentences after we process the material using the improved process.

Acknowledgements

The work presented here was conducted with funding by the University of Helsinki and the Academy of Finland. The SUKI project was funded by the Kone Foundation from 2013 to 2019. We thank the anonymous reviewers for their questions and suggestions.

References

Daniel Abondolo and Riitta-Liisa Valijärvi, editors. forthcoming. *The Uralic Languages*. London: Routledge, 2nd edition.

Daniel Abondolo, editor. 1998. *The Uralic languages*. London: Routledge.

Ahmed Ali, Stephan Vogel, and Steve Renals. 2017. Speech recognition challenge in the wild: Arabic MGB-3. In *2017 IEEE Automatic Speech Recognition and Understanding Workshop (ASRU)*, pages 316–322.

Timofey Arkhangelskiy. 2019. Corpora of social media in minority Uralic languages. In *Proceedings of the Fifth International Workshop on Computational Linguistics for Uralic Languages*, pages 125–140. Tartu.

Marianne Bakró-Nagy, Johanna Laakso, and Elena Skribnik, editors. forthcoming. *The Oxford Guide to the Uralic Languages*. Oxford: Oxford University Press.

---

[23]https://nds.wikipedia.org/wiki/Plattdüütsch
[24]https://nds-nl.wikipedia.org/wiki/Nedersaksisch

Timothy Baldwin and Marco Lui. 2010. Multilingual Language Identification: ALTW 2010 Shared Task Dataset. pages 5–7, Melbourne, Australia.

Yves Bestgen. 2017. Improving the Character Ngram Model for the DSL Task with BM25 Weighting and Less Frequently Used Feature Sets. In *Proceedings of the Fourth Workshop on NLP for Similar Languages, Varieties and Dialects (VarDial)*, pages 115–123, Valencia, Spain.

Cagri Çöltekin and Taraka Rama. 2016. Discriminating Similar Languages: Experiments with Linear SVMs and Neural Networks. In *Proceedings of the Third Workshop on NLP for Similar Languages, Varieties and Dialects (VarDial)*, pages 15–24, Osaka, Japan.

Timothy Feist. 2015. *A grammar of Skolt Saami*. Number 273 in Mémoires de la Société Finno-Ougrienne. Finno-Ugrian Society.

Dirk Goldhahn, Thomas Eckart, and Uwe Quasthoff. 2012. Building large monolingual dictionaries at the leipzig corpora collection: From 100 to 200 languages. In *LREC*, volume 29, pages 31–43.

Cyril Goutte and Serge Léger. 2015. Experiments in Discriminating Similar Languages. In *Proceedings of the Joint Workshop on Language Technology for Closely Related Languages, Varieties and Dialects (LT4VarDial)*, pages 78–84, Hissar, Bulgaria.

Lenore A Grenoble. 2003. *Language policy in the Soviet Union*. Kluwer Academic Publishers.

Cyril Grouin, Dominic Forest, Lyne Da Sylva, Patrick Paroubek, and Pierre Zweigenbaum. 2011. Présentation et Résultats du Défi Fouille de Texte DEFT2010 Où et Quand un Article de Presse a-t-il Été Écrit? In *Actes du sixième Défi Fouille de Textes*, pages 3–14, Montpellier, France.

Heidi Jauhiainen, Tommi Jauhiainen, and Krister Lindén. 2015a. The Finno-Ugric Languages and The Internet Project. In *Proceedings of the 1st International Workshop on Computational Linguistics for Uralic Languages (IWCLUL 2015)*, number 2 in Septentrio Conference Series, pages 87–98.

Tommi Jauhiainen, Heidi Jauhiainen, and Krister Lindén. 2015b. Discriminating Similar Languages with Token-Based Backoff. In *Proceedings of the Joint Workshop on Language Technology for Closely Related Languages, Varieties and Dialects (LT4VarDial)*, pages 44–51, Hissar, Bulgaria.

Tommi Jauhiainen, Krister Lindén, and Heidi Jauhiainen. 2015c. Language Set Identification in Noisy Synthetic Multilingual Documents. In A. Gelbukh, editor, *Proceedings of the Computational Linguistics and Intelligent Text Processing 16th International Conference, (CICLing 2015)*, Part I of Lecture Notes in Computer Science, pages 633–643, Cairo, Egypt. Springer.

Tommi Jauhiainen, Krister Lindén, and Heidi Jauhiainen. 2016. HeLI, a Word-Based Backoff Method for Language Identification. In *Proceedings of the Third Workshop on NLP for Similar Languages, Varieties and Dialects (VarDial3)*, pages 153–162, Osaka, Japan.

Tommi Jauhiainen, Krister Lindén, and Heidi Jauhiainen. 2017a. Evaluating HeLI with Non-Linear Mappings. In *Proceedings of the 4th Workshop on NLP for Similar Languages, Varieties and Dialects (VarDial 2017)*, pages 102–108, Valencia, Spain.

Tommi Jauhiainen, Krister Lindén, and Heidi Jauhiainen. 2017b. Evaluation of Language Identification Methods Using 285 Languages. In *Proceedings of the 21st Nordic Conference on Computational Linguistics (NoDaLiDa 2017)*, pages 183–191, Gothenburg, Sweden.

Heidi Jauhiainen, Tommi Jauhiainen, and Krister Linden. 2019a. Wanca in Korp: Text corpora for underresourced Uralic languages. In Jarmo Harri Jantunen, Sisko Brunni, Niina Kunnas, Santeri Palviainen, and Katja Västi, editors, *Proceedings of the Research data and humanities (RDHUM) 2019 conference*, number 17 in Studia Humaniora Ouluensia, pages 21–40, Finland. University of Oulu.

Tommi Jauhiainen, Marco Lui, Marcos Zampieri, Timothy Baldwin, and Krister Lindén. 2019b. Automatic Language Identification in Texts: A Survey. *Journal of Artificial Intelligence Research*, 65:675–782.

Heidi Jauhiainen, Tommi Jauhiainen, and Krister Lindén. 2020. Building web corpora for minority languages. In *Proceedings of the 12th Web as Corpus Workshop*, pages 23–32.

Tommi Jauhiainen. 2019. *Language identification in texts*. Ph.D. thesis, University of Helsinki, Finland.

Philipp Koehn. 2005. Europarl: A Parallel Corpus for Statistical Machine Translation. pages 79–86, Phuket, Thailand.

Irina Krylova, Boris Orekhov, Ekaterina Stepanova, and Lyudmila Zaydelman. 2015. Languages of Russia. In *Russian Summer School in Information Retrieval*, pages 179–185.

Shervin Malmasi and Mark Dras. 2015. Language Identification using Classifier Ensembles. In *Proceedings of the Joint Workshop on Language Technology for Closely Related Languages, Varieties and Dialects (LT4VarDial)*, pages 35–43, Hissar, Bulgaria.

Shervin Malmasi, Marcos Zampieri, Nikola Ljubešić, Preslav Nakov, Ahmed Ali, and Jörg Tiedemann. 2016. Discriminating Between Similar Languages and Arabic Dialect Identification: A Report on the Third DSL Shared Task. In *Proceedings of the Third Workshop on NLP for Similar Languages, Varieties and Dialects*, pages 1–14, Osaka, Japan.

Andrei Mikheev. 2002. Periods, Capitalized Words, etc. *Computational Linguistics*, 28(13):289–318.

Gordon Mohr, Michael Stack, Igor Rnitovic, Dan Avery, and Michele Kimpton. 2004. Introduction to Heritrix. 4th International Web Archiving Workshop (at ECDL2004).

Irina Nikolaeva. 2014. *A grammar of Tundra Nenets*, volume 65. Walter de Gruyter GmbH & Co KG.

Boris Orekhov, Irina Krylova, I. Popov, L. Stepanova, and Lyudmila Zaydelman. 2016. Russian minority languages on the web. In *Computational Linguistics and Intellectual Technologies: Proceedings of the International Conference "Dialogue 2016*, pages 498–508.

Niko Partanen, Rogier Blokland, KyungTae Lim, Thierry Poibeau, and Michael Rießler. 2018. The first Komi-Zyrian universal dependencies treebanks. In *Second Workshop on Universal Dependencies (UDW 2018), November 2018, Brussels, Belgium*, pages 126–132.

Tommi A Pirinen. 2019. Building minority dependency treebanks, dictionaries and computational grammars at the same time—an experiment in Karelian treebanking. In *Proceedings of the Third Workshop on Universal Dependencies (UDW, SyntaxFest 2019)*, pages 132–136.

Francisco Rangel, Paolo Rosso, Martin Potthast, and Benno Stein. 2017. Overview of the 5th Author Profiling Task at PAN 2017: Gender and Language Variety Identification in Twitter. In Linda Cappellato, Nicola Ferro, Lorraine Goeuriot, and Thomas Mandl, editors, *Working Notes Papers of CLEF 2017 Evaluation Labs and Workshop*, Dublin, Ireland, September. CEUR-WS.org.

Jack Michael Rueter and Francis M Tyers. 2018. Towards an open-source universal-dependency treebank for Erzya. In *International Workshop for Computational Linguistics of Uralic Languages*.

Jack Rueter, Niko Partanen, and Larisa Ponomareva. 2020. On the questions in developing computational infrastructure for Komi-Permyak. In *Proceedings of the Sixth International Workshop on Computational Linguistics of Uralic Languages*, pages 15–25.

Jack Rueter, Mika Hämäläinen, and Niko Partanen. in press. Open-source morphology for endangered mordvinic languages. In *Proceedings of the 2nd Workshop for Natural Language Processing Open Source Software (NLP-OSS)*.

Florian Siegl and Michael Rießler. 2015. Uneven steps to literacy. In *Cultural and Linguistic Minorities in the Russian Federation and the European Union*, pages 189–230. Springer.

Denis Sinor, editor. 1988. *The Uralic languages: Description, history and foreign influences*, volume 1. Brill Academic Publishers.

Thamar Solorio, Elizabeth Blair, Suraj Maharjan, Steven Bethard, Mona Diab, Mahmoud Gohneim, Abdelati Hawwari, Fahad AlGhamdi, Julia Hirschberg, Alison Chang, and Pascale Fung. 2014. Overview for the First Shared Task on Language Identification in Code-Switched Data. In *Proceedings of The First Workshop on Computational Approaches to Code Switching*, pages 62–72, Doha, Qatar, October.

Francis Tyers and Mariya Sheyanova. 2017. Annotation schemes in north sàmi dependency parsing. In *Proceedings of the Third Workshop on Computational Linguistics for Uralic Languages*, pages 66–75.

Francis M Tyers, Jonathan North Washington, Ilnar Salimzyanov, and Rustam Batalov. 2012. A prototype machine translation system for tatar and bashkir based on free/open-source components. In *First Workshop on Language Resources and Technologies for Turkic Languages*, page 11.

Beáta Wagner-Nagy. 2018. *A grammar of Nganasan*. Brill.

Marcos Zampieri, Liling Tan, Nikola Ljubešić, and Jörg Tiedemann. 2014. A Report on the DSL Shared Task 2014. In *Proceedings of the First Workshop on Applying NLP Tools to Similar Languages, Varieties and Dialects*, pages 58–67, Dublin, Ireland.

Marcos Zampieri, Liling Tan, Nikola Ljubešić, Jörg Tiedemann, and Preslav Nakov. 2015. Overview of the DSL Shared Task 2015. In *Proceedings of the Joint Workshop on Language Technology for Closely Related Languages, Varieties and Dialects (LT4VarDial)*, pages 1–9, Hissar, Bulgaria.

Marcos Zampieri, Shervin Malmasi, Nikola Ljubešic, Preslav Nakov, Ahmed Ali, Jörg Tiedemann, Yves Scherrer, and Noëmi Aepli. 2017. Findings of the VarDial Evaluation Campaign 2017. In *Proceedings of the Fourth Workshop on NLP for Similar Languages, Varieties and Dialects*, pages 1–15, Valencia, Spain.

Marcos Zampieri, Shervin Malmasi, Preslav Nakov, Ahmed Ali, Suwon Shon, James Glass, Yves Scherrer, Tanja Samardžić, Nikola Ljubešić, Jörg Tiedemann, Chris van der Lee, Stefan Grondelaers, Nelleke Oostdijk, Antal van den Bosch, Ritesh Kumar, Bornini Lahiri, and Mayank Jain. 2018. Language Identification and Morphosyntactic Tagging: The Second VarDial Evaluation Campaign. In *Proceedings of the Fifth Workshop on NLP for Similar Languages, Varieties and Dialects (VarDial)*, Santa Fe, USA.

Marcos Zampieri, Shervin Malmasi, Yves Scherrer, Tanja Samardžić, Francis Tyers, Miikka Silfverberg, Natalia Klyueva, Tung-Le Pan, Chu-Ren Huang, Radu Tudor Ionescu, Andrei Butnaru, and Tommi Jauhiainen. 2019. A Report on the Third VarDial Evaluation Campaign. In *Proceedings of the Sixth Workshop on NLP for Similar Languages, Varieties and Dialects (VarDial)*. Association for Computational Linguistics.

Arkaitz Zubiaga, Inaki San Vicente, Pablo Gamallo, José Ramom Pichel, Inaki Alegria, Nora Aranberri, Aitzol Ezeiza, and Víctor Fresno. 2014. Overview of TweetLID: Tweet Language Identification at SEPLN 2014. In *Proceedings of the Tweet Language Identification Workshop 2014 co-located with 30th Conference of the Spanish Society for Natural Language Processing (SEPLN 2014)*, pages 1–11, Girona, Spain, September.

Ènn Èrnits. 2006. Ob oboznačenii zvukov v vodskom literaturnom âzyke. *Linguistica Uralica*, 42(1):1–9.

Dialect Identification under Domain Shift:
Experiments with Discriminating Romanian and Moldavian

Çağrı Çöltekin
University of Tübingen
Department of Linguistics
`ccoltekin@sfs.uni-tuebingen.de`

Abstract

This paper describes a set of experiments for discriminating between two closely related language varieties, Moldavian and Romanian, under a substantial domain shift. The experiments were conducted as part of the Romanian dialect identification task in the VarDial 2020 evaluation campaign. Our best system based on linear SVM classifier obtained the first position in the shared task with an F1 score of 0.79, supporting the earlier results showing (unexpected) success of machine learning systems in this task. The additional experiments reported in this paper also show that adapting to the test set is useful when the training set is from another domain. However, the benefit of adaptation becomes doubtful even when using a small amount of data from the target domain.

1   Introduction

Language identification can be performed with near-perfect accuracy from a short text in many settings (Jauhiainen et al., 2019, for a recent survey of the solutions). However, automatic discrimination of texts from closely related languages or dialects remains to be a challenging task. The successful discrimination of texts between closely related language varieties may improve language identification for practical applications, as well as providing further insights into the differences between these linguistic varieties. Recent VarDial evaluation campaigns have featured discrimination challenges between related languages (Zampieri et al., 2017; Zampieri et al., 2018; Zampieri et al., 2019). The present study is conducted within the scope of the VarDial 2020 (Găman et al., 2020) Romanian Dialect Identification (RDI) task.

Romanian and Moldavian are two closely related language varieties spoken in Romania and the Republic of Moldavia respectively. The languages, particularly in written form, are very similar – to the extent that discrimination by human annotators is barely above chance levels (Găman and Ionescu, 2020). However, as evidenced by the last year's evaluation campaign (Zampieri et al., 2019), the machine learning methods applied to the task seem to be more successful (Chifu, 2019; Onose et al., 2019; Tudoreanu, 2019; Wu et al., 2019). The MOROCO corpus (Butnaru and Ionescu, 2019) used in last year's RDI shared task consists of texts from online news. Although the data is fairly balanced with respect to the topics, and some of the obvious non-linguistic cues (e.g., named entities) are removed from the data, the data may still contain some unintended non-dialectal cues (e.g., style differences between the newspapers in two countries). A natural question that arises is whether the machine learning methods tap into such non-obvious cues not relevant to linguistic differences, or the data contains a strong signal for identifying the linguistic variation. To this end, the present shared task includes data from two different domains (or genres). The source domain is the MOROCO corpus of newspaper text, and the target domain texts consist of a newly collected data set gathered from Twitter.

The systems used in the current study are based on ensembles of linear SVM models with a simple adaptation mechanism that retrains the model(s) with the data augmented by the test instances that are classified by a base classifier with high confidence. Besides the adaptation to the test set at prediction time, we also experiment with a training set selection method based on reverse-prediction. This method is

This work is licensed under a Creative Commons Attribution 4.0 International License.
License details: `http://creativecommons.org/licenses/by/4.0/`.

Proceedings of the 7th VarDial Workshop on NLP for Similar Languages, Varieties and Dialects, pages 186–192
Barcelona, Spain (Online), December 13, 2020

based on training a classifier on a small target data (development set) and selecting the training instances
which the classifier predicts with high confidence.

In the remainder of this paper, we describe the system, present the results, and provide a discussion
with brief conclusions.

2 System Description

The main task at hand is predicting the language variety (Romanian or Moldavian) under domain shift.
The participants were provided with a large annotated corpus from the source domain (newspaper text)
and a small annotated development set from the target domain. The evaluation is based on the performance of the systems on the target domain.

All experiments reported in this study are performed using linear SVM classifiers with sparse character
and word n-gram features. Overlapping character and word n-gram features (for all 'n' from 1 to a
maximum value, determined during tuning) are combined into a single feature set, and weighted using
BM25 (Robertson et al., 2009). The input is tokenized using a simple regular expression tokenizer that
treats any contiguous alphabetic or non-space character sequence as a token. Except for (optional) case
normalization (treated as a hyperparameter), and filtering based on low document frequency (also another
hyperparameter), no preprocessing or filtering is performed. The same system has been used with minor
differences for discriminating similar languages in the earlier VarDial evaluation campaigns (Çöltekin
and Rama, 2016; Çöltekin and Rama, 2017; Çöltekin et al., 2018), and obtained top or near-top results.
The detailed description of the approach can be found in these papers.

For some of the experiments, we use an ensemble of linear SVM classifiers described above trained
on different, non-overlapping parts of the data. The predictions of the individual classifiers are combined
using weighted majority voting where the distances from the decision boundary are used as weights.

Another interesting aspect of the system is an adaptation technique used during prediction. The adaptation method is similar to the adaptation method used in a few systems in earlier VarDial shared tasks
(Jauhiainen et al., 2018a; Jauhiainen et al., 2018b; Wu et al., 2019). The method relies on a base classifier
trained on the training data. During testing, the test instances for which the base classifier is confident in
its decisions are added to the training set and the classifier is retrained with this augmented training set.

One of the differences between the source and the target domain is the average length of the documents.
On average, the source domain newspaper texts are naturally longer than the tweets (target domain).
Although the feature weighting method we use (BM25) counteracts the sensitivity to document size to
some extent, we split the source domain documents to sentences. In all of the shared task submissions,
the source domain documents were split before training the models.

Another aspect of some of our systems is filtering large source domain data based on what we call
'reverse-prediction'. With the assumption that the features relevant for the target domain can be captured
well by a classifier trained on the small target domain development set, we first tune and train a classifier
on the development set. We use this classifier to predict the labels of the large training set. We select
the predictions with high confidence that match the gold-standard labels. In this paper, we consider the
test instances with a distance of more that 1.0 from the decision boundary as confident predictions. The
intuition is that, despite reduced data size, the selected training instances may include features better
tuned to the target domain.

3 Experiments and Results

3.1 Data

The data for this task comes from two different sources. The first data set, the MOROCO (Butnaru
and Ionescu, 2019) corpus, is used as the source domain (or genre) in this task. The target corpus is
collected from Twitter by Găman and Ionescu (2020). The source corpus is provided with a training–
development set division. In most of our experiments we combine training and development sets, and
split the documents into sentences,[1] labeling each sentence with the label of the document. During the

---

[1]Version 1.4 of the Python `sentence-splitter` library was used with defaults for splitting the documents into sentences (`https://pypi.org/project/sentence-splitter/`).

Data set	instances	μ_{char}	σ_{char}	μ_{token}	σ_{token}	RO/MD
Source						
Development	5923	1718.55	1746.34	391.88	393.94	1.18
Training	33 564	1714.99	1847.48	390.11	410.18	1.18
Train+dev sentences	424 383	158.81	141.72	36.34	36.04	1.45
Selection (documents)	21 376	1853.36	2122.72	420.26	469.18	0.95
Selection (sentences)	243 904	161.40	144.75	36.83	36.19	1.30
Target						
Development	215	91.43	20.01	24.09	6.39	0.90
Test	5022	92.09	18.86	23.66	6.04	1.01

Table 1: Summary of the data. The columns μ_{char} and μ_{token} indicate average number of characters and tokens, σ_{char} and σ_{token} indicate standard deviations of respective measures. 'RO/MD' is the ratio of Romanian instances to Moldavian instances, provided as a measure of class imbalance.

competition, only a small development set from the target domain was released, and the test data with labels were provided after the competition. The statistics on the data sets are provided in Table 1.

The source domain contains a slight class imbalance. Also because of the fact that the Romanian documents are longer on average, sentence splitting amplifies this imbalance. The target domain is much more balanced, and contains shorter documents on average, even compared to sentence-split version. The document lengths of the target domain are less varied. The Twitter data set is also more balanced. We apply training instance selection with reverse-prediction to the whole documents, then use the sentence split version in the experiments reported below. The resulting data contains approximately half of the training and development instances. One notable aspect is that the resulting data sets have longer texts, likely because the classifier is more confident on longer texts. Furthermore, the selection process reverses the class imbalance on documents. However, since Romanian documents are longer on average, the balance is again in favor of Romanian in the sentence-split data.

3.2 Experimental setup

All classifiers we use were tuned on the respective data sets. We tune the following hyperparameters: SVM margin/regularization constant 'C' in range $[0.01, 4.0]$; maximum character n-gram order in range $[0, 7]$; maximum token n-gram order in range $[0, 4]$; document frequency cutoff in range $[1, 5]$; and whether to apply case normalization to tokens or not. The BM25 parameters were kept at their default values suggested by Robertson et al. (2009). For each classifier trained, we draw 1000 random hyperparameter combinations, train and test it using 10-fold cross validation and record the average macro-averaged F1 score over the cross validation folds.

For large data sets (of the source domain), during prediction, we combine the output of 20 classifiers trained on non-overlapping equal parts of the training set, and the use the majority vote weighted by the distance from the decision boundary as the final decision. For small data sets, we also employ a less-effective form of ensembling. We train 5 separate models on the same data set using the top-five hyperparameter settings, and combine their decisions the same way. The implementation is based on Python scikit-learn library (Pedregosa et al., 2011).

3.3 Shared Task Results

We submitted three runs to the competition. The first run used only the target development set as training data. We tune a model with random search over the hyperparameters listed above using 10-fold cross validation on the target development set, we re-train 5 classifiers with the best hyperparameter settings on the complete target development data, and use their combined (with weighted voting) decisions on the test set as final predictions.

For the second run, we used the complete source data (after sentence segmentation). We first tune the classifier on a random 1/20th sample of the whole data. Then, re-train 20 classifiers on the non-

Data set	Precision	Recall	F1 Score
Target dev	84.04 (8.50)	84.77 (8.28)	84.01 (8.52)
Target dev+test	89.29 (0.92)	89.31 (0.91)	89.29 (0.92)
Source sentences	86.36 (0.19)	85.73 (0.18)	86.01 (0.18)
Source documents	96.37 (0.27)	96.51 (0.26)	96.26 (0.28)

Table 2: In-domain results. All scores are macro-averaged, and presented as percentages. The values in the parentheses are the standard deviations of the scores over the folds of in 10-fold cross validation experiments.

overlapping parts of the complete source data set (development and training sets), and use the weighted vote as final predictions.

The third run is based on selection of the sentences from the source data which were predicted confidently by a classifier trained on the target development set. In particular, for run 3, we select the sentences from the source data whose distance to the decision boundary is 1.00 or larger. The tuning and prediction follows the same procedure as the second run.

All systems used the test set adaptation method, where all test instances with distances 0.50 or higher from the decision boundary of the base classifier were added to the training set, and the predictions are obtained from a classifier trained on this augmented data set.

Our first two runs obtained the first two ranks among 19 submissions in the competition with macro-averaged F1 scores of 0.788 and 0.784 respectively. The final run, with training data selection, obtained the fifth rank with an macro-averaged F1 score of 0.756.

The results indicate that, given a large test set to adapt to, even a small amount of target training data is effective. When shifting the domains, it seems crucial to have more data. Even a carefully selected subset of out-of-domain data leads to inferior performance in comparison to small in-domain data.

3.4 In-domain Experiments

Besides the experiments with the systems for the shared task participation, we present a set of in-domain experiments without adaptation. For the source domain, we present both results with and without sentence splitting. For the target domain, we present results obtained on the small development set (215 tweets), and combination of both development and test sets. All performance scores are average scores on 10-fold cross validation on the indicated data sets. For each setting, the SVM classifier was trained with 1000 random draws from the hyperparameter space indicated above, and the highest scores were reported.

Table 2 presents the results of the in-domain experiments. The in-domain performance of the system on the source data is in-line with the last year's competition. The scores on source documents are almost the same as the post-competition result reported by Wu et al. (2019), which was 6.70 percentage points higher than the official winner. Training and testing the system on source sentences causes a performance drop of approximately 10 %. Presumably, the decrease of performance is due to increased ambiguity as a result of decreased length of the documents. In fact, tuning and training the classifier on sentences (of the official training set), and testing it on the documents (of the official development set) results in comparable scores (macro-averaged F1 score is 95.04) – despite the mismatch of text length between development splits and the test set.

The results on the target domain are also impressive. Using only 215 tweets in a cross-validation setup, the average F1 score over cross-validation folds is 84.01. And more data definitely helps, both for increasing the performance, and reducing the variance. Once we have about 5000 instances, the average F1-score on 10-fold cross validation is close to the scores obtained on the news domain. And, interestingly, despite the smaller data set and shorter texts (even in comparison to news sentences), the model is more successful on tweets than the news sentences. In fact, running the same experiments on the source domain with the 5000 instances reduces the F1 score of the classifier to 93.80 and 73.96 for source documents and sentences respectively.

Training set	Precision		Recall		F1 Score	
	-adapt	+adapt	-adapt	+adapt	-adapt	+adapt
Target dev	78.20	78.83	78.20	78.76	78.20	78.76
Source all	76.63	78.44	76.57	78.43	76.57	78.43
Source select	74.54	75.66	74.54	75.65	74.53	75.65

Table 3: Comparison of systems with (+adapt) and without (-adapt) adaptation to the test set. All scores are macro-averaged, and presented as percentages.

3.5 Adaptation to the Test Data

All of our official submissions included the test set adaptation method described in Section 2. To show the effects of the adaptation method, we present the scores both with and without adaptation in this section. Table 3 presents the scores on the test set with and without domain adaptation. The results with domain adaptation are the scores of the official submissions. The results without domain adaptation is calculated on the test set released by the organizers after the competition.

The adaptation has little effect when training data is in-domain. This is perhaps not surprising as training and test domains are identical. However, considering the small amount of training data (target dev set), one hopes to get additional benefits from increased training set because of domain adaptation. When training data comes from a different text type, domain adaptation seem to be more effective, increasing the scores close to two percentage points. The increase is less helpful for the training set selected through reverse-prediction. This may be because of the fact that the reverse-prediction already does the part of the job of the test set adaptation. Nevertheless, the most successful method is the one trained on small in-domain data with a small margin in comparison to full source data with adaptation. When trained with out-of-domain data, domain adaptation is clearly useful. Selecting training instances based on reverse-prediction does not seem to be helpful. This may be due to decrease in training data size, but the selection procedure may have also resulted in over-tuning to the development set. Indeed, the training documents selected with reverse-prediction has a 'RO/MD' ratio of 0.95, closer to the development set distribution (0.90) than the training set distribution (1.18).

4 General Discussion

This paper presented results from (ensembles of) linear SVM classifiers on the task of cross-domain discrimination of Moldavian and Romanian. Our systems obtained top positions on the official competition. The results indicate that linear SVMs are (still) one of the best solutions in certain settings. Furthermore, the cross-domain success of the system supports findings of Găman and Ionescu (2020), that better-than-human achievement of the machine learning models is based on dialect differences, and not due to some correlated hidden variable in the data set.

The in-domain experiments indicate that if the training sizes are similar, the discrimination is better on the Twitter data in comparison to the newspaper text. The in-domain experiment on Twitter corpus yield better discrimination than the in-domain experiment with with news sentences despite smaller training set size. This probably indicates that non-standard texts contain more cues to dialectal differences, since they do not necessarily follow common literary and stylistic traditions expected from more formal texts.

The adaptation method based on test set augmentation was found to be useful when training and test domains are different. The benefit of the test set adaptation method is not clear when the training and tests are from the same domain, even when the training set is very small.

The training data selection experiments resulted in worse results than expected. A potential reason for the failure is the fact that most training instances selected by the procedure contain the features that already occur in the target development set, hence, not providing additional information expected from a large data set. Although the training set selection method as used in this study seems to have failed, methods involving relevant, yet diverse instance may be helpful in adapting to a new domain.

References

Andrei Butnaru and Radu Tudor Ionescu. 2019. MOROCO: The Moldavian and Romanian dialectal corpus. In *Proceedings of the 57th Annual Meeting of the Association for Computational Linguistics*, pages 688–698, Florence, Italy, July. Association for Computational Linguistics.

Adrian-Gabriel Chifu. 2019. The R2I_LIS team proposes majority vote for VarDial's MRC task. In *Proceedings of the Sixth Workshop on NLP for Similar Languages, Varieties and Dialects*, pages 138–143, Ann Arbor, Michigan, June. Association for Computational Linguistics.

Çağrı Çöltekin and Taraka Rama. 2016. Discriminating similar languages with linear SVMs and neural networks. In *Proceedings of the Third Workshop on NLP for Similar Languages, Varieties and Dialects (VarDial3)*, pages 15–24, Osaka, Japan.

Çağrı Çöltekin and Taraka Rama. 2017. Tübingen system in VarDial 2017 shared task: experiments with language identification and cross-lingual parsing. In *Proceedings of the Fourth Workshop on NLP for Similar Languages, Varieties and Dialects (VarDial)*, pages 146–155, Valencia, Spain.

Çağrı Çöltekin, Taraka Rama, and Verena Blaschke. 2018. Tübingen-Oslo team at the VarDial 2018 evaluation campaign: An analysis of n-gram features in language variety identification. In *Proceedings of the Fifth Workshop on NLP for Similar Languages, Varieties and Dialects (VarDial 2018)*, pages 55–65.

Mihaela Găman and Radu Tudor Ionescu. 2020. The unreasonable effectiveness of machine learning in Moldavian versus Romanian dialect identification. *arXiv preprint arXiv:2007.15700*.

Mihaela Găman, Dirk Hovy, Radu Tudor Ionescu, Heidi Jauhiainen, Tommi Jauhiainen, Krister Lindén, Nikola Ljubešić, Niko Partanen, Christoph Purschke, Yves Scherrer, and Marcos Zampieri. 2020. A Report on the VarDial Evaluation Campaign 2020. In *Proceedings of the Seventh Workshop on NLP for Similar Languages, Varieties and Dialects (VarDial)*.

Tommi Jauhiainen, Heidi Jauhiainen, and Krister Lindén. 2018a. HeLI-based experiments in Swiss German dialect identification. In *Proceedings of the Fifth Workshop on NLP for Similar Languages, Varieties and Dialects (VarDial 2018)*, pages 254–262, Santa Fe, New Mexico, USA, August. Association for Computational Linguistics.

Tommi Jauhiainen, Heidi Jauhiainen, and Krister Lindén. 2018b. Iterative language model adaptation for Indo-Aryan language identification. In *Proceedings of the Fifth Workshop on NLP for Similar Languages, Varieties and Dialects (VarDial 2018)*, pages 66–75, Santa Fe, New Mexico, USA, August. Association for Computational Linguistics.

Tommi Sakari Jauhiainen, Marco Lui, Marcos Zampieri, Timothy Baldwin, and Krister Lindén. 2019. Automatic language identification in texts: A survey. *Journal of Artificial Intelligence Research*, 65:675–782.

Cristian Onose, Dumitru-Clementin Cercel, and Stefan Trausan-Matu. 2019. SC-UPB at the VarDial 2019 evaluation campaign: Moldavian vs. Romanian cross-dialect topic identification. In *Proceedings of the Sixth Workshop on NLP for Similar Languages, Varieties and Dialects*, pages 172–177, Ann Arbor, Michigan, June. Association for Computational Linguistics.

Fabian Pedregosa, Gaël Varoquaux, Alexandre Gramfort, Vincent Michel, Bertrand Thirion, Olivier Grisel, Mathieu Blondel, Peter Prettenhofer, Ron Weiss, Vincent Dubourg, Jake Vanderplas, Alexandre Passos, David Cournapeau, Matthieu Brucher, Matthieu Perrot, and Édouard Duchesnay. 2011. Scikit-learn: Machine learning in Python. *Journal of Machine Learning Research*, 12:2825–2830.

Stephen Robertson, Hugo Zaragoza, et al. 2009. The probabilistic relevance framework: BM25 and beyond. *Foundations and Trends® in Information Retrieval*, 3(4):333–389.

Diana Tudoreanu. 2019. DTeam @ VarDial 2019: Ensemble based on skip-gram and triplet loss neural networks for Moldavian vs. Romanian cross-dialect topic identification. In *Proceedings of the Sixth Workshop on NLP for Similar Languages, Varieties and Dialects*, pages 202–208, Ann Arbor, Michigan, June. Association for Computational Linguistics.

Nianheng Wu, Eric DeMattos, Kwok Him So, Pin-zhen Chen, and Çağrı Çöltekin. 2019. Language discrimination and transfer learning for similar languages: Experiments with feature combinations and adaptation. In *Proceedings of the Sixth Workshop on NLP for Similar Languages, Varieties and Dialects*, pages 54–63, Ann Arbor, Michigan, June. Association for Computational Linguistics.

Marcos Zampieri, Shervin Malmasi, Nikola Ljubešić, Preslav Nakov, Ahmed Ali, Jörg Tiedemann, Yves Scherrer, and Noëmi Aepli. 2017. Findings of the VarDial evaluation campaign 2017. In *Proceedings of the Fourth Workshop on NLP for Similar Languages, Varieties and Dialects (VarDial)*, pages 1–15, Valencia, Spain, April. Association for Computational Linguistics.

Marcos Zampieri, Shervin Malmasi, Preslav Nakov, Ahmed Ali, Suwon Shon, James Glass, Yves Scherrer, Tanja Samardžić, Nikola Ljubešić, Jörg Tiedemann, Chris van der Lee, Stefan Grondelaers, Nelleke Oostdijk, Dirk Speelman, Antal van den Bosch, Ritesh Kumar, Bornini Lahiri, and Mayank Jain. 2018. Language identification and morphosyntactic tagging: The second VarDial evaluation campaign. In *Proceedings of the Fifth Workshop on NLP for Similar Languages, Varieties and Dialects (VarDial 2018)*, pages 1–17, Santa Fe, New Mexico, USA, August. Association for Computational Linguistics.

Marcos Zampieri, Shervin Malmasi, Yves Scherrer, Tanja Samardžić, Francis Tyers, Miikka Silfverberg, Natalia Klyueva, Tung-Le Pan, Chu-Ren Huang, Radu Tudor Ionescu, Andrei M. Butnaru, and Tommi Jauhiainen. 2019. A report on the third VarDial evaluation campaign. In *Proceedings of the Sixth Workshop on NLP for Similar Languages, Varieties and Dialects*, pages 1–16, Ann Arbor, Michigan, June. Association for Computational Linguistics.

Applying Multilingual and Monolingual Transformer-Based Models for Dialect Identification

Cristian Popa, Vlad Ștefănescu
University Politehnica of Bucharest
`{cristian.viorel.popa, vlad.a.stefanescu}@gmail.com`

Abstract

We study the ability of large fine-tuned transformer models to solve a binary classification task of dialect identification, with a special interest in comparing the performance of multilingual to monolingual ones. The corpus analyzed contains Romanian and Moldavian samples from the news domain, as well as tweets for assessing the performance. We find that the monolingual models are superior to the multilingual ones and the best results are obtained using an SVM ensemble of 5 different transformer-based models. We provide our experimental results and an analysis of the attention mechanisms of the best-performing individual classifiers to explain their decisions. The code we used was released under an open-source license.

1 Introduction

Dialect Identification is a Natural Language Processing (NLP) task that started receiving more interest in recent years, in part due to VarDial, the workshop on NLP for Similar Languages, Varieties and Dialects (Nakov et al., 2017; Zampieri et al., 2018b; Zampieri et al., 2019b) and its organized evaluation campaigns (Zampieri et al., 2017; Zampieri et al., 2018a; Zampieri et al., 2019a).

This paper presents our solution to the RDI shared task of VarDial 2020 (Găman et al., 2020) on behalf of team "Anumiți". The problem we focus on is the binary classification of Moldavian and Romanian samples, training on the MOROCO (Butnaru and Ionescu, 2019) corpus and a small number of collected tweets, and testing afterwards on an additional set of tweets. Multiple experiments were done on this corpus (Găman and Ionescu, 2020; Tudoreanu, 2019; Chifu, 2019; Wu et al., 2019; Onose et al., 2019), but we are, to the best of our knowledge, the first ones to apply some of the models in this paper to solve the task.

We study the performance of 3 multilingual models, trained on Romanian corpora, and 2 other BERT-based models trained only on Romanian data. The results show clearly that the ones explicitly trained for Romanian tasks are superior for the dialect identification task at hand. We present the results of the different individual classifiers and an SVM ensemble of them, as well as the words that the Romanian-trained ones pay attention to, in order to differentiate between the two dialects. We released all the code under an open-source license: `https://github.com/CristianViorelPopa/transformers-dialect-identification`.

2 Related Work

Considerable progress was made in the NLP field in recent years with the introduction of attention models (Bahdanau et al., 2014) and, later on, transformers (Vaswani et al., 2017), deep neural networks that use an encoder-decoder architecture. A multitude of models (Devlin et al., 2019; Radford et al., 2019; Liu et al., 2019; Lewis et al., 2019) that make use of the transformer architecture emerged and achieved state-of-the-art performance on a large number of NLP tasks through transfer learning. These are pre-trained on large amounts of textual data in order to encompass general knowledge of the target language(s) to later be fine-tuned on downstream tasks, such as question-answering (Rajpurkar et al.,

This work is licensed under a Creative Commons Attribution 4.0 International License. License details: `http://creativecommons.org/licenses/by/4.0/`.

Proceedings of the 7th VarDial Workshop on NLP for Similar Languages, Varieties and Dialects, pages 193–201
Barcelona, Spain (Online), December 13, 2020

2016). This allows for better results on small datasets, where previously deep learning was not a viable solution. The architecture of the transformer-based models features multiple layers of transformers with multi-head attention, which allow the model to jointly attend to information from different representation subspaces at different positions (Vaswani et al., 2017).

A short time after, multilingual transformer-based models made an appearance. These are trained on multiple languages in order to solve suitable problems, such as cross-lingual sentence classification (Conneau et al., 2018). The multilingual BERT model (*mBERT*) uses the original BERT architecture and training objectives, but is trained on corpora of up to 104 languages, including Romanian. The model learns to infer masked tokens in the input sequences (*Masked Language Modeling*) and ignores the binary classification (*Next Sentence Prediction*) objective of the initial BERT. *XLM* (Lample and Conneau, 2019) is a cross-lingual model employs multiple language modeling objectives, including a modified variant of the BERT Masked Language Modeling supporting text streams with an arbitrary number of sentences and subsampling of frequent tokens. *XLM-RoBERTa* (*XLM-R*) (Conneau et al., 2019) is an update of XLM that is additionally trained on 2.5TB of newly cleaned CommonCrawl (Wenzek et al., 2019) data. Both XLM and XLM-R are trained on 100 languages, including Romanian.

In addition to the multilingual models, there is also the possibility of training transformer models, such as BERT, from scratch using only monolingual data for the specific task. Such progress has been made in the case of the Romanian language (Dumitrescu et al., 2020). These are trained on the OPUS (Tiedemann and Nygaard, 2004), OSCAR (Suárez et al., 2019) and Romanian Wikipedia corpora.

The popularity of transformer-based models determined a lot of research to be done for explaining their inside attention mechanisms (Tenney et al., 2019; Michel et al., 2019; Rogers et al., 2020; Clark et al., 2019). This growing field of study is called "BERTology."

3   Method

Our research focuses entirely on pre-trained transformer-based models fine-tuned using the same textual data and similar hyper-parameters.

3.1   Corpus Pre-processing

The training, validation and test datasets have two distinct categories of data: extracts from the news domain and tweets. The training set contains 33,564 news extracts and no tweets, the validation set has 5,923 news extracts and 215 tweets, while the test set consists of 5,022 tweets and no news extracts.

We apply multiple pre-processing techniques on these datasets. First of all, we remove recurring JavaScript artifacts. This only applies for the news samples. Further on, we attempt to remove unnecessary whitespaces, such as the ones before commas and periods. Additionally, we normalize the usage of punctuation, as there are multiple similar ASCII characters for the same punctuation symbol and there is the possibility of one symbol being equivalent to multiple ones (e.g. "…" as a single ASCII symbol and "..." as three period symbols).

The named entities in the given corpus are all replaced by the tokens "NE." We make the decision to replace these with "[MASK]" tokens, which are relevant in the language modeling objective of models such as BERT.

Finally, the two types of data are very distinct in regards to their sample size, with news extracts in the training set having an average character length of 1715, while the tweets in the test set have an average length of 92. For this reason, we observed that using the training data in its original state does not achieve satisfying results on tweets. To fix this, we split each news extract into sentences.[1] This brings the number of training samples to 366,628, more than 10 times the initial size of the dataset. We showcase the huge boost in performance this attains in a later section.

---

[1]To do this, we use the sentence segmentation available in the spaCy package (Honnibal and Montani, 2017)

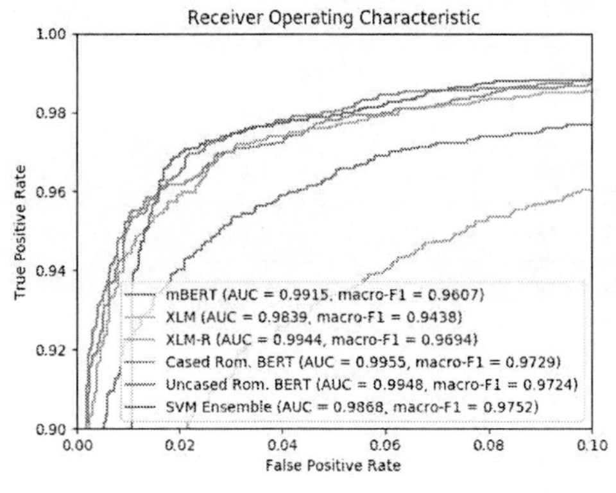

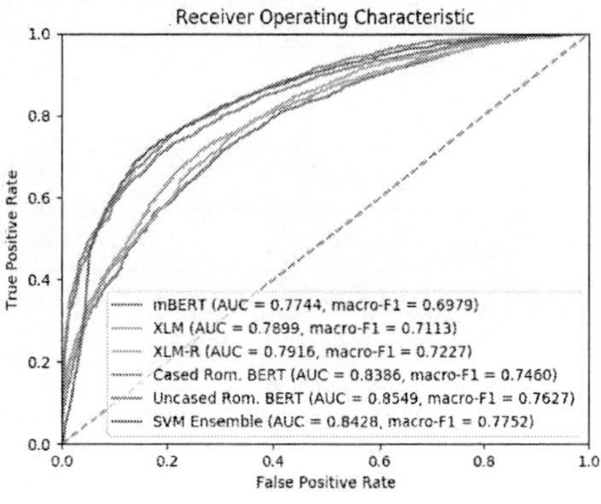

(a) Performance of all models on news extracts.   (b) Performance of all models on tweets.

Figure 1: Performance comparison between all transformer models and the SVM ensemble.

3.2 Training the Models

We use 3 multilingual models and 2 monolingual models in our experiments. The multilingual models are the base (12-layer, 12-heads) cased variant of mBERT[2], the 16-layer, 16-heads XLM trained on 100 languages, and the large (24-layer, 16-heads) XLM-R[3]. The monolingual models use the BERT architecture, are trained only on Romanian data and employ 12 layers and 12 heads, similar to the mBERT model (Dumitrescu et al., 2020). They vary by the data tokenizer they use (cased vs. uncased).[4] We refer to the latter as cased/uncased Romanian BERT.

There are potential advantages and disadvantages to using both monolingual and multilingual models. The former are more specifically trained for the task, while the latter may encompass better linguistic knowledge. Nonetheless, neither the multilingual models, nor the monolingual ones do not explicitly incorporate Moldavian corpora during their initial training.

For the dialect identification task, an additional classification layer is added. All the models are fine-tuned under similar conditions. We use an Adam optimizer (Kingma and Ba, 2014) with a learning rate of 2e-5 and a warmup of 6% of total steps for 2 epochs. The input samples are truncated to 128 tokens. Note that this favors our initial decision of splitting the news extracts into sentences, as a large chunk of information would be lost otherwise. Due to hardware limitations, the XLM and XLM-R models use a batch size of 16, compared to the 32 of the other models, as these are significantly larger.[5] This is the only difference in hyper-parameters for the fine-tuning. The models are only trained on the news extracts in the training set. We choose the decision threshold for each model to be the one that maximizes the macro-F1 score.

A final SVM ensemble is trained from the probabilities generated by the 5 transformer-based models on every sample. We split the 215 tweets in the validation set into 108 samples that we use to train the ensemble and 107 samples to test its performance and determine the optimal threshold with the same objective as before. The best hyper-parameters of the SVM are found using a simple grid search, given the low dimensionality of the dataset, comprising only 5 numerical features. The kernel chosen following it was the radial basis function.

4 Experimental Results

In the results presented further, the metrics we analyze are the Area Under Curve (AUC) and macro-averaged F1 score, which requires a decision threshold to clearly distinguish Romanian-predicted sam-

---

[2] https://github.com/google-research/bert/blob/master/multilingual.md
[3] https://github.com/facebookresearch/XLM
[4] https://github.com/dumitrescustefan/Romanian-Transformers
[5] We use the HuggingFace Transformers (Wolf et al., 2019) library for our experiments.

Table 1: Qualitative results of all the models used.

Models	News Extracts		Tweets	
	AUC	Macro-F1	AUC	Macro-F1
mBERT	0.9915	0.9607	0.7744	0.6979
XLM	0.9839	0.9438	0.7899	0.7113
XLM-R	0.9944	0.9694	0.7916	0.7227
Cased Rom. BERT	**0.9955**	0.9729	0.8386	0.7460
Uncased Rom. BERT	0.9948	0.9724	**0.8549**	0.7627
SVM Ensemble	0.9868	**0.9752**	0.8428	**0.7752**

Table 2: Best macro-F1 scores for all the submissions on the RDI shared task.

Models	Macro-F1
Tubingen	0.787592
Anumiți (SVM Ensemble)	**0.775178**
Phlyers	0.666090
SUKI	0.658437
UPB	0.647577
UAIC	0.555044
akanksha	0.481325
The Linguistadors	0.429412

ples from Moldavian ones. We choose to study the AUC since we believe it is stronger than the F1 score for showcasing the underlying potential of the model, as it is based on all the possible decision thresholds. The news extracts and tweets have distinct enough samples that the performance varies greatly. For this reason, we consider both results relevant and showcase them separately. For the news extracts, we assess the performance on the 5,923 extracts in the validation set, with the threshold being set based on the same samples. For the tweets, we determine the threshold based on the 215 samples in the validation set, while we are interested in the performance of the larger test set with 5,022 samples. The SVM ensemble is an exception to this rule, as it is trained on half of the validation tweets, while the other half is used to determine the best threshold.

Because the performance on the news extracts is very good and the AUC quickly approaches 1.0 for all models, we only showcase a specific area of the ROC with False Positive Rate (FPR) between 0.0 and 0.1, as well as True Positive Rate (TPR) between 0.9 and 1.0. This way, we are able to present a clearer comparison between the models.

4.1 Comparison of the Models

First of all, we investigate the performance of all the individual models and the SVM ensemble on the two types of datasets. The ROC of each one can be seen in Figure 1 and the numeric values of the metrics are recorded in Table 1. We notice some clear differences in behaviour between the two cases. For the news extracts, the two Romanian variants of BERT and XLM-R are closely competing, while mBERT is performing slightly worse and XLM is the obvious loser. In regards to the tweets, we see that the monolingual models are superior to all the multilingual ones, with the uncased version coming out on top. In both cases, the SVM ensemble is not the best according to the AUC, but still achieves the

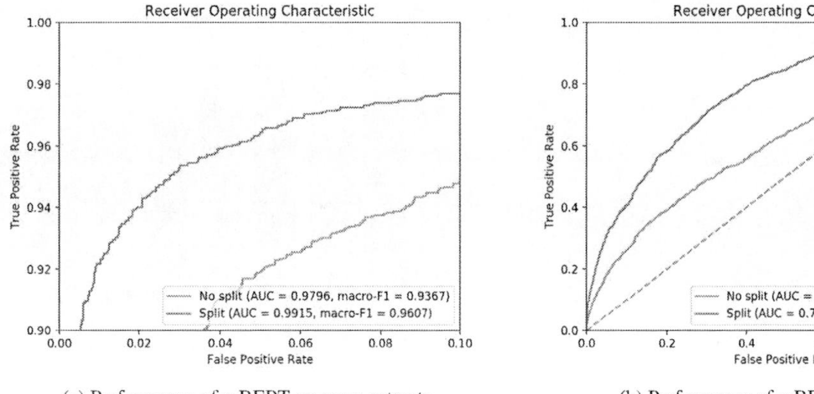

(a) Performance of mBERT on news extracts.   (b) Performance of mBERT on tweets.

Figure 2: Performance comparison for mBERT trained on split vs. unsplit samples.

highest macro-F1 score. The three runs we submitted were the ones with the highest macro-F1 scores on the "Tweets" set, namely the two Romanian BERT models, along with the SVM ensemble. Table 2 displays the best macro-F1 scores obtained by the teams participating in the RDI shared task of VarDial 2020. We closely trail the first place submission, validating that transformer-based models are viable and competitive in classifying dialects.

Given that the Romanian BERT models achieve the best results on both the news extracts and the tweets, we may conclude that for identifying between Romanian and Moldavian dialects, monolingual models trained on Romanian corpora are better than their multilingual counterparts trained on a large number of languages.

4.2 Improvement of Splitting

As mentioned previously, the decision to split the extracts from the news domain into sentences and use those instead as training samples brought a huge improvement to our models. We showcase this with the mBERT model in Figure 2. Notice that the performance on the tweets was greatly enhanced and there is an additional small boost on the news extracts as well.

4.3 Analysis of the Attention Mechanism

Inspired by the works of Clark et al. (2019), we attempt to explain the decisions of some of our models, namely the monolingual ones, as they proved to achieve the best results. We are interested in finding the tokens most important in differentiating between the two dialects, based on the attention that is being paid to them inside the transformer modules. The encoder in the transformer architecture (Vaswani et al., 2017) features multiple attention heads where each token in the input attends to the others with a certain degree of attention. Each layer in the BERT architecture is such an encoder employing multi-head attention. In our case, the monolingual models comprise 12 layers of encoders, each one having 12 attention heads.

We define the importance of a token in classifying a sample as the total amount of attention that is being paid to it over all layers and attention heads, divided by the number of instances it is being encountered in. Mathematically, the importance of a token t_{target} in a corpus C it is defined as follows:

$$Importance(t_{target}) = \frac{\sum_{i=1}^{n_l} \sum_{j=1}^{n_h} \sum_{s \in C} \sum_{t_a \in s} \sum_{t_b \in s} \begin{cases} attn_{ij}(t_a, t_b), t_b = t_{target} \\ 0, t_b \neq t_{target} \end{cases}}{\sum_{i=1}^{n_l} \sum_{j=1}^{n_h} \sum_{s \in C} \sum_{t_a \in s} \sum_{t_b \in s} \begin{cases} 1, t_b = t_{target} \\ 0, t_b \neq t_{target} \end{cases}} \tag{1}$$

197

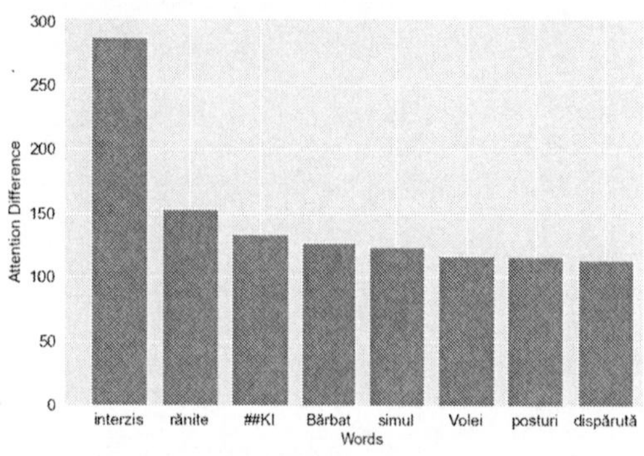
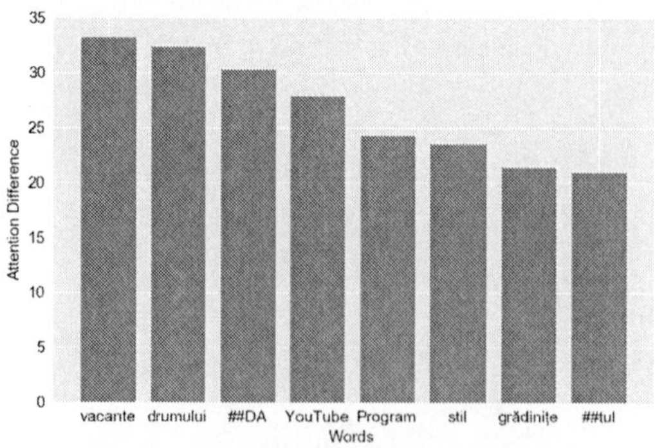

(a) Differentiating tokens for the Romanian dialect.   (b) Differentiating tokens for the Moldavian dialect.

Figure 3: Differentiating tokens for both dialects extracted from the cased Romanian BERT.

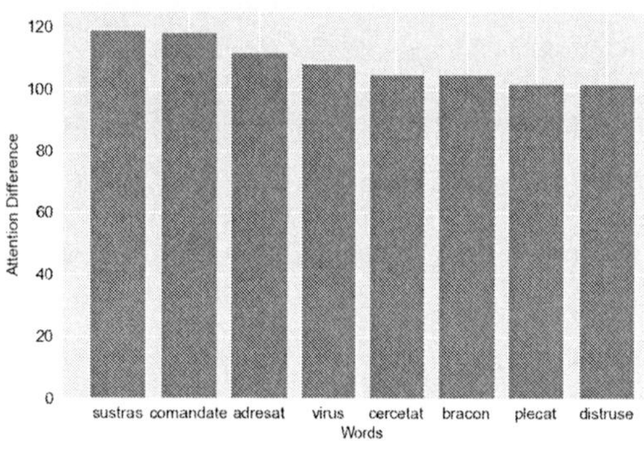
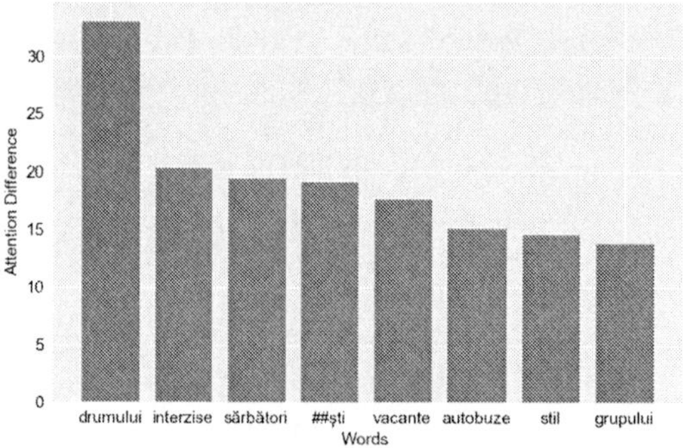

(a) Differentiating tokens for the Romanian dialect.   (b) Differentiating tokens for the Moldavian dialect.

Figure 4: Differentiating tokens for both dialects extracted from the uncased Romanian BERT.

where $attn_{ij}(t_a, t_b)$ is the attention that token t_a pays to token t_b in layer i and head j, n_l is the total number of layers and n_h is the number of attention heads per layer.

The importance of a token is computed for Romanian and Moldavian samples separately. The difference between them for a single token represents its capacity to distinguish the Romanian dialect from the Moldavian one (Romanian-biased) and vice-versa (Moldavian-biased). We refer to these tokens as "*differentiating tokens*" and extract them only from the tweets in the test set. Instead of the real labels, we choose to use the ones predicted by the models. The plots in Figures 3 and 4 showcase the top-8 differentiating tokens found in all cases and their corresponding difference in attention between the two dialects. The "##" symbols indicate that the token is a continuation of a previous one for the same word (e.g. "*##face*" for "*preface*"). Table 3 contains the number of appearances for each of these tokens in the Romanian and Moldavian samples.

One first observation that can be made is that the attention being paid to Romanian-biased differentiating tokens has a higher magnitude than the Moldavian-biased ones. As we expect, with few exceptions, the tokens are encountered multiple times in the dialect they are biased towards and usually once in the other dialect (note that we only consider tokens present in both). This means that the models are able to pay attention to meaningful tokens, that are favored by one dialect, even though these may well be used by both, such as "*virus.*" As native speakers of the Romanian language, with minor knowledge of Moldavian-specific constructs, we don't find these tokens particularly related to grammar, but rather to trends in the media. For instance, the token "*Volei*" may be prevalent in Romanian samples due to the

Table 3: Differentiating tokens for the Romanian BERT models (top half - tokens biased toward Romanian samples; bottom half - tokens biased toward Moldavian samples; left half - cased version; right half - uncased version) and their corresponding number of appearances in the corpora, based on predicted label.

Tokens	RO Count	MD Count	Tokens	RO Count	MD Count
interzis	1	3	sustras	9	2
rănite	9	2	comandate	1	1
##KI	3	1	adresat	1	1
Bărbat	12	1	virus	5	1
simul	1	1	cercetat	10	1
Volei	4	1	bracon	6	1
posturi	3	1	plecat	8	1
dispărută	2	1	distruse	1	1
vacante	1	5	drumului	1	5
drumului	1	5	interzise	1	4
##DA	2	36	sărbători	1	5
YouTube	6	96	##şti	1	3
Program	1	6	vacante	1	5
stil	1	7	autobuze	2	7
grădinițe	1	10	stil	1	7
##tul	1	4	grupului	1	12

popularity of their national Volleyball team. An interesting takeaway is that Romanian media tends to utilize more adjectives, compared to the Moldavian one making use of nouns for the most part. This indicates that expressiveness was favored in the Romanian samples.

5 Conclusion

In this paper, we analyzed a total of 3 multilingual and 2 monolingual transformer-based models fine-tuned on a task of dialect identification between Romanian and Moldavian dialects. We present our methodology for pre-processing the data and found that the monolingual models outclass the multilingual ones on data originating from two different sources, with an SVM ensemble combining them all that achieves the best macro-F1 score. Lastly, we provide a study on the explainability of the best models, focusing on the tokens that these classifiers find the most important in distinguishing the dialects.

References

Dzmitry Bahdanau, Kyunghyun Cho, and Yoshua Bengio. 2014. Neural machine translation by jointly learning to align and translate. *arXiv preprint arXiv:1409.0473*.

Andrei Butnaru and Radu Tudor Ionescu. 2019. MOROCO: The Moldavian and Romanian dialectal corpus. In *Proceedings of the 57th Annual Meeting of the Association for Computational Linguistics*, pages 688–698, Florence, Italy, July. Association for Computational Linguistics.

Adrian-Gabriel Chifu. 2019. The R2I_LIS team proposes majority vote for VarDial's MRC task. In *Proceedings of the Sixth Workshop on NLP for Similar Languages, Varieties and Dialects*, pages 138–143, Ann Arbor, Michigan, June. Association for Computational Linguistics.

Kevin Clark, Urvashi Khandelwal, Omer Levy, and Christopher D. Manning. 2019. What Does BERT Look At? An Analysis of BERT's Attention. In *BlackBoxNLP@ACL*.

Alexis Conneau, Ruty Rinott, Guillaume Lample, Adina Williams, Samuel R. Bowman, Holger Schwenk, and Veselin Stoyanov. 2018. XNLI: Evaluating Cross-lingual Sentence Representations. In *Proceedings of the 2018 Conference on Empirical Methods in Natural Language Processing*. Association for Computational Linguistics.

Alexis Conneau, Kartikay Khandelwal, Naman Goyal, Vishrav Chaudhary, Guillaume Wenzek, Francisco Guzmán, Edouard Grave, Myle Ott, Luke Zettlemoyer, and Veselin Stoyanov. 2019. Unsupervised Cross-lingual Representation Learning at Scale. *arXiv preprint arXiv:1911.02116*.

Jacob Devlin, Ming-Wei Chang, Kenton Lee, and Kristina Toutanova. 2019. BERT: Pre-training of deep bidirectional transformers for language understanding. In *Proceedings of the 2019 Conference of the North American Chapter of the Association for Computational Linguistics: Human Language Technologies, Volume 1 (Long and Short Papers)*, pages 4171–4186, Minneapolis, Minnesota, June. Association for Computational Linguistics.

Stefan Daniel Dumitrescu, Andrei-Marius Avram, and Sampo Pyysalo. 2020. The birth of Romanian BERT.

Mihaela Găman and Radu Tudor Ionescu. 2020. The Unreasonable Effectiveness of Machine Learning in Moldavian versus Romanian Dialect Identification. *arXiv preprint arXiv:2007.15700*.

Mihaela Găman, Dirk Hovy, Radu Tudor Ionescu, Heidi Jauhiainen, Tommi Jauhiainen, Krister Lindén, Nikola Ljubešić, Niko Partanen, Christoph Purschke, Yves Scherrer, and Marcos Zampieri. 2020. A Report on the VarDial Evaluation Campaign 2020. In *Proceedings of the Seventh Workshop on NLP for Similar Languages, Varieties and Dialects (VarDial)*.

Matthew Honnibal and Ines Montani. 2017. spaCy 2: Natural language understanding with Bloom embeddings, convolutional neural networks and incremental parsing. To appear.

Diederik P Kingma and Jimmy Ba. 2014. Adam: A method for stochastic optimization. *arXiv preprint arXiv:1412.6980*.

Guillaume Lample and Alexis Conneau. 2019. Cross-lingual Language Model Pretraining. *Advances in Neural Information Processing Systems (NeurIPS)*.

Mike Lewis, Yinhan Liu, Naman Goyal, Marjan Ghazvininejad, Abdelrahman Mohamed, Omer Levy, Ves Stoyanov, and Luke Zettlemoyer. 2019. Bart: Denoising sequence-to-sequence pre-training for natural language generation, translation, and comprehension. *arXiv preprint arXiv:1910.13461*.

Yinhan Liu, Myle Ott, Naman Goyal, Jingfei Du, Mandar Joshi, Danqi Chen, Omer Levy, Mike Lewis, Luke Zettlemoyer, and Veselin Stoyanov. 2019. RoBERTa: A Robustly Optimized BERT Pretraining Approach. *arXiv preprint arXiv:1907.11692*.

Paul Michel, Omer Levy, and Graham Neubig. 2019. Are sixteen heads really better than one? In *Advances in Neural Information Processing Systems*, pages 14014–14024.

Preslav Nakov, Marcos Zampieri, Nikola Ljubešić, Jörg Tiedemann, Shevin Malmasi, and Ahmed Ali, editors. 2017. *Proceedings of the Fourth Workshop on NLP for Similar Languages, Varieties and Dialects (VarDial)*, Valencia, Spain, April. Association for Computational Linguistics.

Cristian Onose, Dumitru-Clementin Cercel, and Stefan Trausan-Matu. 2019. SC-UPB at the VarDial 2019 evaluation campaign: Moldavian vs. Romanian cross-dialect topic identification. In *Proceedings of the Sixth Workshop on NLP for Similar Languages, Varieties and Dialects*, pages 172–177, Ann Arbor, Michigan, June. Association for Computational Linguistics.

Alec Radford, Jeffrey Wu, Rewon Child, David Luan, Dario Amodei, and Ilya Sutskever. 2019. Language models are unsupervised multitask learners.

Pranav Rajpurkar, Jian Zhang, Konstantin Lopyrev, and Percy Liang. 2016. Squad: 100,000+ questions for machine comprehension of text. *arXiv preprint arXiv:1606.05250*.

Anna Rogers, Olga Kovaleva, and Anna Rumshisky. 2020. A primer in BERTology: What we know about how BERT works. *arXiv preprint arXiv:2002.12327*.

Pedro Javier Ortiz Suárez, Benoît Sagot, and Laurent Romary. 2019. Asynchronous pipeline for processing huge corpora on medium to low resource infrastructures. In *7th Workshop on the Challenges in the Management of Large Corpora (CMLC-7)*. Leibniz-Institut für Deutsche Sprache.

Ian Tenney, Dipanjan Das, and Ellie Pavlick. 2019. BERT rediscovers the classical NLP pipeline. In *Proceedings of the 57th Annual Meeting of the Association for Computational Linguistics*, pages 4593–4601, Florence, Italy, July. Association for Computational Linguistics.

Jörg Tiedemann and Lars Nygaard. 2004. The OPUS corpus - parallel and free: `http://logos.uio.no/opus`. In *Proceedings of the Fourth International Conference on Language Resources and Evaluation (LREC'04)*, Lisbon, Portugal, May. European Language Resources Association (ELRA).

Diana Tudoreanu. 2019. DTeam @ VarDial 2019: Ensemble based on skip-gram and triplet loss neural networks for moldavian vs. Romanian cross-dialect topic identification. In *Proceedings of the Sixth Workshop on NLP for Similar Languages, Varieties and Dialects*, pages 202–208, Ann Arbor, Michigan, June. Association for Computational Linguistics.

Ashish Vaswani, Noam Shazeer, Niki Parmar, Jakob Uszkoreit, Llion Jones, Aidan N Gomez, Łukasz Kaiser, and Illia Polosukhin. 2017. Attention is all you need. In *Advances in neural information processing systems*, pages 5998–6008.

Guillaume Wenzek, Marie-Anne Lachaux, Alexis Conneau, Vishrav Chaudhary, Francisco Guzmán, Armand Joulin, and Edouard Grave. 2019. Ccnet: Extracting high quality monolingual datasets from web crawl data. *arXiv preprint arXiv:1911.00359*.

Thomas Wolf, Lysandre Debut, Victor Sanh, Julien Chaumond, Clement Delangue, Anthony Moi, Pierric Cistac, Tim Rault, R'emi Louf, Morgan Funtowicz, and Jamie Brew. 2019. HuggingFace's Transformers: State-of-the-art Natural Language Processing. *ArXiv*, abs/1910.03771.

Nianheng Wu, Eric DeMattos, Kwok Him So, Pin-zhen Chen, and Çağrı Çöltekin. 2019. Language Discrimination and Transfer Learning for Similar Languages: Experiments with Feature Combinations and Adaptation. In *Proceedings of the Sixth Workshop on NLP for Similar Languages, Varieties and Dialects*, pages 54–63, Ann Arbor, Michigan, June. Association for Computational Linguistics.

Marcos Zampieri, Shervin Malmasi, Nikola Ljubešić, Preslav Nakov, Ahmed Ali, Jörg Tiedemann, Yves Scherrer, and Noëmi Aepli. 2017. Findings of the VarDial evaluation campaign 2017. In *Proceedings of the Fourth Workshop on NLP for Similar Languages, Varieties and Dialects (VarDial)*, pages 1–15, Valencia, Spain, April. Association for Computational Linguistics.

Marcos Zampieri, Shervin Malmasi, Preslav Nakov, Ahmed Ali, Suwon Shon, James Glass, Yves Scherrer, Tanja Samardžić, Nikola Ljubešić, Jörg Tiedemann, Chris van der Lee, Stefan Grondelaers, Nelleke Oostdijk, Dirk Speelman, Antal van den Bosch, Ritesh Kumar, Bornini Lahiri, and Mayank Jain. 2018a. Language identification and morphosyntactic tagging: The second VarDial evaluation campaign. In *Proceedings of the Fifth Workshop on NLP for Similar Languages, Varieties and Dialects (VarDial 2018)*, pages 1–17, Santa Fe, New Mexico, USA, August. Association for Computational Linguistics.

Marcos Zampieri, Preslav Nakov, Nikola Ljubešić, Jörg Tiedemann, Shervin Malmasi, and Ahmed Ali, editors. 2018b. *Proceedings of the Fifth Workshop on NLP for Similar Languages, Varieties and Dialects (VarDial 2018)*, Santa Fe, New Mexico, USA, August. Association for Computational Linguistics.

Marcos Zampieri, Shervin Malmasi, Yves Scherrer, Tanja Samardžić, Francis Tyers, Miikka Silfverberg, Natalia Klyueva, Tung-Le Pan, Chu-Ren Huang, Radu Tudor Ionescu, Andrei M. Butnaru, and Tommi Jauhiainen. 2019a. A report on the third VarDial evaluation campaign. In *Proceedings of the Sixth Workshop on NLP for Similar Languages, Varieties and Dialects*, pages 1–16, Ann Arbor, Michigan, June. Association for Computational Linguistics.

Marcos Zampieri, Preslav Nakov, Shervin Malmasi, Nikola Ljubešić, Jörg Tiedemann, and Ahmed Ali, editors. 2019b. *Proceedings of the Sixth Workshop on NLP for Similar Languages, Varieties and Dialects*, Ann Arbor, Michigan, June. Association for Computational Linguistics.

HeLju@VarDial 2020:
Social Media Variety Geolocation with BERT Models

Yves Scherrer
Department of Digital Humanities
University of Helsinki
yves.scherrer@helsinki.fi

Nikola Ljubešić
Department of Knowledge Technologies
Jožef Stefan Institute
nikola.ljubesic@ijs.si

Abstract

This paper describes the Helsinki–Ljubljana contribution to the VarDial shared task on social media variety geolocation. Our solutions are based on the BERT Transformer models, the constrained versions of our models reaching 1st place in two subtasks and 3rd place in one subtask, while our unconstrained models outperform all the constrained systems by a large margin. We show in our analyses that Transformer-based models outperform traditional models by far, and that improvements obtained by pre-training models on large quantities of (mostly standard) text are significant, but not drastic, with single-language models also outperforming multilingual models. Our manual analysis shows that two types of signals are the most crucial for a (mis)prediction: named entities and dialectal features, both of which are handled well by our models.

1 Introduction

Until 2019, all VarDial evaluation campaigns have focused on classification tasks where the number of linguistic varieties was defined beforehand by the task organizers. The 2020 SMG task breaks with this tradition and asks the participants to predict latitude-longitude coordinates, i.e., two output values on a continuous scale. The SMG task is divided in three subtasks focusing on different linguistic areas: the Bosnian-Croatian-Montenegrin-Serbian (BCMS) language area, the German-speaking area of Germany and Austria (DEAT), and German-speaking Switzerland (CH). All three datasets are based on social media data, Twitter in the case of BCMS and Jodel in the case of DEAT and CH.

This paper describes the HeLju (Helsinki–Ljubljana) submission to the SMG task. Our motivation was to investigate how existing classification and regression approaches can be adapted to a double regression task. Most of our work is based on the BERT sentence classification architecture in both constrained and unconstrained settings. We experiment with various pre-trained models, different types of coordinate encoding and other hyperparameters. Finally, we manually analyze the development set predictions made with our best-performing models.

2 Related work

One of the first works focusing on predicting geolocation from social media text is Han et al. (2012). The authors investigate feature (token) selection methods for location prediction, showing that traditional predictive algorithms yield significantly better results if feature selection is performed.

There has been already a shared task on geolocation prediction at WNUT 2016 (Han et al., 2016). The task focused not only on predicting geolocation from text, but also from various user metadata. The best performing systems were combining the available information via feedforward networks or ensembles.

Thomas and Hennig (2018) report significant improvements over the winner of the WNUT-16 shared task by learning separately text and metadata embeddings via different neural network architectures

This work is licensed under a Creative Commons Attribution 4.0 International Licence. Licence details: http://creativecommons.org/licenses/by/4.0/.

Proceedings of the 7th VarDial Workshop on NLP for Similar Languages, Varieties and Dialects, pages 202–211
Barcelona, Spain (Online), December 13, 2020

	BCMS	DEAT	CH
Training instances	320 042	336 983	22 600
Development instances	39 750	46 582	3 068
Test instances	39 723	48 239	3 097
Median instance length	12	45	47
Maximum instance length	44	272	129

Table 1: Data characteristics. Instance length statistics are computed on space-separated token count of the training sets.

(LSTM, feedforward), merging those embeddings and performing the final classification via a softmax layer.

To the best of our knowledge, large pre-trained language models such as BERT have not yet been applied to the problem of geolocation prediction, but just to language identification (Bernier-Colborne et al., 2019).

3 Data

The VarDial evaluation campaign provides training, development and test data for the three subtasks. Table 1 gives an overview of the data. It can be seen that the BCMS and DEAT datasets are roughly equivalent in size, whereas the CH dataset is more than one order of magnitude smaller. The instances from the Twitter dataset (BCMS) correspond to single tweets, while the instances from the Jodel datasets correspond to entire conversations and are thus much longer on average.

The task organizers also provide a simple baseline for the geolocation task. They compute the centroid ("average location") of all instances in the training data and then predict the coordinates of this centroid for all development or test instances (see Table 2, first row).

4 Experiments

The geolocation task takes text as input and produces two real-valued outputs, the predicted latitude and longitude. The two outputs can be produced by independently trained models or by a single model that benefits from some form of parameter sharing.

4.1 Traditional machine learning approaches

In dialect classification, one of the most popular and successful approaches relies on an SVM classifier that is trained on character n-grams. It has also been shown beneficial to weight the n-gram frequencies, e.g. using the TF-IDF weighting scheme (Jauhiainen et al., 2019; Martinc and Pollak, 2019). We adapted this setup by substituting the SVM classifier by two independent SVR regression models, one for latitude and one for longitude.[1] As input features, we used TF-IDF-weighted n-grams of length 3 to 6 occurring at least 5 times in the training corpus. For this and all other experiments presented in the paper, we train and test our systems on lower-cased data, as we found no evidence that casing information would be relevant for geolocation. No further pre-processing was applied to the data. Table 2 (second row) shows that this approach easily beats the centroid baseline for all three subtasks.

4.2 Neural machine learning approaches

In recent years, pre-trained language representations have become very successful for various downstream tasks. BERT (Devlin et al., 2019) is currently one of the most popular pre-trained language representation frameworks and is based on the Transformer neural network architecture (Vaswani et al., 2017). Typically, a BERT model is created in two phases. In the pre-training phase, a Transformer is trained from scratch using a masked language modeling task. This task only requires unlabeled data. A

---

[1] We used the *MultiOutputRegressor* class of the Scikit-Learn toolkit (Pedregosa et al., 2011) to combine the two models.

	Median distance (km)		
Model	BCMS	DEAT	CH
Centroid baseline	107.1	201.3	41.4
SVR with TF-IDF character n-grams	82.2	168.7	29.7
Constrained BERT	48.1	159.2	17.8
Multilingual BERT	44.9	150.7	16.6
Language-specific BERT	42.7	146.5	15.6

Table 2: Median distances (lower is better) of different models on the development set.

wide variety of pre-trained models have been made publicly available. Since the Transformer architecture requires a fixed-size vocabulary, each pre-trained model also comes with a pre-trained tokenizer that splits infrequent words into subword units. In the fine-tuning phase, a pre-trained model is adapted to a particular downstream task. For example, in an instance classification task, the output representation of the special [CLS] token is fed into a separate fully-connected layer that predicts the output class. In this phase, training data with gold class labels are required. Bernier-Colborne et al. (2019) have successfully used BERT for dialect identification. The fine-tuning step can be adapted easily from a classification to a regression problem by removing the sigmoid function and choosing an appropriate loss function. Likewise, double regression can be implemented by producing two-dimensional output vectors.[2]

We report three preliminary experiments with the BERT architecture here.[3] In the first experiment, we pre-train a BERT model from scratch on the VarDial SMG training data (without the coordinates),[4] and then fine-tune it on the regression task with the SMG training data (including the coordinates). Just like the SVR setup, this is a constrained setup in the sense that no data sources other than the ones provided by VarDial are used. The third row in Table 2 shows that BERT outperforms the SVR massively on all three tasks despite using exactly the same data. In particular, the median distances are reduced by more than 40% for the BCMS and CH tasks.

In the second experiment, we use the pre-trained `bert-base-multilingual-uncased` model[5] and fine-tune it on the VarDial data; we use the provided tokenizer without any adaptation. This model has been pre-trained on about 100 languages, including German, Croatian and Serbian. However, we do not expect it to be particularly well adapted to our task for two reasons. First, massively multilingual models are prone to capacity dilution: at constant model capacity, the part allocated to each language is inversely proportional to the number of languages covered by the model (Conneau et al., 2020). Second, its tokenizer is trained on all the languages it supports, yielding therefore suboptimal text splitting in comparison to language-specific tokenizers. Despite these shortcomings, the distances (Table 2, fourth row) are further reduced by 5–7% compared to the constrained setup. Note that in preliminary experiments, we also tested the XLM-RoBERTa model (Conneau et al., 2020), but found no benefits compared with the original multilingual BERT.

For the third experiment, we looked for alternative pre-trained models that overcome the limitations of multilingual BERT and specifically cover the languages of the three subtasks. For BCMS, we use the `crosloengual-bert` model provided by Embeddia (Ulčar and Robnik-Šikonja, 2020).[6] For DEAT, we use the `bert-base-german-dbmdz-uncased` model provided by the Bavarian State Library.[7] As we were not able to find a pre-trained model for Swiss German, we started with the German BERT

---

[2] For our experiments, we adapt the *simpletransformers* library (https://simpletransformers.ai/), which already supports single regression fine-tuning. This library is built on top of the HuggingFace *Transformers* library (Wolf et al., 2019).

[3] For all BERT experiments reported in this section, we use the hyperparameters specified in Sections 4.3 and 4.4, but report numbers from single runs.

[4] We pre-trained the models for 50 000 steps with a batch size of 32, for all three models. For each model, a WordPiece tokenizer with vocabulary size 30 000 is trained on the same data.

[5] https://huggingface.co/bert-base-multilingual-uncased

[6] https://huggingface.co/EMBEDDIA/crosloengual-bert

[7] https://huggingface.co/dbmdz/bert-base-german-uncased

and continued pre-training for another five epochs on the SwissCrawl corpus (Linder et al., 2020). For all three tasks, we rely on the provided tokenizers without modifications. This third setup further improves geolocation results (see last line of Table 2).

Our final submissions are based on the first BERT setup for the constrained setting, and on the third BERT setup for the unconstrained setting.

4.3 Hyperparameter tuning

During our initial experiments, we found the BERT models to be quite sensitive to some hyperparameter settings. We found that the optimal batch sizes for the fine-tuning step depended on the amount of available training data. We obtained the best results with batch sizes of 64 for BCMS, 128 for DEAT, and 32 for CH.

Although the pre-trained BERT models support maximum sequence lengths of up to 512 tokens, we found a smaller maximum length of 128 tokens to work equally well for the BCMS and CH task, while for DEAT the optimal maximum sequence length was 256 tokens, both of which reduced the GPU memory requirements.[8] The *simpletransformers* library also provides a sliding window option that splits long instances into pieces instead of just cutting them off at the maximum length. We did not see any beneficial effect of this option, which suggests that the beginning of each conversation is most indicative of its geographic localization.[9]

During fine-tuning, intermediate models were saved every 2000 training steps and the savepoint with the lowest median distance value measured on the development set was selected. The best models were generally obtained around epoch 8 for BCMS, epoch 4 for DEAT, and epoch 50 for CH. All models tended to overfit to the training data thereafter.

4.4 Coordinate encoding and loss functions

Fine-tuning a BERT model on a regression task requires the selection of an appropriate loss function. This loss function should ideally correspond to the evaluation measure used in the task. The official evaluation measure is median distance measured with the Haversine formula (which assumes that the Earth is a perfect sphere with a radius of 6371 km). While it is possible to train models using the Haversine loss function, we found it more promising to apply some conversions to the coordinates and to use standard regression loss functions instead. We explored various configurations:

Coordinate projections The raw latitude and longitude coordinates have some properties that make them potentially hard to learn: (1) one latitude degree does not amount to the same number of kilometers than one longitude degree; (2) one longitude (East-West) degree corresponds to a larger number of kilometers near the Equator than near the poles. We propose three alternative projections that can be used in conjunction with standard loss functions:

- **Cosine-adjusted longitude:** All longitude values are multiplied by the cosine of their corresponding latitude. The latitude values remain unchanged.[10]

- **UTM projection:** The latitude-longitude coordinates are converted to the UTM coordinate system. This system is based on rectangular zones where each point is represented as the metric distance from the origin of the zone. We chose zone 34T for BCMS, 32U for DEAT, and 32T for CH.[11]

- **Cartesian coordinate system:** The latitude-longitude coordinates are converted into a triple of X, Y and Z coordinates in a 3-dimensional space where the origin corresponds to the center of the Earth.

---

[8]Note that this sequence length is computed after tokenization. While the median instance length before tokenization lies between 12 and 47 (see Table 1), the median instance length after tokenization varies between 24 and 78. The chosen threshold lies thus still well above the median.

[9]This may also be an artifact of the collection method for DEAT and CH, where each conversation is assigned the coordinate of its first message.

[10]See https://stackoverflow.com/a/1664836.

[11]See https://en.wikipedia.org/wiki/Universal_Transverse_Mercator_coordinate_system.

| | | Average median distances (↓) | | | Average relative distance |
		BCMS	DEAT	CH	reduction to baseline (↑)
Projection	Lat-Lon	49.86	**149.30**	15.92	46.9%
	Cos-adj. Lat	50.57	150.80	15.93	46.5%
	UTM	49.61	149.95	**15.86**	**47.0%**
	Cartesian	**49.41**	149.63	15.90	**47.0%**
Loss function	MSE	56.36	151.84	16.04	44.4%
	MAE	**43.36**	**148.00**	**15.76**	**49.3%**
Scaling	Independent	**49.72**	150.18	**15.87**	**46.9%**
	Joint	50.00	**149.65**	15.93	46.8%

Table 3: Results of parameter search experiments. The rightmost column represents averages over the three tasks in the form of relative distance reduction percentages, i.e. higher values are better.

Loss functions We experiment with two commonly used regression loss functions, mean absolute error (MAE/L1) and mean square error (MSE/L2). The former corresponds to Manhattan distance, whereas the latter corresponds to Euclidean distance. While both loss functions apply equally well to multi-dimensional regression, we expect Euclidean distance to be more appropriate for geographic space.

Loss reduction Commonly, the individual losses of a batch are reduced to a single value by taking their mean or sum. Since the official evaluation measure is based on the median, we tried a median reduction as well, but with consistently poor results. We therefore continue to use the mean reduction.

Centering and scaling Neural networks tend not to converge well if the output values are large or not well distributed. A common solution for this problem consists in standardizing the values by centering (i.e., subtracting the mean of the training data) and scaling (i.e., dividing by the standard deviation of the training data). Since our data is two-dimensional, standardizing the values of both dimensions independently may lead to distortion, as (assuming both value distributions are normal) the coordinates are being forced into a square even though the original space is not square-shaped. To prevent this, we propose joint standardization, where the mean is computed independently for each dimension, but the standard deviation is computed jointly on all (mean-removed) values.

Leaving aside the median reductions, which underperformed in preliminary experiments, we trained a total of 48 models (3 tasks × 4 projections × 2 loss functions × 2 scalings) and evaluated each on the respective development set.

The first three columns of Table 3 show average median distances taken over all models of a task, keeping one of the parameters fixed. The last column shows an average over the three tasks; in order to make the numbers comparable, we convert the median distances to distance reduction percentages relative to the task-specific baseline and report the mean reduction percentages over the three tasks.

In terms of projection, we find that the cosine-adjusted latitude encoding performs worse than the other three, even though it satisfies the same requirements as UTM, for example. Surprisingly, raw latitude and longitude do not perform worse than the metric coordinate systems. In terms of loss function, the results show a clear and consistent advantage for MAE loss. We currently do not have an explanation for this result, as the MSE loss should capture geographic distances better.[12] Finally, the two scaling methods are indistinguishable. We also tested for interactions between parameters using a mixed-effects regression model, but did not obtain any statistically significant effects. For our final models (both constrained and unconstrained), we opted for raw latitude-longitude, MAE loss and joint scaling.

These findings seem to contradict several intuitions of geographic modelling: (1) some amount of distortion in the coordinate space does not seem to be an issue, since distortion-free projections such as

---

[12]Note that the same advantage for MAE obtains when evaluated on mean distance instead of median distance.

System name	Constrained	Rankings	Median distance (km)		
			BCMS	DEAT	CH
HeLju 1	no	1,2,2	41.54	143.85	15.72
HeLju 2	no	2,1,1	41.61	143.30	15.45
HeLju 3	yes	1,1,3	48.99	159.59	17.97

Table 4: Final results of our submitted three runs in median distances (lower is better).

UTM or Cartesian do not perform better than raw latitude-longitude, and (2) Manhattan distance seems more appropriate than Euclidean distance. We conclude from this that the geolocation task does not require a geographically faithful modelling of the output space. This suggests that the models do not infer the dialect landscape as a continuum that spreads in two dimensions, but rather as a set of distinct zones (presumably urban areas) whose exact geographic relationships to each other are to some extent arbitrary. We will come back to this hypothesis in Section 5.

4.5   Test-time adaptations

It is well known that neural-network-based models can be sensitive to weight initialization. Therefore, we trained four identical models per task with different random seeds and selected the one with the lowest development set distance for producing the test output.

Furthermore, given that the development sets are rather generous in size, we hypothesized that the information contained therein might be more useful for training than for validation. Therefore, we produced an alternative data split in which the development set is reduced to 3000 (BCMS), 6000 (DEAT) and 1000 (CH) instances respectively, and the remainder is added to the training set. We again train four models per task with this extended data split.

4.6   Results

We submitted three systems per track: an unconstrained system with the default data split (*HeLju 1*), an unconstrained system with the extended data split (*HeLju 2*), and a constrained system with the default data split (*HeLju 3*).

The results of our three submitted systems, with their ranking among all submitted systems, are given in Table 4. Our first observation is that the overall results are very close to the results obtained on dev data, which shows that the dev and test data are quite probably coming from the same distribution. The two unconstrained systems (the only two of their kind among the submitted systems) outperform the constrained version significantly, with the two unconstrained systems performing very similarly, showing that extending the training data with parts of the dev data did not give the extra push that we were hoping for.

The constrained system obtained best results in two out of three subtasks, yielding only third place in the CH subtask that had one order of magnitude less training data than the two other tasks, which also gives the most probable reason for its not-superior performance. In the two tasks where our constrained system won, we we outperformed the second ranked system by an absolute difference in median distance of 8.25 kilometers for the BCMS subtask and 24.4 kilometers for the DEAT subtask. In the CH subtask, the winning system outperformed ours with an absolute difference of 2.04 kilometers.

5   Error analysis

Figure 1 shows the spatial distribution of the development set instances of the three tasks. The plots on the left show the predicted locations, with the color indicating the distance to the true locations. In all three plots, high-accuracy zones can be distinguished (colored in red), which correspond to urban areas. Furthermore, instances that are hard to classify are put into a "default" zone close to the centroid location, in order to minimize distances.

The plots on the right show the true locations, with the color indicating the distance to the predicted

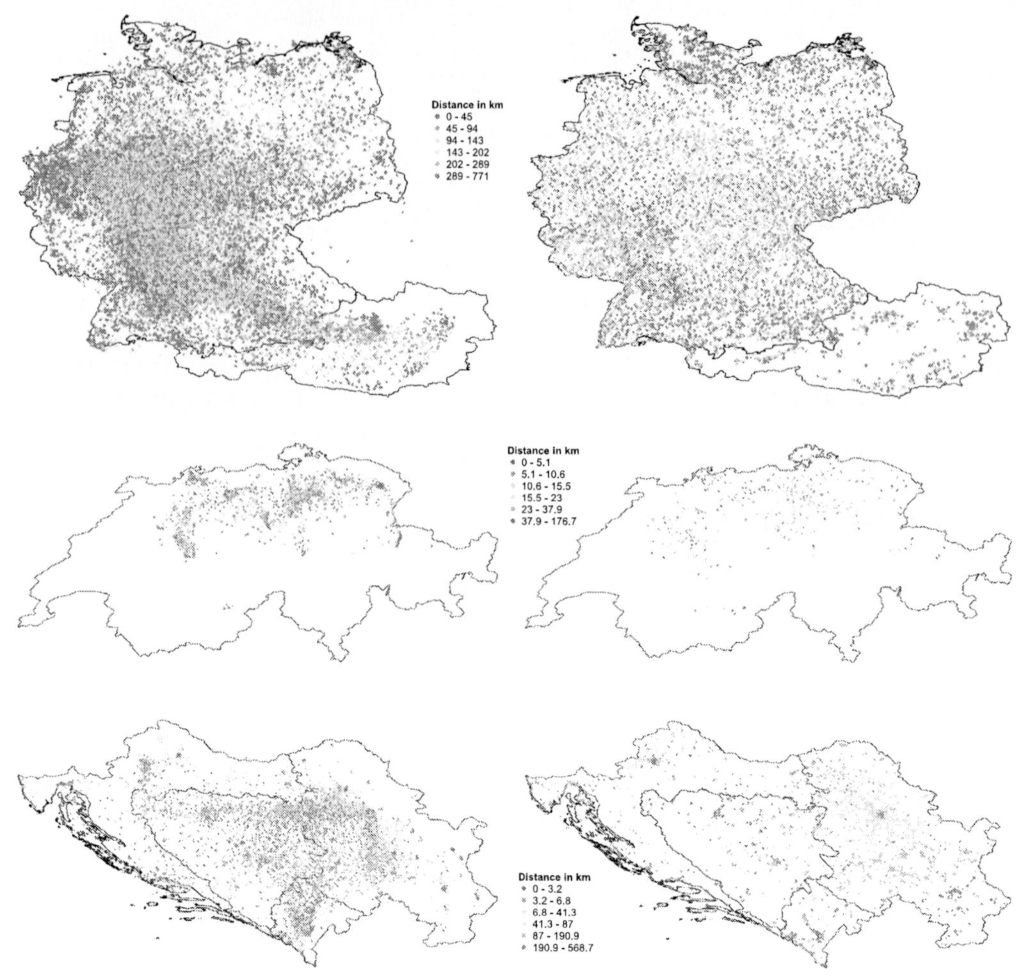

Figure 1: Visualization of development set predictions. Left: instances are placed at their predicted place, the color shows the distance to the true place. Right: instances are placed at their true place, the color shows the distance to the predicted place. Red color stands for small distances, blue color for large distances.

locations. For the DEAT task, red and blue dots occur simultaneously in the same areas. For BCMS, the major urban areas can again be distinguished easily.

We manually analyzed a subset of development set instances for each task. To this end, we chose two areas per task that can be delimited easily and that lie outside of the "default area". We then selected at most 50 "good" and 50 "bad" predictions, on the basis of a task-specific threshold set according to a natural break occurring in the data. We then counted how many of these instances contain dialectal features and named entities (mostly place names, but also names of well known locations, people, institutions or businesses), and whether these features were used consistently (e.g. an instance located in Berlin mentions *Berlin*) or inconsistently (e.g. an instance located in Berlin mentions *Köln*). Table 5 lists some consistent and inconsistent dialectal features, whereas Table 6 shows the results of this analysis.

This small-scale analysis shows some striking differences between the tasks. For the CH task, good prediction performance is mainly associated with the presence of consistent dialectal features, whereas for the DEAT task, prediction almost exclusively relies on the presence of consistent named entities. The BCMS task lies between those two, with both named entity and dialectal signal being present in good

Task	Region	Consistent features	Inconsistent features
BCMS	Zagreb	*Kolindin ili Josipovicev fejk osmijeh*	*Cao cao #svenasvetu* *da uvik slikaju iste pičine*
	Belgrade	*letnji pljusak je okej* *Ustala sam posle 3 meseca pre 4 sata*	*volio bih da ti kazem* *Upravo sam saznao ovu pretužnu vijest*
CH	Wallis	*Und wier chännes miterläbu!* *ich sägu minum botsch ästagsch öi h.* *Sust nu jemand moru en Statisterolla?*	*Hahaha je confirme y a trop …* *Hans liebte Franz doch Franz …* *Da isch en Aargaueri[n] uf de …*
	Chur	*leid tuats miar glich abitz* *Wär muos am 3.7 nach Airolo irucka?* *Liabi Lüüt fahrend doch eifach 50*	*Bisch demfau z frouefäud?* *Wulewu kuschee awek mua?* *wo konn men do heint fortgian?*
DEAT	Berlin	*dat* *nüscht*	*isch*
	Vienna	*spoats eichs bitte ma jt zu sagen* *Also is bei mir doch nicht so fad* *eine ur schirche kartoffelnase*	–

Table 5: Examples of consistent and inconsistent dialect features.

Task	Region	Criterion	N	Named entities		Dialectal features	
				Consistent	Inconsistent	Consistent	Inconsistent
BCMS	Zagreb	< 20 km	50	54%	0%	40%	4%
		> 100 km	50	4%	10%	0%	16%
	Belgrade	< 20 km	50	24%	0%	48%	0%
		> 100 km	50	4%	4%	0%	20%
CH	Wallis	< 20 km	12	8%	0%	100%	0%
		> 50 km	11	27%	9%	73%	27%
	Chur	< 50 km	106	23%	6%	99%	5%
		> 70 km	6	17%	17%	67%	50%
DEAT	Berlin/ Potsdam	< 70 km	47	94%	11%	2%	0%
		> 400 km	50	8%	10%	4%	2%
	Vienna	< 70 km	13	92%	8%	23%	0%
		> 600 km	50	0%	6%	4%	0%

Table 6: Presence of named entities and dialectal features in well and badly classified subsets of the development set.

predictions.

Bad performance is hard to predict for CH, but seems to be related to inconsistent usage of dialectal features. For DEAT, bad performance seems to be due almost exclusively to the absence of named entities. In the DEAT dataset, dialectal and regional features – consistent or not – are extremely rare. In the BCMS dataset bad prediction performance is mostly to be followed back to lack of useful named entity and dialectal signal, as well as a significant amount of misleading dialectal signal, which is to be followed back to the fact that the two selected regions are the two largest cities in the whole area that are surely visited or inhabited by speakers from around the area.

6 Conclusion

In this paper we have presented the first use of the popular Transformer-based BERT systems on geolocation prediction that ensured a very strong first place in the unconstrained version of the VarDial 2020 SMG shared task and the first place in two out of three subtasks in the constrained version of the shared task.

We have shown that pre-trained models perform drastically better than the usual traditional machine learning approaches, even if both are based on the same significant amount of data available. Models pre-trained on large amounts of text do outperform those pre-trained on the training data only, but not with a drastic difference. This lack of a larger difference might probably be followed back to the lack of dialectal features in the large pre-training data.

Language-specific pre-trained models do outperform multilingual models, but not as drastically as one would expect. This lack of a larger difference can probably again be followed back to the lack of dialectal features in the pre-training data. Finally, performing various target transformations from the original (latitude, longitude) space does not improve results.

Our error analysis has shown that the three subtasks are quite different regarding the useful signal available. While the DEAT decisions mostly rely on named entities, and the CH decisions on dialectal features, the BCMS subtask lies somewhere in the middle, with both signals having similar importance. By having such a diverse test bed, we believe that we have shown that the current state-of-the art natural language models produce also the best results on this task, regardless of the type of the useful signal, as long as a significant amount of data (around million instances) is available for pre-training and fine-tuning.

Acknowledgements

This work has been supported by the FoTran project, funded by the European Research Council (ERC) under the European Union's Horizon 2020 research and innovation programme (grant agreement No 771113), and the Slovenian Research Agency through research core funding No. P6-0411 "Language resources and technologies for Slovene language" and the research project ARRS N6-0099 and FWO G070619N "The linguistic landscape of hate speech on social media".

References

Gabriel Bernier-Colborne, Cyril Goutte, and Serge Léger. 2019. Improving cuneiform language identification with BERT. In *Proceedings of the Sixth Workshop on NLP for Similar Languages, Varieties and Dialects*, pages 17–25, Ann Arbor, Michigan, June. Association for Computational Linguistics.

Alexis Conneau, Kartikay Khandelwal, Naman Goyal, Vishrav Chaudhary, Guillaume Wenzek, Francisco Guzmán, Edouard Grave, Myle Ott, Luke Zettlemoyer, and Veselin Stoyanov. 2020. Unsupervised cross-lingual representation learning at scale. In *Proceedings of the 58th Annual Meeting of the Association for Computational Linguistics*, pages 8440–8451, Online, July. Association for Computational Linguistics.

Jacob Devlin, Ming-Wei Chang, Kenton Lee, and Kristina Toutanova. 2019. BERT: Pre-training of deep bidirectional transformers for language understanding. In *Proceedings of the 2019 Conference of the North American Chapter of the Association for Computational Linguistics: Human Language Technologies, Volume 1 (Long and Short Papers)*, pages 4171–4186, Minneapolis, Minnesota, June. Association for Computational Linguistics.

Bo Han, Paul Cook, and Timothy Baldwin. 2012. Geolocation prediction in social media data by finding location indicative words. In *Proceedings of COLING 2012*, pages 1045–1062, Mumbai, India, December. The COLING 2012 Organizing Committee.

Bo Han, Afshin Rahimi, Leon Derczynski, and Timothy Baldwin. 2016. Twitter geolocation prediction shared task of the 2016 workshop on noisy user-generated text. In *Proceedings of the 2nd Workshop on Noisy User-generated Text (WNUT)*, pages 213–217, Osaka, Japan, December. The COLING 2016 Organizing Committee.

Tommi Jauhiainen, Marco Lui, Marcos Zampieri, Timothy Baldwin, and Krister Lindén. 2019. Automatic language identification in texts: A survey. *Journal of Artificial Intelligence Research*, 65:675–782.

Lucy Linder, Michael Jungo, Jean Hennebert, Claudiu Cristian Musat, and Andreas Fischer. 2020. Automatic creation of text corpora for low-resource languages from the internet: The case of Swiss German. In *Proceedings of The 12th Language Resources and Evaluation Conference*, pages 2706–2711, Marseille, France, May. European Language Resources Association.

Matej Martinc and Senja Pollak. 2019. Combining n-grams and deep convolutional features for language variety classification. *Natural Language Engineering*, 25(5):607–632.

F. Pedregosa, G. Varoquaux, A. Gramfort, V. Michel, B. Thirion, O. Grisel, M. Blondel, P. Prettenhofer, R. Weiss, V. Dubourg, J. Vanderplas, A. Passos, D. Cournapeau, M. Brucher, M. Perrot, and E. Duchesnay. 2011. Scikit-learn: Machine learning in Python. *Journal of Machine Learning Research*, 12:2825–2830.

Philippe Thomas and Leonhard Hennig. 2018. Twitter geolocation prediction using neural networks. In Georg Rehm and Thierry Declerck, editors, *Language Technologies for the Challenges of the Digital Age*, pages 248–255, Cham. Springer International Publishing.

Matej Ulčar and Marko Robnik-Šikonja. 2020. FinEst BERT and CroSloEngual BERT: less is more in multilingual models.

Ashish Vaswani, Noam Shazeer, Niki Parmar, Jakob Uszkoreit, Llion Jones, Aidan N Gomez, Łukasz Kaiser, and Illia Polosukhin. 2017. Attention is all you need. In I. Guyon, U. V. Luxburg, S. Bengio, H. Wallach, R. Fergus, S. Vishwanathan, and R. Garnett, editors, *Advances in Neural Information Processing Systems 30*, pages 5998–6008. Curran Associates, Inc.

Thomas Wolf, Lysandre Debut, Victor Sanh, Julien Chaumond, Clement Delangue, Anthony Moi, Pierric Cistac, Tim Rault, Rémi Louf, Morgan Funtowicz, and Jamie Brew. 2019. HuggingFace's Transformers: State-of-the-art natural language processing. *ArXiv*, abs/1910.03771.

A dual-encoding system for dialect classification

Petru Rebeja
Faculty of Computer Science,
"Alexandru Ioan Cuza" University
16 Berthelot St., Iași
petru.rebeja@gmail.com

Dan Cristea
Faculty of Computer Science,
"Alexandru Ioan Cuza" University
16 Berthelot St., Iași
Institute for Computer Science,
Iași branch of the Romanian Academy
2 Codrescu St., Iași
danu.cristea@gmail.com

Abstract

In this paper we present the architecture, processing pipeline and results of the ensemble model developed for Romanian Dialect Identification task. The ensemble model consists of two TF-IDF encoders and a deep learning model aimed together at classifying input samples based on the writing patterns which are specific to each of the two dialects. Although the model performs well on the training set, its performance degrades heavily on the evaluation set. The drop in performance is due to the design decision which makes the model put too much weight on presence/lack of textual marks when determining the sample label.

1 Introduction

The VarDial evaluation campaign (Zampieri et al., 2017; Zampieri et al., 2018; Zampieri et al., 2019) proposes several tasks related to the study of language variations across geographical regions.

One of its oldest challenges is the is the identification of some specific dialects which, throughout the years, was tackled using several tasks. The challenge started initially with Arabic Dialect Identification in the third edition of VarDial (Malmasi et al., 2016). The fourth edition (Zampieri et al., 2017) expands the family of dialect identification tasks with German Dialect Identification. The sixth edition (Zampieri et al., 2019) comes with yet another task named Moldavian vs. Romanian Cross-dialect Topic identification.

The current edition of the evaluation campaign (Găman et al., 2020) introduces the task of Romanian Dialect Identification (RDI). This is a closed task which is aimed at classifying a text sentence as whether it pertains to the Moldavian idiom[1] or one of the other idioms of Romanian language.

For this task, our team proposes a simple[2] ensemble model which is built on the idea of exploiting the known differences in writing between the two dialects and on emphasizing such differences for classification.

This paper describes the architecture of the proposed model, the setup for training experiments, the processing pipeline, and the results obtained for the RDI task. Towards the end of the paper we also provide some insights into how we can easily tear-down and recreate the whole environment used for our experiments.

The paper is structured as follows: Section 2 presents some of the previous approaches in dialect identification tasks which bear a resemblance to our approach, Section 3 briefly introduces the dataset used for the model, Section 4 describes the architecture of the model, Section 5 describes the experiments and the results, and in the end, Section 6 presents the conclusions and future work.

2 Related Work

The task of discriminating between dialects of the same language has been the subject of various approaches that employ feature engineering, shallow or deep learning, and/or a combination of the afore-

---

[1]Less than a dialect, but in the following we will refer to them as being dialects.

[2]The model architecture (see Section 4) contains relatively few layers.

This work is licensed under a Creative Commons Attribution 4.0 International License. License details: http://creativecommons.org/licenses/by/4.0/.

Proceedings of the 7th VarDial Workshop on NLP for Similar Languages, Varieties and Dialects, pages 212–219
Barcelona, Spain (Online), December 13, 2020

mentioned.

One such example of using deep learning models for dialect classification is the Word-Based Convolutional Neural Network (Elaraby and Abdul-Mageed, 2018), developed for Arabic Dialect Identification. As authors note, their model "is conceptually similar" to the model described in (Kim, 2014). This model uses pretrained and fine-tuned word embeddings as the input to of a convolutional layer with max-pooling, followed by a fully-connected (dense) layer with softmax activation.

Another approach for dialect classification is to use ensemble models. Examples of such models include a Meta-classifier (Malmasi and Zampieri, 2017) for Arabic Dialect Identification, which leverages the collective knowledge of a cluster of individual classifiers by predicting the dialect based on their individual decisions, and an equally-weighted voting schema between a character-level convolutional network, a Long Short-Term Memory network and a string-kernel model for German Dialect Identification (Butnaru, 2019).

At the previous edition of VarDial (Zampieri et al., 2019), the highest-scoring model for the Moldavian vs Romanian Cross-dialect Topic Identification task, was also an ensemble model (Tudoreanu, 2019). The model consists of a triplet loss network, a skip-gram network and a SVM classifier. The SVM classifier receives the concatenated representations learned by each network and based on these makes the prediction of the dialect.

Unlike the model presented in (Tudoreanu, 2019) where the architecture emphasizes the learning of representation for taking a decision, the model presented herein uses shallow representations and puts more weight learning the distinction between them when deciding which label to predict.

3   Dataset

The data source for Romanian Dialect Identification task is the MOROCO dataset (Butnaru and Ionescu, 2019) which consists of short text sentences (one per line) from both Romanian and Moldavian dialects of the Romanian language. The sentences were extracted from various news articles and besides the already mentioned dialect labels, the dataset also provides additional labels for the topic within each sentence falls: culture, finance, politics, science, sports, and tech.

The novelty of the current evaluation campaign is that a supplementary corpus was used for evaluation: MOROCO Tweets (Găman and Ionescu, 2020), containing tweets as data samples instead of sentences from news articles.

Loading Data and Preprocessing. Our approach to working with the data from MOROCO dataset is to construct an in-memory table, using Pandas library[3] with four columns: sample id, dialect label, topic label, and the sample itself.

After loading the dataset in memory, we perform on the fly, simple preprocessing on it. First, the sample text is converted to lowercase, then the tokenization mechanism splits it into its component words.

4   Model Architecture

The model we developed for the RDI task is an ensemble of three parts: two encoders and a deep-learning model consisting of five layers excluding the output layer. The entire architecture of the ensemble model is shown in Figure 1.

As stated in Section 1, at the core of our model lies the intuition that the peculiarities of each of the two Romanian dialects involved in the RDI task can be detected by spotting the differences in writing.

One of the most obvious examples of this intuition lies in how each dialect deals with writing words such as *atât*. The official rules stated by Romanian Academy say that in the middle of the words the character *â* should be used whereas the Moldavian dialect uses the form *î* for the same sound, thus the same word — *atât* — is written in Moldavian dialect as *atît*. Our model aims to capture such differences and exploit them in the classification.

Each input sentence is transformed into two different encodings where each encoding is obtained from the Term Frequency-Inverse Document Frequency (Salton and Buckley, 1988) (TF-IDF) representation

---

[3]https://pandas.pydata.org/

of the sentence in each of the two dialects. In other words, each sentence gets two TF-IDF representations — one for each dialect.

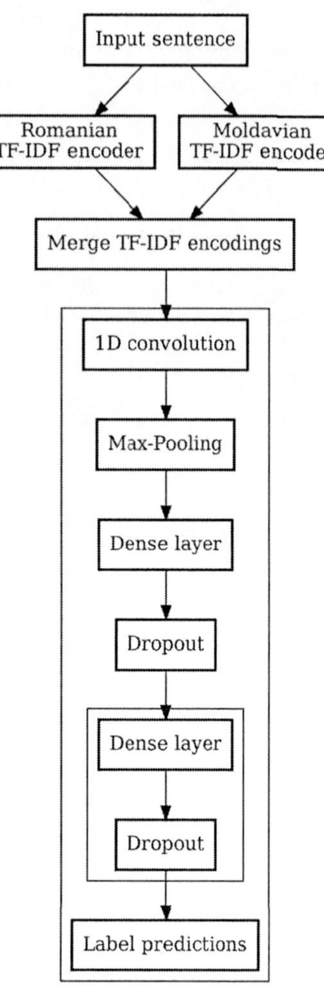

Figure 1: The architecture of our ensemble model for Romanian Dialects Classification task.

After obtaining the TF-IDF encodings for an input sentence, the encodings are merged into a single matrix by concatenating columns. Although this operation (represented by the *Merge TF-IDF encodings* node in the model diagram) is represented by a separate node it is a *logical* operation in the sense that it is not part of the model architecture.

The tensor containing concatenated encodings is passed through a one-dimensional convolutional layer aimed at identifying the prominent features from each of the two encodings of the dialects. The Global Max-Pooling layer that follows the convolutional layer picks the aforementioned features and send them to the following layers.

The results of the Global Max-Pooling layer are then passed through a Dense layer followed by a Dropout (Srivastava et al., 2014) layer with Rectified Linear Unit (Nair and Hinton, 2010) (ReLU) activation. Then the results pass through yet another group consisting of a Dense and Dropout with ReLU activation layers after which, the final Dense layer outputs the predictions for each of the RDI labels. A single dropout rate was used for both Dropout layers whereas the Dense layers are shrinking in size towards the final layer (see Table 1).

Lastly, the predictions of the output layer, together with the expected output are fed to a categorical crossentropy loss function and an Adam (Kingma and Ba, 2014) optimizer is used to find the global minimum.

4.1 Hyper-Parameters

Since the hardware we used to train our ensemble model has relatively low resources the training process was affected by high memory usage, which led to longer training sessions. Under such hardware and time constraints it was prohibitive for us to perform a full-blown hyper-parameter tuning session of the model.

As such, we were forced to settle for the best-performing set of hyper-parameters from a small set of variations.

We present the parameters and their associated values for the best results on evaluation set in Table 1.

5 Experiments and Results

We approach training of the full ensemble model in three separate stages: one training stage per each TF-IDF encoder (for Romanian and Moldavian dialects) and a third and final stage for training the deep-learning classification model.

All of these stages are performed in a single run, as part of a training pipeline that follows closely the architecture of the model presented in Section 4 (Figure 1) with the exception that TF-IDF encoders were trained one after the other rather than in parallel. We describe each of these stages in the following subsections.

In training the whole ensemble model we followed the classical recipe: the model was trained on the train data and validated against the validation set. We report the accuracy on training and validation sets and the score obtained on evaluation set in Section 5.4.

5.1 Training TF-IDF Encoders

We start training the TF-IDF encoders for each dialect by building a global vocabulary from the train data. Having a unified vocabulary ensures that both of the encoders properly encode the same features of the input sample and thus both encodings can be compared against writing regularities such as the one mentioned in the beginning of Section 4.

In other words, when working on the same vocabulary, the Romanian TF-IDF encoder would give a lower score to the word *atît* and high score to the word *atât* whereas the Moldavian TF-IDF encoder would assign scores inversely.

To build the common vocabulary, we make a full pass over the training set. Once the vocabulary is built, we split the training data into two sets according to its dialect label: a set consisting solely of samples for Romanian dialect and another one consisting of samples for Moldavian dialect. Finally, a TF-IDF encoder is trained on each of these two sets, resulting in the encoders presented in Figure 1.

5.2 Generating Batches On-the-Fly

Due to hardware constraints mentioned in Section 4.1, we were unable to load the whole training set into memory after encoding it using the aforementioned TF-IDF dialect encoders.

In order to be able to perform the training we decided to create a custom batch generator that would build each batch of training/validation samples on the fly.

The batch generator has references to the collection of training samples and their associated labels alongside the two TF-IDF encoders for Romanian and Moldavian dialects. It then determines the total number of batches according to the batch size parameter specified when starting the training. After determining the total number of batches to be generated, the generator then encodes each batch of samples on request.

The encoding process itself is performed as follows: for each sample indexed between the start and end indices of the batch, a TF-IDF encoding is computed for both Romanian and Moldavian dialects. We will denote those encodings with $\mathbf{RO_{TF-IDF}}$ and $\mathbf{MD_{TF-IDF}}$ respectively. Afterwards, the encodings are concatenated column-wise to form the tensor $\mathbf{x} = [\mathbf{RO_{TF-IDF}} \quad \mathbf{MD_{TF-IDF}}]$ which will be sent to the deep-learning model. Practically, the batch generator encapsulates the *Merge TF-IDF encodings* node from Figure 1 in Section 4.

At the end of each training epoch, the batch generator shuffles the samples to prevent overfitting.

5.3 Dialect Classification Model

For each of the submitted runs of the RDI task, we created a variation of the dialect classification model, where the changes applied for migrating a model from a prior to posterior versions consist of adding more layers.

Parameter name	Value
1D convolution	
Number of filters	512
Kernel size	7
Dropout rate	
All layers	0.3
Output dimensions	
Dense layer 1	128
Dense layer 2	32
Adam optimizer	
Learning rate	0.001
Decay rate β_1	0.9
Decay rate β_2	0.999

Table 1: The hyper-parameters used for training the deep-learning model which obtained the best results on the evaluation set.

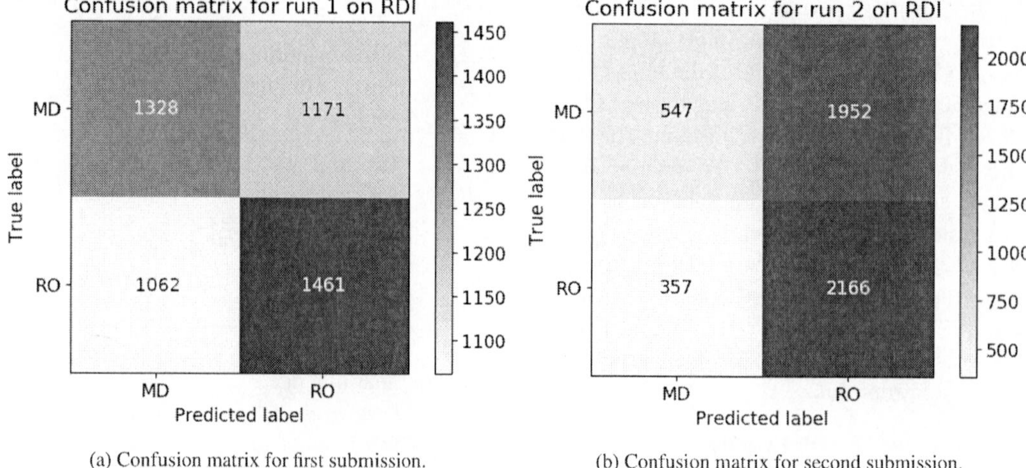

(a) Confusion matrix for first submission.　　　(b) Confusion matrix for second submission.

Figure 2: Confusion matrices for our ensemble model on the RDI task for first run and second run. The images were edited to improve readability.

For the first submission of results we started with a model containing a smaller number of layers, namely: a *1-dimensional convolution* layer, a *Global Max-Pooling* layer, a *Dense* layer, a *Dropout* layer, and an output layer.

In the second version of our model we introduced another group of layers consisting of a second *Dense* layer followed by a *Dropout* layer.

The architecture presented in Figure 1 depicts the changes applied when upgrading from first version of the model to second version by encapsulating them into the innermost rectangle.

5.4 Results and Interpretation

For each of the two submitted runs, the ensemble model was trained for 25 epochs with a batch size of 32 samples. We programmed the model to save its weights each time there was an improvement in the accuracy score thus the results presented in this section are obtained using the highest performing weights for each run.

For the first submission, the ensemble model obtained a 0.8091 accuracy on the training set, 0.7988 accuracy on the validation set and 0.5553 accuracy on the evaluation set. For the second submission, the scores were 0.8220 on training set, 0.8106 on validation set, and 0.5402 for evaluation set respectively. The accuracy scores for each run are also presented in Table 2.

Looking at both the results presented in Table 2 and the confusion matrices presented in Figure 2, it seems that our ensemble model suffers from overfitting.

	Model accuracy		
Run	Train	Validation	Evaluation
1	0.8091	0.7988	0.5553
2	0.8220	0.8106	0.5402

Table 2: Accuracy scores of our ensemble model for both of the submitted runs.

The overfitting phenomenon is also suggested by the inverse correlation between model parameters, accuracy scores on train and validation data and accuracy scores on evaluation set obtained in each submission. The total number of parameters of the model has increased from first submission to second submission due to adding more layers and also widening the existing *Dense* layers. This change, as can be seen from Table 2 led to an increase in accuracy on training and evaluation sets but in the same time we can see the performance on the evaluation set degrading from first to second submission, which is a clear indication of overfitting.

However, we consider the poor performance of the model to be based on its designed intention. As

216

described in Section 4, the core intention of our model is to identify text patterns which are specific for each of the two dialects and discriminate the samples based on identified patterns.

If we are to compare the confusion matrix from first submission (Figure 2a) with the confusion matrix from the second submission (Figure 2b) we can see that for the second submission the model fails to detect the text peculiarities of the Moldavian dialect. Another observation that can be made from comparing the confusion matrices from Figure 2 is that in the second submission the model heavily favors the Romanian dialect.

Since the training data is relatively balanced (there are slightly more samples from Romanian dialect than from Moldavian), we cannot attribute such heavy favoring of the Romanian dialect to a skewed dataset thus, the conclusion is that the model fails to detect discriminatory patterns in the evaluation samples which leads to improper classification. Although we did not evaluate the TF-IDF encodings computed by both encoders in any way, we consider the idea of improper TF-IDF encodings as being highly unlikely.

Rather, we consider the poor performance in identifying the discriminatory text patterns to be caused by the lack of thereof. We were not able to find in the evaluation set a sufficiently large amount of samples that exhibit markings which would allow for immediate discrimination. Furthermore, we observed multiple samples labeled as pertaining to Moldavian dialect that rather than obeying the rule of using the character *î* inside the words were using the *â* character which is a characteristic of the Romanian dialect.

As such, it becomes clear that our design decision on discriminating predominantly based on text markings is not sufficient alone to properly discriminate between Romanian and Moldavian dialects and the model needs additional signals to perform proper classification.

5.5 A Note on Experiment Reproducibility

Since our initial runs of the experiments required switching from a development machine to a more powerful machine used for training we asked ourselves the question on how to reproduce the same environment in training as used for development.

Although `Python` provides a way to recreate a virtual environment by using a file from which to install the required packages, we needed a bit more choreography in order to synchronize the environments on the machines used for developing and training the model such as: having a predefined directory structure from where to load the data and where to save the output, the need to activate the virtual environment for `Python` etc.

In order to fulfill the need for homogeneous environments, we turned ourselves to the Docker platform[4] which allows for full replication of an environment onto different machines.

Thus, for our environments we created a Docker image which contains not only the packages required by `Python` but also the system-wide packages required for loading and reading the data and training the model. This way, the entire experiment can be reproduced at any time by following three simple steps: building the Docker image from the provided file, starting a container with mounted volumes for directories containing data, and run the training.

The source-code of our ensemble, including the `Dockerfile` used for building the image is available on GitHub[5].

6 Conclusions and Future Work

In this paper we describe the architecture of an ensemble model designed to classify an input sentence as pertaining to Romanian or Moldavian dialects based primarily on the text markings which make the distinction between those two dialects. Alongside the model architecture and performance we describe the processing pipeline used for training the model and the setup of the training environment which allowed us to easily replicate the training environment on the machine where training was performed.

To our great disappointment, the results of the evaluation set shown both in Table 2 and in Figure 2 indicate that the design decision of identifying textual marks and discriminating primarily on those marks

---

[4]https://www.docker.com/. We used the freely available Community Edition.
[5]https://github.com/RePierre/vardial2020

leads to poor performance. Our main conclusion in regards to the model performance is that relying only on such marks and differences in text is not enough to discriminate real-world examples because — as data from the evaluation set shows — only some input samples display such marks, not all of them. Furthermore, as our subsequent analysis revealed, some of the marks which the model sought for are lacking (e.g. *Sfântul NE NE este a doua finalistă a ediției inaugurale a NE NE NE* — pertaining to Moldavian dialect but uses *â* instead of *î*), which blurs even more the lines between Romanian and Moldavian dialects and points to a tendency of the Moldavian dialect to adhere to the writing norms of its Romanian counterpart. In such case, the model doesn't learn to properly discriminate between the two dialects.

Even though our model makes use of techniques such as *Dropout* (Srivastava et al., 2014) which are meant to prevent overfitting and boost generalization, the model generalizes poorly and its confidence drops when the input sample lacks the strong textual marks it was trained to look for.

In order to improve results — as one might expect — the future work should heavily concentrate on the classification model part of the ensemble presented herein. First and foremost, we need to investigate what is the root cause of long training time and improve the part responsible for it. This will allow us to test multiple variations of the model and perform a proper hyper-parameter tuning. However, if our investigation will conclude that there is no single part responsible for the most of the incurred delay in training, it make sense to consider rewriting the whole model architecture.

References

Andrei Butnaru and Radu Tudor Ionescu. 2019. Moroco: The moldavian and romanian dialectal corpus. In *Proceedings of the 57th Annual Meeting of the Association for Computational Linguistics*, pages 688–698.

Andrei Butnaru. 2019. Bam: A combination of deep and shallow models for german dialect identification. In *Proceedings of the Sixth Workshop on NLP for Similar Languages, Varieties and Dialects*, pages 128–137.

Mohamed Elaraby and Muhammad Abdul-Mageed. 2018. Deep models for arabic dialect identification on benchmarked data. In *Proceedings of the Fifth Workshop on NLP for Similar Languages, Varieties and Dialects (VarDial 2018)*, pages 263–274.

Mihaela Găman and Radu Tudor Ionescu. 2020. The unreasonable effectiveness of machine learning in moldavian versus romanian dialect identification. *arXiv preprint arXiv:2007.15700*.

Mihaela Găman, Dirk Hovy, Radu Tudor Ionescu, Heidi Jauhiainen, Tommi Jauhiainen, Krister Lindén, Nikola Ljubešić, Niko Partanen, Christoph Purschke, Yves Scherrer, and Marcos Zampieri. 2020. A Report on the VarDial Evaluation Campaign 2020. In *Proceedings of the Seventh Workshop on NLP for Similar Languages, Varieties and Dialects (VarDial)*.

Yoon Kim. 2014. Convolutional neural networks for sentence classification. *arXiv preprint arXiv:1408.5882*.

Diederik P Kingma and Jimmy Ba. 2014. Adam: A method for stochastic optimization. *arXiv preprint arXiv:1412.6980*.

Shervin Malmasi and Marcos Zampieri. 2017. Arabic dialect identification using ivectors and asr transcripts. In *Proceedings of the Fourth Workshop on NLP for Similar Languages, Varieties and Dialects (VarDial)*, pages 178–183.

Shervin Malmasi, Marcos Zampieri, Nikola Ljubešić, Preslav Nakov, Ahmed Ali, and Jörg Tiedemann. 2016. Discriminating between similar languages and arabic dialect identification: A report on the third dsl shared task. In *Proceedings of the Third Workshop on NLP for Similar Languages, Varieties and Dialects (VarDial3)*, pages 1–14, Osaka, Japan, December.

Vinod Nair and Geoffrey E. Hinton. 2010. Rectified linear units improve restricted boltzmann machines. In *Proceedings of the 27th International Conference on International Conference on Machine Learning*, ICML'10, page 807–814, Madison, WI, USA. Omnipress.

Gerard Salton and Christopher Buckley. 1988. Term-weighting approaches in automatic text retrieval. *Information processing & management*, 24(5):513–523.

Nitish Srivastava, Geoffrey Hinton, Alex Krizhevsky, Ilya Sutskever, and Ruslan Salakhutdinov. 2014. Dropout: a simple way to prevent neural networks from overfitting. *The journal of machine learning research*, 15(1):1929–1958.

Diana Tudoreanu. 2019. Dteam@ vardial 2019: Ensemble based on skip-gram and triplet loss neural networks for moldavian vs. romanian cross-dialect topic identification. In *Proceedings of the Sixth Workshop on NLP for Similar Languages, Varieties and Dialects*, pages 202–208.

Marcos Zampieri, Shervin Malmasi, Nikola Ljubešić, Preslav Nakov, Ahmed Ali, Jörg Tiedemann, Yves Scherrer, and Noëmi Aepli. 2017. Findings of the VarDial Evaluation Campaign 2017. In *Proceedings of the Fourth Workshop on NLP for Similar Languages, Varieties and Dialects (VarDial)*, Valencia, Spain.

Marcos Zampieri, Shervin Malmasi, Preslav Nakov, Ahmed Ali, Suwon Shuon, James Glass, Yves Scherrer, Tanja Samardžić, Nikola Ljubešić, Jörg Tiedemann, Chris van der Lee, Stefan Grondelaers, Nelleke Oostdijk, Antal van den Bosch, Ritesh Kumar, Bornini Lahiri, and Mayank Jain. 2018. Language Identification and Morphosyntactic Tagging: The Second VarDial Evaluation Campaign. In *Proceedings of the Fifth Workshop on NLP for Similar Languages, Varieties and Dialects (VarDial)*, Santa Fe, USA.

Marcos Zampieri, Shervin Malmasi, Yves Scherrer, Tanja Samardžić, Francis Tyers, Miikka Silfverberg, Natalia Klyueva, Tung-Le Pan, Chu-Ren Huang, Radu Tudor Ionescu, Andrei Butnaru, and Tommi Jauhiainen. 2019. A Report on the Third VarDial Evaluation Campaign. In *Proceedings of the Sixth Workshop on NLP for Similar Languages, Varieties and Dialects (VarDial)*. Association for Computational Linguistics.

Experiments in Language Variety Geolocation and Dialect Identification

Tommi Jauhiainen
Department of Digital Humanities
University of Helsinki
tommi.jauhiainen@helsinki.fi

Heidi Jauhiainen
Department of Digital Humanities
University of Helsinki
heidi.jauhiainen@helsinki.fi

Krister Lindén
Department of Digital Humanities
University of Helsinki
krister.linden@helsinki.fi

Abstract

In this paper we describe the systems we used when participating in the VarDial Evaluation Campaign organized as part of the 7th workshop on NLP for similar languages, varieties and dialects. The shared tasks we participated in were the second edition of the Romanian Dialect Identification (RDI) and the first edition of the Social Media Variety Geolocation (SMG). The submissions of our SUKI team used generative language models based on Naive Bayes and character n-grams.

1 Introduction

We first took part in the related language identification shared tasks in 2015 (Jauhiainen et al., 2015) and we have been using the same team name *SUKI* ever since. The shared tasks have been organized as part of the VarDial workshops dealing with computational methods and language resources for closely related languages, language varieties, and dialects. The 2020 VarDial Evaluation Campaign contained three separate shared tasks (Găman et al., 2020).[1] We participated in the Romanian Dialect Identification (RDI) and the Social Media Variety Geolocation (SMG) shared tasks. We did not participate in the third task, Uralic Language Identification (ULI), as we were part of the team organizing it (Jauhiainen et al., 2020).

In this paper, we first introduce some previous work related to these shared tasks, to language identification and to identification of Romanian dialects in particular as well as to geolocation of texts. Then we describe the RDI and the SMG shared tasks, their datasets and the systems we used in our submissions as well as the results of the shared tasks.

2 Related work

2.1 Shared tasks

The RDI and the SMG shared tasks were organized as a part of the VarDial Evaluation Campaign 2020, which continued the tradition of shared tasks focusing on close languages for the seventh consecutive year (Zampieri et al., 2014; Zampieri et al., 2015; Malmasi et al., 2016; Zampieri et al., 2017; Zampieri et al., 2018; Zampieri et al., 2019). The RDI shared task was a continuation of the first track of the Moldavian vs. Romanian Cross-dialect Topic identification (MRC) shared task organized in 2019 (Zampieri et al., 2019). The SGM was the first shared task of its kind and the first language identification shared task where the aim was to pin a text to a location.

---

[1]https://sites.google.com/view/vardial2020/evaluation-campaign

This work is licensed under a Creative Commons Attribution 4.0 International License. License details: http://creativecommons.org/licenses/by/4.0/.

Proceedings of the 7th VarDial Workshop on NLP for Similar Languages, Varieties and Dialects, pages 220–231
Barcelona, Spain (Online), December 13, 2020

2.2 Language identification in texts

Automatic language identification in texts was first introduced in the 1960s (Mustonen, 1965). A recent survey by Jauhiainen et al. (2019d) introduces the different aspects of language identification as well as most of the methods used for it during the past 50 years. The methods used for the task of language identification are mostly shared with other classification tasks as almost any modern machine learning method can be trained to distinguish between different languages (Jauhiainen, 2019). Support Vector Machines (SVM) are among the most popular and successful machine learning algorithms that have been applied to language identification and have traditionally been very competetive in language identification shared tasks, winning many of them (Goutte et al., 2014; Malmasi and Dras, 2015; Çöltekin and Rama, 2016; Malmasi and Zampieri, 2016; Bestgen, 2017; Malmasi and Zampieri, 2017; Çöltekin et al., 2018; Wu et al., 2019). Deep learning methods have traditionally been less successful in language identification than in other classification tasks (Çöltekin and Rama, 2016; Gamallo et al., 2016; Medvedeva et al., 2017). The first time a language identification shared task was won using deep learning was in the Cuneiform Language Identification (CLI) shared task we organized in 2019 (Zampieri et al., 2019; Jauhiainen et al., 2019a) when it was won by Bernier-Colborne et al. (2019) using BERT-based classifier (Devlin et al., 2018).

In our submissions for the shared tasks, we used language identifiers based on the product of relative frequencies we had developed for the VarDial Evaluation campaign of the previous year (Jauhiainen et al., 2019a; Jauhiainen et al., 2019b). The method is basically the same as Naive Bayes (NB) using the observed relative frequencies of character n-grams as probabilities.

2.3 Identification of Romanian dialects

The RDI shared task focused on distinguishing between Moldavian and Romanian. Romanian and Moldavian are coupled together as dialects of the Romanian language (ron) in the ISO 639-3 standard (SIL, 2020).[2]

The shared task debuted as one of the tracks of the MRC shared task of the VarDial Evaluation Campaign 2019 (Zampieri et al., 2019). The aim was to maximize the macro-averaged F_1 score for the two dialects. When macro-averaging, the F_1 score of each individual dialect is calculated first and the result is the average of those F_1 scores. The dataset of the shared task was published as the Moldavian and Romanian Dialectal Corpus (MOROCO) (Butnaru and Ionescu, 2019).

The 2019 edition was officially won by Tudoreanu (2019) using two character-level neural networks which were combined as an ensemble using SVM in the manner of Stacked Generalisation (Wolpert, 1992). Some of the participants had problems producing the correct number of lines for their submissions (Zampieri et al., 2019) and produced corrected results after the end of the shared task for their system description papers (Onose et al., 2019; Wu et al., 2019).

Some additional experiments using the MOROCO data have also been reported (Tudoreanu, 2019; Onose et al., 2019; Găman and Ionescu, 2020; Georgescu et al., 2020). Găman and Ionescu (2020) conducted an evaluation of the data and compared the performance of several methods with the annotations done by native speakers of the dialects. They noted that the machine learning methods were superior to humans in distinguishing between the two dialects and concluded that the models were better at finding character level clues than human annotators.

The results of all these experiments were not available together, so we collected them in Table 1. The first column describes the method used as well as the possible MRC team name in parentheses. The second column gives the Macro F_1 score and the third lists the source for the information. The methods used include SVMs, Kernel Ridge Regression (KRR), Convolutional Neural Networks (CNN), Hierarchical Attention Networks (HAN) (Yang et al., 2016), Bidirectional Gated Recurrent Units (BiGRU), Long Short-Term Memory cells (LSTM), and Recurrent Neural Networks (RNN). The MRC shared task was supposed to be closed, i.e. no task external data was to be used. However, pre-trained word vectors were used during the competition and have also been used in some of the later experiments. The pre-trained word vectors used are from Common Crawl (Grave et al., 2018), Romanian Language Corpus (CoRoLa)

---

[2]https://iso639-3.sil.org/code/ron

(Mititelu et al., 2018), and the Nordic Language Processing Laboratory "NLPL" (Kutuzov et al., 2017) and they have been indicated in Table 1.

Method	Macro F_1	Reported by
Linear SVM classifier with LM adaptation (tearsofjoy)	0.962	Wu et al. (2019)
Stacking with 12 classifiers	0.945	Găman and Ionescu (2020)
KRR with string kernels	0.943	Găman and Ionescu (2020)
KRR	0.941	Butnaru and Ionescu (2019)
CNN+SE with ADA activation	0.940	Georgescu et al. (2020)
SVM with string kernels	0.939	Găman and Ionescu (2020)
CNN with ADA activation	0.937	Georgescu et al. (2020)
CNN+SE+PyNADA with ReLU and ADA activations	0.937	Georgescu et al. (2020)
CNN with ReLU and ADA activations	0.936	Georgescu et al. (2020)
Ensemble (DTeam)	0.934	Tudoreanu (2019)
Neural network based on softmax loss (DTeam)	0.933	Tudoreanu (2019)
CNN+SE with leaky ReLU activation	0.931	Georgescu et al. (2020)
HAN with FastText Common Crawl word vectors (SC-UPB)	0.930	Onose et al. (2019)
CNN+SE with ReLU activation	0.930	Georgescu et al. (2020)
CNN+SE	0.929	Butnaru and Ionescu (2019)
CNN with characters	0.929	Găman and Ionescu (2020)
Voting between 12 classifiers	0.929	Găman and Ionescu (2020)
CNN with leaky ReLU activation	0.929	Georgescu et al. (2020)
CNN (DTeam)	0.928	Tudoreanu (2019)
CNN with ReLU activation	0.928	Georgescu et al. (2020)
CNN	0.927	Butnaru and Ionescu (2019)
BiGRU with FastText Common Crawl word vectors (SC-UPB)	0.903	Onose et al. (2019)
Two skip-gram CNNs stacked using SVM (DTeam)	*0.895*	*Zampieri et al. (2019)*
LSTM with CoRoLa word vectors	0.895	Găman and Ionescu (2020)
Neural network based on triplet loss (DTeam)	0.869	Tudoreanu (2019)
BiGRU with CoRoLa word vectors	0.868	Onose et al. (2019)
BiGRU with Common Crawl word vectors	0.865	Găman and Ionescu (2020)
LSTM with NLPL word vectors	0.852	Găman and Ionescu (2020)
LSTM with FastText Common Crawl word vectors (SC-UPB)	0.847	Onose et al. (2019)
BiGRU with NLPL word vectors (SC-UPB)	0.834	Onose et al. (2019)
LSTM with CoRoLa word vectors (SC-UPB)	0.825	Onose et al. (2019)
LSTM with NLPL word vectors (SC-UPB)	0.798	Onose et al. (2019)
Majority voting between 5 classifiers on 40 features (R2I_LIS) (train+dev)	*0.796*	*Zampieri et al. (2019)*
Majority voting between 5 classifiers on 40 features (R2I_LIS) (train+dev)	0.778	Chifu (2019)
Majority voting between 5 classifiers on 40 features (R2I_LIS) (train)	0.776	Chifu (2019)
Linear SVM classifier (tearsofjoy)	*0.757*	*Zampieri et al. (2019)*
Word-level bigrams with add-one smoothing (lonewolf)	*0.735*	*Zampieri et al. (2019)*
RNN with GRUs and pre-trained FastText model (SC-UPB)	*0.709*	*Zampieri et al. (2019)*
HAN with CoRoLa word vectors	0.697	Găman and Ionescu (2020)
HAN with NLPL word vectors	0.694	Găman and Ionescu (2020)
HAN with Common Crawl word vectors	0.694	Găman and Ionescu (2020)
Character-level bigrams with add-one smoothing (lonewolf)	0.656	Chifu (2019)
Word-level bigrams with Good-Turing smoothing (lonewolf)	0.608	Chifu (2019)
HAN with FastText Common Crawl word vectors (SC-UPB)	0.508	Onose et al. (2019)

Table 1: The Macro F_1 scores for Romanian dialect identification on the MOROCO dataset reported by various papers. The official submissions of each team is in italics.

2.4 Geolocation of texts

Many datasets of social media texts come with some sort of location attached to each text. People living close to each other tend to speak and write in similar ways and about common subjects. This makes identification of the location of a tweet[3] or a jodel[4] possible by just looking at the text produced. In addition to a text itself, many geolocation detection methods use, for example, the metadata of the user profile (Huang and Carley, 2017) or other texts produced by the same user (Chong and Lim, 2019). In the context of the SMG shared task, the aim was to distinguish dialectal differences based on just the text of the tweet or jodel itself. In many studies, the aim has been to pinpoint a correct city (Huang and Carley, 2017; Snyder et al., 2019), a country (Huang and Carley, 2017), or even a specific venue, like

---

[3]https://twitter.com

[4]https://jodel.com

a restaurant or a shop (Chong and Lim, 2019). In the SMG shared task the exact coordinates for each mystery text were required.

3 Romanian Dialect Identification (RDI) shared task

The RDI shared task was a two-way classification task between texts written in the Moldavian or Romanian dialects of the Romanian language. Each participating team was allowed to submit three runs and the runs were evaluated based on the macro-averaged F_1 score. We experimented with three classification techniques and in the end we submitted only one run to the shared task gaining fourth place among the eight teams submitting results.

3.1 Test setup

In order to train their models, the participants were provided with the MOROCO data set (Butnaru and Ionescu, 2019). The original MOROCO data set is divided into training, validation, and testing, but for this shared task, all the 33,564 samples of text were to be used for training. All in all, there were 15,403 texts for Moldavian and 18,161 texts for Romanian.

For validation, two different sets of texts were provided. The first validation set *dev-source* was in-domain with the training data (texts were from the news domain) while the second validation set *dev-target* was out-of domain (the texts were tweets). The *dev-source* contained 2,718 additional texts for Moldavian and 3,205 texts for Romanian. However, the *dev-target* was considerably smaller with only 113 texts for Moldavian and 102 texts for Romanian.

The test set included 5,022 lines of texts without language labels. The participants were informed that they were tweets similar to those of the second validation set *dev-target*. The average length of a line was 98 characters. In all of the three datasets, the named entities had been transformed to "\$NE\$" tags. Butnaru and Ionescu (2019) do not specify how the named entity removal was performed in practice or whether it was automatic or manual.

3.2 Experiments on the development set

The participants were informed beforehand that the shared task test set would consist of tweets. For this reason, we focused our experiments on the out-of-domain validation set *dev-target*. Thus, we combined the MOROCO dataset and the in-domain validation data *dev-source* as the training data for our experiments.

For this task, we set out to experiment with the same methods as we did for the baseline of the CLI shared task in 2019 (Jauhiainen et al., 2019a). We used the product of relative frequencies method and its adaptive version also in the German Dialect Identification (GDI) and Discriminating between the Mainland and Taiwan variation of Mandarin Chinese (DMT) shared tasks of the VarDial Evaluation campaign 2019 (Jauhiainen et al., 2019b). With the adaptive version, we won the DMT track for traditional Chinese (Zampieri et al., 2019). Without adaptation, the results of our implementation of the NB classifier were comparable to other methods not using language model adaptation, e.g. SVM ensembles or deep neural networks such as RNN, CNN, and LSTM (Jauhiainen et al., 2019b). Unfortunately, in this years campaign, we did not have time to experiment with the HeLI method (Jauhiainen et al., 2016).

For the CLI task, one of the methods produced best results using character n-grams up to 15 characters and we started experimenting using similar very long character sequences. It was soon evident, that our server environment was not capable of processing the training data with such long n-grams and we ended up using a maximum of 12 character sequences.[5] The three methods we evaluated on the RDI training and development data were the sum of relative frequencies, the simple-scoring, and the product of relative frequencies methods. In all of the three methods, the language models for the two dialects consist of all the possible character n-grams extracted from their training data.

3.2.1 Sum of relative frequencies

In the sum of relative frequencies, the character n-grams extracted from the mystery text to be identified M are compared with the language models $dom(O(C_g))$ of the two dialects g, and for each n-gram found

---

[5]The problem was mainly with the memory usage: we used a maximum of 60 gigabytes as our Java memory heap.

in a language model, the score $R_{sum}(g, M)$ is increased by the respective relative frequency. The dialect gaining the highest score is selected. Jauhiainen et al. (2019d) formulate the method as in Equation 1:

$$R_{sum}(g, M) = \sum_{i=1}^{l_{MF}} \frac{c(C_g, f_i)}{l_{C_g^F}}$$

(1)

where l_{MF} is the number of individual features in the text M and $c(C_g, f_i)$ is the count of its ith feature f_i in the training corpus.

All the possible combinations of character n-grams from 1 to 12 were evaluated. The best results with a macro F_1 of 0.4848 were obtained using only character 12-grams. The score was very low considering that the task was a simple binary classification between two dialects.

3.2.2 Simple scoring

In simple scoring, the character n-grams from the text to be identified (M) are compared with the language models and the scores of the dialects are increased by one for each one found. The dialect with the highest score is predicted. Jauhiainen et al. (2019d) formulate the method as in Equation 2:

$$R_{simple}(g, M) = \sum_{i=1}^{l_{MF}} \left\{ \begin{array}{ll} 1 & \text{, if } f_i \in dom(O(C_g)) \\ 0 & \text{, otherwise} \end{array} \right.$$

(2)

Again we experimented with all the possible combinations of character n-grams from 1 to 12. The results were much more promising than when using the sum of relative frequencies method. Table 2 shows some of the best character n-gram combinations from these experiments. The column "n Min" tells the minimum length of the character n-grams used and the "n Max" the maximum length.

n Min	n Max	Macro F_1
1-2	12	0.6099
3 or 5	12	0.6142
4	12	0.6193
1-3	11	0.6193
4	11	0.6099
1-3	10	0.5978

Table 2: Experiments with the simple scoring method on the RDI validation target.

As can be noticed, four combinations gave exactly the same highest result of 0.6193. The reason for arriving at the exact same score was that the *dev-target* was a relatively small set only totaling 215 texts.

3.2.3 Product of relative frequencies

The third method evaluated was the product of relative frequencies. We used the same implementation of this method in last years Evaluation Campaign (Jauhiainen et al., 2019a; Jauhiainen et al., 2019b). In this method, the relative frequencies are multiplied together. Jauhiainen et al. (2019d) formulate the method as in Equation 3:

$$R_{prod}(g, M) = \prod_{i}^{l_{MF}} \frac{c(C_g, f_i)}{l_{C_g^F}}$$

(3)

In case the feature f_i was not found in the training corpus of a dialect C_g, a smoothing value was used. The smoothing value was the relative frequency of a feature found only once in the training corpus. In the actual implementation of the algorithm, the sum of negative logarithms of the relative frequencies were used. The smoothing value was multiplied by a penalty modifier determined using the development set.

We experimented with several combinations of values for the minimum and maximum lengths of character n-grams as well as the penalty modifiers. The best results were obtained using character n-grams from five to eigth with a penalty modifier of 1.18. These results together with the results of some nearby parameter combinations can be seen in Table 3. The results using the product of relative frequencies were clearly superior to the results of the two previous methods so we decided to do some more experiments with this method.

n Min	n Max	Penalty modifier	Macro F_1
5	8	1.18	0.6528
5	8	1.19	0.6485
5	8	1.17	0.6475
4	8	1.25-1.26	0.6451
5	9	1.25-1.29	0.6451

Table 3: Experiments with the product of relative frequencies method on the RDI validation target.

So far the results were obtained using the training and validation sets without any preprocessing. First we experimented with removing the "NE" tags representing named entities from the datasets before training and evaluation. There was a clear increase in the F_1 score as evidenced in Table 4.

n Min	n Max	Penalty modifier	Macro F_1
4	7	1.14	0.6706
4	7	1.11-1.13	0.6656
3	7	1.15-1.18	0.6656
4	7	1.15	0.6663
4	8	1.12	0.6598

Table 4: Experiments with the product of relative frequencies method on the RDI validation target with the named entity tags removed.

We further experimented with removing all non-alphabetic characters, which again increased the F_1-score (Table 5). As "alphabetic" characters we considered all characters included in the character set of any language according to Java regular expressions.[6]

n Min	n Max	Penalty modifier	Macro F_1
4	5	1.35-1.36	0.6877
4	6	1.40-1.48	0.6836
4	5	1.37-1.39	0.6832
4	5	1.34	0.6829
3	5	1.40-1.42	0.6648

Table 5: Experiments with the product of relative frequencies method on the RDI validation target using only alphabetic characters.

The next preprocessing step was lowercasing all characters (Table 6). This ended up giving a further boost of 2.1% to the Macro F_1 score. All in all, using these three simple pre-processing steps increased the F_1 score by 7.6%.

In the two previous VarDial Evaluation campaigns we were able to gain good results using language model adaptation together with the product of relative frequencies and the HeLI methods (Jauhiainen et al., 2018a; Jauhiainen et al., 2018b; Jauhiainen et al., 2019b; Jauhiainen et al., 2019c). We did evaluate using the product of relative frequencies with the best parameters from the previous trials together with language model adaptation. This combination did not further increase the score, instead with various parameters the scores were actually lower. Thus, we decided not to use language model adaptation in the actual run.

3.3 Results

We removed the named entity tags from the test set and used only lowercased alphabetic characters. We ended up with two lines for which our language identifier returned an unknown language. This was due to both lines being a single "a" after preprocessing and the classifier using a minimum length of four for the character n-grams. We changed them to Moldavian (MD) as we were not allowed to submit any

---

[6]For the exact regular expression see line 241 of HeLI.java at https://github.com/tosaja/HeLI/blob/master/HeLI.java

n Min	n Max	Penalty modifier	Macro F_1
4	5	1.39-1.41	0.7023
4	5	1.33-1.38 and 1.42-1.48	0.6976
3	5	1.21-1.22	0.6976
4	6	1.21-1.24	0.6879

Table 6: Experiments with the product of relative frequencies method on the RDI validation target using only lowercased alphabetic characters.

other tags than one of the two Romanian dialects. We submitted these results as our only run to the RDI shared task.

Rank	Team	run	Macro F_1
1	Tubingen	1	0.7876
2	Anumiti	3	0.7751
3	Phlyers	1	0.6661
4	**SUKI**	**1**	**0.6584**
5	UPB	1	0.6476
6	UAIC	1	0.5550
7	akanksha	1	0.4813
8	The_Linguistadors	2	0.4294

Table 7: The best results of each team participating on the RDI 2020 shared task.

Our final score of 0.6584 on the test set was in line with what can be expected from gaining an F-score around 0.70 on the development set. The score gave us the fourth place in the shared task (Table 7).

4 Social Media Variety Geolocation (SMG) shared task

This task was divided into three separate tracks, each focusing on its own geographic area. The first track, DE-AT, included Jodel conversations in standard German from Germany and Austria. Second track, CH, focused on Swiss German Jodel conversations from Switzerland. The third track, BCMS, featured tweets from Croatia, Bosnia and Herzegovia, Montenegro, and Serbia. All the tracks were scored using the median distance in kilometers of all the predicted locations to the actual ones.

4.1 The datasets for the shared task

Before the testing period the participants were provided with training and development data for each of the tracks. The data for the DE-AT and CH tracks came from a mobile chat application called Jodel, where users can chat anonymously with others in the same area (Hovy and Purschke, 2018) while the data for the BCMS track consisted of tweets (Ljubešić et al., 2016). The sizes of each dataset are shown in Table 8. The reason why the BCMS data is divided between many more locations than the DE-AT and CH data is that the coordinates of the locations are given in much more detail (with up to 8 decimal places in BCMS and only 2 decimal places for DE-AT and CH).

Track	Set	#Texts	Average length in tokens	Number of unique locations
DE-AT	Training	336,983	71	5,228
DE-AT	Development	46,582	71	6,512
DE-AT	Test	48,239	69	???
CH	Training	22,600	55	222
CH	Development	3,068	57	339
CH	Test	3,097	55	???
BCMS	Training	320,042	13	264,741
BCMS	Development	39,750	13	36,992
BCMS	Test	39,723	13	???

Table 8: The sizes of the datasets for the SMG shared task.

4.2 The methods used

We opted for a simple approach of dividing the given geographic areas into 81 equally sized geographical areas. For both longitude and latitude, the distance between maximum and minimum points in the datasets was divided by 9. Each of the 100 unique corner coordinates of the 81 areas functioned as a gathering point. All the jodels or tweets in the training data were gathered at their nearest gathering point. After that the location of each gathering point was adjusted to be in the center of the original positions of the tweets or jodels gathered at the point. We only had resources to try different divisions with the Swiss German data and we experimented with dividing by 8 or 10 instead of 9, but this did not improve the results.

Not all of the points gathered texts, but for all those that included texts, a language model was created. That language model was then used with a language identifier. While experimenting, we calculated our results using average distance instead of median distance. The distance we used was based on coordinate points and as the longitude and latitude are not equal in kilometers, our optimization was not perfect. We used the same product of relative frequencies classifier in language identification, which was described earlier with regard to the RDI shared task (Equation 3). The parameters we used with each track can be seen in Table 9.

Track	n Min	n Max	Penalty modifier
DEAT	1	5	1.9
CH	2	3	2.35
BCMS	1	7	3.5

Table 9: Parameters used in the submissions for the three SMG tracks.

4.3 Results

Table 10 shows the results of the teams participating in the SMG 2020 shared task DEAT track. Our submission was clearly the least efficient of all submitted systems.

Rank	Team	Median distance	Mean distance
1	helsinki-ljubljana	159.59	183.97
2	Piyush_Mishra	183.99	204.93
3	CUBoulder-UBC	198.27	218.51
4	ZHAW	205.81	230.78
5	**SUKI**	**243.12**	**266.85**

Table 10: The best results of each team participating in the SMG 2020 shared task DEAT track.

Table 11 shows the results of the teams participating in the SMG 2020 shared task Swiss German track.

Rank	Team	Median distance	Mean distance
1	ZHAW	15.93	25.06
2	helsinki-ljubljana	17.66	26.21
3	CUBoulder-UBC	19.49	27.63
4	**SUKI**	**23.96**	**34.59**
5	UnibucKernel	25.57	30.52
6	The_lingustadors	26.70	31.21
7	Piyush_Mishra	27.31	33.20

Table 11: The best results of each team participating in the SMG 2020 shared task Swiss German track.

Table 12 shows the results of the teams participating in the SMG 2020 shared task BCMS track. Our submission gave us the third position which was our best ranking among the tracks. The winning helsinki-ljubljana teams median distance was in a league of its own, but we were relatively close to the ZHAW teams result.

Rank	Team	Median distance	Mean distance
1	helsinki-ljubljana	48.99	86.83
2	ZHAW	57.24	100.42
3	**SUKI**	**61.01**	**105.11**
4	CUBoulder-UBC	64.76	106.67
5	Piyush_Mishra	85.70	112.65
6	The_lingustadors	97.16	141.88

Table 12: The best results of each team participating on the SMG 2020 shared task BCMS track.

5 Conclusions and future work

In this paper, we presented the systems we experimented with when participating in two of the shared tasks organized as part of the VarDial Evaluation Campaign 2020. Our systems did not reach the state of the art in any of the tracks of the shared tasks.

There is clearly some room for improvement in the approaches we used. We did not have time to experiment with using adaptive language models in the SMG shared task. Using them might have improved the identification accuracy considerably. Also, using 100 coordinate points might not have been optimal in the DEAT and BCMS tracks as the areas where those texts came from were larger than the CH track but we only optimized the division using the CH track training data. There is also room for improvement in how we optimized the parameters for the SMG shared task as we used the average distance and the distance "unit" we used were coordinate points instead of kilometers.

References

Gabriel Bernier-Colborne, Cyril Goutte, and Serge Léger. 2019. Improving cuneiform language identification with bert. In *Proceedings of the Sixth Workshop on NLP for Similar Languages, Varieties and Dialects*, pages 17–25.

Yves Bestgen. 2017. Improving the Character Ngram Model for the DSL Task with BM25 Weighting and Less Frequently Used Feature Sets. In *Proceedings of the Fourth Workshop on NLP for Similar Languages, Varieties and Dialects (VarDial)*, pages 115–123, Valencia, Spain.

Andrei Butnaru and Radu Tudor Ionescu. 2019. Moroco: The Moldavian and Romanian dialectal corpus. In *Proceedings of the 57th Annual Meeting of the Association for Computational Linguistics*, pages 688–698.

Cagri Çöltekin and Taraka Rama. 2016. Discriminating Similar Languages: Experiments with Linear SVMs and Neural Networks. In *Proceedings of the Third Workshop on NLP for Similar Languages, Varieties and Dialects (VarDial)*, pages 15–24, Osaka, Japan.

Adrian-Gabriel Chifu. 2019. The R2I_LIS team proposes majority vote for VarDial's MRC task. In *Proceedings of the Sixth Workshop on NLP for Similar Languages, Varieties and Dialects*, pages 138–143.

Wen-Haw Chong and Ee-Peng Lim. 2019. Fine-grained geolocation of tweets in temporal proximity. *ACM Transactions on Information Systems (TOIS)*, 37(2):1–33.

Çağrı Çöltekin, Taraka Rama, and Verena Blaschke. 2018. Tübingen-Oslo team at the VarDial 2018 evaluation campaign: An analysis of n-gram features in language variety identification. In *Proceedings of the Fifth Workshop on NLP for Similar Languages, Varieties and Dialects (VarDial 2018)*, pages 55–65.

Jacob Devlin, Ming-Wei Chang, Kenton Lee, and Kristina Toutanova. 2018. Bert: Pre-training of deep bidirectional transformers for language understanding. *arXiv preprint arXiv:1810.04805*.

Pablo Gamallo, José Ramom Pichel, Iñaki Alegria, and Manex Agirrezabal. 2016. Comparing two Basic Methods for Discriminating Between Similar Languages and Varieties. In *Proceedings of the Third Workshop on NLP for Similar Languages, Varieties and Dialects (VarDial)*, pages 170–177, Osaka, Japan.

Mihaela Găman and Radu Tudor Ionescu. 2020. The unreasonable effectiveness of machine learning in Moldavian versus Romanian dialect identification. *arXiv preprint arXiv:2007.15700*.

Mariana-Iuliana Georgescu, Radu Tudor Ionescu, Nicolae-Catalin Ristea, and Nicu Sebe. 2020. Non-linear neurons with human-like apical dendrite activations. *arXiv preprint arXiv:2003.03229*.

Cyril Goutte, Serge Léger, and Marine Carpuat. 2014. The NRC System for Discriminating Similar Languages. In *Proceedings of the First Workshop on Applying NLP Tools to Similar Languages, Varieties and Dialects (VarDial)*, pages 139–145, Dublin, Ireland.

Edouard Grave, Piotr Bojanowski, Prakhar Gupta, Armand Joulin, and Tomas Mikolov. 2018. Learning word vectors for 157 languages. In *Language Resources and Evaluation Conference*, number CONF.

Mihaela Găman, Dirk Hovy, Radu Tudor Ionescu, Heidi Jauhiainen, Tommi Jauhiainen, Krister Lindén, Nikola Ljubešić, Niko Partanen, Christoph Purschke, Yves Scherrer, and Marcos Zampieri. 2020. A Report on the VarDial Evaluation Campaign 2020. In *Proceedings of the Seventh Workshop on NLP for Similar Languages, Varieties and Dialects (VarDial)*.

Dirk Hovy and Christoph Purschke. 2018. Capturing regional variation with distributed place representations and geographic retrofitting. In *Proceedings of the 2018 Conference on Empirical Methods in Natural Language Processing*, pages 4383–4394, Brussels, Belgium. Association for Computational Linguistics.

Binxuan Huang and Kathleen M Carley. 2017. On predicting geolocation of tweets using convolutional neural networks. In *International conference on social computing, behavioral-cultural modeling and prediction and behavior representation in modeling and simulation*, pages 281–291. Springer.

Tommi Jauhiainen, Heidi Jauhiainen, and Krister Lindén. 2015. Discriminating Similar Languages with Token-based Backoff. In *Proceedings of the Joint Workshop on Language Technology for Closely Related Languages, Varieties and Dialects (LT4VarDial)*, pages 44–51, Hissar, Bulgaria.

Tommi Jauhiainen, Krister Lindén, and Heidi Jauhiainen. 2016. HeLI, a Word-Based Backoff Method for Language Identification. In *Proceedings of the Third Workshop on NLP for Similar Languages, Varieties and Dialects (VarDial3)*, pages 153–162, Osaka, Japan.

Tommi Jauhiainen, Heidi Jauhiainen, and Krister Lindén. 2018a. HeLI-based Experiments in Swiss German Dialect Identification. In *Proceedings of the Fifth Workshop on NLP for Similar Languages, Varieties and Dialects (VarDial)*, pages 254–262, Santa Fe, NM.

Tommi Jauhiainen, Heidi Jauhiainen, and Krister Lindén. 2018b. Iterative Language Model Adaptation for Indo-Aryan Language Identification. In *Proceedings of the Fifth Workshop on NLP for Similar Languages, Varieties and Dialects (VarDial)*, pages 66–75, Santa Fe, NM.

Tommi Jauhiainen, Heidi Jauhiainen, Tero Alstola, and Krister Lindén. 2019a. Language and dialect identification of cuneiform texts. In *Proceedings of the Sixth Workshop on NLP for Similar Languages, Varieties and Dialects*, pages 89–98. Association for Computational Linguistics.

Tommi Jauhiainen, Heidi Jauhiainen, and Krister Lindén. 2019b. Discriminating between Mandarin Chinese and Swiss-German varieties using adaptive language models. In *Proceedings of the 6th Workshop on NLP for Similar Languages, Varieties and Dialects (VarDial 2019)*, pages 178–187, Minneapolis, Minnesota.

Tommi Jauhiainen, Krister Lindén, and Heidi Jauhiainen. 2019c. Language model adaptation for language and dialect identification of text. *Natural Language Engineering*, 25(5):561–583.

Tommi Jauhiainen, Marco Lui, Marcos Zampieri, Timothy Baldwin, and Krister Lindén. 2019d. Automatic Language Identification in Texts: A Survey. *Journal of Artificial Intelligence Research*, 65:675–782.

Tommi Jauhiainen, Heidi Jauhiainen, Niko Partanen, and Krister Lindén. 2020. Uralic Language Identification (ULI) 2020 shared task dataset and the Wanca 2017 corpora. In *Proceedings of the Seventh Workshop on NLP for Similar Languages, Varieties and Dialects (VarDial)*.

Tommi Jauhiainen. 2019. *Language identification in texts*. Ph.D. thesis, University of Helsinki, Finland.

Andrei Kutuzov, Murhaf Fares, Stephan Oepen, and Erik Velldal. 2017. Word vectors, reuse, and replicability: Towards a community repository of large-text resources. In *Proceedings of the 58th Conference on Simulation and Modelling*, pages 271–276. Linköping University Electronic Press.

Nikola Ljubešić, Tanja Samardžić, and Curdin Derungs. 2016. TweetGeo - a tool for collecting, processing and analysing geo-encoded linguistic data. In *Proceedings of COLING 2016, the 26th International Conference on Computational Linguistics: Technical Papers*, pages 3412–3421, Osaka, Japan, December. The COLING 2016 Organizing Committee.

Shervin Malmasi and Mark Dras. 2015. Language Identification using Classifier Ensembles. In *Proceedings of the Joint Workshop on Language Technology for Closely Related Languages, Varieties and Dialects (LT4VarDial)*, pages 35–43, Hissar, Bulgaria.

Shervin Malmasi and Marcos Zampieri. 2016. Arabic Dialect Identification in Speech Transcripts. In *Proceedings of the Third Workshop on NLP for Similar Languages, Varieties and Dialects (VarDial)*, pages 106–113, Osaka, Japan.

Shervin Malmasi and Marcos Zampieri. 2017. German Dialect Identification in Interview Transcriptions. In *Proceedings of the Fourth Workshop on NLP for Similar Languages, Varieties and Dialects (VarDial)*, pages 164–169, Valencia, Spain.

Shervin Malmasi, Marcos Zampieri, Nikola Ljubešić, Preslav Nakov, Ahmed Ali, and Jörg Tiedemann. 2016. Discriminating Between Similar Languages and Arabic Dialect Identification: A Report on the Third DSL Shared Task. In *Proceedings of the Third Workshop on NLP for Similar Languages, Varieties and Dialects*, pages 1–14, Osaka, Japan.

Maria Medvedeva, Martin Kroon, and Barbara Plank. 2017. When Sparse Traditional Models Outperform Dense Neural Networks: the Curious Case of Discriminating between Similar Languages. In *Proceedings of the Fourth Workshop on NLP for Similar Languages, Varieties and Dialects (VarDial)*, pages 156–163, Valencia, Spain.

Verginica Barbu Mititelu, Dan Tufiş, and Elena Irimia. 2018. The reference corpus of the contemporary Romanian language (CoRoLa). In *Proceedings of the Eleventh International Conference on Language Resources and Evaluation (LREC 2018)*.

Seppo Mustonen. 1965. Multiple Discriminant Analysis in Linguistic Problems. *Statistical Methods in Linguistics*, 4:37–44.

Cristian Onose, Dumitru-Clementin Cercel, and Stefan Trausan-Matu. 2019. SC-UPB at the VarDial 2019 evaluation campaign: Moldavian vs. Romanian cross-dialect topic identification. In *Proceedings of the Sixth Workshop on NLP for Similar Languages, Varieties and Dialects*, pages 172–177.

SIL. 2020. *ISO 639-3 Codes for the representation of names of languages*. SIL International.

Luke S Snyder, Morteza Karimzadeh, Ray Chen, and David S Ebert. 2019. City-level geolocation of tweets for real-time visual analytics. In *Proceedings of the 3rd ACM SIGSPATIAL International Workshop on AI for Geographic Knowledge Discovery*, pages 85–88.

Diana Tudoreanu. 2019. DTeam@ VarDial 2019: Ensemble based on skip-gram and triplet loss neural networks for Moldavian vs. Romanian cross-dialect topic identification. In *Proceedings of the Sixth Workshop on NLP for Similar Languages, Varieties and Dialects*, pages 202–208.

David H. Wolpert. 1992. Stacked Generalization. *Neural Networks*, 5(2):241–259.

Nianheng Wu, Eric DeMattos, Kwok Him So, Pin-zhen Chen, and Çağrı Çöltekin. 2019. Language discrimination and transfer learning for similar languages: experiments with feature combinations and adaptation. In *Proceedings of the Sixth Workshop on NLP for Similar Languages, Varieties and Dialects*, pages 54–63.

Zichao Yang, Diyi Yang, Chris Dyer, Xiaodong He, Alex Smola, and Eduard Hovy. 2016. Hierarchical attention networks for document classification. In *Proceedings of the 2016 conference of the North American chapter of the association for computational linguistics: human language technologies*, pages 1480–1489.

Marcos Zampieri, Liling Tan, Nikola Ljubešić, and Jörg Tiedemann. 2014. A Report on the DSL Shared Task 2014. In *Proceedings of the First Workshop on Applying NLP Tools to Similar Languages, Varieties and Dialects*, pages 58–67, Dublin, Ireland.

Marcos Zampieri, Liling Tan, Nikola Ljubešić, Jörg Tiedemann, and Preslav Nakov. 2015. Overview of the DSL Shared Task 2015. In *Proceedings of the Joint Workshop on Language Technology for Closely Related Languages, Varieties and Dialects (LT4VarDial)*, pages 1–9, Hissar, Bulgaria.

Marcos Zampieri, Shervin Malmasi, Nikola Ljubešic, Preslav Nakov, Ahmed Ali, Jörg Tiedemann, Yves Scherrer, and Noëmi Aepli. 2017. Findings of the VarDial Evaluation Campaign 2017. In *Proceedings of the Fourth Workshop on NLP for Similar Languages, Varieties and Dialects*, pages 1–15, Valencia, Spain.

Marcos Zampieri, Shervin Malmasi, Preslav Nakov, Ahmed Ali, Suwon Shon, James Glass, Yves Scherrer, Tanja Samardžić, Nikola Ljubešić, Jörg Tiedemann, Chris van der Lee, Stefan Grondelaers, Nelleke Oostdijk, Antal van den Bosch, Ritesh Kumar, Bornini Lahiri, and Mayank Jain. 2018. Language Identification and Morphosyntactic Tagging: The Second VarDial Evaluation Campaign. In *Proceedings of the Fifth Workshop on NLP for Similar Languages, Varieties and Dialects (VarDial)*, Santa Fe, USA.

Marcos Zampieri, Shervin Malmasi, Yves Scherrer, Tanja Samardžić, Francis Tyers, Miikka Silfverberg, Natalia Klyueva, Tung-Le Pan, Chu-Ren Huang, Radu Tudor Ionescu, Andrei Butnaru, and Tommi Jauhiainen. 2019. A Report on the Third VarDial Evaluation Campaign. In *Proceedings of the Sixth Workshop on NLP for Similar Languages, Varieties and Dialects (VarDial)*. Association for Computational Linguistics.

Exploring the Power of Romanian BERT for Dialect Identification

George-Eduard Zaharia[1*], Andrei-Marius Avram[1,2*],
Dumitru-Clementin Cercel[1], Traian Rebedea[1]
University Politehnica of Bucharest, Faculty of Automatic Control and Computers[1]
Research Institute for Artificial Intelligence, Romanian Academy[2]
{george.zaharia0806, andrei_marius.avram}@stud.acs.upb.ro
{dumitru.cercel, traian.rebedea}@upb.ro

Abstract

Dialect identification represents a key aspect for improving a series of tasks, such as opinion mining, considering that the location of the speaker can greatly influence the attitude towards a subject. In this work, we describe the systems developed by our team for VarDial 2020: Romanian Dialect Identification, a task specifically created for challenging participants to solve the dialect identification problem for an under-resourced language, such as Romanian. More specifically, we introduce a series of neural architectures based on Transformers, that combine a BERT model exclusively pre-trained on the Romanian language with several other techniques, such as adversarial training or character-level embeddings. By using a custom Romanian BERT model, we were able to reach a macro-F1 score of 64.75 on the test dataset, thus allowing us to be ranked 5th out of 8 participant teams. Moreover, we improved the F1-scores reported by the authors of MOROCO with over 1.7%, obtaining a 96.23% macro-F1 score, alongside micro and weighted F1 scores of 96.25%.

1 Introduction

Currently, the Romanian language is still considered an under-resourced language, although in the recent years, several datasets were created that tried to mitigate this problem such as the reference corpus of the Contemporary Romanian Language (CoRoLa) (Mititelu et al., 2018), the Romanian Named Entity Corpus (RONEC) (Dumitrescu and Avram, 2019), the Biomedical Gold Standard Corpus (MoNERo) (Mitrofan et al., 2019), the Romanian Speech Corpus (RSC) (Georgescu et al., 2020), and the Romanian WordNet (Dumitrescu et al., 2018). With the rise of attention-based language models, the first Romanian Bidirectional Encoder Representations from Transformer (Ro-BERT) appeared and it outperformed Multilingual BERT (M-BERT) (Pires et al., 2019) on all the evaluation tasks (Dumitrescu et al., 2020)[1].

One of the most addressed and challenging tasks in natural language processing research is text dialect identification. As a response to this challenge, Butnaru and Ionescu (2019) introduced the Moldavian and Romanian Dialectal Corpus (MOROCO), a dataset that contains 33,564 samples of text collected from news websites, grouped in two dialects using the top level domain of the websites: Romanian and Moldavian (".ro" and ".md"). Moreover, a shared task, called Romanian Dialect Identification (RDI), was proposed at VarDial 2020 (Găman et al., 2020) and it aimed to evaluate the performance of each participant system on this corpus.

Starting from the MOROCO dataset, the RDI competition introduces the challenge of properly identifying the Romanian or Moldavian dialect, considering that the test dataset is from a different domain. That is, the validation dataset contains long texts, written in either the Romanian or the Moldavian dialect, while the test dataset is composed of short entries, based on tweets. Therefore, this difference

---

*These authors contributed equally.

This work is licensed under a Creative Commons Attribution 4.0 International License.
License details: http://creativecommons.org/licenses/by/4.0/.

[1]Romanian BERT comes in the cased and uncased variants, that are open-sourced at:
https://github.com/dumitrescustefan/Romanian-Transformers

Proceedings of the 7th VarDial Workshop on NLP for Similar Languages, Varieties and Dialects, pages 232–241
Barcelona, Spain (Online), December 13, 2020

influenced the performance of our models, considering that we were able to obtain a 97.04% macro-F1
score on the validation set, while the evaluation on the test set yielded a 64.75% macro-F1 score.

This work is structured as follows. In Section 2, we perform an analysis of existing solutions for
closely related dialect identification tasks. Section 3 outlines our solutions for the dialect identification
issue, while Section 4 details the performed experiments, experimental setup, and error analysis. Finally,
we draw conclusions in Section 5.

2   Related Work

There are various approaches regarding the language dialect identification task. Some of them are cen-
tered around the Romanian language, while others are focused on different ones, such as the Arabic or
German dialects. However, they are equally important, considering that some techniques can cross the
language barrier and be used as universal dialect identification methods.

2.1   Romanian Dialect Identification

For example, previous work (Onose et al., 2019) in Romanian dialect identification employed the usage
of various deep learning models, including Recurrent Neural Networks (RNNs) (Elaraby and Abdul-
Mageed, 2018a), Long Short-Term Memory (LSTM) networks (Hochreiter and Schmidhuber, 1997),
and Gated Recurrent Units (GRUs) (Cho et al., 2014), alongside various word embeddings. Furthermore,
Tudoreanu (2019) applied an ensemble of neural networks that uses a triplet loss alongside Convolutional
Neural Networks (CNNs) (Kim, 2014), with the purpose of maximizing the distance between an anchor
sample and a negative example while minimizing the difference between the anchor and the positive
example. Wu et al. (2019) also considered Support Vector Machines (Cortes and Vapnik, 1995), but
paired with character n-grams.

2.2   Dialect Identification for Other Languages

Aiming to tackle the Arab dialect identification problem by participating at the MADAR shared
task (Bouamor et al., 2019), Abdul-Mageed et al. (2019) introduced a series of solutions based on traditional, deep learning, Natural Language Processing (NLP) techniques, like GRUs and, at the same time,
state-of-the-art, Transformer-based methods, i.e., BERT (Zhang and Abdul-Mageed, 2019). Moreover,
Salameh et al. (2018) engaged in the same problem by employing a solution based on features, including character and word n-grams and applying a Multinomial Naive Bayes classifier. Similar traditional
methods were also applied by Elaraby and Abdul-Mageed (2018b) using logistic regression, SVMs, and,
moreover, models based on RNNs. Other work (Butnaru and Ionescu, 2018) proposed string kernel functions (Lodhi et al., 2002) that capture the similarity between text samples based on character n-grams,
while a different approach (Ali, 2018) simply implies the usage of CNNs.

Employing similar techniques, but switching the language, Malmasi and Zampieri (2017) addressed
the German dialect identification issue by also using traditional machine learning techniques, but, furthermore, adding different ensemble classifiers. Further focusing on the German language, Gaman and
Ionescu (2020) proposed several methods for approaching the previously mentioned subject, including
character-level CNNs, Support Vector Regressors based on string kernels and ensemble learning systems (Chen and Guestrin, 2016).

3   Methods

We focused our approaches around Transformers (Vaswani et al., 2017), considering that they represent
state-of-the-art solutions for solving NLP problems.

3.1   Vanilla Transformer-based Solutions

3.1.1   Multilingual BERT

Aimed for multilingual NLP problems, M-BERT is a variant of BERT (Devlin et al., 2018), pre-trained
on over 100 languages, thus ensuring good performance for all of them, not only for the English language.

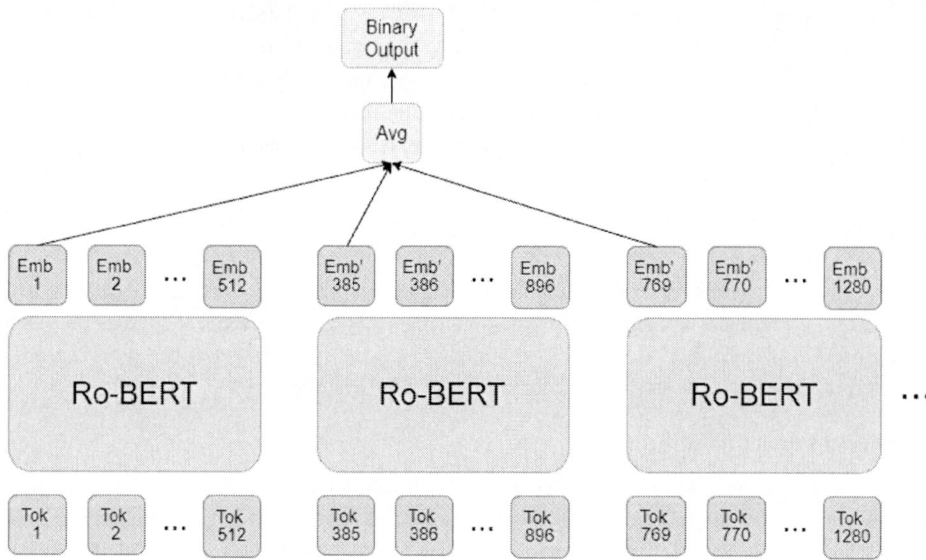

Figure 1: The architecture of Custom-Ro-BERT-FT. The *Emb'* notation shows that the respective embedding is different from the embedding obtained on the same tokens, on the previous sequence.

M-BERT can be used for a wide array of tasks, including sequence classification, therefore allowing us to fine-tune the model for our problem, dialect identification in Romanian.

3.1.2 Romanian BERT

We also experimented with the embeddings obtained from the Ro-BERT model. Ro-BERT was trained on three publicly available corpora: OPUS (Tiedemann, 2012), OSCAR (Suárez et al., 2019), and Wikipedia, using masked language modeling and next sentence prediction as training objectives. To validate the resulted model, the performance of Ro-BERT was compared with the performance of M-BERT on three tasks from Romanian corpora: (1) Simple Universal Dependencies - the models had to predict independently the Universal Part-of-Speech (UPOS) and the eXtended Part-of-Speech, (2) Joint Universal Dependencies - the models had to jointly predict the UPOS, Universal Features, Lemmas and Dependency Parsing, and (3) Named Entity Recognition - the models had to predict the BIO labels. For the first two tasks, the authors used the Romanian RRT corpus (Barbu Mititelu et al., 2016), while for the last one RONEC (Dumitrescu and Avram, 2019). The evaluation results showed that Ro-BERT outperformed M-BERT on all tasks with values ranging between 1% and 3%.

3.2 Proposed Approaches

3.2.1 Custom Ro-BERT Fine-tuning

To use the Transformer-based language models on the competition dataset, we firstly tokenized the sentences by using the Byte-Pair Encoding (BPE) tokenizer with the additional NE token. As depicted in Table 1, some of the sequences can be very long, so applying the model directly on them as described in Devlin et al. (2018) is not optimal. To mitigate this problem, we applied the model on consecutive sequences of 512 tokens that share the first 128 tokens with the previous sequence. Then, to create a binary output, we averaged the embeddings of all tokens out of each 512 token sequence and projected it into a scalar. This process is further depicted in Figure 1. We will further reference this system under the name of Custom-Ro-BERT-FT.

3.2.2 Embedding Concatenation

Next, we intended to enhance the word representations with information at the morpheme-level, therefore, we needed to use character-level embeddings. By breaking each word into a sequence of characters,

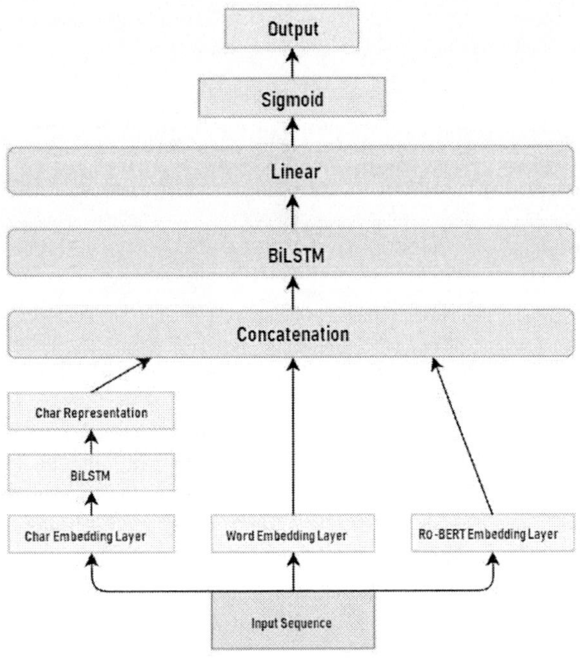

Figure 2: The architecture of the EC model.

then mapping them to a series of indexes and then feeding them into a Bidirectional LSTM (BiLSTM), we were able to obtain another set of representations for the inputs. The character-level embeddings allowed us to identify structural similarities between different words, an important aspect when tackling a dialect identification problem.

Furthermore, we also added pre-trained fastText word embeddings (Bojanowski et al., 2017). The three representations (i.e., Transformer embeddings, word embeddings, and character embeddings) were concatenated, making sure that the first dimension is identical for all of them, representing the number of input tokens. The resulted tensor was then fed to a BiLSTM network and then to a linear layer, thus obtaining the final representation for the input sequence. Finally, we used the sigmoid activation function for obtaining the final class. Figure 2 depicts the previously described architecture, called EC.

3.2.3 Adversarial Training

Initially applied for improving computer vision solutions, adversarial training (Goodfellow et al., 2014) represents a technique that intentionally alters a percentage of training entries with perturbations. Even though the changes are minimal, the effects on the performance of the system can be major, since the perturbations can lead to missclassifications. The previously mentioned process can be applied to both text and image models. Because of the generalization it creates, it can lead to improved performance for the first category. Therefore, language models achieve better results when trained under this approach.

Since we intended to also maximize the performance of our models, we resorted to an adversarial training technique. Therefore, we used FreeLB (Zhu et al., 2019), an enhanced adversarial training method for natural language models. FreeLB performs adversarial training by introducing adversarial perturbations at word-level embeddings and then minimizing the adversarial loss resulted from the input samples. The model receives training data in batches that are affected by the adversarial algorithm, namely, they are augmented with extra adversarial entries. Each iteration creates some outputs, the purpose of the FreeLB algorithm being to take the gradients of these outputs and to average them. Furthermore, FreeLB minimizes the maximum risk at each ascent step, with the advantage of creating an insignificant overhead.

4   Experiments

4.1   Dataset Analysis

Dataset	White Space Tokenizer		Ro-BERT Tokenizer		M-BERT Tokenizer	
	Avg. Tokens	Max. Tokens	Avg. Tokens	Max. Tokens	Avg. Tokens	Max. Tokens
Train (MOROCO)	310.04	15988	356.08	18456	449.70	24169
Valid (MOROCO)	309.92	10809	355.87	12578	450.02	16676
Test (MOROCO)	313.65	13213	360.87	15313	455.50	20151
Test (RDI)	15.63	25	21.71	42	26.65	44

Table 1: Statistics of the datasets we used in our experiments, MOROCO-RDI and RDI.

MOROCO was created by collecting texts from the top news websites in Romania and Moldavia, and by automatically labeling them using the Internet domain, resulting in 33,564 samples (45.89% Moldavian and 54.11% Romanian) having a total of more than 10 million tokens. The news were selected from six domains: culture, finance, politics, science, sports, and tech. The authors further processed the text by removing all HTML tags and by replacing the named entities with the NE token in order to prevent the models from classifying based on features that are not specific to the dialect, but to the environment in which the dialect is used. Moreover, in order to provide a proper comparison with other similar corpora, five tasks were created on the MOROCO data set: binary classification by dialect (MOROCO-RDI), intra-dialect classification by topic using the Romanian or the Moldavian samples, and cross-dialect topic classification by training a model on the samples of one dialect and testing on the other dialect set of samples. The dataset was also split into training, validation and testing, resulting in subsets that contained 21,719, 5,921 and 5,924 number of samples.

At the evaluation phase of the RDI task, a new data set was used to evaluate the performance of the submitted models. The new set contained 5,022 samples, mostly taken from social media.

Further, we analyzed the two datasets (MOROCO and RDI) in Table 1 by computing the average number of tokens and the maximum number of tokens, using the white space tokenizer, the Romanian BERT uncased tokenizer, and the M-BERT uncased tokenizer. We note that the change in domain led to a significant difference in the number of tokens, of several orders of magnitude, which in turn made our models to perform much worse on the RDI test set than we initially estimated on the MOROCO test set.

4.2   Implementation Details

For the EC solution, we considered the Adam optimizer (Kingma and Ba, 2014) with a 0.001 learning rate. Furthermore, the BiLSTM hidden size is 500, while the input maximum length is 280 tokens. We trained the model for 8 epochs, by using an early stopping policy. At the same time, for the adversarial training method, we used an initial learning rate of 5e-5, alongside the Adam optimizer. Moreover, the weight decay and the epsilon parameters were kept with their default values 0.0 and 1e-8 respectively, and the training process spanned over 12 epochs. For the standard Ro-BERT and also for the custom Ro-BERT fine-tuning process, we employed the Adam with weight decay (AdamW) optimizer (Loshchilov and Hutter, 2017) with a 2e-5 learning rate, for 4 epochs.

4.3   Custom Language Model Comparison

The first experiment we conducted was a comparison between M-BERT and Ro-BERT on the MOROCO-RDI test dataset in order to choose a language model to work with. At this stage, because the entries had a high number of tokens, we also experimented with various N, i.e., the number of consecutive sequences with 512 tokens that share 128 tokens with the previous sequence, on which the language model is applied. The maximum number of tokens (determined by N) and by using the Ro-BERT and M-BERT tokenizers is presented in Table 2, together with the percentage of samples that have fewer tokens than the maximum. Also, the results are depicted in Figure 3. The left figure presents the case where all samples that have more tokens than the maximum allowed, are dropped both from the train set

No. of Apply (N)	No. of Tokens	M-BERT Perc.	Ro-BERT Perc.
1	512	72.38%	83.60%
2	896	92.28%	95.50%
3	1280	96.62%	98.04%
4	1536	97.78%	98.64%

Table 2: Maximum number of tokens allowed for a given N and the percentage of samples that satisfy this condition.

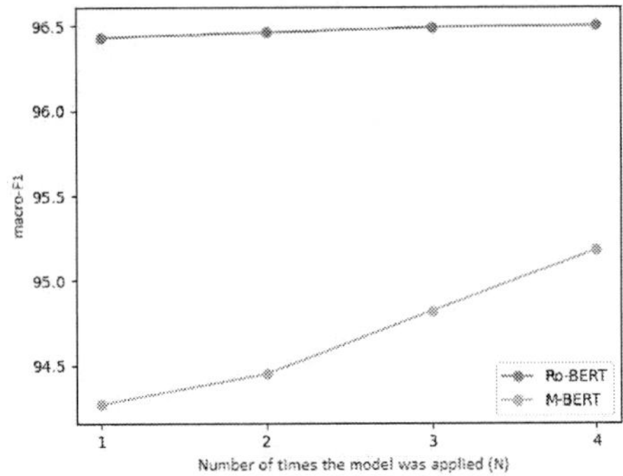
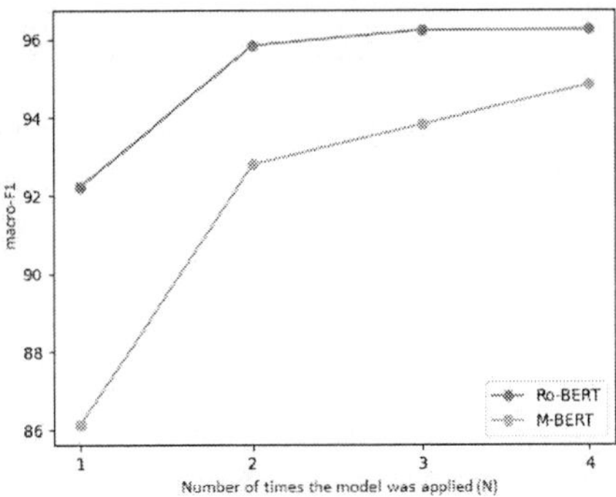

Figure 3: M-BERT and Ro-BERT comparison with various N - the number of times each language model is applied, trained on the MOROCO-RDI dataset and tested on samples from the test set that do not have a token length longer than the maximum allowed in the training set (left) or on the whole test set (right).

and the test set, while the right figure keeps all the samples from the test set, but also drops the samples from the training set that do not meet the requirements. It can be observed that in both cases Ro-BERT offers a better performance for all values of N and that the rate of change in performance of M-BERT improves faster than the performance of Ro-BERT, maybe even surpassing Ro-BERT for a large number of tokens[2].

At evaluation time, for the RDI dataset, the sequences were much smaller than the ones from the initial dataset (MOROCO-RDI), and in order to avoid overfitting on long sequences, we used the system that applies Ro-BERT only 3 times instead of 4 times. Moreover, our choice is further motivated by the fact that the difference in performance between $N = 3$ and $N = 4$ is rather small (0.6%).

4.4 Submitted Results

Next, we experimented with four different types of architectures, out of which we used the best three for our VarDial submissions. Table 3 presents the results obtained on the entire test datasets. The MOROCO-RDI dataset contains entries similar to the ones used for training and validation. On the other hand, the RDI shared task counterpart contains much shorter entries, obtained from tweets.

The best results obtained for the RDI dataset are yielded by using the Custom-Ro-BERT-FT technique, with a weighted-F1 score of 64.80%, alongside a 64.75% micro-F1 and a 67.10% macro-F1. The closest result further obtained by our experiments comes at a difference of 8.41% in terms of weighted-F1 score, provided by the FreeLB technique, with a value of 56.39%. Also, the same experiment produced a 60.77% micro-F1 score and a 56.32% macro-F1 score. Furthermore, the EC solution proves to offer poorer results, considering the increased width and depth of the neural network and thus the large number of parameters that needed to be fine-tuned. The main metric, the weighted-F1 score, has a value of 46.59%, while the others, the macro and micro F1 measures, have values of 46.48% and 55.07%,

---

[2]Unfortunately, we could not make this analysis due to the lack of computational resources.

Task	Method	Micro-F1	Weighted-F1	Macro-F1
RDI	Standard Ro-BERT Fine-tuning	60.77	55.82	55.74
	Custom-Ro-BERT-FT	**67.10**	**64.80**	**64.75**
	FreeLB	60.77	56.39	56.32
	EC	55.07	46.59	46.48
	Top Model	78.75	78.76	78.77
MOROCO-RDI	Standard BERT Fine-tuning	94.48	94.52	94.51
	Custom-Ro-BERT-FT	**96.25**	**96.25**	**96.23**
	FreeLB	96.15	96.15	96.12
	EC	86.17	86.43	86.31
	Butnaru and Ionescu (2019)	94.60	94.11	94.50

Table 3: Results obtained by our models on the test sets.

respectively.

If we focus our attention on the MOROCO-RDI test dataset format, we can see that the performance difference is considerable. With a 96.25% weighted-F1 score and very close values for macro and micro F1, the Custom-Ro-BERT-FT technique offers the best results, closely followed by FreeLB at a margin of 0.1% in weighted-F1 score, with a value of 96.15%. Moreover, the micro and macro F1 scores have values of 96.15% and 96.12%, respectively. The EC model offers a value of 86.43% weighted-F1 alongside 86.17% and 86.31% micro and macro F1 scores. Furthermore, the standard Ro-BERT fine-tuning comes second to last in terms of performance, with a 1.73% difference in weighted-F1 score when compared to the Custom-Ro-BERT-FT model.

4.5 Error Analysis

Table 4 presents examples of entries correctly or wrongly classified. As seen, most of the incorrect entries are part of the Moldavian dialect. The main reason behind the misclassifications is represented by the domain and length differences between the train and development datasets and the evaluation dataset. For training and validation, the average number of tokens is about 310, while for the evaluation dataset, the number is around 15. This discrepancy does not allow the models to properly detect the dialect form the test entries, considering that, in some situations, there are no proper key features that can point towards a Romanian or a Moldavian dialect. For example, the last two examples of misclassified entries from Table 4 do not show any defining aspects of either one of the dialects. Moreover, the fourth one contains only one proper word, "Primele" (eng. "The first"), while the other words are masked by the NE token. This may be an important problem for the task and dataset at hand, as the differences between Moldavian and Romanian are minor and might not arise in short fragments of text such as tweets. For future versions, these datasets should be manually curated to contain more relevant samples.

On the other hand, some entries have clear indicators that point towards a certain dialect. As an example, the root word "raion" (eng. "district"), specific to the Moldavian dialect, is a clear indicator of the origin of that input. Additionally, some named entities are not masked and are also present in the training dataset, thus clearing the origin of the including text (e.g., the named entities "Dodon" or "Chicu" in the first two correctly classified samples).

5 Conclusion and Future Work

This paper presented our approaches regarding the Romanian Dialect Identification task, organized by VarDial 2020. We proposed a series of Transformer-based architectures that intended to solve the dialect identification issue. All the solutions employ the usage of Ro-BERT, a Transformer model pre-trained on Romanian language corpora. By fine-tuning Ro-BERT with two different techniques, standard and custom, we were able to achieve good scores on both the MOROCO-RDI test dataset and the RDI dataset, used for this year's competition. Also, by using an adversarial training technique (FreeLB) on Ro-BERT, we improved the state-of-the-art score on the MOROCO-RDI dataset, while the performance

Category	Entry	True label
Correct	1) Dodon: NEavut în trecut un guvern, un stat capturat, a urmat un NE condus de NE Dodon: In the past, NE had a government, a captured state, followed by a NE lead by NE	MD
	2) Chicu crede crearea platformelor industriale în fiecare centru raional o soluție de renaștere a economiei naționale Chicu believes that the creation of industrial platforms in each district center represents a solution for the rebirth of the national economy	MD
	3) Seri de tango și saloane de flori la un spital de psihiatrie din NE Un psiholog aduce speranță unor oameni ca Tango evenings and flower salons at a psychiatric hospital in NE A psychologist brings hope to people like	RO
Wrong	1) Pericol pentru NE NE vor revenirea a NE NE de militari ruși în zona de securitate Danger to NE NE want the return of NE NE Russian military in the security zone	MD
	2) FOTO NE NE NE iarna a devenit primăvară. Un arbust ornamental a înflorit, NE de vremea caldă PHOTO NE NE NE winter has become spring. An ornamental shrub bloomed, NE because of the warm weather	RO
	3) Cum te protejezi împotriva coronavirusului NE How to protect yourself against the coronavirus NE	MD
	4) Primele NE NE NE NE NE NE The first NE NE NE NE NE NE	MD

Table 4: Examples of correctly and wrongly classified entries. MD: Moldavian, RO: Romanian.

decreased on the RDI set. Moreover, employing an embedding concatenation technique does not help with performance, yielding the poorest results among the four techniques we experimented with.

For future work, we intend to also experiment with multi-task learning approaches (Caruana, 1997), considering that, usually, an auxiliary task can help the model to detect additional features that can lead to increased performance. Another aspect we plan to test are CoRoLA-based word embeddings, which can replace their counterpart in the embedding concatenation experiment.

References

Muhammad Abdul-Mageed, Chiyu Zhang, AbdelRahim Elmadany, Arun Rajendran, and Lyle Ungar. 2019. Dianet: Bert and hierarchical attention multi-task learning of fine-grained dialect. *arXiv preprint arXiv:1910.14243*.

Mohamed Ali. 2018. Character level convolutional neural network for arabic dialect identification. In *Proceedings of the Fifth Workshop on NLP for Similar Languages, Varieties and Dialects (VarDial 2018)*, pages 122–127.

V Barbu Mititelu, Radu Ion, Radu Simionescu, Elana Irimia, and Cenel-Augusto Perez. 2016. The romanian treebank annotated according to universal dependencies. In *Proceedings of the tenth international conference on natural language processing (hrtal2016)*.

Piotr Bojanowski, Edouard Grave, Armand Joulin, and Tomas Mikolov. 2017. Enriching word vectors with subword information. *Transactions of the Association for Computational Linguistics*, 5:135–146.

Houda Bouamor, Sabit Hassan, and Nizar Habash. 2019. The madar shared task on arabic fine-grained dialect identification. In *Proceedings of the Fourth Arabic Natural Language Processing Workshop*, pages 199–207.

Andrei M Butnaru and Radu Tudor Ionescu. 2018. Unibuckernel reloaded: First place in arabic dialect identification for the second year in a row. *arXiv preprint arXiv:1805.04876*.

Andrei Butnaru and Radu Tudor Ionescu. 2019. Moroco: The moldavian and romanian dialectal corpus. In *Proceedings of the 57th Annual Meeting of the Association for Computational Linguistics*, pages 688–698.

Rich Caruana. 1997. Multitask learning. *Machine learning*, 28(1):41–75.

Tianqi Chen and Carlos Guestrin. 2016. Xgboost: A scalable tree boosting system. In *Proceedings of the 22nd acm sigkdd international conference on knowledge discovery and data mining*, pages 785–794.

Kyunghyun Cho, Bart Van Merriënboer, Caglar Gulcehre, Dzmitry Bahdanau, Fethi Bougares, Holger Schwenk, and Yoshua Bengio. 2014. Learning phrase representations using rnn encoder-decoder for statistical machine translation. *arXiv preprint arXiv:1406.1078*.

Corinna Cortes and Vladimir Vapnik. 1995. Support vector machine. *Machine learning*, 20(3):273–297.

Jacob Devlin, Ming-Wei Chang, Kenton Lee, and Kristina Toutanova. 2018. Bert: Pre-training of deep bidirectional transformers for language understanding. *arXiv preprint arXiv:1810.04805*.

Stefan Daniel Dumitrescu and Andrei-Marius Avram. 2019. Introducing ronec–the romanian named entity corpus. *arXiv preprint arXiv:1909.01247*.

Stefan Daniel Dumitrescu, Andrei Marius Avram, Luciana Morogan, and Stefan-Adrian Toma. 2018. Rowordnet– a python api for the romanian wordnet. In *2018 10th International Conference on Electronics, Computers and Artificial Intelligence (ECAI)*, pages 1–6. IEEE.

Stefan Daniel Dumitrescu, Andrei-Marius Avram, and Sampo Pyysalo. 2020. The birth of romanian bert. *arXiv preprint arXiv:2009.08712*.

Mohamed Elaraby and Muhammad Abdul-Mageed. 2018a. Deep models for arabic dialect identification on benchmarked data. In *Proceedings of the Fifth Workshop on NLP for Similar Languages, Varieties and Dialects (VarDial 2018)*, pages 263–274.

Mohamed Elaraby and Muhammad Abdul-Mageed. 2018b. Deep models for arabic dialect identification on benchmarked data. In *Proceedings of the Fifth Workshop on NLP for Similar Languages, Varieties and Dialects (VarDial 2018)*, pages 263–274.

Mihaela Gaman and Radu Tudor Ionescu. 2020. Combining deep learning and string kernels for the localization of swiss german tweets. *arXiv preprint arXiv:2010.03614*.

Alexandru-Lucian Georgescu, Horia Cucu, Andi Buzo, and Corneliu Burileanu. 2020. Rsc: A romanian read speech corpus for automatic speech recognition. In *Proceedings of The 12th Language Resources and Evaluation Conference*, pages 6606–6612.

Ian Goodfellow, Jean Pouget-Abadie, Mehdi Mirza, Bing Xu, David Warde-Farley, Sherjil Ozair, Aaron Courville, and Yoshua Bengio. 2014. Generative adversarial nets. In *Advances in neural information processing systems*, pages 2672–2680.

Mihaela Găman, Dirk Hovy, Radu Tudor Ionescu, Heidi Jauhiainen, Tommi Jauhiainen, Krister Lindén, Nikola Ljubešić, Niko Partanen, Christoph Purschke, Yves Scherrer, and Marcos Zampieri. 2020. A Report on the VarDial Evaluation Campaign 2020. In *Proceedings of the Seventh Workshop on NLP for Similar Languages, Varieties and Dialects (VarDial)*.

Sepp Hochreiter and Jürgen Schmidhuber. 1997. Long short-term memory. *Neural computation*, 9(8):1735–1780.

Yoon Kim. 2014. Convolutional neural networks for sentence classification. *arXiv preprint arXiv:1408.5882*.

Diederik P Kingma and Jimmy Ba. 2014. Adam: A method for stochastic optimization. *arXiv preprint arXiv:1412.6980*.

Huma Lodhi, Craig Saunders, John Shawe-Taylor, Nello Cristianini, and Chris Watkins. 2002. Text classification using string kernels. *Journal of Machine Learning Research*, 2(Feb):419–444.

Ilya Loshchilov and Frank Hutter. 2017. Decoupled weight decay regularization. *arXiv preprint arXiv:1711.05101*.

Shervin Malmasi and Marcos Zampieri. 2017. German dialect identification in interview transcriptions. In *Proceedings of the Fourth Workshop on NLP for Similar Languages, Varieties and Dialects (VarDial)*, pages 164–169.

Verginica Barbu Mititelu, Dan Tufiş, and Elena Irimia. 2018. The reference corpus of the contemporary romanian language (corola). In *Proceedings of the Eleventh International Conference on Language Resources and Evaluation (LREC 2018)*.

Maria Mitrofan, Verginica Barbu Mititelu, and Grigorina Mitrofan. 2019. Monero: a biomedical gold standard corpus for the romanian language. In *Proceedings of the 18th BioNLP Workshop and Shared Task*, pages 71–79.

Cristian Onose, Dumitru-Clementin Cercel, and Stefan Trausan-Matu. 2019. Sc-upb at the vardial 2019 evaluation campaign: Moldavian vs. romanian cross-dialect topic identification. In *Proceedings of the Sixth Workshop on NLP for Similar Languages, Varieties and Dialects*, pages 172–177.

Telmo Pires, Eva Schlinger, and Dan Garrette. 2019. How multilingual is multilingual bert? *arXiv preprint arXiv:1906.01502*.

Mohammad Salameh, Houda Bouamor, and Nizar Habash. 2018. Fine-grained arabic dialect identification. In *Proceedings of the 27th International Conference on Computational Linguistics*, pages 1332–1344.

Pedro Javier Ortiz Suárez, Benoît Sagot, and Laurent Romary. 2019. Asynchronous pipeline for processing huge corpora on medium to low resource infrastructures. In *7th Workshop on the Challenges in the Management of Large Corpora (CMLC-7)*. Leibniz-Institut für Deutsche Sprache.

Jörg Tiedemann. 2012. Parallel data, tools and interfaces in opus. In *Lrec*, volume 2012, pages 2214–2218.

Diana Tudoreanu. 2019. Dteam@ vardial 2019: Ensemble based on skip-gram and triplet loss neural networks for moldavian vs. romanian cross-dialect topic identification. In *Proceedings of the Sixth Workshop on NLP for Similar Languages, Varieties and Dialects*, pages 202–208.

Ashish Vaswani, Noam Shazeer, Niki Parmar, Jakob Uszkoreit, Llion Jones, Aidan N Gomez, Łukasz Kaiser, and Illia Polosukhin. 2017. Attention is all you need. In *Advances in neural information processing systems*, pages 5998–6008.

Nianheng Wu, Eric DeMattos, Kwok Him So, Pin-zhen Chen, and Çağrı Çöltekin. 2019. Language discrimination and transfer learning for similar languages: experiments with feature combinations and adaptation. In *Proceedings of the Sixth Workshop on NLP for Similar Languages, Varieties and Dialects*, pages 54–63.

Chiyu Zhang and Muhammad Abdul-Mageed. 2019. No army, no navy: Bert semi-supervised learning of arabic dialects. In *Proceedings of the Fourth Arabic Natural Language Processing Workshop*, pages 279–284.

Chen Zhu, Yu Cheng, Zhe Gan, Siqi Sun, Tom Goldstein, and Jingjing Liu. 2019. Freelb: Enhanced adversarial training for natural language understanding. In *International Conference on Learning Representations*.

Combining Deep Learning and String Kernels for the Localization of Swiss German Tweets

Mihaela Găman
Department of Computer Science
University of Bucharest
14 Academiei, Bucharest, Romania
mp.gaman@gmail.com

Radu Tudor Ionescu
Department of Computer Science
Romanian Young Academy
University of Bucharest
14 Academiei, Bucharest, Romania
raducu.ionescu@gmail.com

Abstract

In this work, we introduce the methods proposed by the UnibucKernel team in solving the Social Media Variety Geolocation task featured in the 2020 VarDial Evaluation Campaign. We address only the second subtask, which targets a data set composed of nearly 30 thousand Swiss German Jodels. The dialect identification task is about accurately predicting the latitude and longitude of test samples. We frame the task as a double regression problem, employing a variety of machine learning approaches to predict both latitude and longitude. From simple models for regression, such as Support Vector Regression, to deep neural networks, such as Long Short-Term Memory networks and character-level convolutional neural networks, and, finally, to ensemble models based on meta-learners, such as XGBoost, our interest is focused on approaching the problem from a few different perspectives, in an attempt to minimize the prediction error. With the same goal in mind, we also considered many types of features, from high-level features, such as BERT embeddings, to low-level features, such as characters n-grams, which are known to provide good results in dialect identification. Our empirical results indicate that the handcrafted model based on string kernels outperforms the deep learning approaches. Nevertheless, our best performance is given by the ensemble model that combines both handcrafted and deep learning models.

1 Introduction

The organizers of the 2020 VarDial Evaluation Campaign (Găman et al., 2020) proposed a shared task targeted towards the geolocation of short texts, e.g. tweets, namely the Social Media Variety Geolocation (SMG) task. Typically formulated as a double regression problem, the task is about predicting the location, expressed in latitude and longitude, from where the text received as input was posted on a certain social media platform. Twitter and Jodel are the platforms used for data collection, divided by the language area in three subtasks, namely:

- Standard German Jodels (DE-AT) - formed of conversations initiated in Germany and Austria in regional dialectal forms (Hovy and Purschke, 2018).

- Swiss German Jodels (CH) - based on a smaller number of Jodel conversations from Switzerland (Hovy and Purschke, 2018).

- BCMS Tweets - from the area of Bosnia and Herzegovina, Croatia, Montenegro and Serbia where the macro-language used is BCMS, with both similarities and a fair share of variation among the component languages (Ljubešić et al., 2016).

In this paper, we focus only on the second subtask, SMG-CH, proposing a variety of handcrafted and deep learning models, as well as an ensemble model that combines all our previous models through meta-learning. Our first model is a Support Vector Regression (SVR) classifier (Chang and Lin, 2002) based on string kernels, which are known to perform well in other dialect identification tasks (Butnaru

This work is licensed under a Creative Commons Attribution 4.0 International License. License details: http://creativecommons.org/licenses/by/4.0/.

Proceedings of the 7th VarDial Workshop on NLP for Similar Languages, Varieties and Dialects, pages 242–253
Barcelona, Spain (Online), December 13, 2020

and Ionescu, 2018b; Ionescu and Popescu, 2016; Ionescu and Butnaru, 2017). Our second model is a character-level convolutional neural network (CNN) (Zhang et al., 2015), which is also known to provide good results in dialect identification (Butnaru and Ionescu, 2019; Tudoreanu, 2019). Due to the high popularity and the outstanding results of Bidirectional Encoder Representations from Transformers (BERT) (Devlin et al., 2019) in solving mainstream NLP tasks, we decided to try out a Long Short-Term Memory (LSTM) network (Hochreiter and Schmidhuber, 1997) based on German BERT embeddings as our third model. Lastly, we combine our three models into an ensemble that employs Extreme Gradient Boosting (XGBoost) (Chen and Guestrin, 2016) as meta-learner. We conducted experiments on the development set provided by the organizers, in order to decide which models to choose for our three submissions for the SMG-CH subtask. Our results indicate that the ensemble model attains the best results. Perhaps surprisingly, our shallow approach based on string kernels outperforms both deep learning models. Our observations are consistent across the development and the test sets provided by the organizers.

The rest of this paper is organized as follows. We present related work on dialect identification and geolocation of short texts in Section 2. Our approaches are described in more detail in Section 3. We present the experiments and empirical results in Section 4. Finally, our conclusions are drawn in Section 5.

2   Related Work

One of the initial works on text-based geotagging (Ding et al., 2000) aims at automatically finding the geographic scope of web pages, in a classification setup relying on named location entities such as cities and states. The authors used gazetteers as the source of the location mappings, proposing a rather heuristic approach. Gazetteers, constitute a tool used in one of the three general approaches taken so far in text-based geolocation, this tool being adopted in a number of works (Lieberman et al., 2010; Quercini et al., 2010; Cheng et al., 2010). In this line of research, some researchers employed rule-based methods (Bilhaut et al., 2003), while others plugged named entity recognition into various machine learning techniques (Gelernter and Mushegian, 2011; Qin et al., 2010). The main disadvantage of these methods is that they rely on the existence of specific mentions of locations in text, rather than inferring them in a not so straightforward manner. These direct mentions of places do not represent a safe assumption, especially when it comes to social media platforms such as Twitter, which is used as the data source in some of these studies (Cheng et al., 2010). The other two main categories of approaches for text-based geolocation rely on either unsupervised learning (Ahmed et al., 2013; Hong et al., 2012; Eisenstein et al., 2010) or supervised classification (Wing and Baldridge, 2011; Kinsella et al., 2011). The unsupervised methods can be described in large part as clustering techniques based on topic models.

There are some studies on user geolocation in social media, that look at this task from a supervised learning perspective (Rout et al., 2013) and can be included in the second set of approaches for geotagging. However, in such works, other details (e.g. social ties) in the users profile have been considered rather than their written content. Although these works cover geolocation prediction in social media, they do not use text as input. Our current interest in studying language variation for the geolocation of users in social media has been covered in the literature in a series of works (Rahimi et al., 2017; Han et al., 2014; Doyle, 2014; Roller et al., 2012; Eisenstein et al., 2010), employing various machine learning techniques, that range from probabilistic graphical models (Eisenstein et al., 2010) and adaptive grid search (Roller et al., 2012) to Bayesian methods (Doyle, 2014) and neural networks (Rahimi et al., 2017).

The related work to date covers a wide range of languages and dialects, including Dutch (Wieling et al., 2011), British (Szmrecsanyi, 2008), American (Huang et al., 2016; Eisenstein et al., 2010) and even African American Vernacular English (Jones, 2015). Most related to our work is the study of Hovy and Purschke (2018), which targets the German language and its variations and, in addition to the previously mentioned endeavours, performs a quantitative analysis against a dialect map. Moreover, Hovy and Purschke (2018) collected 16.8 million online posts from the German-speaking area with the aim of learning document representations of cities. Among these posts, some were from the German speaking side of Switzerland, being part of the SMG shared task, more specifically the SMG-CH subtask that we are addressing. The authors aimed at capturing enough regional variations in the written language, serving as input in automatically distinguishing the geographical region of speakers. The focus was on larger regions covering a given dialect, the proposed approach being based on clustering. Given the shared task formulation, we take a different approach and use the provided data in a double regression setup, addressing the problem both from a shallow perspective and a deep learning perspective, respectively.

3 Methods

3.1 ν-Support Vector Regression based on String Kernels.

String Kernels. Lodhi et al. (2001) introduced string kernels as a means of comparing two documents, based on the inner product generated by all substrings of length n, typically known as character n-grams. Since then, string kernels have found many applications, from sentiment analysis (Giménez-Pérez et al., 2017; Ionescu and Butnaru, 2018; Popescu et al., 2017), automated essay scoring (Cozma et al., 2018) and sentence selection (Masala et al., 2017) to native language identification (Ionescu et al., 2014; Ionescu et al., 2016; Ionescu and Popescu, 2017; Popescu and Ionescu, 2013) and dialect identification (Butnaru and Ionescu, 2018b; Butnaru and Ionescu, 2019; Ionescu and Butnaru, 2017).

In this work, we employ string kernels as described in (Butnaru and Ionescu, 2019), specifically using the efficient algorithm for building string kernels of Popescu et al. (2017). We note that the number of character n-grams is usually much higher than the number of samples, so representing the text samples as feature vectors may require a lot of space. String kernels provide an efficient way to avoid storing and using the feature vectors (primal form), by representing the data though a kernel matrix (dual form). Each cell in the kernel matrix represents the similarity between some text samples x_i and x_j. In our experiments, we use the presence bits string kernel (Popescu and Ionescu, 2013) as the similarity function. For two strings x_i and x_j over a set of characters S, the presence bits string kernel is defined as follows:

$$k^{0/1}(x_i, x_j) = \sum_{g \in S^n} \#(x_i, g) \cdot \#(x_j, g), \tag{1}$$

where n is the length of n-grams and $\#(x, g)$ is a function that returns 1 when the number of occurrences of n-gram g in x is greater than 1, and 0 otherwise.

ν-Support Vector Regression. Support Vector Machines (SVM) (Cortes and Vapnik, 1995) represent a popular method initially designed for binary classification, which was subsequently repurposed for regression, under the SVR (Drucker et al., 1997) acronym (i.e. Support Vector Regression). Similar to SVM, SVR uses the notion of support vectors and margin in order to find an optimal estimator. In the original ϵ-SVR formulation (Drucker et al., 1997), there is an ϵ-insensitive region, i.e. ϵ tube, defined in the optimization function. The goal is to find the flattest tube containing most of the training samples, while also minimizing the prediction error and model complexity. Different from linear regression, ϵ-SVR fits the error within the maximum margin ϵ, instead of minimizing the error directly (Smola and Schölkopf, 2004). In our experiments, we employ an equivalent SVR formulation known as ν-SVR (Chang and Lin, 2002), where ν is the configurable proportion of support vectors to keep with respect to the number of samples in the data set. In ν-SVR, the margin ϵ is automatically estimated to its optimal value. Using ν-SVR, the optimal solution can converge to a small model, with only a few support vectors. This is especially useful in our use case, as the data set provided in the SMG-CH subtask does not contain too many samples. Another reason to employ ν-SVR in our regression task is that it was found to surpass other regression methods in complex word identification (Butnaru and Ionescu, 2018a).

3.2 Character-Level Convolutional Neural Network

Character Embeddings. From the pioneering works in language modelling at the character level (Gasthaus et al., 2010; Wood et al., 2009) to date (Georgescu et al., 2020), a broad range of neural architectures rely on characters as features. Among these, we can mention Recurrent Neural Networks (RNNs) (Sutskever et al., 2011), LSTM networks (Ballesteros et al., 2015), CNNs (Kim et al., 2016; Zhang et al., 2015) and transformer models (Al-Rfou et al., 2019). Characters are the base units in building words that exist in the vocabulary of most languages. Knowledge of words, semantic structure or syntax is not required when working with characters. Robustness to spelling errors and words that are outside the vocabulary (Ballesteros et al., 2015) constitute other advantages explaining the growing interest in using characters as features. In our paper, we employ a convolutional neural network working at the character level (Zhang et al., 2015). The employed CNN is equipped with a character embedding layer, automatically learning a 2D representation of text formed of character embedding vectors, that is further processed by the convolutional layers.

Convolutional Neural Networks. Inspired by the visual cortex of mammals (Fukushima, 1980), CNNs have been extensively used in image classification (LeCun et al., 1989; LeCun et al., 2004; Krizhevsky et al., 2012), subsequently being adapted for various NLP tasks (Kim, 2014; Zhang et al., 2015). CNNs are composed of convolutional blocks, consisting of convolutions and pooling operations, usually followed by a sequence of dense layers and ending with an output layer, with the number of neurons equal to the number of values that we are interested in predicting. In the experiments, we employ a character-level CNN (Zhang et al., 2015) with squeeze-and-excitation (SE) blocks, introduced by Butnaru and Ionescu (2019). Since this method has been previously applied in Romanian dialect identification with good results (Butnaru and Ionescu, 2019; Tudoreanu, 2019), we consider it a good candidate for our text geolocation task. We therefore change the original architecture by replacing the Softmax classification layer with a regression layer formed of two units, one predicting the latitude and one predicting the longitude, respectively. We train our character-level CNN towards minimizing the mean squared error (MSE) loss function with respect to the ground-truth latitude and longitude.

3.3 Long Short-Term Memory Networks based on BERT Embeddings

BERT Embeddings. Transformers (Vaswani et al., 2017) represent a very important advance in Natural Language Processing, with many benefits over the traditional sequential neural architectures. Based on an encoder-decoder architecture with attention, transformers proved to be better at modelling long-term dependencies in sequences, while being effectively trained as the sequential dependency of previous tokens is removed. Unlike other contemporary attempts at using transformers in language modelling (Radford et al., 2018), BERT (Devlin et al., 2019) incorporates context from both directions in the process of building deep language representations, in a self-supervised fashion. The masked language modeling technique enables BERT to pre-train these deep bidirectional representations, that can be further fine-tuned and adapted for a variety of tasks, without significant architectural updates. We also make use of this property in the current work, employing a TensorFlow version of a German BERT model[1]. The model has been trained on the latest German Wikipedia dump, the OpenLegalData dump and a collection of news articles, summing up to a total of 12 GB of text files. We add the pre-trained German BERT model to be fine-tuned in an end-to-end fashion along with our LSTM architecture for geolocation of Swiss German short texts.

Long Short-Term Memory Networks. RNNs (Werbos, 1988) operate at the sequence level, attaining state-of-the-art performance on various problems involving time series (Weiss et al., 2018). Major drawbacks in regular RNNs are the phenomenons of exploding and vanishing gradients, which can be caused by an increase in the length of the input sequence (Hochreiter et al., 2001). LSTM networks (Hochreiter and Schmidhuber, 1997) represent a flavour of RNN, designed to overcome the aforementioned challenges faced when working with RNNs. An LSTM unit has a more complex structure, including a memory cell to remember dependencies in the input and three gates acting as regulators: input, output and, in more recent versions, forget gates, which enable the cell to reset its state (Gers et al., 2000). The LSTM architecture used in this work is inspired by the one described in (Onose et al., 2019), which has been successfully employed in Romanian dialect identification. We train our LSTM model using the mean squared logarithmic error as loss function. We opted for the aforementioned loss in favor of the mean squared error, as the latter loss function did not produce optimal results for our LSTM.

---

[1] `https://github.com/deepset-ai/FARM`

3.4 Ensemble Learning

XGBoost. Gradient tree boosting (Friedman, 2001) is based on training a tree ensemble model in an additive fashion. This technique has been successfully used in classification (Li, 2010) and ranking (Burges, 2010) problems, obtaining notable results in reputed competitions such as the Netflix Challenge (Bennett et al., 2007). Furthermore, gradient tree boosting is the ensemble method of choice in real-world pipelines running in production (He et al., 2014). XGBoost (Chen and Guestrin, 2016) is a tree boosting model targeted at solving large-scale tasks with limited computational resources. This approach aims at parallelizing tree learning while also trying to handle various sparsity patterns. Overfitting is addressed through shrinkage and column subsampling. Shrinkage acts as a learning rate, reducing the influence of each individual tree. Column subsampling is borrowed from Random Forests (Breiman, 2001), bearing the advantage of speeding up the computations. In the experiments, we employ XGBoost as a meta-learner over the individual predictions of each of the models described above. We opted for XGBoost in detriment of average voting and a ν-SVR meta-learner, both providing comparatively lower performance levels in a set of preliminary ensemble experiments.

4 Experiments

4.1 Data Set

The data set for the SMG-CH subtask contains a training set of 22,600 samples, with one sample per line, each formed of a piece of text and a pair of coordinates representing the position on Earth, i.e. latitude and longitude. The development set is composed of 3,086 samples, provided in the same format. The test set consists in 3,097 samples without coordinates. We note that the centroid computed on the training data has a latitude of 47.26 degrees and a longitude of 8.33 degrees, confirming that the average location is on the territory of Switzerland.

4.2 Parameter Tuning

ν-SVR based on string kernels. In the experiments, we use ν-SVR with a pre-computed string kernel, employing the efficient algorithm proposed in (Popescu et al., 2017). In a set of preliminary experiments, we employed various blended spectrum string kernels based on various n-gram ranges that include n-grams from 3 to 7 characters long. The best performance in terms of both mean absolute error (MAE) and mean squared error (MSE) were attained by a string kernel based on the blended spectrum of 3 to 5 character n-grams. These results are consistent with those reported by Ionescu and Butnaru (2017), suggesting that the 3-5 n-gram range is optimal for German dialect identification. The resulting kernel matrix is used as input in a double regression setup, with a ν-SVR model for predicting the latitude (in degrees), and another ν-SVR model for predicting the longitude (in degrees), respectively. We tried out values ranging from 10^{-4} to 10^4 for the regularization penalty C, during the hyperparameter tuning phase. Similarly, for the proportion of support vectors ν, we considered 10 values covering the interval $(0, 1]$ with a step of 0.1. For both regression models, the best value for the parameter C is 10. As for the parameter ν, the default value of 0.5 seems to yield the best results.

Character-level CNN. Except for the last layer, the architecture used in our experiments is identical to the architecture employed by Butnaru and Ionescu (2019) for Romanian dialect identification. An input of maximum 5000 characters (zero-padding is used as necessary) is expected into the network, with the characters initially encoded with their position in the vocabulary. For each character, a vectorial representation of 128 elements is learned in the embedding layer. Three convolutional blocks follow, each being composed of a convolutional layer with 128 one-dimensional filters of size 7 for the first two blocks, and of size 3 for the last block, resptectively. Each convolutional block also performs downsampling through max-pooling operations with a filter of size 3. Squeeze-and-excitation (SE) attention modules are integrated after each pooling layer. The outputs are then flattened and given as input into the regression layer, containing two neurons, one for predicting the latitude and the other for predicting the longitude. Adam (Kingma and Ba, 2015) is used as the optimization algorithm, in an attempt to minimize the MSE loss. We trained our model on mini-batches of 128 samples for 100 epochs with early stopping, using a learning rate of $5 \cdot 10^{-4}$. The network converged in 60 epochs, after observing no improvements for the last 7 epochs.

LSTM based on BERT embeddings. In conjunction with the LSTM, we fine-tuned a BERT model that is pre-trained on a German corpus, as detailed in Section 3.1. Thus, we input the data into a BERT layer, initialized with the corresponding pre-trained parameters. We set the maximum sequence length to 310, which is around the mean sequence length in the SMG-CH data set. The BERT layer is followed by two LSTM layers of size 128 each, both having *tanh* activation. We use dropout for regularization, randomly removing 20% of the neurons. We tried out various optimization algorithms such as Adam, RMSProp and stochastic gradient descent (SGD) with momentum. We obtained the best convergence using SGD with a momentum rate of 0.9 and a learning rate of $\alpha = 10^{-1}$. The training automatically ended after 18 epochs because of early stopping, as there were no more improvements registered for the loss value.

Extreme Gradient Boosting. We employed XGBoost as a meta-learner, training it over the predictions of all the other models. In our case, XGBoost provided the best results with the number of estimators set to 1000, a maximum depth of 10^{-4} and the learning rate $\alpha = 10^{-2}$.

4.3 Preliminary Results

In the development phase, as there was no metric specified in the description of the SMG task, we treated it as any other regression problem and evaluated the predictions in terms of both MAE and MSE. In Table 1, we present the results obtained by our four models on the development set. As the organizers released the ground-truth labels for the test set after the competition, we also include the MAE and the MSE on the test set, for reference.

Method	MAE		MSE	
	Development	Test	Development	Test
ν-SVR + string kernels	0.2306	0.2289	0.1066	0.1049
character-level CNN	0.2937	0.3123	0.1552	0.1633
LSTM + BERT embeddings	0.3594	0.3618	0.2226	0.2259
XGBoost ensemble	0.2234	0.2207	0.1043	0.1017

Table 1: Results in terms of Mean Absolute Error (MAE) and Mean Squared Error (MSE) obtained on the development set and on the test set by the proposed handcrafted, deep and ensemble algorithms. The reported MAE and MSE values represent the average value computed over the latitude and the longitude, both being expressed in degrees.

Considering the results presented in Table 1, it is clear that the algorithm that achieves the best MAE and MSE values is the ensemble based on the XGBoost meta-learner. This does not come as a surprise, as the ensemble combines the predictions of three individual models, each being based on a different type of features and a different learning model. While these aspects are complementary in theory, the results indicate that this is also the case in practice.

Additionally, we note that the performance achieved by ν-SVR comes close to the one attained by the ensemble, leaving behind the two neural models based on characters and fine-tuned BERT embeddings. This confirms the efficiency of string kernels over deep learning approaches observed in related works (Butnaru and Ionescu, 2019; Găman and Ionescu, 2020), which seems to be independent of the task to be solved.

Another comment regarding the results outlined in Table 1 is that the errors on the development set do not fall far from the ones obtained on the test set. However, the ensemble model as well as the ν-SVR based on string kernels obtain slightly lower errors at test time compared to the errors reported on the development set. The opposite seems to happen with the deep models, as both the LSTM based on BERT embeddings and the character-level CNN yield slightly higher errors on the test data than on the development data.

Every participant was allowed to make three submissions to compete against other shared task participants. Based on the results reported on the development set, we have decided to choose the character-

Figure 1: Distances between ground-truth locations (blue) and predicted locations (red) for a subset of 100 Swiss German Jodels randomly selected from the official test set. Best viewed in color.

level CNN, the ν-SVR based on string kernels and the XGBoost ensemble as candidates for the SMG-CH challenge. We excluded the LSTM based on BERT embeddings, since it attains the highest errors among the considered models.

4.4 Final Results

Method	Submission	Median distance	Mean distance	Clustering Accuracy
character-level CNN	#1	40.23	42.87	29.79%
ν-SVR + string kernels	#2	26.78	31.49	51.13%
XGBoost ensemble	#3	25.57	30.52	53.88%

Table 2: The final results of our team (UnibucKernel) obtained in the SMG-CH subtask, with the metrics picked by the organizers, oriented on clustering by city and on distances expressed in kilometers.

Table 2 shows our final results obtained on the test set, considering the metrics chosen by the organizers, which are oriented on distances (in kilometers) and on clustering accuracy. Considering the official metrics, our best submission placed us in the top six participants.

We observe that our best performing algorithm, namely the XGBoost ensemble combining the predictions of both deep and shallow methods based on various types of features, achieves a median distance of 25.57 km, a mean distance of 30.52 km and a clustering accuracy of 53.88%. Consistent with our findings on the development set, the ν-SVR based on string kernels does not fall far behind the XGBoost ensemble, obtaining a mean distance and median distance that is about one kilometer higher and a clustering accuracy that is nearly 2.75% lower. The deep character-level CNN seems significantly worse, with around 15 km and more than 10 km higher errors in terms of the median and the mean distances as compared to the other two submitted models, and around 21% lower clustering accuracy. In our opinion, these results stand proof that neural networks might not be the holy grail in every possible situation.

We believe that the proposed methods attain decent results, given the challenging nature of the problem at hand. However, it is clear to us that they could benefit from some improvements, considering the values obtained in the final evaluation phase. One important step in this direction is to visualize the errors, at scale, on the map of Switzerland, for a better understanding of the patterns that our best performing algorithm drew with its predictions. Thus, we overlap the predicted and the ground-truth locations on the map of Switzerland, illustrating the result in Figure 1. The points depicted on the map are described by their 2D coordinates, latitude and longitude, as in the data set provided for the task. The ground-truth locations are colored in blue, while the predictions are illustrated in red. For each pair of ground-truth and predicted location, there is a line connecting the two points, giving us a better idea regarding the errors made by the XGBoost ensemble, in terms of distance. For the visualization presented in Figure 1, we have randomly selected a subset of 100 points from the test set, with non-overlapping ground-truth locations. We hereby notice that including all the data points from the test set would generate a visualization that is too cluttered and hard to understand. Hence, we opted for a smaller number of points for a better visualization experience. Considering the annotated map illustrated in Figure 1, we observe that our predictions tend to be clustered around the main cities in the German-speaking side of Switzerland, such as Zürich, Bern, Lucerne and Basel. This bias towards the mentioned cities might be induced by the data samples from the training set, likely not having a well-distributed variance in terms of the locations or the texts used in the learning process. We also observe that the ground-truth locations exhibit a higher variance than the predicted locations. One possible solution would to manually adjust the variance of the predicted location to match the variance of the actual locations.

5 Conclusion

In the current work, we tackled the SMG-CH shared subtask of the 2020 VarDial Evaluation Campaign. We addressed this challenge from a shallow perspective, with handcrafted models such as a ν-SVR based on string kernels, as well as from a deep learning perspective, with neural models such as an LSTM based on BERT embeddings and a character-level CNN, respectively. Additionally, we combined the proposed models into an ensemble, employing the XGBoost meta-learner. We obtained our best results with the XGBoost ensemble, which benefits from complementary information from the handcrafted and deep models. We therefore brought one more proof regarding the effectiveness of ensemble learning in general, and of XGBoost, in particular. Another important conclusion is that our shallow model based on string kernels outperforms the two deep neural networks. We consider this as yet another indicator of the high discriminative power that string kernels can bring to a fairly standard learning model, i.e. the ν-SVR.

In future work, we aim to explore ways to improve our performance with respect to the metrics proposed by the shared task organizers. Currently, it seems that training the models to simply minimize the MSE or the MAE values is not effective, as our best model was significantly outperformed by the model proposed by the shared task organizers themselves.

Acknowledgements

This work was supported by a grant of the Romanian Ministry of Education and Research, CNCS - UEFISCDI, project number PN-III-P1-1.1-TE-2019-0235, within PNCDI III. This article has also benefited from the support of the Romanian Young Academy, which is funded by Stiftung Mercator and the Alexander von Humboldt Foundation for the period 2020-2022.

References

Amr Ahmed, Liangjie Hong, and Alex J. Smola. 2013. Hierarchical geographical modeling of user locations from social media posts. In *Proceedings of WWW*, pages 25–36.

Rami Al-Rfou, Dokook Choe, Noah Constant, Mandy Guo, and Llion Jones. 2019. Character-Level Language Modeling with Deeper Self-Attention. In *Proceedings of AAAI*, pages 3159–3166.

Miguel Ballesteros, Chris Dyer, and Noah A. Smith. 2015. Improved Transition-Based Parsing by Modeling Characters instead of Words with LSTMs. In *Proceedings of EMNLP 2015*, pages 349–59.

James Bennett, Stan Lanning, et al. 2007. The Netflix Prize. In *Proceedings of KDD*, volume 2007, page 35.

Frédérik Bilhaut, Thierry Charnois, Patrice Enjalbert, and Yann Mathet. 2003. Geographic reference analysis for geographic document querying. In *Proceedings of HLT-NAACL-GEOREF*, pages 55–62.

Leo Breiman. 2001. Random forests. *Machine learning*, 45(1):5–32.

Christopher J.C. Burges. 2010. From RankNet to LambdaRank to LambdaMART: An Overview. *Learning*, 11(23-581):81.

Andrei Butnaru and Radu Tudor Ionescu. 2018a. UnibucKernel: A kernel-based learning method for complex word identification. In *Proceedings of BEA-13*, pages 175–183.

Andrei M. Butnaru and Radu Tudor Ionescu. 2018b. UnibucKernel Reloaded: First Place in Arabic Dialect Identification for the Second Year in a Row. In *Proceedings of VarDial*, pages 77–87.

Andrei M. Butnaru and Radu Tudor Ionescu. 2019. MOROCO: The Moldavian and Romanian Dialectal Corpus. In *Proceedings of ACL*, pages 688–698.

Chih-Chung Chang and Chih-Jen Lin. 2002. Training ν-Support Vector Regression: Theory and Algorithms. *Neural Computation*, 14:1959–1977.

Tianqi Chen and Carlos Guestrin. 2016. XGBoost: A scalable tree boosting system. In *Proceedings of KDD*, pages 785–794.

Zhiyuan Cheng, James Caverlee, and Kyumin Lee. 2010. You are where you tweet: a content-based approach to geo-locating twitter users. In *Proceedings of CIKM*, pages 759–768.

Corinna Cortes and Vladimir Vapnik. 1995. Support-vector networks. *Machine Learning*, 20(3):273–297.

Mădălina Cozma, Andrei Butnaru, and Radu Tudor Ionescu. 2018. Automated essay scoring with string kernels and word embeddings. In *Proceedings of ACL*, pages 503–509.

Jacob Devlin, Ming-Wei Chang, Kenton Lee, and Kristina Toutanova. 2019. BERT: Pre-training of Deep Bidirectional Transformers for Language Understanding. In *Proceedings of NAACL*, pages 4171–4186.

Junyan Ding, Luis Gravano, and Narayanan Shivakumar. 2000. Computing geographical scopes of web resources. In *Proceedings of VLDV*.

Gabriel Doyle. 2014. Mapping dialectal variation by querying social media. In *Proceedings of EACL 2014*, pages 98–106.

Harris Drucker, Christopher J.C. Burges, Linda Kaufman, Alex J. Smola, and Vladimir Vapnik. 1997. Support vector regression machines. In *Proceedings of NIPS*, pages 155–161.

Jacob Eisenstein, Brendan O'Connor, Noah A Smith, and Eric Xing. 2010. A latent variable model for geographic lexical variation. In *Proceedings of EMNLP 2010*, pages 1277–1287.

Jerome H Friedman. 2001. Greedy function approximation: a gradient boosting machine. *Annals of statistics*, pages 1189–1232.

Kunihiko Fukushima. 1980. Neocognitron: A self-organizing neural network model for a mechanism of pattern recognition unaffected by shift in position. *Biological cybernetics*, 36(4):193–202.

Jan Gasthaus, Frank Wood, and Yee Whye Teh. 2010. Lossless Compression Based on the Sequence Memoizer. In *Proceedings of DCC*, page 337–345.

Judith Gelernter and Nikolai Mushegian. 2011. Geo-parsing messages from microtext. *Transactions in GIS*, 15(6):753–773.

Mariana-Iuliana Georgescu, Radu Tudor Ionescu, Nicolae-Catalin Ristea, and Nicu Sebe. 2020. Non-linear Neurons with Human-like Apical Dendrite Activations. *arXiv preprint arXiv:2003.03229*.

Felix A. Gers, Jürgen Schmidhuber, and Fred Cummins. 2000. Learning to forget: Continual prediction with LSTM. *Neural Computation*, 12(10):2451–2471.

Rosa M. Giménez-Pérez, Marc Franco-Salvador, and Paolo Rosso. 2017. Single and Cross-domain Polarity Classification using String Kernels. In *Proceedings of EACL*, pages 558–563.

Mihaela Găman and Radu Tudor Ionescu. 2020. The Unreasonable Effectiveness of Machine Learning in Moldavian versus Romanian Dialect Identification. *journal=arXiv preprint arXiv:2007.15700*.

Mihaela Găman, Dirk Hovy, Radu Tudor Ionescu, Heidi Jauhiainen, Tommi Jauhiainen, Krister Lindén, Nikola Ljubešić, Niko Partanen, Christoph Purschke, Yves Scherrer, and Marcos Zampieri. 2020. A Report on the VarDial Evaluation Campaign 2020. In *Proceedings of VarDial*.

Bo Han, Paul Cook, and Timothy Baldwin. 2014. Text-based twitter user geolocation prediction. *Journal of Artificial Intelligence Research*, 49:451–500.

Xinran He, Junfeng Pan, Ou Jin, Tianbing Xu, Bo Liu, Tao Xu, Yanxin Shi, Antoine Atallah, Ralf Herbrich, Stuart Bowers, et al. 2014. Practical lessons from predicting clicks on ads at facebook. In *Proceedings of ADKDD*, pages 1–9.

Sepp Hochreiter and Jürgen Schmidhuber. 1997. Long Short-Term Memory. *Neural Computation*, 9(8):1735–1780.

Sepp Hochreiter, Yoshua Bengio, Paolo Frasconi, Jürgen Schmidhuber, et al. 2001. Gradient flow in recurrent nets: the difficulty of learning long-term dependencies. *A Field Guide to Dynamical Recurrent Neural Networks*, pages 237–244.

Liangjie Hong, Amr Ahmed, Siva Gurumurthy, Alex J. Smola, and Kostas Tsioutsiouliklis. 2012. Discovering geographical topics in the twitter stream. In *Proceedings of WWW*, pages 769–778.

Dirk Hovy and Christoph Purschke. 2018. Capturing Regional Variation with Distributed Place Representations and Geographic Retrofitting. In *Proceedings of EMNLP*, pages 4383–4394.

Yuan Huang, Diansheng Guo, Alice Kasakoff, and Jack Grieve. 2016. Understanding us regional linguistic variation with twitter data analysis. *Computers, Environment and Urban Systems*, 59:244–255.

Radu Tudor Ionescu and Andrei M. Butnaru. 2017. Learning to Identify Arabic and German Dialects using Multiple Kernels. In *Proceedings of VarDial*, pages 200–209.

Radu Tudor Ionescu and Andrei M. Butnaru. 2018. Improving the results of string kernels in sentiment analysis and Arabic dialect identification by adapting them to your test set. In *Proceedings of EMNLP*, pages 1084–1090.

Radu Tudor Ionescu and Marius Popescu. 2016. UnibucKernel: An Approach for Arabic Dialect Identification based on Multiple String Kernels. In *Proceedings of VarDial*, pages 135–144.

Radu Tudor Ionescu and Marius Popescu. 2017. Can string kernels pass the test of time in native language identification? In *Proceedings of BEA-12*, pages 224–234.

Radu Tudor Ionescu, Marius Popescu, and Aoife Cahill. 2014. Can characters reveal your native language? A language-independent approach to native language identification. In *Proceedings of EMNLP*, pages 1363–1373.

Radu Tudor Ionescu, Marius Popescu, and Aoife Cahill. 2016. String kernels for native language identification: Insights from behind the curtains. *Computational Linguistics*, 42(3):491–525.

Taylor Jones. 2015. Toward a description of African American Vernacular English dialect regions using "Black Twitter". *American Speech*, 90(4):403–440.

Yoon Kim, Yacine Jernite, David Sontag, and Alexander M. Rush. 2016. Character-Aware Neural Language Models. In *Proceedings of AAAI*, pages 2741–2749.

Yoon Kim. 2014. Convolutional Neural Networks for Sentence Classification. In *Proceedings of EMNLP*, pages 1746–1751.

Diederik P. Kingma and Jimmy Ba. 2015. Adam: A method for stochastic optimization. In *Proceedings of ICLR*.

Sheila Kinsella, Vanessa Murdock, and Neil O'Hare. 2011. "I'm eating a sandwich in Glasgow" modeling locations with tweets. In *Proceedings of SMUC*, pages 61–68.

Alex Krizhevsky, Ilya Sutskever, and Geoffrey E. Hinton. 2012. ImageNet Classification with Deep Convolutional Neural Networks. In *Proceddings of NIPS*, pages 1097–1105.

Yann LeCun, Bernhard Boser, John S. Denker, Donnie Henderson, Richard E. Howard, Wayne Hubbard, and Lawrence D. Jackel. 1989. Backpropagation Applied to Handwritten Zip Code Recognition. *Neural Computation*, 1(4):541–551.

Yann LeCun, Fu Jie Huang, and Leon Bottou. 2004. Learning methods for generic object recognition with invariance to pose and lighting. In *Proceedings of CVPR*, volume 2, pages II–104.

Ping Li. 2010. Robust Logitboost and Adaptive Base Class (ABC) Logitboost. In *Proceedings of UAI*, pages 302–311.

Michael D Lieberman, Hanan Samet, and Jagan Sankaranarayanan. 2010. Geotagging with local lexicons to build indexes for textually-specified spatial data. In *In Proceedings of ICDE*, pages 201–212.

Nikola Ljubešić, Tanja Samardžić, and Curdin Derungs. 2016. TweetGeo - A Tool for Collecting, Processing and Analysing Geo-encoded Linguistic Data. In *Proceedings of COLING*, pages 3412–3421.

Huma Lodhi, John Shawe-Taylor, Nello Cristianini, and Christopher J.C.H. Watkins. 2001. Text Classification Using String Kernels. In *Proceedings of NIPS*, pages 563–569.

Mihai Masala, Stefan Ruseti, and Traian Rebedea. 2017. Sentence selection with neural networks using string kernels. In *Proceedings of KES*, pages 1774–1782.

Cristian Onose, Dumitru-Clementin Cercel, and Ştefan Trăuşan-Matu. 2019. SC-UPB at the VarDial 2019 Evaluation Campaign: Moldavian vs. Romanian Cross-Dialect Topic Identification. In *Proceedings of VarDial*, pages 172–177.

Marius Popescu and Radu Tudor Ionescu. 2013. The Story of the Characters, the DNA and the Native Language. In *Proceedings of BEA-8*, pages 270–278.

Marius Popescu, Cristian Grozea, and Radu Tudor Ionescu. 2017. HASKER: An efficient algorithm for string kernels. Application to polarity classification in various languages. In *Proceedings of KES*, pages 1755–1763.

Teng Qin, Rong Xiao, Lei Fang, Xing Xie, and Lei Zhang. 2010. An efficient location extraction algorithm by leveraging web contextual information. In *Proceedings of GIS*, pages 53–60.

Gianluca Quercini, Hanan Samet, Jagan Sankaranarayanan, and Michael D Lieberman. 2010. Determining the spatial reader scopes of news sources using local lexicons. In *Proceedings of GIS*, pages 43–52.

Alec Radford, Karthik Narasimhan, Tim Salimans, and Ilya Sutskever. 2018. Improving language understanding with unsupervised learning. *Technical report, OpenAI*.

Afshin Rahimi, Trevor Cohn, and Timothy Baldwin. 2017. A neural model for user geolocation and lexical dialectology. *arXiv preprint arXiv:1704.04008*.

Stephen Roller, Michael Speriosu, Sarat Rallapalli, Benjamin Wing, and Jason Baldridge. 2012. Supervised text-based geolocation using language models on an adaptive grid. In *Proceedings of EMNLP*, pages 1500–1510.

Dominic Rout, Kalina Bontcheva, Daniel Preoţiuc-Pietro, and Trevor Cohn. 2013. Where's@ wally? A Classification Approach to Geolocating Users Based on their Social Ties. In *Proceedings of HT*, pages 11–20.

Alex J. Smola and Bernhard Schölkopf. 2004. A tutorial on support vector regression. *Statistics and computing*, 14(3):199–222.

Ilya Sutskever, James Martens, and Geoffrey Hinton. 2011. Generating Text with Recurrent Neural Networks. In *Proceedings of ICML*, pages 1017–1024.

Benedikt Szmrecsanyi. 2008. Corpus-based dialectometry: Aggregate morphosyntactic variability in british english dialects. *International Journal of Humanities and Arts Computing*, 2(1-2):279–296.

Diana Tudoreanu. 2019. DTeam @ VarDial 2019: Ensemble based on skip-gram and triplet loss neural networks for Moldavian vs. Romanian cross-dialect topic identification. In *Proceedings of VarDial*, pages 202–208.

Ashish Vaswani, Noam Shazeer, Niki Parmar, Jakob Uszkoreit, Llion Jones, Aidan N Gomez, Łukasz Kaiser, and Illia Polosukhin. 2017. Attention is all you need. In *Proceedings of NIPS*, pages 5998–6008.

Gail Weiss, Yoav Goldberg, and Eran Yahav. 2018. On the Practical Computational Power of Finite Precision RNNs for Language Recognition. In *Proceedings of ACL*, pages 740–745.

Paul J. Werbos. 1988. Generalization of backpropagation with application to a recurrent gas market model. *Neural Networks*, 1(4):339–356.

Martijn Wieling, John Nerbonne, and R. Harald Baayen. 2011. Quantitative social dialectology: Explaining linguistic variation geographically and socially. *PloS One*, 6(9):e23613.

Benjamin Wing and Jason Baldridge. 2011. Simple supervised document geolocation with geodesic grids. In *Proceedings of ACL*, pages 955–964.

Frank Wood, Cédric Archambeau, Jan Gasthaus, Lancelot James, and Yee Whye Teh. 2009. A Stochastic Memoizer for Sequence Data. In *Proceedings of ICML*, pages 1129–1136.

Xiang Zhang, Junbo Zhao, and Yann LeCun. 2015. Character-level Convolutional Networks for Text Classification. In *Proceedings of NIPS*, pages 649–657.

ZHAW-InIT - Social Media Geolocation at VarDial 2020

Fernando Benites
benf@zhaw.ch

Manuela Hürlimann
hueu@zhaw.ch

Pius von Däniken
vode@zhaw.ch

Mark Cieliebak
mc@spinningbytes.com

Zurich University of
Applied Sciences,
Switzerland

Zurich University of
Applied Sciences,
Switzerland

Zurich University of
Applied Sciences,
Switzerland

SpinningBytes AG,
Switzerland

Abstract

We describe our approaches for the Social Media Geolocation (SMG) task at the VarDial Evaluation Campaign 2020. The goal was to predict geographical location (latitudes and longitudes) given an input text. There were three subtasks corresponding to German-speaking Switzerland (CH), Germany and Austria (DE-AT), and Croatia, Bosnia and Herzegovina, Montenegro and Serbia (BCMS). We submitted solutions to all subtasks but focused our development efforts on the CH subtask, where we achieved third place out of 16 submissions with a median distance of 15.93 km and had the best result of 14 unconstrained systems. In the DE-AT subtask, we ranked sixth out of ten submissions (fourth of 8 unconstrained systems) and for BCMS we achieved fourth place out of 13 submissions (second of 11 unconstrained systems).

1 Introduction

The 7th Workshop on NLP for Similar Languages, Varieties and Dialects (Găman et al., 2020) introduced a new task on *Social Media Geolocation (SMG)*: Given a social media post, a system has to predict the latitude and longitude of where it was written. This is an extension to previous evaluation campaigns (Zampieri et al., 2019; Zampieri et al., 2018; Zampieri et al., 2017), which focused on dialect identification, assigning a discrete label – usually corresponding to a geographic region – to a piece of text. Geolocation prediction allows for a more fine-grained assessment of dialectal varieties without the need to define hard and somewhat arbitrary boundaries within dialect continua.

Our motivation for participating in the SMG shared task was to gain more knowledge about real-world, noisy, digital data. More specifically, we seek to mine written texts for different Swiss German Dialects and would profit from being able to place them geographically, particularly in the context of our other projects on Swiss German.

We submitted solutions to all three sub-tasks (see Results in Section 4) and, in light of our motivation, focused specifically on the Swiss sub-task during development. Our submissions are based on three different models (see Section 3): an SVM meta-classifier combining different classifiers based on word and character features for CH (see Section 3.4); a single SVM with fewer features and no meta-classifer for DE-AT and BCMS (see Section 3.6); and a language modelling approach (see Section 3.5) which was applied to all subtasks. We furthermore experimented with character-level Convolutional Neural Networks (CNNs) (see Section 3.7). For all systems, we cluster geolocations to get a number of discrete labels to predict.

2 Related Work

The central focus of the evaluation campaign at VarDial is to identify dialects of various languages. There have been three previous editions, which laid the basis for dialect identification in Swiss German (Zampieri et al., 2019; Zampieri et al., 2018; Zampieri et al., 2017). Dialect classification is useful for many tasks and applications, e.g. for POS-tagging of dialectal data (Hollenstein and Aepli, 2014), for

This work is licensed under a Creative Commons Attribution 4.0 International Licence. Licence details: http://creativecommons.org/licenses/by/4.0/.

Proceedings of the 7th VarDial Workshop on NLP for Similar Languages, Varieties and Dialects, pages 254–264
Barcelona, Spain (Online), December 13, 2020

compilation of German dialect corpora (Hollenstein and Aepli, 2015), or for automatic speech recognition of Swiss German.

Past VarDial campaigns have led to the creation of diverse datasets for language and dialect identification, for example: Samardžić et al. (2016) provide a Swiss German dialect data set based on the Archi-Mob corpus, Jauhiainen et al. (2019) present a collection of cuneiform texts derived from a larger open access collection, and Huang et al. (2000) and McEnery and Xiao (2003) created data sets for Taiwanese and Mandarin Chinese. The 2020 SMG task is based on social media posts from Twitter (Ljubešić et al., 2016) and Jodel (Hovy and Purschke, 2018), annotated with geolocations (see Section 3.1).

Many studies addressed the problem of language and dialect identification, creating a noticeable amount of related work, summarised in the evaluation campaign reports (Zampieri et al., 2019; Zampieri et al., 2018; Zampieri et al., 2017) and Jauhiainen et al. (2018b). A typical approach uses Support Vector Machines (SVMs) with different feature extraction methods. The use of character language models for language identification has previously been studied by Vatanen et al. (2010).

Over the years various models have been proposed for text-based geolocation prediction (Han et al., 2014; Kinsella et al., 2011; Rahimi et al., 2017b; Rahimi et al., 2017a).

As for discretization of geolocations, Wing and Baldridge (2014) propose a hierarchical approach to divide the earth into a grid with different levels of granularity. Similarly to Duong-Trung et al. (2017), we use a K-Means clustering approach to subdivide the space, which is more data-driven than a grid.

Our main focus is the CH subtask, where our approach is, from a text classification point of view, most similar to MAZA, which was proposed at VarDial 2017 (Malmasi and Zampieri, 2017). MAZA uses Term Frequency (TF) on character n-grams and word unigram features to train several SVMs. Then it uses a Random Forest meta-classifier with 10-fold cross-validation on the predictions of the SVMs. We extended this approach and used Term Frequency-Inverse Document Frequency (TF-IDF) on word and on character level. We used an SVM as a meta-classifier, and concatenated the output of the base classifiers (see Section 3.4). This solution approach was motivated by the fact that we have already applied similar architectures successfully in a wide range of tasks (Benites de Azevedo e Souza et al., 2019; Benites et al., 2018b; Benites, 2019), especially in (Benites et al., 2018a) we established empirically that for (Swiss German) dialect recognition TF-IDF is better than just TF.

For the BCMS and DE-AT subtasks, we used a single SVM with word- and character-level TF-IDF features (see Section 3.6). We also made submissions using a variant of the HeLI method by Jauhiainen et al. (2016; Jauhiainen et al. (2018a), which we extended with a voting mechanism that takes the centre of the top predicted coordinates in case of low confidence (see Section 3.5).

3 Method

3.1 Task Definition

The shared task data was collected from the social media platforms *Jodel*[1] and *Twitter*[2]. Jodel posts were collected from Germany and Austria (DE-AT), as well as German-speaking Switzerland (CH) (Hovy and Purschke, 2018). Tweets were sourced from Bosnia and Herzegovina, Croatia, Montenegro, and Serbia (BCMS) (Ljubešić et al., 2016). Every sample contains, in addition to the text, latitude and longitude coordinates as set by the users of the respective platform (Jodel or Twitter).

While Tweets are usually authored by a single person, the Jodel samples consist of short conversations involving multiple speakers. This leads to some samples containing multiple dialects. Similarly, we observed samples containing indirect speech in non-local dialects.

For evaluation, two metrics were defined by the organizers: the *median* and the *mean* distances between predicted and real geolocations across all texts in the test set, with the former being the official metric of the SMG shared task.

We opted to frame the task as a text classification problem, by combining locations into discrete clusters and predicting cluster identities.

---

[1] https://jodel.com/
[2] https://twitter.com/

3.2 Label Clustering

In order to obtain a small number of classes, we use K-Means clustering (Lloyd, 1982) to cluster the geolocations. This allows standard classification methods to tackle the problem, since a certain number of samples per class can then be guaranteed. Generalization is increased, while resolution suffers from the somewhat coarser view. We experimented with different values of k, which will be discussed in subsequent sections. In order to generate coordinates for prediction, we used the centroid coordinate of the predicted cluster.

3.3 Text Preprocessing

The basic preprocessing step common to all systems consisted in splitting the sentences into words on whitespaces. No stopword removal or lemmatization was performed since these steps have been shown to erase features which are useful for differentiating between the dialects (Maharjan et al., 2014). Afterwards, multiple feature extraction methods were applied, as explained in the next sections.

3.4 System 1: SVM-CV

3.4.1 Feature Extraction

Feature Set	Token Type	Case-Sensitive	N-gram Range	Number of Features
1	word	no	1 - 3	70000
2	word	no	1 - 5	70000
3	char	no	1 - 7	30000
4	char	no	2 - 3	50000
5	char	yes	2 - 3	50000
6	char_wb	no	1 - 5	60000
7	char_wb	no	1 - 7	60000
8	char_wb	yes	2 - 3	50000

Table 1: Overview of the different feature sets used by the SVM-CV system. See text for details.

We use a collection of different feature sets based on the TF-IDF representation (Manning et al., 2008). They vary by the type of tokens considered (words, characters, and characters ignoring whitespace), case-sensitivity, the range of n-grams, and the maximum number of features in the set. Table 1 gives an overview of the feature sets that were used. Note that the token type *char_wb* refers to character tokens ignoring whitespace between words. We use the implementation provided by the *scikit-learn*[3] library to extract these features.

3.4.2 Classifiers

For every feature set we train separate linear one-vs-rest SVM classifiers with the discrete cluster identities as target labels. We then use the distances to the decision boundaries of every classifier for every feature set as a new feature vector for another linear SVM meta-classifier.

During training every base classifier is trained via 5-fold cross-validation, and predictions on the held-out fold are used to train the meta-classifier.

Figure 1 illustrates the approach, and we refer to Benites et al. (2018a) for a detailed description.

During prediction, we usually output the geolocation corresponding to the result of our meta-classifier. However, if a sample is below a certain confidence threshold (see also Section 3.8), we assign it the mean latitude and longitude from the complete training data, instead of the location of the predicted cluster center, so the error would be equally distributed and not skewed.

3.5 System 2: LM

Our second approach is a language modelling system and is heavily modelled on the HeLI submission to the VarDial 2018 GDI task (Jauhiainen et al., 2018a). The full method is described in Jauhiainen et al.

---

[3] https://scikit-learn.org/stable/

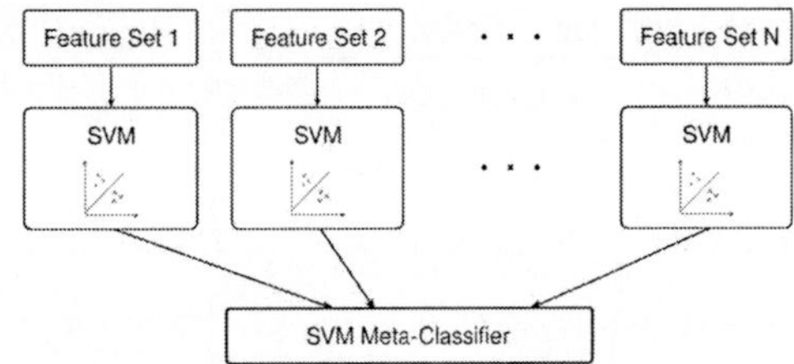

Figure 1: Overview of the SVM-CV classifier

(2016), to which we refer the interested reader.

3.5.1 Corpora and Language Models

We first created local corpora using the same K-Means clustering procedure as outlined in 3.2. We then create character-level language models for each of the corpora using the scoring procedure defined in Jauhiainen et al. (2018a): the text is split into words at whitespaces and relative n-gram frequencies are calculated within each word (including the preceding and following space characters). The score associated with an n-gram of a dialect is the negative decadic logarithm of its relative frequency within that dialect's subcorpus, meaning that n-grams with a high relative frequency have low scores.

3.5.2 Prediction

In order to make a prediction for an unseen input text, a score is calculated for each dialect based on the language models. The text is split into words at whitespaces, and for each word (again including leading and trailing space) the mean of its n-gram scores is calculated. If an n-gram is not present in the model of this dialect, a penalty term is assigned instead. The score of the text is calculated as the mean of its word-level scores, and the dialect with the lowest score is selected as output.

3.5.3 Voting Mechanism

We define the confidence of a prediction in line with Jauhiainen et al. (2018a) as the difference in scores between the second best and the best dialect. For samples that have low confidence, we introduce a voting mechanism where we use the centre of the V highest-confidence clusters as the prediction, whose coordinate is represented by the mean of the V longitudes and the mean of the V latitudes. In section 4.1.2, the value V is represented by v.

3.5.4 Parameters and Tuning

The tunable hyperparameters of this method are: the number of clusters (k), the n-gram order of the language models (n), whether case is preserved in the input to the language models, the penalty term (we assume the same term for all languages) (p), the confidence threshold below which to apply voting, and the number of clusters to use when determining the centre during voting.

We briefly experimented with using a maximum number of features per dialect (called "cutoff" by Jauhiainen et al. (2018a)) but found no improvement.

We used neither the backoff procedure to lower-order n-grams from Jauhiainen et al. (2016) nor the highly promising semi-supervised language model adaptation (Jauhiainen et al., 2018a) due to lack of time.

3.6 System 3: SVM-Base

For the larger DE-AT and BCMS datasets, we did not have sufficient time to train and tune SVM-CV. Instead, we used a simple linear SVM classifier for these languages with the feature sets shown in Table 2. Feature sets 1, 2 and 3 are also used for SVM-CV, corresponding to rows 1, 2 and 5 in Table 1, while set 4 is unique to SVM-Base.

Feature Set	Token Type	Case-Sensitive	N-gram Range	Number of Features
1	word	no	1 - 3	70000
2	word	no	1 - 5	70000
3	char	yes	2 - 3	50000
4	char_wb	yes	1 - 3	150000

Table 2: Overview of the different feature sets used by the SVM-Base system.

3.7 System 4: CNN

We also experimented with a character-wise Convolutional Neural Network (CNN) (Zhang et al., 2015), which we did not submit. We include it as a neural baseline to compare our other approaches against. The network was composed of multiple convolutions in parallel with filter size and width of $\{(128,2),$ $(96,2), (96,4), (64,3), (64,4)\}$ with dropout set at 0.1 and maxpooling. The output of the convolutional layers are subsequently concatenated. Afterwards a 3-layer fully connected network is applied with 100, 100 and 50 neurons per layer, respectively. The activation function on all layers was ReLU, except for the last where softmax was applied. As output, and so as the number of classes, the number of clusters is used, similarly to the approach of SVMs. We used the Adam optimizer (Kingma and Ba, 2014) with the learning rate set to 0.001 and minimizing the binary cross entropy loss. The network is then trained for 100 epochs.

3.8 Handling Outliers

We discovered one text in French in the development set and decided to use the language detection library *langdetect*[4]. If the language is detected as French we set the coordinates to (46.67, 7.0), the center of the French-speaking part of Switzerland. In case the prediction score is very low (below -0.9 for SVM-CV and -0.8 for SVM-Base) we assign the text to the center of the training data with coordinates (47.26, 8.3).

4 Results

In the following, we evaluate the performance of our four systems plus the two simple baseline systems. Since we were primarily focusing on the CH subtaks, we present the detailed analysis for these data. Later on, we briefly present how our systems performed on the other subtasks.

4.1 CH subtask

4.1.1 Optimizing Number of K-Means Centroids on CH data

One of the most important parameters when using clustering to discretize geographical data, is the number of centroids k for the K-Means algorithm. This determines the upper bound on performance as well as the number of samples per class and the number of classes. Usually, classification performance decreases rapidly with an increasing number of classes, which most probably negatively affects the median distance[5], the main metric of this competition.

We analyzed the reconstruction error with different numbers of clusters on the training set, over ten runs for each setting, i.e. we clustered the locations of the training samples and then calculate the distance between the cluster centroid to the actual location of the sample assigned to this centroid. The results are depicted in Table 3, where we show median and mean distances for 10, 20, 35, 50, 75 and 100 clusters, along with their variances. We see that the largest relative drop is between 50 and 75 ($\frac{0.79}{0.09}$=878%), but the difference is almost negligible in terms of geographical dialectal difference. The drop between 35 and 50 is also interesting, although it might be difficult to argue that there are about 50 dialectal hotspots. We chose 35 to use as k parameter for the K-Means algorithm, since it promised the least error for the most generalization capacity, i.e. lower risk of overfitting.

---

[4] https://github.com/Mimino666/langdetect

[5] We judge the probability very low for the case when a finer-grained division (more clusters, e.g. cluster a is subdivided into subcluster b, c and d), allows a finer resolution, and a misclassification might still decrease the mean distance (e.g. b is right, but d is predicted, however subcluster c cause that the center of a is far distant than the target (which would lie within b)).

Nr. Clusters	Median	Var	Mean	Var
10	10.61	± 0.16	11.33	± 0.01
20	5.65	± 0.29	6.91	± 0.04
35	3.19	± 0.02	3.91	± 0.01
50	0.79	± 0.10	1.72	±0.00
75	0.09	± 0.00	0.42	± 0.00
100	0.04	± 0.00	0.15	± 0.00

Table 3: Reconstruction error depending on the number of clusters for CH-subtask training data, for 10 runs

Nr.	k	p	med-dv	mean-dv
1	60	5.5	18.33	27.27
2	60	5.6	18.33	27.30
3	70	5.8	18.33	27.42
4	70	5.6	18.42	27.52
5	70	5.9	18.49	27.37
6	70	5.5	18.64	27.61
7	70	5.7	18.64	27.64
8	60	5.8	18.70	27.47
9	60	5.9	18.70	27.41
10	60	5.4	18.73	27.28

Table 4: Tuning results for LM-CH: first step, n=4, cs=no

Nr.	cs	v	vt	Dev median	Dev mean	Test median	Test mean
	no	0	n/a	18.33	27.27	19.05	27.97
1	yes	3	0.01	**17.17**	26.06	17.66	26.21
2	yes	3	0.02	17.30	25.76	17.75	25.79
3	no	3	0.01	17.41	25.87	17.84	26.44
4	no	3	0.02	17.42	25.33	**17.56**	25.77
5	yes	2	0.01	17.47	26.38	18.35	26.63
6	yes	2	0.02	17.49	26.09	18.44	26.41
7	no	4	0.01	17.53	25.81	18.07	26.30
8	yes	4	0.01	17.78	26.16	17.87	26.15
9	no	4	0.02	17.81	25.32	18.04	25.55
10	yes	4	0.02	18.01	25.87	18.24	25.74

Table 5: Tuning results for LM-CH: second step; best relevant results marked in bold

4.1.2 LM Parameter Tuning

We proceeded in two steps for tuning the parameters of the LM system. First, we searched over the n-gram-level ($n \in \{4, 5, 6\}$), number of clusters ($c \in \{35, 40, 50, 60, 70\}$), penalty ($p \in \{5, 5.1, 5.2, \ldots, 6\}$), and case-sensitivity (cs), of which we selected the best configuration. Using this parameter set, we fine-tuned the parameters relating to voting (see Section 3.5.3) in a second step , i.e. the number of voters ($v \in \{0, 2, 3, 4, 5\}$) and the voting confidence threshold ($vt \in \{0.001, 0.01, 0.02, 0.05, 0.1\}$).

Please refer to Section 3.5.4 for the description of the parameters.

In Table 4, we report the results of the first step, showing the ten configurations with the best results in descending order by median distance error. The best-performing n-gram order is 4, which is in line with results obtained by Jauhiainen et al. (2018a). We can also see that larger numbers of clusters and penalties above 5.4 are beneficial. The best models are not sensitive to case; we hypothesize that this is because lower-casing helps overcome data sparsity.

Table 5 shows the results of the second step using n-gram-level of 4 (n=4), cluster size of 60 (k=60), and penalty to 5.5 (p=5.5), with the best ten results by median distance on the development set. We tune the voting-related parameters v and vt. We also tune case-sensitivity cs again, since the voting scenario could equalize the more sparse data. We can see that the voting mechanism significantly improves performance on both development and test set. The most successful configuration for CH uses three voters and a confidence threshold of 0.01, leading to a median distance of 17.66 km on the test set, which corresponds to the fourth best submission for this subtask.

		Dev		Test		
System	Clusters	Median	Mean	Median	Mean	Submitted
Baseline: Center	-	43.13	48.10	43.13	48.47	
Baseline: SVM-Base-Unigram	10	21.29	28.58	19.99	27.94	
Baseline: SVM-Base-Unigram	20	**19.53**	29.23	19.02	28.06	
Baseline: SVM-Base-Unigram	35	19.86	29.30	**18.64**	28.70	
Baseline: SVM-Base-Unigram	50	19.93	29.65	18.83	28.54	
Baseline: SVM-Base-Unigram	100	20.13	29.67	19.06	29.06	
System 1: SVM-CV	20	17.80	25.60	17.83	25.46	
System 1: SVM-CV	35	16.83	26.36	15.93	25.05	x
System 1: SVM-CV	50	**16.68**	25.27	**15.59**	24.39	
System 1: SVM-CV	100	16.83	25.65	15.93	24.30	
System 2: LM	10	19.74	27.81	19.55	28.25	
System 2: LM	20	19.05	27.48	19.69	27.76	
System 2: LM	35	18.97	27.22	18.33	26.97	
System 2: LM	50	17.50	26.87	**17.51**	26.47	
System 2: LM	60	**17.17**	26.06	17.66	26.21	x
System 2: LM	70	17.53	26.40	18.07	26.49	
System 2: LM	100	17.62	26.39	18.27	26.44	
System 3: SVM-Base	20	**19.62**	28.63	19.69	28.18	
System 3: SVM-Base	35	19.68	29.22	18.80	28.17	
System 3: SVM-Base	50	19.90	29.39	**18.32**	28.02	
System 3: SVM-Base	100	20.03	28.83	19.06	28.48	
System 4: CNN	20	**24.66**	33.12	24.68	33.21	
System 4: CNN	35	25.78	35.19	23.30	32.00	

Table 6: Results for CH subtask for different systems on development and test sets

4.1.3 Comparison of the Different Systems on the CH subtask

We report the results for the various systems with different numbers of clusters in Table 6. In addition to the systems described in Section 3 we include 2 baselines: *Center* predicting the geographic center of the training set for every sample, and *SVM-Base-Unigram* which is a version of SVM-Base using only unigram word features. The parameters of LM are set according to the best setting presented in 4.1.2 and only the number of clusters is varied.

CNNs give relatively good results which would score about 10-11th place in the competition. A simple SVM-TF-IDF baseline with Unigram feature extraction would already be among the best 10 places with a median distance of about 20km. Increasing the number of clusters from 10 to 20 makes it better, but then the error distance increases for *SVM-Base-Unigram*. *SVM-Base* has comparable performance to *SVM-Base-Unigram* which could point to simple word/features being already good indications of geographic locations.

The LM method (System 2) benefits from a larger number of clusters than the SVM- and CNN based ones, peaking at 50 clusters on the test set and 60 on the development set.

For the SVM-CV system we see a drop of about 2 points compared to *SVM-Base*. Using the optimum number of clusters we get very close to the winning system.

Geographical Error Analysis of SVM-CV   We can see from Figure 2a that the hotspots around Zurich with the most texts were predicted with good quality. Problematic were the borders where there were regions containing smaller number of texts. For example, the Basel region (top left) was very well predicted, whereas the regions of Schaffhausen (top most) and St. Galler Rheintal (right most) were often wrongly predicted by a large distance.

In Figure 2b, we can see the confusion of the largest errors (more than 5 km). We can clearly see a confusion between the region of Bern (left most) and St. Gallen (top right). Also St. Gallen and Schwyz (red spot below in the middle).

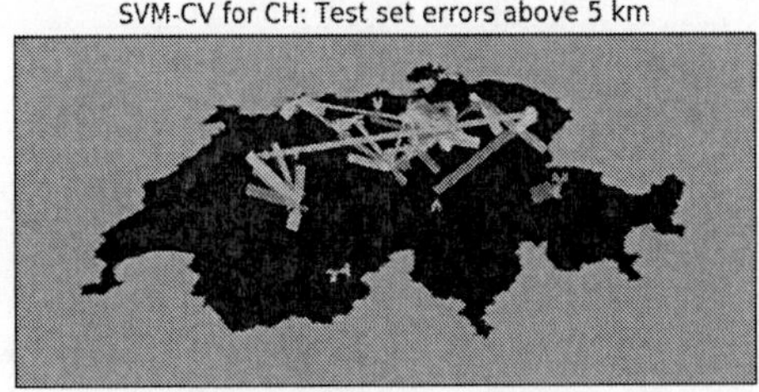

(a) Errors of SVM-CV classifier for CH. (b) Errors of SVM-CV classifier for CH.

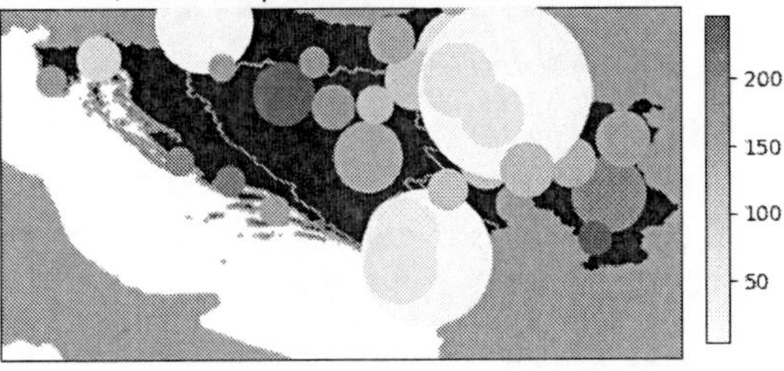

(a) Errors of SVM-Base classifier for BCMS. (b) Errors of SVM-Base classifier for BCMS.

4.2 BCMS subtask

System 2: LM We tuned the same parameters as described in Section 4.1.2 for CH and found the best setting to be identical to CH, except for the absence of case-sensitivity, and using five voters instead of three, which resulted in a development set median distance of 109.86 km. The LM-based approach performed rather poorly in the evaluation, scoring last place out of all submissions with 111.4 km median distance.

System 3: SVM-Base The SVM-Base system performed somewhat better. We evaluated different numbers of clusters: 25, 35, 50, 75 and 100, which yielded development set results within 3 km (59.02 with 35 clusters to 62.05 km with 100 clusters). Hence, our submission was based on 35 clusters. It achieved fourth rank in terms of submissions (second by teams), with 57.2 km median distance, more than 15 km behind the winning submission of 41.54 km.

System 1: SVM-CV: Addendum After the competition, the gold labels were released and we had time to run the SVM-CV system on all sub-tasks. We also calculated the predictions for System 1 with 35 Cluster which took roughly 2 days. We achieved a better result than the first placed (41.54 km) approach with a median distance of 36.79 km but a worse mean distance of 83.08 km (80.89 km for the first place). An analysis why this system performed better in this dataset in comparison to the other competitors in the other two datasets would be interesting, but we leave this for future work.

Geographical error analysis Figures 3a and 3b visualise the errors of the SVM-Base system on the BCMS subtask. We can see that areas with many samples, mostly around the capital cities of the respective countries, are predicted accurately (Figure 3a), but also that there is a strong trend of assigning False Positives to them (Figure 3b).

4.3 DE-AT subtask

System 2: LM We used the same parameters of BCMS subtask System 2 for the DE-AT. On the development set, this achieved 229.46 km, while on the test set the result was 217.8 km, 8th place among submissions and a large margin behind the best submission of 143.3 km.

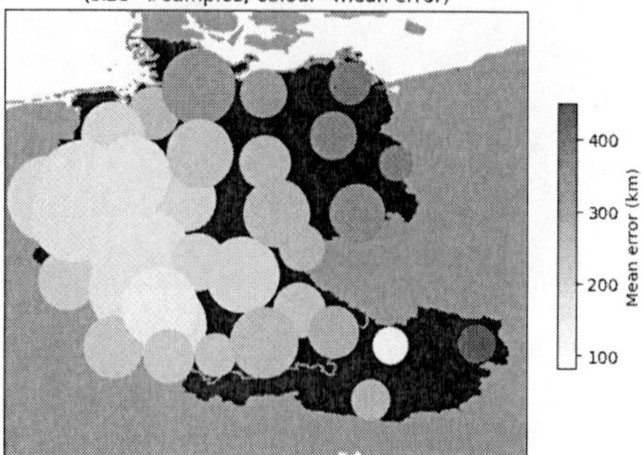

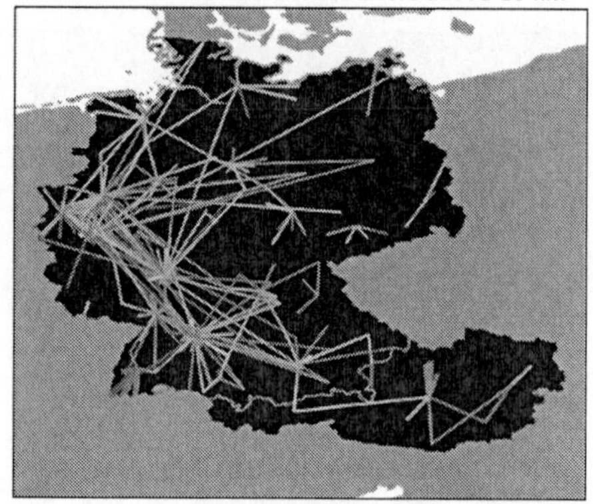

<table>
<tr><td>(a) Errors of SVM-Base classifier for DE-AT.</td><td>(b) Errors of SVM-Base classifier for DE-AT.</td></tr>
</table>

System 3: SVM-Base Due to lack of time we evaluated only 25, 35 and 50 clusters, of which 25 clusters performed the best on the development set, resulting in a median distance of 200.81 km. The test set result of 205.81 km ranked sixth, markedly behind the top three submissions.

System 1: SVM-CV: Addendum As pointed out before in Section 4.2, after the competition, we ran System 1 on all sub-tasks. This took for DE-AT roughly 5 days to finish. The prediction quality achieved with 35 clusters yielded a median distance of 167.01 km (first place: 143.3 km) and a mean distance of 193.32 km (first place: 166.64 km).

Geographical error analysis We visualize the results of the better submission which was again SVM-Base. As can be seen in Figure 4a, the main difficulties of the system are in the regions of Eastern Germany and Eastern Austria. In Figure 4b, we can see that texts from these problematic regions tend to be assigned more to the west; but also that many smaller errors are accumulated in the more populous areas along the Rhine.

5   Conclusion

We presented our approach to the VarDial 2020 SMG shared task, focusing on the submission for the CH subtask. Despite the expected noise, caused by people moving between different regions without adjusting their writing, a meta algorithm on top of SVMs with different n-grams weighted by TF-IDF performs impressively well, particularly for Switzerland (CH subtask). We achieve the second rank in terms of teams and the third by submissions with a median distance error of only 15.93 km. Deep learning approaches combining CNN and K-Means also showed interesting results but are still far behind a simple Unigram-TF-IDF with K-Means.

Acknowledgements

We thank the task organizers for their support and the reviewers for their detailed and helpful feedback. This research has been funded by the Swiss Innovation Agency project no. 28190.1 PFES-ES and by SpinningBytes AG, Switzerland.

References

Fernando Benites, Ralf Grubenmann, Pius von Däniken, Dirk von Grünigen, Jan Deriu, and Mark Cieliebak. 2018a. Twist Bytes-German Dialect Identification with Data Mining Optimization. In *Proceedings of the Fifth Workshop on NLP for Similar Languages, Varieties and Dialects (VarDial 2018)*, pages 218–227.

Fernando Benites, Shervin Malmasi, and Marcos Zampieri. 2018b. Classifying patent applications with ensemble methods. *arXiv preprint arXiv:1811.04695*.

Fernando Benites de Azevedo e Souza, Pius von Däniken, and Mark Cieliebak. 2019. Twistbytes-identification of cuneiform languages and german dialects at vardial 2019. In *6th Workshop on NLP for Similar Languages, Varieties and Dialects, VarDial 2019, Minneapolis, United States, 7 June 2019*, pages 194–201. Association for Computational Linguistics.

Fernando Benites. 2019. Twistbytes–hierarchical classification at germeval 2019: walking the fine line (of recall and precision). *arXiv preprint arXiv:1908.06493*.

Nghia Duong-Trung, Nicolas Schilling, Lucas Rego Drumond, and Lars Schmidt-Thieme. 2017. An effective approach for geolocation prediction in twitter streams using clustering based discretization.

Mihaela Găman, Dirk Hovy, Radu Tudor Ionescu, Heidi Jauhiainen, Tommi Jauhiainen, Krister Lindén, Nikola Ljubešić, Niko Partanen, Christoph Purschke, Yves Scherrer, and Marcos Zampieri. 2020. A Report on the VarDial Evaluation Campaign 2020. In *Proceedings of the Seventh Workshop on NLP for Similar Languages, Varieties and Dialects (VarDial)*.

Bo Han, Paul Cook, and Timothy Baldwin. 2014. Text-based twitter user geolocation prediction. *J. Artif. Int. Res.*, 49(1):451–500, January.

Nora Hollenstein and Noëmi Aepli. 2014. Compilation of a Swiss German dialect corpus and its application to PoS tagging. In *Proceedings of the First Workshop on Applying NLP Tools to Similar Languages, Varieties and Dialects*, pages 85–94.

Nora Hollenstein and Noëmi Aepli. 2015. A Resource for Natural Language Processing of Swiss German Dialects. In *GSCL*.

Dirk Hovy and Christoph Purschke. 2018. Capturing regional variation with distributed place representations and geographic retrofitting. In *Proceedings of the 2018 Conference on Empirical Methods in Natural Language Processing*, pages 4383–4394, Brussels, Belgium. Association for Computational Linguistics.

Chu-Ren Huang, Feng-Yi Chen, Keh-Jiann Chen, Zhao-ming Gao, and Kuang-Yu Chen. 2000. Sinica treebank: Design criteria, annotation guidelines, and on-line interface. In *Proceedings of the Second Workshop on Chinese Language Processing: Held in Conjunction with the 38th Annual Meeting of the Association for Computational Linguistics - Volume 12*, CLPW '00, pages 29–37, Stroudsburg, PA, USA. Association for Computational Linguistics.

Tommi Sakari Jauhiainen, Bo Krister Johan Linden, Heidi Annika Jauhiainen, et al. 2016. Heli, a word-based backoff method for language identification. In *Proceedings of the Third Workshop on NLP for Similar Languages, Varieties and Dialects VarDial3, Osaka, Japan, December 12 2016*.

Tommi Jauhiainen, Heidi Jauhiainen, and Krister Lindén. 2018a. Heli-based experiments in swiss german dialect identification. In *Proceedings of the Fifth Workshop on NLP for Similar Languages, Varieties and Dialects (VarDial 2018)*, pages 254–262.

Tommi Jauhiainen, Marco Lui, Marcos Zampieri, Timothy Baldwin, and Krister Lindén. 2018b. Automatic language identification in texts: A survey. *arXiv preprint arXiv:1804.08186*.

Tommi Jauhiainen, Heidi Jauhiainen, Tero Alstola, and Krister Lindén. 2019. Language and Dialect Identification of Cuneiform Texts. *arXiv preprint*, arXiv:1903.01891.

Diederik P Kingma and Jimmy Ba. 2014. Adam: A method for stochastic optimization. *arXiv preprint arXiv:1412.6980*.

Sheila Kinsella, Vanessa Murdock, and Neil O'Hare. 2011. "i'm eating a sandwich in glasgow": Modeling locations with tweets. In *Proceedings of the 3rd International Workshop on Search and Mining User-Generated Contents*, SMUC '11, page 61–68, New York, NY, USA. Association for Computing Machinery.

Nikola Ljubešić, Tanja Samardžić, and Curdin Derungs. 2016. TweetGeo - a tool for collecting, processing and analysing geo-encoded linguistic data. In *Proceedings of COLING 2016, the 26th International Conference on Computational Linguistics: Technical Papers*, pages 3412–3421, Osaka, Japan, December. The COLING 2016 Organizing Committee.

Stuart Lloyd. 1982. Least squares quantization in pcm. *IEEE transactions on information theory*, 28(2):129–137.

Suraj Maharjan, Prasha Shrestha, and Thamar Solorio. 2014. A Simple Approach to Author Profiling in MapReduce. In *CLEF*.

Shervin Malmasi and Marcos Zampieri. 2017. German Dialect Identification in Interview Transcriptions. In *Proceedings of the Fourth Workshop on NLP for Similar Languages, Varieties and Dialects (VarDial)*, pages 164–169, Valencia, Spain, April.

Christopher D. Manning, Prabhakar Raghavan, and Hinrich Schütze. 2008. *Introduction to Information Retrieval*. Cambridge University Press, New York, NY, USA.

A. M. McEnery and R. Z. Xiao. 2003. The lancaster corpus of mandarin chinese., 12.

Afshin Rahimi, Timothy Baldwin, and Trevor Cohn. 2017a. Continuous representation of location for geolocation and lexical dialectology using mixture density networks. In *Proceedings of the 2017 Conference on Empirical Methods in Natural Language Processing*, pages 167–176, Copenhagen, Denmark, September. Association for Computational Linguistics.

Afshin Rahimi, Trevor Cohn, and Timothy Baldwin. 2017b. A neural model for user geolocation and lexical dialectology. In *Proceedings of the 55th Annual Meeting of the Association for Computational Linguistics (Volume 2: Short Papers)*, pages 209–216, Vancouver, Canada, July. Association for Computational Linguistics.

Tanja Samardžić, Yves Scherrer, and Elvira Glaser. 2016. ArchiMob – a corpus of spoken Swiss German. In *Proceedings of LREC*.

Tommi Vatanen, Jaakko J. Väyrynen, and Sami Virpioja. 2010. Language Identification of Short Text Segments with N-gram Models. In Nicoletta Calzolari (Conference Chair), Khalid Choukri, Bente Maegaard, Joseph Mariani, Jan Odijk, Stelios Piperidis, Mike Rosner, and Daniel Tapias, editors, *Proceedings of the Seventh International Conference on Language Resources and Evaluation (LREC'10)*, Valletta, Malta, may. European Language Resources Association (ELRA).

Benjamin Wing and Jason Baldridge. 2014. Hierarchical discriminative classification for text-based geolocation. In *Proceedings of the 2014 conference on empirical methods in natural language processing (EMNLP)*, pages 336–348.

Marcos Zampieri, Shervin Malmasi, Nikola Ljubešić, Preslav Nakov, Ahmed Ali, Jörg Tiedemann, Yves Scherrer, and Noëmi Aepli. 2017. Findings of the VarDial Evaluation Campaign 2017. In *Proceedings of the Fourth Workshop on NLP for Similar Languages, Varieties and Dialects (VarDial)*, Valencia, Spain.

Marcos Zampieri, Shervin Malmasi, Preslav Nakov, Ahmed Ali, Suwon Shuon, James Glass, Yves Scherrer, Tanja Samardžić, Nikola Ljubešić, Jörg Tiedemann, Chris van der Lee, Stefan Grondelaers, Nelleke Oostdijk, Antal van den Bosch, Ritesh Kumar, Bornini Lahiri, and Mayank Jain. 2018. Language Identification and Morphosyntactic Tagging: The Second VarDial Evaluation Campaign. In *Proceedings of the Fifth Workshop on NLP for Similar Languages, Varieties and Dialects (VarDial)*, Santa Fe, USA.

Marcos Zampieri, Shervin Malmasi, Yves Scherrer, Tanja Samardžić, Francis Tyers, Miikka Silfverberg, Natalia Klyueva, Tung-Le Pan, Chu-Ren Huang, Radu Tudor Ionescu, Andrei Butnaru, and Tommi Jauhiainen. 2019. A Report on the Third VarDial Evaluation Campaign. In *Proceedings of the Sixth Workshop on NLP for Similar Languages, Varieties and Dialects (VarDial)*. Association for Computational Linguistics.

Xiang Zhang, Junbo Jake Zhao, and Yann LeCun. 2015. Character-level convolutional networks for text classification. *CoRR*, abs/1509.01626.

Discriminating between standard Romanian and Moldavian tweets using filtered character ngrams

Andrea Ceolin
University of Pennsylvania
`ceolin@sas.upenn.edu`

Hong Zhang
University of Pennsylvania
`zhangho@sas.upenn.edu`

Abstract

We applied word unigram models, character ngram models, and CNNs to the task of distinguishing tweets of two related dialects of Romanian (standard Romanian and Moldavian) for the VarDial 2020 RDI shared task (Găman et al., 2020). The main challenge of the task was to perform cross-genre text classification: specifically, the models must be trained using text from news articles, and be used to predict tweets. Our best model was a Naïve Bayes model trained on character ngrams, with the most common ngrams filtered out. We also applied SVMs and CNNs, but while they yielded the best performance on an evaluation dataset of news article, their accuracy significantly dropped when they were used to predict tweets. Our best model reached an F1 score of 0.715 on the evaluation dataset of tweets, and 0.667 on the held-out test dataset. The model ended up in the third place in the shared task.

1 Introduction

Language identification can be challenging for NLP techniques when languages are hardly distinguishable. One example of this challenge is the identification of Moldavian, a dialect of Romanian which exhibits almost no difference with standard Romanian. The distinction between Romanian and Moldavian is only motivated by the presence of a political boundary, which corresponds to no real isogloss. In spelling, the two languages are almost identical, with a minor exception involving the distribution of the letters 'â' and 'î', although other grammatical distinctions can be found in number, gender and case morphology, and in lexical choices. In particular, the lexical divergence was the result of Moldavian being under the influence of Russian, in the years in which it was part of the Soviet Union.

An additional challenge for language identification is that existing resources might belong to domains that are different from the domain on which one needs to perform a classification task. For instance, in certain cases one can find data from textbooks, encyclopedias and newspaper articles, but not from social media, even though language identification is often used to classify online messages (Tromp and Pechenizkiy, 2011; Bergsma et al., 2012; Barman et al., 2014; Lui and Baldwin, 2014). This raises the question of how to use out-of-domain data when performing language identification in a restricted domain.

The VarDial 2020 RDI shared task (Găman et al., 2020) invited participants to perform cross-genre language identification by training a classifier on newspaper articles, and using it to distinguish standard Romanian from Moldavian tweets. In this paper, we present the contribution of the team Phlyers to the task.

2 Methods

Previous methods used for language identification typically involve bag-of-words models (Huang and Lee, 2008), Naïve Bayes models applied to word and character ngrams (Jauhiainen et al., 2016) and Support Vector Machines (Zampieri et al., 2019). Deep learning methods based on CNNs and LSTMs

This work is licensed under a Creative Commons Attribution 4.0 International Licence. Licence details: `http://creativecommons.org/licenses/by/4.0/`. The code for the models employed in this work is found at `https://github.com/AndreaCeolin/VarDial2020`. We thank Monica-Alexandrina Irimia for comments about the project.

Proceedings of the 7th VarDial Workshop on NLP for Similar Languages, Varieties and Dialects, pages 265–272
Barcelona, Spain (Online), December 13, 2020

have also been successfully applied to similar tasks (Jaech et al., 2016; Butnaru and Ionescu, 2019; Hu et al., 2019; Tudoreanu, 2019).

Last year's VarDial edition (Zampieri et al., 2019) proposed the first shared task based on distinguishing standard Romanian from Moldavian. The best model achieved an F1 score of 0.895 on the test set, using an ensemble method based on CNNs and Support Vector Machines (Tudoreanu, 2019). The task consisted in training a classifier on news article in Romanian and Moldavian from the MOROCO corpus (Butnaru and Ionescu, 2019), and using it to classify other news articles yet to be added to the corpus.

This year's task asked participants to train a classifier on the news articles of the MOROCO corpus in order to distinguish standard Romanian from Moldavian in a test dataset of tweets (Găman and Ionescu, 2020). The task was particularly challenging because the organizers provided a large evaluation dataset based on news articles (5923) and a small evaluation dataset based on tweets (215) (cf. Table 1). This made the evaluation stage particularly delicate, because on the one hand a good model tested on the news evaluation dataset could fail to generalize to a different domain, while on the other hand the size of the tweets evaluation dataset was so small that the risk of overfitting was considerable.

VarDial (2020) RDI Shared task	Sentences
Training (News)	33564
Evaluation (News)	5923
Evaluation (Tweets)	215
Test (Tweets)	5022

Table 1: Summary statistics of the VarDial 2020 shared task.

We decided to train a variety of models, and to study their generizability to genres different from those in the training data. The models that we trained for the task are the following:

- **Multinomial Naïve Bayes - Words**. This is a standard Naïve Bayes model applied to word unigrams. The best performance on the news evaluation dataset was reached by using a TFIDF matrix instead of word counts. The optimal alpha was 0.0001 for both the unigram- and the TFIDF- based model.

- **Multinomial Naïve Bayes - Character Ngrams**. This is a standard Naïve Bayes model applied to character ngrams. The best performance on the news evaluation set was reached by a model which calculates ngrams in the window [5-8], with alpha=0.0001. Padding symbols (n-1) are added both before and after each word in order to retrieve ngrams for each value of n.

- **Linear SVM - Words**. This is a standard Support Vector Machine model with a linear kernel. The best performance on the news evaluation set was reached by using a TFIDF matrix instead of word counts. The optimal regularization parameter C was 2.

- **Linear SVM - Character Ngrams**. Our best Support Vector Machine model with a linear kernel uses character ngrams in the window [6-8], with C=1. Padding symbols (n-1) are added both before and after each word in order to retrieve ngrams for each value of n.

- **Character CNN**. We used the character-based CNN proposed in Zhang et al. (2015), and modified it according to the baseline model in Butnaru and Ionescu (2019). We created an alphabet of 76 symbols representing all the characters that appear at least 50 times in the training data, plus a 'NA' symbol, and then we used one-hot encoding vectors as input to the CNN. The three hyperparameters we fine-tuned were the batch size (10), the learning rate (0.0001), and the size of the fully-connected layers (1000), while the other parameters were taken from Butnaru and Ionescu (2019). Training was performed for 20 epochs. See Figure 1 for a summary of the model.

- **Character TDNN**. Inspired by the research in speech recognition community, we implemented a Time Delay Neural Network (TDNN) (Peddinti et al., 2015), in order to better capture the morphological features of the two languages. Our model contains 2 stacked convolution blocks. Each block

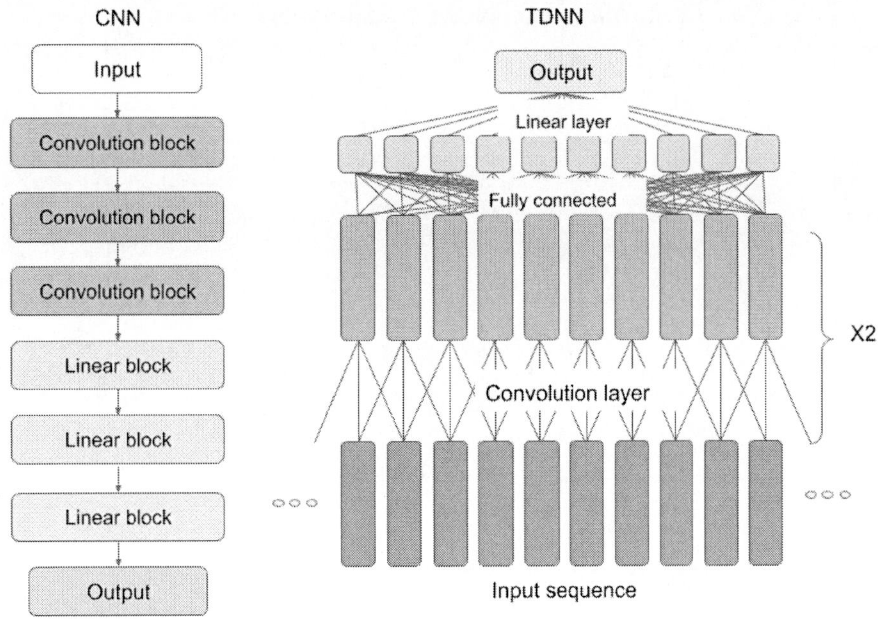

Figure 1: The architectures of our neural network models (CNN on the left, TDNN on the right).

learns 100 k-by-3 filter banks, where k is the dimension of the input vectors and 3 is the window length, that maps a trigram character window to a scalar. Input sequences were padded to equal length. The output 1-by-n vector, where n is the input sequence length, is then passed through a fully connected layer. Subsampling was not performed in training. Training was performed for 50 epochs.

The architectures of the CNN and the TDNN are shown in Figure 1.

3 Results

3.1 Evaluation

The results of the models are summarized in Table 2. All the models exhibit a drop in performance when used to classify tweets instead of news articles (Figure 2). The best model on the news evaluation dataset is the Linear SVM model trained on TFIDF transformed word unigrams, with an F1 score of 0.942. By inspecting the weight matrix, we were able to identify the words which have the highest contribution in determining the class of the news articles. Among the best words that are used to identify the Moldavian class, 'sînt' ('are') and 'cînd' ('when') have the largest weights. These are frequent words which are spelled differently in Romanian ('sunt' and 'când'). As for Romanian, 'news' and 'foto', which are loanwords, as well as the frequent word 'sâmbătă' ('Saturday'), which has a different spelling in Moldavian, ('sîmbătă'), carry the largest weights.

The CNN model reaches a similar accuracy (F1 score: 0.931), which is almost identical to the accuracy obtained by Butnaru and Ionescu (2019) on the same dataset. An interesting observation for the neural network-based models is that although the accuracy of the models on the news dataset increases by iterating through the training set, the improvement does not generalize to the testing domain (see Figure 3). The lack of cross-domain generalizability might indicate that naive implementations of deep neural network architectures are not well-suited for cross-genre classifications.

The models that best generalize to Twitter data are the Multinomial Naïve Bayes (MNB) models trained on TFIDF transformed word unigrams (F1 score=0.892) and character ngrams (F1 score=0.883). In particular, the highest accuracy is reached by the character ngram model, which yields an F1 score of

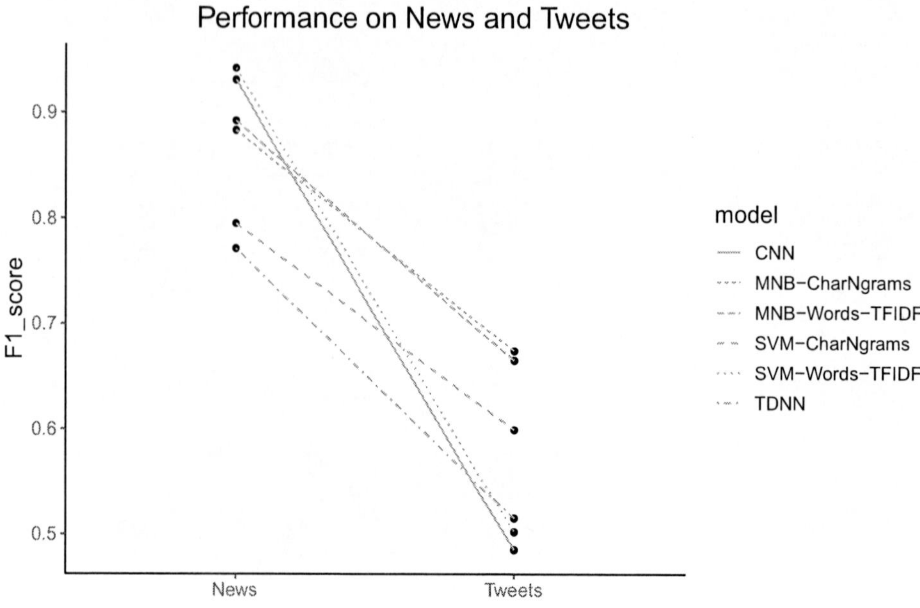

Figure 2: Drop in performance of the best performing models from the News development set to the Tweets development set.

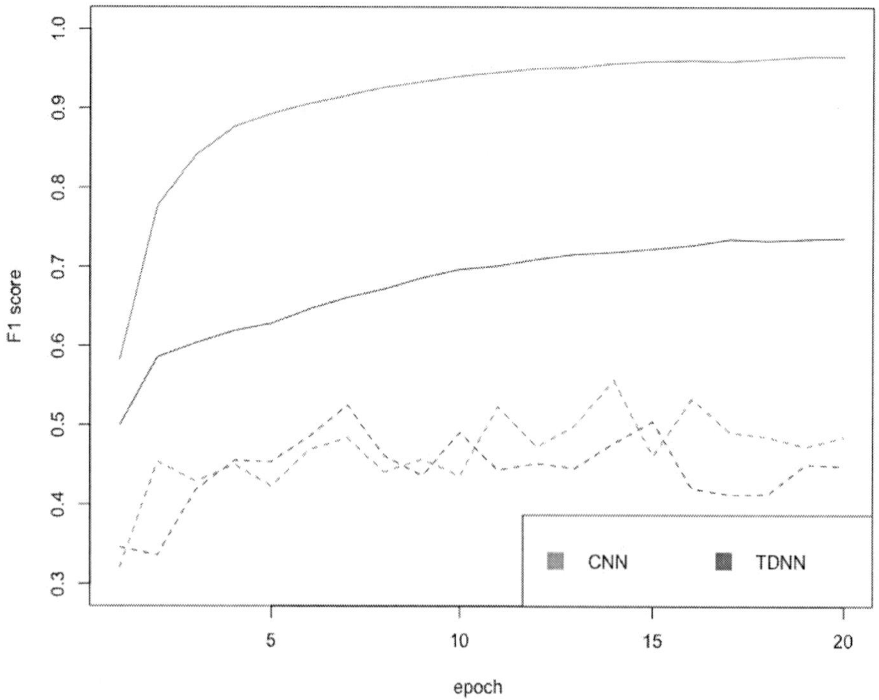

Figure 3: Comparing the training and validation performance measured by F1 score after 20 epochs of training. Solid line: validation score on news articles; dotted line: validation score on tweets.

	News articles (2019)	Tweets (2020)
MNB - Word unigrams	0.891	0.637
MNB - Word unigrams- TFIDF	0.892	0.665
MNB - Char. ngrams [5-8]	0.883	**0.674**
MNB - Char. ngrams [5-8] - TFIDF	0.351	0.322
Linear SVM - Word unigrams	0.693	0.504
Linear SVM - Word unigrams - TFIDF	**0.942**	0.502
Linear SVM - Char. ngrams [6-8]	0.795	0.599
Linear SVM - Char. ngrams [6-8] - TFIDF	0.351	0.345
CNN	0.931	0.485
TDNN	0.771	0.515

Table 2: Performance of the models tested (F1 scores).

0.674 on the tweets dataset.

For these reasons, we decided to use the Multinomian Naïve Bayes model based on character ngrams for the task, and we proceeded to the fine-tuning stage.

3.2 Fine-tuning on the News set

We fine-tuned the MNB character ngram model on the tweets dataset (Table 3). We noticed that by removing the most common ngrams, performance improved. In particular, removing all the ngrams which appeared more than 1000 times overall improved the performance up to an F1 score of 0.890 on the news dataset (see Figure 4). On the contrary, removing less frequent ngrams did not improve performance. This result is interesting, because usually performance is increased by removing the tail of the frequency distribution, not the head: in this case, since the TFIDF transformation was not sufficient to normalize the behavior of high-frequency ngrams, removing them turned out to be a better strategy to increase the performance of the classifier.

Filter applied based on total occurences	Ch-ngram filtered	News articles (19)	Tweets (20)
MNB - Char. ngrams [5-8], filter < 5000	1638 (0.2%)	0.884	0.674
MNB - Char. ngrams [5-8], filter < 3000	3580 (0.4%)	0.888	0.674
MNB - Char. ngrams [5-8], filter < 1000	13766 (1.5%)	**0.890**	0.683
MNB - Char. ngrams [5-8], filter < 500	26384 (2.8%)	0.887	**0.702**
MNB - Char. ngrams [5-8], filter < 250	45102 (4.8%)	0.877	0.692
MNB - Char. ngrams [5-8], filter > 4	564021 (60.5%)	0.876	0.692
MNB - Char. ngrams [5-8], filter > 3	523377 (56.7%)	0.878	0.683
MNB - Char. ngrams [5-8], filter > 2	461784 (49.6%)	0.881	0.684
MNB - Char. ngrams [5-8], filter > 1	340764 (36.7%)	0.882	0.674

Table 3: Fine-tuning of the models tested. Total char. ngrams: 931786.

3.3 Fine-tuning on the Tweets set

After further fine-tuning of the ngram window and the threshold of ngrams to filter, we obtained two best models on the tweets dataset (Table 4). Both models reached an F1 score of 0.715. The performance did not improve after including in the training set the data coming from the evaluation set containing news articles. The two best models had the following settings:

- MNB - Char. ngrams, [6-8], filter <250, alpha=0.001

- MNB - Char. ngrams, [5-7], filter <200, alpha=0.001

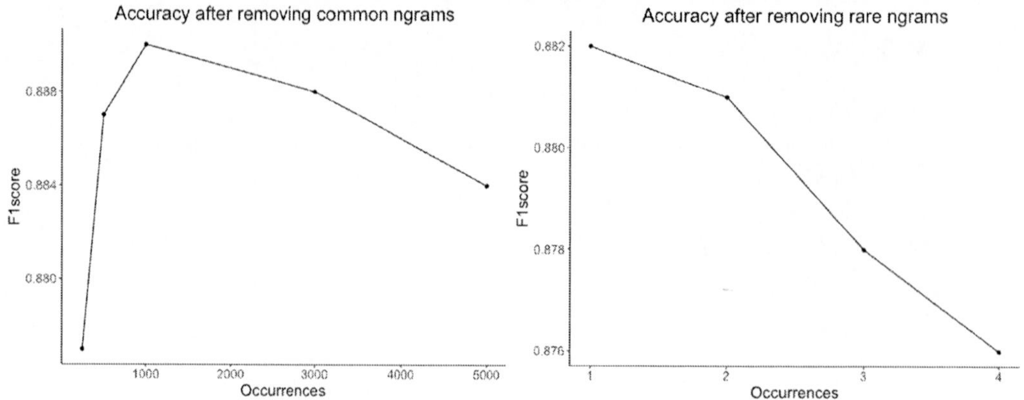

Figure 4: Accuracy change on the news evaluation dataset after ngram filtering. Left: common ngrams removed; right: common ngrams preserved.

Tweets (2020)		
	Train	Train+Dev1
MNB - Char. ngrams [6-8], filter <250	**0.715**	**0.715**
MNB - Char. ngrams [5-7], filter <200	**0.715**	**0.715**

Table 4: Final performance on the tweets evaluation dataset after fine-tuning the parameters of the MNB - ngrams model.

3.4 VarDial 2020 - RDI Shared Task

We submitted three runs to the VarDial 2020 RDI shared task:

1. **MNB - Char. ngrams, [5-8], filter <1000, alpha=0.0001.** This was the best ngram model on the news articles.

2. **MNB - Char. ngrams, [6-8], filter <250, alpha=0.001.** This was one of the two best models on the tweets evaluation data set.

3. **MNB - Char. ngrams, [5-7], filter <200, alpha=0.001.** This was one of the two best models on the tweets evaluation dataset.

The results for our models on the test dataset of the task are summarized in Table 5. The best model was the one which was fine-tuned on the news dataset. This result suggests that our fine-tuning strategy on the tweets dataset led to overfitting on the news articles, and thus poorer performance on tweets. Additionally, after our submissions, we realized that the tweets in the test data had not being preprocessed to remove punctuation, numbers and other symbols. Preprocessing increases the submission F1 score up to 0.692.

Both the Multinomial Naïve Bayes model based on TFIDF word unigrams, which was the second best model on the tweets dataset, and the one based on unfiltered character ngrams, performed worse than the best model submitted. The same was true for the Linear SVM model based on character ngrams.

4 Conclusion

We applied word unigram models, character ngram models, and two neural network models to classify tweets of two related dialects (standard Romanian and Moldavian) for the VarDial 2020 RDI shared task (Găman et al., 2020), with training data from a different domain. Two of the models we proposed, a Linear SVM model based on TFIDF word unigrams and a CNN model, reached a high accuracy on the news evaluation dataset, but failed to generalize to the tweets evaluation dataset. On the contrary,

Model	Tweets (2020) test data results	
	no preprocessing, submitted	preprocessing
1. MNB - Char. ngrams [5-8], filter <1000	**0.666**	**0.692**
2. MNB - Char. ngrams [6-8], filter <250	0.651	0.678
3. MNB - Char. ngrams [5-7], filter <200	0.645	0.675
MNB - Word unigrams - TFIDF	0.630	0.677
MNB - Char. ngrams [5-8]	0.651	0.676
Linear SVM - *n*grams [6-8]	0.593	0.590

Table 5: Results on the test dataset.

Multinomial Naïve Bayes models turned out to be the best performing models on the task. The more complex neural network models suffered from the problem of poor generalizability. In addition, we showed that removing high frequency ngrams can be a valid alternative when working on datasets for which a TFIDF transformation does not improve classification accuracy.

References

Utsab Barman, Amitava Das, Joachim Wagner, and Jennifer Foster. 2014. Code mixing: A challenge for language identification in the language of social media. In *Proceedings of the first workshop on computational approaches to code switching*, pages 13–23.

Shane Bergsma, Paul McNamee, Mossaab Bagdouri, Clayton Fink, and Theresa Wilson. 2012. Language identification for creating language-specific twitter collections. In *Proceedings of the second workshop on language in social media*, pages 65–74.

Andrei M Butnaru and Radu Tudor Ionescu. 2019. Moroco: The Moldavian and Romanian dialectal corpus. *arXiv preprint arXiv:1901.06543*.

Mihaela Găman and Radu Tudor Ionescu. 2020. The Unreasonable Effectiveness of Machine Learning in Moldavian versus Romanian Dialect Identification. *arXiv preprint arXiv:2007.15700*.

Mihaela Găman, Dirk Hovy, Radu Tudor Ionescu, Heidi Jauhiainen, Tommi Jauhiainen, Krister Lindén, Nikola Ljubešić, Niko Partanen, Christoph Purschke, Yves Scherrer, and Marcos Zampieri. 2020. A Report on the VarDial Evaluation Campaign 2020. In *Proceedings of the Seventh Workshop on NLP for Similar Languages, Varieties and Dialects (VarDial)*.

Hai Hu, Wen Li, He Zhou, Zuoyu Tian, Yiwen Zhang, and Liang Zou. 2019. Ensemble Methods to Distinguish Mainland and Taiwan Chinese. In *Proceedings of the Sixth Workshop on NLP for Similar Languages, Varieties and Dialects*, pages 165–171.

Chu-Ren Huang and Lung-Hao Lee. 2008. Contrastive approach towards text source classification based on top-bag-of-word similarity. In *Proceedings of the 22nd Pacific Asia conference on language, information and computation*, pages 404–410.

Aaron Jaech, George Mulcaire, Mari Ostendorf, and Noah A Smith. 2016. A neural model for language identification in code-switched tweets. In *Proceedings of The Second Workshop on Computational Approaches to Code Switching*, pages 60–64.

Tommi Sakari Jauhiainen, Bo Krister Johan Linden, Heidi Annika Jauhiainen, et al. 2016. HeLI, a word-based backoff method for language identification. In *Proceedings of the Third Workshop on NLP for Similar Languages, Varieties and Dialects (VarDial 2016)*.

Marco Lui and Timothy Baldwin. 2014. Accurate language identification of twitter messages. In *Proceedings of the 5th workshop on language analysis for social media (LASM)*, pages 17–25.

Vijayaditya Peddinti, Daniel Povey, and Sanjeev Khudanpur. 2015. A time delay neural network architecture for efficient modeling of long temporal contexts. In *Sixteenth Annual Conference of the International Speech Communication Association*.

Erik Tromp and Mykola Pechenizkiy. 2011. Graph-based n-gram language identification on short texts. In *Proc. 20th Machine Learning conference of Belgium and The Netherlands*, pages 27–34.

Diana Tudoreanu. 2019. DTeam@ VarDial 2019: Ensemble based on skip-gram and triplet loss neural networks for Moldavian vs. Romanian cross-dialect topic identification. In *Proceedings of the Sixth Workshop on NLP for Similar Languages, Varieties and Dialects*, pages 202–208.

Marcos Zampieri, Shervin Malmasi, Yves Scherrer, Tanja Samardžic, Francis Tyers, Miikka Pietari Silfverberg, Natalia Klyueva, Tung-Le Pan, Chu-Ren Huang, Radu Tudor Ionescu, et al. 2019. A report on the third VarDial evaluation campaign. In *Proceedings of the Sixth Workshop on NLP for Similar Languages, Varieties and Dialects (VarDial 2019)*. The Association for Computational Linguistics.

Xiang Zhang, Junbo Zhao, and Yann LeCun. 2015. Character-level convolutional networks for text classification. In *Advances in neural information processing systems*, pages 649–657.

Challenges in Neural Language Identification: NRC at VarDial 2020

Gabriel Bernier-Colborne, Cyril Goutte
National Research Council Canada
{Gabriel.Bernier-Colborne, Cyril.Goutte}@nrc-cnrc.gc.ca

Abstract

We describe the systems developed by the National Research Council Canada for the Uralic language identification shared task at the 2020 VarDial evaluation campaign. Although our official results were well below the baseline, we show in this paper that this was not due to the neural approach to language identification in general, but to a flaw in the function we used to sample data for training and evaluation purposes. Preliminary experiments conducted after the evaluation period suggest that our neural approach to language identification can achieve state-of-the-art results on this task, although further experimentation is required.

1 Introduction

The goal of the Uralic language identification (ULI) shared task at VarDial 2020 (Găman et al., 2020) was to identify and discriminate 29 Uralic language varieties. This involves distinguishing the relevant languages from a large set of non-relevant languages and discriminating between these languages.

To solve this task, we used an approach similar to the one we developed for the cuneiform language identification shared task at VarDial 2019 (Bernier-Colborne et al., 2019). This approach was ranked first in that competition, which was one of the first times a language identification shared task was won by a neural network (Zampieri et al., 2019). It is a deep learning approach based on character embeddings and a transformer network (Vaswani et al., 2017) trained in a similar fashion to BERT (Devlin et al., 2019).

On this year's ULI shared task, we did not have the same level of success using this neural approach to language identification, as our accuracy scores on the held-out test set were significantly lower than the baseline scores.

In this paper, we explore the challenges presented by the ULI task and explain the reasons for the low accuracy scores achieved by our model in the official evaluation. We then show that neural language identification can produce much better results if trained and tuned correctly.

2 Task Definition and Data

The goal of this language identification task is simply to identify the language of a given text, which is typically a single sentence. If more than one language is used in the text (e.g. code switching), the main language must be identified. Since there are both relevant and non-relevant languages in the test set, the task involves not only discriminating amongst the relevant languages, but also distinguishing them from the non-relevant languages. The shared task was closed, so no data could be used except for the training set provided.

The task was subdivided into three tracks. The training and test data is the same for all three tracks, the difference being the way in which evaluation metrics are computed. For tracks 1 and 2, only test cases where either the predicted or true label is a relevant language are evaluated, using macro-averaged and micro-averaged F1 score respectively. For track 3, all test cases are evaluated, using the macro-averaged F1 score.

This work is licensed under a Creative Commons Attribution 4.0 International Licence. Licence details: http:// creativecommons.org/licenses/by/4.0/.

Proceedings of the 7th VarDial Workshop on NLP for Similar Languages, Varieties and Dialects, pages 273–282
Barcelona, Spain (Online), December 13, 2020

The 29 relevant languages for this task are part of the Uralic group of languages, which are spoken mainly in northern Eurasia. Some of these languages are very under-resourced, and some are already extinct, e.g. Kemi Saami, which was represented in this task.

Also included in the test set are 149 other languages considered non-relevant. These include the three largest Uralic languages (i.e. Estonian, Finnish, and Hungarian), as well as a wide variety of other languages. In total, 178 languages or language varieties were represented in this task, the highest number covered so far in a language identification shared task.

The training set provided contains 646,043 examples for the relevant languages and 63,772,445 examples for the non-relevant ones. Thus, there is much less data for the relevant languages, on average. Both the relevant and non-relevant portions of the training set are (highly) unbalanced. The class frequencies in the relevant training data range from 19 (Kemi Saami) to 214,225 (Northern Saami). The non-relevant portion of the dataset contains anywhere from 10,000 to 3,000,000 examples per class (i.e. language).

The training set was compiled from 2 different sources: data for the relevant languages comes from the Wanca 2016 corpus (Jauhiainen et al., 2019a), whereas the non-relevant data was extracted from the Leipzig corpus (Goldhahn et al., 2012). The relevant data in the held-out test set comes from the Wanca 2017 dataset. For more information on the dataset, the task, and the baseline scores, refer to Jauhiainen et al. (2020).

Regarding the length of the texts, for relevant languages, 86% of the texts contain 128 characters or less, and only 1.2% are longer than 256 characters. For non-relevant languages, 70% of texts contain 128 characters or less, and 0.02% are longer than 256 characters.

Note that there are no duplicates in the relevant training data. In the non-relevant training data, less than 0.5% of examples appear more than once (whether in the same language or different languages).

2.1 Challenges

The ULI shared task presented many challenges. Some of these challenges are inherent to language identification in general. For instance, some of the target languages are very closely related, such as Ingrian, Ludian, and Karelian (Jauhiainen et al., 2020). This can make it hard to distinguish between such languages. Furthermore, some languages are spoken and written much more frequently than others, such that there are often large class imbalances in datasets for language identification. In the case of the ULI task, some language varieties have so little data available that it was announced at the outset that some relevant languages would not be present in the held-out test set. In general, detecting very rare languages is challenging, especially if they are closely related to other languages present in the training data.

The ULI shared task presented its own specific challenges. There are not only large class imbalances within the relevant and non-relevant groups, but also a large discrepancy between these two groups, as there is about 100 times more training data for the non-relevant languages, meaning that their frequency is about 20 times greater on average than the relevant languages (as there are about 5 times more non-relevant than relevant languages). These large and complex class imbalances make this a tricky task to learn.

The training set is also quite large, so simply processing all that data may incur a high computational cost. Using a neural model such as a large transformer network, simply encoding all the texts may take a long time. So finding a way to efficiently train and tune a model on such a large dataset may be challenging.

Another potential challenge posed by the ULI task is the presence of noise (i.e. incorrectly labeled sentences) in the training data, as the corpora were produced in part using automatic web crawling and language identification methods.

Finally, a challenge that turned out to have a huge impact on our results is the fact that the organizers decided not to provide a dedicated development set; just a training set. This is a legitimate design decision for such a competition, which entails that participants must create their own development set from the training data. The adequacy of this development set is very important to estimate the accuracy that the model will achieve on the held-out test data, and select the best models.

3 A Neural Approach to Language Identification

The neural approach we used for this task is similar to the one we developed for the cuneiform language identification shared task at VarDial 2019. The model is a deep neural network which takes sequences of characters as input. The model is trained in two stages: (partially) self-supervised pre-training, and supervised fine-tuning. Typically, when training this type of model, the pre-training phase would exploit large amounts of unlabeled text data, then the subsequent fine-tuning phase would exploit a much smaller amount of labeled data. Since the ULI shared task was a closed one, we used the same training set for both pre-training and fine-tuning.

The network is composed of a stack of bidirectional transformer modules (Vaswani et al., 2017) which encode the input sequence. The output of this encoder is fed to one or more output layers, which depend on the tasks used for pre-training and fine-tuning.

First, we pre-train the model using 2 pre-training tasks: masked language modeling (MLM) and sentence pair classification (SPC). The MLM task is exactly as described by Devlin et al. (2019). The objective is to predict tokens (in this case, characters) chosen at random based on all the other tokens in the text. This produces a model that can predict characters in context for any of the languages represented in the training data (with varying degrees of accuracy), and must therefore have learned the specific patterns of each language (or at least some of them).

As for the SPC pre-training task, it is similar to the next sentence prediction task proposed by Devlin et al. (2019), but we adapted it for language identification. Instead of predicting whether two sequences follow each other in the training corpus, we predict whether two sequences are in the same language. This introduces a supervised signal into the pre-training task (whereas MLM is self-supervised), as we use the labels in the training data in order to label pairs of texts as belonging to the same language or not. Learning to predict whether two texts belong to the same language should be helpful to predict the language used in a specific text, when we fine-tune the model on this task later on.

Thus, the pre-training phase uses two different output layers, one for MLM and one for SPC. The first is a simple softmax over the vocabulary, which is composed of characters in this case. The input of this layer is the encoding of a character in the sequence that has been masked beforehand: before feeding the sequence to the encoder, we pick some characters at random and replace them with a special masking token. Based on the encoding of a masked token (which encodes information about the other tokens in the sequence), the softmax layer is used to predict the most likely character. For more details on the implementation of masked language modeling, refer to Devlin et al. (2019).

The second output layer is a binary classifier which applies average pooling over the final hidden states of the encoder for each of the two input texts (separately), then computes the dot product of the two pooled encodings, then predicts whether the two input texts belong to the same language based on this similarity function. Texts whose pooled encodings are similar will therefore be predicted to belong to the same language. Note that this bi-encoding approach to SPC has a lower computational cost than the cross-encoding approach we used for cuneiform language identification at VarDial 2019, where both sequences are concatenated and encoded together. The cost remains quadratic with respect to the length of the sequence, but the sequence is half as long, and we encode two sequences instead of one.

Once the model is pre-trained, we fine-tune it on the target task, which is to predict the language of each text, using the labeled training data. For this, we use the pre-trained encoder, and add a new output layer for language identification, which is simply a softmax over the 178 languages.

The loss function used to learn all tasks is cross-entropy, which is commonly used for multi-class classification problems, averaged across examples in a batch. We did not assign class-specific cost weights, but we did experiment with oversampling of the training data during fine-tuning, which plays a similar role in alleviating class imbalances (see related work in Sec. 7). In cases where we used multiple tasks at once for training, losses were summed.

The vocabulary (or alphabet) of symbols for which we learn embeddings is composed of every character in the training set whose frequency is greater than some threshold, plus a few reserved symbols (e.g. unknown characters and padding). In the experiments we carried out on our own train/dev/test split, we computed the vocab on the training portion only. Using a minimum frequency of 2, this produced a vocab of about 15K characters. Input characters that are not part of the vocabulary are mapped to a special symbol for unknown characters.

For efficiency, we used a small architecture containing only 8 transformer layers, rather than the 12 layers of the "base" architecture proposed by Devlin et al. (2019). Our other hyperparameter settings for pre-training largely follow their recommendations:

- Nb transformer layers: 8

- Nb attention heads: 12

- Hidden layer size: 768

- Feed forward/filter size: 3072

- Hidden activation: gelu

- Dropout probability: 0.1

- Optimizer: Adam (with $\beta_1 = \beta_2 = 0.9$)

- Learning rate: 1e-4

- Warmup steps for pre-training: 10K

- Maximum input length: 128

For fine-tuning, we experimented with different values for the batch size and learning rate. We also tested a longer maximum input length of 256. In this case, the position embeddings that were not used during pre-training, and are therefore still randomly initialized, are learned on the fly during fine-tuning.

Note that no pre-processing was applied to the input text (e.g. word or sub-word tokenization, character normalization, etc.).

We used a single GPU (Nvidia K80 or V100, depending on the experiment) with 12 GB of memory for both pre-training and fine-tuning. Note that simply producing the predictions of the model on the held-out test set, containing over 1.5 million examples, took about 8 hours on a V100 (with a batch size of 64 and a maximum sequence length of 256).

Our code, which exploits the Transformers library by HuggingFace (Wolf et al., 2020), is available is at `https://www.github.com/gbcolborne/vardial2020`.

4 Methodology

To produce our systems for the ULI task, we experimented with various training tasks and hyperparameter settings, and selected the models that seemed to perform best. Before we could do this, we first had to create a dev set, as none was provided for this task. A dev set was necessary to tune the hyperparameters of the model and to estimate the accuracy we could expect to achieve on the held-out test set. To get an unbiased estimate of held-out accuracy, we created two dev sets, one used to tune hyperparameters, and the other to evaluate the fully tuned model. We will call the former 'dev' and the latter 'dev-test' when needed to distinguish the two. In the following sections, we explain how we split the training data to obtain these dev sets, then provide an overview of our model selection experiments.

4.1 Splitting the Data

Before sampling a dev set from the ULI training data, we have to consider the fact that there is 20 times more data for the non-relevant languages than the relevant ones, on average, and that both the relevant and non-relevant data are unbalanced. If we sampled examples at random, without considering the relative class frequencies, we would have to sample a very large number of examples in order to get a decent coverage of all the languages in the training data.

For our dev sets, we had the following desiderata:

- They should be large enough to estimate the evaluation metrics accurately, yet not so large that running the evaluation would be prohibitively expensive in terms of computation time. Something on the order of 10,000-100,000 examples seemed reasonable.

- They should cover most of the relevant languages, but not necessarily all of them, as we knew from the outset that some relevant languages would not appear in the held-out test set. We decided to ensure that a few of the rarest languages would be absent from our dev sets.

We also thought it might be helpful to sample the three non-relevant Uralic languages more frequently than the other non-relevant languages. The motivation was that these three languages would likely be the hardest to distinguish from the 29 relevant languages.

To sample our dev sets, we computed the relative class frequencies separately for these three groups: relevant, non-relevant Uralic, and non-relevant non-Uralic. Then, we sampled from each of these three groups independently, by setting the sampling probability of each language in a group to its relative frequency. We sampled two dev sets containing 12,000 examples each. In each of them, three of the relevant languages were absent.

After the official evaluation, we figured out that there was a major flaw in the way we sampled data to create the dev sets. By analyzing the class distribution of these dev sets, we observed that the three non-relevant Uralic languages were being sampled much more often than either the relevant languages or the 146 other non-relevant languages. This was because we sampled uniformly from the 3 groups, ignoring the fact that there were far fewer languages in the non-relevant Uralic group. This made our dev sets bad estimators of held-out test accuracy. This would affect not only model selection, but also the training itself, as we used a similar function to resample the training data. More details on the effect of this mistake are provided in Sec. 5.

4.2 Model Selection

While developing our system, we empirically investigated questions such as:

- Does doing SPC along with MLM during pre-training improve classification accuracy after fine-tuning?

- Does doing MLM on the labeled training data along with language identification during fine-tuning improve classification accuracy?

- Does doing MLM on the unlabeled dev or test data during fine-tuning (to adapt the encoder to the unlabeled data) improve classification accuracy?

- What are the optimal settings of those hyperparameters of the BERT method that are known to have a significant impact on accuracy (e.g. batch size, learning rate, number of training steps, etc.).

- Does increasing the maximum input length to 256 during fine-tuning improve classification accuracy?

- Does damping the relative class frequencies used for sampling improve accuracy?

We will not go into the details of these experiments here. Because of the flaw in the sampling function we used to sample our dev sets, the results of these experiments are of little interest.

We ended up submitting the predictions of three different systems for each of the three tracks. For each track, we submitted the predictions of:

- A model trained on all the training data, using the optimal settings for a given track according to our model selection experiments. This model was pre-trained with both MLM and SPC, and fine-tuned with both MLM and language identification.

- Same as the previous model, but during fine-tuning, we ran MLM on the unlabeled, held-out test set alongside MLM and language identification on the labeled training data.

- An ensemble of 6 models, i.e. the two previous models for each of the three tracks. We used plurality voting. To break ties, we favoured the model tuned for a given track (with adaptation to the unlabeled test data).

5   Official Results

We were the only team who participated in the ULI task (perhaps because of some of the challenges we have outlined in this paper), therefore we can only compare our results to the baseline scores computed by the organizers. The baseline scores were computed using the HeLI method (Jauhiainen et al., 2017).

System	Track 1 (macro F1, rel.)	Track 2 (micro F1, rel.)	Track 3 (macro F1, all)
Best run	0.300	0.260	0.675
Baseline	0.802	0.973	0.926

Table 1: Score of our best run on the held-out test set. For tracks 1 and 2, only the test cases where either the predicted or true label is a relevant language are evaluated. For track 3, all test cases are evaluated. Also shown are the scores of the baseline system, i.e. HeLI.

Our best score on each of the three tracks is shown Table 1 along with the baselines. It is obvious from these results that our models performed very poorly on the held-out test set. Our scores were not only much lower than the baseline, but also much lower than the scores we had estimated on our own dev sets.

Looking at our precision and recall scores on track 2, we observed that recall was relatively high (0.895), but precision was very low (0.085), indicating that our model was badly over-detecting relevant languages.

Faced with these results, we set about figuring out what went wrong. Was this neural approach simply inadequate for this language identification task or was there some flaw in the way we trained and selected our models? The fact that our dev sets had significantly overestimated our held-out accuracy suggested that the latter explanation was plausible.

6   Post-evaluation Experiments

To confirm our suspicion that our dev sets were bad estimators of held-out test accuracy, we evaluated the baseline method, i.e. HeLI, on our split of the training data. We used a different implementation of HeLI than the organizers, but our settings were similar to those reported by Jauhiainen et al. (2020). We used the implementation that is publicly available at `https://github.com/tosaja/HeLI`, and modified the settings in the `HeLI.java` class as follows: we only used lower-case features, all feature count thresholds were increased from the default 1000 to 300,000, the maximum n-gram length was set to 6, and the penalty was set to 7.

System	Track 1 (macro F1, rel.)	Track 2 (micro F1, rel.)	Track 3 (macro F1, all)
Best run	0.705	0.783	0.655
Baseline	0.659	0.735	0.611

Table 2: Scores on our dev set before the sampling flaw was corrected.

The baseline scores we obtained on our dev set are shown in Table 2, along with the best dev score we observed when training the neural models. These results indicated that the baseline system's scores were similar to those of our neural network, and much lower than the scores achieved by the baseline system on the held-out test set. This corroborated our suspicion that there was a flaw in the function we used to sample the dev sets, which made them bad estimators of held-out test accuracy.

Since we used a similar function to sample the training data, optimization of the parameters of the neural network was also affected. The combination of these two factors explains why our system's scores were so much lower than the baseline scores in the official evaluation.

Equipped with this knowledge, we set about re-evaluating our neural approach to see if it could achieve a similar level of accuracy as the baseline method on a more representative dev set. Due to time constraints, we were not able to conduct a thorough assessment of this question, but we report the results of our preliminary experiments below.

6.1 Fixing the Sampling Function

We produced new dev sets using a corrected sampling procedure. First, we compute relative frequencies of relevant and non-relevant languages separately. Then we compute sampling probabilities of the languages in the two groups using the following function:

$$P_i(x) = \frac{f_i(x)^\alpha}{\sum_{x'} f_i(x')^\alpha}$$

where $P_i(x)$ is the sampling probability of language x in group i (relevant or non-relevant), $f_i(x)$ returns the relative frequency of x within its group, α is a damping factor between 0 and 1 (with 0 producing a uniform distribution), and the denominator of the term on the right normalizes over all the languages in the group.

To get a distribution over all languages, we combine the distributions for relevant and non-relevant languages. The probability of language x is given by computing the score $s(x)$ as follows and renormalizing:

$$s(x) = \begin{cases} \gamma P_{\text{relevant}}(x), & \text{if } x \text{ is relevant} \\ P_{\text{non-relevant}}(x), & \text{otherwise} \end{cases}$$

$$P(x) = \frac{s(x)}{\sum_{x'} s(x')}$$

Here, γ is the relative weight of relevant examples with respect to non-relevant ones, e.g. $\gamma = 2$ means we would sample relevant examples approximately twice as often as non-relevant ones. So this is basically interpolating between a distribution where only non-relevant languages have non-zero probability (with $\gamma = 0$) and a distribution where the opposite is true (as $\gamma \to \infty$).

Using this probability distribution, with $\alpha = 1$ and $\gamma = 1$, we sampled a dev set containing 20,000 examples and a dev-test set containing 100,000 examples.

6.2 Experiments

We first tested the baseline system on our new split of the training data. Scores are shown in Table 3. These scores are similar to the baseline scores computed on the held-out test set by the organizers. This indicated that our new dev sets were good (or at least better) estimators of held-out test accuracy.

Evaluation Data	Track 1 (macro F1, rel.)	Track 2 (micro F1, rel.)	Track 3 (macro F1, all)
Dev	0.971	0.985	0.950
Dev-test	0.912	0.984	0.942

Table 3: Scores of the baseline system (i.e. HeLI) on our corrected dev sets.

We then trained our neural model using the corrected sampling function to sample training examples. After pre-training the model on our training set for about 700,000 steps, we did a small fine-tuning grid search in order to begin exploring the following questions:

- Does damping the sampling probabilities for training (with $\alpha < 1$) help?

- Does sampling relevant examples more often than non-relevant ones during training (with $\gamma > 1$) help?

- Does doing MLM along with language identification help?

- Should we fine-tune the whole model or freeze the weights of the encoder?

Accordingly, we tested every combination of the following settings:

- $\alpha = \{ 1, 0.75 \}$

- $\gamma = \{ 1, 2 \}$

- Tasks = { SPC only (frozen encoder), SPC only (full fine-tuning), MLM+SPC (full fine-tuning) }

As for the other hyperparameters, we used the following settings, which had worked well in our previous experiments: maximum input length = 128, learning rate = 3e-5, batch size = 32. When the encoder was frozen, batch size was increased to 128. We fine-tuned the 12 models for as long as possible given the time left before the deadline to submit this paper. We used early stopping for model selection, optimizing for track 3 when $\gamma = 1$ and for track 1 when $\gamma = 2$; we did not optimize any models for track 2.

Score optimized	Evaluation data	Track 1 (macro F1, rel.)	Track 2 (micro F1, rel.)	Track 3 (macro F1, all)
Track 1	Dev	0.961	0.983	0.743
	Dev-test	0.928	0.982	0.757
Track 3	Dev	0.899	0.973	0.844
	Dev-test	0.894	0.974	0.836

Table 4: Scores of the neural model on our corrected dev sets. Score on 'dev' is the best dev score achieved for a given track during training. Score on 'dev-test' is the score of the corresponding (early-stopped) model on our 'dev-test' set.

The best dev scores and the scores of the corresponding (early-stopped) models on the dev-test set are shown in Table 4. Comparing these results to the baseline scores in Table 3, we can see that the neural model achieved a higher score on the dev-test set for track 1 (0.928 vs. 0.912), a slightly lower score for track 2 (0.982 vs. 0.984), and a significantly lower score for track 3 (0.836 vs. 0.942). Below, we briefly investigate why our track 3 score is still well below that of the baseline method.

The hyperparameter settings that were optimal for track 1 according to the grid search were: SPC only (full fine-tuning), $\alpha = 0.75$, $\gamma = 2$. The best dev score was achieved after 510,000 steps. As for track 3, the optimal settings were: SPC only (with frozen encoder), $\alpha = 0.75$, $\gamma = 1$. The best dev score was achieved after 715,000 steps.

These results suggest that damping the relative class frequencies when computing the sampling probabilities for training was effective, and that sampling relevant examples more often was helpful for track 1, where we only evaluate test cases where either the gold or predicted label is a relevant language. It also appears that doing MLM alongside SPC during fine-tuning was not helpful, although more extensive experiments would be required to confirm this. Finally, freezing the encoder was helpful for track 3, perhaps because in this case we increased the batch size from 32 to 128, which allowed the model to observe more training data.

Given the time available, we were only able to fine-tune for about 750,000 steps, and the best track 3 dev score was achieved near the end of this, after step 715,000. Given that the batch size was 128 and $\gamma = 1$, the model was able to observe about 45M non-relevant examples in total, which is about 3/4 of the available training data for non-relevant languages. As it is usually recommended to do 3 or 4 epochs during fine-tuning, it seems likely that training longer would improve accuracy. Further tuning the hyperparameters, including those of the sampling function, would also be required to fully assess this method.

In summary, results suggest the neural approach can achieve scores close to and perhaps better than those of the baseline system, but further experimentation is required to establish this.

7 Related Work

Jauhiainen et al. (2019b) provide a thorough survey of research on language identification. Regarding the state-of-the-art, they point out that linear SVMs exploiting character n-grams as features have been highly successful in shared tasks on language identification. The HeLI method has also achieved much success, and has been shown to be robust to class imbalances in the training data.

It was only recently shown that neural networks could achieve state-of-the-art results on language identification tasks. Regarding the system we developed for the cuneiform language identification task at VarDial 2019, Zampieri et al. (2019, p. 13) stated that "to the best of our knowledge, this is the first time a language identification shared task has been won using neural networks in addition to the first MRC [Moldavian vs. Romanian Cross-dialect Topic identification] subtask."

Regarding the challenge posed by class imbalances, an extensive survey on rare event detection by Haixiang et al. (2017) showed that imbalanced learning was a common issue in many different fields of research. Their study indicated that resampling (i.e. oversampling or subsampling) the training data to alleviate or eliminate the imbalance is the most commonly used technique to deal with this issue.

Buda et al. (2018) compared various methods of dealing with class imbalance in a deep learning context, using convolutional neural networks. They investigated two different types of imbalance, one where the class size is equal among the minority and majority classes, but the majority classes are larger, and another where class size increases linearly from the smallest to the largest class. Note that the class imbalances in the ULI dataset are much more complex than this: the class sizes in the non-relevant training data increase in steps (e.g. 33 classes have 10K members, 28 classes have 30K members, 17 classes have 100K members, etc.), whereas the class sizes in the relevant data can not easily be reduced to a simple function, and the class sizes are about 20 times smaller for the relevant data on average. At any rate, Buda et al. (2018) showed that oversampling was helpful in almost all their experiments. Note that the specific method of oversampling they use, which equalizes all class sizes, would result in a very, very large epoch size in the case of the ULI training data, as we would have to sample about 3 million examples for each of the 178 languages.

Madabushi et al. (2020) found that BERT could handle imbalanced training data well without requiring data augmentation, another technique used to alleviate this issue. However, they were dealing with fewer classes than we did in this work (i.e. they focused on a binary classification task), and their data exhibited smaller imbalances between classes (e.g. 28% vs. 72% in the binary classification task). Still, they did observe that random oversampling provided a gain in accuracy, as did cost-sensitive training, which plays a similar role in addressing class imbalance, by assigning different "cost" weights to the different classes (e.g. a higher cost for less frequent classes).

8 Concluding Remarks

In this paper, we described the systems built by the NRC team for the Uralic language identification shared task at the 2020 VarDial evaluation campaign. Our official results were well below the baseline, and we subsequently identified the reason for this, which turned out to be a flaw in the function we used to sample data for both training and evaluation purposes. The preliminary experiments we were able to conduct after correcting this flaw suggest that a neural network can achieve state-of-the-art results on this language identification task, but further experimentation is required to establish this.

We plan on conducting more extensive experiments on our neural approach to language identification, and re-evaluating it on the held-out ULI test set if the organizers make it available. We also plan on exploring different classification architectures, in order to improve efficiency and accuracy. Future work might also touch on ways to reduce noise in the training data, or its effect on classification accuracy.

Acknowledgements

We thank the organizers for their work developing and running this shared task, and the anonymous reviewers for their helpful comments on this paper.

References

Gabriel Bernier-Colborne, Cyril Goutte, and Serge Léger. 2019. Improving cuneiform language identification with BERT. In *Proceedings of VarDial*, pages 17–25.

Mateusz Buda, Atsuto Maki, and Maciej A. Mazurowski. 2018. A systematic study of the class imbalance problem in convolutional neural networks. *Neural Networks*, 106:249 – 259.

Jacob Devlin, Ming-Wei Chang, Kenton Lee, and Kristina Toutanova. 2019. BERT: Pre-training of deep bidirectional transformers for language understanding. In *Proceedings of NAACL*, pages 4171–4186.

Dirk Goldhahn, Thomas Eckart, and Uwe Quasthoff. 2012. Building large monolingual dictionaries at the Leipzig corpora collection: From 100 to 200 languages. In *Proceedings of LREC*, pages 759–765, Istanbul, Turkey, May.

Mihaela Găman, Dirk Hovy, Radu Tudor Ionescu, Heidi Jauhiainen, Tommi Jauhiainen, Krister Lindén, Nikola Ljubešić, Niko Partanen, Christoph Purschke, Yves Scherrer, and Marcos Zampieri. 2020. A Report on the VarDial Evaluation Campaign 2020. In *Proceedings of VarDial*.

Guo Haixiang, Li Yijing, Jennifer Shang, Gu Mingyun, Huang Yuanyue, and Gong Bing. 2017. Learning from class-imbalanced data: Review of methods and applications. *Expert Systems with Applications*, 73:220 – 239.

Tommi Jauhiainen, Krister Lindén, and Heidi Jauhiainen. 2017. Evaluation of language identification methods using 285 languages. In *Proceedings of the 21st Nordic Conference on Computational Linguistics*, pages 183–191.

Heidi Jauhiainen, Tommi Jauhiainen, and Krister Linden. 2019a. Wanca in Korp: Text corpora for underresourced Uralic languages. In Jarmo Harri Jantunen, Sisko Brunni, Niina Kunnas, Santeri Palviainen, and Katja Västi, editors, *Proceedings of the Research data and humanities (RDHUM) 2019 conference*, number 17 in Studia Humaniora Ouluensia, pages 21–40, Finland. University of Oulu.

Tommi Jauhiainen, Marco Lui, Marcos Zampieri, Timothy Baldwin, and Krister Lindén. 2019b. Automatic Language Identification in Texts: A Survey. *Journal of Artificial Intelligence Research*, 65:675–782.

Tommi Jauhiainen, Heidi Jauhiainen, Niko Partanen, and Krister Lindén. 2020. Uralic Language Identification (ULI) 2020 shared task dataset and the Wanca 2017 corpora. In *Proceedings of VarDial*.

Harish Tayyar Madabushi, Elena Kochkina, and Michael Castelle. 2020. Cost-sensitive BERT for generalisable sentence classification with imbalanced data.

Ashish Vaswani, Noam Shazeer, Niki Parmar, Jakob Uszkoreit, Llion Jones, Aidan N Gomez, Łukasz Kaiser, and Illia Polosukhin. 2017. Attention is all you need. In *Advances in Neural Information Processing Systems*, pages 5998–6008.

Thomas Wolf, Lysandre Debut, Victor Sanh, Julien Chaumond, Clement Delangue, Anthony Moi, Pierric Cistac, Tim Rault, Rémi Louf, Morgan Funtowicz, Joe Davison, Sam Shleifer, Patrick von Platen, Clara Ma, Yacine Jernite, Julien Plu, Canwen Xu, Teven Le Scao, Sylvain Gugger, Mariama Drame, Quentin Lhoest, and Alexander M. Rush. 2020. HuggingFace's Transformers: State-of-the-art natural language processing.

Marcos Zampieri, Shervin Malmasi, Yves Scherrer, Tanja Samardžic, Francis Tyers, Miikka Pietari Silfverberg, Natalia Klyueva, Tung-Le Pan, Chu-Ren Huang, Radu Tudor Ionescu, et al. 2019. A report on the third VarDial evaluation campaign. In *Proceedings of VarDial*.

Geolocation of Tweets with a BiLSTM Regression Model

Piyush Mishra
University of Colorado
`first.last@colorado.edu`

Abstract

Identifying a user's location can be useful for recommendation systems, demographic analyses, and disaster outbreak monitoring. Although Twitter allows users to voluntarily reveal their location, such information isn't universally available. Analyzing a tweet can provide a general estimation of a tweet location while giving insight into the dialect of the user and other linguistic markers. Such linguistic attributes can be used to provide a regional approximation of tweet origins. In this paper, we present a neural regression model that can identify the linguistic intricacies of a tweet to predict the location of the user. The final model identifies the dialect embedded in the tweet and predicts the location of the tweet.

1   Introduction

Social media platforms are useful sources for doing data analysis on linguistic patterns. Twitter is one such platform and allows access to tweets posted by the users via APIs. While the metadata of a tweet is accessible, only 3% of tweets include geotagging information (Jurgens et al., 2015). This severely limits the use of a metadata-based approach for location identification. Even if a geolocation model performs well with such metadata, it will fail in the absence of such information. Since tweets are rich in information, a model that relies only on the textual content of tweets will have a better chance of performing consistently.

The location prediction task can be addressed either as a classification problem or a regression problem. The former can be implemented in two ways; by treating known locations as classes or by dividing the entire region at hand into a grid and using the center of the sub-regions as classes. A regression approach can be seen as a simple double regression task where a model predicts the latitude and longitude of a tweet separately, based on its features. Previous studies have shown that tweets, along with their metadata, can be used to predict a user's location (Han et al., 2014). Neural models have been used to better utilize the metadata, along with the tweets (Thomas and Hennig, 2017).

This paper presents an approach to predict the location of a user using a neural model trained solely on the tweets' text content, without any external knowledge sources. This allows the model to generalize more easily to new domains and languages. This paper intends to get justifiable results at a low cost and with limited resources.

The remainder of this paper is organized as follows: The first section provides an overview of related works on location prediction. Section 3 described the datasets used. Section 4 describes the details of the neural network architecture. Results on the validation set are shown in Section 5. Finally, Section 6 concludes the paper with possible future work.

2   Related Work

One of the earliest works on text-based geotagging (Ding et al., 2000) used named entities such as cities, states, etc. mentioned in the text to identify the geographic scope of the web pages in a classification setup. Later, rule-based methods were employed to identify the locations (Bilhaut et al., 2003), while

This work is licensed under a Creative Commons Attribution 4.0 International Licence. Licence details: `http://creativecommons.org/licenses/by/4.0/`.

Proceedings of the 7th VarDial Workshop on NLP for Similar Languages, Varieties and Dialects, pages 283–289
Barcelona, Spain (Online), December 13, 2020

others used named entity recognition in combination with various machine learning techniques (Qin et al., 2010). All these approaches rely on the fact that there is a mention of some location in the text which may not always be the case. Other approaches include supervised classification (Kinsella et al., 2011; Wing and Baldridge, 2011) using words as features and unsupervised learning, where clustering techniques are employed based on topic modeling (Ahmed et al., 2013; Hong et al., 2012).

Some of the previous research has focused on leveraging the metadata associated with the tweet to improve the performance. Many results submitted in the Workshop on Noisy User-generated Text (WNUT2016) (Han et al., 2014) used such metadata heavily. Models were built that focused on user-declared locations, timezone values, and user self-descriptions in addition to the content of the tweet itself (Miura et al., 2016). As part of feature pre-processing, tweet-level geo coordinates were repalced with geo coordinates of the corresponding tweet cities using several mapping services such as GeoNames and time zone boundaries. Finally, neural networks were trained using the FastText n-gram model (Joulin et al., 2017) on posted text, user location, user descriptions, and user timezones.

Ensemble methods are also common, often relying on several information resources like text, user location text, user time zone information, messenger source, and reverse country look-ups for URL mentions. Jayasinghe et al. (2016) relies on specific URL mentions and screened website metadata for geographic coordinates.

Multinomial naïve Bayes methods have been employed that focused on the use of textual features (i.e., location indicative words, GeoNames gazetteers, user mentions, and hashtags) (Chi et al., 2016). Since the authors are using location indicative words, city/country names, hashtags and @mentions as a combined feature set, even though it relies on textual data more than the metadata, dialect related information isn't covered.

Related work to date covers a wide range of languages and dialects including Dutch (Wieling et al., 2011), British (Szmrecsanyi, 2008), American English (Huang et al., 2015; Eisenstein et al., 2010) and African American Vernacular English (Jones, 2015).

3   Data Set

We use the data provided for SMG sub-task (Ljubešić et al., 2016) (Hovy and Purschke, 2018) of the VarDial 2020 shared task is used for the training and testing purpose of the model (Găman et al., 2020). Using data from social media platforms like Twitter and Jodel, three language areas are covered. Each language has a training, a validation, and a test file. Each file contains entries separated by newlines and each entry contains a latitude, a longitude, and a text tuple, separated by tabs.

- Standard German Jodels (DE-AT): Jodel conversations initiated in Germany and Austria, which are written in standard German but commonly contain regional and dialectal forms.

- Swiss German Jodels (CH): Jodel conversations from Switzerland, in Swiss German dialects.

- BCMS Tweets (BCMS): Geo-located tweets published in the area of Croatia, Bosnia and Herzegovina, Montenegro, and Serbia.

The distribution of all three datasets across latitudes and longitudes are shown in Figure 1, Figure 2, and Figure 3 below.

Language	Training Set	Validation Set	Test Set
DE-AT	336983	46582	48239
CH	22600	3068	3097
BCMS	320042	39750	39723

Table 1: Number of data points per set per language

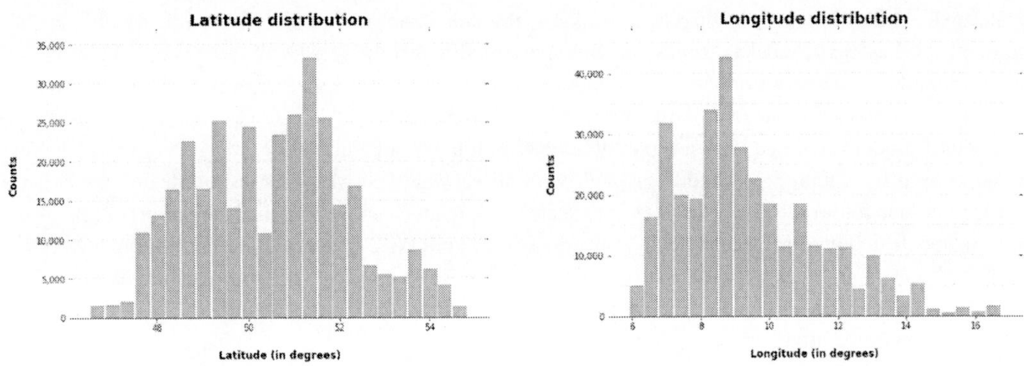

Figure 1: Dataset distribution of DE-AT Jodels across latitudes and longitudes

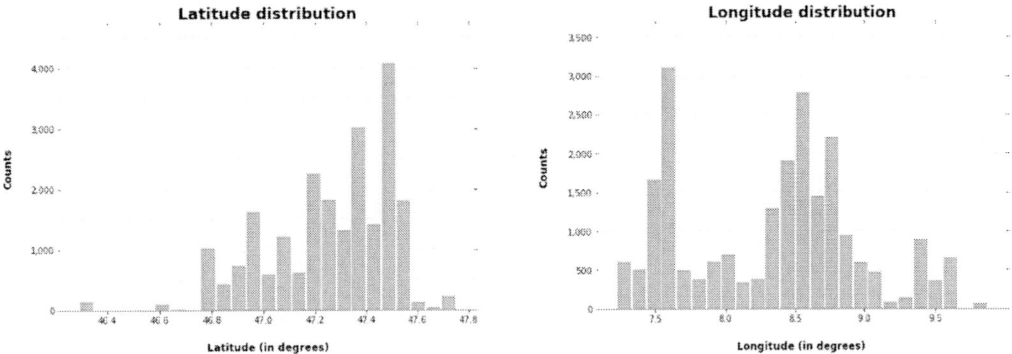

Figure 2: Dataset distribution of CH Jodels across latitudes and longitudes

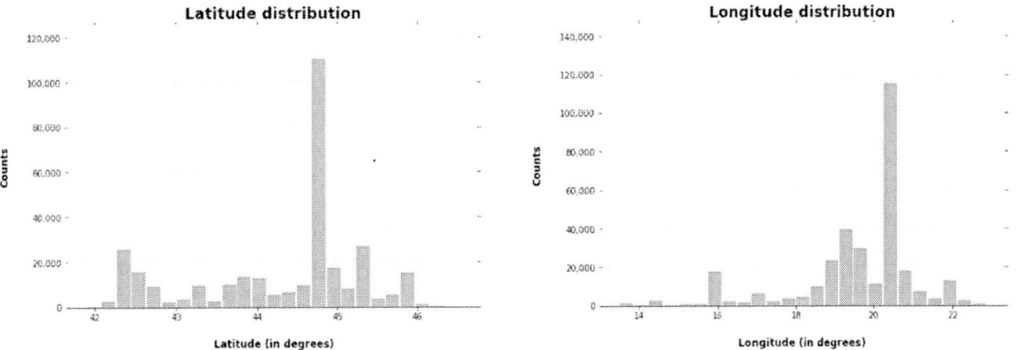

Figure 3: Dataset distribution of BCMS Tweets across latitudes and longitudes

4 Architecture

To identify the location of a given tweet, a double regression approach has been taken. The model will identify the latitude and longitude separately for a given text and the distance between the actual and predicted location will be used to measure its performance. For this purpose, we are using two bidirectional LSTM models.

For text pre-processing, we use a tweet tokenizer as part of the cleanup, to remove unwanted punctuation and lower-case conversion. We use a list of German stopwords to further clean the DE-AT dataset. We decided to keep the stopwords for Swiss German due to the smaller size of the dataset. For BCMS, stopwords from multiple languages are needed which are not as consistent as German, so those are included in the dataset as well. Using TF-IDF weighting allows us to focus on the highly relevant tokens

285

in the text. Using this new set of relevant tokens, the tweets are updated so that irrelevant tokens are removed. A FastText model is trained on this new, modified training set, unsupervised. This trained FastText model is used to produce an embedding matrix. The unsupervised training allows the overall model to be implemented in a similar fashion for all 3 languages.

A neural model is created with a trainable embedding layer, an embedding matrix from the FastText model is used for obtaining embeddings, and two bidirectional LSTM layers are used, one for latitude training and one for longitude. Using a trainable embedding layer with the embedding matrix reduces the training epochs required for the model to converge. Since both LSTM layers share a common embedding layer, both have to rely on the same set of embeddings for learning. Two dense layers are added before the output layer. This allows the model to adjust the weights better for a gradual change. A visual representation of the architecture is presented in Fig. 4.

Figure 4: Neural model architecture

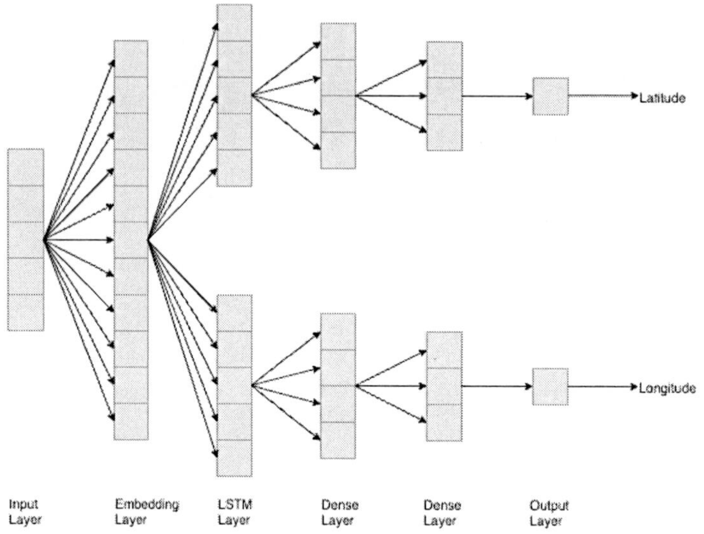

Because the evaluation metric for this task is the median distance loss over the test data, Quantile function with 0.5 as alpha is used as the loss function. While a neural model with MSE or MAE as the loss function predicts better for individual tweets, the distance loss over the entire set becomes greater than the quantile function. On the other hand quantile function takes into account the distribution of the dataset while training and, with alpha set to 0.5, it estimates the median instead of mean. For regularization, since L1 brings weights of unimportant features to zero, only contributing features remain. This helps in better feature selection. We use ReLU as activation functions and Adagrad as the optimizer for adaptive updates of frequently and infrequently occurring feature parameters.

5   Results

The performance of the model on validation and test data is shown in Table 2. Median loss (distance in km) has been used as the metric.

Language	Validation Set	Test Set
DE-AT	174.049	183.99
CH	27.39	27.31
BCMS	95.318	85.70

Table 2: Median distance (in kilometers) over the dataset.

Language	Min Latitude	Max Latitude	Min Longitude	Max Longitude
DE-AT	46.53	54.84	5.92	16.72
CH	46.29	47.75	7.23	9.87
BCMS	41.88730403	46.52582591	13.49204277	22.8606

Table 3: Ranges of latitudes and longitudes with respect to the dataset

Rank	Team	Median distance	Mean distance
1	helsinki-ljubljana	159.59	183.97
2	**This work**	**183.99**	**204.93**
3	CUBoulder-UBC	198.27	218.51
4	ZHAW	205.81	230.78
5	SUKI	243.12	266.85

Table 4: The best results of each team participating on the SMG 2020 shared task DEAT track.

Rank	Team	Median distance	Mean distance
1	ZHAW	15.93	25.06
2	helsinki-ljubljana	17.66	26.21
3	CUBoulder-UBC	19.49	27.63
4	SUKI	23.96	34.59
5	UnibucKernel	25.57	30.52
6	The lingustadors	26.70	31.21
7	**This work**	**27.31**	**33.20**

Table 5: The best results of each team participating on the SMG 2020 shared task Swiss German track.

Rank	Team	Median distance	Mean distance
1	helsinki-ljubljana	48.99	86.83
2	ZHAW	57.24	100.42
3	SUKI	61.01	105.11
4	CUBoulder-UBC	64.76	106.67
5	**This work**	**85.70**	**112.65**
6	The lingustadors	97.16	141.88

Table 6: The best results of each team participating on the SMG 2020 shared task BCMS track.

It can be observed that the deviation of validation and test result is not more than 10km for DE-AT and BCMS dataset and much smaller for the CH dataset. The marginal deviation on the CH dataset can be attributed to the small size of the dataset. Another factor responsible for the scale of deviation for DE-AT and BCMS vs CH is the range of latitudes and longitudes. Below is the range of latitudes and longitudes for all 3 datasets.

From Table 2, it can be observed that, with minimal configuration and constrained training, the model is performing equally well or even better for test data than the validation data. In constrained submissions, our model gave the second-best result for the DE-AT dataset. The performance of all the participating teams for the SMG shared task is shown in Table 4, Table 5, and Table 6.

6   Conclusion and Future Work

We have presented a neural network architecture that addresses the tweet location prediction as a dual regression task. No custom processing of the text was done besides a generic tweet tokenization. As part of the cleanup, stopwords were removed from the Standard German dataset only. No pre-trained model or embedding was used which made the model generic enough to be used for any dataset. The model was trained on Google colab with limited GPU access with a maximum training time was around 8hrs.

In the future, we aim to use the distance between the predicted and actual locations as the main loss parameter to train the model. This should give a better insight into the usage of quantile function since this task focused on median distance loss as the performance metric. We will also analyze the performance of our model against a classification model where the known tweet-emission locations are used as a constrained set of labels.

References

Amr Ahmed, Liangjie Hong, and Alexander Smola. 2013. Hierarchical geographical modeling of user locations from social media posts. pages 25–36, 05.

Frédérik Bilhaut, Thierry Charnois, Patrice Enjalbert, and Yann Mathet. 2003. Geographic reference analysis for geographic document querying. In *Proceedings of the HLT-NAACL 2003 workshop on Analysis of geographic references*, pages 55–62.

Lianhua Chi, K. Lim, N. Alam, and C. Butler. 2016. Geolocation prediction in twitter using location indicative words and textual features. In *NUT@COLING*.

Junyan Ding, Luis Gravano, and Narayanan Shivakumar. 2000. Computing geographical scopes of web resources. *Proceedings of the 26th VLDB Conference*, 12.

Jacob Eisenstein, Brendan O'Connor, Noah A. Smith, and Eric Xing. 2010. A latent variable model for geographic lexical variation. In *Proceedings of the 2010 conference on empirical methods in natural language processing (EMNLP)*, pages 1277–1287.

Mihaela Găman, Dirk Hovy, Radu Tudor Ionescu, Heidi Jauhiainen, Tommi Jauhiainen, Krister Lindén, Nikola Ljubešić, Niko Partanen, Christoph Purschke, Yves Scherrer, and Marcos Zampieri. 2020. A Report on the VarDial Evaluation Campaign 2020. In *Proceedings of the Seventh Workshop on NLP for Similar Languages, Varieties and Dialects (VarDial)*.

Bo Han, Paul Cook, and Timothy Baldwin. 2014. Text-based twitter user geolocation prediction. *J. Artif. Intell. Res.*, 49:451–500.

Liangjie Hong, Amr Ahmed, Siva Gurumurthy, Alexander Smola, and Kostas Tsioutsiouliklis. 2012. Discovering geographical topics from twitter streams. In *Proceedings of The 21st International World Wide Web conference (WWW)*, 04.

Dirk Hovy and Christoph Purschke. 2018. Capturing regional variation with distributed place representations and geographic retrofitting. In *Proceedings of the 2018 Conference on Empirical Methods in Natural Language Processing*, pages 4383–4394, Brussels, Belgium. Association for Computational Linguistics.

Yuan Huang, Diansheng Guo, Alice Kasakoff, and Jack Grieve. 2015. Understanding U.S. regional linguistic variation with Twitter data analysis. *Computers, Environment and Urban Systems*, 54, 12.

Gaya Jayasinghe, Brian Jin, J. McHugh, B. Robinson, and Stephen Wan. 2016. CSIRO Data61 at the WNUT Geo Shared Task. In *Proceedings of the 2nd Workshop on Noisy User-generated Text (WNUT)*, pages 218–226.

Taylor Jones. 2015. Toward a description of African American Vernacular English dialect regions using "Black Twitter". *American Speech*, 90:403–440, 11.

Armand Joulin, E. Grave, P. Bojanowski, and Tomas Mikolov. 2017. Bag of tricks for efficient text classification. *ArXiv*, abs/1607.01759.

David Jurgens, T. Finethy, James McCorriston, Yi Tian Xu, and D. Ruths. 2015. Geolocation prediction in twitter using social networks: A critical analysis and review of current practice. In *ICWSM*.

Sheila Kinsella, Vanessa Murdock, and Neil O'Hare. 2011. "i'm eating a sandwich in Glasgow": modeling locations with tweets. In *Proceedings of the 3rd international workshop on Search and mining user-generated contents*, pages 61–68.

Nikola Ljubešić, Tanja Samardžić, and Curdin Derungs. 2016. TweetGeo - a tool for collecting, processing and analysing geo-encoded linguistic data. In *Proceedings of COLING 2016, the 26th International Conference on Computational Linguistics: Technical Papers*, pages 3412–3421, Osaka, Japan, December. The COLING 2016 Organizing Committee.

Yasuhide Miura, Motoki Taniguchi, Tomoki Taniguchi, and Tomoko Ohkuma. 2016. A simple scalable neural networks based model for geolocation prediction in Twitter. In *Proceedings of the 2nd Workshop on Noisy User-generated Text (WNUT)*.

Teng Qin, Rong Xiao, Lei Fang, Xing Xie, and Lei Zhang. 2010. An efficient location extraction algorithm by leveraging web contextual information. In *Proceedings of the 18th SIGSPATIAL International Conference on Advances in Geographic Information Systems*, pages 53–60.

Benedikt Szmrecsanyi. 2008. Corpus-based dialectometry: Aggregate morphosyntactic variability in British English dialects. *International Journal of Humanities and Arts Computing*, 2:279–296, 10.

Philippe Thomas and Leonhard Hennig. 2017. Twitter geolocation prediction using neural networks. In *International Conference of the German Society for Computational Linguistics and Language Technology*, pages 248–255. Springer.

Martijn Wieling, John Nerbonne, and R. Harald Baayen. 2011. Quantitative social dialectology: Explaining linguistic variation geographically and socially. *PloS one*, 6(9).

Benjamin Wing and Jason Baldridge. 2011. Simple supervised document geolocation with geodesic grids. In *Proceedings of the 49th annual meeting of the Association for Computational Linguistics: Human Language Technologies*, pages 955–964.